£34.50 (NET)

The Weimar Era and Hitler 1918-1933

The Weimar Era and Hitler 1918-1933

A Critical Bibliography by Peter D. Stachura

CLIO PRESS · OXFORD

British Library Cataloguing in Publication Data

Stachura, Peter D.
  The Weimar era and Hitler, 1918—1933.
  1. Germany — History — 1918—1933 —
    Bibliography
  2. Germany — Politics and government — 1918—
    1933 — Bibliography
016.943085   Z2240

  ISBN 0—903450—08—9

Designed by Bernard Crossland
Typeset at the Alden Press, Oxford London and
Northampton
Printed in Great Britain at
the Alden Press, Oxford

Clio Press Ltd.,
Woodside House,
Hinksey Hill,
Oxford, OX1 5BE,
England

American Bibliographical Center-Clio Press,
2040 Alameda Padre Serra,
Santa Barbara,
California 93103
U.S.A.

For Kay and Gregory

Contents

Contents

Part II. The Rise of National Socialism

Introduction

Students of the Weimar Republic and of National Socialism are confronted by a relentlessly expanding volume of secondary literature on a wide range of historical problems and experiences relating to the 1918—33 period. While this development has the advantage of allowing access to more and more detailed information, even the most conscientious and best organized of us are beginning to feel not a little overawed by the sheer weight of scholarly output in these fields. The specialist finds himself spending an increasing proportion of his time back-checking secondary data relevant to his research interest, while the undergraduate is often intimidated by the task of compiling a book list on a Weimar theme.

In these circumstances, and in response to a clearly articulated demand, I felt the moment apposite to undertake the preparation of a reliable, up-to-date bibliography of secondary literature covering the Weimar Republic; such a book breaks new ground in incorporating between two covers a detailed and critically annotated bibliography of that literature. The need for an easily available bibliographical study of this kind is pressing because, until the present, scholars have been unable to turn to one identifiable source for reference consultation. Hitherto, the sources of bibliographical knowledge have been confined to the following:

(*a*) Bibliographies published in monographs and general textbooks. This is unsatisfactory because there is no single book which furnishes an exhaustive and thoroughly detailed bibliography. Moreover, the vast majority of books list only those publications which were used by the author in connection with a particularly specialized area of research. Selective book lists are plentiful but they are hardly more than a tentative solution to a large and increasingly complex problem.

(*b*) The bibliographical supplements published by the outstanding West German academic journal,

the *Vierteljahrshefte für Zeitgeschichte*. These partially solve the problem, but apart from the fact that many students, especially undergraduates, cannot read German, the *Vierteljahrshefte für Zeitgeschichte* is expensive to buy and is not always available, even in university libraries. Also, the supplements contain works published between certain dates, such as between 1971 and 1973, and do not therefore provide a single, compact reference source, and in any case the citations are unannotated.

(*c*) Various publications appearing at regular intervals in the Federal Republic. Most of the published work on the Weimar era emanates from Germany and these publications, which include among others the *Jahrbuch der historischen Forschung*, the *Literaturverzeichnis der politischen Wissenschaften*, the *Deutsches Buchverzeichnis* and the *Deutsche Nationalbibliographie*, carry detailed bibliographical data. However, these are not usually within easy reach of Anglo-Saxon readers, and, of course, catalogue only German works.

(*d*) The bibliography compiled by the Wiener Library entitled: *From Weimar to Hitler: Germany 1918—33* (London: Vallentine Mitchell, revised and enlarged edition 1964). At the time, this volume of some 3000 entries constituted a good reference source, but it is now more than a decade out of date. Even so, it was not so much a comprehensive bibliography as a record of the extensive holdings of the Library on Weimar history. As such, there are a relatively large number of notable omissions, particularly articles. Unfortunately, the Wiener Library no longer publishes updated book lists.

(*e*) Several leading scholarly periodicals, including the *American Historical Review* and the *Historische Zeitschrift*, include a section listing recently published articles, and these are exceptionally useful.

But the articles are not assessed as to content or merit, and in order to establish what has been written over a longer period of time on German history between 1918 and 1933, one is again faced with the problem of ploughing through many issues of the journals. Furthermore, neither of the two aforementioned journals provide a corresponding catalogue of book and monograph publications.

The latter qualification also applies to the most authoritative reference source in respect of articles, *Historical Abstracts*, published by the American Bibliographical Center. Not only does it collate material from the widest possible range of major and minor journals, but all citations are carefully annotated by a team of specialists and are comprehensively indexed.

This evidence spotlights the serious lacuna in the tools necessary for a study of the Weimar period and the problem will only grow in magnitude as time goes on. It is therefore the primary purpose of this book to offer a preliminary study which, while not claiming to be anything like complete, does provide a reasonably comprehensive and critically assessed bibliography. The students and specialists to whom this work is mainly addressed will hopefully find it useful and moderately rewarding. If so, then my aim will have been fulfilled.

I am well aware of the pitfalls and hazards in writing a bibliography of this type, particularly in an area of research as intense and highly competitive as German history 1918—33. In view of the vast quantity of published work covering this period, there must be a possibility of some significant titles being overlooked. Every effort has been made to ensure that omissions have been reduced to an acceptable level. More important perhaps, the provision of a critical assessment of virtually every citation was done with a considerable degree of trepidation on my part, not least because such an exercise might be regarded as pretentious by some. By way of self-justification, I would only state that I believe the bibliography as a whole is much more valuable where each item's worth is indicated. Some specialists will doubtless take exception to a number of my reviews, but it must be an occupational hazard for a reviewer not to have his critiques unanimously accepted. The opinions expressed in this study are based on a thorough reading of every entry and at all times my aim has been to be scrupulously fair and objective. Although I have often been aware of other scholars' appraisals of certain works, I have not allowed these unduly to influence my own judgement. In this way, full responsibility for the views given here is borne by me alone.

The bibliography contains only works published between the end of the Second World War in May 1945, and the early Spring of 1975, effectively, thirty years of publishing in the field of the Weimar Republic and the early National Socialist movement. Only exceptionally, in section 24 (Early Writings of National Socialist Leaders), have works published before 1945 been included, and then only because it was felt that this section usefully complemented other sections in Part II of the bibliography.

The general criterion adopted in organizing the bibliography has been thematic but I have tried to adhere as far as possible at the same time to a chronological pattern. The bibliography comprises monographs, *Festschriften*, documentary collections, articles, pamphlets and unpublished dissertations and theses which have made a contribution to our understanding of a crucial and absorbing period in modern German history. Few general historical surveys have been admitted. The overwhelming majority of the entries have been published in Germany, the United States of America, Canada, Great Britain and Australia, but where deemed appropriate, French and occasionally East European publications are also cited.

It should also be pointed out that I have not sought artificially to limit the number of East German entries, most of which will be unknown to students and indeed to many specialists. East German works have been treated in this bibliography in exactly the same way as publications from the Federal Republic. Even if readers find unacceptable the rather inflexible ideological/political framework within which most East German historians present their findings, they should still be informed about the nature and extent of historical research and writing in the other part of divided Germany.

A reservation must be made regarding German university dissertations. Those cited from East Germany have been severely restricted in number, largely because copies of many were unobtainable in the time at my disposal in Germany: I decided against listing those that I was unable to review. In any case, these dissertations are not usually available outside Germany unless through the lengthy channels of the international section of the Inter-Library Loan Service. As regards West German dissertations, I have included only those which I was able to read personally, so there will be some notable omissions, especially where *Habilitationsschriften* are concerned. For these blemishes, the reader has my apologies.

Acknowledgements

It would not have been possible to undertake and complete this work without the generous assistance and cooperation of many libraries and their staffs both at home and abroad. I am very grateful, in the first instance, to the University of Stirling Library, especially Miss Lynne Mitchell, who dealt with my numerous inter-library loan requests with admirable efficiency and cheerfulness; the libraries of the universities of Glasgow and Edinburgh, as well as the National Library (Edinburgh); the Institute of Contemporary History and Wiener Library (London); the Institut für Zeitgeschichte, the Bayerische Staatsbibliothek, and the Universitätsbibliothek — all of Munich; and finally, the Archiv der deutschen Jugendbewegung (Burg Ludwigstein). Of the fellow scholars with whom I discussed this project at various stages, I would like to mention in particular Professor Volker R. Berghahn, who read an advanced version of the manuscript and provided many perceptive and valuable comments. This should in no way detract, of course, from my own responsibility for the entire contents of the work.

I am heavily obligated to Miss E.G. West and her colleagues for undertaking the typing of a difficult manuscript and subsequent alterations to it. My most substantial debt, however, is to my wife and son whose contribution to the making of this book was in a very special sense of deep importance.

PETER D. STACHURA

Stirling, March 1977

List of Periodicals Consulted

Agricultural History
Agricultural History Review
American Economic Review
American Historical Review
American Journal of Economics and Sociology
American Journal of Sociology
American Philosophical Quarterly
American Political Science Review
American Slavic and East European Review
American Sociological Review
American Sociologist
Annals of the American Academy of Political
  and Social Science
Archiv für Kommunalwissenschaft
Archiv für Kulturgeschichte
Archiv für Rechts- und Sozialphilosophie
Archiv für Sozialgeschichte
Aussenpolitik
Australian Economic History Review
Australian Journal of Philosophy
Australian Journal of Political History
Australian Journal of Politics and History
Australian & New Zealand Journal of Sociology
Australian Outlook
Austrian Historical Newsletter
Austrian History Yearbook

Beiträge zur Geschichte der Deutschen
  Arbeiterbewegung
Blätter für Deutsche Landesgeschichte
Blätter für Deutsche und Internationale Politik
British Journal for the Philosophy of Science
British Journal of Political Science
British Journal of Sociology
Bulletin of the Institute of Historical Research
Bulletin des Leo Baeck Instituts
Bulletin of the Society for the Study of Labour
  History
Business History
Business History Review

Cahiers d'Histoire de la Guerre
Cambridge Historical Journal
Canadian Historical Review
Canadian Journal of Economics
Canadian Journal of History
Canadian Journal of Philosophy
Canadian Slavic Studies
Catholic Historical Review
Central European History
Comparative Political Studies
Comparative Politics
Comparative Studies in Society and History
Contemporary Review
Current History

Deutsche Aussenpolitik
Deutsche Rundschau

Encounter
English Historical Review
European Economic Review
European Review
European Studies Review
Explorations in Economic History

Foreign Affairs
Forschungen zur Osteuropäischen Geschichte
Frankfurter Hefte

German Life and Letters
German Quarterly
Germanic Review
Geschichte in Wissenschaft und Unterricht
Gesellschaft, Staat, Erziehung

Hessisches Jahrbuch für Landesgeschichte
Historical Journal

List of Periodicals Consulted

Historisches Jahrbuch
Historische Zeitschrift
History
History of Political Economy
History and Theory
History Today
Hochland

International Affairs (London)
International Economic Review
International Labour Review
International Review
International Review of Social History
International Social Science Journal
Internationale Wissenschaftliche Korrespondenz
    zur Geschichte der Deutschen Arbeiterbewegung
Irish Historical Studies (Proceedings of the Irish
    Historical Conference)
Irish University Studies

Jahrbuch des Archivs der Deutschen Jugend-
    bewegung
Jahrbuch für Geschichte
Jahrbuch für die Geschichte Mittel- und
    Ostdeutschlands
Jahrbücher für Geschichte Osteuropas
Jahrbuch für Sozialwissenschaft
Jahrbuch für Wirtschaftsgeschichte
Jewish Historical Studies
Jewish Social Studies
Journal of Central European Affairs
Journal of Contemporary History
Journal of Ecclesiastical History
Journal of Economic History
Journal of Economic Studies
Journal of Economic Theory
Journal of European Economic History
Journal of European Studies
Journal of the History of Ideas
Journal of the History of Philosophy
Journal of Interdisciplinary History
Journal of International Affairs
Journal of International Economics
Journal of Modern History
Journal of Peasant Studies
Journal of Philosophy
Journal of Political Economy
Journal of Politics
Journal of Religious History
Journal of Social History
Journal of World History

Kölner Zeitschrift für Soziologie und Sozial-
    psychologie
Kyklos

Labour History

Merkur
Militärgeschichtliche Mitteilungen

Minerva
Modern Age

Die Neue Gesellschaft
Neue Politische Literatur

Osteuropa
Oxford German Studies

Das Parlament: Aus Politik und Zeitgeschichte
Past and Present
Philosophy
Philosophical Journal
Philosophical Quarterly
Philosophical Review
Philosophical Studies
Polish Western Affairs
Political Science Quarterly
Political Studies
Political Quarterly
Die Politische Meinung
Politische Studien
Politische Vierteljahrsschrift
Proceedings of the British Academy
Psychoanalytic Quarterly
Public Opinion Quarterly
Publizistik

Quarterly Journal of Economics

Renaissance and Modern Studies
Review of Economic Studies
Review of Politics
Revue des Deux Mondes
Revue d'Histoire de la Deuxième Guerre Mondiale
Revue Historique
Revue d'Histoire Moderne et Contemporaine
Revue Française de Science Politique
Round Table
Rural Sociology
Russian Review

Scandinavian Economic History Review
Scottish Historical Review
Scottish Journal of Political Economy
Scottish Studies
Slavic Review
Slavonic and East European Review
Social Research
Sociology
Sociological Review
Soviet Studies
St. Antony's Papers
Survey: a Journal of East-West Studies

Transactions of the Royal Historical Society

Vierteljahrshefte für Zeitgeschichte
Vierteljahrsschrift für Sozial- und Wirtschaftsgeschichte

Wehrwissenschaftliche Rundschau
Weimarer Beiträge
Die Welt als Geschichte
Western Political Quarterly
Wiener Library Bulletin
William and Mary Quarterly
Wissenschaftliche Zeitschrift der Friedrich-Schiller-Universität Jena
World Politics

Yearbook of the Leo Baeck Institute

Zeitschrift für Bayerische Landesgeschichte
Zeitschrift für die Gesamte Staatswissenschaft
Zeitschrift für die Geschichte der Juden
Zeitschrift für die Geschichte des Oberrheins
Zeitschrift für Geschichtswissenschaft
Zeitschrift für Militärgeschichte
Zeitschrift für Ostforschung
Zeitschrift für Politik

The Weimar Republic

General Studies

1

ARETIN, Erwein Freiherr von.
Krone und Ketten: Erinnerungen eines bayerischen Edelmannes. Edited by Karl Buchheim and Kurt Otmar von Aretin. Munich: Süddeutscher Verlag (1954), 443 pp.
These memoirs of a Bavarian monarchist in the Weimar era are generally informative and free of apologetics. They cover the period between December 1930 and the summer of 1934, and are particularly useful for the author's description of that section of Bavarian political opinion which was suspicious of any co-operation between the Centre Party and the SPD. Aretin's hostility to von Papen is clearly expressed, as is his belief in Bavarian states' rights *vis-à-vis* the Berlin government and his support for the Wittelsbach cause. The description of the political situation in Bavaria just prior to the *Machtergreifung* is perceptive.

ARETIN, Kurt O. Freiherr von; FAUTH, Gerhard.
Die Entwicklung Deutschlands zur totalitären Diktatur 1918—1934. Munich: Bayerische Landeszentrale für Heimatdienst (1959), 127pp.
A general survey of some of the main developments in the Weimar Republic and first year of Nazi rule. Designed for mainly educational purposes, it now needs to be substantially revised.

AY, Karl-Ludwig.
"Die deutsche Revolution 1914—1948: Bemerkungen über gesellschaftlichen Wandel und Epochenbegriff". *Zeitschrift für Bayerische Landesgeschichte*, vol. 36, pt. 2 (1973), p. 877—96.
Discusses, among other points, the character and aims of Hitler and the different interpretations of him that have been offered by scholars. A worthwhile paper.

BADIA, Gilbert.
La Fin de la république allemande (1929—1933). Paris: Editions Sociales (1958), 136pp.
A brief account of the last days of Weimar. The author's analysis of the factors involved in the Republic's collapse, however, is rather superficial.

BARIÉTY, Jacques; DROZ, Jacques.
République de Weimar et régime hitlérien, 1918—1945. Paris: Hatier (1973), 224 pp.
An excellent synthesis of the most recent research on Germany between the wars. Concisely written, it is consistently relevant and balanced and can be highly recommended for undergraduates. Bariéty has written the section on Weimar and he includes an appendix which contains a few hitherto unpublished documents of importance, for example, the foreign policy programme of the *Reichsverband der deutschen Industrie* of October 1922, and a record of a meeting between Stresemann and Minister Presidents of the *Länder* in July 1924 at which the Foreign Minister explained the principles of his policy.

BECK, Reinhart.
Die Geschichte der Weimarer Republik im Spiegel der sowjetzonalen Geschichtsschreibung. Dissertation, Erlangen University (1963).
An interesting study of the interdependent factors of politics and Marxist ideology in the East German approach to the history of the Weimar Republic. The author suggests that ideological considerations often prevail over objective assessment.

BECKENBACH, Ralf.
Der Staat im Faschismus: Ökonomie und Politik im deutschen Reich, 1920—1945. West Berlin: Verlag für das Studium der Arbeiterbewegung (1974), 134 pp.
A rather unsophisticated and generally unconvincing attempt to establish that fascism was the inevitable outgrowth of capitalism. The author does not seem aware of previous important studies in this field, for example, the work of Henry A. Turner.

BEHR, Hermann.
Die goldener Zwanziger Jahre: das fesselnde Panorama einer entfesselten Zeit. Hamburg: Hammerich & Lesser (1964), 144 pp.
Contains some desultory observations of the 1920s. Useful perhaps for introductory reading to the period, though the author provides no new perspectives or interpretations.

BENZ, Wolfgang.
Quellen zur Zeitgeschichte: Personen und Sachregister. 2 vols. Stuttgart: Deutsche Verlagsanstalt (1973), 366 pp.
An up-to-date and very reliable work of reference for students and scholars alike.

3

BERGHAHN, Volker R.
"Die Harzburger Front und die Kandidatur
Hindenburgs für die Präsidentschaftswahlen 1932".
Vierteljahrshefte für Zeitgeschichte, vol. 13, pt. 1
(1965), p. 64—82.
Based almost entirely on unpublished archival material,
much of it from the *Deutsches Zentralarchiv* in Potsdam,
Berghahn has presented a closely argued essay which throws
fresh light on an important episode of the Republic's last
phase. Concentrating on the period between the establishment of the Harzburg Front in autumn 1931 and the
announcement of candidates for the presidential election in
February 1932, he skilfully analyses the complexities of the
politics pursued by the *Stahlhelm*, General Schleicher,
Hindenburg and Hitler. Above all, the author demonstrates
that Brüning's dismissal in May 1932 could have happened
several months earlier, in February 1932, if Schleicher and
Hindenburg had had their way.

BESSON, Wolfgang; **HILLER** von **GAERT-
RINGEN**, Friedrich (eds.).
Geschichte und Gegenwartsbewusstsein: historische
Betrachtungen und Untersuchungen; Festschrift
für Hans Rothfels zum 70. Geburtstag. Göttingen:
Vandenhoeck & Ruprecht (1963), 526 pp.
A *Festschrift* of 20 papers for Professor Rothfels dealing
with the various fields of historical study in which he has
worked. Papers on contemporary history include one by
Hiller von Gaertringen on the *Dolchstoss* myth. See under
Hiller von Gaertringen in 4A (v).

BOSL, Karl; **FRANZ**, Günther; **HOFMANN**,
Hanns H. (eds.).
Biographisches Wörterbuch zur deutschen
Geschichte. 3 vols. Munich: Francke Verlag (1973
—1975).
The three volumes are the second revised edition of the
Handbook of German History founded by Hellmuth
Rössler and Günther Franz (see under Rössler and Franz
later in this section). Hofmann deals with National
Socialism, but his entries retain the same unfortunate
nationalist bias of the first edition. Hitler has the largest
entry in volume 1 (which covers A—H) and here at least
Hofmann provides a competent summary of the state of
present research on him. In general terms, the three
volumes constitute a handy and reasonably well organized
source of reference.

BRACHER, Karl Dietrich.
Das deutsche Dilemma: Leidenswege der
politischen Emanzipation. Munich: Piper (1971),
470 pp. (English ed.: **The German Dilemma: the
Relationship of State and Democracy**. New York:
Praeger (1975).)
Mature reflections of a leading authority on Germany's long
and painful road to parliamentary democracy.

BRACHER, Karl Dietrich.
Die Auflösung der Weimarer Republik: eine
Studie zum Problem des Machtverfalls in der
Demokratie. Villingen: Ring-Verlag (1960), 809 pp.
Enlarged and new ed.
Still the standard work on the collapse of the Republic. A
truly monumental work of brilliant scholarship which treats
virtually every aspect of the disintegration of pluralism in
Germany before 1933. Bracher provides a penetrating and
richly documented analysis of the structural defects of the
republican system and the degree to which these defects
contributed to Weimar's final collapse. An excellent 40-
page bibliography is appended. Essential reading.

BRACHER, Karl Dietrich.
"Parteienstaat, Präsidialsystem, Notstand: zum
Problem der Weimarer Staatskrise". *Politische
Vierteljahrsschrift*, vol. 3, pt. 3 (1962), p. 212—24.

An outline of the author's understanding of the nature of
the political crisis in Germany 1930—32, emphasizing the
notion of a power vacuum being filled by more and more
authoritarianism.

BRACHER, Karl Dietrich.
Deutschland zwischen Demokratie und Diktatur:
Beiträge zur neueren Politik und Geschichte.
Munich: Scherz (1964), 415 pp.
Another outstanding contribution, in which Bracher deals
most expertly with the problem for democracy presented by
the very nature of the Weimar constitution, as well as on a
more empirical level by the character of certain institutions,
such as the civil service and the officer corps. This volume
should be read in conjunction with the author's *Die Auflösung der Weimarer Republik*.

BRACHER, Karl Dietrich.
"Auflösung einer Demokratie: das Ende der
Weimarer Republik als Forschungsproblem". In
*Faktoren der Machtbildung: wissenschaftliche
Studien zur Politik*. Edited by A.R. Gurland.
Berlin: Duncker & Humblot (1952), p. 39—98.
Bracher sets out his priorities regarding the historical prob-
lem of the collapse of the Weimar Republic. Not only his
ideas and perspectives, but also his methodological approach
are discussed in a paper which clearly anticipates the
general orientation of his *Die Auflösung der Weimarer
Republik*.

BRANDT, Willy; **LOWENTHAL**, Richard.
Ernst Reuter: ein Leben für die Freiheit. Munich:
Kindler-Verlag (1957), 759 pp.
A sympathetic and sometimes valuable account of Reuter
who is perhaps best known as the courageous Mayor of
Berlin in the early days after 1945. Non-German readers
will be surprised to learn that Reuter held a top post in the
early German Communist Party (KPD) after 1918 before
switching to the Social Democrats. Reuter subsequently
held the office of Mayor of Magdeburg before 1933. Apart
from details of Reuter's colourful career, the book provides
useful background information on the Weimar era.

BRAUBACH, Max.
"Weimar, Hitler, Widerstand: ein Bericht über
Neuerscheinungen zur Geschichte der Jahre 1918
bis 1945". *Historisches Jahrbuch*, vol. 90 (1970),
p. 81—159.
A critical review of new books on the period. The author's
comments are balanced and scholarly.

BRAUBACH, Max.
"Vom Ersten bis zum Ende des Zweiten
Weltkrieges: Bericht über Veröffentlichungen der
Jahre 1971—1974". *Historiches Jahrbuch*, vol. 94
(1974), p. 247—332.
A well-informed critical review. The first section, "Vom
Kampf um Neuordnung und Demokratie" (p. 247—56)
deals with recent publications on the Weimar era, while the
second section, "Hitler-Renaissance" (p. 256—73) looks at
the avalanche of published material on Hitler.

BRAUN, Otto.
Von Weimar zu Hitler. Hamburg: Norddeutsche
Verlags-anstalt (1949), 458 pp.
The somewhat disappointing memoirs of the former SPD
Minister-President of Prussia (1919—32). It is helpful for
general background of the period as seen through the eyes
of a right-wing Social Democrat, but the volume does not
furnish detailed information on internal developments within the SPD itself.

BRECHT, Arnold.
Vorspiel zum Schweigen: das Ende der deutschen Republik. Vienna: Verlag für Geschichte und Politik (1948). (English edition: **Prelude to Silence: the End of the German Republic.** London: Oxford University Press (1944), 156 pp.)
A useful description of the last phase (1930—33) of the Republic from a person who at that time was a top official in the civil service and who was able to observe the workings of government from close at hand. He was in frequent contact with ministers and helped draft important legislation. He writes as one who was genuinely sorry to see parliamentary democracy being systematically undermined, but his admiration for Brüning as Chancellor is striking. He makes the distinction between the traditional conservative-nationalists and the National Socialists, but does not concede that the attitudes of the former were as much to blame for the Republic's collapse as National Socialism. His treatment of the Papen and Schleicher administrations is rather cursory.

BRECHT, Arnold.
"Die Auflösung der Weimarer Republik und die politische Wissenschaft". *Zeitschrift für Politik*, vol. 2, pt. 4, (1955), p. 291—308.
A critical review of Bracher's *Die Auflösung der Weimarer Republik* whose fundamental importance Brecht freely admits. Brecht adds his own comments to some of the detailed points in the book, including the Papen coup of 20 July 1932 in Prussia.

BRECHT, Arnold.
Aus nächster Nähe: Lebenserinnerungen eines beteiligten Beobachters, 1884—1927. Stuttgart: Deutsche Verlagsanstalt (1966), 526 pp.
Part I of the fascinating autobiography of this informed and perceptive observer of German political developments. His account of the complex situation in the Chancellory on the eve of the November Revolution is valuable, as are his reflections on general political developments in early Weimar.

BRECHT, Arnold.
Mit der Kraft des Geistes: Lebenserinnerungen, zweite Hälfte, 1927—1967 Stuttgart: Deutsche Verlagsanstalt (1967), 496 pp.
Part II of Brecht's autobiography is no less interesting than the first, and contains his account of Weimar's collapse. Many of these points have, of course, been made in his previous studies.

BRECHT, Arnold.
The Political Education of Arnold Brecht: an Autobiography 1884—1970. Princeton: Princeton University Press (1970), 544 pp.
The English version of his autobiography. Unfortunately, this edition has been considerably shortened from the original.

BUCHHEIM, Karl.
Die Weimarer Republik: Grundlagen und politische Entwicklung. Munich: Kösel-Verlag (1960), 141 pp.
This succinct review of the development and collapse of the Republic needs to be revised. It is sounder on the 1919—24 than the 1929—33 period. In any case, this book is intended only for the general reader.

BUCHHEIM, Karl.
"Die Tragödie der Weimarer Republik". *Hochland* vol. 49, pt. 6 (1957), p. 515—27.
The author's theme is that the Republic never had a sound foundation on which to build.

CARLEBACH, Emil.
Von Brüning zu Hitler: das Geheimnis faschistischer Machtergreifung. Frankfurt: Röderberg (1971), 63 pp.
The author appears to subscribe to fanciful conspiracy theories in this poor and non-serious pamphlet.

CASTELLAN, Georges.
"Histoire de l'Allemagne depuis 1918". *Revue Historique*, vol. 243 (1970), p. 367—414.
A very sound critical survey of primary and documentary sources for research into modern German history. The author also gives a critique of a few selected monographs.

CASTELLAN, Georges.
L'Allemagne de Weimar, 1918—1933. Paris: Libraire Armand Colin (1969), 443 pp.
A full and generally reliable study of political and constitutional developments, but weak on economic, social, and cultural aspects.

CHANADY, Attila.
"Erich Koch-Weser and the Weimar Republic". *Canadian Journal of History*, vol. 7, pt. 1 (1972), p. 51—63.
A paper of no particular importance.

CHILDS, David.
Germany since 1918. London: Batsford (1971), 308 pp.
A well-written introduction to twentieth century German history 1918—70. It is packed with relevant information, though the author does not explore the interdependence of economic, domestic and foreign policies. This fault is noticeable particularly in the section dealing with the Weimar Republic.

CONZE, Werner.
"Die Weimarer Republik". In *Deutsche Geschichte im Überblick: ein Handbuch.* Edited by Peter Rassow. Stuttgart: Metzler (1953), p. 616—66.
Intended for the general reader, it is now hopelessly out of date.

CONZE, Werner.
Die Zeit Wilhelms II und die Weimarer Republik: deutsche Geschichte 1890—1933. Stuttgart: Metzler (1964), 270 pp.
The author's treatment of the Weimar Republic shows that he has taken cognizance of research completed since his earlier publication (see above). But again, the volume is designed for a non-specialist audience, and of course now requires still further revision.

CONZE, Werner.
"Zur deutschen Geschichte, 1918—1933". *Neue Politische Literatur*, vol. 2, pt. 12 (1957), p. 926—35.
A review of some new books published at that time on Weimar themes. The author takes a special look at studies concerning Stresemann and Groener.

CONZE, Werner; RAUPACH, Hans (eds.).
Die Staats- und Wirtschaftskrise des deutschen Reiches 1929/33. Stuttgart: Klett (1967), 255 pp.
A very useful collection of articles by six historians on various aspects of the economy in Weimar Germany. See under authors Hans Raupach (section 13A(iii) (a)); Dietmar Keese (section 13A(ii) (e)); Wilhelm Treue (section 13A(ii)

(a)); Ursula Hüllbüsch (section 14); Werner Conze (section 4F).

CURTIUS, Julius.
Sechs Jahre Minister der deutschen Republik.
Heidelberg: Carl Winter Verlag (1948), 275 pp.
The author was Minister of Economics 1926—29 and Foreign Minister in succession to Stresemann 1929—31. In the first part of the book he deals with economic policy, and in the second part with foreign affairs. Neither part contains anything of real importance, and, overall, these dry memoirs add very little to our knowledge of either the Republic or Weimar government. Moreover, the book is badly written and is based on an extremely narrow range of sources.

DEDERKE, Karlheinz.
Reich und Republik: Deutschland 1917—1933.
Stuttgart: Klett (1969), 320 pp.
A well composed synthesis of the main social, political and economic aspects of the period. Although designed for use in schools, the author has included (in his narrative) the most up-to-date research of specialists. For example, in his discussion of the reasons for the National Socialist triumph in 1933, he stresses the aid given to Hitler by big business, agrarians, etc. The sections on social and economic developments are especially well done. Many undergraduates would profit by reading this attractively presented volume.

DELMER, Sefton.
Trail Sinister: an Autobiography. 2 vols. London: Secker & Warburg (1961), 423 pp.
The former correspondent of the London *Daily Express* has a few chapters on Weimar, but they are highly impressionistic and tell us nothing of interest or significance. In fact, the book as a whole is exceptionally dull.

DITTMANN, Wilhelm.
Das politische Deutschland vor Hitler. Nach dem amtlichen Material des Statistischen Reichsamtes in Berlin. Zurich: Europa Verlag (1945), 44 pp.
A handy collection of tables, charts, diagrams, and miscellaneous statistical data on German politics before 1933.

DÖBLIN, Alfred.
Schriften zur Politik und Gesellschaft. Freiburg im Breisgau: Walter-Verlag (1972), 532 pp.
A selection of Döblin's critical writings. Most of them are concerned with aspects of Weimar society and politics. Interesting offerings from the writer who made his name as the author of *Berliner Alexanderplatz.*

DÖBLIN, Alfred.
Der deutsche Maskenball von Linke Poot: Wissen und Verändern. Freiburg im Breisgau: Walter-Verlag (1972), 321 pp.
A further collection of Döblin's writings on Weimar. His strongly nonconformist outlook comes across very clearly.

DRAPER, Theodore.
"The Spectre of Weimar". *Social Research,* vol. 39, pt. 2 (1972), p. 322—40.
The author tries to establish whether it is valid to draw an analogy between the Weimar Republic and the United States of the late 1960s, which he considers to be suffering a severe crisis and possibly heading for fascism. He examines the analogy in specific terms under various headings like "heritage", "youth" and so on. Not surprisingly, he concludes that there are significant differences between the two countries and that the Weimar experience does not provide too many lessons for the United States. Altogether this paper is a rather futile exercise.

ERDMANN, Karl Dietrich.
"Die Weimarer Republik". In Bruno Gebhardt (ed.). *Handbuch der deutschen Geschichte. Vol. IV: Die Zeit der Weltkriege.* Stuttgart: Union-Verlag (1973), 329 pp. 9th new ed.
Can be recommended as one of the most competent and readable general histories of the Weimar era.

ERDMANN, Karl Dietrich.
"Die Geschichte der Weimarer Republik als Problem der Wissenschaft". *Vierteljahrshefte für Zeitgeschichte,* vol. 3, pt. 1 (1955), p. 1—19.
Erdmann argues that the legacy of the *Obrigkeitsstaat* was the principal reason for the Republic's collapse. He adds that the weight of Germany's conservative and authoritarian past was too much for the Republic from the outset; his implied conclusion is that Weimar was doomed from the beginning — a pessimistic view not shared unanimously by historians.

ERNST, Fritz.
Die Deutschen und ihre jüngste Geschichte: Beobachtungen und Bemerkungen zum deutschen Schicksal der letzten fünfzig Jahre (1911—1961). Stuttgart: Kohlhammer (1963), 162 pp. (English edition: **The Germans and their Modern History.** New York: Columbia University Press (1966), 164 pp.)
Based on a series of lectures which the author delivered at Heidelberg University in 1961/62 in which he reflects on Germany's recent past in the aftermath of the Nazi catastrophe. The real purpose of the book is to help re-educate the German public about their own historical experience, and on this account the book caused some controversy in Germany when it first appeared. Non-German readers may wonder at this because Ernst does not say anything of a startling nature. The volume, however, serves as a useful introduction to the subject for students.

ESCHENBURG, Theodor (ed.).
Die improvisierte Demokratie: gesammelte Aufsätze zur Weimarer Republik. Munich: Piper-Verlag (1962), 306 pp. (English edition, translated by Lawrence Wilson: **The Road to Dictatorship: Germany 1918—1933.** London: Oswald Wolff (1964), 174 pp.).
The editor regards the continued existence of the *Obrigkeitsstaat* and its feudal-conservative-militarist supporters as the main reason for the Republic's collapse. Against this array of reactionary forces, democratic elements had no real opportunity to strike deep roots. Of the 10 articles included in this volume, those dealing with the Weimar era are readable but intended for a general audience: Ernst Fraenkel on the "Historical Handicaps of German Parliamentarianism"; Kurt Sontheimer, "Anti-Democratic Thought in the Weimar Republic"; Erich Matthias, "Social Democracy and the Power in the State"; Rudolf Morsey, "The Centre Party between the Fronts"; and Ossip K. Flechtheim, "The Role of the Communist Party".

ESCHENBURG, Theodor.
"Die Rolle der Persönlichkeit in der Krise der Weimarer Republik: Hindenburg, Brüning, Groener, Schleicher". *Vierteljahrshefte für Zeitgeschichte,* vol. 9, pt. 1 (1961), p. 1—29.
An analysis of the motives, ideas, and actions of the personalities whom the author considers to have dictated the pace and style of German politics between March 1930 and May 1932. A balanced and informative assessment is given of each person, none of whom come out very well. At the same time, the paper provides a valuable analysis of the political scene during the Brüning era. Unfortunately, there are no footnote references.

ESCHENBURG, Theodor.
"The Collapse of Democratic Régimes between the First and the Second World War". In L. Wilson (translator). *The Road to Dictatorship: Germany 1918—1933*. London: Oswald Wolff (1964), p. 7—23.

EYCK, Erich.
A History of the Weimar Republic. 2 vols. Cambridge (Mass.): Harvard University Press (1962 —63). (German edition: Geschichte der Weimarer Republik, Vol. I: Vom Zusammembruch des Kaisertums bis zur Wahl Hindenburgs 1918—25. Vol. II: Von der Konferenz von Locarno bis zu Hitlers Machtübernahme, 1925—33. Zurich: Reutsch-Verlag (1954—56).)

Still one of the most lucid general histories of the period, though it concentrates heavily on political and constitutional narrative and neglects social and economic factors to a large extent. The weaknesses of the constitution and of the political parties are probably the best descriptive parts of the book, even though the author's judgement is often subjective. The work is based entirely on printed secondary sources. A general criticism is that Eyck prefers to narrate rather than analyse.

FEDERAU, Fritz.
Von Versailles bis Moskau: Politik und Wirtschaft in Deutschland 1919—1970; ein Dokumentarbericht. Berlin: Haude & Spener (1971), 248 pp.

Not particularly useful for the Weimar period in view of the great deal of scholarly interest in the interaction of politics and the economy (especially big business) during the 1918 —39 period.

FEUCHTWANGER, E. J. (ed.).
Upheaval and Continuity: a Century of German History. London: Oswald Wolff (1973), 192 pp.

A useful compendium of 12 papers originally delivered at the University of London in 1971—72, with an appropriate introduction by the editor. The volume is meant to provide a concise treatment of major political and social themes in German history 1870—1960. Articles of note are those by Kurt Sontheimer, Francis L. Carsten, and Martin Broszat (listed under individual authors).

FLAKE, Otto.
Die Deutschen: Aufsätze zur Literatur und Zeitgeschichte. Hamburg: Rütten & Loening (1963), 270 pp.

Most of the essays collected here were in fact written during the Weimar era and deal with contemporary political problems. Of curiosity value more than anything else.

FRANÇOIS-PONCET, André.
The Fateful Years: Memoirs of a French Ambassador in Berlin. London: Victor Gollancz (1948).

Valuable memoirs of a sharp and perceptive observer of the German political scene 1931—38. The rise of National Socialism is a major theme, and the author is critical of democratic forces for not coming together in a united front to check Hitler. Schleicher comes in for particularly severe rebuke. Contains also useful notes on the National Socialist leadership and Hitler's charisma.

FREYH, Richard.
Stärke und Schwäche der Weimarer Republik. Hanover: Verlag für Literatur und Zeitgeschehen (1960), 63 pp.

An inadequate attempt to draw up a balance sheet of the Republic. The idea of such a "reckoning" is in itself rather futile, especially when dealt with so briefly.

FRIEDENSBURG, Ferdinand.
Die Weimarer Republik. Hanover: Norddeutscher Verlagsanstalt (1957), 295 pp. New ed.

Written by a former democratically minded Vice-President of the Berlin Police in Weimar, it is too apologetic of the Republic and its "achievements". He blames the fall of democracy on the depression and the political immaturity of the German people, making them vulnerable to the totalitarianisms of left and right, and allowing the army to play a decisive role in politics. A limited but moderately interesting work.

GATZKE, Hans W.
"The Republic of Weimar". *Current History*, vol. 28, pt. 2 (1955), p. 217—22.
Unimportant.

GEISS, Imanuel; WENDT, Bernd J. (eds.).
Deutschland in der Weltpolitik des 19. und 20. Jahrhunderts: Fritz Fischer zum 65. Geburtstag. Düsseldorf: Bertelsmann (1973), 596 pp.

A *Festschrift* for the well-known Hamburg professor consisting of 29 essays written by former pupils and colleagues. Many of the essays had been published previously. Although the period covered is from the French Revolution to the present Federal Republic, there is a particular emphasis on Imperial Germany 1871—1914. The only paper of note touching on Weimar is that by Imanuel Geiss, who writes on the colourful career of Kurt Riezler, Bethmann-Hollweg's intimate advisor, who, after 1918, advocated a German foreign policy of peace and reconciliation.

GÖHRING, Martin.
Bismarcks Erben, 1890—1945: Deutschlands Weg von Wilhelm II bis Adolf Hitler. Wiesbaden: Steiner (1958), 386 pp.

A straightforward narrative for the general reader. It is clearly written and succinct, but requires to be updated.

GORDON, Harold J.
"Politischer Terror und Versailles Abrüstungsklausel in der Weimarer Republic". *Wehrwissenschaftliche Rundschau*, vol. 16, pt. 1 (1966), p. 36—54.

An interesting discussion of a major characteristic of the Weimar political scene and its military/disarmament implications.

GOSSWEILER, Kurt.
"Karl Dietrich's Auflösung der Weimarer Republik". *Zeitschrift für Geschichtswissenschaft*, vol. 6, pt. 3 (1958), p. 508—57.

A bitterly hostile review of K. D. Bracher's major work (note Gossweiler's error over Bracher's name). The main reason for the hostility is simply Bracher's failure to write from a Marxist-Leninist perspective!

GRENZMANN, Robert.
Generation ohne Hoffnung: Aufzeichnungen aus den Jahren 1913—1933. Edited by Klaus Simmer-Jochem. Hanover: Pfeiffer (1968), 365 pp.

Pleasantly written, readable, but not very informative about Weimar politics.

HAFERKORN, Katja.
"Die bürgerliche westdeutsche Historiographie über das Ende der Weimarer Republik". *Zeitschrift für Geschichtswissenschaft*, vol. 18, pt. 6 (1970), 1003—22.
The author is concerned to show that West German historians are somehow agents of the Federal Republic's "imperialism", rather than to provide a scholarly appraisal of studies on Weimar. The paper indeed amounts to a political polemic against the Bonn government and its "reactionary monopolistic bourgeois" supporters.

HALLGARTEN, George W. F.
Als die Schatten fielen: Erinnerungen vom Jahrhundertbeginn zur Jahrtausendwende. Berlin: Ullstein (1969), 367 pp.
Memoirs of the leading American historian who vividly recounts his impressions of the numerous political personalities he met in Germany before his emigration in 1933.

HALPERIN, S. William.
Germany Tried Democracy: a Political History of the Reich from 1918 to 1933. New ed. New York: Norton Library (1965), 567 pp.
A very good general history; well organized, concise, balanced and thoughtful. Unfortunately, the book does not have an overall coherent thesis. Recommended for undergraduates.

HARTUNG, Fritz.
"Zur Geschichte der Weimarer Republik".
Historische Zeitschrift, vol. 181 (1956).
A general survey of developments to 1924 only. Not especially valuable.

HEIBER, Helmut.
Die Republik von Weimar. Munich: Deutscher Taschenbuch Verlag (1966), 283 pp.
A chronologically arranged survey of considerable competence. The chapters dealing with the middle years of the Republic (4—7) are very informative. The bibliography, however, is sketchy.

HERMANN, Alfred (ed.).
Aus Geschichte und Politik: Festschrift zum 70. Geburtstag von Ludwig Bergsträsser. Düsseldorf: Droste (1954), 326 pp.
The papers, contributed by 18 historians, differ widely in quality and topicality. Noteworthy is the editor's own article on Stresemann.

HERMANN, Hans H.
Weimar: Bestandsaufnahme einer Republik.
Reinbek bei Hamburg: Rowohlt (1969), 172 pp.
A volume of no special virtue; it attempts yet another stocktaking of major events in the 1919—33 period.

HERMENS, Ferdinand; SCHIEDER, Theodor (eds.).
Staat, Wirtschaft und Politik in der Weimarer Republik: Festschrift für Heinrich Brüning. Berlin: Duncker & Humblot (1967), 507 pp.
An admirable volume of articles whose theme is the Republic, and in particular the Brüning era. See under individual authors — Ferdinand Hermens on the Brüning government and the depression; Ernst Deuerlein on Heinrich Brauns; and Helmut Unkelbach on the causes of Weimar's collapse.

HERZFELD, Hans.
"Germany: after the Catastrophe". *Journal of Contemporary History*, vol. 2, pt. 1 (1967), p. 79—91.
A brief but scholarly review of research trends since the end of the Second World War on Germany's recent history.

HERZFELD, Hans.
Ausgewählte Aufsätze: dargebracht als Festgabe zum siebzigsten Geburtstage. Berlin: de Gruyter (1962), 460 pp.
A collection of 14 papers, most of which were written by the author since 1945. Apart from studies of the army and Johannes Popitz (see sections on the army and civil service respectively), he has a stimulating piece on "State and Nation in German Historiography during the Weimar Era".

HERZFELD, Hans.
Die Weimarer Republik. Frankfurt: Ullstein (1966), 156 pp.
A compact and smoothly written work for the general reader.

HERZFELD, Hans.
Die moderne Welt 1789—1945. Part II: Weltmächte und Weltkriege: die Geschichte unserer Epoche 1890—1945. Brunswick: Westermann Verlag (1957), 376 pp.
A more general study which is marred by a series of elementary factual errors and a few rather bizarre interpretations. Nonetheless, moderately useful for the non-specialist.

HERZOG, Wilhelm.
Menschen denen ich begegnete. Frankfurt: Francke-Verlag (1959), 494 pp.
Impressions of Rathenau, Kurt Eisner, and Max Liebermann among others are included in an otherwise mediocre work.

HESS, Jürgen C.
Theodor Heuss vor 1933: ein Beitrag zur Geschichte des demokratischen Denkens in Deutschland. Stuttgart: Klett Verlag (1973), 231 pp.
An appreciative and sympathetic description of Heuss as an upholder of parliamentary democracy. However, Heuss is rightly depicted as a critical believer in Weimar democracy and as someone who freely acknowledged its many failings. A worthwhile study.

HEUSS, Theodor.
Erinnerungen 1905—1933. Tübingen: Wunderlich Verlag (1963), 460 pp.
The clear and dispassionate memoirs of a Weimar democrat who later became President of the Federal Republic. He provides sharp and interesting insights into Weimar politics and impressions of leading figures, including Hitler.

HIDEN, J. W.
The Weimar Republic. London: Longman (1974), 114 pp.
Designed as an introduction to seminar discussion on the subject for university students, it is too brief and superficial to adequately fulfil even that modest purpose. The volume is perhaps better suited for school certificate candidates.

HILLGRUBER, Andreas.
Die Auflösung der Weimarer Republik. Hanover: Verlag für Literatur und Zeitgeschehen (1960), 72 pp.
A mature assessment of the causes of Weimar's collapse, but it now needs to be revised.

HIRSCH, Helmut.
Experiment in Demokratie: zur Geschichte der Weimarer Republik. Wuppertal: Hammer-Verlag (1972), 184 pp.

A collection of 10 somewhat disjointed and unconvincing papers on leading personalities who exerted important influence on the development of the Republic. Rosa Luxemburg, Friedrich Ebert, Hugo Stinnes, Gustav Stresemann and Hitler are among those considered. Hirsch offers no new interpretations of his subjects and has merely regurgitated the views of previous studies.

HIRSCHFELD, Hans E.; REICHHARDT, Hans J. (eds.).
Ernst Reuter: Schriften, Reden, vol. 2. Berlin: Propyläen-Verlag (1973), 870 pp.
A well-edited collection of Reuter's letters, speeches, and articles from 1922—46.

HOEGENER, Wilhelm.
"Weimar aus der Sicht des Politikers". *Politische Studien*, vol. 9 (1958), p. 500—62.
Not very profound reflections from a former Weimar politician on Weimar.

HOEGENER, Wilhelm.
Der politische Radikalismus in Deutschland 1919—1933. Munich: Günter Olzog Verlag (1966), 256 pp.
Does not say anything new or important.

HOEGENER, Wilhelm.
Die verratene Republik: Geschichte der deutschen Gegenrevolution. Munich: Isar-Verlag (1958), 397 pp.
Written from a pronounced Social Democratic viewpoint, this is a mundane account of the main steps leading to the collapse of the Republic. The best section of the book is where the author, who was chairman of the Bavarian Legislature's committee of investigation into the 1923 Hitler Putsch, describes the Bavarian political situation in that year, and Bavaria's relationship with the Berlin government. Not an objective study, it is essentially composed of his personal recollections.

HOEGENER, Wilhelm.
Der schwierige Aussenseiter: Erinnerungen eines Abgeordneten, Emigranten und Minister-präsidenten. Munich: Isar-Verlag (1959), 344 pp.
The full autobiography of the SPD politician who in 1954—57 was Minister President of Bavaria. He outlines the aims of the Weimar SPD and relates some of the crises overtaking the party. Hoegener, however, is not well informed on other aspects of Weimar politics, especially other parties. The volume, which is divided into three sections (pre-1933; 1933—45; and post-1945), is of strictly limited usefulness.

HOHLFELD, Johannes (ed.).
Dokumente der deutschen Politik und Geschichte von 1848 bis zur Gegenwart: ein Quellenwerk für die politische Bildung und Staatsbürgerliche Erziehung. Vol. III: Die Weimarer Republik 1919—1933. Berlin: Wendler (1949), 476 pp.
This volume does not rank with the best documentary collections for the Weimar period.

HOFFMANN, Joachim.
Die grossen Krisen, 1917—1933. Frankfurt: Diesterweg (1962), 144 pp.
Superficial and too full of factual errors and dubious interpretations.

HOLL, Karl; WILD, Adolf (eds.).
Ein Demokrat kommentiert Weimar: die Berichte Hellmut von Gerlachs an die Carnegie-Friedens-stiftung in New York 1922—1930. Bremen: Schünemann (1973), 268 pp.
Gerlach, the left-wing editor of the weekly *Die Welt am Montag*, sent monthly reports on the German political scene to the Carnegie Foundation for International Peace 1922—30. The reports are written with some journalistic flair but often tend to simplify events. Moreover, Gerlach was not too perceptive, for he consistently overrated the strength of the SPD and underestimated Hitler. However, the volume is of interest in that it gives the views of a non-Marxist left-wing intellectual in Weimar.

HOLL, Karl.
"Europapolitik im Vorfeld der deutschen Regierungspolitik: zur Tätigkeit proeuropäischer Organisationen in der Weimarer Republic". *Historische Zeitschrift*, vol. 219 (1974), p. 33—94.
The author describes in considerable detail the development, aims and activities of pro-European groups in Weimar. Especially interesting is his analysis of their connections with foreign countries and the involvement of the German foreign office. The reasons for the failure of these organizations are also given.

HUNT, Richard N. (ed.).
The Creation of the Weimar Republic: Stillborn Democracy? Lexington (Mass.): Heath (1969), 106 pp.
Another volume in the excellent Problems in European Civilization series. The format is as before, with a number of leading specialists giving their views on why the Republic failed. The editor provides a competent introduction. Undergraduates should take note.

JASPER, Gotthard.
Der Schutz der Republik: Studien zur staatlichen Sicherung der Demokratie in der Weimarer Republik 1922—1930. Tübingen: Mohr (1963), 337 pp.
Concerned with the formulation and application of the "Law for the Protection of the Republic", passed shortly after the murder by right-wing extremists of Walther Rathenau in 1922. He considers the law to have been a failure because it was applied leniently to the Right and harshly to the Left. For this, he blames conservatives in the civil service and judiciary. The book's usefulness is reduced by some factual errors and a tendency to oversimplify and, more importantly, by the author's indiscriminate use of polemical contemporary sources.

JASPER, Gotthard (ed.).
Von Weimar zu Hitler, 1930 bis 1933. Cologne: Kiepenheuer & Witsch (1968), 527 pp.
A collection of papers on various themes of Weimar development, none of which add anything original.

JASPER, Gotthard.
"Das innere Gefüge der Weimarer Republik". *Neue Politische Literatur*, vol. 9 (1964), p. 512—20.
A look at a few recent publications in the field.

JONAS, Klaus W.
The Life of Crown Prince William. London: Routledge & Kegan Paul (1961), 252 pp.
Chapter VIII deals with Prince William's life as a private citizen in the Weimar Republic.

JONES, Larry E.
"The Dying Middle": Weimar Germany and the Failure of Bourgeois Unity 1924—1930. Dissertation, University of Wisconsin (1970).
The central theme, "The Dying Middle", refers to the political decline of the middle class parties and to the social and economic decline of the bourgeoisie in general. The author emphasizes the political aspects and in particular the attempt to create a united liberal bourgeois party. The *Liberale Vereinigung* was founded in 1924 to promote an amalgamation of the German Democratic Party (DDP) and the German Peoples' Party (DVP), but it was never effective. Jones also considers the German State Party, founded in 1930 on the demise of the DDP, and the role played here by the *Jungdeutsche Orden*. The main value of the study is that the author has worked up a good deal of previously unpublished material, especially from private papers.

JONES, Larry E.
" 'The Dying Middle': Weimar Germany and the Fragmentation of Bourgeois Politics". *Central European History*, vol. 5, pt. 1 (1972), p. 23—54.
Jones presents here the main conclusions of his doctoral thesis.

KALTEFLEITER, Werner.
Wirtschaft und Politik in Deutschland: Konjunktur als Bestimmungsfaktor des Parteiensystems. Cologne: Westdeutscher Verlag (1966), 170 pp.
An impressively integrated work which states that an interdependence of politics and economics together with other factors such as tradition accounts for the sweeping economic changes in Germany during the depression of the early 1930s. Convincing statistical data back up the author's hypothesis.

KARL, Heinz; RUGE, Wolfgang.
"Forschungen zur Geschichte der Weimarer Republik". *Zeitschrift für Geschichtswissenschaft*, vol. 18, special number (1970), p. 515—51.
A critical and politically slanted discussion of recent literature.

KEIL, Wilhelm.
Erlebnisse eines Sozialdemokraten. 2 vols. Stuttgart: Deutsche Verlagsanstalt (1948).
Rather boring and uninformative memoirs of a former SPD politician. Parts 1—4 of the second volume deal with Weimar.

KESSLER, Harry G.
Tagebücher 1918—37. Edited by Wolfgang Pfeiffer-Belli. Frankfurt: Insel-Verlag (1961), 799 pp.
These diaries of the friend and biographer of Rathenau are an important contribution to the history of Weimar. From his liberal and democratic standpoint, he records the November Revolution in Berlin, his own activity in the DDP and pacifist movements, his estimate of politicians, and his reactions to the ascent of National Socialism. A judicious and entertaining work.

KESSLER, Harry G.
Gesichter und Zeiten: Erinnerungen. Berlin: Fischer (1962), 267 pp. New ed.
Written with style and marked by the same high degree of perceptiveness displayed in the author's previous work. Most interesting memoirs of a cultivated and attractive personality.

KOCHAN, Lionel.
The Struggle for Germany 1914—1945. Edinburgh: Edinburgh University Press (1963), 150 pp.

The theme is the struggle of the Western powers and of Russia for a controlling influence in Germany; at the same time, the Germans themselves were divided into pro-Western and pro-Eastern attitudes. The final outcome was Germany's partition in 1945 which the author believes was the logical result of the power struggle over Germany. Kochan skilfully blends ideological, diplomatic and military factors into his argument, which is well documented and essentially convincing.

KOHN, Hans (ed.).
German History: Some New German Views. London: Allen & Unwin (1954), 224 pp.
Contains 11 papers by prominent German historians on themes of modern German history. The volume as a whole needs to be handled with some caution because it clearly serves more of a political than a purely historical role. One of the papers is by Ludwig Dehio who provides a concise analysis of Germany's position between the two world wars.

KOLLMANN, Eric C.
"Reinterpreting Modern German History: the Weimar Republic". *Journal of Central European Affairs*, vol. 21, pt. 4 (1961—62), p. 434—51.
A valuable discussion of general trends in the postwar historiography of the Weimar Republic, considering changes of opinion on the historical position of the Republic (an epilogue to the Wilhelmine era; an interlude between the Second and Third Reichs; or a genuine experiment in democracy?), the nature of the November Revolution, the causes of Weimar's collapse, etc. Within this context, the author ably reviews major works that have appeared since 1945 on the Weimar era.

KOZA, Ingeborg.
Die erste deutsche Republik im Spiegel des politischen Memoirenschrifttums: Untersuchungen zum Selbstverständnis und zur Selbstkritik bei den politisch Handelnden aus den Reihen der staatsbejahenden Parteien zur Zeit der 1. deutschen Republik. Wuppertal: Henn (1971), 167 pp.
A generally unhelpful attempt to evaluate the contribution of politically based memoirs to an understanding of the Weimar Republic and its problems.

KRUMMACHER, Friedrich A; WUCHER, Albert (eds.).
Die Weimarer Republik. Munich: Desch (1965), 428 pp.
Designed for the general public. A history of Weimar presented through a collection of photographs and documentary texts; the latter form the only interesting part of the book.

LEBER, Annelore; MOLTKE, Greya G. von.
Für und wider: Entscheidungen in Deutschland 1918—1945. Berlin: Mosaik-Verlag (1961), 287 pp.
Useful general work; Part I deals with Weimar.

LEHMANN, Hans.
Die Weimarer Republik: Darstellung und Dokumente. Munich: Günter Olzog Verlag (1960), 96 pp.
A popular history, though the origins of the *Dolchstoss* myth are given in some detail.

LEITHÄUSER, Joachim.
Wilhelm Leuschner: ein Leben für die Republik. Cologne: Bund-Verlag (1962), 264 pp.
A factual account of a former Minister for Home Affairs in Hesse before 1933, who is better known as a leading socialist member of the anti-Nazi resistance. Not very helpful for understanding major events in Weimar.

LÖBE, Paul.
Der Weg war lang: Erinnerungen eines Reichstags-
präsidenten. Berlin: Arani (1949), 173 pp.
(Revised and enlarged edition, Berlin: Arani
(1954), 302 pp.)
Cannot be rated as an important contribution to either the
history of the SPD or the Republic — especially disappointing in view of the fact that the author was President of the
Reichstag from 1920—32. The memoirs are sketchy and
vague and mainly serve to reveal how indecisive Löbe
himself was as a politician.

LOCHNER, Louis P.
Always the Unexpected: a Book of Reminiscences.
New York: Macmillan (1956), 339 pp.
A readable description of the author's experiences while
working in the Berlin office of Associated Press 1924—41.
He met many politicians and statesmen, including Strese-
mann, and records his impressions. Contains also some use-
ful observations on Weimar political life.

LÖWENSTEIN, Hubertus zu.
Botschafter ohne Auftrag: Lebensbericht. Düsseldorf: Droste (1973), 331 pp.
Moderately interesting memoirs of the so-called "Red
Prince" who, however, seems to have vastly overrated his
own importance as a political and diplomatic figure. There
are a few worthwhile remarks about Weimar, but he himself comes over as something of a bore.

LÜDERS, Marie-Elizabeth.
Fürchte dich nicht: Persönliches und Politisches
aus mehr als 80 Jahren 1878—1962. Cologne:
Westdeutscher Verlag (1963), 247 pp.
Touches on Weimar, but says nothing of interest.

LUTHER, Hans.
Politiker ohne Partei: Erinnerungen. Stuttgart:
Deutsche Verlagsanstalt (1960), 437 pp.
Generally disappointing memoirs of the former Reich
Chancellor. In fact, this account extends only to the end of
his first period in office in December 1925. He spends
much of the time discussing economic and financial
matters, but does so rather ineffectively.

LUTHER, Hans.
Weimar und Bonn: zwei Vorträge. Munich: Isar
Verlag (1951), 48 pp.
The text of two unremarkable lectures given at Munich's
Hochschule für Politische Wissenschaften in January 1951.

MANGOLDT, Ursula von.
Auf der Schwelle zwischen gestern und morgen:
Begegnungen und Erlebnisse. Weilheim: Barth-
Verlag (1963), 241 pp.
Memoirs containing useful sketches of a few well-known
personalities in politics and the arts during the Weimar era.

MANN, Golo.
Deutsche Geschichte 1919—1945. Frankfurt:
Fischer (1961), 197 pp.
Highly competent survey for the general reader.

MATTHIAS, Erich.
"Zur Geschichte der Weimarer Republik: ein
Literaturbericht", *Die Neue Gesellschaft,* vol. 3,
pt. 4 (1956).
In this scholarly review of recent publications, Matthias
disagrees with the view (expressed by K. D. Erdmann,
among others) that the legacy of the conservative-authoritarian state (*Obrigkeitsstaat*) made the collapse of the
Republic inevitable.

MATTHIAS, Erich.
"Hindenburg zwischen den Fronten: zur Vorges-
chichte der Reichspräsidentenwahlen von 1932".
Vierteljahrshefte für Zeitgeschichte, vol. 8, pt. 1
(1960), p. 75—84.
Contains revealing documentation on this important and
complex aspect of late Weimar politics.

MATULL, Wilhelm.
Otto Braun, preussischer Ministerpräsident der Wei-
marer Zeit: Gedenkrede anlässlich seines 100.
Geburtstages am 4. März 1972. Dortmund:
Ostdeutsche Forschungsstelle (1973), 44 pp.
A somewhat over-appreciative summary of Braun's political
work.

McKENZIE, John R.
Weimar Germany 1918—1933. London: Blandford
Press (1971), 269 pp.
An uninspiring, dullish work which is little more than a
school textbook.

MEINECKE, Friedrich.
The German Catastrophe: Reflections and Recoll-
ections. Boston: Beacon Press (1963), 121 pp.
New ed.
A masterful and objective study of the social and historical
forces in Germany in the nineteenth and twentieth centuries
which produced National Socialism and led to Germany's
destruction in 1945. The author rejects the notion that the
triumph of Hitler was inevitable, arguing that there were
forces in Weimar which could have saved the Republic.

MEISSNER, Otto.
Staatssekretär unter Ebert-Hindenburg-Hitler:
der Schicksalsweg des deutschen Volkes von 1918
—1945, wie ich ihn erlebte. Hamburg: Hoffmann &
Campe (1950), 643 pp.
A valuable and revealing account, especially of the last
phase of the Republic and the top level intrigues (in
which Meissner himself figured prominently) which finally
brought Hitler to power.

MEYER, Henry C. (ed.).
The Long Generation: Germany from Empire to
Ruin, 1913—1945. New York: Harper & Row
(1973), 359 pp.
Consists of extracts from secondary works on major political, social and economic themes in Germany. Without an
accompanying critical commentary, the value of such an
approach is not readily perceptible. The editor's introduction is banal and does not attempt to put an overall
interpretation on the selected extracts.

MEYER, Henry C. (ed.).
Weimar and Nazi Germany. New York: Harper &
Row, (196?).
A volume in the Documentary History of Western Civil-
ization series which succeeds in presenting some illuminat-
ing documentary texts on the Weimar Republic. As editor,
Meyer has little of importance to say.

MEYER, Henry C.
Mitteleuropa in German Thought and Action, 1815
—1945. The Hague: Martinus Nijhoff (1955),
378 pp.
A much more satisfying volume than the same author's
aforementioned works. He fully explores and documents

11

the development of the *Mitteleuropa* concept in Germany, making clear the differences between this concept and Pan-Germanism and National Socialism. After 1918, *Mittel-europa* thought incorporated the idea of *Anschluss*, but in Weimar more radical racist and nationalistic ideas super-seded it. This objective study's main thesis that the *Mittel-europa* concept was of no practical importance is success-fully argued.

MICHAELIS, Herbert; SCHRAEPLER, Ernst;
SCHEEL, Günter (eds.).
Ursachen und Folgen: vom deutschen Zusammen-bruch 1918 und 1945 bis zur staatlichen Neuord-nung Deutschlands in der Gegenwart — eine Urkunden- und Dokumentensammlung zur Zeitges-chichte. 9 vols.
Berlin: Wendler (1958—64).
An important and extremely useful documentary source. Vols. IV—VIII are devoted to Weimar, the latter entitled "Das Ende des parlamentarischen Systems: Brüning — Papen — Schleicher 1930—33".

MIELCKE, Karl (ed.).
Dokumente zur Geschichte der Weimarer Republik. Brunswick: Verlag Limbach (1961), 110 pp.
A useful collection of documents on domestic and foreign policy matters. The deliberations of the National Assembly are well illustrated and the inaugural proclamations of the leading political parties are included. Germany's entry into the League of Nations is given considerable emphasis, though the 1930—33 period is largely neglected. There is no accompanying editorial commentary on the documents — a serious omission.

MIELCKE, Karl.
Geschichte der Weimarer Republik. Brunswick: Verlag Limbach (1951), 150 pp.
A dry narrative, now hopelessly outdated.

MORSEY, Rudolf.
"Vom Kommunalpolitiker zum Kanzler: die politische Rolle Adenauers in der Zeit der Weimarer Republik und in der Ära der Besatzungs-herrschaft (1919—1949)", In *Konrad Adenauer: Ziele und Wege*. Mainz: Hase & Koehler (1972), p. 13—81.
An authoritative and balanced (but not entirely un-sympathetic) analysis of Adenauer's early political career, including his controversial role in the Rhineland in the 1920s.

MUCKERMANN, Friedrich.
Im Kampf zwischen zwei Epochen: Lebenserinner-ungen. Edited by Nicolaus Junk. Mainz: Matthias-Grünewald-Verlag (1973), 667 pp.
Lively memoirs of a Jesuit priest who became a prominent opponent of the Third Reich. In Weimar, he was a leading protagonist of Catholic cultural ideas, but his book discusses wider aspects of the Republic's political and intell-ectual scene.

MÜLLER, Karl A.
Erinnerungen: im Wandel einer Welt, 1919—1932.
Vol. 3. Munich: Süddeutscher Verlag (1966), 334 pp.
The author was the brother-in-law of leading National Socialist Gottfried Feder, and had good connections with the NSDAP. Writing from a radical conservative stand-point, he offers some interesting notes on Weimar politics, especially in Bavaria.

MULLER, Klaus-Jürgen.
Schicksalsjahre deutscher Geschichte. Boppard: Boldt (1964), 304 pp.
The author constructs his competent narrative around what in his view were the "years of destiny" for Germany, 1914, 1939, and 1944.

MUTH, Heinrich.
"Literaturberichte: Zeitgeschichte: die innere Entwicklung der Weimarer Republik". *Geschichte in Wissenschaft und Unterricht*, vol. 7, pt. 7 (1956), p. 592—7.
A rather uninformative review of books on Weimar.

MUTH, Heinrich.
"Zeitgeschichte: Innenpolitik 1918—1933".
Geschichte in Wissenschaft und Unterricht, vol. 11, pt. 6 (1960), p. 498—511.
His selection of books is not exhaustive.

MUTH, Heinrich.
"Zeitgeschichte: Innenpolitik 1918—1933".
Geschichte in Wissenschaft und Unterricht, vol. 13 pt. 3 (1962), p. 311—28.
Same approach as noted above.

MUTH, Heinrich.
"Zeitgeschichte: Innenpolitik 1918—1933".
Geschichte in Wissenschaft und Unterricht, vol. 16 (1965), p. 582—96, 640—50.
A rather fuller review.

MUTH, Heinrich.
"Zeitgeschichte: Innenpolitik 1918—1933".
Geschichte in Wissenschaft und Unterricht, vol. 22 (1971), p. 562—76, 623—40.
The most complete review of literature on Weimar that the author has contributed in this series.

NEWMAN, Karl J.
"Multikausale und interdependente Faktoren des Weimarer Verfalls und des totalitären Sieges".
In F.A. Hermens & T. Schieder (eds.). *Staat, Wirtschaft und Politik in der Weimarer Republik: Festschrift für Heinrich Brüning*. Berlin: Duncker & Humblot (1967), p. 431—47.
An essay in historical methodology rather than one in historical analysis. The author comes to the unsurprising conclusion that the collapse of the Republic cannot be properly understood in terms of single factors.

NICHOLLS, Anthony J.
Weimar and the Rise of Hitler. London: Macmillan (1968), 203 pp.
Not much on National Socialism, but a good and clearly written narrative of major developments in the Republic. Intended for the general reader and junior undergraduates, this slim volume admirably fills that aim.

NICHOLLS, Anthony J.; MATTHIAS, Erich (eds.).
German Democracy and the Triumph of Hitler: Essays in Recent German History. London: Allen & Unwin (1971), 271 pp.
All eleven essays in this volume are thoughtful and inform-ative, and were first presented at seminars at the University of Mannheim and St. Antony's College, Oxford. See under individual authors: Erich Matthias, Lothar Albertin,

Michael Stürmer, Hans Boldt, Anthony Nicholls, Robin Lenman, Jill McIntyre, Tim Mason, and Werner Link.

NIEKISCH, Ernst.
Die Legende von der Weimarer Republik. Cologne: Verlag Wissenschaft und Politik (1968), 238 pp.
Readable reflections on Weimar politics by the famous National Bolshevik.

NISSEN, Rudolf.
Helle Blätter, dunkle Blätter. Stuttgart: Deutsche Verlagsanstalt (1969).
A fascinating autobiography of a medical specialist who was deeply interested in political and social themes during Weimar. In particular, he skilfully depicts the general atmosphere of Weimar and how the younger generation was affected.

PAPEN, Franz von.
Memoirs. London: André Deutsch (1952), 630 pp.
As perhaps was to be expected, the volume is thoroughly apologetic in tone; otherwise the book does not provide the kind of detailed information one might have anticipated from a former Chancellor and intriguer *par excellence*.

PAPEN, Franz von.
Vom Scheitern einer Demokratie, 1930—1933. Mainz: Hase & Koehler (1968), 408 pp.
This, his second set of memoirs, is not entirely free of the major faults of the first. Papen appears unaware of the major works already published on the collapse of the Republic, so that his own perspectives are largely out of focus. Moreover, his facts are not always reliable. To be treated very cautiously.

PHELPS, Reginald H.
The Crisis of the German Republic, 1930—32: Its Background and Course. Dissertation, Harvard University (1947).
No longer useful.

PLESSNER, Helmuth.
"Die Legende von den zwanziger Jahren". *Merkur,* vol. 16, pt. 1 (1962), p. 33—46.
Reflects somewhat ruefully on the present fascination with the 1920s and laments that the intellectual and cultural effort of the period was not put to more constructive use in view of what was to come after 1933. An impressionistic but thoughtful essay.

PROSS, Harry (ed.).
Die Zerstörung der deutschen Politik: Dokumente 1871—1933. Frankfurt: Fischer (1959), 380 pp.
The documents are carefully selected and edited.

PÜNDER, Hermann.
Politik in der Reichskanzlei: Aufzeichnungen aus den Jahren 1929—1932. Edited by Thilo Vogelsang. Stuttgart: Deutsche Verlagsanstalt (1961), 179 pp.
These diaries of State Secretary Pünder, who served in the Prussian and Reich civil service 1919—32 and who in 1926—32 was the senior ranking official in the Reich Chancellory, are an important source for the last years of Weimar (October 1929—October 1932). Particularly edifying are his comments on the Brüning era and on the Chancellor himself whom he admired. The diaries do not say much, however, about Hindenburg or the National Socialists.

PÜNDER, Hermann.
Von Preussen nach Europa: Lebenserinnerungen. Stuttgart: Deutsche Verlagsanstalt (1968).

Like the diaries, these memoirs make very interesting reading, especially, of course, for the Weimar period of which he has intimate knowledge.

RADBRUCH, Gustav.
Briefe. Göttingen: Vandenhoeck & Ruprecht (1968), 345 pp.
Radbruch was a former Minister of Justice in the Weimar period and he presents in this volume 284 letters written by him 1898—1943. Some of the correspondence was with leading public figures, but Radbruch's comments on the Republic and its politics are not perceptive.

RITTER, Gerhard.
Das deutsche Problem: Grundfragen deutschen Staatsleben gestern und heute. Munich: Oldenbourg (1962), 218 pp. (English ed.: **The German Problem: Basic Questions of German Political Life, Past and Present.** Columbus, Ohio: Ohio State U.P. (1965).)
A discussion of trends in recent German history whose purpose is to set National Socialism in a European rather than an exclusively German context. This leads the author to a very useful analysis of the causes of Weimar's demise.

RITTER, Gerhard (ed.).
Entstehung und Wandel der modernen Gesellschaft: Festschrift für Hans Rosenberg zum 65. Geburtstag. Berlin: de Gruyter (1970), 384 pp.
A collection of eleven papers divided into two parts: the first deals with the field of the theory and historiography of industrial society; the second concentrates on social groups and institutions. Of note for our purposes are articles by G.D. Feldman on the origins of the Stinnes-Legien agreement of November 1918, and by Ritter on the early Weimar party system (see under Feldman and Ritter respectively).

RITTER, Gerhard; ZIEBURA, Gilbert (eds.).
Faktoren der politischen Entscheidung: Festgabe für Ernst Fraenkel zum 65. Geburtstag. Berlin: de Gruyter (1963), 151 pp.
Sixteen papers of which only Wolfgang Scheffler's need concern us (see under Scheffler).

RÖHL, John C. G.
From Bismarck to Hitler: the Problem of Continuity in German History. London: Longman (1970), 191 pp.
A series of extracts from mainly secondary sources to illustrate major problems of German history 1870—1945. Part I is devoted to "The Roots of National Socialism"; Part II deals among other subjects with the 1918 Revolution, the foreign policy of the Weimar Republic, and the rise of National Socialism. A fuller and more explicit commentary would have enhanced the value of the book, which is designed for use by undergraduates.

ROSENBERG, Arthur.
Entstehung der Weimarer Republik. Frankfurt: Europäische Verlagsanstalt (1961), 265 pp. New ed.

ROSENBERG, Arthur.
Geschichte der Weimarer Republik. Frankfurt: Europäische Verlagsanstalt (1961), 258 pp.
Originally published in the 1930s, Rosenberg's work remains a stimulating but tendentious account of the rise and fall of the Republic. He writes from a Marxist viewpoint, emphasizing the significance of class in Weimar's political development. The study ends in 1930 because by then, he believes, the Republic's democratic system was finished and replaced by an authoritarian system which inevitably led to Hitler.

ROSSITER, Clinton L.
Constitutional Dictatorship: Crisis Government in the Modern Democracies. Princeton: Princeton University Press (1948), 432 pp.
A very general narrative of the western democracies and the Weimar Republic; on the latter, the author is not well informed.

RÖSSLER, Hellmuth; FRANZ, Günther (eds.).
Sachwörterbuch zur deutschen Geschichte. Munich: Oldenbourg (1956—58), 1472 pp.
This large volume is meant to be an objective and reliable reference source for events, personalities, parties, etc. in German history; it is thick on detail, but sparse on analysis. Yet there are significant factual errors in the treatment of some Weimar themes. More regrettably, there is considerable evidence of nationalistic and even anti-semitic bias.

ROTHFELS, Hans.
Zeitgeschichtliche Betrachtungen: Vorträge und Aufsätze. Göttingen: Vandenhoeck & Ruprecht (1959), 263 pp.
A collection of previously published lectures and articles by this outstanding German scholar. The themes are wide-ranging, but all relate to modern history.

RUGE, Wolfgang.
"Zur bürgerlichen Geschichtsschreibung der BRD über die Weimarer Republic". *Zeitschrift für Geschichtswissenschaft*, vol. 22, pt. 7 (1974), p. 677—700.
The leading East German historian severely castigates "bourgeois" West German historians for failing to get the perspectives and priorities right in their approach to the problems of the Weimar Republic. Above all, the lessons of Marxist-Leninism are lost on them, he declares.

RYDER, A. J.
Twentieth Century Germany: from Bismarck to Brandt. London: Macmillan (1973), 656 pp.
A careful, penetrating, and fluent synthesis. The section on Weimar is informed and balanced. Recommended for the general reader and undergraduates.

SALDERN, Adelheid von.
Hermann Dietrich: ein Staatsmann der Weimarer Republik. Boppard: Boldt (1966), 226 pp.
An able biography of Dietrich (1879—1954), a member of the German State Party and a Minister of Finance in the Brüning administration. Some of the observations on the general Weimar political situation are unsound.

SAPINSLEY, Barbara.
From Kaiser to Hitler: the Life and Death of a Democracy, 1919—1933. New York: Grosset (1968), 163 pp.
Superficial and lacking in conceptual framework.

SCHACHT, Hjalmar.
Sechsundsiebzig Jahre meines Lebens. Bad Wörishofen: Kindler und Schiermayer (1953), 689 pp.
Not uniformly interesting, but contains some observations on the Weimar era and financial policy which are worthy of attention. Schacht himself, vain, ambitious, and cunning, appears to have been a monumental bore.

SCHACHT, Hjalmar.
1933: wie eine Demokratie stirbt. Düsseldorf: Econ-Verlag (1968), 179 pp.

Schacht gives his reasons for the collapse of Weimar. They add little to what is already known.

SCHEELE, Godfrey.
The Weimar Republic: Overture to the Third Reich. London: Faber & Faber (1946), 360 pp.
The author's main hypothesis that the Third Reich was inchoate in the Weimar Republic, that the Republic was in effect doomed to failure, is doubtful. Otherwise, this is a vigorous and, in most respects, compelling critique of Weimar, above all of the capitalists, militarists, and bureaucrats who formed the backbone of the anti-democratic counter-revolution. A provocative study which presents one of the first revisionist interpretations of why the Republic collapsed.

SCHIEDER, Theodor.
Staat und Gesellschaft im Wandel unserer Zeit: Studien zur Geschichte des 19. und 20. Jahrhunderts. Munich: Oldenbourg (1958), 207 pp.
A volume of his articles, most of which have been published elsewhere. His major theme is the complex and fluctuating relationship between state and society in Germany during the nineteenth and twentieth centuries. The essays are philosophically oriented and are clearly influenced by the ideas of Max Weber. There is nothing specific on the Weimar period.

SCHIEDER, Theodor (ed.).
Beiträge zur Geschichte der Weimarer Republik. Munich: Oldenbourg (1971), 147 pp.
A collection of essays of which Heinrich Muth's study of Carl Schmitt is the most noteworthy (see under Muth in section 2).

SCHMOLKE, Michael.
"Reden und Redner vor den Reichspräsidentschaftswahlen im Jahre 1932". *Publizistik*, vol. 4, pt. 2 (1959), p. 97—117.
Principally concerned with an analysis of four major speeches during the campaign, by Goebbels, Kurt Walter, Ulbricht, and Brüning. Also examines the rhetorical methods employed by the NSDAP and in particular Hitler's opening speech of the campaign in the Berlin *Sportpalast* on 27 February. Informative, but Schmolke does not use any of the archival material that is available.

SCHOEPS, Hans J. (ed.).
Zeitgeist im Wandel. Vol. II: Zeitgeist der Weimarer Republik. Stuttgart: Klett (1968), 279 pp.
A general book which discusses a number of Weimar themes, the November Revolution, the position of the arts and education, and the role of the Churches. Appropriate for background reading.

SCHOEPS, Hans J.
Rückblicke: die letzten dreissig Jahre (1925—1955) und danach. Berlin: Haude & Spener (1963), 241 pp.
The author, a German Jew, records his admiration for the traditions of Prussianism, strange as it may seem. Most of the book revolves around this misplaced nostalgia, so that the only worthwhile sections are those in which he talks about the Jewish question and the *Bündische* youth movement.

SCHOEPS, Hans J.
"Das letzte Vierteljahr der Weimarer Republik im Zeitschriftenecho". *Geschichte in Wissenschaft und Unterricht*, vol. 7 (1956), p. 464—72.
A cursory look at how contemporary journals reported the last few months before the Republic's collapse.

SCHREEB, Gerhard.
**Demokratie in Deutschland: Weimarer Republik —
Bundesrepublik; ein Vergleich.** Osnabrück: Fromm
(1962), 106 pp.
An unconvincing attempt to compare the substance and
structure of the two democratic periods in twentieth century German history.

SCHREIBER, Georg.
**Zwischen Demokratie und Diktatur: persönliche
Erinnerungen an die Politik und Kultur des Reiches
(1919—1944).** Regensberg: Regensbergsche Verlags-
buchhandlung (1949), 149 pp.
Unrevealing and badly written memoirs.

SCHREINER, Albert.
**"Zu einigen Fragen der neuesten deutschen
Geschichte".** *Zeitschrift für Geschichtswissenschaft,*
vol. 3, pt. 3 (1955), p. 374—430.
The well-known East German historian adopts a typically
rigid Marxist-Leninist line in this general discussion of the
Second Reich and the Weimar Republic. He is at pains to
criticize the SPD's "betrayal" of the German working class
in the face of fascism. Best forgotten.

SCHULZ, Gerhard.
**"Der 'Nationale Klub von 1919' zu Berlin: zum
politischen Zerfall einer Gesellschaft".** *Jahrbuch
zur Geschichte Mittel- und Ostdeutschlands,* vol.
11 (1962), p. 207—37.
The most authoritative account available on the steady
decline of this aristocratic/conservative establishment.
Schulz argues that its decline was a reflection of wider
political and social changes in Weimar.

SCHULZ, Gerhard.
"Die grosse Krise in der Zeitgeschichte". *Neue
Politische Literatur,* vol. 4 (1959).
Too general to be of use in comprehending Weimar develop-
ments.

SCHWARZ, Albert (ed.).
"Die Weimarer Republik". In Brandt-Meyer-Just
(eds.). *Handbuch der Deutschen Geschichte. Vol.
IV.* Konstanz: Akademische Verlagsgesellschaft
(1958), 232 pp.
A sound book, valuable for a detailed and knowledgeable
exposition of Weimar's economic and financial development. The author also writes well on cultural aspects. The
main emphasis is on the 1919—23 period and all major
themes therein are handled admirably. He believes the depression was the fundamental cause of Weimar's collapse.

SCHWARZ, Gotthart.
**"Krise des Parteienstaates oder Problematik des
Präsidialsystems? Zur Kontroverse um die 'Auflö-
sung der Weimarer Republik'".** *Geschichte in
Wissenschaft und Unterricht,* vol. 20, pt. 11—12
(1969), p. 683—9.
A brief look at the debate over where the main emphasis
should be put in the factors causing the Republic's collapse.
For the non-specialist.

SELL, Friedrich C.
Die Tragödie des deutschen Liberalismus. Stuttgart:
Deutsche Verlagsanstalt (1953).
A very broad but generally helpful survey of the problems
of liberal and parliamentary development in modern
Germany.

SEVERING, Carl.
Mein Lebensweg. 2 vols. Cologne: Verlag Greven
(1950).
Volume I of the former SPD minister's important memoirs
extends to 1923; Volume II covers 1924—50. A record of
his struggle against the foes of democracy in Prussia and the
Reich before 1933.

SMITH, David.
Left and Right in Twentieth Century Europe.
London: Longman (1970), 117 pp.
The theme of extremist political movements battling for
power is very apt for the Weimar situation. In some respects,
this book complements Lionel Kochan's *The Struggle for
Germany 1914—45* (see earlier in this section).

SNYDER, Louis L.
**The Weimar Republic: a History of Germany from
Ebert to Hitler.** New York: Van Nostrand (1966),
223 pp.
Too general, though it does contain a fairly useful docu-
mentary section which includes extracts from the Spartacist
Manifesto of November 1918, the Treaty of Versailles, the
Rapallo Pact, and Hitler's Düsseldorf speech to Rhenish
industrialists in January 1932.

SNYDER, Louis L. (ed.).
Documents of German History. New Brunswick:
Rutgers University Press (1958), 642 pp.
Half the book is devoted to the 1900—60 period, though
Weimar is covered in a mere twenty-two pages. Even then,
the documents selected do little to illustrate the nature of
Weimar's political development.

SONTHEIMER, Kurt.
**"The Weimar Republic — Failure and Prospects of
German Democracy".** In E. J. Feuchtwanger (ed.).
*Upheaval and Continuity: a Century of German
History.* London: Oswald Wolff (1973),
p. 101—15.
A brief survey (without footnotes) of the chances of
democracy and the challenges it faced in Weimar. The
author argues that the Republic had certain things in its
favour in the beginning, including the support of a majority
of Germans, but concedes it was an improvization which
was almost immediately confronted by towering odds. He
concludes by reflecting on the healthier state of democracy
in the present Federal Republic.

SONTHEIMER, Kurt.
**Deutschland zwischen Demokratie und Antidemo-
kratie.** Munich: Nymphenburger Verlagshandlung
(1971), 275 pp.
A mature discussion of the development of political consciousness in Germany and the traditional struggle for
supremacy between the forces of democracy and reaction.

SONTHEIMER, Kurt.
**"Weimar — ein deutsches Kaleidoskop. Mit einem
Nachwort über Bonn".** *Merkur,* vol. 27 (1973),
p. 505—17.
Virtually the same essay as noted above.

STAMPFER, Friedrich.
Die ersten 14 Jahre der deutschen Republik.
Hamburg: Auerdrück Verlag (1952), 690 pp.
The author was a moderate member of the SPD and his
narrative, full but somewhat discursive, faithfully mirrors
that outlook. His analysis of the reasons for Weimar's
collapse and the victory of Hitler is ingenuous.

STAMPFER, Friedrich.
Erfahrungen und Erkenntnisse: Aufzeichnungen aus meinem Leben. Cologne: Verlag für Politik und Wirtschaft (1957), 299 pp.
These memoirs are valuable for insights into the history and development of the SPD in Weimar. As a one-time chief editor of *Vorwärts*, Stampfer was well placed to gain a thorough understanding of party policy and tactics.

STEINBERGER, Walter.
Die Entwicklung der Demokratie in Deutschland von 1918—1933. Dissertation, University of Munich (1951).
A competent survey in its day, but now hopelessly out of date, of course.

STERN, Fritz.
"Adenauer and a Crisis in Weimar Democracy". *Political Science Quarterly*, vol. 73, pt. 1 (1958), p 1—27.
Explains why Adenauer and Stresemann could not stand the sight of each other following a bitter quarrel.

STRIBRNY, Wolfgang.
"Kronprinz Wilhelm und den Reichspräsidentswahl 1932". In *Geschichte in der Gegenwart: Festschrift für Kurt Kluxen.* Edited by Ernst Heinen and Hans J. Schoeps. Paderborn: Ferdinand Schöningh Verlag (1972).
Deals with the Crown Prince's candidature for the Reich Presidency in 1932. The Kaiser eventually persuaded him to drop the idea. What is interesting, however, is the evidence that the Crown Prince's aim was to approximate to the NSDAP and perhaps play a role *vis-à-vis* Hitler similar to the Mussolini-King Victor Emmanuel III relationship. The author's apologetic conclusion seems sadly out of place.

TORMIN, Walter (ed.).
Die Weimarer Republik. Hanover: Verlag für Literatur und Zeitgeschehen (1962), 306 pp.
Yet another collection of articles by various hands, none of which is particularly noteworthy.

UNKELBACH, Helmut.
"Ursachen des Zusammenbruchs der Weimarer Republik und ihre Lehren". In F. A. Hermens & T. Schieder (eds.). *Staat, Wirtschaft, und Politik in der Weimarer Republik: Festschrift für Heinrich Brüning.* Berlin: Duncker & Humblot (1967), p. 393—429.
This is the first time this reviewer has come across a case where a historical problem is dealt with in terms of mathematical formulae. Unkelbach uses a series of symbols to work out the causes of the Republic's collapse, so that anyone looking for a conventionally presented essay will be disappointed. His approach, novel though it may be, is unhelpful to say the least, for, at the end of the mathematical juggling, Unkelbach does not come up with any new ideas.

VERMEIL, Edmond.
Doctrinaires de la révolution allemande (1918—1938). Paris: Nouvelles Editions Latines (1948), 333 pp.
Fairly ordinary portraits of leading Weimar personalities including Rathenau, Hitler, and Spengler.

VERMEIL, Edmond.
Germany's Three Reichs: Their History and Culture. London: Andrew Dakers (1945), 420 pp.

Chapter VII is entitled "Weimar Republic and National Socialist Party", but there is hardly anything on the former.

VERMEIL, Edmond.
Germany in the Twentieth Century: a Political and Cultural History of the Weimar Republic and the Third Reich. New York: Praeger (1956), 288 pp.
Not to be counted among the best general histories of Weimar and even less so than of Hitler's Germany.

VIERHAUS, Rudolf.
"Die politische Mitte in der Weimarer Republik". *Geschichte in Wissenschaft und Unterricht*, vol. 15, pt. 3 (1964), p. 133—49.
Rather sketchy; compares unfavourably with the work in this field of Larry Jones (see earlier in this section).

VIETSCH, Eberhard von.
Wilhelm Solf, Botschafter zwischen den Zeiten. Tübingen: Wunderlich Verlag (1961), 403 pp.
Absorbing in places but not when he discusses the Weimar period (p. 194—312).

VOGELSANG, Thilo.
"Neuere Literatur zur Geschichte der Weimarer Republik". *Vierteljahrshefte für Zeitgeschichte*, vol. 9, pt. 2 (1961), p. 211—24.
A critical review of some literature on Weimar political history published 1946—60. Judicious, and containing an excellent appraisal of *Das Ende der Parteien*, edited by Erich Matthias and Rudolf Morsey.

VOGELSANG, Thilo.
"Zur Geschichte der Weimarer Republik". *Neue Politische Literatur*, vol. 3, pt. 6 (1958), p. 421—30.
Another review of new books on Weimar. Brief but reveals, as usual, uncanny judgement.

VOGT, Hannah.
The Burden of Guilt: a Short History of Germany 1914—1945. London: Oxford University Press (1964), 318 pp.
Marked by an unusually bitter tone, this volume leaves much to be desired in terms of scholarly objectivity.

VOLKMANN, Hans-Erich.
Die russische Emigration in Deutschland 1919—1929. Würzburg: Holzner (1966), 154 pp.
Treats that part of the Russian emigration to Europe after 1917 which settled in Germany and, in particular, those émigrés of monarchist sympathies. The author discusses their political and social attitudes and the manner in which successive German governments regarded them. Not an exhaustive study, but a diligently prepared introduction to a complex topic.

WEHLER, Hans-Ulrich (ed.).
Eckart Kehr, der Primat der Innenpolitik: gesammelte Aufsätze zur preussisch-deutschen Sozialgeschichte im 19. u. 20. Jahrhundert. Berlin: de Gruyter (1965), 292 pp.
A well edited collection of Kehr's brilliant essays, whose major theme is a sharp assessment of the socio-economic basis of German domestic and military policy in the modern period. Topics discussed include the officer corps, the Prussian bureaucracy, and the armaments industry; there is also a paper on German historiography in the Weimar era in which he roundly criticizes Meinecke's *Ideengeschichte*. Original, provocative, and highly recommended.

WERESZYCKI, Henryk.
"From Bismarck to Hitler: the Problems of
Continuity from the Second to the Third Reich".
Polish Western Affairs, vol. 14, pt. 1 (1973), p.
19—32.
A valuable and thought-provoking contribution to a much
debated theme.

WHEATON, Eliot B.
Prelude to Calamity: the Nazi Revolution 1933—
1935. With a Background Survey of the Weimar
Era. London: Victor Gollancz (1969), 523 pp.
The Weimar section (p. 3—182) has taken account of the
findings of most important studies. A useful synthesis for
the junior undergraduate.

WHEELER-BENNETT, John W.
"The End of the Weimar Republic". *Foreign
Affairs*, vol. 50, pt. 2 (1972), p. 351—71.
A review of the causes of Weimar's collapse without refer-
ence to footnotes or archival sources. He concludes that
"the tragedy of Brüning is the tragedy of Weimar"; the
Chancellor's fatal error was to have trusted Hindenburg.

WIEDNER, Wolfgang.
Theodor Heuss: das Demokratie- und
Staatsverständnis im Zeitablauf; Betrachtungen der
Jahre 1902—1963. Ratingen: Henn (1973), 200 pp.
Elegantly written and sensitive study, with sensible things
to say about Weimar politics.

WILLIAMS, Robert C.
Culture in Exile: Russian Émigrés in Germany
1881—1941. London: Cornell University Press
(1972), 404 pp.
A detailed and informative study which goes much deeper
into the political and social situation of the *émigrés* than
Volkmann's book (see above). Particular stress is laid on the
activities of Jews and Baltic Germans, the author considering the latter to have exerted significant influence in the
early NSDAP. The political attitudes of the *émigrés* as a
whole, however, ranged from extreme left to extreme right.
There are unfortunately a large number of factual errors,
and a tendency to simplify certain issues, notably in the
second part of the book which covers the period 1923—41.

ZECHLIN, Walter.
Pressechef bei Ebert, Hindenburg und Kopf:
Erlebnisse eines Pressechef und Diplomaten.
Hanover: Verlag Schlüter (1956), 234 pp.
Provides a few details, none of them of great moment,
about the work of the Reich Presidents.

ZONDEK, Hermann.
"Recollections from the Days of Weimar". *Year-
book of the Leo Baeck Institute*, vol. 12 (1967),
p. 213—26.
The author was one of Weimar's most outstanding physic-
ians and endocrinologists. He records his impressions of
Stresemann, the Kellogg Pact, a lecture tour he made to
Russia in 1932, and Schleicher (who was also a patient).

2

Constitutional and Political History and Theory

ALBERTIN, Lothar.
"Parlamentarismus — Forschung zwischen Theorie und Praxis". *Neue Politische Literatur*, vol. 15 (1970), p. 332—42.
The author's main purpose is to discuss the functioning of the parliamentary system 1923—28.

ALBERTIN, Lothar.
"Kabinette ohne politische Perspective". *Neue Politische Literatur*, vol. 17 (1972), p. 490—500.
A brief discussion of the failings of a number of cabinets in Weimar, including the *Rat der Volksbeauftragten*, the Müller cabinets of the early 1920s, as well as those of Fehrenbach (1920—21) and Cuno (1922—23).

APELT, Willibalt.
Geschichte der Weimarer Verfassung. Munich: Beck (1964), 461 pp. Second ed.
Useful as an introduction to the topic.

ARETIN, Kurt O. von.
"Die Verfassungstreue am Ende der Weimarer Republik". *Frankfurter Hefte*, vol. 22, pt. 3 (1967), p. 161—8.[1]
Argues that loyalty to the constitution had been so debilitated by January 1933 that Hitler had no problems in destroying it. For this state of affairs, Brüning must bear considerable responsibility because, according to the author, his monarchist sympaties caused him to plan the overthrow of the constitutional order in the Republic. The conclusion is sound.

BAUER, Wolfram.
Wertrelativismus und Wertbestimmtheit im Kampf um die Weimarer Demokratie: zur Politologie des Methodenstreites der Staatsrechtslehrer. Berlin: Duncker & Humblot (1968), 462 pp.
A searching analysis of the inadequacies of the discipline of *Staatsrechtslehre* as a contributory factor to the eventual collapse of the Republic, principally because the discipline saddled the Republic with a fundamental and permanent doubt about its legitimacy. The resulting discrepancy between its legality and legitimacy allowed its political opponents greater latitude than would have been normal in attacking republican institutions. This involved work discusses the discipline with regard to the ideas of four leading students of *Staatsrechtslehre*, Erich Kaufmann, Hermann Heller, Rudolf Smend, and Hans Kelsen.

1. Republished as "Verfassung und Verfassungsuntreu" in the same journal, vol. 30, pt. 1 (1975), p. 19—26.

BAUER, Wolfram.
"Wertrelativismus und Wertbestimmtheit im Kampf um die Weimarer Demokratie: zum Methodenstreit der Staatsrechtslehrer und seiner Bedeutung für die Politologie". *Vierteljahrshefte für Zeitgeschichte*, vol. 16, pt. 3 (1968), p. 209—29.
Contains a summary of the main conclusions reached in Bauer's monograph.

BAY, Jürgen.
Der Preussenkonflikt 1932—33: ein Kapitel aus der Verfassungsgeschichte der Weimarer Republik. Erlangen: Hogl-Verlag (1965), 283 pp.
An adequate examination of the main constitutional and legal implications of Papen's coup against Prussia. To be read in conjunction with broader studies of the topic (see section 4G).

BEERK, Georg.
Das parlamentarische System der Weimarer Reichsverfassung. Dissertation, University of Hamburg (1948).
A theoretical work which explores the legalistic and *staatswissenschaftliche* aspects of the Weimar constitution.

BENDERSKY, Joseph W.
The Politics of an Intellectual: the Political Activity and Ideas of Carl Schmitt 1910—1945. Dissertation, Michigan State University (1975), 389 pp.
A self-styled "revisionist" interpretation which tries to see Schmitt's work in a wider perspective and not only in relation to his links with National Socialism. On the basis of some new material, it is argued that Schmitt, far from being a proponent of National Socialism before 1933, actually worked for the stabilization of the Weimar Republic. This hypothesis needs further elaboration and evidence before it can be taken seriously.

BESSON, Waldemar.
"Zur Frage der Staatsführung in der Weimarer Republik". *Vierteljahrshefte für Zeitgeschichte*, vol. 7, pt. 1 (1959), p. 85—111.
The author provides the text of a talk given to the *Deutsche Hochschule für Politik* on 5 July 1929 by sociologist Alexander Rüstrow, as well as a record of part of the discussion which followed among various intellectuals and

18

politicians, including Theodor Heuss. The problem they were dealing with was how to secure the state's authority in a free democratic society, and Rüstrow's remarks anticipated the presidential cabinet system which replaced parliamentary democracy in March 1930.

BOOKBINDER, Paul.
From the "other judge" to the "other German": Carl Schmitt 1910—1936. Dissertation, Brandeis University (1972).
A brief and not altogether satisfactory look at some aspects of Schmitt's thought. The author considers the basis of Schmitt's gradual disillusionment with the Republic and with liberal parliamentarianism, and his growing propensity to National Socialism. In place of democracy, Schmitt came to place his faith in a radical brand of totalitarian democracy.

BRACHER, Karl-Dietrich.
Die Entstehung der Weimarer Verfassung. Hanover: Hannoversche Druck- und Verlagsgesellschaft (1963), 66 pp.
A short but incisive study of how the constitution finally came about.

FIJALKOWSKI, Jürgen.
Die Wendung zum Führerstaat: ideologische Komponenten der politischen Philosophie Carl Schmitts. Cologne: Westdeutscher Verlag (1958), 222 pp.
An excellent, objective and scholarly investigation of a daunting task, namely, an analysis of Schmitt's ideas on social structure and constitutional problems and his later support for totalitarianism. The author pinpoints where Schmitt went wrong in his thinking and how, paradoxically, his errors eventually led him to the conclusion he had wanted from the beginning, that democracy had no future in Weimar and that a totalitarian solution was necessary. Hence, his acceptance of the *Führerstaat*.

FROMME, Friedrich K.
Von der Weimarer Verfassung zum Bonner Grundgesetz: die verfassungspolitischen Folgerungen des parlamentarischen Rates aus Weimarer Republik und nationalsozialistischer Diktatur. Tübingen: Mohr (1960), 243 pp.
A thoroughly researched work which demonstrates in clear detail the precise nature of the Weimar constitution's influence on the shaping of the Bonn "Basic Law" of 1949. That influence was considerable, for the men of 1949 were determined to learn the constitutional lessons of the Weimar era. The author also furnishes a balanced analysis of the ways in which constitutional defects hastened the fall of Weimar.

GRASSMANN, Siegfried.
Hugo Preuss und die deutsche Selbstverwaltung. Lübeck: Matthiesen (1965), 130 pp.
An assessment of the origins and development of Preuss's political and administrative ideas, in which an important influence was Otto von Gierke's theory of the organic nature of state institutions. Adequate but by no means exhaustive.

GREEN, Allen T.
Hugo Preuss and the Weimar Constitution. Dissertation, Emory University (1965).
Treats his career and development of ideas on constitutional theory before 1918, and examines his role in the making of the Weimar constitution. Green argues that Preuss wielded most influence in the preparatory stages of the drafting process, but that his influence declined thereafter as Ebert was obliged to make concessions to the forces of particularism. He therefore concludes that the final draft actually reflected very few of Preuss's original conceptions. A thought-provoking study.

GROSSER, Dieter.
Volker Nietzschke und Jochen Winkler: die Weimarer Verfassung. Sarstedt: Sarstedter Verlag (1960), 44 pp.
Wholly inconsequential.

HARTUNG, Fritz.
Deutsche Verfassungsgeschichte vom 15. Jahrhundert bis zur Gegenwart. Stuttgart: Koehler (1950), 375 pp.
Gives a brief survey of developments concerning the Weimar constitution (p. 315—43).

HERZFELD, Hans.
Demokratie und Selbstverwaltung in der Weimarer Epoche. Stuttgart: Kohlhammer (1957), 51 pp.
Discusses the origins of communal self-government in Germany and how it basically functioned in Weimar. He also analyses communal self-government's relation to democracy.

HOFMANN, Hasso.
Legitimität gegen Legalität: der Weg der politischen Philosophie Carl Schmitts. Neuwied: Luchterhand (1964), 304 pp.
A thoroughly documented and scholarly appraisal of the work and theories of Schmitt. Hofmann rejects the notion that Schmitt was an opportunist, arguing that in fact he developed intellectually as a reactionary political theorist and ideologue.

HOFMANN, Wolfgang.
Zwischen Rathaus und Reichskanzlei: die Oberbürgermeister in der Kommunal- und Staatspolitik des deutschen Reiches von 1890—1933. Stuttgart: Kohlhammer (1974).
The most authoritative and comprehensive study of the constitutional position of the office of mayor in German local government. In Weimar, his role was made extremely difficult by the competing authorities of state and national government, but he retained considerable importance.

HOFMANN, Wolfgang.
"Plebiszitäre Demokratie und kommunale Selbstverwaltung in der Weimarer Republik". *Archiv für Kommunalwissenschaft*, vol. 4 (1965), p. 264—81.
Examines the implications for communal self-government of the concept of plebiscitary democracy. Heavy but rewarding.

HUBER, Ernst R. (ed.).
Quellen zum Staatsrecht der Neuzeit. Vol. 2: Deutsche Verfassungsdokumente der Gegenwart (1919—1951). Lübeck: Matthiesen (1951), 694 pp.
A most valuable and well organized documentary collection.

JEPSEN, C. H.
The Influence of the Multi-Party System on Representative Government in Germany under the Weimar Constitution. Dissertation, University of Oxford (1956).
Hardly conclusive since it is not based on very extensive source material.

KNOLL, J. H.
"Der autoritäre Staat, Konservative Ideologie und Staatstheorie am Ende der Weimarer Republik". *Politische Studien*, vol. 10, pt. 1 (1959), p. 159—64.
A superficial examination of authoritarian attitudes towards the state during the last phase of the Republic.

KODALLE, Klaus-Michael.
Politik als Macht und Mythos: Carl Schmitts Politische Theologie. Stuttgart: Kohlhammer (1973), 154 pp.
Updates Fijalkowski's work slightly, but does not supersede it.

KRIEGER, Leonard; STERN, Fritz (eds.).
The Responsibility of Power. New York: Doubleday (1967), 464 pp.
A collection of 24 essays whose main theme is political power, its application in theory and practice; the book's third section is entitled "The Dilemma of Power in the Democratic Age", and includes illustrations from Weimar. Useful for background reading to the political and constitutional problems confronting the Republic.

KROCKOW, Christian.
Die Entscheidung: eine Untersuchung über Ernst Jünger, Carl Schmitt, Martin Heidegger. Stuttgart: Ferdinand Enke Verlag (1958), 164 pp.
An unsuccessful attempt to describe, compare and contrast the ideas of these different brands of right-wing political theorists.

LOEWENSTEIN, Karl.
"Max Weber als 'Ahnherr' des plebiszitären Führerstaates". *Kölner Zeitschrift für Soziologie- und Sozialpsychologie*, vol. 13 (1961), p. 275—89.
A stimulating and fair discussion of the relation of Weber's ideas to authoritarian modes of government.

MASTE, Ernst.
"Hugo Preuss: Vater der Weimarer Verfassung. Zur 100. Wiederkehr des Geburtstages von Hugo Preuss am 28. Oktober". *Das Parlament: Aus Politik und Zeitgeschichte*, B43/60 (26.10.1960).
A brief appreciation of Preuss's role in the making of the constitution.

MASTE, Ernst.
Die Republik der Nachbarn: die Nachbarschaft und der Staatsgedanke Artur Mahraums. Giessen: Walltor-Verlag (1957), 219 pp.
A study of the constitutional theories of the former leader of the *Jungdeutsche Orden* under whose influence the group forsook extreme nationalism and came to accept democracy.

MOMMSEN, Wolfgang.
"Zum Begriff der 'plebiszitären Führerdemokratie' bei Max Weber". *Kölner Zeitschrift für Soziologie- und Sozial-psychologie*, vol. 15 (1963), p. 295—322.
An excellent paper, best read in conjunction with Karl Loewenstein's work on the same topic (see earlier).

MOMMSEN, Wolfgang.
Max Weber und die deutsche Politik 1890—1920. Tübingen: Mohr (1974), 586 pp. New ed.
A definitive analysis of Weber's ideas and career written with rare understanding and penetration. He explains the nationalist and expansionist outlook of Weber in foreign policy, and the retardative influence of his philosophy on democratic development at home.

MUTH, Heinrich.
"Carl Schmitt in der deutschen Innenpolitik des Sommers 1932". In T. Schieder (ed.). *Beiträge zur Geschichte der Weimarer Republik.* Supplement to *Historische Zeitschrift* (1971), p. 75—147.
Admirably documented, the essay establishes the importance of Schmitt's influence on constitutional questions in the hectic summer of 1932.

NEEDLER, Martin.
"Theory of the Weimar Presidency". *Review of Politics*, vol. 21 (1959), p. 692—9.
Concerned with explaining the origins and evolution of the office of Reich President, and discusses his role in constitutional theory and practice 1930—33, stressing the peculiar problem of the presidential cabinet which was able to emerge due to fundamental weaknesses in the constitution. Concludes that the development of the presidential cabinet was implicit in the ambiguous position of the cabinet in the constitution. Needler raises a number of interesting points but does not sufficiently develop any of them. The paper is altogether too brief for the importance of the theme.

PIKART, Eberhard.
"Ein Brief Kurt Riezlers an den Hamburger Bürgermeister Petersen vom 1. Februar 1924". *Vierteljahrshefte für Zeitgeschichte*, vol. 15, pt. 2 (1967), p. 211—18.
The letter from Riezler to a political friend, Carl Wilhelm Petersen (1868—1933), *Reichstag* deputy, one-time chairman of the DDP, and Mayor of Hamburg 1924—27 and 1931—33. Riezler argues for a revision of the Weimar constitution, incorporating aspects of the Prussian-Reich relationship of the Bismarckian constitution. *Coup d'état* methods should be used to effect this change if necessary, he adds. The letter reveals that even true democrats like Riezler were dissatisfied with the constitution as it stood.

POLAK, Karl.
Die Weimarer Verfassung: ihre Errungenschaften und Mängel. East Berlin: Kongress-Verlag (1952), 64 pp.
Of little value.

PORTNER, Ernst.
Die Verfassungspolitik der Liberalen 1919: ein Beitrag zur Deutung der Weimarer Reichsverfassung. Bonn: Röhrscheid (1973), 278 pp.
An important study of liberal/democratic attitudes to constitutional questions at the outset of the Republic. Carefully researched and powerfully argued.

PORTNER, Ernst.
"Koch-Wesers Verfassungsentwurf: ein Beitrag zur Ideengeschichte der deutschen Emigration". *Vierteljahrshefte für Zeitgeschichte*, vol. 14, pt. 3 (1966), p. 280—98.
A sympathetic and informative essay on the career of Erich Koch-Weser (1879—1944), former DDP leader and chairman of its parliamentary faction. He was an influential member of the committee which drew up the Weimar constitution, and Portner discusses his constitutional ideas on government. Koch-Weser emerges as one of the most perceptive, humane and moderate politicians of the Weimar era.

POTTHOFF, Heinrich.
"Das Weimarerverfassungswerk und die deutsche Linke". *Archiv für Sozialgeschichte*, vol. 12 (1972), p. 433—83.
Analyses the demands relating to a new constitution in 1918—19 made by various groups, including the Indepen-

dent Social Democrats (USPD). In an extremely detailed and vigorously argued paper, Potthoff demonstrates the gulf between the final version of the constitution and what the socialist Left had actually wanted. The essay is in addition one of the best up-to-date discussions of the strengths and weaknesses of the constitution.

PÜNDER, Hermann.
Der Reichspräsident in der Weimarer Republik.
Frankfurt: Athenäum-Verlag (1961), 27 pp.
An outline of the function and significance of the office.

REVERMANN, Klaus.
Die stufenweise Durchbrechung des Verfassungs-systems der Weimarer Republik in den Jahren 1930 bis 1933: eine staatsrechtliche und historisch-politische Analyse. Münster: Aschendorff (1959), 175 pp.
An incisive monograph which, in analysing the period March 1930—March 1933, concludes that the Republic collapsed not so much because of the weaknesses of the constitutional and party systems, but because of the human failings of the political and governmental leadership. They did not do enough to defend democracy, and this the author believes was fundamentally due to a lack of demo-cratic spirit among the German people at large.

RIBHEGGE, Wilhelm.
"Die Systemfunktion der Gemeinden: zur deutschen Kommunalgeschichte seit 1918". *Das Parlament: Aus Politik und Zeitgeschichte*, B47 (24.11.1973).
A rounded discussion of a number of themes relating to communal self-government, including communal democracy during the November Revolution, the development of communal self-government in Weimar and the attitudes of the major parties to it.

SCHEUNER, Ulrich.
"Die Anwendung des Artikels 48 der Weimarer Reichsverfassung unter den Präsidentschaften von Ebert und Hindenburg". In F. A. Hermens & T. Schieder (eds.). *Staat, Wirtschaft und Politik in der Weimarer Republik: Festschrift für Heinrich Brüning* (1967), p. 249—86.
Compares and contrasts the use made of Article 48 by Ebert and Hindenburg, the one to defend democracy in the early 1920s, the other to help destroy democracy in the early 1930s. His discussion of Ebert's implementation of the Article is the most useful part of the paper because his explanation of Hindenburg's abuses adds nothing new to our understanding of the presidential cabinet phenomenon.

SCHIEDER, Theodor.
"Das Verhältnis von politischer und gesellschaft-licher Verfassung und die Krise des bürgerlichen Liberalismus". *Historische Zeitschrift*, vol. 177 (1954), p. 49—74.
A valuable and in some respects provocative essay.

SCHIFFERS, Reinhard.
Elemente direkter Demokratie im Weimarer Regierungssystem. Düsseldorf: Droste (1971), 323 pp.
A solid but in places rather dull contribution. The author examines the various procedures of direct democracy set up by the constitution, the different views of their appropriat-ness taken by leading Weimar politicians and intellectuals, and the influence of South German constitutions in these respects on the Reich constitution. He is critical of the political parties for abusing direct democratic institutions for selfish ends, and there can be little quarrel with that conclusion.

SCHLUCHTER, Wolfgang.
Entscheidung für den sozialen Rechtsstaat: Hermann Heller und die staatstheoretische Diskussion in der Weimarer Republik. Cologne: Kiepenheuer & Witsch (1968), 300 pp.
Heller, a socialist, was an original but obscure political theorist in the Weimar era who was fascinated by the dynamics of power. The author adequately outlines the substance of Heller's theories though not always as clearly as one would have wished.

SCHMITT, Carl.
Verfassungsrechtliche Aufsätze aus den Jahren 1924—1954. Berlin: Duncker & Humblot (1958), 517 pp.
The essays gathered together in this volume provide a thoroughly representative selection of Schmitt's constitut-ional and political theories.

SCHÖNE, Siegfried.
Von der Reichskanzlei zum Bundeskanzleramt. Berlin: Duncker & Humblot (1968).
A perceptive analysis of the reasons why the Reich Chan-cellor 1890—1933 did not exercise effective control over the government. Many of the restrictions on his power were legacies from the Wilhelmine era; the influence of the army, the absence of stable *Reichstag* support, and the competing authority of the Reich President all combined to weaken the Chancellor's position. The study broadens our know-ledge of the manner in which central government worked in Weimar.

SCHULZ, Gerhard.
Zwischen Demokratie und Diktatur: Verfassung-spolitik und Reichsreform in der Weimarer Republik. Berlin: de Gruyter (1963), 678 pp.
A voluminous, detailed, and on the whole penetrating inves-tigation of Weimar's constitutional history 1919—30, with emphasis on the complex problems of federalism and unitarianism; the author shows how a compromise of sorts was reached between the two. He illustrates his discussion by analysing the series of crises in Reich-*Länder* relations, including those involving Bavaria. The role of the *Reichsrat* in the Reich-*Land* conflict is shown to have been surpris-ingly effective. Finally, the whole question of *Reichsreform* is amply documented.

SONTHEIMER, Kurt.
"Der antiliberale Staatsgedanke in der Weimarer Republik". *Politische Vierteljahrsschrift*, vol. 3, pt. 1 (1962), p. 25—42.
A theme which the author elaborates on in his outstanding study of anti-democratic thought in Weimar. Here, he out-lines the main lines of argument of that standpoint.

SONTHEIMER, Kurt.
"Die Idee des Reiches im politischen Denken der Weimarer Republik". *Geschichte in Wissenschaft und Unterricht*, vol. 13, pt. 4 (1962), p. 205—21.
An able exposition of different political attitudes to the concept of a Reich.

SONTHEIMER, Kurt.
"Zur Grundlagenproblematik der deutschen Staatsrechtslehre in der Weimarer Republik". *Archiv für Rechts- und Sozialphilosophie*, vol. 46, pt. 1 (1960), p. 39—71.
A clear and mature consideration of the main problems surrounding the role of the *Staatsrechtslehre* discipline in the constitutional history of Weimar.

STEINBORN, Peter.
Grundlagen und Grundzüge Münchener Kommun-
alpolitik in den Jahren der Weimarer Republik.
Munich: Wölfle (1968), 604 pp.
The most thorough and detailed monograph available on
the subject, and particularly useful for the 1920s.

STÜRMER, Michael.
"Der unvollendete Parteienstaat: zur Vorgeschichte
des Präsidialregimes am Ende der Weimarer
Republik". *Vierteljahrshefte für Zeitgeschichte,*
vol. 21, pt. 2 (1973), p. 119—26.
In seeking the roots of the presidential cabinet system
1930—32, Stürmer first of all reminds us of the historical
factors inhibiting a healthy evolution of parliamentarianism
in Germany since 1871. As for the 1920s, he rightly points
out the deficiencies of party and political development
and concludes that there were certain ominous developments during the period which paved the way for the presidential cabinet. In short, the presidential cabinet was
implicit in the nature of Weimar politics. An important
idea, but one only wishes that it was developed more fully.

WEBER, Günter.
Die wichtigsten Reformpläne zur Weimarer
Reichsverfassung betreffend das Verhältnis Reich-
Länder. Dissertation, University of Cologne (1948).
A discussion of the conflict between federalism and uni-
tarianism.

WINKLER, Hans-Joachim.
Die Weimarer Demokratie: eine politische Analyse
der Verfassung und der Wirklichkeit. Berlin:
Colloquium Verlag (1963), 111 pp.
An appraisal of the Weimar constitution from a political
viewpoint, and also of democracy as a practical system of
government. The political repercussions of the constitution's weaknesses form the substance of a clearly written
essay.

3

The Institutional Framework of the State

A. THE REICHSTAG AND REICHSTAG ELECTIONS

BRACHER, Karl D.
"Probleme der Wahlentwicklung in der Weimarer Republik". In *Spiegel der Geschichte: Festgabe für Max Braubach zum 10. April 1964.* Edited by Konrad Repgen and Stephan Skalweit. Munster: Aschendorff (1964), p. 858—86.
A very informative discussion of the principal factors determining voting preferences and electoral patterns.

CREEKMORE, Marion.
The German Reichstag Election of 1928. Dissertation, University of Tulane (1968).
An evaluation of this election's significance in Weimar electoral and political history. The results of the election are scrutinized and the author ties this in with an analysis of the strengths and weaknesses of the *Reichstag*, the parties, and the voting public. Certainly a useful study.

DEUERLEIN, Ernst (ed.).
Der Reichstag: Aufsätze, Protokolle, und Darstellungen zur Geschichte der parlamentarischen Vertretung des deutschen Volkes 1871—1933.
Frankfurt: Athenäum Verlag (1963), 307 pp.
In the first part of this valuable volume, several authors examine various aspects of the *Reichstag* 1871—1933, and include Ernst Deuerlein on "Der Reichstag in Verfassungsrecht und Verfassungswirklichkeit", Alfred Milatz on "Wahlrecht, Wahlergebnisse und Parteien des Reichstags" (an excellent paper), Albert Schwarz on "Die Volksvertretung der ersten Republik 1920—1933", and Marie-Elizabeth Lüders on "Aus der Frauenarbeit des Reichstags 1919—1933". The second half of the book contains stenographic reports of the more important and dramatic parliamentary sessions.

FRAENKEL, Ernst.
"Historical Handicaps of German Parliamentarianism". In Lawrence Wilson (translator), *The Road to Dictatorship: Germany 1918—1933.* London: Oswald Wolff (1964), p. 27—37.
A brief outline of some of the main reasons why the Germans found it so difficult, and by 1933 impossible, to successfully adopt parliamentary democracy in their form of government. The author stresses the failure of the political parties to fulfil the important responsibilities devolving upon them in a pluralistic parliamentary democracy.

GERMANY.
Reichstag: Verhandlungen des Reichstages. Vols. 1 —458 (1867—1933). Washington D.C.: NCR Microcard Editions (1969).
Naturally indispensable source of documentary records.

HAGMANN, Meinrad.
Der Weg ins Verhängnis: Reichstagswahlergebnisse 1919 bis 1933, besonders aus Bayern. Munich: Beckstein (1946), 38 pp.
Very useful, but all too brief.

HALLGRING, Louis.
The German Reichstag Elections of September 1930. Dissertation, Columbia University (1950).
Much more restricted in scope and depth than Creekmore's study of the 1928 election. Hallgring relies mainly on American newspaper reports on the election.

JÄCKEL, Eberhard; JUNKER, Detlef; KUHN, Axel (eds.).
Deutsche Parlamentsdebatten. Vol. 2: 1919—1933. Frankfurt: Fischer (1971), 297 pp.
Selective extracts, but fills a gap in published documentary records of the *Reichstag*.

KING-HALL, Stephen; ULLMANN, Richard K.
German Parliaments: a Study of the Development of Representative Institutions in Germany.
London: The Hansard Society (1954), 162 pp.
Chapter V is entitled "The Most Liberal of all Constitutions" and discusses the intrinsic values of the *Reichstag* and the constitutional principles on which it rested. Rather too general.

MARKMANN, Heinz.
Das Abstimmungsverhalten der Parteifraktionen in deutschen Parlamenten. Meisenheim: Hain (1955), 205 pp.
Looks at the voting preferences of the parties in the *Reichstag* 1924—32, as well as in the federal and state parlia-

ments 1945—51. The author discusses the question of how party factions are controlled and disciplined, and how members regard the rules of parliamentary democracy. For the Weimar period, he shows that the KPD and NSDAP were the most cohesive factions in the *Reichstag.*

MICK, Guenter.
See his work in section 9D (Trier).

MILATZ, Alfred.
Wähler und Wahlen in der Weimarer Republik.
Bonn: Bundeszentrale für politische Bildung (1965), 152 pp.
An invaluable and detailed statistical analysis of elections and voting patterns, in which sociological, economic, traditional, and confessional factors are emphasized. The major Weimar parties are each given individual treatment, and then seen in the context of election results 1920—33. The author has provided excellent tables and diagrams and an appendix of superbly constructed maps.

MISCH, Axel.
Das Wahlsystem zwischen Theorie und Taktik: zur Frage von Mehrheitswahl und Verhältniswahl in der Programmatik der Sozialdemokratie bis 1933.
Berlin: Duncker & Humblot (1974), 290 pp.
For review see section 6B(i).

PRATT, Samuel A.
The Social Basis of Nazism and Communism in Urban Germany: a Correlational Study of the July 31, 1932, Reichstag Elections in Germany. Dissertation, Michigan State College (1948).
Not very comprehensive in scope and its conclusions must be regarded as tentative.

RITTER, Gerhard A. (ed.).
Gesellschaft, Parlament und Regierung: zur Geschichte des Parlamentarismus in Deutschland.
Düsseldorf: Droste (1974).
A useful collection of essays by various hands on the weaknesses of nineteenth and twentieth century parliamentary development in Germany.

SCHÄFER, Friedrich.
"Zur Frage des Wahlrechts in der Weimarer Republik". In F. A. Hermens & T. Schieder (eds.). *Staat, Wirtschaft und Politik in der Weimarer Republik: Festschrift für Heinrich Brüning.* Berlin: Duncker & Humblot (1967), p. 119—40.
A thought-provoking examination of the Weimar electoral system, particularly the early hopes that accompanied the system of proportional representation as the most democratic system available, and the quick disillusionment with that system. He argues that PR contributed significantly to the constitutional breakdown of the Republic, adding controversially that the government had a responsibility to create a new electoral law which would produce a viable *Reichstag.*

SCHMITT, Veit.
Die Stellungnahme der Deutschnationalen Volkspartei, des Zentrums, und der Sozialdemokratischen Partei im Reichstag zur Steuerreform von 1925.
Dissertation, University of Erlangen (1951).
An examination (incomplete) of the parties' record on tax reforms in parliament.

SCHUMACHER, Martin (ed.).
Parlamentspraxis in der Weimarer Republik: die Tagungsberichte der Vereinigung der deutschen Parlamentsdirektoren 1925 bis 1933. Düsseldorf: Droste (1974), 272 pp.
A record of the minutes of the sessions of the German parliamentary directorate which in 1925—29 met only five times, but more frequently 1929—33. The volume throws light on the technical-administrative practices of the *Reichstag* and individual state parliaments and constitutes therefore an excellent source for procedural etiquette in the parliamentary system.

SCHWARZ, Max (ed.).
M.d.R. Biographisches Handbuch der deutschen Reichstage. Hanover: Verlag für Literatur und Zeitgeschehen (1965), 832 pp.
A very handy reference work which provides brief biographical sketches of all former deputies of the *Reichstag* (numbering 5,370 names in all), though the deputies supplied their own information. The book is divided into three parts, covering the 1848—49, 1867—1918, and 1919—33 periods respectively.

SHIVELY, W. Phillips.
"Party Identification, Party Choice, and Voting Stability: the Weimar Case", *American Political Science Review*, vol. 66, pt. 4 (1972), p. 1203—25.
An engrossing and revisionist study of voting patterns and the nature of party affiliations in Weimar politics. Using graphs and charts as aids, the author examines the voting preferences of certain social groups distinguished by sex, religion and environment, dividing his material into two periods, 1924—28 and 1928—33. The main conclusion is that party identification was not an important factor in Weimar. Voting was determined largely by social and economic structures. Interestingly, it is also stipulated that NSDAP gains 1928—33 did not come disproportionately from among previous non-voters.

STRIEFLER, Heinrich.
Deutsche Wahlen in Bilden und Zahlen: eine soziographische Studie über die Reichstagswahlen der Weimarer Republik. Düsseldorf: Wende Verlag (1946), 64 pp.
Contains some very good graphs, but is not nearly thorough enough.

ZIEGLER, Donald J.
Prelude to Democracy: a Study of Proportional Representation and the Heritage of Weimar Germany, 1871—1920. Lincoln (Nebr.): University of Nebraska Press (1958), 134 pp.
Weighs up the pros and cons of PR in Weimar and the Second Reich and attempts to show how social and political conditions before 1918 influenced the later development of PR. The author believes PR was used to discriminate against democratic groups, especially the socialists. But the book as a whole says nothing new and adds little to an important constitutional debate. There are some bad factual errors and he exaggerates the degree to which the limitations of the constitution caused Weimar's downfall.

B. THE CIVIL SERVICE (BUREAUCRACY)

BEHREND, H.-K.
"Zur Personalpolitik des preussischen Ministeriums des Innern". *Jahrbuch für die Geschichte Mittel- und Ostdeutschlands*, vol. 6 (1957), p. 109—30.
An informative insight into the priorities and decision-making of an important ministry.

DANNER, Lothar.
Ordnungspolizei Hamburg: Betrachtungen zu
ihrer Geschichte 1918 bis 1933. Hamburg: Verlag
Deutsche Polizei (1958), 252 pp.
A reasonable addition to our knowledge of how government
administration worked in Hamburg, though the influence of
political pressure groups is overlooked.

DIECKMANN, Hildemarie.
Johannes Popitz: Entwicklung und Wirksamkeit in
der Zeit der Weimarer Republik. Berlin: Colloquium
Verlag (1960), 157 pp.
Popitz was a leading expert in public finance and played a
significant part in helping the Republic overcome the inflation of the early 1920s. He also made a name for himself
through his creation of an important tax law in 1925. This
account of his activities as a financial expert in the Prussian
and Reich civil service is sound and detailed, and is also a
worthwhile contribution to the administrative and fiscal
history of the Republic.

DIECKMANN, Hildemarie.
"Johannes Popitz als Finanzpolitiker und
Rechtswissenschafter in der Zeit der Weimarer
Republik". *Jahrbuch für die Geschichte Mittel-*
und Ostdeutschlands, vol. 8 (1959), p. 265–317.
Spotlights Popitz's ideas for fiscal and administrative
reform. These are incorporated into the author's book (see
above).

HERZFELD, Hans.
"Johannes Popitz: ein Beitrag zum Schicksal des
deutschen Beamtentums". In *Forschungen zu*
Staat und Verfassung: Festschrift für Fritz Hartung.
Berlin (1958), p. 345–65.
Considers the significance of Popitz's career for the nature
and development of the civil service in general.

HETTLAGE, K. M.
"Johannes Popitz 1884–1945". In *Männer der*
deutschen Verwaltung. Cologne (1963), p. 329–47.
A brief survey of the highlights of his career, which culminated in Popitz becoming a member of the German resistance
movement to Hitler in 1944.

HOFFMANN, Gabriele.
Sozialdemokratie und Berufsbeamtentum: zur
Frage nach Wandel und Kontinuität im Verhältnis
der Sozialdemokratie zum Berufsbeamtentum in
der Weimarer Zeit. Hamburg: Buske Verlag (1972),
289 pp.
See section 6B(i) for review.

KNIGHT, Maxwell E.
The German Executive, 1890–1933. Stanford:
Stanford University Press (1952), 52 pp.
Shows that the aristocracy and upper classes dominated the
key posts in German administration until 1933. The
November Revolution and Weimar experience resulted in
only a small number of lower class people entering the
upper reaches of the service, so that this study is a useful
contribution to the "continuity" debate in modern German
history. Provides many tables containing interesting statistical data.

LIANG, Hsi-Huey.
The Berlin Police Force in the Weimar Republic.
Berkeley: University of California Press (1970),
252 pp.
The major theme of this pioneering study is the composition,
organization, activities and function of the Berlin *Schutz-*
polizei and *Kriminalpolizei* forces. He argues that they were
at no time a wholly reliable instrument of the Republic,
that most members tended to be politically right-wing and
therefore less enthusiastic about tackling violence from the
political Right. The author, however, has not made the
most of an intriguing subject; he neglects important themes
pertaining to his principal subject but above all he has not
satisfactorily related the role of the police to the wider
context of Weimar politics. The usefulness of the book is
therefore limited.

LIANG, Hsi-Huey.
"The Berlin Police and the Weimar Republic".
Journal of Contemporary History, vol. 4, pt. 4
(1969), p. 157–72.
An extract from the author's book which depicts the Berlin
police force as a kind of barometer for the capital's
changing social habits in the 1920s.

MOMMSEN, Hans.
"Die Stellung der Beamtenschaft in Reich, Ländern,
und Gemeinden in der Ära Bruening". *Vierteljahrs-*
hefte für Zeitgeschichte, vol. 21, pt. 2 (1973),
p. 151–65.
In a stimulating paper, the author recalls the initial enthusiasm among the conservative-minded *Beamtenschaft* for the
presidential cabinet style of government, and how this
attitude changed once Brüning's economy measures began
to hit the *Beamten.* The presidential system did not trans-
fer political power from parliamentary bodies to the state
bureaucracy as the *Beamten* had hoped. Hence, they soon
believed the Brüning government was undermining their
position throughout the bureaucratic structure with the
result that each side became distrustful and suspicious of
the other. This paper examines the fundamentals of
Brüning's policy towards the *Beamtenschaft,* and the influence of the *Beamten* in politics, concluding that due to
his alienation of the bureaucracy Brüning lost the chance
of "an authoritarian stabilization of the Republic".

PIKART, Eberhard.
"Preussische Beamtenpolitik 1918–1933". *Viertel-*
jahrshefte für Zeitgeschichte, vol. 6, pt. 2 (1958),
p. 119–37.
A penetrating examination of the policies and wide-ranging
attitudes of the bureaucracy in Prussia, whose position was
complicated and made more and more anomalous, not only
because of the pressures of Prussian-Reich dualism, but also
because of the fact that Prussia had a democratic government until 1932. The author skilfully unravels the tangled
situation most convincingly.

PIKART, Eberhard.
"Berufsbeamtentum und Parteienstaat: eine
Fallstudie". *Zeitschrift für Politik,* vol. 7 (1960),
p. 225–40.
Examines the attitude of career civil servants to the party
system and to parliamentary government. Most officials did
not openly oppose the Republic but few wholeheartedly
supported it, and instead maintained a generally ambivalent
and tentative attitude. The author illustrates this point with
reference to the relationship between the coalition government and civil servants of the Prussian Finance Ministry
shortly after the Kapp Putsch.

PRYCE, Donald B.
German Government Policy toward the Radical
Left 1919–1923. Dissertation, Stanford University
(1970).
An examination of how the Reich government formulated
and implemented its policies towards the radical Left, in
particular the role of the various bureaucratic agencies
responsible for dealing with political subversion. Concludes
that the government was weak in this sphere and was therefore dependent on the army to put down disorder.

RUNGE, Wolfgang.
Politik und Beamtentum im Parteienstaat: die Demokratisierung der politischen Beamten in Preussen zwischen 1918 und 1933. Stuttgart: Klett (1965), 292 pp.
A pioneering study of the attempts to make the higher administrative civil service in Prussia safe for democracy. The author examines a series of case studies concerning the extent to which efforts aimed at democratization were actually implemented in Westphalia, Hesse-Nassau, and the Rhineland. He shows that most of these attempts were only partially successful.

SAGERER, G.; SCHULER, Emil.
Die Bayerische Landespolizei von 1919—1935. Munich: Selbstverlag (1954).
A brief outline history of the development of this organization which does not take sufficient account of the political *ambience* in which it operated. The study does not add much to our knowledge of either Bavarian or national politics.

SCHULER, Emil.
Die Bayerische Landespolizei, 1919—1935. Munich: Selbstverlag (1964).
Supplements the earlier joint work with Sagerer by adding some more detail. The limitations of the former book remain nonetheless.

C. THE JUDICIARY, THE COURTS, AND JUSTICE

FRAENKEL, Ernst.
Zur Soziologie der Klassenjustiz und Aufsätze zur Verfassungskrise 1931—32. Darmstadt: Wissenschaftliche Buchgesellschaft (1968), 103 pp.
A brief but learned study which illuminates some important features of the judicial process and the extent to which social pressures were involved.

FREY, Erich.
Ich beantrage Freispruch: aus den Erinnerungen des Strafverteidiges. Hamburg: Blüchert (1959), 492 pp.
Interesting memoirs of a leading defence lawyer of the Weimar era, with detailed insights into the functioning of the legal system.

GRABERT, Herbert (ed.).
Friedrich Grimm: ein Leben für das Recht. Tatsachen und Dokumente zur Erinnerung an das Wirken eines grossen Anwalts und Patrioten. Tübingen: Verlag der deutschen Hochschullehrer-Zeitung (1961), 77 pp.
A sympathetic biography of the pro-*völkisch* and right-wing nationalist lawyer who among other briefs acted as the principal defence lawyer for those accused of the Feme murders in Weimar days. Indeed, in places the study amounts to a panegyric of Grimm and cannot be taken seriously.

GRIMM, Friedrich.
Politische Justiz, die Krankheit unserer Zeit: 40 Jahre Dienst am Recht. Bonn: Universitäts-Buchdruckerei (1953), 184 pp.
Memoirs of the right-wing lawyer who had good connections with leading National Socialists, including Gregor Strasser. However, he does not give very much away in Chapters V—VII, which deal with the Weimar period. Disappointing.

GROSSHUT, F. S.
Staatsnot, Recht, und Gewalt. Nuremberg: Glock und Lutz (1962), 334 pp.
Contains (p. 56—249) a good general discussion of how far justice was influenced by politics in Weimar.

GUMBEL, Emil J.
Vom Fememord zur Reichskanzlei. Heidelberg: Verlag Schneider (1962), 90 pp.
Describes some of the most notorious examples of political justice in the Republic. Too many lawyers and judges were anti-republican and hence tended to hear right-wing defendents with leniency. A familiar theme. The more complex implications of this problem are not considered at all here.

HANNOVER, Heinrich; HANNOVER, Elizabeth.
Politische Justiz 1919—1933. Frankfurt: Fischer (1966), 335 pp.
An excellent scholarly analysis of the whole question of political justice in the Republic. They trace the development of judicial attitudes towards politically motivated crime from the November Revolution. through the horrors of the Bavarian Revolution, the Kapp Putsch, the murder of Rathenau and Erzberger, the *Fememord*, and treason trials, to the Potempa incident in 1932. A full chapter is devoted to the use of the courts against the Communists, and a separate chapter also to the relationship between the courts and National Socialism.

HANNOVER, Elizabeth; HANNOVER, Heinrich.
Der Mord an Rosa Luxemburg und Karl Liebknecht: Dokumentation eines politischen Verbrechens. Frankfurt: Suhrkampf (1967), 185 pp.
A clinical and authoritative study of two of the most notorious political murders of the Weimar era.

HAUSSMANN, Wolfgang (ed.).
Hugo Marx: Werdegang eines jüdischen Staatsanwalts und Richters in Baden (1892—1933); ein soziologisch-politisches Zeitbild. Villingen: Neckar-Verlag (1965), 240 pp.
Helpful in explaining some of the dilemmas facing the legal profession when political considerations begin to impinge on the administration of justice. Marx's career, however, may not have been typical.

JASPER, Gotthard.
See his work (*Der Schutz der Republik*) in section 1.

JASPER, Gotthard.
"Aus den Akten der Prozesse gegen die Erzberger-Mörder". *Vierteljahrshefte für Zeitgeschichte*, vol. 10, pt. 4 (1962), p. 430—53.
The author provides important documents relating to the murder of Erzberger in 1921 by members of the Organization Consul. The documents provide an instructive insight into the organization and its membership, and its reason for killing Erzberger. He was hated in nationalist circles for his *Erfüllungspolitik*, but his murder was designed to help provoke a left-wing reaction which would lead to army intervention against the Left, and then the opportunity to set up a nationalist government. Though this plan sounds incredible, the fanatical Right often forsook logic in their plans.

KAUL, Friedrich K.
Der Pitaval der Weimarer Republik. 3 vols. East
Berlin: Verlag Das Neue Berlin (1954–62).
The first volume is entitled "Justiz wird zum Verbrechen"
and is concerned with political justice in Weimar. Notorious
cases are discussed, including those of Felix Fechenbach,
who was active in the Bavarian revolution, and *Oberleutnant*
Paul Schulz, who spent some years in prison after being
convicted as a Feme murderer. The work is not free from
political sloganizing, and, in any case, does not reach the
standard of the book by the Hannovers (see earlier).

NEUSEL, Werner.
**Die Spruchtätigkeit der Strafsenate des Reichs-
gerichts in politischen Strafsachen in der Zeit der
Weimarer Republik.** Marburg: Görich &
Weiershäuser (1971), 128 pp.
A full-scale study is needed of the approach of the Supreme
Court at Leipzig to the question of political justice. This
slim volume begins to ask the right kind of questions, but
does not come up with definitive answers.

NIEWYK, Donald L.
See his article in section 11.

RADBRUCH, Gustav.
Der innere Weg: Aufrisz meines Lebens. Göttingen:
Vandenhoeck & Ruprecht (1961), 163 pp.
This autobiography of a former Minister of Justice in the
Republic is at its best when discussing his specialist role in
the legal system. Radbruch cannot be regarded as a typical
personality of the legal profession on account of his odd
outlook which was made up of Kantian, patriotic, and
socialist ideas.

SCHILD, Hermann.
**Friedrich Grimm: mit offenem Visier — aus den
Lebenserinnerungen eines deutschen Rechtsanwalts.**
Leoni am Starnberger See: Drüffel-Verlag (1961),
283 pp.
Another grossly apologetic work on the right-wing lawyer.
Should not be taken seriously.

SINZHEIMER, Hugo; FRAENKEL, Ernst.
Die Justiz in der Weimarer Republik: eine Chronik.
Neuwied: Luchterhand (1968), 486 pp.
A fully documented narrative and analysis of the problems
affecting the administration of justice in Weimar. Although
more detailed in many respects than the Hannover work, it
is heavier to read and not as well organized.

STERN, Howard.
Political Crime and Justice in the Weimar Republic.
Dissertation, Johns Hopkins University (1966).
A discussion of the phenomenon of right- and left-wing
political crime in 1919–23, which examines in detail cases
brought before the courts. The author argues that they dis-
criminated against the Left, while right-wingers were
thought to have acted out of "national" motives. He concludes, however, that judicial institutions became more
neutral after 1923, though this proposition is not substantiated.

4

Political Events

A. THE NOVEMBER REVOLUTION

(i) Immediate Origins

BERMBACH, Udo.
Vorformen parlamentarischer Kabinettsbildung in Deutschland: der interfraktionelle Ausschuss 1917/18 und die Parlamentarisierung der Reichsregierung. Cologne: Westdeutscher Verlag (1967), 389 pp.
The author convincingly demonstrates that the initial advances towards parliamentary government achieved by the Inter-Party Committee in 1917—18 were a valuable preparation for the establishment of the Weimar Republic. Although badly written and organized, this is an adequate but not definitive work on the Committee, and needs to be supplemented by the studies of Erich Matthias and Rudolf Morsey (see below).

GRUNDMANN, Elizabeth; KROHN, Claus-Dieter.
"Die Einführung des parlamentarischen Systems in Deutschland 1918". *Das Parlament: Aus Politik und Zeitgeschichte,* B 12 (20.3.1971).
Discusses the moves towards parliamentarization in government, the parties, and the army — the creation of a new administration. Also considers the objectives of this process, the constitutional reforms and their impracticality.

HANSSEN, Peter.
Diary of a Dying Empire. Bloomington: Indiana University Press (1955), 409 pp.
Hanssen was a *Reichstag* deputy of North Schleswig and his diary covers the years 1914—18. Contains his notes on the relative impotence of the *Reichstag* and for 1918 his observations of how Germans reacted to the prospect of losing the war. The diary offers a valuable insight into aspects of the German collapse and the early days of the November Revolution.

KAMNITZER, Heinz; MAMMACH, Klaus.
"Aus Dokumenten zur Vorgeschichte der deutschen Novemberrevolution". *Zeitschrift für Geschichtswissenschaft,* vol. 1, pt. 5 (1953), p. 789—810.
Presents material provided by the *Sächsische Landeshauptarchiv*'s collection of documents from the former Saxon Ministry of the Interior, consisting of memoranda, police reports and pamphlets. The authors claim the documents show the "outstanding importance" of the influence of the Russian revolutionary movement and the October Revolution on the German working class movement's struggle against imperialism and war.

KRUMMACHER, Fritz.
Die Auflösung der Monarchie. Hanover: Verlag für Literatur und Zeitgeschehen (1960), 72 pp.
An outline of the last tortured days of the Kaiser and his entourage.

MATTHIAS, Erich; MORSEY, Rudolf (eds.).
Die Regierung des Prinzen Max von Baden. Düsseldorf: Droste (1962), 699 pp.
This large volume contains important source material illuminating the reform movement in the *Reichstag* before November 1918, including the Majority Committee of *Reichstag* members, and the protocols of cabinet meetings held during Baden's chancellorship. The editors furnish a learned introduction and have organized the source material very effectively indeed.

MATTHIAS, Erich; MORSEY, Rudolf (eds.).
Der interfraktionelle Ausschuss 1917—1918. 2 vols. Düsseldorf: Droste (1959), 642, 893 pp.
Another high quality documentary collection. The two volumes contain all available source material on the meetings of the Majority Committee of *Reichstag* members (6 July 1917 onwards). The question of reform in Prussia and the Reich and war aims are among the subjects treated. Complements the editors' volume on the Baden administration.

SCHREINER, Albert (ed.).
Revolutionäre Ereignisse und Probleme in Deutschland während der Periode der Grossen Sozialistischen Oktoberrevolution 1917/18. East Berlin: Akademie-Verlag (1957), 353 pp.
A rather rigid Marxist-Leninist interpretation of events leading up to the German collapse. To be treated with caution.

WESTARP, Kuno Graf von.
Das Ende der Monarchie am 9. November 1918: abschliessender Bericht nach den Aussagen der Beteiligten. Berlin: Rauschenbach (1952), 216 pp.
Chronicles the events at Spa immediately preceding the

Kaiser's abdication. The author's monarchist sympathies are inevitably very apparent and his strictures against the socialists and republican elements, among whom he evidently places Max of Baden, are not unexpected. Of little value.

(ii) The Naval Mutinies

DEIST, Wilhelm.
"Die Politik der Seekriegsleitung und die Rebellion der Flotte Ende Oktober 1918". *Vierteljahrshefte für Zeitgeschichte*, vol. 14, pt. 4 (1966), p. 341—68.
A richly detailed essay which takes a revealing look at power struggles and political manoeuvring in the upper echelons of the naval command, and the political and military consequences, particularly in so far as these were linked to the mutinies at the end of the war. He focuses on the creation of a completely new command structure in the autumn of 1918, the *Seekriegsleitung* (SKL) under Admiral Scheer. The increasing politicization of a large part of the naval officer corps is also treated.

WOODWARD, David.
"The Mutiny at Kiel, November 1918". *History Today*, vol. 18, pt. 12 (1968), p. 829—35.
A popular, dramatized account of the mutiny with illustrations, one of which is a poster of the infamous Peoples' Marine Brigade.

WOODWARD, David.
"Mutiny at Wilhelmshaven 1918". *History Today*, vol. 18, pt. 11 (1968), p. 779—85.
Another popular account with the usual pictorial aids.

WROBEL, Kurt.
Die Volksmarinedivision. East Berlin: Verlag des Ministeriums für Nationale Verteidigung (1957), 144pp.
A brief study of the naval mutinies and of the part played by the "red shock troops" of the Peoples' Marine Brigade. The book is hopelessly tendentious.

ZEISLER, Kurt.
Aufstand in der deutschen Flotte: die revolutionäre Matrosenerhebung im Herbst 1918. East Berlin: Verlag des Ministeriums für Nationale Verteidigung (1956), 92 pp.
More of a propaganda pamphlet than an objective historical study.

(iii) The Revolution — General

ANGRESS, Werner T.
"Juden im politischen Leben der Revolutionszeit". In W. E. Mosse & A. Paucker (eds.). *Deutsches Judentum in Krieg und Revolution, 1916—1923: ein Sammelband.* Tübingen: Mohr (1971).
See section 11, on The Jews and Anti-Semitism, for review.

ARNS, Günter.
"Erich Koch-Wesers Aufzeichnungen vom 13. Februar 1919". *Vierteljahrshefte für Zeitgeschichte*, vol. 17, pt. 1 (1969), p. 96—115.
Extracts from Koch-Weser's diary which provide a detailed outline of Germany's internal and external political situation in February 1919. Koch-Weser pinpoints with uncanny accuracy the problems with which the politicians of the early Republic were faced.

ASCHER, Abraham.
"Russian Marxism and the German Revolution, 1917—1920". *Archiv für Sozialgeschichte*, vol. 7 (1967), p. 391—439.
An interesting and detailed examination of Russian Marxist attitudes to the German Revolution. Ascher shows that their judgements were hopelessly out of touch with the realities of the German situation and that their standpoint caused them to modify their basic creed, though they did not acknowledge that any modifications took place. Also, Russian Marxist appraisals of the situation in Germany varied considerably from one group to another, and changes in their opinions usually resulted from developments in Russia itself rather than from Germany. Russian ignorance about Germany, the author concludes, persisted throughout the Weimar era.

AUFHÄUSER, Siegfried.
"Der 9. November 1918: persönliche Erinnerungen an eine deutsche Revolution". *Neue Gesellschaft*, vol. 15 (1968), p. 459—62.
A republican supporter recalls from fragmented memoirs the heady days of 9—11 November in Berlin. He was a trade union official whose task was to act as liaison man with the workers' and soldiers' councils.

BASSLER, Gerhard P.
"The Communist Movement in the German Revolution, 1918—1919: a Problem of Historical Typology?". *Central European History*, vol. 6, pt. 3 (1973), p. 233—77.
See in section 6B(vii) for a review.

BAUER, Roland.
"Zur Einschätzung des Charakters der deutschen Novemberrevolution 1918—19". *Zeitschrift für Geschichtswissenschaft*, vol. 6, pt. 1 (1958), p. 134—69.
He blames right-wing social democrats and their bourgeois allies for robbing the Revolution of its true proletarian character. A familiar Marxist interpretation.

BERTHOLD, Lothar; NEEF, Helmut.
Militarismus und Opportunismus gegen die Novemberrevolution: das Bündnis der rechten SPD-Führung mit der Obersten Heeresleitung November und Dezember 1918. East Berlin: Rütten & Loening (1958), 218 pp.
A lengthy introduction provides an orthodox Marxist interpretation of the Revolution. The second part of the book consists of documentation relating to the understanding between the Majority Socialists and the army leadership. This is a useful section and adds to the scholarly debate on this controversial aspect of the Revolution.

BOOMS, Hans.
"Die Novemberereignisse 1918: Ursachen und Bedeutung einer Revolution". *Geschichte in Wissenschaft und Unterricht*, vol. 20, pt. 10 (1969), p. 577—604.
A balanced re-appraisal of the causes and significance of the Revolution fifty years after, in which Booms shows acquaintance with the major schools of thought on the subject.

BREHME, Gerhard.
Die sogenannte Sozialisierungs-gesetzgebung der Weimarer Republik. East Berlin: Deutscher Zentralverlag (1960), 174 pp.
This book discusses a relatively neglected aspect of the November Revolution, namely, the part played by socialization and the "socialization laws" of 1919. The author examines the positions taken up on the issue by the left-wing parties and criticizes the SPD for allowing itself to be used by the bourgeoisie to wreck the socialization process. The KPD, needless to say, passes his scrutiny with flying colours.

BURDICK, Charles B.; LUTZ, Ralph H. (eds.).
The Political Institutions of the German Revolution 1918—1919. New York: Praeger (1966), 305 pp.
A collection of documents on the political institutions which played some part in the Revolution, the workers' and soldiers' councils, the *Vollzugsrat*, the *Zentralrat*, the Council of Peoples' Commissars, and the Reich government. The documents consist of the minutes of the meetings of these bodies. Although selective, the collection is far-ranging and constitutes a valuable source of information.

CARSTEN, Francis L.
Revolution in Central Europe 1918—1919. Berkeley: University of California Press (1972), 360 pp.
The author is primarily concerned with a comparative study of revolution in Germany and Austria, and only in passing with the Hungarian and Czechoslovakian experience. He examines the role of the workers' and soldiers' councils as well as the attitudes of the various parties involved in the revolutionary situation. Carsten underestimates the radical nature of the councils and exaggerates their importance. His thesis that there was a genuine revolution in Germany which failed because of what he refers to as "the circuitous course of German history" is, of course, highly debatable. Although Carsten in general tends to describe rather than analyse, the book fulfils a valuable role in providing a well documented and comprehensive history of the Revolution in Germany and Austria.

CASTELLAN, Georges.
"La Révolution allemande de novembre 1918 (November-revolution)". *Revue d'Histoire Moderne et Contemporaine*, vol. 16 (1969), p. 40—51.
An intelligent review of the historiography pertaining to some controversial aspects of the November Revolution, notably the extent to which the Bolshevik Revolution influenced the German situation, and the policies of the Majority Socialists.

COPER, Rudolf.
Failure of a Revolution: Germany in 1918—1919. London: Cambridge University Press (1955), 294 pp.
A disappointing book. Badly organized, frivolous, tendentious, and polemical, it has no pretensions to being an academic work. There is no overall hypothesis and the book is in fact composed of a series of random and ill-informed observations.

COPPING, David.
German Socialists and the Revolution of 1918—1919. Dissertation, Stanford University (1952).
A competent survey at the time, but no longer satisfactory.

DECKER, Alexander.
"Die Novemberrevolution und die Geschichtswissenschaft in der DDR". *Internationale Wissenschaftliche Korrespondenz zur Geschichte der Deutschen Arbeiterbewegung*, vol. 10, pt. 3 (1974), p. 269—99.
An informative discussion which reveals some sympathy for the East German position.

DIECKMANN, Johannes (ed.).
Die Grosse Sozialistische Oktoberrevolution und Deutschland. 2 vols. East Berlin: Dietz Verlag (1967), 638, 508 pp.
A collection of papers, all of which are written from an unyielding Marxist-Leninist standpoint, on the nature and extent of the October Revolution's impact on the November Revolution, and subsequent Weimar developments, including the performance of the major parties. A poor quality product.

DIEHL, Ernst.
"Die Bedeutung der Novemberrevolution 1918". *Zeitschrift für Geschichtswissenschaft*, vol. 17, pt. 1 (1969), p. 14—32.
The author affirms it was a bourgeois-democratic revolution which was carried through to a certain degree by proletarian methods. Failure was due to the terror tactics of the counter-revolution, which was supported by the Majority Socialists; but, argues Diehl, the events of 1918 laid the basis for the establishment of the German Democratic Republic!

DRABKIN, J. S.
Die November-Revolution 1918 in Deutschland. East Berlin: Deutscher Verlag der Wissenschaften (1968), 593 pp.
Originally published in Russia in 1958, this book provides much useful detailed information, though naturally within a Marxist-Leninist framework of argument.

DREETZ, Dieter.
"Zur Entwicklung der Soldatenräte des Heimatheeres (November 1918 bis März 1919)". *Zeitschrift für Militärgeschichte*, vol. 9, pt. 4 (1970), p. 429—38.
Contains some previously unpublished archival material on an important aspect of the Revolution. Certainly a worthwhile paper.

DREETZ, Dieter.
"Bestrebungen der OHL zur Rettung des Kerns der imperialistischen deutschen Armee in der Novemberrevolution". *Zeitschrift für Militärgeschichte*, vol. 8, pt. 1 (1969), p. 50—66.
Prints four important documents which throw further light on the army attitude to the Revolution and, in particular, the concern of the army command to preserve intact the nucleus of the troops as a basis for later expansion. The first document publishes in full an extract from the diary of the "internal political department" of the army command for the period 9 November 1918 to 9 January 1919. The fourth document relates to an army regiment preparing to take the offensive against the revolutionary Berlin workers in early 1919. Very revealing.

EINHORN, Marion.
"Zur Rolle der Räte in November and Dezember 1918". *Zeitschrift für Geschichtswissenschaft*, vol. 4, pt. 3 (1956), p. 545—59.
The author argues without producing nearly enough evidence that initially the councils incorporated the revolutionary-democratic power of the workers and peasants, but later were betrayed by the SPD government. She exaggerates

when stating that at first the councils were able to inflict severe damage to the power structure of the bourgeoisie. Her ideas are worth attention, but they remain unsubstantiated.

ELBEN, Wolfgang.
Das Problem der Kontinuität in der deutschen Revolution 1918—1919: die Politik der Staatssekretäre und der militärischen Führung von November 1918 bis Februar 1919. Düsseldorf: Droste (1965), 194 pp.
Examines the relations between the new political leadership and the bureaucracy on a national and provincial level. The SPD's unpreparedness for revolution and governmental responsibility is well brought out, as is the unyielding attitude of the civil service and army. A thoroughly documented and imaginative work.

FELDMAN, Gerald D.
"Economic and Social Problems of the German Demobilisation 1918—19" *Journal of Modern History*, vol. 47, pt. 1 (1975), p. 1—47.
See section 13A (ii) (e) for review.

FELDNER, Rolf.
"Zwischen kaiserlichen Armee und Reichswehr: das Problem der Machtverteilung in der revolutionären Übergangsphase". *Das Parlament: Aus Politik und Zeitgeschichte*, B50 (11.12.71).
Discusses the problems facing the army in 1918—19; how to overcome defeat, the abdication of the Kaiser, relations with the new government, the soldiers' councils, conflicts over the organization and build-up of the army. Concludes by providing an overview of the army's development until the beginning of the Seeckt era.

FLEMMING, Jens.
"Parlamentarische Kontrolle in der Novemberrevolution: zur Rolle und Politik des Zentralrats zwischen erstem und zweitem Rätekongress (Dezember 1918 bis April 1919). *Archiv für Sozialgeschichte*, vol. 11 (1971), p. 69—139.
A fundamental and important study of the organization, policies, and influence of the Central Council of the German Socialist Republic, the institutional figurehead of the council movement in the Revolution. The author concentrates on relations between the Central Council and the Reich parliamentary government, and on individual problems like the future of the army, the January uprising in Berlin, and socialization.

FRIEDLANDER, Henry E.
The German Revolution 1918—1919. Dissertation, University of Pennsylvania (1968).
A long dissertation stressing the large degree to which the failure of the Revolution handicapped the Weimar Republic. A comprehensive treatment of the Revolution which says little that is new.

FRIEDLANDER, Henry E.
"Conflict of Revolutionary Authority: Provisional Government vs. Berlin Soviet, November-December 1918". *International Review of Social History*, vol. 7 (1962), p. 163—76.
Examines the competing authorities of the Council of Peoples' Representatives and the Executive Council of the Berlin workers' and soldiers' councils (*Vollzugsrat*). The paper seeks to find out why the Berlin Soviet lost power to the former after only five weeks. Among the reasons was that the Council of Peoples' Representatives came to be seen as representing the legitimate interests of the nation and was extended recognition by the Allies. The Berlin

Soviet, on the other hand, was regarded as anti-democratic, inexperienced, weakly led, and pro-Russian. A clearly argued, but too brief paper.

GÖRLITZ, Walter.
November 1918: Bericht über die deutsche Revolution. Oldenburg: Stalling (1968), 210 pp.
A conservative-oriented general view of the revolutionary events and their significance. Cannot be rated one of the better studies on this subject.

GRAU, Roland.
"Zur Rolle der Soldatenräte der Fronttruppen in der Novemberrevolution". *Zeitschrift für Militärgeschichte*, vol. 7, pt. 4 (1968), p. 550—64.
Heavily laden with slogans and political jibes. The author sees the soldiers' councils as at first part of the proletarian revolutionary front against the capitalist-imperial system, encouraged in their activities by the example of the Russian workers and peasants. But soon they were taken over by Social Democratic and petty bourgeois forces. Essentially a paper of ideological propaganda.

GRIEBEL, Alexander.
"Das Jahr 1918 im Lichte neuer Publikationen". *Vierteljahrshefte für Zeitgeschichte*, vol. 6, pt. 4 (1958), p. 361—79.
A useful review of important new books on the collapse and Revolution.

GROH, Dieter.
"Remarques sur la révolution de novembre en Allemagne". *Revue d'Histoire Moderne et Contemporaine*, vol. 16 (1969), p. 51—7.
Does not say anything original or important.

GROTEWOHL, Otto.
Dreissig Jahre später: die Novemberrevolution und die Lehren der Geschichte der deutschen Arbeiterbewegung. East Berlin: Dietz (1952), 168 pp.
A heavily politicized interpretation, completely lacking scholarly objectivity.

HABEDANK, Heinz.
Um Mitbestimmung und Nationalisierung während der Novemberrevolution und im Frühjahr 1919. East Berlin: Verlag Tribüne (1968), 359 pp.
Discusses in some detail important economic and social aspects of the Revolution. A useful work in a relatively neglected field.

HAFFNER, Sebastian.
Failure of a Revolution: Germany 1918—1919. London: André Deutsch (1973).
A popular work, with no footnotes or bibliography, but fluently written. His untenable thesis is that Ebert betrayed a genuine revolutionary mass movement. A superficial and unconvincing work.

HELLIGE, Hans-Dieter.
"Die Sozialisierungsfrage in der deutschen Revolution von 1918/19". *Internationale Wissenschaftliche Korrespondenz zur Geschichte der Deutschen Arbeiterbewegung*, vol. 11, pt. 1 (1975).
A none too enlightening review of several recent studies concerned with the socialization issue.

HERTZMAN, Lewis.
"Farmers' League and November Revolution:
Two Letters of Gustav Roesicke". *International
Review of Social History*, vol. 11, pt. 1 (1966),
p. 108—12.
Two letters written on 10 December 1918 by Roesicke,
deputy leader of the *Bund der Landwirte*, reveal the uncertainty in right-wing interest groups compelled to adjust
to the revolutionary situation. Roesicke shows more scepti-
cism over Count Westarp's proposals for reconstituting
traditional Prussian values in the DNVP, and in any case
his main aim was to safeguard the integrity of the *Bund der
Landwirte*.

HERWIG, Holger H.
"The First German Congress of Workers' and
Soldiers' Councils and the Problem of Military
Reforms". *Central European History*, vol. 1, pt.2
(1968), p. 150—65.
The first Congress was held in Berlin on 16—21 December
1918. This article looks at a relatively forgotten aspect of
its deliberations, the problem of the military. The membership of the Congress was for the most part non-revolutionary
but still produced thorough reform proposals (the
Hamburger Punkte), which the army rejected. Ebert eventually upheld this objection even though the SPD had voted
in favour of the reform at the Congress. Although the
article contains noteworthy material, it includes a few unwarranted conclusions, and fails to explain why Ebert re-
pudiated the decision of Congress.

HINTZE, Peter.
"Zur Frage des Charakters der Arbeiter- und
Soldatenräte in der Novemberrevolution".
Zeitschrift für Geschichtswissenschaft, vol. 5, pt. 2
(1957), p. 264—77.
Concludes with regret that these councils were largely
non-Communist.

HOMBURG, Heidrun.
Gewerkschaften: Unternehmer und Staat in der
Demobilmachungsphase (November 1918—Mai
1919); Überlegungen am Beispiel des Düsseldorfer
Regierungsbezirks. Dissertation, University of
Freiburg (1973).
See section 13A(ii)(e) for review.

HONHART, Michael W.
The Incomplete Revolution: the Social Democrats'
Failure to Transform the German Economy 1918—
1920. Dissertation, Duke University (1972).
See section 13A(ii)(e) for review.

HUNT, Richard N.
"F. Ebert and the German Revolution of 1918".
In L. Krieger & F. Stern (eds.). *The Responsibility
of Power*. London: Macmillan (1968), p. 315—34.
An objective and for the most part fair appraisal of Ebert's
strengths and weaknesses in the Revolution.

HÜRTEN, Heinz.
"Soldatenräte in der deutschen Novemberrevolution
1918", *Historisches Jahrbuch*, vol. 90 (1970),
p. 299—328.
An important article. The author discusses the reasons why
the soldiers' councils were not revolutionary and instead
willing to co-operate with the army command and the
Ebert government. Also, he pays particular attention to the
conflict between the Executive of the soldiers' and workers'
councils in Berlin and the soldiers' councils in the West over
control of political and military policy.

JESSEN-KLINGENBERG, Manfred.
"Die-Ausrufung der Republik durch Philipp
Scheidemann am 9. November 1918". *Geschichte
in Wissenschaft und Unterricht*, vol. 19, pt. 11
(1968), p. 649—56.
A brief review of the circumstances in which Scheidemann
made his famous but unplanned proclamation.

KLEEN, Walter.
"Über die Rolle der Räte in der Novemberrevolution". *Zeitschrift für Geschichtswissenschaft*,
vol. 4, pt. 2 (1956), p. 326—31.
Provides a commentary on several documents pertaining to
the activities of the soldiers' and workers' councils in the
Erfurt area. Argues that the councils were under bourgeois
domination from beginning to end, and that the Revolution
failed because of the absence of a mass-based working
class party.

KLUGE, Ulrich.
Soldatenräte und Revolution: Studien zur Militärpolitik in Deutschland 1918/19. Göttingen: Vandenhoeck & Ruprecht (1975), 480 pp.
This is the first systematic analysis of the military council
movement in the Revolution. The author traces its origins
and development, discusses the movement's relations with
the left-wing parties, and examines its military, political,
and constitutional aims and how far these aims were
realized. Based on wide sources, this is a significant and
well researched work.

KOLB, Eberhard; RÜRUP, Reinhard (eds.).
Der Zentralrat der deutschen sozialistischen
Republik 1918—1919: Quellen zur Geschichte der
Rätebewegung in Deutschland 1918/19. Leiden:
Brill (1968), 830 pp.
An excellently edited and full documentary collection on
the Central Council, established in December 1918. The
volume consists mainly of the minutes of the Council's
sessions as well as the minutes of the combined sessions
with the *Volksbeauftragte* and the Berlin *Vollzugsrat*. This
is an indispensable work for an understanding of the council
movement in general.

KOLB, Eberhard (ed.).
Vom Kaiserreich zur Weimarer Republik.
Cologne: Kiepenheuer & Witsch (1972), 437 pp.
A collection of papers on various aspects of Germany in
1918—19, with the emphasis on diversity of view and
interpretation. Kolb outlines the major trends in the
historiography of the Revolution. The nature of the Revolution, the course of the Revolution, and the Versailles
negotiations are all covered. In the fourth and final section
of the book, there are assessments of what historians have
written on the 1918—19 period over the last fifty years.

KOLB, Eberhard.
Die Arbeiterräte in der deutschen Innenpolitik
1918—1919. Düsseldorf: Droste (1962), 432 pp.
This is probably the best treatment of the workers' councils,
and the attitude towards them adopted by the trade unions
and the socialist parties. The author shows that only the
Spartacists wholeheartedly supported the councils which,
however, declined once the radical Left and the shop
stewards' movement were defeated. A compelling and
authoritative study.

KOLB, Eberhard.
"Rätewirklichkeit und Räteideologie". In Hans
Neubauer (ed.). *Deutschland und die russische
Revolution*. Stuttgart: Deutsche Verlagsanstalt
(1968).
A brief review of the aims and aspirations of the council
movement.

KÖNNEMANN, Erwin.
"Die Einschätzung der politischen Lage durch die OHL nach den Märzkämpfen 1919". *Zeitschrift für Militärgeschichte*, vol. 11, pt. 1 (1972), p. 61–71.
Publishes a record of a meeting of the *Oberste Heersleitung* on 22 March 1919 in which Groener spoke on the domestic situation and the threat of Bolshevism. The document is from the Seeckt papers.

LINDAU, Rudolf.
Revolutionäre Kämpfe 1918–1919: Aufsätze und Chronik. East Berlin: Dietz Verlag (1960), 268 pp.
An anthology of previously published essays by Marxist writers on aspects of the November Revolution. The "revisionist" SPD is heavily criticized throughout, of course, but there are some details to be picked up about the risings in Hamburg, Munich, and central Germany.

LINDEMANN, Albert S.
The "Red Years": European Socialism vs. Bolshevism 1919–1921. Berkeley: University of California Press (1974), 376 pp.
A broad treatment of the threat or alleged threat of Bolshevism in Western Europe. Unfortunately, Germany is not handled particularly well.

LINSE, Ulrich.
"Hochschulrevolution: zur Ideologie und Praxis sozialistischer Studentengruppen während der deutschen Revolutionszeit 1918/19". *Archiv für Sozialgeschichte*, vol. 14 (1974), p. 1–114.
An excellent analysis of the ideological aims and activities of the socialist groups and their splinter groups which emerged in German universities at the end of the war. Basically, they wanted to introduce new social criteria and democratization into the rather inflexible and tradition-bound universities; most of these efforts, however, failed largely because most students and authorities were conservative in outlook. The socialist students themselves could not agree on which political party to support, and inevitably split into factions.

LÖSCHE, Peter.
"Rätesysteme im historischen Vergleich".
Politische Vierteljahresschrift, Special Number 2 (1971).
A comparative study of the council movement, including that thrown up by the November Revolution.

MAIER, Charles.
Recasting Bourgeois Europe: Stabilization in France, Germany, and Italy in the Decade after World War I. Princeton: Princeton University Press (1975), 703 pp.
An important book which in using a comparative model attempts to show that the actions of the immediate postwar governments in these countries resulted in a restoration of fundamental elements of pre-1914 bourgeois society. The line of continuity is indisputable, he argues. The work has notable deficiencies, however; he does not define what constituted "bourgeois" society, and he certainly underestimates the changes brought about by war between 1914 and 1918.

MALANOWSKI, Wolfgang.
November Revolution 1918: die Rolle der SPD.
Frankfurt: Ullstein (1969), 189 pp.
A highly competent narrative of the main aspects of the Revolution; it is also carefully organized and lucidly written.

MAMMACH, Klaus.
"Die Bedeutung der Novemberrevolution". *Zeitschrift für Geschichtswissenschaft*, vol. 17, pt. 1 (1969), p. 209–12.
Briefly outlines some of the problems which still need to be researched in this "important sphere of the history of the German working class movement", including the nature and development of the factory councils, their changing character, and the influence of the SPD.

MATTHIAS, Erich.
Zwischen Räten und Geheimräten: die deutsche Revolutionsregierung 1918/19. Düsseldorf: Droste (1970), 178 pp.
This is a separate edition of Matthias's outstanding introduction to his book co-edited with Susanne Miller, *Die Regierung der Volksbeauftragten 1918/19* (see below).

MATTHIAS, Erich; MILLER, Susanne (eds.).
Die Regierung der Volksbeauftragten 1918/19.
2 vols. Düsseldorf: Droste (1969), 399, 408 pp.
An indispensable source for the Revolution; the volumes contain the minutes of the cabinet sessions of the Council of Peoples' Representatives. Many other relevant sources, including the minutes of the proceedings of meetings and discussions which the Council held with members of the Berlin *Vollzugsrat* and the Central Executive of the workers' and soldiers' councils, are also presented. The massive detail throws important light on the attitudes and policies of Ebert and the SPD, the extent of SPD influence in the workers' and soldiers' councils, and the SPD fears of Bolshevism. Among other topics are the socialization of industry and the army. Matthias provides an excellent introduction in which he discusses the authority of the bureaucracy before 1918, the army leadership, and the opportunities for a third course in 1918–19 between the radical Left and the Majority Socialists.

MUTH, Heinrich.
"Die Entstehung der Bauern- und Landarbeiterräte im November 1918 und die Politik des Bundes der Landwirte". *Vierteljahrshefte für Zeitgeschichte*, vol. 21, pt. 1 (1973), p. 1–38.
A much needed paper on the role of the peasants' councils in the Revolution. Most scholars have dismissed these as being insignificant in comparison with the workers' councils; this absorbing study redresses the balance. The author establishes that in several important respects the peasants' councils were different; politically they were on the whole right-wing, and the attitude of a local council was invariably determined by the local leadership. In contrast, the workers' councils were left-wing, and their degree of radicalism was determined more by local conditions and the rank and file membership. The author has used a great deal of new archival material.

NEUBAUER, Hans (ed.).
Deutschland und die russische Revolution.
Stuttgart: Deutsche Verlagsanstalt (1968).
A collection of previously published essays, including a study already noted above, Eberhard Kolb's "Rätewirklichkeit und Räteideologie".

NIMTZ, Walter.
Die Novemberrevolution 1918 in Deutschland. Mit einem Dokumentenanhang. East Berlin: Dietz Verlag (1962), 248 pp.
The narrative part of the book is based on a series of lectures originally delivered by the author at an East German Communist Party training school. Consequently his contribution makes no serious attempt to be objective. The documentary section, on the other hand, is useful.

NIMTZ, Walter.
"Über den Charakter der Novemberrevolution von 1918/19 in Deutschland". *Zeitschrift für Geschichtswissenschaft*, vol. 6, pt. 3 (1958), p. 687—715.
Contains nothing we have not read before from East German sources. The paper rigidly adheres to the party line.

OECKEL, Heinz.
Die revolutionäre Volkswehr 1918/19: die deutsche Arbeiterklasse im Kampf um die revolutionäre Volkswehr (November 1918 bis Mai 1919). East Berlin: Deutscher Militärverlag (1968), 326 pp.
A study which has made use of significant documentary material, but this has been interpreted within a Marxist-Leninist framework. Nonetheless, many new details are provided on the organization and activity of the left-wing military forces in 1918—19.

OEHME, Walter.
Damals in der Reichskanzlei: Erinnerungen aus den Jahren 1918—19. East Berlin: Kongress-Verlag (1958), 366 pp.
There are interesting details in these memoirs of a former staff member of the Reich Chancellory. The book also contains notes on the Berlin revolutionary movement.

OERTZEN, Peter von.
"Die grossen Streiks der Ruhrbergarbeiterschaft im Frühjahr 1919: ein Beitrag zur Diskussion über die revolutionäre Entstehungsphase der Weimarer Republik". *Vierteljahrshefte für Zeitgeschichte*, vol. 6, pt. 3 (1958), p. 231—62.
See section 14 for review.

OERTZEN, Peter von.
Betriebsräte in der Novemberrevolution: eine politikwissenschaftliche Untersuchung über Ideengehalt und Struktur der betrieblichen und wirtschaftlichen Arbeiterräte in der deutschen Revolution 1918—19. Düsseldorf: Droste (1963), 377 pp.
A richly detailed narrative of the factory council movement, including its function as a working class organization in the factories. The book lacks something in straight objectivity because the author's pro-council sympathies are clearly evident throughout.

OPEL, Fritz.
Der Deutsche Metallarbeiter-Verband während der Ersten Weltkrieges und der Revolution. Hanover: Norddeutsche Verlagsanstalt (1957), 144 pp.
See section 14 for review.

PETERSEN, Jens.
"1918—1968: der fünfzigste Jahrestag der Novemberrevolution im Spiegel der deutschen Presse". *Geschichte in Wissenschaft und Unterricht*, vol. 20, pt. 8 (1969), p. 454—79.
A collection of extracts from West German newspapers and magazines on the occasion of the fiftieth anniversary of the Revolution. These extracts represent a cross-section of attitudes on the most important and debated aspects of the Revolution, and help clarify the new Germany's vision of its recent past.

PHILIPP, Kurt.
The Independent Socialists' Attempts to Govern Germany, November-December 1918. Dissertation, University of Kansas (1969).
Investigates the neglected topic of the Independent Socialists' activity in the government of the Council of Peoples' Representatives (Nov.—Dec. 1918). The author analyses why the Majority Socialists and the Independents soon fell out by explaining their different outlook on militarism, the future political structure of Germany, foreign affairs, and socialization. Most disagreement, however, was over the date for national elections. He stresses that the USPD did not present a cohesive front *vis-à-vis* the Majority Socialists, nor did it clarify its policies sufficiently, so the party did not attract enough working class support in 1918. A good survey.

RAASE, Werner.
Die Entwicklung der deutschen Gewerkschaftsbewegung in der Zeit der revolutionären Nachkriegskrise. East Berlin: Verlag Tribüne (1967), 166 pp.
See section 14 for review.

RICHTER, Werner.
Gewerkschaften, Monopolkapital und Staat im Ersten Weltkrieg und in der Novemberrevolution 1914—1919. East Berlin: Verlag Tribüne (1959), 403 pp.
See section 14 for review.

RIEZLER, Kurt.
Tagebücher, Aufsätze, Dokumente. Edited by K. D. Erdmann. Göttingen: Vandenhoeck & Ruprecht (1972), 766 pp.
An important source for the period between the collapse of the monarchy and the establishment of the Republic. Riezler's observations are perceptive and shrewd.

RITTER, Gerhard; MILLER, Susanne (eds.).
Die deutsche Revolution, 1918—1919. Frankfurt: Fischer (1968), 380 pp.
A commemorative volume of the fiftieth anniversary of the Revolution. Contains documentary extracts on different aspects of the Revolution and its development.

RUGE, Wolfgang.
"Neue Dokumente über den Soldatenrat bei der Obersten Heeresverwaltung". *Zeitschrift für Geschichtswissenschaft*, vol. 16, pt. 11 (1968), p. 1402—20.
Some new and illuminating documentary material concerning the impact of the Revolution on the upper reaches of the army command structure.

RUGE, Wolfgang.
"Zur Taktik der deutschen Monopolbourgeoisie im Frühjahr und Sommer 1919". *Zeitschrift für Geschichtswissenschaft*, vol. 11, pt. 6 (1963), p. 1088—1109.
A prejudiced view of the role of class in the Revolution, the alleged endeavours of the "monopolistic bourgeoisie" to defeat the radical aims of the Revolution.

RÜRUP, Reinhard.
Probleme der Revolution in Deutschland 1918/19. Wiesbaden: Steiner (1968), 59 pp.
A succinct and well informed review of the problems facing scholars of the November Revolution, and a critical look at some publications.

RÜRUP, Reinhard.
"Problems of the German Revolution, 1918—19".
Journal of Contemporary History, vol. 3, pt. 4
(1968), p. 109—35.
An incisive review of the different phases in the historiography of the Revolution. The author stresses that the Revolution was an opportunity missed; that is, an opportunity to establish a firm democratic state. Hence, the government failed to make the necessary reforms of institutions that would make a parliamentary system viable, and consequently the Republic was severely weakened from the beginning.

RYDER, A. J.
The German Revolution of 1918: a Study of German Socialism in War and Revolt. London: Cambridge University Press (1967), 303 pp.
A thoroughly researched and very sound study of the vicissitudes of German socialism (SPD and USPD) in war and revolution, and of the November Revolution. The author criticizes the circumspection of Ebert and the Majority Socialists in the Revolution and states that a more adventurous policy by them would have given the Republic a better chance of survival in the long run.

RYDER, A. J.
The German Revolution 1918—1919. London: Routledge & Kegan Paul (1959), 29 pp.
A pamphlet specially written for the English Historical Association's series. Provides a compact narrative, but is too superficial to be helpful to anyone but the general reader and school certificate candidates. The series seems to be designed for that readership in any case.

SCHMIDT, Günter.
"Zur Staats- und Machtfrage in der Novemberrevolution". *Jahrbuch für Geschichte*, vol. 2 (1967), p. 249—82.
See section 13A (ii) (e) for review.

SCHNIEDER, Dieter; KUDA, Rudolf.
Arbeiterräte in der Novemberrevolution: Ideen, Wirkungen, Dokumente. Frankfurt: Suhrkampf (1968), 172 pp.
The commentary does not offer any original interpretations of the role and importance of the workers' councils, nor does the documentary section provide new evidence.

SCHREINER, Albert.
"Zur Frage der Räte in der Novemberrevolution 1918". *Zeitschrift für Geschichtswissenschaft*, vol. 4, pt. 4 (1956), p. 735—8.
Mainly concerned with an over-critical look at Walter Tormin's book (see below) on the subject.

SCHULZ, Gerhard.
Revolutions and Peace Treaties 1917—1920. London: Methuen (1972), 258 pp. (Original German edition: Munich: Deutscher Taschenbuch-verlag (1967)).
Presents in clear fashion a general summary of political and social upheavals in 1917—18 and an analysis of the international peace treaties of 1919—20. Not intended for specialists, the study contains no new ideas, but the author has admirably condensed a good deal of often controversial material. There is a good bibliography attached.

SNELL, John L.
"Die Republik aus Versäumnissen". *Die Welt als Geschichte*, vol. 15, pt. 3—4 (1955), p. 196—219.
The author's theme is the cause of the monarchy's collapse in 1918. Apart from the ambiguous nature of President Wilson's demands on Germany, and the loyalty and tenacity of the non-socialist parties *vis-à-vis* the monarchy, he argues that the principal cause of collapse was the blindness of the Kaiser himself. The thesis is untenable because it ignores constitutional, political and social trends in Germany during the war which were of much greater importance in 1918.

STREISAND, Joachim.
"La Révolution de 1918 en Allemagne". *Revue d'Histoire Moderne et Contemporaine*, vol. 16, pt. 1 (1969), p. 57—63.
Says nothing of note.

TÖPNER, Kurt.
Gelehrte Politiker und politisierende Gelehrte: die Revolution von 1918 im Urteil deutscher Hochschullehrer. Göttingen: Musterschmidt (1970), 290 pp.
An interesting survey of the by no means unanimous reaction of German university teachers to the Revolution, though the large majority were unfavourably disposed to it. Indeed, reaction against the Revolution helped stiffen their resistance to the Weimar Republic after 1919.

TORMIN, Walter.
Zwischen Rätediktatur und sozialer Demokratie: die Geschichte der Rätebewegung in der deutschen Revolution 1918/19. Düsseldorf: Droste (1954), 148 pp.
Competent to a degree, but contains few new ideas and has been superseded in the meantime by more challenging and thorough studies. His main point is that the workers' and soldiers' councils were anti-Communist in the main.

WALLWITZ, Alice G. (ed.).
Panorama 1918: ein Jahr im Spiegel der Presse. Munich: Scherz (1968), 159 pp.
Contains a fairly random selection of newspaper and magazine extracts on the November Revolution; of no special value.

WATT, Richard M.
The Kings Depart: the Tragedy of Germany — Versailles and the German Revolution. London: Weidenfeld & Nicolson (1969), 604 pp.
A popular work for the general reader only, often written in the historic present tense to achieve a dramatic effect.

WINCKLER, Lutz.
"Die Novemberrevolution in der Geschichtsschreibung der DDR". *Geschichte in Wissenschaft und Unterricht*, vol. 21, pt. 4 (1970), p. 216—34.
A very useful and informative review of the work of leading East German historians on the Revolution. Winckler is rightly critical and not dismissive in tone.

(iv) The Revolution — Regional

(a) Bavaria

ALBRECHT, Willy.
Landtag und Regierung in Bayern am Vorabend der Revolution von 1918: Studien zur gesellschaftlichen und staatlichen Entwicklung Deutschlands von 1912—1918. Berlin: Duncker & Humblot (1968), 487 pp.
A detailed history of political development in Bavaria as seen from the vantage point of the 1918 Revolution. The

author concentrates on the activities and deliberations of the Bavarian government and *Landtag*, but reveals also the diversity of intellectual and political opinion in Bavaria at the end of the war. Moreover, large sections of the population had become alienated from the Berlin government long before 1918, thus setting the stage for the Bavarian-Reich crises of the 1918—23 period. He concludes that the Revolution in Bavaria was as much due to the weakness of the government as anything else.

AY, Karl-Ludwig.
Die Entstehung einer Revolution: die Volksstimm-ung in Bayern während des Ersten Weltkrieges.
Berlin: Duncker & Humblot (1968).
Analyses public opinion in Bavaria before 1918 and certain trends which contributed to the Revolution. Stresses the hostility towards the Berlin authorities, anti-Prussianism, and growing apathy as the war dragged on. The study forms a handy introduction to the Revolution proper in Bavaria.

AY, Karl-Ludwig.
Appelle einer Revolution: Dokumente aus Bayern zum Jahre 1918/1919. Das Ende der Monarchie. Das revolutionäre Interregnum. Die Rätezeit.
Munich: Süddeutcher Verlag (1968), 38 pp.
Over one hundred brief documents consisting of newspaper clippings, proclamations, pamphlet extracts and the like on the collapse of the Wittelsbachs, the revolutionary period of Eisner, and the Soviet Republic are presented in this slender volume. The documents are meant to illustrate the attitude of the major political parties to these events. The general reader may find something of interest here.

BADIA, Gilbert.
"Allemagne, November 1918: Kurt Eisner devant le Comité Exécutif des Conseils Berlinois". *Revue d'Histoire Moderne et Contemporaine*, vol. 15 (1968), p. 340—61.
Prints the verbatim report of Kurt Eisner's debate with the Executive Committee of the Berlin *Arbeiter-und Soldatenrat* on 25 November 1918. The report helps clarify the objections of Munich to domination by Berlin.

BEYER, Hans.
Von der Novemberrevolution zur Räterepublik in München. East Berlin: Rütten & Loening (1957), 185 pp.
An impressive array of primary and secondary sources have been used for this study. Unfortunately, the author's interpretation of his material is strictly in accordance with Marxist-Leninism; he maintains that the Bavarian workers' and soldiers' councils were genuinely committed to the setting up of a proletarian dictatorship, but were betrayed by the Majority Socialists.

BEYER, Hans.
München 1919: der Kampf der Roten Armee in Bayern, 1919. East Berlin: Verlag des Ministeriums für Nationale Verteidigung (1956), 54 pp.
A wholly tendentious study in favour of the extreme Left.

BEYER, Hans.
"Die bayerische Räterepublik 1919". *Zeitschrift für Geschichtswissenschaft*, vol. 2, pt. 2 (1954), p. 175—215.
Attacks Eisner as a reformist and his régime as "bourgeois", and totally distorts the role of the KPD in the Soviet Republic as well as exaggerating the extent to which the Bavarian working class was revolutionary. Beyer is not an historian but an unsophisticated political propagandist.

BIRNBAUM, I.
"Juden in der Münchener Räterepublik". In Hans Lamm (ed.). *Von Juden in München.* Munich, 1958.
Discusses the activities of Jewish leaders like Max Levien, Eugen Leviné-Nissen and Tobias Axelrod who were prominent in the Soviet Republic period.

BOSL, Karl (ed.).
Bayern im Umbruch: die Revolution von 1918.
Munich: Oldenbourg (1969), 603 pp.
The causes, course and consequences of the Bavarian Revolution are assessed with considerable skill in this volume. There are fourteen studies on aspects of the revolutionary situation, and they serve as an admirable introduction to the topic.

DORST, Tankred (ed.).
Die Münchener Räterepublik: Zeugnisse und Kommentar. Frankfurt: Suhrkampf (1966), 192 pp.
A general work, which also contains a number of interesting extracts from reports of various descriptions relating to the Soviet Republic.

GRUNBERGER, Richard.
Red Rising in Bavaria. London: Arthur Barker (1973), 164 pp.
A synthesis of previously published work on the revolutionary period, with no footnotes or bibliography. Intended for the general reader, it is doubtful whether this book fulfils even that modest aim; it is unreliable in detail, contains too many simple factual errors, distorts events and the role of personalities, and is too crudely biased in favour of the Left. In short, the book is virtually a total failure.

HILLMAYER, H.
Roter und Weiss Terror in Bayern nach 1918.
Munich: Nusser (1974), 216 pp.
The theme is the extensive use of violence and terror tactics during the revolutionary period in Bavaria; the author tries to find an explanation for this situation, describes the forms the violence assumed, and sums up the short- and long-term consequences. A useful addition to the field.

HÜTTL, Ludwig.
"Die Stellungnahme der katholischen Kirche und Publizistik zur Revolution in Bayern 1918/19". *Zeitschrift für Bayerische Landesgeschichte*, vol. 34, pt. 2 (1971), p. 652—95.
The author begins this illuminating study by reviewing the development of the Church and Church-state relations in Bavaria 1914—18. Following a period of neutrality at the beginning of the revolutionary period, the Church adopted a sharply hostile attitude towards the Revolution because of Eisner's radical cultural policies. The events of the Soviet Republic strengthened this hostility. Afterwards, the Church became involved in disputes with the Republic over the question of the monarchy, Church-state relations, and school education. In all, he concludes, the Church did not make a positive contribution to democracy.

KALMER, Georg.
"Die 'Massen' in der Revolution 1918/19: die Unterschichten als Problem der bayerischen Revolutionsforschung". *Zeitschrift für Bayerische Landesgeschichte*, vol. 34, pt. 1 (1971), p. 316—57.
Kalmer turns to the problem of "radicalization"; he examines Bavaria's political structure, with very good charts showing the fortunes of various parties 1912—20. He also discusses the differences in the Communist and bourgeois interpretations of the Revolution, and concludes with an outline of the future tasks of scholarship.

KLUGE, Ulrich.
"Die Militär- und Räterepublik der bayerischen Regierungen Eisner und Hoffmann 1918/19".
Militärgeschichtliche Mitteilungen, vol. 13, pt. 1 (1973), p. 7—58.
A detailed and powerfully argued paper which presents a fair measure of previously unpublished material.

KOLB, Eberhard.
"Geschichte und Vorgeschichte der Revolution von 1918/19 in Bayern". *Neue Politische Literatur*, vol. 16 (1971), p. 383—94.
A scholarly appraisal of works on the pre-history and development of the Bavarian Revolution, paying particular attention to its origins and the radicalization of the bourgeoisie.

KÜHNL, Reinhard.
"Die Revolution in Bayern 1918: Voraussetzungen der Revolution", *Geschichte in Wissenschaft und Unterricht*, vol. 14 (1963), p. 681—93.
The author enquires how it was that the Bavarian people, regarded as conservative, Christian and monarchist, could succumb so relatively easily to revolution in 1918. He examines political, social, economic and ideological factors in the Bavarian situation which combined in 1918 to create a general disposition favourable to revolution, and describes in detail the last few days in the province before revolution broke out.

KÜHNL, Reinhard.
"Die Regierung Eisner in Bayern 1918/19: die Situation nach dem 7. November". *Geschichte in Wissenschaft und Unterricht*, vol. 15, pt. 7 (1964), p. 398—410.
A detailed account of the immediate pre- and post-revolutionary days and an outline of the political dilemmas confronting the Eisner régime, and the attitudes of the political parties. The author is sympathetic towards Eisner.

LASCHITZA, Annelies.
"Kurt Eisner, Kriegsgegner und Feind der Reaktion: zu seinem 100. Geburtstag". *Beiträge zur Geschichte der Deutschen Arbeiterbewegung*, vol. 9 (1967), p. 454—89.
An appreciative review of Eisner's anti-war activities and his efforts at introducing a more democratic type of government in Bavaria.

LINSE, Ulrich.
"Gemeinde im Wandel: die Novemberrevolution 1918/19 in Burghausen a.d. Salzach als Konflikt zwischen bürgerlicher Gewerbestadt und moderner Industriewelt". *Zeitschrift für Bayerische Landesgeschichte*, vol. 33, pt. 1 (1970), p. 355—423.
A very valuable local study of a small town in Bavaria in pre- and revolutionary times. Examines the main contours of the town's political and economic development before 1914, the growing conflict, accentuated by the war, between the idea of *Bürgerliche Ordnung* and industrialism, and the social antagonism between bourgeoisie and industrial workers, that were engendered by the 1918 Revolution. The role of the major parties, the BVP and SPD, is considered, and also the consequences of the counter-revolution.

MEYER-LEVINÉ, Rosa.
Leviné: Leben und Tod eines Revolutionärs — Erinnerungen. Mit einem dokumentarischen Anhang. Munich: Carl Hauser Verlag (1972), 297 pp.

Leviné's widow presents a generally balanced book of memoirs which contains a good description of his role in the Munich Soviet in 1919. A documentary appendix includes documents pertaining to Leviné's political career.

MITCHELL, Allen.
Revolution in Bavaria 1918—1919: the Eisner Régime and the Soviet Republic. Princeton: Princeton University Press (1965), 374 pp.
The main strength of this monograph is the author's description of the Bavarian workers' and soldiers' councils and his assessment of Eisner. He thinks the latter was a naive idealist who believed in a modified form of parliamentary democracy. The period of the Soviet Republic, however, is less well treated. Overall, well worth reading.

MORENTZ, Ludwig (ed.).
Revolution und Räteherrschaft in München: aus der Stadtchronik 1918/1919. Munich: Georg Müller Verlag (1969), 136 pp.
The editor provides a sound commentary linking a selection of extracts from official government documents of the period, private letters, and reports relating to the Bavarian Revolution. The attitudes and reactions of many participants in these events are also recorded.

NEUBAUER, Helmut.
München und Moskau 1918/1919: zur Geschichte der Rätebewegung in Bayern. Munich: Isar-Verlag (1958), 100 pp.
An objective and well-documented analysis of the ideological and political influence of Russian Bolsheviks on the Munich and Bavarian revolutionary situation. The interventions by Lenin and other Russian leaders are discussed in detail and make fascinating reading. The author also rejects Hans Beyer's thesis that the councils were genuinely dedicated to the idea of a proletarian dictatorship.

PÖRTNER, Paul.
"The Writers' Revolution: Munich 1918—19".
Journal of Contemporary History, vol. 3, pt. 4 (1968), p. 137—51.
Concerned with the political involvement of a handful of German writers in the Bavarian Revolution, where a radically leftist Council of Intellectual Workers (*Rat geistiger Arbeiter*) was formed by Kurt Hiller. Also relates the political activities of Gustav Landauer and Ernst Toller, both of whom were, of course, prominent in the Soviet Republic. However, Pörtner does not show that the role of any intellectual apart from Eisner was significant. The article is indeed rather thin on material and weak in argument.

RAATJES, John.
The Role of Communism during the Munich Revolutionary Period, November 1918—May 1919. Dissertation, University of Illinois (1958).
Rather tentative, and does not explain why the revolutionary situation radicalized so much in Spring 1919.

RICHTER, Armin.
"Rat Murat und die Sozialisierung der Presse: neue Daten und Materialien zum revolutionären Pressekampf vor und während der Münchener Räterepublik". *Publizistik*, vol. 16, pt. 3 (1971), p. 279—93.
A description of the attempted socialization of the press during the Revolution, and of the counter-efforts of the bourgeois press. The well-known novelist of the time B. Traven (pseud. Rat Murat) played a conspicuous role in the struggle against the right-wing press and in the fight to achieve socialization.

SCHADE, Franz.
Kurt Eisner und die bayerische Sozialdemokratie.
Hanover: Verlag für Literatur und Zeitgeschehen
(1961), 200 pp.
The book deals with three main themes: the development
of the social democratic movement in Bavaria, and its
relation to the state; the Revolution in Bavaria; and the
role of Eisner. Only on the latter subject does the author
have anything worthwhile to say. He sees Eisner as a sort of
neo-Kantian figure.

SCHMOLZE, Renate; SCHMOLZE, Gerhard (eds.).
Kurt Eisner: die halbe Macht den Räten —
ausgewählte Aufsätze und Reden. Cologne: Verlag
Hegner (1969), 292 pp.
Contains a representative selection of Eisner's writings
and the editors also provide an evaluation of his political
career and thought. They do not regard him as a forceful
enough leader, arguing that in fact he had few qualities of
leadership. However, he is depicted as an idealistic and
humane philosopher.

SCHMOLZE, Gerhard (ed.).
Revolution und Räterepublik in München 1918/
19 in Augenzeugenberichten. Düsseldorf: Karl
Rauch Verlag (1969), 426 pp.
A comprehensive, sound and informative treatment of the
Bavarian Revolution. The atmosphere of the period is
effectively recreated by a judicious selection of eye-witness
reports of people who were actively involved. A biographical
index of many revolutionaries and counter-revolutionaries
is a welcome addition to the study.

SCHWARZ, Klaus-Dieter.
Weltkrieg und Revolution in Nürnberg: ein
Beitrag zur Geschichte der deutschen Arbeiter-
bewegung. Stuttgart: Klett (1971), 336 pp.
Most of the book is devoted to the war years with only the
last chapter on the Revolution in Nuremberg. Unfortunately,
Schwarz does not link the revolutionary events of 1918—19
with the development of Nuremberg as a right-wing and
racialist citadel in the early 1920s, in which, of course,
Julius Streicher was prominent.

SUTTERLIN, Siegfried.
Foreign Political Tendencies in Bavaria, 1917—
1919: a Study in the Old and New Diplomacy.
Dissertation, University of Minnesota (1974).
A study of the diplomatic activities of the Bavarian government as defeat in the First World War loomed for Germany,
and of the new diplomacy of the revolutionary period.
Profound disagreement arose by 1917 between Munich and
Berlin over certain war issues, a situation which eventually
led Eisner to try to negotiate separately with the Allies and
effect a reconciliation with them. When the Allies failed to
reciprocate, Munich broke with them and Berlin, and, during the Soviet Republic in particular, turned to Russia.
But, concludes the author, this orientation merely served
to strengthen the counter-revolutionary forces in 1919
and later. An interesting contribution on an often neglected aspect of the Bavarian revolutionary era.

(b) Berlin

BEY-HEARD, Franke.
Hauptstadt und Staatsumwälzung: Berlin 1919;
Problematik und Scheitern der Rätebewegung in
der Berliner Kommunalverwaltung. Stuttgart:
Kohlhammer (1969), 262 pp.
An important book which examines relations between
Adolf Wermuth, Mayor of Berlin 1912—20, and the representatives of the councils and their approach to the
problems of democratization. A lot of their deliberations
also concerned the question of making communal government more effective.

CARR, Edward H.
"Radek's 'political salon' in Berlin 1919", *Soviet
Studies*, vol. 3, pt. 4 (1952), p. 411—30.
Some interesting details here on Radek's political influence
in the Berlin revolutionary situation.

FISCHER, Kurt.
Die Berliner Abwehrkampf 1918—19. East Berlin:
Verlag des Ministeriums für Nationale Verteidigung
(1956), 47 pp.
More of a propaganda sheet than anything else on the
struggles of the Berlin proletariat in the Revolution.

KÖNNEMANN, Erwin.
"Der Truppeneinmarsch am 10. Dezember 1918 in
Berlin: neue Dokumente zur Novemberrevolution".
Zeitschrift für Geschichtswissenschaft, vol. 16, pt.
12 (1968), p. 1592—609.
Publishes four documents from the Schleicher *Nachlass* and
dated 1.12.1918 (a Schleicher letter), 9.12.1918 (a Groener
telegram to General Lequis), and 24.12.1918 (two reports
by Major Harbon). These throw light on the political ideas
of the Army Command, and in particular the army's collaboration with the Majority Socialists in suppressing the
radical Left.

LUTHER, Karl H.
"Die nachrevolutionären Machtkämpfe in Berlin,
November 1918—März 1919". *Jahrbuch zur
Geschichte Mittel- und Ostdeutschlands*, vol. 8
(1959), p. 187—221.
One of the best and most detailed studies of the political
and military struggles for power in the capital. Pays special
attention to the involvement of the radical Left.

RASMUSS, Hainer.
Die Januarkämpfe 1919 in Berlin. East Berlin:
Verlag des Ministeriums für Nationale Verteidigung
(1956), 56 pp.
Concerned with the Spartacist uprising, but this is not an
objective work.

WALDMAN, Eric.
The Spartacist Uprising of 1919 and the Crisis of
the German Socialist Movement: a Study of the
Relation of Political Theory and Party Practice.
Milwaukee: Marquette University Press (1958),
248 pp.
A sound and comprehensive analysis of the rising and its
broader implications. The rising permanently divided the
German working class in Weimar. The author shows that no
one planned the revolt, that it arose out of the highly
charged political atmosphere in Berlin and was occasioned
by the dismissal of a Berlin Police Chief, Emil Eichhorn.
Subsequent protest meetings developed into a rising. The
author's main thesis, which he adduces with great skill, is
that the rising was the outcome of long-standing tensions
in the socialist movement.

(c) Others (Bremen — Württemberg)

BERTHOLD, Walter.
"Die Kämpfe der Chemnitzer Arbeiter gegen die militaristische Konterrevolution im August 1919". *Beiträge zur Geschichte der Deutschen Arbeiterbewegung*, vol. 4, pt. 1 (1962), p. 127—38.
Gives the erroneous impression that the workers in this Saxon city (now called Karl-Marx-Stadt) were influenced by the KPD.

BÜNEMANN, Richard.
Hamburg in der deutschen Revolution von 1918/ 19. Dissertation, University of Hamburg (1951).
Based on rather scanty sources and fails to fill many important gaps.

COMFORT, Richard A.
"The Political Role of the Free Unions and the Failure of Council Government in Hamburg, November 1918 to March 1919". *International Review of Social History*, vol. 9, pt. 1 (1964), p. 47—64.
See section 14 for review.

FACIUS, Friedrich.
"Das Ende der kleinstaatlichen Monarchien Thüringens 1918: ein Überblick". In Walter Schlesinger (ed.). *Festschrift für Friedrich von Zahn.* Cologne: Mitteldeutsche Forschungen (1969), p. 50—64.
Brief but informed look at revolution in Thuringia.

HATCH, William.
Württemberg and the November 1918 Revolution: a Study of the Struggle between the Moderate and Radical Socialists for Control of the Revolution 1918—1919. Dissertation, Stanford University (1973).
The author seeks to establish whether the Württemberg revolutionary experience showed any important variations from the national norm. He claims there were political and institutional differences, for example, the socialist government of Wilhelm Blos dealt with the radical left-wing threat without bloodshed and without army support. Otherwise, Hatch does not produce further evidence for the differences he claims existed.

KASSING, Heinz-Herbert.
Die Rätebewegung während der Revolution 1918/ 19 in Braunschweig. Manuscript, Göttingen (1973), 172 pp.
A descriptive narrative rather than an analysis, but sets out the principal facts of the matter.

KLUGE, Ulrich.
"Das 'württembergische Volksheer' 1918—1919: zum Problem der bewaffneten Macht in der deutschen Revolution". In *Klassenjustiz und Pluralismus: Festschrift für Ernst Fraenkel zum 75. Geburtstag.* Hamburg: Hoffmann & Campe (1973), p. 92—130.
A much more valuable contribution to the Württemberg Revolution than Hatch's study. Kluge presents much new archival material to document in detail an important feature of the radical movement. He is also able to view his subject in a wider perspective.

KRAUSE, Hartfrid.
Revolution und Konterrevolution 1918/19, am Beispiel Hanau. Kronberg i. Taunus: Scripter-Verlag (1974), 403 pp.
Detailed and interesting account of this Hessian town, though the author's conclusions regarding the long-term consequences of the revolutionary period in Hesse are open to debate.

KUCKUCK, Peter (ed.).
Revolution und Räterepublik in Bremen. Frankfurt: Suhrkampf (1969), 176 pp.
A series of papers on important political and social aspects of the Revolution.

LUCAS, Erhard.
Frankfurt unter der Herrschaft des Arbeiter- und Soldatenrates 1918/19. Frankfurt: Verlag Neue Kritik (1972), 180 pp.
A competent and informative survey, sympathetic to the revolutionary cause.

RÜRUP, Reinhard (ed.).
Arbeiter-Soldatenräte im rheinisch-westfälischen Industrie-Gebiet: Studien zur Geschichte der Revolution 1918/19. Wuppertal: Hammer-Verlag (1975), 403 pp.
An informative and interesting collective work which, in examining in detail the impact of the Revolution in different localities of an industrial area, maintains a high standard of scholarship throughout.

SCHUMANN, Wolfgang.
"Zur Rolle der Räte in der Novemberrevolution in Oberschlesien". *Zeitschrift für Geschichtswissenschaft*, vol. 4, pt. 4 (1956), p. 738—50.
The author uses mostly archival material to examine the role of the councils in the Oppeln district. He believes the workers' and soldiers' councils were revolutionary-democratic organs of the workers and peasants only during the first part of the Revolution in Oppeln. In Upper Silesia as a whole, some councils were immediately under bourgeois control, while some were taken over by them only later. In any case, the article serves to underline the complexity of the council movement.

WIEDERHÖFT, Hani.
"Der Arbeiter- und Soldatenrat in Hamburg und das sowjetische Konsulat im November 1918". *Zeitschrift für Geschichtswissenschaft*, vol. 21, pt. 3 (1973), p. 426—40.
The most interesting section of the paper is that in which sixteen documents are presented indicating the extent of connections between the workers' and soldiers' councils.

WILHELMUS, Wolfgang.
"Die Auswirkungen der Oktoberrevolution auf die revolutionäre Bewegung in Vorpommern bis zum I. Rätekongress im Dezember 1918". In Albert Schreiner (ed.). *Die Oktoberrevolution und Deutschland.* East Berlin: Rütten & Loening (1958).
The author grossly exaggerates the extent to which the radical Left in Germany in 1918/19 was directly influenced by the events and example of the Bolshevik Revolution.

WILHELMUS, Wolfgang.
"Die Rolle der Räte in Vorpommern". *Zeitschrift für Geschichtswissenschaft*, vol. 4, pt. 5 (1956), p. 964—89.

The author begins by charting the "anti-revolutionary" course of the SPD and its success in halting the Revolution and serving the interests of the bourgeoisie. The councils, he believes, were controlled from the beginning by petty bourgeois elements. However, the essay is useful for details on the Revolution in this agrarian region, including developments in Stettin.

(v) The Dolchstoss Myth

BOTJER, George.
A Judicial Effort to Determine the Causes of the German Defeat in 1918: Dolchstossprozess Cossmann-Gruber (1925). Dissertation, Florida State University (1973).

An analysis of the famous *Dolchstoss* trial in 1925 which arose out of reports in the *Süddeutsche Monatshefte* (Cossmann being its publisher) in support of the legend. Martin Gruber, editor of the pro-Social Democratic *Münchener Post* opposed this view on the grounds that it constituted a threat to the SPD in forthcoming elections (*Reichstag* elections of December 1924). Discussion of the merits and demerits of the *Dolchstoss* myth dominated the trial. Gruber's allegations that Cossmann had distorted history were declared unfounded, and Cossmann was awarded heavy damages. The author does not examine the question of political justice in connection with this trial which is a surprising omission.

HILLER von GAERTRINGEN, Friedrich.
" 'Dolchstoss'-Diskussion und 'Dolchstosslegende' im Wandel von vier Jahrzehnten". In Waldemar Besson & Friedrich Hiller von Gaertringen (eds.). *Geschichte und Gegenwarts-Bewusstsein: Festschrift für Hans Rothfels zum 70. Geburtstag.* Göttingen: Vandenhoeck & Ruprecht (1963), p. 122—60.

The author examines the influence of the myth on the course of German history and the changing assessments of the degree of that influence from 1918 to 1960. He rightly affirms that this fallacious myth prevented the German people from properly evaluating their true historical position because it falsified interpretation of that position. The origins of the myth, its development, and the reasons for its wide acceptance, are explained. An objective and lucid exposition.

JOHNSTONE, Theodore.
Dolchstoss: the Making of a Legend 1890—1919. Dissertation, University of Kansas (1974).

The author investigates the genesis and development of certain trends which culminated in 1918 in the legend, and its impact on German society and politics. He argues that the basis for the legend existed in the Wilhelmine era and needed only defeat in war to crystallize the basis into a myth, nurtured by the former establishment of imperial Germany. Thus, the myth resulted from the establishment's crisis of identity before 1914 as well as from defeat in 1918. This is a challenging and profoundly interesting thesis, although it tells us more about Wilhelmine Germany than it does of the Weimar Republic.

PETZOLD, Joachim.
Die Dolchstosslegende: eine Geschichtsfälschung im Dienst des deutschen Imperialismus und Militarismus. East Berlin: Akademie Verlag (1963), 148 pp. 3rd ed.

A polemical and politically oriented work which has no pretensions to being a scholarly objective undertaking. This is not to deny that the author provides some interesting detail on the theme, but the hypothesis that the myth was a tool of militarist-capitalist-imperial cliques is advocated in a crude fashion.

RUDOLPH, Ludwig Ritter von.
Die Lüge die nicht Stirbt: die "Dolchstosslegende" von 1918. Nuremberg: Glock & Lutz (1958), 146 pp.

A competent description of the baleful effect of the myth on German political development after 1918.

SCHRÖDER, Heinz.
Das Ende der Dolchstosslegende: geschichtliche Erkenntnis und politische Verantwortung. Hamburg: Hammerich & Lesser (1946), 80 pp.

Sees 1945 as finally breaking the myth, but as Friedrich Hiller von Gaertringen shows in his study (see above), unscrupulous opportunists in post-1945 German politics have sought to use the myth for their own base ends.

B. THE VERSAILLES PEACE SETTLEMENT

(i) The Paris Peace Conference

ALBEE, Parker B.
American and Allied Policies at the Paris Peace Conference: the Drawing of the Polish-German Frontier. Dissertation, Duke University (1968).

A study of the decision-making process that led to the redrawing of the controversial Polish-German frontier in 1919. The emphasis is firmly on the policies and approach of the United States to the problem, as well as on the Council of Ten and the Council of Four which took the decisions. Wilson's sympathies for Poland are well narrated, but the author correctly shows that at the end of the day the Poles lost important concessions previously promised them (largely due to Lloyd George's objections).

BURNETT, Robert A.
Georges Clemenceau in the Paris Peace Conference 1919. Dissertation, University of North Carolina (1968).

An assessment of the extent of Clemenceau's influence on the decisions of the Conference. The author does not see him as an arch-opponent of Wilson or as an anti-German chauvinist, but as a responsible statesman who wanted a just peace. Somehow, the argument on this last score does not carry much conviction.

CAHEN, Fritz M.
Der Weg nach Versailles: Erinnerungen 1912—1919; Schicksalsepoche einer Generation. Boppard: Boldt (1963), 383 pp.

Fairly useful observations, which also contain an assessment of Brockdorff-Rantzau, the head of the German delegation at the Peace Conference.

CZERNIN, Ferdinand.
Die Friedensstifter (Versailles 1919): Männer und Mächte um den Versailles Vertrag. Munich: Scherz (1968), 390 pp.

A comprehensive narrative, reliable for the most part as regards factual detail, of the leading personalities and states at the Conference.

DICKMANN, Fritz.
Die Kriegsschuldfrage auf der Friedenskonferenz von Paris 1919". *Historische Zeitschrift*, no. 197 (1963), p. 1—101.
Perhaps the most authoritative and incisive account available of the controversial war-guilt question; he explains in detail the attitudes of the Allied powers and the reasons why the Treaty eventually incorporated the war-guilt clause.

DÖBLIN, Alfred.
Sieger und Besiegte: eine wahre Geschichte.
Hamburg: Aurora Verlag (1946), 110 pp.
A brief and unimpressive description of the Conference.

ELCOCK, Howard.
Portrait of a Decision: the Council of Four and the Treaty of Versailles. London: Eyre Methuen (1972), 286 pp.
Purports to offer a comprehensive re-evaluation, but this is an exceedingly disappointing book. The research has been clearly perfunctory, the ideas are second-hand, and as a whole the book is colourless. The author fails to come to terms with the complexity of the peace negotiations so that the heart of his narrative is superficial. The work regrettably does not increase our knowledge of the topic.

EPSTEIN, Fritz T.
"Zwischen Compiègne und Versailles: geheime amerikanische Militärdiplomatie in der Period des Waffenstillstandes 1918/19". *Vierteljahrshefte für Zeitgeschichte*, vol. 3, pt. 4 (1955), p. 412—45.
An excellent exposition of an important aspect of the peacemaking process. Epstein's main theme is the significance of the part played in the secret diplomacy of the United States by Colonel Arthur L. Couger.

GOLDBERG, George.
The Peace to End the Peace: the Paris Peace Conference of 1919. New York: Harcourt, Brace & World (1969), 221 pp.
A well informed, rounded description, but intended as an introduction to the topic rather than a definitive study.

GUNZENHÄUSER, Max.
Die Pariser Friedenskonferenz 1919 und die Friedensverträge 1919—1920: Literaturbericht und Bibliographie. Frankfurt: Bernard & Graefe (1970), 287 pp.
A general survey of the Conference and the various peace treaties that followed. The most useful part of the book is its comprehensive bibliography.

HANKEY, Maurice.
The Supreme Control at the Paris Peace Conference, 1919. London: Allen & Unwin (1963), 206 pp.
The memoirs of Lord Hankey, secretary of the Imperial War Cabinet in 1918 and secretary of the United Kingdom delegation to the Conference. In Part II of the book he records his impressions of the Conference, but they contain no major revelations.

HAUPTS, Leo.
"Zur deutschen und britischen Friedenspolitik in der Krise der Pariser Friedenskonferenz: britischdeutsche Separatverhandlungen im April/Mai 1919". *Historische Zeitschrift*, no. 217 (1973), p. 54—98.
A good paper on the Anglo-German negotiations at the Hague in Spring 1919. Supporting his arguments with fresh archival material, the author shows clearly that neither the Germans nor the British took their meetings seriously.

HEADLAM-MORLEY, James.
A Memoir of the Paris Peace Conference 1919. Edited by Agnes Headlam-Morley and others. London: Methuen (1972), 230 pp.
Headlam-Morley was a member of the United Kingdom delegation to the Conference, and was regarded as the British specialist on Central and Eastern Europe. He was personally involved in many of the most important decisions taken at the Conference, including those relating to Germany's eastern frontiers. His memoirs present interesting and detailed observations of various aspects of the Conference and of leading statesmen attending. As a whole, the memoirs usefully convey the essence of official British attitudes to the question of peacemaking.

HELDE, Thomas T.
The Blockade of Germany, November 1918—July 1919. Dissertation, Yale University (1949).
Does not fully explore the blockade's political implications for the Peace Conference.

HERZFELD, Hans.
"Nach vierzig Jahren, die Pariser Friedensschlüsse". *Politische Studien*, vol. 10 (1959), p. 425—34.
The author briefly reviews international scholarly opinion on the work of the Peace Conference and the Versailles Treaty, and examines the motives and hopes of those who made the Peace. He also assesses the contribution of Versailles to the outbreak of the Second World War. A suitably detached approach is employed by the author to all these topics.

HIRSCH, Helmut.
Die Saar in Versailles: die Saarfrage auf der Friedenskonferenz von 1919. Bonn: Röhrscheid (1952), 72 pp.
A short and unsatisfactory look at the Conference's handling of the Saar question. Dismisses too cavalierly the German proposals, which in the long term were seen to have been much sounder than those of the Allies.

HUSTON, James A.
"The Allied Blockade of Germany 1918—1919". *Journal of Central European Affairs*, vol. 10, pt. 2 (1950), p. 145—66.
The blockade was a means employed by the Allies to compel Germany's fulfilment of the peace terms. France in particular ignored the humanitarian angle, and the blockade was not lifted until June 1919 when the Germans reluctantly accepted what had been decided at Paris. This article has only sketched the Allied attitudes towards the blockade and there is virtually nothing on how Germany saw it. An inconclusive paper.

KING, Jere C.
Foch versus Clemenceau: France and German Disarmament 1918—1919. London: Oxford University Press (1960), 137 pp.
A clearly argued account of the Foch-Clemenceau struggle over the question of whether the Rhineland should be separated from Germany and this incorporated into the peace treaty. The militarists around Foch actively encouraged the separatists in 1918—19 while Clemenceau, knowing that Great Britain and the United States were against separatism, was concerned to maintain Allied unity and settle for a compromise. The theme of separatism is treated well, but the conflict between Foch and Clemenceau is not. Nor is it shown in detail why Clemenceau's views finally prevailed.

KITSIKIS, Dimitri.
Le Rôle des experts à la conférence de la paix de 1919: gestation d'une technocratie en politique internationale. Ottawa: Editions de l'Université d'Ottawa (1972), 227 pp.
This study draws attention to the work of hundreds of technical experts, including historians and lawyers, which was necessary for the running of the Conference. Organizational and procedural problems were on a particularly vast scale. However, the author has chosen to overlook the complexities of the situation, and has instead strung together a series of vague generalizations.

LEVIN, N. Gordon.
Woodrow Wilson and World Politics. New York (1968).
A very competent study which also contains a good discussion of Wilson's approach to the Peace Conference.

LOW, Alfred D.
See his work in section 19E (i).

MANTOUX, Paul.
Paris Peace Conference 1919: Proceedings of the Council of Four (March 24 — April 18). Geneva: Droz (1964).
The author was an interpreter at the Conference. By covering the period 24 March—18 April, his book usefully complements Hankey's account (see above) which leaves out this period.

MAYER, Arno J.
Politics and Diplomacy of Peacemaking: Containment and Counter-Revolution at Versailles 1918—1919. New York: Knopf (1968), 918 pp.
A scholarly and challenging work whose main thesis is that ideological considerations and the problem of revolution (Bolshevism) rather than the peace terms themselves were the primary concern of the statesmen. Mayer also examines Wilson's role and concludes that as a peacemaker he failed. The atmosphere in Europe in 1918—19 is vividly described and it is within this context that the author analyses the threat of revolution which, he maintains, was uppermost in the minds of the Allies as they deliberated on the future boundaries of European nations. This claim, though powerfully asserted by Mayer, is not supported by sufficient evidence. He is more convincing when discussing radical leftist policies and movements in Europe 1918—19.

NELSON, Harold J.
Land and Power: British and Allied Policy on Germany's Frontiers, 1916—1919. Newton Abbot: David & Charles (1973), 402 pp. New ed.
An informative study which investigates British, French and American policies in preparing the postwar territorial settlement with Germany. He reveals the significant differences of opinion among the Allies at the outset, but by 1919 most of these had been resolved.

RÖSSLER, Hellmuth (ed.).
Ideologie und Machtpolitik 1919: Plan und Werk der Pariser Friedenskonferenz 1919. Göttingen: Musterschmidt (1966), 273 pp.
A collection of articles by various scholars on aspects of the peacemaking process and Versailles. The editor himself writes on how Germany approached these issues.

SCHÜDDEKOPF, Otto-Ernst.
"German Foreign Policy between Compiègne and Versailles". *Journal of Contemporary History*, vol. 4, pt. 2 (1969), p. 181—97.
A discussion of Germany's attempt at shaping a new foreign policy between the collapse of the monarchy and the pro-

mulgation of the Peacy Treaty. The author examines the men and institutions that were involved, among them, the Foreign Ministry and the Supreme Army Command (in particular, Count Brockdorff-Rantzau and General Groener respectively). He affirms that Germany pursued an active foreign policy 1918—19 and that the foundations of later Weimar policy were laid at this time. An illuminating paper.

SCHWABE, Klaus.
Deutsche Revolution und Wilson-Frieden: die amerikanische und deutsche Friedensstrategie zwischen Ideologie und Machtpolitik 1918—19. Düsseldorf: Droste (1971), 711 pp.
An analysis of German-American relations between January 1918 and June 1919. The author is mainly concerned to reconcile the two major interpretations of Versailles: that it was a case where Wilson betrayed his idealistic principles to help saddle Germany with a *Diktat*, or that the Treaty was really meant to destroy the threat of Bolshevism (as Arno Mayer suggests). Schwabe offers a synthesis of these views, in which the German negotiating method is criticized sharply for adding to the general confusion and for trying to use Bolshevism as a bargaining ploy — a policy which Schwabe condemns as counter-productive. The author has carried out massive research, but much of his material is not original; moreover, the book makes for heavy reading, concerned as it is with facts. Nonetheless, he tries to present a balanced interpretation.

SNELL, John L.
"Wilson on Germany and the Fourteen Points". *Journal of Modern History*, vol. 26, pt. 4 (1954), p. 364—9.
Publishes a document of 16 October 1918 which reveals, more than any other, Wilson's thoughts on the constitutional reforms of the German government in October 1918. The document also provides Wilson's own interpretation of many of his fourteen points at the time when Germany accepted them as a basis for peace negotiations.

UNITED STATES GOVERNMENT.
Papers Relating to the Foreign Relations of the United States: the Paris Peace Conference 1919. Washington D.C.: U.S. Government Printing Office (1942—47).
A valuable documentary record, containing the minutes of the Council of Heads of Delegations (the governing body of the Peace Conference after the signing of the Treaty with Germany) from 1 July to 28 August 1919.

WATSON, D. R.
"The Making of the Treaty of Versailles". In N. Waites (ed.). *Troubled Neighbours: Franco-British Relations in the Twentieth Century.* London: Weidenfeld & Nicolson (1971).
Does not say anything that is new.

WHITEMAN, Harold (ed.).
Charles Seymour: Letters from the Paris Peace Conference. New Haven: Yale University Press (1966), 289 pp.
A collection of private letters from Seymour, the United Kingdom's specialist in Austria-Hungary at the Conference, to his wife and his parents-in-law. They are chiefly useful for the vivid evocation of the atmosphere in which the Conference took place.

(ii) The Treaty of Versailles

BAILEY, Gordon.
Dry Run for the Hangman: the Versailles-Leipzig Fiasco 1919—1921, Feeble Foreshadow of Nuremberg. Dissertation, University of Maryland (1971).

Examines futile attempts by the Allies to have a war crimes trial against Germans after the war. The Supreme Court in Leipzig took over the administration of the procedure, but only a small minority of the 900 accused were convicted. The author's point is that Leipzig was therefore the forerunner of Nuremberg though the Allies in 1919—21 learned something about planning, procedure and diplomacy in preparing an international judicial body.

BAUMGART, Winfried.
Vom Europäischen Konzert zum Völkerbund.
Darmstadt: Wissenschaftliche Buchgesellschaft (1974), 181 pp.
Provides a summary of previous research on a number of international treaties, including the Paris Peace Conference and Versailles, and discusses such themes as national self-determination, the war-guilt question, and reparations. A work for the general reader.

BAUMGART, Winfried.
"Brest-Litovsk und Versailles: ein Vergleich zweier Friedenschlüsse". *Historische Zeitschrift*, no. 210 (1970), p. 583—619.
A highly detailed comparison of the two treaties. The author is unwilling to see either as an undiluted *Diktat*, stating that in fact both represented compromises between opposing ideologies. A spirited argument, but not entirely convincing.

BRETTON, Henry L.
Stresemann and the Revision of Versailles: a Fight for Reason. Stanford: Stanford University Press (1953), 199 pp.
See section 19A (i) for review.

BRÜGEL, J. W.
"Das Schicksal der Strafbestimmungen des Versailles Vertrags". *Vierteljahrshefte für Zeitgeschichte*, vol. 6, pt. 3 (1958), p. 263—70.
A brief look at a little noticed aspect of the Treaty.

EPSTEIN, Fritz T.
"Zur Interpretation des Versailler Vertrages: der von Polen 1919—1922 erhobene Reparationsanspruch". *Jahrbücher für Geschichte Osteuropas*, vol. 5 (1957), p. 315—35.
Considers another dark aspect of postwar German-Polish relations, the dispute over whether Poland was due reparations payments from Germany. The Versailles Treaty was ambiguous on this issue.

HERZFELD, Hans.
Erster Weltkrieg und Friede von Versailles. Berlin: Propyläen-Verlag (1960), 127 pp.
A general, interpretative survey, designed for primary reading on the subject.

HIRSCH, Helmut.
Die Saar von Genf: die Saarfrage während des Völkerbundregimes von 1920—35. Bonn: Röhrscheid (1954), 96 pp.
Complements the author's earlier volume (see section 4B (i)). In this short study he merely outlines French attitudes to and connections with the Saar. The problem still awaits its historian.

LANGER, William.
"The Well-Spring of our Discontents", *Journal of Contemporary History*, vol. 3, pt. 4 (1968), p. 3—17.
A reassessment of the impact of the First World War and Versailles on the subsequent course of European history. Many other factors influenced the course — population change, technological innovation, urbanization, and the phenomenon of the Industrial Revolution — all of which had their origins in pre-1914 Europe. The author condemns reparations as an "international calamity" for victors and vanquished alike; the Treaty, he states, markedly contributed to the growth of National Socialism. In all, he condemns Versailles because it did not work. Many of the interpretations in this paper are controversial and are unlikely to gain wide support.

LEDERER, Ivo J. (ed.).
The Versailles Settlement: Was it Foredoomed to Failure? Boston: D.C. Heath & Co. (1960), 116 pp.
A volume in the Problems in European Civilization series, with the usual format of a selection of scholarly views, summarized in the editor's introduction. Most helpful for undergraduates.

LUCKAU, Alma.
"Unconditional Acceptance of the Treaty of Versailles by the German Government, June 22—28, 1919". *Journal of Modern History*, vol. 17, pt. 3 (1945), p. 215—20.
Publishes a memorandum dated 6 July 1919 of meetings of the German cabinet and party leaders on 22 and 23 June 1919 to discuss the signing of the Versailles Treaty. The first part of the memorandum explains the events preceding unconditional acceptance of the Treaty by the National Assembly on 23 June; the second part reveals the procedure by which the two signatories to the Treaty from the German side were chosen.

MANTOUX, Étienne.
The Carthaginian Peace, or the Economic Consequences of Mr. Keynes. London: Oxford University Press (1946), 210 pp.
A French indictment of Keynes' ideas; however, the book is not incisive enough, and is besides rather dull.

MATTHIAS, Erich.
"The Influence of the Versailles Treaty on the Internal Development of the Weimar Republic". In A. J. Nicholls and E. Matthias (eds.). *German Democracy and the Triumph of Hitler.* London: Allen & Unwin (1971), p. 13—28.
A balanced interpretation of the consequences of the Versailles Treaty for the development of Weimar politics. Domestic factors were more important in causing the collapse of the Republic and it was the psychological rather than the material consequences of Versailles that did most harm in Germany. But Versailles did place a heavy burden on the Republic and its constituent elements (e.g. the Dawes and Young Plans) were used as weapons in the domestic political struggle. Ultimately, not only the avowed enemies of the Republic but also its so-called democratic supporters must share the blame for the failure of democracy in 1933. Very worthwhile paper, whose opinions reflect current scholarly views.

MIQUEL, Pierre.
"Versailles im politischen Meinungsstreit Frankreichs 1919—1926". *Vierteljahrshefte für Zeitgeschichte*, vol. 20, pt. 1 (1972), p. 1—15.
A consideration of the different attitudes adopted by political groups in France towards the meaning and implementation of the Treaty.

MURALT, Leonard von.
From Versailles to Potsdam. Hinsdale (Illinois):
Regnery (1948), 93 pp.
A concise account of post-1918 peace treaties. The author
is critical of Versailles for lacking a conceptual framework,
and of the statesmen for not knowing or caring anything
of Europe. Hence, he argues, the Treaty was a disaster for
both sides. A stimulating work.

NAUMANN, Hans-Günter.
**"Über die wirtschaftlichen Auswirkungen des
Versailles Vertrages".** *Geschichte in Wissenschaft
und Unterricht,* vol. 21 (1970), p. 420—37.
A critical look at just how much, financially, Germany was
penalized by the economic clauses of the Treaty. Naumann
does his arithmetic and concludes that Germany did not
suffer unduly. Indeed, after 1923, the economic burden on
her was "astonishingly slight" (p. 436).

NICOLSON, Harold.
"Peacemaking at Paris: Success, Failure, or Farce?".
Foreign Affairs, vol. 25, pt. 2 (1947), p. 190—203.
Reflects on the lessons for the Western powers of the Peace
Conference which had elements of success, failure and farce
combined.

RÖSSLER, Hellmuth (ed.).
Die Folgen von Versailles 1919—1924. Göttingen:
Musterschmidt (1969), 195 pp.
A collection of articles by different scholars on matters
pertaining to the results of the Treaty. Georg Kotowski ex-
amines the effect of Versailles on the Weimar Republic, and
Maurice Baumont writes on French security problems 1920
—24.

RUGE, Wolfgang.
**"Zur chauvinistischen Propaganda gegen den
Versailles Vertrag 1919—1929".** *Jahrbuch für
Geschichte,* vol. 1 (1967), p. 65—106.
Contains a good deal of valuable information on the right-
wing campaign against Versailles. Ruge also pinpoints some
of the contradictions in the policies of the DNVP, for ex-
ample. Very useful.

RUMPF, Helmut.
"Fünfzig Jahre Versailler Vertrag". *Aussenpolitik,*
vol. 20, pt. 6 (1969), p. 368—78.
A brief review of changing views on the significance and
effect of the Treaty for the development of Germany and
Europe.

SCHMIDT, Royal J.
Versailles and the Ruhr: Seedbed of World War II.
The Hague: Nijhoff (1968), 310 pp.
For review see section 19B (i).

SCHULZE, Hagen.
"Der Oststaat-Plan 1919". *Vierteljahrshefte für
Zeitgeschichte,* vol. 18, pt. 2 (1970), p. 123—63.
One of the most preposterous ideas circulating in the con-
fusion of post-1918 Germany was that of establishing a
German state based on the eastern provinces as the best
way of preserving *Deutschtum.* The idea originated in east
German political circles in the face of aggressive designs by
the Poles on some German provinces (including East and
West Prussia). This detailed article, in investigating the plan,
also illuminates the high degree of tension between Germans and Poles in the east at the end of the war.

SHARP, A. J.
**Britain and France and the Execution of the Peace
of Versailles (sic), 1919—23, with Special Reference
to Disarmament and Reparations.** Dissertation,
University of Nottingham (1975).
Weak on the German side.

UNITED STATES GOVERNMENT.
**The Treaty of Versailles and after: Annotations
of the Text of the Treaty.** Washington, D.C.: U.S.
Government Printing Office (1947), 1018 pp.
A valuable aid to interpreting the numerous and some-
times ambiguous clauses of the Treaty.

WÜEST, Erich.
**Der Vertrag von Versailles im Licht und Schatten
der Kritik.** Zürich: Europa Verlag (1962), 277 pp.
The primary concern of the author is to examine the bitter
controversy over the economic and financial consequences
of the Treaty for Germany. His conclusion is now the
orthodox view; that Germany fared much better than contemporaries believed, and was not seriously hindered economically by reparations.

C. THE EARLY WEIMAR REPUBLIC (1919–1923)

(i) General

ANGRESS, Werner T.
**"Weimar Coalition and Ruhr Insurrection,
March—April 1920: a Study of Government
Policy".** *Journal of Modern History,* vol. 29, pt.1
(1957), p. 1--20.
An examination of an aspect of the political background to
the *Reichstag* election of June 1920 at which the "Weimar
Coalition" parties irrevocably lost their majority. One of
the immediate causes of this defeat, according to the author,
was the authorities' clumsy handling of the radical left-wing
revolt in the Ruhr in early spring 1920. He examines the
origins and course of this rising, which was suppressed by
the *Reichswehr.* Angress criticizes the government, and
Severing in particular, for failing to act as swiftly or as
decisively in the Ruhr as it had done against the Kapp
Putsch. A neatly argued piece.

ARNS, Günter.
**Regierungsbildung und Koalitionspolitik in der
Weimarer Republik 1919—1924.** Clausthal-
Zellerfeld: Bönecke Verlag (1971), 334 pp.
An excellent study, based on considerable primary research.
The complex factors involved in cabinet formation after
1920, when the Weimar coalition parties (SPD, DDP,
Centre) lost their majority, are particularly well analysed.
The rivalries and petty interests of the parties are vividly
described.

BIRKENFELD, Wolfgang.
**"Der Rufmord am Reichspräsidenten: zu
Grenzformen des politischen Kampfes gegen die
frühe Weimarer Republik 1919—1925".** *Archiv für
Sozialgeschichte,* vol. 5 (1965), p. 453—500.
An analysis of the politically inspired legal actions arising
from attacks by the Left and Right against the office of
Reich President and its first incumbent, Friedrich Ebert.
There were altogether 173 court actions 1919—25, involving
slander, defamation, libel, murder threats, etc. The author
gives a breakdown of the newspapers, magazines, and

personnel involved. A large documentary appendix contains details relating to the actions brought by Ebert, and extracts from threatening letters he received. The paper provides an interesting footnote to early Weimar history.

BROUÉ, Pierre.
"L'Allemagne des révolutions (1918–1923)".
Revue d'Histoire Moderne et Contemporaine,
vol. 12 (1965), p. 141–52.
A none too enlightening review of literature published since 1960 on the early Weimar period.

BROUÉ, Pierre.
Die deutsche Revolution, 1918–1923. Berlin:
Verlag Neuer Kurs (1973), 142 pp.
A far too superficial and simplistic narrative of the November Revolution and early developments in Weimar.

BUNDESZENTRALE FÜR HEIMATDIENST (ed.).
Die Weimarer Nationalversammlung. Bonn:
Selbstverlag (1960), 198 pp.
A reference book full of reliable and useful information about the composition and deliberations of the National Assembly.

HARBECK, Karlheinz (ed.).
Das Kabinett Cuno: 22. November 1922–
12. August 1923. (Akten der Reichskanzlei:
Weimarer Republik.) Boppard: Boldt (1968),
799 pp.
Contains selected reports of cabinet meetings, ministerial reports, memoranda and correspondence of the Reich Chancellor's office. They touch on the main concerns of the Cuno government, the struggle with the French in the Ruhr, reparations, and inflation. This is another well edited volume in this splendid documentary series.

KROHN, Claus-Dieter.
"Helfferich contra Hilferding: konservative Geldpolitik und die sozialen Folgen der deutschen Inflation 1918–1922". *Vierteljahrsschrift für Sozial- und Wirtschaftsgeschichte*, vol. 62, pt. 1 (1975), p. 62–92.
See section 13A (iv) for review.

KRUSCH, Hans-Joachim.
Um die Einheitsfront und eine Arbeiter-regierung.
East Berlin: Verlag Tribüne (1966), 399 pp.
See section 14 for review.

LAUBACH, Ernst.
Die Politik der Kabinette Wirth 1921–1922.
Lübeck: Matthiesen (1968), 344 pp.
This book deals mainly with Wirth's handling of foreign policy and reparations in particular. The author is objective and concludes that the Chancellor's record on these counts is satisfactory. On other themes, such as inflation, disarmament and domestic affairs, the book is much less impressive, for Laubach simply repeats in a synthesized form the opinions of others. Though the book is a valuable contribution to reparations studies, it is too descriptive as a whole.

OEHME, Walter.
Die Weimarer Nationalversammlung 1919:
Erinnerungen. East Berlin: Rütten & Loening
(1962), 403 pp.
Memoirs which betray the author's ideological and political

commitments rather too obviously. He is mainly concerned to convince his readers that the Republic was a tool of capitalism and that the SPD sabotaged the Revolution.

PRÜFER, Guntram; TORMIN, Walter.
Die Entstehung und Entwicklung der Weimarer Republik bis zu Eberts Tod. Hanover: Verlag für Literatur und Zeitgeschehen (1962), 66 pp. 4th ed.
A review of the November Revolution, the new party structure, economic and constitutional problems facing Weimar, and other important features of the 1918–23 era. To be used as an introduction to the period.

SCHULTZENDORFF, Walther von.
Proletarier und Prätorianer:
Bürgerkriegssituationen aus der Frühzeit der Weimarer Republik. Cologne: Markus-Verlag (1966), 211 pp.
The pressure exerted by the Left and Right on the early Republic is the theme of this general survey. He has not included any new material, nor does he offer fresh interpretations, but the narrative is smooth and free of howlers.

SCHULZE, Hagen (ed.).
Das Kabinett Scheidemann: 13. Februar bis 20.
Juni 1919. (Akten der Reichskanzlei: Weimarer Republik.) Boppard: Boldt (1971), 554 pp.
This volume contains a great deal of documentary material on the Scheidemann cabinet taken from the files of the Reich Chancellory. The editor supplies a competent introduction and the text is usefully footnoted.

SCHULZE-BIDLINGMAIER, Ingrid (ed.).
Das Kabinett Wirth I und II: 10. Mai 1921 bis 26. Oktober 1921; 26. Oktober 1921 bis 22. November 1922. (Akten der Reichskanzlei: Weimarer Republik.) 2 vols. Boppard: Boldt (1974), 1231 pp.
Another excellent contribution in the series. Rich in important documentation relating to cabinet meetings, meetings with party leaders and with government officials.

VOGT, Martin (ed.).
Das Kabinett Müller I: 27. März bis 21. Juni 1920.
(Akten der Reichskanzlei: Weimarer Republik.)
Boppard: Boldt (1971), 375 pp.
On the same lines as other volumes in the series and as well edited.

WILLIAMSON, John G.
Karl Helfferich 1872–1924: Economist, Financier, Politician. Princeton: Princeton University Press (1971), 439 pp.
See section 13A (iv) for review.

WITT, Peter-Christian.
"Reichsfinanzminister und Reichsfinanzverwaltung". *Vierteljahrshefte für Zeitgeschichte*, vol. 23, pt. 1 (1975), p. 1–61.
See section 13A (iv) for review.

WULF, Peter (ed.).
Das Kabinett Fehrenbach, 25. Juni 1920 bis 4. Mai 1921. (Akten der Reichskanzlei: Weimarer Republik.) Boppard: Boldt (1972), 720 pp.
The Fehrenbach minority cabinet was mainly involved with the reparations question over which it eventually collapsed. Most of the documentation in this volume throws light on reparations. An excellent documentary source.

(ii) Kapp Putsch

ELIASBERG, George
Der Ruhrkrieg von 1920. Bad Godesberg: Verlag
Neue Gesellschaft (1974), 304 pp.
One of the best studies available on this theme. The author
examines the contribution of the labour movement to the
defeat of the Putsch, but argues that this was a hollow
victory because the substance of the anti-democratic
counter-revolution in Weimar remained intact. Eliasberg
argues that the Putsch era in 1920 afforded the Republic a
second opportunity (the first being the November Revolution) to achieve a solid democratic order, but once again
the chance was lost. The author successfully presents new
ideas in this monograph.

ELIASBERG, George
**"Der Ruhrkrieg 1920: zum Problem von Organ-
isation und Spontaneität in einem Massenaufstand
und zur Dimension der Weimarer Krise".** *Archiv
für Sozialgeschichte*, vol. 10 (1970), p. 291—377.
Most of the material here is to be found in one form or
another in his book. He discusses the possibilities of
democratizing the Republic, and expertly examines the
political, economic, and social conditions in the Ruhr
region which gave rise to the civil war in 1920. The reasons
why the proletariat was unable to maintain a common front
for long are amply documented.

ERGER, Johannes.
**Der Kapp-Lüttwitz-Putsch: ein Beitrag zur
deutschen Innenpolitik 1919—20.** Düsseldorf:
Droste (1967), 365 pp.
An important study, thoroughly documented, but concentrates only on Berlin. The author argues that the Putsch was
a largely military affair initiated by Lüttwitz; his analysis of
the weaknesses of the government and strengths of the
labour movement is good, though he tends to play down
the political significance of the general strike. Moreover,
Erger goes some way towards offering an apologia for the
Reichswehr.

FELDMAN, Gerald D.
"Big Business and the Kapp Putsch". *Central
European History*, vol. 4, pt. 2 (1971), p. 99—130.
A detailed and valuable study of the response of big business
to the Kapp Putsch, which thus provides also an insight into
how this influential group viewed the Republic in general.
The author discusses pre-1920 efforts to depoliticize capital-
labour disputes and the role of organizations like the
Reichsverband der deutschen Industrie and the *Zentral-
arbeitsgemeinschaft*. Most businessmen rejected the Putsch,
but for the wrong reasons and in a way that did little to
strengthen the Republic. Although anti-republican in outlook they considered the time inappropriate for a putsch.

HAMMER, Franz
**Freistaat Gotha im Kapp-Putsch, nach Doku-
menten und Erinnerungen alter Mitkämpfer erzählt.**
East Berlin: Verlag Neues Leben (1955), 123 pp.
Provides details on the local situation and resistance to the
Putschists, but it is questionable how far this account,
based on the testimony of former activists, is reliable.

HELLFAIER, Karl.
**"Die vereinigte Friedrichs-Universität in Halle-
Wittenberg und der Kapp-Putsch: Quellen zur
Geschichte der Weimarer Republik".** *Archiv für
Sozialgeschichte*, vol. 2 (1962), p. 359—68.

Publishes interesting contemporary documents which
reveal the attempts of the university authorities to remain
neutral in the conflict.

HENNICKE, Otto.
Die rote Ruhrarmee. East Berlin: Verlag des
Ministeriums für Nationale Verteidigung (1956),
118 pp.
A misleading account which tries to propagate the myth of
the unity of the working class in the Ruhr in 1920 under
the leadership of the KPD. The author's arguments otherwise adhere closely to the party line. Very much inferior to
Eliasberg's work.

HERBER, Hugo.
**Vor 40 Jahren: Niederschlagung des Kapp-Putsches
in Südthüringen.** East Berlin: Institut für
Marxismus-Leninismus (1962).
An unreliable study which contains exaggerated claims on
the role of the KPD in defeating the Putschists.

INSTITUT FÜR MARXISMUS-LENINISMUS.
**Arbeitereinheit siegt über Militaristen:
Erinnerungen an der Niederschlagung des Kapp-
Putsches, März 1920.** East Berlin: Dietz Verlag
(1960), 203 pp.
Does not even attempt to offer an objective, scholarly
appraisal of the working class role in defeating the Putsch.
The KPD is alloted unwarranted prominence.

KOENEN, Wilhelm.
**"Zur Frage der Möglichkeit einer Arbeiterregierung
nach dem Kapp-Putsch."** *Beiträge zur Geschichte
der Deutschen Arbeiterbewegung*, vol. 4 (1962),
p. 342—52.
Highly speculative, and claiming absurdly that the SPD was
the principal obstacle to a working class government in
1920. For one thing, the author conveniently forgets that
the proletariat was by no means united after the Putsch, as
events in the Ruhr clearly revealed.

KÖNNEMANN, Erwin (ed.).
**Arbeiterklasse siegt über Kapp und Lüttwitz:
Quellen.** 2 vols. East Berlin: Akademie-Verlag
(1971), 948 pp.
An impressive documentary collection, much of the material
from East German archives in Potsdam and Merseburg, with
emphasis naturally on the response of the working class and
the KPD to the Putsch. The editorial comments reflect a
familiar political tone. Nonetheless, the volumes must be
regarded as a standard source of reference.

KÖNNEMANN, Erwin; KRUSCH, Hans-Joachim.
**Aktionseinheit contra Kapp Putsch: der Kapp
Putsch im März 1920 und der Kampf der
deutschen Arbeiterklasse.** East Berlin: Dietz Verlag
(1972), 575 pp.
A highly propagandistic work which sees the united front
presented by the working classes against the Putsch
reaching its logical climax in the establishment of the
German Democratic Republic. The volume does, however,
provide interesting extracts from contemporary speeches,
proclamations, and party statements, as well as detailed
information on reactions to the Putsch in many large towns.

KRAUSE, Fritz (ed.).
**Arbeitereinheit rettet die Republik: Dokumente
und Materialien zur Niederschlagung des Kapp-
Putsches im März 1920.** Frankfurt: Verlag
Marxistische Blätter (1970), 181 pp.
The editor's political bias is evident throughout this book.

He exaggerates the longevity of working class unity in 1920 and he ignores the fact that it was not only the workers who helped defeat the Putsch. The eighty documents included are, however, interesting, throwing light, for example, on the warnings of the KPD in 1920 against a right-wing putsch, and on the ruthlessness of the *Reichswehr* in the Ruhr.

KRUPPA, Reinhold.
Die Niederlausitz griff zur Waffe: die Abwehr des Kapp-Putsches in der Niederlausitz. East Berlin: Verlag des Ministeriums für Nationale Verteidigung (1957), 78 pp.
This local study does not change our interpretation of the nature and extent of the resistance to the Putsch, but it furnishes a few noteworthy details for the Lower Lausitz area.

LUCAS, Erhard.
Märzrevolution 1920. Vol. I: Vom Generalstreik gegen den Militärputsch zum bewaffneten Arbeiteraufstand. Vol. II: Der bewaffnete Arbeiteraufstand im Ruhrgebiet . . . zu den Klassenkämpfen in den verschiedenen Regionen des Reiches. Frankfurt: Verlag Roter Stern (1973—74), 251, 364 pp.
Volume I is particularly heavily documented on the Putsch, the general strike and the war in the Ruhr. Volume II provides extensive detail on the events throughout Germany, but above all in Berlin. All in all, the documentation reaches a very high standard, but the author's interpretations are frequently rather odd. He is critical of the left-wing parties and of displays of local patriotism by workers.

LUCAS, Erhard.
"Die Widerstandsbewegung gegen den Kapp-Putsch in der DDR-Historiographie". *International nationale Wissenschaftliche Korrespondenz zur Geschichte der Deutschen Arbeiterbewegung*, vol. 18, pt. 1 (1973), p. 72—9.
A brief but illuminating discussion.

LUCKAU, Alma.
"Kapp Putsch — Success or Failure?" *Journal of Central European Affairs*, vol. 7, pt. 4 (1948), p. 394—405.
Besides looking at the broader aspects of the Putsch, the author tries to account for the ambiguous role of Seeckt and some of his colleagues in the Ministry of Defence. She argues that the army was in any case strengthened as a result of the affair, with Seeckt being the "real victor". In a long-term perspective, she sees the Putsch as allowing the army to begin developing as a "state within a state". Some scholars might predate this development.

PFOTENHAUER, Otto.
März 1920: die Niederschlagung des Kapp-Putsches durch die Einheitsaktion der Weimarer Republik. Weimar: Stadtmuseen (1973), 32 pp.
Another pamphlet which seeks to promote the erroneous myth of working class unity before, during, and after the Putsch.

POLZIN, Martin.
Kapp-Putsch in Mecklenburg: Junkertum und Landproletariat in der revolutionaren Krise nach dem 1. Weltkrieg. Rostock: Hinstorff Verlag (1966), 333 pp.

The author shows that the Putschists received considerable backing from the traditionally conservative-nationalist landowners of Mecklenburg, while, he argues, the urban working class and rural peasantry resisted the Putschists. He certainly distorts the outlook of the peasantry which notoriously followed the political attitudes of their landowners and later flocked to the NSDAP.

SCHLOTTNER, Erich H.
Stresemann, der Kapp-Putsch, und die Ereignisse in Mitteldeutschland und in Bayern im Herbst 1923: ein Beitrag zur Geschichte der Weimarer Republik. Dissertation, University of Frankfurt/Main (1948).
Rather too ambitious in scope, but containing some interesting detail.

SCHUNKE. Joachim.
Schlacht um Halle: die Abwehr des Kapp-Putsches in Halle und Umgebung. East Berlin: Verlag des Ministeriums für Nationale Verteidigung (1956), 111 pp.
A useful local study, though inevitably prone to exaggerating the organizing influence of the KPD.

D. THE "YEARS OF STABILITY" (1924—1928).

ABRAMOWSKI, Günter (ed.).
Das Kabinett Marx I und II: 30. November 1923 bis 3. Juni 1924; 3. Juni 1924 bis 15. Januar 1925. (Akten der Reichskanzlei: Weimarer Republik.) 2 vols. Boppard: Boldt (1973), 1406 pp.
Continues the exemplary standard of previous volumes in the series. A rich collection of documentary sources.

BAUMGARTEN, Dieter.
Deutsche Finanzpolitik 1924—1928. Berlin: Ernst-Reuter-Gesellschaft (1965), 223 pp.
For review, see section 13A (iv).

BLUNCK, Jürgen.
Der Gedanke der Grossen Koalition in den Jahren 1923—1928. Dissertation, University of Kiel (1961).
Undistinguished.

FRAENKEL, Ernst.
"Der Ruhreisenstreit 1928—1929 in historisch-politischer Sicht". In F.A. Hermens & T. Schieder (eds.). *Staat, Wirtschaft, und Politik in der Weimarer Republik: Festschrift für Heinrich Brüning.* Berlin: Duncker & Humblot (1967), p. 97—118.
See section 14 for review.

HAUNGS, Peter.
Reichspräsident und parlamentarische Kabinettsbildung: eine Studie zum Regierungssystem der Weimarer Republik in den Jahren 1924 bis 1929. Cologne: Westdeutscher Verlag (1968), 362 pp.
An examination of how the government system functioned 1924—29 from the perspective of relations between the

Reich President, cabinet and coalition. The author provides a careful analysis therefore of the six cabinets 1924—29, with a case study of the fourth one, the Marx government. He stresses the important role of the President, yet seems to contradict this view when he refers to the dualism in competence between the President and the cabinet. Haungs also fails to discuss adequately the different attitudes towards government of the political parties. This is a serious omission in a book which is of uneven quality.

KROHN, Claus-Dieter.
Stabilisierung und ökonomische Interessen: die Finanzpolitik des deutschen Reiches 1923—1927.
Düsseldorf: Bertelsmann (1974), 287 pp.
See section 13A (iv) for review.

NETZBAND, Karl-Bernhard; WIDMAIER, Hans P.
Wahrungs- und Finanzpolitik der Ära Luther 1923—1925. Tübingen: Mohr (1964), 286 pp.
For review, see section 13A (iv)

SCHINKEL, Harald.
Entstehung und Zerfall der Regierung Luther.
Dissertation, Free University of Berlin (1959).
A competent narrative, which has some interesting notes on Stresemann.

STOCKHAUSEN, Max von.
Sechs Jahre Reichskanzlei: Erinnerungen und Tagebuchnotizen 1922—1927. Edited by Walter Goerlitz. Bonn: Athenäum Verlag (1954), 279 pp.
The author was the recorder of the minutes of Reich Chancellory meetings and the personal aide to many Weimar chancellors. Based on his notes and diaries, this memoir provides a rather incomplete narrative of German politics in the 1920s, and as a whole the book does not increase our knowledge of the period to any extent. His recollections of personalities are also fragmentary.

STÜRMER, Michael.
Koalition und Opposition in der Weimarer Republik 1924—28. Düsseldorf: Droste (1967), 319 pp.
By far the most authoritative political history of these middle years. Detailed and penetrating, the author's analysis reveals the many elements of instability and uncertainty during the period in government, the parties, civil service, and the army. As a result, the formation of cabinets was a frequent exercise for the politicians as one minority administration followed another. The author has used much new archival material for this study.

STÜRMER, Michael.
"Parliamentary Government in Weimar Germany 1924—1928". In A. J. Nicholls & E. Matthias (eds.). *German Democracy and the Triumph of Hitler.* London: Allen & Unwin (1971), p. 59—77.
A review of the economic, ideological, and political problems which bedevilled the minority cabinets of these years. Most of the problems were inherited from the pre-1924 period and remained unsolved throughout this time because of the fluctuating state of government and coalition.

STÜRMER, Michael.
"Probleme der parlamentarischen Mehrheitsbildung in der Stabilisierungsphase der Weimarer Republik". *Politische Vierteljahrsschrift,* vol. 8, pt. 1 (1967), p. 71—87.
An informative analysis of the conflicting political interests which made the achievement of cabinet stability an impossibility from 1924 to 1928.

WEST, Franklin.
The Parties, the Princes, and the People: a Study of the German Referendum of June 20, 1926. Dissertation, University of California (1970).
The question of whether properties of the former royal houses should be confiscated by the state aroused passionate controversy in Germany in 1925—26. The author examines both sides of the campaign, and the attitudes of the major political parties in the country and in the *Reichstag.* His main point is that this affair represented a breakdown of parliamentary democracy and the abuse of democratic institutions. A valuable study.

E. THE "GRAND COALITION" ERA (1928—1930)

CONZE, Werner.
"Die Krise des Parteienstaates in Deutschland 1929/30". *Historische Zeitschrift,* no. 178 (1954), p. 47—83.
An excellent analysis of the reasons for the collapse of the parliamentary system in March 1930. Sees the fundamental cause as lying in the structural weakness of the Republic from the beginning; the immediate causes of collapse, especially the social and political antagonisms engendered by the economic depression, should not be stressed too much. Not all historians would accept this line of thought.

DRESS, Hans; HAMPEL, Manfred; IMIG, Werner.
"Zur Politik der Hermann-Müller-Regierung 1928—1930". *Zeitschrift für Geschichtswissenschaft,* vol. 10, pt. 8 (1962), p. 1871—90.
Concerned with attacking SPD intellectual Willi Eichler for allegedly falsifying SPD party history. The authors argue that Eichler has tried to conceal the true picture of Müller's "aggressive" and "imperialist" policies. This sounds most dubious indeed.

HOLZER, Jerzy.
Parteien und Massen: die politische Krise in Deutschland 1928—1930. Wiesbaden: Steiner (1975), 106 pp.
A carefully documented study of the nature of the political crisis and the factors and trends affecting the situation. Examines in particular the effects of the 1928 and 1930 *Reichstag* election results on the major political parties. Many useful tables are given.

JASPER, Gotthard.
"Zur innerpolitischen Lage in Deutschland im Herbst 1929". *Vierteljahrshefte für Zeitgeschichte,* vol. 8, pt. 3 (1960), p. 280—9.
Publishes an interesting memorandum written by Carl Severing in December 1929 on political excesses.

LOHE, Eilert.
Der Bruch der Grossen Koalition und die Anfänge der Regierung Brüning im Urteil englischer Diplomaten. Dissertation, Free University of Berlin (1961).
An examination of the British Ambassador's reports on the German domestic and external situation during the period March 1930 — June 1931. It cannot be said that the reports reveal consistent perceptiveness.

MAMMACH, Klaus.
"Der Sturz der Grossen Koalition im März 1930".
Zeitschrift für Geschichtswissenschaft, vol. 16,
pt. 5 (1968), p. 565–86.
A rather too obviously politically biased paper, in which
the SPD predictably come in for rough treatment.

MAURER, Ilse.
Reichsfinanzen und Grosse Koalition: zur
Geschichte des Reichskabinetts Müller
(1928–1930). Frankfurt: Herbert Lang Verlag
(1973), 269 pp.
The main emphasis is on the financial, social and economic
policies of the Müller "Grand Coalition" government; it was
disagreement over these policies which provided the immediate cause of the cabinet's disintegration. Maurer competently analyses the attitudes of the coalition partners in
these areas and tries to suggest ways in which their differences could have been resolved.

TIMM, Helga.
Die deutsche Sozialpolitik und der Bruch der
Grossen Koalition im März 1930. Düsseldorf:
Droste (1952), 215 pp.
In her examination of why the Müller government collapsed,
the author underlines the significance of social policy as a
divisive factor among the coalition partners. She delves
deeply into the complexities of social policy and discusses
different party attitudes to it since 1918, and also the bitterness the subject caused between the trade unions and
employers. The SPD and DVP represented opposite sides
and, of course, disagreement between these parties over
unemployment insurance premiums came to a head in early
1930. Both sides had a measure of responsibility for this,
but Timm is especially critical of the DVP's intransigence.
An informative study, carefully researched, but badly
written and organized, and containing too many value
judgements.

VOGT, Martin (ed.).
Das Kabinett Müller II. 28. Juni 1928– 27. März
1930. (Akten der Reichskanzlei: Weimarer
Republik.) 2 vols. Boppard: Boldt (1970),
1682 pp.
A further carefully edited and valuable volume in this series.
In his introduction, Vogt discusses the nature of the crisis
of the party state and the main problems confronting the
Müller cabinet. The documentation is well arranged and
provides an indispensable fund of material on this important
period.

VOGT, Martin (ed.).
Die Entstehung des Youngplans; dargestellt vom
Reichsarchiv 1931–1933. Boppard: Boldt (1970),
396 pp.
Complements the above-mentioned documentary collection.
This is an account of the origins of the Young Plan com-
missioned by the German government in 1931 to refute
allegations made about the Plan by Hjalmar Schacht in a
book. The commission was not completed until 1933 by
which time it had lost its relevance. The account provides
an insight into official German opinion on the negotiations
preceding the signing of the Plan.

F. THE BRÜNING ERA (1930–1932)

ARETIN, Kurt O. von.
"Brünings ganz andere Rolle: seine Verfassungs-
pläne; Bemerkungen zu den Memoiren".
Frankfurter Hefte, vol. 26, pt. 12 (1971),
p. 931–9
Argues that Brüning's memoirs (see below) confirm what

the author stated in an earlier article (see section 2), namely,
that Brüning's constitutional reform plans not only indicated a shift in official government thinking towards
authoritarianism, but also contributed significantly to the
widespread lack of loyalty to the constitution during the
last days of the Weimar Republic.

AUERBACH, Hellmuth.
"Die Regierung Brüning". *Vierteljahrshefte für
Zeitgeschichte*, vol. 14, pt. 1 (1966), p. 103–4.
This is a report and a summary of the main conclusions
reached at a symposium on the Brüning government in
Cologne in November 1965. Much of the discussion focused
on the question: what kind of government was the Brüning
administration? Was it the last democratic one of the
Republic, or was it an authoritarian forerunner of the
Hitler régime?

BAERWALD, Friedrich.
"Kritische Erinnerungen zu Brünings Memoiren".
Frankfurter Hefte, vol. 26, pt. 10 (1971),
p. 767–74.
Considers that the memoirs are important and should be
essential reading for all politicians, even though Brüning
does not provide any new significant facts. Baerwald also
gives a résumé of the Chancellor's career.

BECKER, Josef.
"Heinrich Brüning in den Krisenjahren der
Weimarer Republik". *Geschichte in Wissenschaft
und Unterricht*, vol. 17, pt. 4 (1966), p. 201–19.
A useful survey of Brüning's political career 1919–30, and
of several important publications on the period of his
chancellorship. Brüning's ideas on various domestic and
foreign policy issues are analysed as are the influences
which helped mould these ideas.

BENNETT, Edward W.
Germany and the Diplomacy of the Financial
Crisis, 1931. Cambridge (Mass.): Harvard
University Press (1962), 345 pp.
See section 19B (v) for review.

BERGHAHN, Volker R.
See his article in section 1.

BORCKE-STARGORDT, Henning.
Der ostdeutsche Landbau zwischen Fortschritt,
Krise und Politik. Würzburg: Holzner (1957),
200 pp.
See section 13A (iii) (a) for review.

BORN, Karl E.
Die deutsche Bankenkrise 1931: Finanzen und
Politik. Munich: Piper (1967), 286 pp.
See section 13A (iv) for review.

BRACHER, Karl Dietrich.
"Brünings unpolitische Politik und die Auflösung
der Weimarer Republik". *Vierteljahrshefte für
Zeitgeschichte*, vol. 19, pt. 2 (1971), p. 113–23.
Bracher writes that interpretations of the Republic's collapse
must now be substantially modified as a result of certain
passages in Brüning's otherwise disappointing memoirs. This
is because the memoirs destroy many illusions not only
about Brüning personally and his policies, but also about
the character and importance of the presidential cabinet
1930–32. The key to the Brüning myth was the assertion
that his course of action offered the only possibility of overcoming the Weimar crisis and saving democracy. Bracher
insists that those who formerly defended the Brüning

experiment, like Werner Conze, must now change their minds. This is the author's main point in his highly critical assessment of the memoirs.

BRECHT, Arnold.
"Gedanken über Brünings Memoiren". *Politische Vierteljahrsschrift*, vol. 12, pt. 4 (1971), p. 607—40.
Reviews all expressed opinions on the memoirs and attempts to sum up. On the whole the author is disappointed with the lack of substantive content, though many themes are touched upon.

BRÜNING, Heinrich.
Memoiren 1918—1934. 2 vols. Stuttgart: Deutsche Verlagsanstalt (1970), 721 pp.
These posthumously published memoirs cover an important period of modern German history, and, in particular, the period of Brüning's chancellorship. He reveals few new facts, and indeed confirms the long-held thesis that during 1930—32 his main efforts were in foreign policy. His descriptions of leading political figures are interesting, and his connections with Gregor Strasser are shown to have been surprisingly firm. Although the overall value of the memoirs is a matter of controversy, they should be essential reading for scholars of Weimar.

BRÜNING, Heinrich.
"Ein Brief". *Deutsche Rundschau*, vol. 70 (July 1947), p. 1—22.
A valuable record of political manoeuvres in the last year of the Republic.

BRÜNING, Heinrich.
Briefe und Gespräche 1934—1945. Edited by Claire Nix. Stuttgart: Deutsche Verlagsanstalt (1974), 556 pp.
More revealing of Brüning's personality than anything else.

BRÜNING, Heinrich.
Briefe 1946—1960. Edited by Claire Nix. Stuttgart: Deutsche Verlagsanstalt (1974), 517 pp.
Contains only fragmentary references to the pre-1933 political situation in Weimar.

BRÜNING, Heinrich.
Reden und Aufsätze eines deutschen Staatsmanns. Edited by Wilhelm Vernekohl. Münster: Verlag Regensberg (1968). 358 pp.
Consists largely of speeches and lectures delivered by Brüning shortly before and during his period in the Chancellor's office, and also after the Second World War (1946—54). The editors provide background information to the contents, but by and large they are too uncritical in their comments.

BUCHHEIM, Karl.
"Heinrich Brüning und das Ende der Weimarer Republik". *Hochland*, vol. 58 (1965—66), p. 501—12.
A brief but considered assessment of Brüning's role in the last year of the Republic and of the impact of his policies on the declining political situation.

BUCHTA, Bruno.
Die Junker und die Weimarer Republik. East Berlin: Deutscher Verlag der Wissenschaften (1959), 176 pp.
See section 13A (iii) (c) for review.

CONZE, Werner.
"Die Regierung Brüning". In F. A. Hermens & T. Schieder (eds.). *Staat, Wirtschaft, und Politik in der Weimarer Republik: Festschrift für Heinrich Brüning.* Berlin: Duncker & Humblot (1967), p. 233—48.
An interpretative analysis of the Brüning government. The author stresses the extremely difficult circumstances in which Brüning not only came to power but also had to govern. His area for manoeuvre was limited and Conze defends his decision to dissolve the *Reichstag* in July 1930. He also argues that the Chancellor's financial and economic policy must be seen as part of his *Gesamtpolitik* and must be judged only on that basis. Finally, Conze affirms his belief in Brüning's assertion that he was only one hundred metres from his goal when he fell from office. The paper is obviously too sympathetic to Brüning, and following the publication of the former Chancellor's memoirs, few will support the views expressed here.

CONZE, Werner.
"Brünings Politik unter dem Druck der grossen Krise". *Historische Zeitschrift*, no. 199 (1964), p. 528—50.
Conze repeats the main argument of the above-cited article, that Brüning performed well amid the most trying circumstances, and that he was removed from office just before attaining his goal.

CONZE, Werner.
"Zum Sturz Brünings". *Vierteljahrshefte für Zeitgeschichte*, vol. 1, pt. 3 (1953), p. 261—88.
Provides important documentation on the reasons for the Chancellor's dismissal from office in May 1932.

CONZE, Werner.
"Brüning als Reichskanzler: eine Zwischenbilanz". *Historische Zeitschrift*, no. 214 (1972), p. 310—34.
Conze presents his interim balance sheet of the historical controversy surrounding Brüning and his government 1930—32. He discusses mainly Brüning's domestic policies, but stresses the fundamental connection between these and his foreign policy. His foreign policy is seen as a continuation of the policies of previous governments in working to liquidate the Versailles Treaty by ending reparations and achieving military equality for Germany. In total, the author does not seem to have drastically modified his previous ideas on the Brüning cabinet.

DEIST, Wilhelm.
"Brüning, Herriot und die Abrüstungsgespräche von Bessinge 1932". *Vierteljahrshefte für Zeitgeschichte*, vol. 5, pt. 3 (1957), p. 265—72.
See section 19B (vi) for review.

GNICHWITZ, S.
Die Presse der bürgerlichen Rechten in der Ära Brüning. Dissertation, University of Münster (1956).
See section 16A (iv) for review.

GOTTO, Klaus.
"Die Memoiren eines Kanzlers". *Die Politische Meinung*, no. 139, vol. 16 (1971), p. 85—91.
A review of the Brüning memoirs.

GRAML, Hermann.
"Präsidialsystem und Aussenpolitik". *Vierteljahrshefte für Zeitgeschichte*, vol. 21, pt. 2 (1973), p. 134—45.
He questions Conze's argument (*Historische Zeitschrift*, no.

214 (1972) — see above) that Brüning's foreign policy was fundamentally no different from that of previous Reich governments in its aim of ending reparations and achieving military equality for Germany. Graml rejects this continuity thesis, arguing there was a new course in foreign policy under Brüning which lent the presidential cabinet special characteristics. He states that like Brüning's constitutional and social-political restorative outlook, his foreign policy revealed a desire to return to the Wilhelmine era. Graml therefore sees Brüning's foreign policy as preparing the way in many respects for Hitler's foreign policy.

HELBICH, Wolfgang.
"Between Stresemann and Hitler: the Foreign Policy of the Brüning Government". *World Politics*, vol. 12, pt. 4 (1959), p. 24—45.
Unsympathetic to Brüning's affirmation of the primacy of foreign policy to the virtual exclusion of domestic policy. Helbich, however, is more concerned with defending the SPD's attitude to Brüning's foreign policy; he does not think the party should be blamed for refusing to give unqualified support to it, that SPD toleration of the government was a big enough concession. Not an entirely convincing argument.

HELBICH, Wolfgang.
Die Reparationen in der Ära Brüning. Berlin: Colloquium Verlag (1962), 139 pp.
Argues that the key to understanding Brüning's policy, especially his economic policy, is the reparations question. Since Brüning stressed the primacy of foreign over domestic policy and since reparations dominated the government's approach, the whole Brüning period must be assessed from the standpoint of reparations; everything else stemmed from this issue, Helbich contends. It also explains, he adds, Brüning's retrenchment policy. A brief but thought-provoking study.

HERMENS, Ferdinand A.
"Das Kabinett Brüning und die Depression". In F.A. Hermens & T. Schieder (eds.). *Staat, Wirtschaft und Politik in der Weimarer Republik: Festschrift für Heinrich Brüning.* Berlin: Duncker & Humblot (1967), p. 287—310.
Presents a revisionist assessment of Brüning's economic, financial and monetary policies which have been the subject of so much criticism. The author argues that certain aspects of Brüning's policies have been misunderstood, while other aspects have not been given proper attention. But his defence of Brüning, though skilful, does not convince, for it relies too heavily on the benefits provided by historical hindsight. He tries to show that the economic situation in Germany in 1930—32, for example, was not as bad as contemporaries made out. Overall, the article is too subjective and is based exclusively on secondary sources.

KADZIK, Konrad.
England und Deutschland 1930—1932: eine Studie über die britische Stellungnahme zu den aussenpolitischen Problemen Deutschlands unter Reichskanzler Heinrich Brüning. Dissertation, Free University of Berlin (1959).
See section 19A (ii) for review.

KNAPP, Thomas A.
"Heinrich Brüning in Exil: Briefe an Wilhelm Sollmann 1940—1946". *Vierteljahrshefte für Zeitgeschichte*, vol. 22, pt. 1 (1974), p. 93—120.
The nine letters reproduced here allow a look into Brüning's work and thoughts during his period of exile in the United States in the 1930s and 1940s. The letters were addressed to the former SPD *Reichstag* deputy (1919—33) and Editor in Chief of the *Rheinische Zeitung* (1920—33), Sollmann. The letters contain, among other things, remarks on political events in Germany 1930—32.

KÖHLER, Henning.
"Arbeitsbeschaffung Siedlung und Reparationen in der Schlussphase der Regierung Brüning". *Vierteljahrshefte für Zeitgeschichte*, vol. 17, pt. 3 (1969), p. 276—307.
See section 13A (ii) (c) for review.

KOOPS, Tilman P.
"Heinrich Brünings 'Politische Erfahrungen'". *Geschichte in Wissenschaft und Unterricht*, vol. 24, pt. 4 (1973), p. 197—221.
A sound, detailed review of Part I of the memoirs.

LOHE, Eilert.
Heinrich Brüning: Offiziere, Staatsmann, Gelehrter. Göttingen: Musterschmidt (1969), 97 pp.
A general survey of Brüning's life and political career which does not raise any of the fundamental problems relating to the former Chancellor.

MIRGELER, Albert.
"Brünings Memoiren". *Hochland*, vol. 63, pt. 2 (1971), p. 201–26.
The author takes a rather more favourable view of Brüning as Chancellor than most. He thinks the memoirs are a "goldmine of political insights". He concedes that Brüning may not have been a genuine political leader, but he was a person of great humanity and one who had an expert understanding of politics.

MOMMSEN, Hans.
"Betrachtungen zu den Memoiren Heinrich Brünings". *Jahrbuch für die Geschichte Mittel- und Ostdeutschlands*, vol. 22 (1973), p. 270—80.
An unflattering review.

MORSEY, Rudolf.
Brüning und Adenauer: zwei deutsche Staatsmänner. Düsseldorf: Droste (1972), 44 pp.
Published version of previous lectures on the two statesmen. Morsey is fair in his appraisal of Brüning.

MORSEY, Rudolf.
Zur Entstehung, Authentizität und Kritik von Brünings "Memoiren 1918—1934". Opladen Westdeutscher Verlag (1975), 54 pp.
A most useful and balanced commentary on the memoirs which is apposite in view of the considerable controversy aroused by them.

MORSEY, Rudolf.
"Neue Quellen zur Vorgeschichte der Reichskanzlerschaft Brünings". In F. A. Hermens & T. Schieder (eds.). *Staat, Wirtschaft und Politik in der Weimarer Republik: Festschrift für Heinrich Brüning.* Berlin: Duncker & Humblot (1967), p. 207—32.
A paper which sets out to lay the basis for an authoritative account of the prelude to Brüning's appointment as Chancellor, and of the rapid formation of his cabinet. Using new material, including the protocols of meetings of the Centre Party's *Reichstag* faction, Hermann Pünder's papers, protocols of cabinet meetings, as well as Brüning's memorandum on his famous talk with Hindenburg on 1 March 1930, Morsey reassesses the part played by Brüning in the downfall of the Müller government. Seven of these new documents are published as an appendix to the text.

MUTH, Heinrich.
"Agrarpolitik und Parteipolitik im Frühjahr 1932".
In F. A. Hermens & T. Schieder (eds.). *Staat,
Wirtschaft und Politik in der Weimarer Republik:
Festschrift für Heinrich Brüning.* Berlin: Duncker
& Humblot (1967), p. 317—60.
See section 13A (iii) (a) for review.

MUTH, Heinrich.
"Zum Sturz Brünings". *Geschichte in Wissenschaft
und Unterricht*, vol. 16, pt. 12 (1965), p. 739—59.
An analysis of the agrarian dimension and its political
ramifications which contributed so importantly to Brüning's
fall from office. This paper is in fact a condensed version of
the above-cited essay by the author.

MUTH, Heinrich.
"Quellen zu Brüning". *Geschichte in Wissenschaft
und Unterricht*, vol. 14, pt. 3 (1963), p. 221—36.
A most informative review and assessment of the archival
material in the *Bundesarchiv* Koblenz relating to Brüning's
political role 1930—32. The author publishes three letters
from *Nachlass* Schleicher; three documents relating to the
dismissal of Prussian Minister of Culture, Josef Becker, in
January 1930; and a further four letters, some sent by or to
Brüning regarding aspects of government policy, 1930—32.

PETZINA, Dieter.
"Elemente der Wirtschaftspolitik in der Spätphase
der Weimarer Republik". *Vierteljahrshefte für
Zeitgeschichte*, vol. 21, pt. 2 (1973), p. 127—33.
See section 13A (ii) (f) for review.

PÜNDER, Hermann.
"Zusammenarbeit mit Heinrich Brüning in der
Reichskanzlei 1930—1932". In F. A. Hermens &
T. Schieder (eds.). *Staat, Wirtschaft und Politik
in der Weimarer Republik: Festschrift für Heinrich
Brüning.* Berlin: Duncker & Humblot (1967),
p. 311—16.
A brief but fond recollection of Brüning from one of his
closest associates in the Reich Chancellory 1930—32. Their
relationship was apparently close, harmonious and trusted.
Pünder, who served under a number of Chancellors, regards
Brüning as the best and also as a statesman of international
standing.

ROESKE, Ulrich.
"Brüning und die Volkskonservativen (1930)".
Zeitschrift für Geschichtswissenschaft, vol. 19,
pt. 7 (1971), p. 904—15.
Brüning had some tentative dealings with this DNVP
splinter group in 1930. Roeske describes these, but draws
unwarranted conclusions from the episode.

RUGE, Wolfgang.
"Die 'Deutsche Allgemeine Zeitung' und die
Brüning-Regierung". *Zeitschrift für Geschichts-
wissenschaft*, vol. 16, pt. 1 (1968), p. 19—53.
See section 13B (iii) for review.

RUGE, Wolfgang.
"Heinrich Brünings posthume Selbstentlarvung".
Zeitschrift für Geschichtswissenschaft, vol. 19,
pt. 10 (1971), p. 1261—73.
A most hostile review of the memoirs.

SCHMOLKE, Michael.
See his work in section 1.

SCHÜTTE, Ernst.
"Über politische Vorurteile — Anmerkungen zu
den 'Memoiren' des Reichskanzlers Heinrich
Brüning". *Die Neue Gesellschaft*, vol. 18, pt. 8
(1971), p. 563—6.
A superficial review of the memoirs.

SCHWERING, Leo.
"Stegerwalds und Brünings Vorstellungen über
Parteireform und Parteiensystem". In F.A. Hermens
& T. Schieder (eds.). *Staat, Wirtschaft, und Politik
in der Weimarer Republik: Festschrift für Heinrich
Brüning.* Berlin: Duncker & Humblot (1967),
p. 23—40.
Schwering's paper aims to show how strongly Adam
Stegerwald's ideas on reform of the party system influenced
Brüning. Stegerwald first put forward his reform programme
in November 1920; its central theme was the need for a
non-confessional Christian party of the middle (a concept
brought to fruition, says Schwering, in the post-1945 CDU
in the Federal Republic). By 1928—29, Brüning shared
Stegerwald's ideas for a new party along these lines, but
after 1930 circumstances did not allow him to take the
matter any further. The article is too uncritical in tone, and
the political propaganda for the CDU is disconcerting to say
the least (the author is a former Centre Party member and
CDU politician).

STRIBRNY, Wolfgang.
See his article in section 1.

TREVIRANUS, Gottfried R.
*Das Ende von Weimar: Heinrich Brüning und seine
Zeit.* Düsseldorf: Econ-Verlag (1968), 431 pp.
A limited study; there is far too much emphasis on personalities and not nearly enough on the fundamental factors
which caused the Republic's collapse. Treviranus is sympathetic towards Brüning and his policies.

VAGTS, Alfred.
"Heinrich Brüning: a Review and a Memoir".
Political Science Quarterly, vol. 87, pt. 1 (1972),
p. 80—9.
Unimportant.

G. THE VON PAPEN ERA (JUNE 1932–NOVEMBER 1932)

BAY, Jürgen.
See his work in section 2.

BENZ, Wolfgang (ed.).
"Papens 'Preussenschlag' und die Länder".
Vierteljahrshefte für Zeitgeschichte, vol. 18, pt. 3
(1970), p. 320—38.
This collection of documents illustrates the involvement
and the reactions of state governments to the Papen coup
of July 1932 against Prussia. The documents relate to a
meeting Papen held three days after the coup with representatives of the state governments. One of the three documents published is Papen's own report on this meeting.

BRAATZ, Werner E.
"Franz von Papen and the Preussenschlag,
20 July 1932: a move by the 'New State' towards
Reichsreform". *European Studies Review*, vol. 3,
pt. 2 (1973), p. 157—80.

An examination of one constitutional aspect of Papen's envisaged "New State" which in fact never materialized. Papen wanted to end the complex and often anomalous constitutional relationship (dualism) between Prussia and the Reich government. In effect, his action in Prussia, far from solving this particular problem, only contributed in the long run to the undermining of the Republic. Although the article describes in detail the immediate origins and results of the coup, it does not have anything original to say about the event.

BRAATZ, Werner E.
Neo-Conservatism in Crisis at the End of the Weimar Republic: Franz von Papen and the Rise and Fall of the "New State", June to December 1932. Dissertation, University of Wisconsin (1969).
Examines the insubstantive theories of von Papen which lay behind the neo-conservative "New State", designed as an authoritarian alternative to parliamentary democracy and dedicated to preserving the mystical *Volksgemeinschaft*. The concept of a "New State" never had much support, although, of course, neo-conservative ideas in general did a great deal to undermine the Weimar Republic and prepare the way for National Socialism.

BRAATZ, Werner E.
"Franz von Papen und die Frage der Reichsreform". *Politische Vierteljahrsschrift*, vol. 16, pt. 3 (1975), p. 319—40.
Contains nothing that is not already given in his two aforementioned articles.

BRAATZ, Werner E.
"Two Neo-Conservative Myths in Germany 1919—32: the 'Third Reich' and the 'New State' ". *Journal of the History of Ideas*, vol. 32, pt. 4 (1971), p. 569—84.
A consideration of some ideas of the *völkisch* movement and the *Jugendbewegung*, both of which were groups closely associated with neo-conservatism. Among the groups mentioned are the *Tatkreis*, the *Juniklub*, and the *Herrenklub*, but the conclusion that there was no neo-conservative third way between democracy and dictatorship is hardly original.

BRACHER, Karl Dietrich.
"Der 20. Juni 1932". *Zeitschrift für Politik*, vol. 3 (1956), p. 243—9.
The author replies in this short paper to criticisms made by Arnold Brecht of Bracher's book *Die Auflösung der Weimarer Republik*, and in particular to Brecht's charge that his discussion of the Papen coup is illogical and contradictory. Bracher repeats his point in unequivocal terms that the coup and the lack of resistance to it was a terrifying symptom of the Republic's basic weakness.

CONZE, Werner.
"Papens Memoiren". *Historische Zeitschrift*, no. 177 (1953), p. 307—17.
A critical review of Papen's memoirs.

DIERSKE, Ludwig.
"War eine Abwehr des 'Preussenschlags' vom 20. Juli 1932 möglich?". *Zeitschrift für Politik*, vol. 17 (1970), p. 197—245.
A broad-ranging examination of the coup based only on secondary sources. The author recounts the immediate circumstances in which the decision was taken by Papen to move against Prussia; he examines Papen's motives, the implementation of the action, the legal implications, the attitude of the population and of the political parties; the paramilitary organizations, the army, and the police are also looked at. He then considers the chances of successful resistance against the coup, and concludes there was no chance. A final section neatly sums up the author's conclusions which, for the most part, are sensible but not original.

ESCHENBURG, Theodor.
"Franz von Papen". *Vierteljahrshefte für Zeitgeschichte*, vol. 1, pt. 2 (1953), p. 153—69.
A scholarly assessment of the former Chancellor's political role in Weimar, prompted by the publication of his memoirs in 1952.

GERVIENS, Wilhelm.
Der 20. Juli 1932 in Wahrheit und Dichtung. Bielefeld (1946).
"Gerviens" is a pseudonym for Carl Severing, the Prussian Minister, who gives here a valuable "insider's" account of the coup.

GOTTWALD, Herbert.
"Franz von Papen und die 'Germania'". *Jahrbuch für Geschichte*, vol. 6 (1972), p. 539—604.
See section 16A (vi) for review.

KÜCKLICH, Erika.
" 'Streik gegen Notverordnungen!'. Zur Gewerkschafts- und Streikpolitik der KPD gegen die staatsmonopolistische Offensive der Regierung Papen im Sommer und Herbst 1932". *Beiträge zur Geschichte der Deutschen Arbeiterbewegung*, vol. 13 (1971), p. 454—69.
See section 6B (vii) for review.

LINDHEIM, Herman von.
"Zu Papens Staatsstreich vom 20. Juli 1932". *Geschichte in Wissenschaft und Unterricht*, vol. 11 (1960), p. 154—64.
A short but valuable discussion of the complex political motives involved and of the possibilities of open resistance to Papen's coup. The author uses fresh material from the Gayl *Nachlass*. The loss of prestige for the SPD on account of its paralysis in the affair is stressed.

MARCON, Helmut.
Arbeitsbeschaffungspolitik der Regierungen von Papen und Schleicher. Frankfurt: Lang (1974), 520 pp.
See section 13A (ii) (c) for review.

MORSEY, Rudolf.
"Zur Geschichte des 'Pressenschlags' am 20. Juli 1932". *Vierteljahrshefte für Zeitgeschichte*, vol. 9, pt. 4 (1961), p. 430—9.
In a brief introduction, Morsey points out that hitherto valuable material in the *Reichskanzlei* files has not been used in the debate over the Papen coup. To prove his point, he publishes three important documents from these files which throw additional light on the affair and on the techniques of modern mass politics.

PETZOLD, Joachim.
"Der Staatsstreich vom 20. Juli 1932 in Preussen". *Zeitschrift für Geschichtswissenschaft*, vol. 4, pt. 6 (1956), p. 1146—86.
He sees the coup as a first decisive move towards establishing a fascist dictatorship as the economic crisis sharpened the class war and brought nearer the possibility of proletarian rule. Thus, the coup was a preventive measure in this respect by capitalists and their allies, Petzold maintains. He stresses the efforts of the KPD to achieve a proletarian

front against reaction and lambasts the SPD for not joining, forgetting to add, of course, that KPD tactics had identified the SPD as its main enemy since 1928—29.

PFEIFFER, R.
Die deutsch-britischen Beziehungen unter den Reichskanzlern von Papen und von Schleicher. Würzburg: Holzner (1971).
See section 19A (ii) for review.

PIKART, Eberhard.
"Zum Problem der Ereignisse des 20. Juli 1932". *Zeitschrift für Politik*, vol. 3 (1956), p. 181—3.
A cursory review of some of the main problems of interpretation, including the question of resistance to the coup.

TRUMPP, Thomas.
Franz von Papen, der preussisch-deutsche Dualismus und die NSDAP in Preussen. Marburg: Görich-Weiershäuser (1963), 235 pp.
A general narrative of the events leading up to the Papen coup. The author discusses the policies and ideas of the Papen government — such as they were — and the complicated constitutional and legal relationship between Prussia and the Reich. He tends to simplify important features of the latter issue, while Trumpp does not deal at all satisfactorily with the National Socialists.

VOGELSANG, Thilo.
"Papen und das aussenpolitische Erbe Brünings: die Lausanner Konferenz 1932". In *Neue Perspektiven aus Wirtschaft und Recht: Festschrift für Hans Schäffer.* Stuttgart (1964), p. 487—507.
See section 19B (v) for review.

VRING, T. von der.
"Ein Dokument zur Haltung der Gewerkschaften gegenüber dem Staatsstreich in Preussen im Jahre 1932". In *Paul Kluke zum 60. Geburtstag.* Frankfurt: Lang (1968), p. 91—110.
A significant document illuminating the curious mixture of anger and apathy that characterized the trade union attitude to the coup.

ZAHN, Manfred.
Öffentliche Meinung und Presse während der Kanzlerschaft von Papens. Dissertation, University of Münster (1953).
A review of press reaction of different political persuasions to major events in the Papen era, including the coup of July 1932.

H. THE LAST PHASE: HITLER'S APPOINTMENT AS CHANCELLOR

BENNECKE, Heinrich.
"Alternativen der Not: Schleicher, Bürgerkrieg oder Hitler?". *Politische Studien*, vol. 14 (1963), p. 444—64.
Bennecke, a former top-ranking SA leader, argues that with the failure of the Schleicher government to attract enough support, Hitler became an obvious candidate for the chancellorship. What finally put him in office was an alleged widespread fear of Communism in the establishment. The hypothesis is well out of date.

BRAUBACH, Max.
"Hitlers Machtergreifung". In *Festschrift für Leo Brandt.* Cologne: Westdeutscher Verlag (1968), p. 443—64.
A scholarly analysis of the reports of the French ambassador to Berlin, Francois-Poncet, on political developments in Germany from July 1932 to July 1933.

BRECHT, Arnold.
"Gedanken zur Verantwortung für Hitlers Ernennung zum deutschen Reichskanzler". In F. A. Hermens & T. Schieder (eds.). *Staat, Wirtschaft und Politik in der Weimarer Republik: Festschrift für Heinrich Brüning.* Berlin: Duncker & Humblot (1967), p. 383—91.
Concludes that although Hindenburg as Reich President must bear ultimate constitutional responsibility for Hitler's appointment, Papen must also bear a considerable moral and political responsibility. Above all, however, the German people and electorate are to blame for not supporting those parties in favour of parliamentary democracy. The paper is very superficial. Obviously the subject needs care and thought, but Brecht does not develop any of his main points.

BUNDESZENTRALE FÜR POLITISCHE BILDUNG.
Rückschau nach 30 Jahren: Hitlers Machtergreifung. Bonn: Selbstverlag (1963), 40 pp.
A number of short papers by leading scholars on various aspects of the German political situation before 1933. Heinz Gollwitzer has an interesting piece entitled "Gedanken zum 30. Januar" and John L. Snell writes on Hitler's success, as seen 30 years afterwards.

CASTELLAN, Georges.
"Von Schleicher, von Papen et l'avènement de Hitler". *Cahiers d'Histoire de la Guerre*, vol. 1, pt. 1 (1949), p. 15—39.
A reconstruction of the last days preceding Hitler's appointment based on the extensive correspondence of the French military attaché in Berlin 1929—34, and documents from the Nuremberg trials. He sees Schleicher as the arch-intriguer who exerted more personal influence on the course of events than anyone else.

FRIEDRICH, Julius.
Wer spielte falsch? Hamburg: Laatzen-Verlag (1949), 83 pp.
An unimpressive examination of the roles of Hindenburg, Hitler, the Crown Prince, Hugenberg and Schleicher. The author does not explain why Papen and Meissner are omitted.

KLEIST-SCHMENZIN, Ewald von.
"Die letzte Möglichkeit: zur Ernennung Hitlers zum Reichskanzler am 30 Jan. 1933". *Politische Studien*, vol. 10 (1959), p. 89—92.
This is an extract from Ewald von Kleist-Schmenzin's diary, in which are recorded his thoughts between 28—30 January 1933. It amounts to a bitter indictment of Hugenberg for failing to heed the advice of his supporters not to accept office in Hitler's cabinet.

KRAUSNICK, Helmut (ed.).
"Ein Brief Thomas Manns vor der Machtergreifung". *Vierteljahrshefte für Zeitgeschichte*, vol. 6, pt. 2 (1958), p. 172—5.
Prints a letter written by Mann which reveals his perceptiveness in the political situation at that time.

MANVELL, Roger; FRAENKEL, Heinrich.
The Hundred Days to Hitler. London: Dent
(1974), 240 pp.
Written in a popular style, the book conveys the dramatic atmosphere in which the Republic finally came to an end. The tension preceding Hitler's appointment is also vividly caught. Otherwise, the narrative is very ordinary and prone to factual error.

MEISSNER, Hans O.; WILDE, Harry W.
Die Machtergreifung: ein Bericht über die Technik des nationalsozialistischen Staatsstreiches.
Stuttgart: Cotta'sche Buchhandlung (1958),
364 pp.
A vividly reconstructed picture of the main events between November 1932 and January-March 1933, with much detail on the intrigues of the major political figures. The authors, however, do not have very much of a profound nature to say about the happenings they describe. Hence as a narrative the book is always interesting, but as an analysis it is extremely disappointing.

RIBBENTROP, Joachim von.
Zwischen London und Moskau. Edited by Annelies von Ribbentrop. Leoni am Starnberger See: Drüffel-Verlag (1954).
Very apologetic throughout and probably rather worthless for understanding international relations, but the book does provide some interesting details on the final act of the Republic, and to the usual intriguers is added Gregor Strasser.

SCHAEFER, Edward.
"Zur Legalität der nationalsozialistischen 'Machtergreifung' ". *Geschichte in Wissenschaft und Unterricht*, vol. 17, pt. 9 (1966), p. 536—54.

A sound analysis of the quasi-legal, constitutional fashion in which the National Socialists were able to come to power. They proved that the spirit of the law could be violated with impunity.

SCHLANGE-SCHÖNINGEN, Hans.
The Morning After. London: Gollancz (1948),
236 pp.
Memoirs of a leading German agriculturalist, providing a sober account of events immediately preceding Hitler's appointment.

TAYLOR, Alan J. P.
"Hitler's Seizure of Power." In A. J. P. Taylor.
Europe: Grandeur and Decline. London: Pelican
(1974), p. 204—19.
A characteristically concise and penetrating analysis of how Hitler came to power; not by a seizure of power, nor by winning over a majority of the German electorate, but by intrigue and fraud.

WUCHER, Albert.
Die Fahne hoch: das Ende der Republik und Hitlers Machtübernahme; ein Dokumentarbericht.
Munich: Süddeutscher Verlag (1963), 254 pp.
A reasonably useful book which includes extracts from contemporary documents illustrating the emotions stimulated by the end of the Weimar Republic and the Nazi triumph: excitement, gloom, optimism, pessimism, etc., are all conveyed.

5

Political Personalities

A. FRIEDRICH EBERT

ARNS, Günter.
"Friedrich Ebert als Reichspräsident". In
Historische Zeitschrift, Supplement I. Beiträge zur
Geschichte der Weimarer Republik. Edited by
Theodor Schieder (1971), p. 11—30.
The author refers to the difficulties of achieving a truly
detailed and objective assessment of Ebert's political
influence due to the lack of primary source material re-
lating to him. He proceeds to consider certain aspects of
Ebert's activity, and in so doing clearly pinpoints the
lacunae in our knowledge of his significance, particularly as
Reich President. However, this paper is an excellent
preliminary evaluation.

BESSON, Waldemar.
Friedrich Ebert: Verdienst und Grenze. Göttingen:
Musterschmidt (1963), 94 pp.
A very sympathetic short biography. The author con-
centrates on his period as Reich President and brings out
Ebert's dilemma as a moderate social democrat having to
find a course between the extremisms of left and right in
a turbulent era.

BUSE, D. K.
"Ebert and the German Crisis 1917--1920".
Central European History, vol. 5, pt. 3 (1972),
p. 234—55.
A critical examination of the responsibility of the SPD,
and Ebert in particular, for the failure to establish a firm
democracy in Germany by 1920. Buse argues that the
SPD failed because it did not or would not entertain
radical alternatives in 1918—19, and he underlines Ebert's
personal influence in causing the party to adopt a non-
revolutionary stance. He suggests therefore that Ebert has
a deep personal responsibility for the failure of the
November Revolution. Not only is this an absurd proposition, but the paper as a whole merely repeats old
arguments.

FRIEDRICH-EBERT-STIFTUNG (ed).
Friedrich Ebert 1871—1925. Bad Godesberg:
Verlag Neue Gesellschaft (1971), 214 pp.
A comprehensive and informative study of his life and
political career.

HASCHKE, George; TÖNNIES, Norbert.
Friedrich Ebert: ein Leben für Deutschland.
Hamburg: Antares-Verlag (1961), 176 pp.
Perhaps too eulogistic a study.

KOTOWSKI, Georg.
Friedrich Ebert: eine politische Biographie. Vol. I.
Der Aufstieg eines deutschen Arbeiterführers
1871—1917. Wiesbaden: Steiner (1963), 280 pp.
A well written first volume in a projected in-depth and
extensive biographical work.

NITZSCHKE, Volker; WEIGT, Peter.
Friedrich Ebert. Berlin: Free University (Otto-
Suhr-Institut) (1960), 48 pp.
Does not add anything new to our appreciation of Ebert.

PETERS, Max.
Friedrich Ebert, erster Präsident der deutschen
Republik: sein Werden und Wirken. Berlin: Arani
Verlag (1950), 113 pp.
An undistinguished effort; not always reliable on matters
of detail, and lacking original perspectives, except where
he describes Ebert as a social revolutionary — a totally
untenable argument.

ROOK, Orville W.
Friedrich Ebert, First President of the German
Weimar Republic. Dissertation, University of
Wisconsin (1958).
Thoroughly mediocre in content and argument.

WITT, Peter-Christian.
Friedrich Ebert: Parteiführer, Reichskanzler,
Volksbeauftragter, Reichspräsident. Bad
Godesberg: Verlag Neue Gesellschaft (1971).
A judicious and informative evaluation, though Witt does
not have anything new to relate about Ebert's activities as
Reich President.

B. MATTHIAS ERZBERGER

EPSTEIN, Klaus.
Matthias Erzberger and the Dilemma of German Democracy. Princeton: Princeton University Press (1959), 486 pp.
A first-rate, scholarly and thorough study, and very close to being the definitive biography of Erzberger. Epstein concentrates on his subject's political life and fully explains and documents the many contrasts and ostensible contradictions in his colourful career. But he stresses that Erzberger's commitment to Catholicism and democracy remained constant. Many previously unpublished materials have been used by the author, including the Erzberger papers.

ESCHENBURG, Theodor.
Matthias Erzberger: der grosse Mann des Parlamentarismus und der Finanzreform. Munich: Piper (1973), 180 pp.
Eschenburg analyses specific aspects of Erzberger's political career, as a parliamentarian and Centre Party politician, and as a financial expert. A judicious and engrossing study.

FRYE, Bruce B.
Matthias Erzberger and German Politics, 1914—21. Dissertation, Stanford University (1953).
A rather poor and uninformative work which fails to get its perspectives right.

HÖFLER, Gustav.
Erzbergers Finanzreform und ihre Rückwirkungen auf die bundesstaatliche Struktur des Reiches. Dissertation, University of Freiburg (1955).
See section 13A (iv) for review.

MÖLLER, Alex.
Reichsfinanzminister Matthias Erzberger und sein Reformwerk. Bonn: Stollfuss-Verlag (1971), 68 pp.
A brief look at Erzberger's reform plans as they affected the powers of the Reich government *vis-à-vis* the *Länder.*.

C. PAUL VON HINDENBURG

BERGHAHN, Volker R.
See his article in section 1.

DORPALEN, Andreas.
Hindenburg and the Weimar Republic. Princeton: Princeton University Press (1964), 506 pp.
A very competent biography which seeks to place Hindenburg in the wider context of the political and constitutional development of the Republic. Although initially he did his best to uphold the constitution after his election as Reich President in 1925, Hindenburg never believed in parliamentary democracy and came more and more under the influence of anti-republican conservative nationalists. The presidential cabinet style of government (which Dorpalen does not treat in enough detail) was a decisive step towards dictatorship. Dorpalen does demonstrate, however, just

how inept and senile Hindenburg became during the last years of Weimar so that more than ever before he was unequal to the task of defending the Republic from its enemies. The book could be pruned somewhat, and Dorpalen does not always write as incisively as one would want, but overall the book is worthwhile.

GÖRLITZ, Walter.
Hindenburg: ein Lebensbild. Bonn: Athenäum-Verlag (1953), 438 pp.
Despite its length, this study is too superficial when dealing with crucial aspects or events of Hindenburg's career, particularly his period in office as Reich President. In general also, Görlitz is not nearly critical enough; for example, some of the nationalist myths surrounding Hindenburg are left untouched.

GRANIER, Gerhard.
"Der Reichspräsident Paul von Hindenburg". *Geschichte in Wissenschaft und Unterricht,* vol. 20, pt. 9 (1969), p. 534—54.
The published version of a lecture delivered at the *Bundesarchiv* in Koblenz, presenting a general review of Hindenburg's career based entirely on secondary sources. The author adds one or two interesting details not widely appreciated, for example, the efforts of certain conservative and aristocratic circles to persuade him to be a candidate for the Reich Presidency in 1919—20. The second half of the paper discusses his period as President and the catastrophic consequences for Germany in having an incompetent ex-general in the most important office of state.

HUBATSCH, Walther.
Hindenburg und der Staat: aus den Papieren des Generalfeldmarschalls und Reichspräsidenten von 1878 bis 1934. Göttingen: Musterschmidt (1966), 397 pp.
An overwhelmingly apologetic work. The main part of the book is in fact composed of 115 documents from the Hindenburg papers, but most of them have been published previously; of the new evidence, virtually all is trivial, so that our overall picture of Hindenburg is hardly changed. The author clearly admires his subject and attempts here to rehabilitate him. The attempt to do so is a lamentable failure.

KALISCHER, Wolfgang.
Hindenburg und das Reichspräsidentenamt im "Nationalen Umbruch" (1932—1934). Dissertation, Free University of Berlin (1957).
An examination of the way in which political developments affected the constitutional powers of the Reich Presidency, and the role of Hindenburg in the situation. An interesting approach, but at the end of the day nothing original comes out of the study.

LUCAS, Friedrich J.
Hindenburg als Reichspräsident. Bonn: Röhrscheid (1959), 157 pp.
The author presents a compact and sensible evaluation of Hindenburg as Reich President 1925—34, without offering any new interpretations. He discusses Hindenburg's conservative and monarchist outlook and his unsuitability for the responsibility of upholding democracy. The author's examination of the presidential cabinet system (1930—32) is cursory, however, and the book contains too many factual errors — none of them serious, it is true. At least the approach is critical, and Lucas attaches a valuable annotated bibliography of works on Hindenburg.

LÜDERS, Martin.
**Der Soldat und das Reich: Paul von Hindenburg,
Generalfeldmarschall und Reichspräsident.** Leoni
am Starnberger See: Drüffel-Verlag (1961),
255 pp.
A pathetic eulogy; makes no serious effort to be objective
and repeats out-of-date legends about the old man's in-
destructibility and patriotism.

LUDWIG, Emil.
Hindenburg: Legende und Wirklichkeit. Munich
(1962), 288 pp.
Originally published in 1935, this study concentrates on
perpetuating the myths while turning a blind eye to
realities; it is superficial and popular and obviously designed
for a different generation.

MARCKS, Erich.
Hindenburg: Feldmarschall und Reichspräsident.
Göttingen: Musterschmidt (1963), 76 pp.
A brief, uncritical panegyric which outdistances all similar
exercises in this respect. The author's main point is that
Hindenburg is best understood as a modern version of
Bismarck.

WHEELER-BENNETT, John.
Hindenburg: the Wooden Titan. New York: St.
Martin's Press (1967), 507 pp. New ed.
Originally published in 1936, this still stands as perhaps the
best all-round biography of Hindenburg. Scholarly and
objective, it captures the curious emptiness of a man who
found it increasingly difficult to take even the simplest
decisions and who therefore had to rely more and more
on his entourage of reactionaries. The book has its faults:
there are a large number of factual errors and not every
important feature of Hindenburg's career is fully investigated.

D. WALTHER RATHENAU

BERGLAR, Peter.
**Walther Rathenau: seine Zeit, sein Werk, seine
Persönlichkeit.** Bremen: Schünemann (1970),
416 pp.
An appreciative, comprehensive, and, on the whole, balanced
study of Rathenau's many roles as financier, industrialist,
intellectual, and politician. His ideas and ideals are fully
discussed on the basis of his voluminous writings.

BERGLAR, Peter.
**"Harden und Rathenau: zur Problematik ihrer
Freundschaft".** *Historische Zeitschrift*, no. 209
(1969), p. 75—94.
See section 16B for review.

BÖTTCHER, Helmuth.
Walther Rathenau: Persönlichkeit und Werk. Bonn:
Athenäum-Verlag (1958), 322 pp.
A competent but somewhat dull book which is more successful in capturing the essence of Rathenau's volatile
personality than in presenting a satisfactory analysis of his
ideas.

BRECHT, Arnold.
Walther Rathenau und das deutsche Volk. Munich:
Nymphenburger Verlag (1950), 24 pp.
A short appreciation of Rathenau's contribution to German
democracy.

EYNERN, M. von (ed.).
**Walther Rathenau, ein preussischer Europäer:
Briefe.** Berlin: Vogt (1955), 468 pp.
An extremely useful and carefully edited collection of
letters, most of them, though, for the pre-1918 period.
They are vividly illustrative of the man's character and
outgoing attitudes.

FELIX, David.
**Walther Rathenau and the Weimar Republic: the
Politics of Reparation.** Baltimore: Johns Hopkins
University Press (1971), 210 pp.
An able study which concentrates on Rathenau's last year
before his murder in 1922. During this time he was Minister
of Reconstruction and then Foreign Minister. Rathenau
became principally involved in the reparations issue and it is
his role here that Felix subjects to close analysis. He believes Rathenau performed an outstanding service to
Germany over reparations, but earned widespread unpopularity because reparations was a delicate problem
touching national sentiment, and also because he was
wealthy, an intellectual with left-wing views, and most
of all because he was a Jew. Felix sees the tragedy of
Rathenau's assassination as epitomizing the sorrows of the
Republic itself.

FELIX, David.
**"Walther Rathenau: German Foreign Minister in
1922".** *History Today*, vol. 20, pt. 9 (1970),
p. 638—47.
A simplified version of some of the points made in the
author's biography, with emphasis on Rathenau's contribution to the Rapallo Treaty.

FELIX, David.
**"Walther Rathenau: the Bad Thinker and His
Uses".** *European Studies Review*, vol. 5, pt. 1
(1975), p. 69—79.
A short assessment of some of Rathenau's political ideas,
concluding that they were "overpoweringly shoddy. . . .
He was one of the worst thinkers ever published". Felix
sees him as essentially a moral philosopher who speculated
on social and economic questions. The article also outlines
aspects of Rathenau's political activity during the First
World War and the early years of Weimar. None of this is
new.

FISHER, Ernest F.
**Road to Rapallo: a Study of Walther Rathenau
and German Foreign Policy 1919—1922.** Dissertation, University of Wisconsin (1972).
See section 19C (ii) for review.

HARTTUNG, Arnold (ed.).
Walther Rathenau: Schriften. Berlin: Berlin Verlag
(1965), 416 pp.
A well chosen selection of Rathenau's political and philosophical writings, but without a helpful editorial commentary.

HENDERSON, W. O.
**"Walther Rathenau: a Pioneer of the Planned
Economy".** *Economic History Review*, vol. 4,
pt. 1 (1951), p. 98—108.
See section 13A (ii) (a) for review.

JOLL, James.
Intellectuals in Politics: Three Biographical Essays.
London: Weidenfeld & Nicolson (1960), 203 pp.
Chapter II is entitled "Walther Rathenau: Prophet without
a Cause" (p. 59—129). Joll, in a fair and not unsympathetic
assessment, criticizes Rathenau's misplaced sense of vo-
cation — hence the subtitle of the essay.

KESSLER, Harry G.
Walther Rathenau: sein Leben und sein Werk.
Wiesbaden: Rheinische Verlagsanstalt (1962),
455 pp. New ed.
Kessler was a close friend and his biography is very appreciative, but also informative; it is also written in a readable
and fluent style.

KOLLMANN, Eric C.
**"Walther Rathenau and German Foreign Policy:
Thoughts and Actions".** *Journal of Modern
History*, vol. 24, pt. 2 (1952), p. 127—42.
Chiefly useful for the author's analysis of how Rathenau's
ideas on foreign policy changed under the influence of
certain events. The First World War was the most important
of such events, causing him to advocate an eastern orientation for Germany when the war in the West became a
stalemate. Rathenau's views on the Western Allies, the
League of Nations and Versailles are also examined.
Kollmann argues that there is a definite pattern in
Rathenau's ideas on foreign policy in the sense that he
argued for an end to the Austrian alliance in favour of
alliance with Russia or France, or both. The final conclusion, which seems balanced, is that Rathenau's ideas
in this sphere were a mixture of shortsightedness and
brilliance.

ORTH, Wilhelm.
Walther Rathenau und der Geist von Rapallo.
East Berlin: Buchverlag der Morgen (1962),
166 pp.
See section 19C (ii) for review.

RATHENAU, Walther.
Tagebuch 1907—1922. Edited by Hartmut Pogge
von Strandmann. Düsseldorf: Droste (1967),
319 pp.
The diary makes fascinating reading and reveals Rathenau's
wide range of important political, business, and intellectual
contacts. Of special note are his record of the 1920 Spa
Conference, a conversation with Wolfgang Kapp during
the 1920 Putsch, and a series of meetings with Allied
diplomats in 1921. The diary also offers further insights
into his political thought and his political activity. The
editorial notes are scholarly and helpful.

RICHTER, Hans W. (ed.).
Walther Rathenau: Schriften und Reden.
Frankfurt: Fischer (1964), 481 pp.
Valuable and ably edited.

SWARSENSKY, Hardi.
"Walther Rathenau: Leben, Werk und Willen".
Zeitschrift für die Geschichte der Juden, vol. 5
(1968), p. 1—20.
A general summary of principal highlights of Rathenau's
career.

WILLIAMSON, D. G.
Walther Rathenau. Dissertation, University of
London (1972).
Reviews Rathenau's political, intellectual and business
ideas and actions without having anything new to say
about them; the author looks at the question of Rathenau's
standing as a whole in Germany 1893—1921 and the
reasons for his unpopularity.

E. GUSTAV STRESEMANN[1]

BERNARD, Henry.
**Gustav Stresemann: ein Beitrag zur Geschichte der
deutschen Freimaurerei.** Krefeld: Verlag der
Freimaurerbriefe (1946), 20 pp.
Insignificant, except for reminding us that Stresemann was
a practising freemason throughout his political life.

BERNARD, Henry.
"Gustav Stresemann: Tatsachen und Legenden".
Das Parlament: Aus Politik und Zeitgeschichte,
B41 (7.10.1959).
Rejects the arguments of the revisionist school of thought
on Stresemann and stoutly defends the myths that surround
him. No one could now find Bernard's defence acceptable.

EYCK, Erich.
"Neues Licht auf Stresemanns Politik". *Deutsche
Rundschau*, vol. 81, pt. 2 (1955), p. 111—19.
Like Bernard, Eyck cannot bring himself to believe the
new picture of Stresemann thrown up by his *Nachlass*
material. He therefore reaffirms many of the legends.

GATZKE, Hans W.
"The Stresemann Papers". *Journal of Modern
History*, vol. 26, pt. 1 (1954), p. 49—59.
A most informative bibliographical paper in which Gatzke
reviews the available literature on Stresemann and points
out the important gaps remaining in the historiography
of the subject. Now, the availability of the Stresemann
Nachlass may allow an objective assessment of the man
to be made. Gatzke expertly weighs up the strengths and
weaknesses of the *Nachlass*, explaining that it throws more
light on German domestic than foreign policy, and little on
Stresemann's personal affairs. A résumé of the contents is
provided.

GATZKE, Hans W.
"Gustav Stresemann: a Bibliographical Article".
Journal of Modern History, vol. 36, pt. 1 (1964),
p. 1—13.
A critical review of postwar studies of Stresemann and a

1. Also refer to section 19 (Foreign Policy) for works dealing with Stresemann's foreign policy.

review of the main sources now available for a full biography of him, with the *Nachlass* of course being the most fruitful source.

GATZKE, Hans W.
"Stresemann und Litwin". *Vierteljahrshefte für Zeitgeschichte*, vol. 5, pt. 1 (1957), p. 76—90.
An analysis of one of Stresemann's less profitable relationships. His contact with Litwin in the business world started off well but quickly became a liability and caused Stresemann considerable trouble.

GÖHRING, Martin.
Stresemann: Mensch, Staatsmann, Europäer.
Wiesbaden: Steiner (1956), 53 pp.
Emphasizes a neglected side of Stresemann; he is not only to be seen as a politician and statesman, but also as a cultivated man with a profound interest in the arts and literature. (Compare this view with Annelise Thimme's version — see below). Göhring also upholds the now refuted idea that Stresemann changed from a fervent German nationalist to an open-minded European.

GÖRLITZ, Walter.
Gustav Stresemann. Heidelberg: Ahren-Verlag (1947), 288 pp.
Now hopelessly out of date.

HERMANN, Alfred.
"Gustav Stresemann". In A. Hermann (ed.). *Aus Geschichte und Politik: Festschrift zum 70. Geburtstag von Ludwig Bergsträsser.* Düsseldorf: Droste (1954), p. 139—51.
Presents the theme that Stresemann was a good European — a view no longer seriously held by anyone. The author glosses over the controversial aspects of Stresemann's career and the paper is altogether too much of a eulogy to be accorded much attention.

HERTZMAN, Lewis.
"Gustav Stresemann: the Problem of Political Leadership in the Weimar Republic". *International Review of Social History*, vol. 5, pt. 3 (1960), p. 361—77.
The author discusses the contrast between Stresemann's success as Foreign Minister and his failure as the political leader of the German Peoples' Party (DVP) — a failure brought about largely because he was unwilling to identify himself exclusively with the narrow interests of the party; he preferred to work for the "national interest". Another contrast is drawn between his hostility to the Revolution and the early Weimar Republic (1918—20), and his subsequent acceptance of the Republic. Stresemann is praised for his achievements as head of government in 1923, which the author asserts laid the groundwork for the state's recovery 1924—29. But within the DVP Stresemann was losing ground all the time before his death in October 1929. For one thing, his party became increasingly opposed to his foreign policies. This is a well argued, thoughtful paper.

HIRSCH, Felix.
Gustav Stresemann: Patriot und Europäer.
Göttingen: Musterschmidt (1964), 112 pp.
The author is too full of praise for his subject — he appears not to have been impressed by the revelations of the

Nachlass and he maintains the myth about Stresemann's European ethos.

HIRSCH, Felix.
"Stresemann and Adenauer: Two Great Leaders of German Democracy in Times of Crisis". In A. O. Sarkissian (ed.). *Studies in Diplomatic History and Historiography.* London: Longman (1961), p. 266—280.
The basic premises regarding Stresemann's and Adenauer's commitment to democracy are suspect to begin with; on Stresemann, the author again demonstrates his ignorance of fundamental truths about the man.

HIRSCH, Felix.
"Stresemann in Historical Perspective". *Review of Politics*, vol. 15, pt. 3 (1953), p. 360—77.
Needless to say, he has got the perspective all wrong; the same uncritical praise for Stresemann again dominates.

KURTH, Liselotte E.
Die literarischen Interessen, Kenntnisse und Leistungen Gustav Stresemanns. M.A. Thesis, Johns Hopkins University (1960).
On the basis of a thorough examination of the *Nachlass* and Stresemann's writings, the author disputes his reputation as an intellectual and man of the arts. She denies that his literary writings add anything of value to literary criticism. For example, she states that Stresemann's essay on Goethe and Napoleon was probably plagiarized from the work of the Swiss author, Andreas Fischer. Thus, she concludes, Stresemann must no longer be regarded as having been a leading specialist on Goethe. In its own way, this is a devastating revisionist interpretation, and deserves a wider readership.

LÖWENSTEIN, Hubertus zu.
Stresemann: das deutsche Schicksal im Spiegel seines Lebens. Frankfurt: Scheffler (1952), 357 pp.
The author somehow sees Stresemann's political career as epitomizing important trends in modern German history, so that Stresemann himself is not depicted as anybody special. This interpretation appears more than a little bizarre, and like most studies published before access to the *Nachlass* became possible, this book wanders too much off the track of historical objectivity.

RUGE, Wolfgang.
Stresemann: ein Lebensbild. East Berlin: Deutscher Verlag der Wissenschaften (1965).
A brief, popular work which adheres to a rigid Marxist-Leninist framework of interpretation. The mandatory obsequious references to the Soviet Union are found in abundance, as are the equally mandatory denunciations of West German revanchists. In between, Ruge manages to say a word or two about his ostensible subject, criticizing Stresemann for promoting German rearmament and big business interests. The book is entirely forgettable.

RUGE, Wolfgang.
"Stresemann — ein Leitbild?" *Blätter für Deutsch- und Internationale Politik*, vol. 14, pt. 5 (1969), p. 468—84.
The author is concerned to show that Stresemann's thoughts and actions in foreign affairs do not deserve to earn him respect in the Federal Republic today. He then

proceeds to a critical review of Stresemann's foreign policy in the 1920s, with special emphasis on its alleged anti-Russian and revanchist orientation. Ruge ends this idiosyncratic paper with the warning that if German politicians want to avoid a nuclear war, they would be better advised to find politicians other than Stresemann to copy!

SCHEIDEL, Joseph (ed.).
Gustav Stresemann. Wiesbaden: Wiesbadener Graphische Betriebe (1960), 168 pp.
This is a *Festschrift* to commemorate the reconstruction of the Stresemann monument in Mainz on 16 October 1960. None of the papers in the volume offer anything new.

STARKULLA, Heinz.
Organisation und Technik der Pressepolitik des Staatsmannes Gustav Stresemann. Dissertation, University of Munich (1951).
See section 16A (i) for review.

STROOMANN, Gerhard.
Aus meinem roten Notizbuch: ein Leben als Ärzt auf Bühlerhöhe. Edited by Heinrich W. Petzet. Frankfurt: Lang (1957).
The memoirs of Stresemann's former doctor; they contain interesting details about his patient's medical history.

THIMME, Annelise.
"Stresemann als Reichskanzler". *Die Welt als Geschichte*, vol. 17, pt. 1 (1957), p. 9—25.
An interesting and detailed examination of Stresemann's short term in office as Chancellor. Using fresh material from the *Nachlass*, the author demonstrates fairly convincingly his development from a party politician to a German politician representing national interests.

THIMME, Annelise.
"Gustav Stresemann, Legende und Wirklichkeit". *Historische Zeitschrift*, no. 181, pt. 2 (1956), p. 287—338.
Fortified by material from the *Nachlass*, Thimme sets about her demolition work on the myths surrounding Stresemann with relish. The result is an important and stimulating paper, in which she shatters most of these legends. But her interpretation of Stresemann's famous letter of 7 September 1925 to Crown Prince Wilhelm involving the controversial subject of his *finanssieren* has been effectively refuted by other authors.

THIMME, Annelise.
Gustav Stresemann: eine politische Biographie zur Geschichte der Weimarer Republik. Hanover: Norddeutsche Verlagsanstalt (1957), 132 pp.
Based on the new material afforded by the *Nachlass*, this is the first full-length political biography of Stresemann.

However, the equally important German Foreign Ministry files were not available to the author. The book is valuable in exploding the myths relating to him, including that of being a "good European", and in explaining his political thought. The author regards him as a political genius, but also as an opportunist. The study is ably argued and extremely readable, but it cannot be said to be definitive.

TURNER, Henry A.
Stresemann and the Politics of the Weimar Republic. Princeton: Princeton University Press (1963), 287 pp.
This work concentrates on Stresemann's domestic rather than foreign policy, and in general succeeds in presenting a well informed, balanced interpretation. The main stages of Stresemann's political development are clearly explained and his failings as leader of the DVP are stressed. His emergence as a *Vernunftrepublikaner*, once he believed that there was a possibility of his conservative and restorationist aims being realized within the republican framework, is especially well covered. This, the first comprehensive treatment of Stresemann's role in domestic politics, is also a valuable contribution to the internal history of the Republic.

VALLENTIN, Antonina.
Stresemann: vom Werden einer Staatsidee. Munich (1948), 303 pp.
Must now be considered so out of date as to be without any real value, except perhaps as a general outline of his career.

WALSDORFF, Martin (ed.).
Bibliographie Gustav Stresemann. Düsseldorf: Droste (1972), 207 pp.
An excellent source of reference which updates Zwoch's earlier compilation (see below).

ZIMMERMANN, Ludwig.
Studien zur Geschichte der Weimarer Republik. Erlangen: Universitätsbund (1956), 68 pp.
Comprises two short essays on Stresemann as a political and as an historical figure. The volume amounts to a revisionist interpretation from a pro-Stresemann and nationalist standpoint. The author sees Stresemann as confronted by agonizing dilemmas in his political career, torn between realism and idealism, but managing in the end to find a moderate middle course. In the second essay, Zimmermann congratulates Stresemann for his priorities in foreign policy and above all has warm words for his patriotism. Although the author has not used the *Nachlass*, this is a provocative survey presented with scholarly detachment.

ZWOCH, Gerhard.
Gustav-Stresemann-Bibliographie. Düsseldorf: Droste (1953), 38 pp.
A comprehensive list of literature on Stresemann that appeared from the 1920s to the time of writing. However, it does not include manuscript sources or press articles.

6

Political Parties

A. GENERAL

BERGSTRÄSSER, Ludwig.
Geschichte der politischen Parteien in Deutschland.
Munich: Isar Verlag (1965), 395 pp.
A standard history of the development of political parties in Germany from the nineteenth century to the present. In addition, an extensive bibliography on the parties is provided (p. 265—335).

BREITLING, Rupert.
"Literatur zur Partei- und Wahlfinanzierung".
Politische Vierteljahresschrift, vol. 9 (1968), p. 99—120.
A review of literature dealing with the question of money and its influence on politics. The second part of the article looks at the situation in Weimar Germany, and how the major parties received funds; particular attention is paid to the NSDAP and DNVP.

BUCHHEIM, Karl.
Geschichte der christlichen Parteien in Deutschland. Munich: Kosel-Verlag (1953), 467 pp.
A competent and reliable general survey, which includes the Centre Party of the Weimar era. The author's main concern is to furnish information rather than provide extensive analysis.

EPSTEIN, Klaus.
"The End of the German Parties in 1933". *Journal of Central European Affairs*, vol. 23, pt. 1 (1963—64), p. 52—76.
A valuable review article of the study *Das Ende der Parteien*, edited by Erich Matthias and Rudolf Morsey (see below). Epstein rightly has nothing but the highest praise for this outstanding contribution.

FRICKE, Dieter (ed.).
Geschichte der bürgerlichen Parteien in Deutschland: Handbuch der Geschichte der bürgerlichen Parteien und anderer bürgerlicher Interessenorganisationen von Vormärz bis zum Jahre 1945.

2 vols. Leipzig: Bibliographisches Institut (1968—70), 806, 974 pp.
An invaluable reference source of non-Marxist parties, organizations and interest groups from before 1848 to 1945. The entries, arranged alphabetically, are surprisingly free of the crude polemics that characterize so much historical writing from the German Democratic Republic. Volume 1 begins with the Pan-German League and ends with the Progressive People's Party; Volume 2 extends from the *Fraktion Augsburger Hof* to the Centre Party (*Zentrum*).

GREBING, Helga.
Geschichte der deutschen Parteien. Wiesbaden: Steiner (1962), 189 pp.
A useful, sound, but too brief appraisal of German political parties from the 19th century onwards. The KPD and NSDAP are dealt with only in passing. Particular stress is laid on the sociological roots of the parties.

MATTHIAS, Erich;MORSEY, Rudolf (eds.).
Das Ende der Parteien 1933. Düsseldorf: Droste (1960), 860 pp.
A scholarly, thoroughly documented, and comprehensively first-rate volume which comprises detailed articles on the demise of the Weimar political parties in 1933. Every major party is treated in separate papers, but all attain a brilliant standard; the volume as a whole constitutes an indispensable contribution to the literature relating to the collapse of the Republic. Matthias writes on the SPD; Morsey on the Centre Party; Karl Schwend on the Bavarian Peoples' Party; Hans Booms on the DVP; Friedrich Hiller von Gaertringen on the DNVP; Siegfried Bahne on the KPD; Alfred Milatz on Weimar elections; Werner Conze on the constitutional position of the parties; and finally Matthias and Morsey jointly on the German State Party.

NEUMANN, Sigmund.
Die Parteien der Weimarer Republik. Stuttgart: Kohlhammer (1965), 148 pp.
One of the best general surveys of the Weimar parties. The main section consists of shrewd individual assessments of the major parties, SPD, Centre, DDP (DSP), DVP, DNVP, NSDAP, and KPD. An extensive bibliography is also given.

PLEVER, Hildegarde.
Politische Werbung in der Weimarer Republik.
Dissertation, University of Munich (1960).
An analysis of political propaganda techniques based on
case studies of the parties and organizations involved in
the campaign for the expropriation of properties belonging
to the former royal houses in 1926, the 1929 campaign on
the so-called "Freedom Law", and the campaign for the
dissolution of the Prussian state parliament in 1931.

RITTER, Gerhard.
**Lebendige Vergangenheit: Beiträge zur historisch-
politischen Selbstbesinnung.** Munich: Oldenbourg
(1958), 331 pp.
Consists of eleven essays all written by Ritter, most of them
relating to nineteenth century themes. Of note for our
purposes is his piece on the "General Character and Historical Foundations of the Nature of Political Parties in
Germany".

RITTER, Gerhard.
**"Kontinuität und Umformung des deutschen
Parteiensystems 1918—1920".** In *Entstehung und
Wandel der modernen Gesellschaft: Festschrift für
Hans Rosenberg zum 65. Geburtstag.* Berlin:
de Gruyter (1970), p. 342—84.
A thought-provoking essay which examines the ways in
which the major parties adapted to the post-war and post-
revolutionary conditions. But the author concludes that
the traumatic events of the war and the November Revolution did not shatter all connections which the parties
had with the past; some became to some extent prisoners
of their own historical legacy. Much useful statistical data
is also presented in the paper.

SCHULEMANN, Max.
Parteien und Reichsreform 1918—1932.
Dissertation, University of Tübingen (1945).
An examination of the attitude of the DNVP, the Centre
Party and the SPD to the problem of constitutional reform
in Weimar. The author's findings have long been superseded
by other studies since 1945.

SONTHEIMER, Kurt.
"Die Parteienkritik in der Weimarer Republik".
Politische Studien, vol. 13 (1962), p. 653—74.
A look at contemporary critics of the party system and the
parties.

TORMIN, Walter.
Geschichte der deutschen Parteien seit 1848.
Stuttgart: Kohlhammer (1966), 304 pp.
Chapters 5—7 deal with the Weimar parties, their place
in the constitution, their memberships, and policies. The
information is fairly detailed and generally accurate.

TREUE, Wolfgang.
Deutsche Parteiprogramme 1861—1956.
Göttingen: Musterschmidt (1961), 404 pp.
Treue provides a good introduction on the history of
political parties in Germany; in a separate section he gives
extracts from party programmes, including those of the
Weimar period. Many tables and diagrams complete a
useful volume.

TREUE, Wolfgang.
Die deutschen Parteien. Wiesbaden: Steiner (1962),
103 pp.
A brief and very general survey of the main parties of the
nineteenth and twentieth centuries. A general textbook for
novices in German history.

B. INDIVIDUAL

(i) The Social Democratic Party (SPD)

ABENDROTH, Wolfgang.
Aufstieg und Krise der deutschen Sozialdemokratie.
Frankfurt: Stimme-Verlag (1964), 143 pp.
A general survey of the social democratic movement in the
nineteenth and twentieth centuries whose hypothesis is that
the major crises in the SPD at various stages in its history
(including 1914 and 1933) have been caused basically by
the erosion of its socialist orientation by capitalism. By
this, Abendroth means that the SPD has diverged from
Marxism, thus losing itself in a no man's land between
socialism and capitalism. The hypothesis is, of course,
controversial, but it is vigorously argued.

ADOLPH, Hans.
**Otto Wels und die Politik der deutschen
Sozialdemokratie 1894—1939: eine politische
Biographie.** Berlin: de Gruyter (1971), 386 pp.
Written in the old-fashioned style of biographical writing,
this volume is disappointing because despite dealing with
one of the most important SPD leaders of the Weimar era,
it adds little that is new or significant on Wels, the SPD, or
indeed the Weimar Republic. The author often wanders
from his principal subject to give a potted party history, a
fault only partly excused by the fact that Wels did not
leave behind personal papers. The author's approach is
sympathetic but uninformative on the whole.

ANDERS, Karl.
**Die ersten hundert Jahre: zur Geschichte einer
demokratischen Partei.** Hanover: Dietz (1963),
326 pp.
A useful sweep through party history from the beginning
to the present, though the book is somewhat uneven in
quality. The pre-1914 period is discussed more skilfully
than the Weimar era.

ARNS, Günter.
**"Die Linke in der SPD-Reichstagsfraktion im
Herbst 1923".** *Vierteljahrshefte für Zeitgeschichte,*
vol. 22, pt. 2 (1974), p. 191—203.
An examination of the composition and extent of the
left-wing opposition within the SPD *Reichstag* faction in
autumn 1923. The Left was in permanent opposition to the
faction's official revisionist policies in the early 1920s.
Although the Left lacked strength and unity it was able
in autumn 1923 with the change of government to render
the SPD faction powerless. The author estimates the leftist
faction to have constituted 30% of the SPD parliamentary
faction (or 55 out of 178 deputies). The vast majority of
these 55 were former USPD members. Informative article
with clear conclusions.

BARTEL, Walter.
Die Linken in der deutschen Sozialdemokratie im Kampf gegen Militarismus und Krieg. East Berlin: Dietz (1958), 640 pp.
Purports to be the first comprehensive Marxist interpretation of the subject, but in fact it is hopelessly tendentious in approach and judgement. The roles of Karl Liebknecht, Rosa Luxemburg and many others are either exaggerated or distorted.

BERLAU, Abraham J.
The German Social Democratic Party 1914—1921. New York: Columbia University Press (1949), 374 pp.
The bulk of the book is concerned with the 1914—18 period. The author has nothing of value to say about the SPD in Weimar. His main point is that during the war the SPD, having already lost its revolutionary impulse, moved further away from socialism, sabotaged the November Revolution and in 1919—21 betrayed the German working class. A book to be dipped into, if at all, with caution.

BORNHARDT, Alfred.
Das Janusgesicht der deutschen Sozialdemokratie: eine wehrpolitische Auseinandersetzung. Stuttgart: Metzler (1953).
Accuses the party of betraying one of its basic principles, antimilitarism, by supporting the overt and covert rearmament of Germany after 1918. Bornhardt, however, has conspicuously failed to document his thesis.

BRANCATO, Albert L.
See his work in section 19E (i)

BRANDT, Willy.
In Exile: Essays, Reflections, and Letters, 1933—1947. London: Oswald Wolff (1971), 264 pp.
The book is of some interest for the pre-1933 period because the ex-Federal Chancellor discusses the difficulties and problems confronting German socialism in Weimar in an interesting fashion. He also remarks on the question of the responsibility of the German people as a whole for the advent of Hitler to power in 1933.

BRAUN, Wilhelm.
Sowjetrussland zwischen SPD und KPD. Dissertation, University of Tübingen (1959).
Looks at the problems in very brief terms of the reciprocal relationship between the SPD and KPD in the last years of the Republic (1930—33) when the Communists were implementing their ultra-left tactics. The problems were very much more complex than the author would lead us to believe.

BREIPOHL, Renate.
Religiöser Sozialismus und bürgerliches Geschichtsbewusstsein zur Zeit der Weimarer Republik. Zürich: Theologischer Verlag (1971), 285 pp.
A full discussion of religious socialism, which was a combination essentially of Christianity and socialism. The author describes and analyses the movement's ideology, its development, the influence of individuals like Paul Tillich, and concludes with a theological critique of religious socialism. She argues it was a failure and degenerated into a kind of bourgeois anti-capitalism. An interesting pioneering work, though her definition of socialism is too rigid, and this upsets the argumentative framework of the book.

BURIAN, Wilhelm.
Reform ohne Massen: zur Entwicklung der Sozialdemokratie seit 1918. Munich: Jugend und Volk Verlag (1974), 70 pp.
Argues that the SPD has drifted away from the concept of a mass-based party since the time of the November Revolution. Seems a rather curious idea.

CALLESEN, Gerd.
Die Schleswig-Frage in den Beziehungen zwischen dänischer und deutscher Sozialdemokratie von 1912 bis 1924. Apenrade: Heimatkundliche Arbeitsgemeinschaft für Nordschleswig (1970), 200 pp.
The Schleswig question was brought to the fore in 1918 with Germany's defeat, and was settled somewhat unsatisfactorily by plebiscite in 1920. The author's point is that neither the Danish nor the German social democratic movement was able to bring about an amicable solution. For this he mainly blames the SPD's progressive retreat from an internationalist outlook and its identification with national interests. On the diplomatic aspects of the Schleswig question, the author is poorly informed.

CASPER, Gustav A.
Die Sozialdemokratische Partei und das deutsche Wehrproblem in den Jahren der Weimarer Republik. Frankfurt (1959).
This is a balanced treatment of a difficult problem, the SPD's attitude to and involvement in German remilitarization after 1918. The author is especially successful in bringing out the fundamental dilemma facing the SPD — how to reconcile long-held party principles with its responsibilities to the nation.

CASPER, Gustav A.
"Die deutsche Sozialdemokratie und die Entstehung der Reichswehr (1918—1921)". *Wehrwissenschaftliche Rundschau*, vol. 8, pt. 4 (1958), p. 194—207.
Based on material available in his book.

COLE, G. D. H.
A History of Socialist Thought. Volume 4: Communism and Social Democracy 1914—1931. Volume 5: Socialism and Fascism 1931—1939. London: Macmillan (1958—60), 940, 351 pp.
Volumes in the author's monumental work on the history of the socialist movement which are as objective, balanced, and scholarly as other parts of this series. In volume 4, he discusses the growing antagonism between Communism and democratic socialism and the rival Internationals. Turning to Germany, Cole is very critical of the SPD's role in Weimar, its weak record on social legislation, its continuing support of the Müller government after Stresemann's death, its attempts to cling to power in Prussia 1930—31, and its lack of leadership during the depression. All this, argues Cole, drove many of the working class into the KPD and NSDAP. Volume 5 describes socialism's reaction to the rise and development of fascism and National Socialism. Germany is dealt with in a separate chapter where he makes the point that National Socialism was not linked to capitalism.

CZISNIK, Ulrich.
Gustav Noske: ein sozialdemokratischer Staatsmann. Göttingen: Musterschmidt (1969), 103 pp.
A generally favourable review of the author's political career with a good discussion of Noske's controversial role in 1919—21.

DIERE, Horst.
Rechtssozialdemokratische Schulpolitik im Dienste des deutschen Imperialismus. East Berlin: Volk und Wissen Volkseigener Verlag (1964), 222 pp.
See section 17C for review.

DRECHSLER, Hanno.
Die Sozialistische Arbeiterpartei Deutschlands (SAPD): ein Beitrag zur Geschichte der deutschen Arbeiterbewegung am Ende der Weimarer Republik. Meisenheim: Hain (1965), 406 pp.
A thorough and richly detailed study not only of the SAPD, but also of the left wing in the SPD 1923—31. (The SAPD was founded in the latter year). The author also discusses other splinter groups between the SPD and KPD, their aims, policies, leaders and following. The SAPD attracted such notables as former KPD stalwart Paul Levi.

ECKERT, G. (ed.).
1863—1963: Hundert Jahre deutsche Sozialdemokratie. Hanover: Dietz (1963).
A work designed for the general reader and the party faithful comprising documents and illustrations relating to SPD history in the last hundred years.

EDINGER, Lewis J.
"German Social Democracy and Hitler's National Revolution of 1933: a Study in Democratic Leadership". *World Politics*, vol. 5, pt. 3 (1953), p. 330—67.
Concerned mainly with the first year of Hitler's régime, with only a few flashbacks to the development of the SPD in Weimar.

EICHLER, Willi.
Hundert Jahre Sozialdemokratie. Bonn: Vorstand der SPD (1962), 85 pp.
A booklet outlining the main strands of party development; p. 45—69 describe in outline the situation in Weimar. Generally uninformative.

EPSTEIN, Klaus.
"Three American Studies of Socialism". *World Politics*, vol. 11 (1959), p. 629—51.
A review of Berlau's book on the SPD (see earlier in this section) and of Peter Gay's *The Dilemma of Democratic Socialism* (1952) and Carl Schorske's *German Social Democracy* (1955).

ERSIL, Wilhelm.
"Über die finanzielle Unterstützung der rechtssozialistischen und bürgerlichen Gewerkschaftsführer durch die Reichsregierung im Jahre 1923". *Zeitschrift für Geschichtswissenschaft*, vol. 6, pt. 6 (1958), p. 1221—48.
Argues that KPD influence in the trade union movement rose dramatically in 1923 during the economic crisis, causing the government to inject massive funds into the unions to enable them to survive the KPD challenge. Ersil grossly exaggerates both the KPD influence and interest in the unions, and he has not produced the documentary evidence to uphold his case.

FLECHTHEIM, Ossip K.
"Die Anpassung der SPD: 1914, 1933, und 1959". *Kölner Zeitschrift für Soziologie und Sozialpsychologie*, vol. 17 (1965), p. 584—604.
An examination of how the SPD reacted to fundamental crises in its history. Compare Flechtheim's views with those of Wolfgang Abendroth (see first entry in this section).

FÜLBERTH, Georg; HARRER, Jürgen.
Die deutsche Sozialdemokratie. Neuwied: Luchterhand (1974), 276 pp.
An able analysis of SPD development from 1890 to 1933.

GATES, Robert A.
"German Socialism and the Crisis of 1929—33". *Central European History*, vol. 7, pt. 4 (1974), p. 332—59.
A very good analysis of the content and relevance of the economic programmes put forward by the SPD and the Free Trade Unions during the depression. The author stresses the complex interrelationship between economic theory and political ideology. He is critical of the serious failings of the SPD policies in particular; above all, the party did not appreciate the importance of having a successful economic policy in a modern industrial democracy. The political consequences of this failure aided the rise of National Socialism.

GATES, Robert A.
The Economic Policies of the German Free Trade Unions and the German Social Democratic Party 1930—1933. Dissertation, University of Oregon (1970).
See section 14 for review.

GIESECKE, Hermann.
"Zur Schulpolitik der Sozialdemokraten in Preussen und im Reich 1918/19". *Vierteljahrshefte für Zeitgeschichte*, vol. 13, pt. 2 (1965), p. 164—77.
See section 17C for review.

GREBING, Helga.
"Hundert Jahre SPD: zwischen Tradition und Fortschritt". *Politische Studien*, vol. 14 (1963), p. 529—42.
A commemorative essay congratulating the SPD on its one hundredth birthday. The author's theme is the synthesis between tradition and progress in the party's development.

GREBING, Helga.
"Die deutsche Sozialdemokratie seit 1914". *Politische Studien*, vol. 9 (1958), p. 849—59.
Criticizes the SPD leadership for its timidity in 1918—19, which resulted in a missed opportunity to firmly establish democracy in Germany. The author also discusses the SPD's dilemma in Weimar: to transform the capitalist system into a socialist-democratic one, yet to fulfil its responsibilities to the state. There is nothing original in this essay.

HARPPRECHT, Klaus.
"Otto Wels und die Sozialdemokratie von
Weimar". *Die Neue Gesellschaft*, vol. 18, pt. 7
(1971), p. 490—3.
A weak, journalistic paper which has nothing of note to
offer.

HEER, Hannes.
Burgfrieden oder Klassenkampf? Zur Politik der
sozialdemokratischen Gewerkschaften 1930—1933.
Neuwied: Luchterhand (1971), 240 pp.
See section 14 for review.

HEIDEGGER, Hermann.
Die deutsche Sozialdemokratie und der nationale
Staat, 1870—1920. Göttingen: Musterschmidt
(1956), 401 pp.
The main thesis is that the SPD became progressively more
and more conservative and nationalist so that the party
after 1918 was a truly national party and could have
fulfilled most of the traditional hopes of the Right. He
unfolds his argument on the basis of the SPD's developing
attitude towards the state before 1914; the party's support
for war credits in the *Reichstag* in 1914 is interpreted as
the logical culmination of its rightward direction. Heidegger
unexpectedly welcomes this development and praises
Ebert and Noske for having defeated Bolshevism in 1918—
19. The reason that the SPD was not accepted as a national
party in Weimar, he adds, is that it failed to identify itself
with Germanic ideals (whatever they may be!) and hence
was not nationalistic enough. An unusual work in many
respects; it contains much factual information, but its
thesis is unbalanced and is not presented with enough
detachment.

HOFFMANN, Gabriele.
Sozialdemokratie und Berufsbeamtentum: zur
Frage nach Wandel und Kontinuität im Verhältnis
der Sozialdemokratie zum Berufbeamtentum in der
Weimarer Zeit. Hamburg: Buske Verlag (1972),
289 pp.
A well documented study of the changing attitudes of the
SPD towards the civil service at a national level in the
Second Empire and Weimar Republic. He argues that
before 1914 the bureaucracy was significantly increasing
its power and strength, which only served to augment
SPD hostility towards it. This hostility was carried over to
the Republic by the party rank and file who continued
to regard the civil service as part of the establishment.
The author casts doubt on the validity of this outlook,
though he seems to overlook the fact that efforts to demo-
cratize the civil service before 1933 largely failed, thus
leaving it staffed by many anti-republicans who also rejected the SPD.

HONHART, Michael.
The Incomplete Revolution: the Social Democrats'
Failure to Transform the German Economy 1918—
1920. Dissertation, Duke University (1972).
Examines why the SPD did not use its power in government
to establish a socialist-based economy. The conservatism of
the party leadership, the party's fear of social revolution,
and the cautiousness of the trade unions are his unoriginal
reasons for this failure. Provides details on the SPD's efforts
to block far-reaching reform in specific instances. There are
few revelations here.

HUNT, Richard N.
German Social Democracy 1918—1933. New
Haven: Yale University Press (1964), 292 pp.
The author does not set out to write a full history of the
SPD. Instead, he concentrates his analysis on the party
organizational structure, the sociology of the membership, relations with the trade unions and internal party
conflicts. The result is a narrowly based but extremely
competent study which stresses the SPD's growing com-
placency, inertness and bureaucratization before 1933.
The leadership is also criticized for being too old and timid.

IHLAU, Olaf.
Die Roten Kämpfer: ein Beitrag zur Geschichte der
Arbeiterbewegung in der Weimarer Republik und
im Dritten Reich. Meisenheim: Hain (1969),
223 pp.
The *Rote Kämpfer* was a radical left-wing socialist group
loosely tied to the SPD but motivated ideologically by the
ultra-leftist view of the KAPD, the Communist splinter
faction, and by another sect, the *Essener Richtung*. The
Rote Kämpfer's views were anti-parliamentarian and anti-
trade union, but pro-workers' council. The author has
admirably unravelled the complexities of the group and the
KAPD to provide a valuable monograph.

KASTNING, Alfred.
Die deutsche Sozialdemokratie zwischen Koalition
und Opposition 1919—1923. Paderborn:
Schöningh (1970), 195 pp.
A study of a major dilemma confronting the SPD in early
Weimar: to join in coalition government with middle
class parties, or to maintain its ideological purity in opposition. Coalition strengthened the Republic to which the
SPD was committed, but weakened the party; opposition
strengthened the party but weakened an already weak state
still further. The author unfortunately does not explain all
the implications of the dilemma. Instead, he looks at the
policy of toleration in detail to determine whether this was
a viable third course. Ultimately, he does not tell us why
the SPD was part of the political structure yet unacceptable
within it.

KITCHEN, Albert B.
Wilhelm Dittmann and German Social Democracy
1918—1933. Dissertation, Auburn University
(1975), 280 pp.
A brief and largely unsatisfactory evaluation of Dittmann's
political career in the USPD (1917—22) and the SPD
(1922—33). The complexities of Weimar politics are not
fully appreciated.

KLINKHAMMER, Reimund.
Die Aussenpolitik der Sozialdemokratischen Partei
Deutschlands in der Zeit der Weimarer Republik.
Freiburg im Breisgau (1955).
A survey of general SPD attitudes in foreign policy, but the
study lacks depth and in any case is poorly informed.

KNUETTER, Hans H.
Die Juden und die deutsche Linke in der Weimarer
Republik 1918—1933. Düsseldorf: Droste (1971),
259 pp.
See section 11 for review.

KOSZYK, Kurt.
Die Presse der deutschen Sozialdemokratie: eine
Bibliographie. Hanover: Verlag für Literatur und
Zeitgeschehen (1966), 404 pp.
See section 16A (ii) for review.

KOSZYK, Kurt.
Zwischen Kaiserreich und Diktatur: die sozial-
demokratische Presse von 1914 bis 1933.
Heidelberg: Quelle & Meyer (1958), 276 pp.
See section 16A (ii) for review.

KUPISCH, Karl.
Das Jahrhundert des Sozialismus und die Kirche.
Berlin: de Gruyter (1958).
See section 10C for review.

LANDAUER, Carl.
European Socialism. Vol. I: From the Industrial
Revolution to the First World War and its After-
math. Vol. II: The Socialist Struggle against
Capitalism and Totalitarianism. 2 vols. Berkeley:
University of California Press (1959).
A good detailed coverage of the SPD in Weimar is given in
volume II. The author places its development in the wider
perspective of the European socialist movement between
the wars.

LANGE, Hermann.
Ideen und Praxis der sozialdemokratischen Aussen-
politik in der deutschen Republik (1918–1926).
Dissertation, University of Erlangen (1949).
Very tentative study, based on an unimpressive selection of
sources. The author skates over too many difficult and
complicated issues.

LÖSCHE, Peter.
Der Bolschewismus im Urteil der deutschen
Sozialdemokratie 1903–1920. Berlin: Colloquium-
Verlag (1967), 306 pp.
Most of the book is concerned with an investigation of the
impact of the October Revolution and its aftermath on
socialist development in Germany. The author sees the
Russian events as having considerably influenced what he
refers to as the "proletarianization" of the German socialist
movement after 1918. Interesting, but not all his interpretations are sound.

MAEHL, William H.
"The Role of Russia in German Socialist Policy,
1914–18". *International Review of Social History*,
vol. 4 (1959), p. 177–98.
Sees Russian influence as decisive in shaping German
socialist policy not only 1914–18, but also after 1918.
In the SPD, the traditional hatred of Russia was intensified
after 1917, causing the party to consolidate its non-revolutionary, western, parliamentary tendencies. In 1918,
therefore, the SPD was unfit to carry out a real revolution.
Regretfully the paper does not have much to say about
either the USPD or KPD.

MAEHL, William H.
"The Anti-Russian Tide in German Socialism
1918–20". *American Slavonic and East European
Review*, vol. 18, pt. 2 (1959), p. 187–96.
Maehl adds a little more detail to his previous argument
that hostility to Russia and the Bolshevik Revolution was
a significant factor in contributing to the SPD's lack of
revolutionary ambition in 1918–20.

MAEHL, William H.
"Recent Literature on the German Socialists,
1891–1932". *Journal of Modern History*, vol. 33,
pt. 3 (1961), p. 292–306.
An incisive critical review of publications on the role of the
SPD, particularly in the Weimar era. He is concerned to
repudiate the general approach of many writers that the
SPD was heavily responsible for the disasters of the Republic by providing a spirited defence of the party's record.
Maehl is especially angered by East German publications on
the topic.

MAEHL, William H.
The German Socialists and the Foreign Policy of
the Reich 1917–1922. Dissertation, University of
Chicago (1947).
Better than most other studies in this sphere, but still
containing too many gaps.

MAEHL, William H.
"The German Socialists and the Foreign Policy
of the Reich from the London Conference to
Rapallo". *Journal of Modern History*, vol. 19,
pt. 1 (1947), p. 35–54.
A discursive, somewhat dated, and altogether too sympathetic an examination and interpretation of SPD attitudes to foreign policy, particularly reparations, 1921–
22. The author praises the SPD for upholding its policy of
fulfilment despite harsh criticism at home and unhelpful
French attitudes abroad. He is also critical of Allied reparation demands, yet praises the SPD's dogged insistence on
meeting these demands. Finally, he explains why the SPD
saw no contradiction between its policy of fulfilment and
its support for the Rapallo Treaty.

MAMMACH, Klaus.
"Die Militärpolitik der SPD-Führung in der
Weimarer Republik in der Sicht der Bundeswehr".
*Beiträge zur Geschichte der Deutschen Arbeiter-
bewegung*, vol. 2 (1960), p. 787–808.
Too politically biased to merit attention.

MANN, Golo.
"Hundert Jahre deutsche Sozialdemokratie".
Die Neue Gesellschaft, vol. 10 (1963), p. 183–9.
A few commemorative remarks on the party's one hun-
dredth anniversary.

MATTHIAS, Erich.
Die deutsche Sozialdemokratie und der Osten
1915–1945: eine Übersicht. Tübingen:
Arbeitsgemeinschaft für Osteuropaforschung
(1954), 128 pp.
The dilemma facing the SPD in this sphere was how to
reconcile its Germanism with its socialism. After 1918, the
party associated itself with nationalists who demanded a

return to Germany of the eastern territories; worse than that, the SPD shared the nationalists' racialist bias against the Poles and Czechs. In fact, the SPD maintained its nationalist posture towards the East throughout the 1918—45 period. This is not one of the author's better works; he is too apologetic on behalf of the SPD, he does not fully explain the paradox in the SPD attitude, and he does not give this question the serious consideration it deserves.

MATTHIAS, Erich.
"German Social Democracy in the Weimar Republic". In A. J. Nicholls & E. Matthias (eds.). *German Democracy and the Triumph of Hitler.* London: Allen & Unwin (1971), p. 47—57.
Contrasts the moderation of the SPD in the German Revolution of 1918 with the power and determination of the Bolsheviks in the October Revolution and with the National Socialists in 1933. The author primarily addresses himself to the questions of why the SPD failed to establish a stable democratic order in 1918—19; how far the SPD was weakened in Weimar by the split in the German working class movement; and what the role of the SPD was as the main party of the new state. Interesting questions, but Matthias does not give himself enough space to answer them all in a fully satisfactory manner.

MATTHIAS, Erich.
"Social Democracy and the Power in the State". In L. Wilson (translator). *The Road to Dictatorship: Germany 1918—33.* London: Oswald Wolff (1964), p. 57—73.
An examination of the extent to which the SPD can be held responsible for the collapse of Weimar, stressing in particular that when the party failed to challenge Papen's coup against Prussia in July 1932, it lost the last chance of saving the Republic. The article appears to be a synthesis of arguments previously put forward by Matthias in other writings.

MATTHIAS, Erich.
"Der Untergang der alten Sozialdemokratie". *Vierteljahrshefte für Zeitgeschichte*, vol. 4, pt. 3 (1956), p. 250—86.
Throws light on the final phase of the SPD prior to dissolution. This article should be read in conjunction with Matthias's chapter on the SPD in his joint work *Das Ende der Parteien* (see section 6A).

MATTHIAS, Erich; PIKART, Eberhard.
Die Reichstagsfraktion der deutschen Sozialdemokratie 1898—1918. 2 vols. Düsseldorf: Droste (1966), 317, 600 pp.
Publishes in full the minutes of the proceedings of the SPD faction in the *Reichstag* until November 1918. A reading of volume II helps one to understand the mentality and character of the party on the eve of the November Revolution.

MATULL, Wilhelm.
Werden und Wesen der deutschen Sozialdemokratie. East Berlin: Dietz (1957), 159 pp.
A general popular survey which covers the SPD in Weimar in one short chapter.

MERKER, Paul.
Sozialdemokratie und Gewerkschaften, 1890—1920. East Berlin: Dietz (1957), 159 pp.
Written from a Communist viewpoint but reliable on detail. The 1918—20 period is dealt with too briefly.

MILLER, Susanne.
"Das Ringen um 'die einzige grossdeutsche Republik'". *Archiv für Sozialgeschichte*, vol. 11 (1971), p. 1—67.
See section 19E (i) for review.

MILLER, Susanne.
"Ideologien und Ideologen: zur Geschichte der deutschen Sozialdemokratie". *Neue Politische Literatur*, vol. 13 (1968), p. 433—42.
Contains some incisive observations on recent publications relating to SPD ideological and political development.

MISCH, Axel.
Das Wahlsystem zwischen Theorie und Taktik: zur Frage von Mehrheitswahl und Verhältniswahl in der Programmatik der Sozialdemokratie bis 1933. Berlin: Duncker & Humblot (1974), 290 pp.
A dry book which looks at the repercussions of the electoral law on the development of the party system. The author analyses the SPD's electoral law policy in three stages: pre-1895; during the First World War; and in the Weimar Republic. The party, he affirms, never seriously questioned the proportional representation system in Weimar since it complemented the compromise nature of the Republic's constitutional system.

MOMMSEN, Hans (ed.).
Sozialdemokratie zwischen Klassenbewegung und Volkspartei. Frankfurt: Fischer (1974), 149 pp.
Contains a number of papers delivered at the German Historians' Meeting in Regensburg in 1972. The theme is the main characteristics of the SPD outlook and policies at different stages of its history from 1863 to 1933. Susanne Miller discusses the difficulties of the party in early Weimar, and Hans Mommsen writes on the SPD's paralysis in the face of the Nazi upsurge.

MOSSE, George L.
"German Socialists and the Jewish Question in the Weimar Republic". *Yearbook of the Leo Baeck Institute*, vol. 16 (1971), p. 123—51.
The author stresses the comparatively small role the Jewish question played in the journalism and propaganda of the German Left, but adds that the relationship between socialist theory and action and the Jewish question goes much deeper. He then proceeds to trace the origins of modern German socialist thought on the Jews to Karl Kautsky. A stimulating discussion.

NIEWYK, Donald.
Socialist, Anti-Semite, and Jew: German Social Democracy Confronts the Problem of Anti-Semitism, 1918—1933. Baton Rouge: Louisiana State University Press (1971), 254 pp.
A carefully documented study of the SPD response to the Jewish question in Weimar. Argues that the party tried its best to combat the rising wave of anti-semitism before 1933, though it mistakenly saw anti-semitism as a political instrument used by the Right to beat the Republic. The party did not appreciate that the phenomenon was more fundamental and sinister.

NOSKE, Gustav.
Aufstieg und Niedergang der deutschen Sozialdemokratie: erlebtes aus Aufstieg und Niedergang einer Demokratie. Offenbach: Bollwerk Verlag (1947), 323 pp.

The memoirs of the former Defence Minister and "Blood-hound of the Revolution". The book includes some shrewd comments on aspects of Weimar politics, but as a whole it disappoints.

NOWKA, Harry.
Das Machtverhältnis zwischen Partei und Fraktion in der SPD: eine historisch-empirische Unter-suchung. Cologne: Carl Heymanns Verlag (1973), 167 pp.
An informative survey of the relationship between the party bureaucracy and membership on one side, and the parliamentary party on the other, during the 1871—1971 period. The section on Weimar is one of the best in the book. The author shows that before 1933 the *Reichstag* faction was firmly under the control of the party prae-sidium and generally acted according to the latter's orders.

OSCHILEWSKI, Walther.
Werden und Wirken: ein Gang durch die Geschichte der Berliner Sozialdemokratie. Berlin: Arani (1954), 144 pp.
Very broad, popular account.

OSTERROTH, Franz; SCHUSTER, Dieter.
Chronik der deutschen Sozialdemokratie.
Hanover: Dietz (1963), 672 pp.
A substantial work of reference for party development from the beginning until 1963. The massive factual infor-mation is arranged chronologically and the accompanying commentary is helpful. Details of election results and the composition of state governments in the Weimar era are given in an appendix. An extensive bibliography of litera-ture on party history completes the volume.

POTTHOFF, Heinrich.
Die Sozialdemokratie von den Anfängen bis 1945.
Bad Godesberg: Verlag Neue Gesellschaft (1974), 229 pp.
One of the best and most up to date of the general histories of the SPD. The major events and controversies that have arisen are discussed in knowledgeable fashion.

ROEHL, Fritzmichael.
Marie Juchacz und die Arbeiterwohlfahrt.
Hanover: Dietz (1961), 204 pp.
A popularly written account of the career and work of Juchacz, founder in 1919 of the socialist welfare organi-zation, the *Arbeiterwohlfahrt*. She also was active in the SPD before 1933.

ROTHFELS, Hans (ed.).
"Die Roten Kämpfer". *Vierteljahrshefte für Zeitgeschichte*, vol. 7, pt. 4 (1959), p. 438—60.
Publishes illuminating documentation on this radical socialist group which even before 1933 went underground. This contribution should be read in conjunction with Ihlau's study (see earlier in this section).

RÜLCKER, Christoph.
"Arbeiterkultur und Kulturpolitik im Blickwinkel des 'Vorwärts 1918—1928". *Archiv für Sozial-geschichte*, vol. 14 (1974), p. 115—55.
See section 16A (ii) for review.

SANGER, Fritz (ed.).
Erich Ollenhauer: Reden und Aufsätze. Hanover: Dietz (1964), 357 pp.
A selection of speeches and writings by the former SPD politician and party leader from 1920 onwards. His idio-syncratic version of the meaning of socialism comes across vividly.

SCHMITT, Veit.
Die Stellungnahme der Deutschnationalen Volks-partei, des Zentrums, und der Sozial-demokratischen Partei im Reichstag zur Steuerreform von 1925. Dissertation, University of Erlangen (1951).
See section 3A for review.

SCHULZE, Hagen (ed.).
Anpassung oder Widerstand: aus den Akten des Parteivorstandes der deutschen Sozialdemokratie 1932/33. Stuttgart: Verlag Neue Gesellschaft (1975), 248 pp.
An important documentary source which throws new light on the dilemma confronting the SPD leadership in the last days of Weimar and early period of the Hitler régime: should it adopt a policy of accommodation or a policy of resistance? The protocols published here further explain why the SPD chose the former.

SCHUSTEREIT, Hartmut.
Linksliberalismus und Sozialdemokratie in der Weimarer Republik. Düsseldorf: Schwann Verlag (1975), 296 pp.
Basically a comparison between the ideas, attitudes, and policies of the DDP and the SPD between 1919 and 1930. Schustereit's line of thought is sometimes a little confused, and confusing, and ultimately our knowledge of neither party is significantly improved.

SHERDAN, Vincent.
The German Social Democratic Party and the League of Nations during the Weimar Republic 1918—1933. Dissertation, Arizona State University (1975), 318 pp.
Shows that despite there being various attitudes within the party to the League, the SPD as a whole supported the official German government position to it throughout the 1920s.

SHIRK-LINDEMANN, Albert.
The Problem of the Communist International for French and German Socialism, 1919—1920.
Dissertation, Harvard University (1968)[1]

SIEMANN, Joachim.
Der sozialdemokratische Arbeiterführer in der Zeit der Weimarer Republik. Dissertation, University of Göttingen (1955).
A sociological study designed to ascertain the background of SPD party leaders. Concludes, not surprisingly, that the vast majority came from the working class (skilled for the most part) and the lower middle class.

1. I was unable to obtain a copy for review.

SUCK, Ernst-August.
Der religiöse Sozialismus in der Weimarer Republik (1918—1933). Dissertation, University of Marburg (1953).
A useful survey of a neglected aspect of socialist history, but superseded by Breipohl's work (see earlier in this section).

THAPE, Ernst.
Von Rot zu Schwarz-Rot-Gold: Lebensweg eines Sozialdemokraten. Hanover: Dietz (1969), 364 pp.
Thape's political career is perhaps not entirely representative of his generation who were SPD members. Spending the First World War in Switzerland, he returned to Magdeburg in 1921 where until 1933 he edited the local social democratic paper, *Volksstimme.* He records his experiences as editor and his contacts with leading SPD party politicians. Though modestly interesting, the memoirs add nothing to our knowledge of either the SPD or the Weimar Republic.

THEIMER, Walter.
Von Bebel zu Ollenhauer: der Weg der deutschen Sozialdemokratie. Munich: Lehnen Verlag (1957).
An undistinguished and error-prone general chronicle of SPD history.

THÖNESSEN, Werner.
Die Frauenemanzipation in Politik und Literatur der deutschen Sozialdemokratie (1893—1933). Berlin (1960).
A useful look at a subject which has also become intellectually fashionable, but much work still has to be done.

TOBIAS, H. J.; SNELL, John L.
"A Soviet Interpretation of the SPD, 1895—1933". *Journal of Central European Affairs,* vol. 13, pt. 1 (1953—54), p. 61—6.
A brief consideration of recent trends in Soviet scholarship, and in particular an appraisal of the work of the Soviet historian, Boris A. Chagin of Leningrad University. In his works on the SPD in Weimar, Chagin accuses the leadership of fostering idealism to check the revolutionary spirit of the workers and to offer resistance to the KPD. By 1933, Chagin states, the SPD had lost its socialist ideology and was dominated by Prussian chauvinism, thus helping to pave the way for fascism. The editors argue that Chagin's work is valuable in some respects; for example, he demonstrates the close relationship between the right-wing socialist theorists and the idealistic philosophy which took hold of the SPD before 1933. He also usefully discusses the influence of neo-Hegelian ideas in the party.

VARAIN, Heinz J.
Freie Gewerkschaften, Sozialdemokratie und Staat: die Politik der Generalkommission unter der Führung Carl Legiens (1890—1920). Düsseldorf: Droste (1956), 207 pp.
See section 14 for review.

VIETZKE, Siegfried.
"Die Kapitulation der rechten SPD-Führung vor dem Hitlerfaschismus Ende Januar/Anfang Februar 1933". *Zeitschrift für Geschichtswissenschaft,* vol. 11, pt. 1 (1963), p. 104—15.
A predictable piece, castigating the SPD as weak (which it was), and traitorous to the working class (which it was not).

WEBER, Hermann.
"Sozialistische Splittergruppen in der Weimarer Republik". *Neue Politische Literatur,* vol. 10 (1965), p. 375—81.
A review of recently published literature on various socialist splinter groups, including the SAPD.

WEBER, Hermann (ed.).
Das Prinzip links: eine Dokumentation; Beiträge zur Diskussion des demokratischen Sozialismus in Deutschland 1847—1973. Hanover: Fackelträger Verlag (1973), 359 pp.
Most of the documents in this collection consist of brief extracts from the writings of leading personalities of the socialist movement in the nineteenth and twentieth centuries. Of note among the documents covering the Weimar period is the programme of the short-lived SPD-KPD coalition in Thuringia in 1923.

WITT, Friedrich W.
Die Hamburger Sozialdemokratie in der Weimarer Republik, unter besonderer Berücksichtigung der Jahre 1929/30—1933. Hanover: Verlag für Literatur und Zeitgeschehen (1971), 219 pp.
The message of this work confirms rather than adds to our understanding of the SPD. The author shows that the party leadership and voters were mainly drawn from skilled workers, a trend accentuated between 1929 and 1933; the unskilled and the unemployed increasingly voted KPD or NSDAP. Witt also indicates that the Hamburg SPD had no real idea of how to cope with the depression or the political crisis, just like the SPD as a whole. Thus, his conclusions merely testify to the validity of the views of previous scholars.

(ii) The Independent Social Democratic Party (USPD)

BALABANOFF, Angelica.
Die Zimmerwalder Bewegung 1914—1919. Frankfurt: Verlag Neue Kritik (1969), 160 pp.
Although originally published in 1928 (Leipzig: Hirschfeld) this is still a valuable inside account of the reformist movement in German socialism.

KRAUSE, Hartfrid.
USPD: zur Geschichte der Unabhängigen Sozialdemokratischen Partei Deutschlands. Frankfurt: Europäische Verlagsanstalt (1975), 397 pp.
A generally valuable and informative account which presents a good deal of new material.

LEDEBOUR, Minna (ed).
Georg Ledebour: Mensch und Kämpfer. Frankfurt: Europa Verlag (1954), 168 pp.
An interesting collection of letters and memoranda relating to the left-wing political activist.

MEIRRITZ, Heinz.
Die Herausbildung einer revolutionären Massenpartei im ehemaligen Land Mecklenburg-Schwerin. Dissertation, University of Rostock (1965).
Concentrates on a discussion of the efforts to create a mass-based party of the working class between 1917 and 1920 by uniting the USPD and the KPD. Some useful material is presented from East German archives, although the tone is tendentious.

MORGAN, David W.
The German Independent Social Democratic Party 1918—1922. Dissertation, University of Oxford (1969).
A very sound overall account based on wide source material.

MORRILL, Don L.
The Independent Social Democratic Party of Germany and the Communist International: March 1919-October 1920. Dissertation, Emory University (1966).
Shows that due to pressure exerted by the Communist International, the left wing of the USPD joined the Third International after giving up its non-alignment policy in October 1920.

MORRILL, Don L.
"The German Independent Socialists at the Second Comintern Congress". *Soviet Studies*, vol. 23, pt. 1 (1971), p. 78—95.
Examines USPD-Comintern relations 1918—20 with special emphasis on the latter's aim of splitting the USPD which was finally brought to a successful conclusion at the Second Comintern Conference in the summer of 1920. The use of the "21 conditions" to split the USPD is described in detail.

MORRILL, Don L.
"The Comintern and the German Independent Social Democratic Party". *Historian*, pt. 2 (1970), p. 191—209.
On the same theme as the aforementioned article, adding nothing new.

NAUMANN, Horst.
Der Kampf des revolutionären Flügels der USPD für den Anschluss an die Kommunistische Internationale und die Vereinigung mit der KPD. Dissertation, Humboldt-Universität, East Berlin (1961).
Naumann has provided a fair amount of useful data from East German archives in this study, which, although not changing the general picture of USPD-Comintern relations, adds interesting detail.

NAUMANN, Horst.
"Die Vereinigung des linken Flügels der USPD mit der KPD". *Zeitschrift für Geschichtswissenschaft*, vol. 19, pt. 11 (1971), p. 1367—84.
Naumann unfortunately turns what could have been a valuable paper into a propaganda piece about the merits of proletarian internationalism and the greatness of the Soviet Union.

NAUMANN, Horst.
"Die USPD und die Kommunistische Internationale". *Zeitschrift für Geschichtswissenschaft*, vol. 19, pt. 8 (1971), p. 1034—44.
A discussion of the preparations for the visit by the USPD delegation to the Second Congress of the Comintern in St. Petersburg and Moscow in July/August 1920.

NAUMANN, Horst.
"Äusserungen des linken Flügels der USPD für den Anschluss an die K.I. und zur Vereinigung mit der KPD im Jahre 1920". *Beiträge zur Geschichte der Deutschen Arbeiterbewegung*, vol. 12, pt. 6 (1970), p. 952—66.
Publishes a series of relevant documents and memoranda expressive of the revolutionary USPD faction's desire to join the Communist International and the KPD.

NAUMANN, Horst.
"Die Bedeutung des II Weltkongresses der Kommunistischen Internationalen für die Vereinigung des revolutionären Flügels der USPD mit der KPD". *Beiträge zur Geschichte der Deutschen Arbeiterbewegung*, vol. 2, pt. 3 (1960), p. 466—87.
Argues the obvious point that the 1920 Congress was the decisive first step towards amalgamation of the USPD's left wing and the KPD.

O'BOYLE, Leonore.
"The German Independent Socialists during the First World War". *American Historical Review*, vol. 56, pt. 1 (1950—51), p. 824—31.
A rather unimpressive, speculative paper. The author argues on the flimsiest of evidence that the USPD could have destroyed the bastions of the old order in 1918 and gone on to make the Weimar Republic a viable democratic state. One wonders what the SPD and KPD would have made of all this.

PÖHLAND, W.
Die Entwicklung der Arbeiterbewegung in Ost-Thüringen von 1914—20. Dissertation, University of Halle (1965).
The author's primary concern is to trace the development of the USPD, particularly its left wing, in South Thuringia.

RATZ, Ursula.
Georg Ledebour, 1850—1947: Weg und Wirken eines sozialistischen Politikers. Berlin: de Gruyter (1969), 281 pp.
A sound biography partly based on the Ledebour papers. Considerable attention is paid to his political activities in Weimar, including his involvement with the USPD 1920—22.

RYDER, A. J.
The Independent Social Democratic Party and the German Revolution 1917—20. Dissertation, University of London (1958).
Not as good as later dissertations on the USPD (see elsewhere in this section for details) which make use of a wider range of sources.

SCHULTZ, Eberhard.
Rolle und Anteil des linken Flügels der USPD in ehemaligen Regierungsbezirk Halle-Merseburg bei der Herausbildung und Entwicklung der KPD zur revolutionären Massenpartei (1917—1920). Dissertation, University of Halle (1969).
A useful local study which incorporates a lot of new but unimportant detail on USPD development.

WHEELER, Robert F.
The Independent Social Democratic Party and the Internationals: an Examination of Socialist Internationalism in Germany 1915 to 1923.
Dissertation, University of Pittsburgh (1970).
A massive thesis which examines how the USPD related to the idea of socialist internationalism and the institutions representative of it. A detailed analysis is given of the USPD-Comintern relationship 1918—20, the efforts of the USPD to found a Social Revolutionary International, and the whole international socialist orientation of the USPD between 1918—23. Very impressively argued and documented.

WHEELER, Robert F.
"Die '21 Bedingungen' und die Spaltung der USPD in Herbst 1920". *Vierteljahrshefte für Zeitgeschichte*, vol. 23, pt. 2 (1975),p. 117—54.
A thorough analysis of the role of the "21 conditions" in finally causing the split in the USPD at the end of 1920. The conditions in fact destroyed what had been until 1920 the largest and best organized workers' party in Germany. The author looks for the first time at the reactions in the USPD to the conditions at the grass-roots level. An important and scholarly paper.

WHEELER, Robert F.
"The Failure of 'Truth and Vanity' at Berne: Kurt Eisner, the Opposition and the Reconstruction of the International". *International Review of Social History*, vol. 18, pt. 2 (1973), p. 173—201.
A valuable reconsideration of the International Labour and Socialist Conference in Berne, January-February 1919, and its importance for the post-1918 development of Marxist internationalism. The Conference influenced the formation and development of the Communist International, but the main theme of the essay is the hitherto underestimated significance of Kurt Eisner's role and that of the left-wing Zimmerwaldian opposition. Wheeler stresses Eisner's role as the "honest broker" mediating between left and right factions and affirms that he saved the Conference. In the long term, however, Eisner's success contributed to the failure of endeavours to resurrect the Second International.

WHEELER, Robert F.
"German Women and the Communist International: the Case of the Independent Social Democrats". *Central European History*, vol. 8, pt. 2 (1975), p. 113—39.
The paper examines in particular differences and similarities in attitudes towards the Comintern among male and female members of the USPD, focusing on their reactions to the "21 Conditions". The discussion is informative but does not make the case that consideration of sex as a variable in political behaviour significantly adds to our understanding of the themes under review in this essay.

(iii) The German National Peoples' Party (DNVP)

CHANADY, A.
"The Disintegration of the German National Peoples' Party, 1924—1930". *Journal of Modern History*, vol. 39, pt. 1 (1967), p. 65—91.
A very competent analysis of the DNVP's development 1924—28, emphasizing the acute strains imposed on the party by its transition during this period from a party of outright opposition to the Republic to one bearing governmental responsibility. As a result, many latent tensions and weaknesses were brought to the surface and were exacerbated after Hugenberg became party leader in 1928. The structural and ideological divisions within the DNVP were revealed by Hugenberg's provocative style of leadership and consequently the party suffered a series of damaging secessions between 1928 and 1930. By the latter date, therefore, the DNVP was already in clear decline.

DIETRICH, Valeska.
Alfred Hugenberg: ein Manager in der Publizistik.
Dissertation, Free University of Berlin (1959).
Examines Hugenberg the press overlord rather than Hugenberg the politician, but his uncompromising outlook in business affords a clue to his brand of radical politics. The dissertation, however, has not fully explored the wider implications of Hugenberg's press and publishing activities.

DIETRICH, Valeska.
"Alfred Hugenberg: das Leben eines Managers". *Politische Studien*, vol. 12 (1961), p. 236—42, 295—301.
The first part of this essay outlines Hugenberg's life and career in industry, where he eventually became a member of the Krupp directorate. He left Krupp in 1919 and began constructing his press empire, and the UFA film concern. The second part describes his involvement in politics as a co-founder of the DNVP, and then as its chairman.

DÖRR, Manfred.
Die Deutschnationale Volkspartei, 1925—1928.
Dissertation, University of Marburg (1964).
A thorough investigation of the party's internal developments, including the increasing tensions which produced an atmosphere conducive to secession. The party's difficulties in finding a coherent policy in government and in opposition are admirably set out. The work constitutes a valuable complement to Hertzman's study (see below).

FRIEDENTHAL, E.
Volksbegehren und Volksentscheid über den Young Plan und die deutschnationale Sezession.
Dissertation, University of Tübingen (1957).
A useful study of the campaign of the "national opposition" against the Young Plan and its relevance to the secession of the farmers and agrarians from the DNVP in 1929. The DNVP's relations with other groups in the campaign, including the NSDAP, are not examined.

GEMEIN, Gisbert J.
Die DNVP in Düsseldorf 1918—1933. Cologne: Gouder und Hansen (1969), 236 pp.
An examination of why a conservative, nationalist, and monarchist party which was supported by overwhelmingly bourgeois sections of the population failed to make a significant impact in an industrial area with a large working class population. Gemein provides details of how the DNVP operated at a regional level, but his conclusions are unremarkable. The party's programme was completely out of touch with the realities of the Düsseldorf situation, the party leadership was weak, the left-wing parties were too powerfully entrenched among the workers, while the Centre Party captured the Catholic vote. Thus from 1930—32, the DNVP's percentage of the vote in the Düsseldorf electoral districts fell to single figures.

GRATHWOL, Robert.
DNVP and European Reconciliation, 1924—1928: a Study of the Conflict between Party Politics and Government Foreign Policy in Weimar Germany. Dissertation, University of Chicago (1968).

A useful exploration of the DNVP's attempts to come to terms with the Stresemann policy of fulfilment towards the Western Allies after 1924. The Dawes Plan and the party's subsequent inclusion in government necessitated a serious rethink of its traditional aims and commitments.

HERTZMAN, Lewis.
DNVP: Right-Wing Opposition in the Weimar Republic, 1918—1924. Lincoln (Nebr.): University of Nebraska Press (1963), 263 pp.

An able but narrowly based analysis of the origins, development, and, above all, the heterogeneity of the DNVP, and the consequent uncertainties and divisions that characterized the party. Thus, from the beginning, the DNVP had a built-in vulnerability to damaging splits. But the author has left a lot of ground uncovered: there is virtually nothing on the sociological composition of the party, on organization, or on the ideas of the leadership.

HERTZMAN, Lewis.
"The Founding of the German National Peoples' Party (DNVP), November 1918—January 1919". *Journal of Modern History*, vol. 30, pt. 1 (1958), p. 24—36.

Traces the origins of the party from November 1918 when the call for a new conservative party was made, until January 1919 when it was finally constituted. Stresses that diverse social groups came together to form the DNVP, which was therefore never a monolithic *Junker* bloc. Hertzman also notes the strongly Lutheran character of most members.

HUGENBERG, Alfred.
Hugenberg und die Hitler Diktatur. 2 vols. Detmold (1949).

Very apologetic in tone, unreliable in detail, and indeed largely worthless.

KUNKLE, Wray.
Gustav Stresemann, the German Peoples' Party, and the German National Peoples' Party 1923—1929. Dissertation, The American University, Washington, D.C. (1969).

See section 6B (iv) for review.

LEOPOLD, John A.
Alfred Hugenberg and German Politics. Dissertation, Catholic University of America (1970).

A rather uninteresting, straightforward chronological narrative of the highlights of Hugenberg's career (1865—1951). The author outlines his political ideas, his nationalism, and business interests in pre-1918 and Weimar Germany. Hugenberg's relationship with Hitler is superficially treated. As a whole, the thesis lacks a conceptual framework.

LEOPOLD, John A.
"The Election of Alfred Hugenberg as Chairman of the German National Peoples' Party". *Canadian Journal of History*, vol. 7, pt. 2 (1972), p. 149—71.

Argues that Hugenberg was able to force his way to the top of the party for three main reasons: his ideological opposition to the Republic, his enormous press and propaganda network which was invaluable, and his financial resources. Personal magnetism he conspicuously lacked.

LIEBE, Werner.
Die Deutschnationale Volkspartei 1918—1924. Düsseldorf: Droste (1956), 190 pp.

Covers more or less the same ground as Hertzman's study, and similarly overlooks many aspects of the party's development. The author concentrates on analysing the heterogeneous ideas which made up the party's outlook, its devotion to the Hohenzollerns, the Fatherland, and its nostalgia for pre-1914 Germany. Liebe rightly argues that the DNVP's policies until 1924 were inherently unstable.

SCHMIDT-HANNOVER, Otto.
Umdenken oder Anarchie: Männer — Schicksale — Lehren. Göttingen: Göttinger Verlagsanstalt (1959), 393 pp.

A semi-biography of Hugenberg, who is portrayed unflatteringly: contains also some interesting comments about internal matters in the DNVP in the 1920s.

SCHMITT, Veit.
Die Stellungnahme der Deutschnationalen Volkspartei, des Zentrums, und der Sozialdemokratischen Partei im Reichstag zur Steuerreform von 1925. Dissertation, University of Erlangen (1951).

See section 3A for review.

STERNER, Siegfried.
Die Stellungnahme der Deutschnationalen Volkspartei zur Sozialpolitik. Dissertation, University of Freiburg (1952).

Sterner paints a negative picture of the DNVP's social policies, even during periods of inflation and depression.

STEUER, Ludwig.
"Hugenberg und die Hitlerdiktatur". In W. Borchmeyer (ed.). *Hugenbergs Ringen in deutschen Schicksalsstunden.* Detmold (1951).

Argues vigorously that Hugenberg did not attempt to use Hitler as a means of attracting and influencing a greater measure of public support.

THIMME, Anneliese.
Flucht in den Mythos: die Deutschnationale Volkspartei und die Niederlage von 1918. Göttingen: Vandenhoeck und Ruprecht (1969), 195 pp.

A perceptive and thought-provoking book whose theme is the contrast between the DNVP's public policies and the real concerns of the conservative nationalists who supported it. The viciousness of its political ideology contrasted with the cultural and political values the German conservative Right thought it personified. The first half of the book provides a competent narrative of the DNVP's history, but it is the second half which puts forward the provocative ideas. The book amounts to a brilliant indictment of the hypocrisy and unreality of the DNVP's position.

WITT, Peter-Christian.
"Eine Denkschrift Otto Hoetzschs vom 5. November 1918". *Vierteljahrshefte für Zeitgeschichte*, vol. 21, pt. 3 (1973), p. 337—53.

Publishes a memorandum of the foreign affairs expert of the conservative newspaper, the *Kreuzzeitung*, in which Hoetzsch sets forth the ideas which he believed had to be implemented if conservatism and a conservative party were to survive the events of 1918—19. The importance of the memorandum lies in that, firstly, it provides a critique of conservative party politics in the last years of the Second Reich, and secondly, in it he lays down plans for developing a conservative mass party after 1918 — the first such plan from a leading conservative.

(iv) The German Peoples' Party (DVP)

ALBERTIN, Lothar.
Liberalismus und Demokratie am Anfang der Weimarer Republik. Düsseldorf: Droste (1972), 466 pp.
See section 6B (v) for review.

DÖHN, Lothar.
Politik und Interesse: die Interessenstruktur der Deutschen Volkspartei. Meisenheim: Hain (1970), 459 pp.
A detailed, balanced, and well integrated monograph which examines the relationship between the policies adopted at different times by the party and the powerful interest groups, notably the industrial lobby, that made up the DVP.

HARTENSTEIN, Wolfgang.
Die Anfänge der Deutschen Volkspartei 1918—1920. Düsseldorf: Droste (1962), 299 pp.
A comprehensive discussion of the origins of the DVP. Much of the party's basic character was shaped at this early time: but many of the weaknesses which caused the party's decline after 1930 were also present from the beginning. The author stresses in particular the party's ambivalent attitude to the Republic which continued despite Stresemann throughout the Weimar era. The least convincing part of the book is that in which Stresemann is depicted as the personification of the DVP.

JONES, Larry E.
"Gustav Stresemann and the Crisis of German Liberalism". *European Studies Review*, vol. 4, pt. 2 (1974), p. 141—63.
Begins by outlining the elements of Stresemann's liberal philosophy which developed before 1914, and contrasts this with the increasing difficulty experienced by him in sustaining his liberal values in the political whirlpool of the early Weimar Republic. However, the article amounts to an unsatisfactory general survey of some of the major events in Stresemann's political life and of his leadership of the DVP. No new insights are presented.

KUNKLE, Wray.
Gustav Stresemann, the German Peoples' Party and the German National Peoples' Party 1923—1929. Dissertation, The American University, Washington, D.C. (1969).
Argues that Stresemann skilfully set Germany limited objectives in foreign policy to correspond to her weakened resources. However, the DVP's support for Stresemann's foreign policy was never consistent. The DNVP gave only limited backing at the best of times. Stresemann is depicted as a "good European" in this thesis, a view which is untenable. The thesis as a whole lacks cohesion in argument and organization.

SCHELM-SPANGENBERG, Ursula.
Die Deutsche Volkspartei im Lande Braunschweig: Gründung, Entwicklung, soziologische Struktur, politische Arbeit. Brunswick: Waisenhaus Verlag (1964), 176 pp.
A useful regional study, though more of a narrative than an analysis. It is not made entirely clear whether the nature of the party's development in Brunswick, where it never had much success, was typical of the party's national development. The work is also weak in explaining the ideas and policies of the party.

THIMME, Roland.
Stresemann und die Deutsche Volkspartei 1923—25. Lübeck: Matthiesen Verlag (1961), 147 pp.
An examination of Stresemann as leader of the DVP; working from this angle, our understanding of him is increased. But the book is better as a history of the DVP in these years, with detailed information provided on its organization, membership and relations with other parties and groups. Stresemann's problem, however, was that he never succeeded in obtaining the full support of his party for his foreign policy so that he never emerged as an outstanding party politician.

(v) The German Democratic Party (DDP)

See section 16A (iii) for references to the liberal-democratic press.

ALBERTIN, Lothar.
"Liberalismus in der Weimarer Republik". *Neue Politische Literatur*, vol. 19 (1974), p. 220—34.
An informative discussion.

ALBERTIN, Lothar.
Liberalismus und Demokratie am Anfang der Weimarer Republik: eine vergleichende Analyse der Deutschen Demokratischen Partei und der Deutschen Volkspartei. Düsseldorf: Droste (1972), 466 pp.
A skilful and detailed analysis of the origins, development, and fall of the two Weimar liberal parties. Organization, membership, aims, policies, leadership, and electorate are aspects discussed; the author argues that each party contributed, to a degree, to the other's decline, since they were competing for money and votes from the same sources. Above all, the main cause of their decline, he contends, was their inability to break clearly with the traditional pattern of liberal politics that had been established before 1914. This invites the question of how and whether the post-1918 liberals could have made a new start, but Albertin does not answer this point. Albertin's study essentially confirms rather than questions previously established conclusions on German liberalism, but does so with a high degree of competence.

ALBERTIN, Lothar.
"Die Verantwortung der liberalen Parteien für das Scheitern der grossen Koalition im Herbst 1921: ökonomische und ideologische Einflüsse auf die Funktionsfähigkeit der parteienstaatlichen Demokratie". *Historische Zeitschrift*, no. 205 (1967), p. 566—627.
A quite excellent paper which demonstrates very clearly that in 1921 neither the DDP nor the DVP had the character to adopt the measures which might have prevented the

occupation of the Ruhr. Economic and ideological influences effectively debilitated the coalition government in a situation of crisis, thereby revealing that even the so-called liberal parties put self-interest before the national interest.

ALBERTIN, Lothar.
"German Liberalism and the Foundation of the Weimar Republic: a Missed Opportunity?". In A. J. Nicholls & E. Matthias (eds.). *German Democracy and the Triumph of Hitler.* London: Allen & Unwin (1971), p. 29—46.

Describes the political activities of liberal politicians and groups in November 1918 as they strove to give the Revolution a liberal character. But Albertin questions whether these efforts contained any real substance because it was soon discovered that the DDP attracted support and funds from restricted sections of society; the party did not succeed during this crucial early period in breaking into the working classes, and never made good this failure. This was, therefore, the first and perhaps most important setback for the liberal cause in Weimar. A clearly argued and stimulating paper.

BOWERS, Peter M.
The Failure of the German Democratic Party 1918—1930. Dissertation, University of Pittsburgh (1973).

Covers ground which is all too familiar in trying to explain why the DDP failed to become an established party of the Protestant liberal bourgeoisie. Adds nothing new.

BRANTZ, Rennie W.
Anton Erkelenz, the Hirsch-Duncker Trade Unions, and the German Democratic Party. Dissertation, Ohio State University (1973).

The author's aim is to explain why the DDP was a political failure through presenting a biography of Anton Erkelenz, an important party leader (1878—1945). Erkelenz, working class and Catholic, had considerable influence in the liberal Hirsch-Duncker unions, and sat in the *Reichstag* (1920—30). His fight to have the DDP break into the working class electorate failed dismally, and Brantz regards his personal failure as symptomatic of the wider failings of the DDP. Brantz does not provide any new ideas on why the DDP declined, but the biographical detail on Erkelenz is useful to have.

CHANADY, Attila.
"The Dissolution of the German Democratic Party in 1930". *American Historical Review*, vol. 73, pt. 5 (1968), p. 1433—53.

An informative but not exhaustive analysis of the major reasons why the DDP collapsed in 1930. The author regards the party's collapse as a significant landmark in the Republic's history and the first overt sign of its impending dissolution, because by that date German liberalism was finished as a viable political force. A survey of the origins, nature, aims, development and conflicts of the DDP 1918—30 is provided, though the real crisis for the party occurred after the *Reichstag* elections of May 1928.

EKSTEINS, Modris.
Theodor Heuss und die Weimarer Republik: ein Beitrag zur Geschichte des deutschen Liberalismus. Stuttgart: Klett (1969), 208 pp.

A compact yet judicious appraisal of the personality, ideas, and importance of one of Weimar's outstanding liberal spokesmen. Not only is the study revealing of Heuss himself, it also provides a perceptive analysis of the weaknesses of liberalism in the republican era.

FISCHENBERG, Günter.
Der deutsche Liberalismus und die Entstehung der Weimarer Republik: die Krise einer politischen Bewegung. Dissertation, University of Münster (1958).

A good study, which analyses in convincing fashion the main reasons why German liberalism did not have an auspicious start to the Weimar era.

FREEMAN, Herbert.
The German Democratic Party 1918—1920. Dissertation, Yale University (1959).

Although covering the same area as Fischenberg's work, this effort is much less satisfactory.

FRYE, Bruce B.
"The German Democratic Party 1918—1930". *Western Political Quarterly*, vol. 16, pt. 1 (1963), p. 167—79.

Reviews why the DDP's middle class support fell away badly after 1920, and why the party was never able to recover. By 1930, it had become a splinter party and ready for dissolution. The author repeats the familiar theme that the failures of the DDP represent in microcosm the failings of German democracy, though he prudently avoids saying that the failure of the DDP was a major cause of Weimar's collapse.

FRYE, Bruce B.
"A Letter from Max Weber". *Journal of Modern History*, vol. 39, pt. 2 (1967), p. 119—25.

In April 1920, Max Weber wrote a letter (published here in full, and in English translation) to Carl Petersen, chairman of the DDP, intimating his resignation as a member of an important DDP committee. He did so because he would not agree to serve as a DDP representative on the reconvened Socialization Committee. The government's compromises with socialism had deeply offended Weber's economic and personal beliefs. Weber's fears were also indicative of the apprehension felt by wider sections of the middle classes faced with the prospect of disadvantageous economic and social legislation.

GOTTSCHALK, Regina.
Die Linksliberalen zwischen Kaiserreich und Weimarer Republik. Mainz: Kubatzki & Probst (1969), 280 pp.

A useful examination of left liberal adaptation of attitudes from the crisis of July 1917 to June 1919. Like previous writers, the author stresses the failure of the liberals to come to terms with the new situation in Germany after November 1918, principally because they were unable to cast off the legacies of the past.

HOLL, Karl.
"Der Austritt Theodor Wolffs aus der Deutschen Demokratischen Partei". *Publizistik*, vol. 16, pt. 3 (1971), p. 294—302.

Provides an interesting exchange of letters between Koch-Weser, chairman of the DDP, and Wolff, chief editor of the *Berliner Tageblatt*. Wolff intimated his resignation from the party because he believed it had failed to maintain a commitment to progressive cultural policies in its attitude in 1926 to a law seeking to protect youth from pornography. The affair illustrates a deeper crisis within the DDP at this time over the degree of its liberalism.

LÜTH, Erich.
See his work in section 9D (Hamburg).

MERZ, Renate.
Die Anfänge der Deutschen Demokratischen Partei in Schleswig-Holstein. Dissertation, University of Kiel (1974) (in photocopy).
Useful for details of local difficulties in setting up a new party, but does not change our general understanding of the early character of the DDP.

OPITZ, Reinhard.
Der deutsche Sozialliberalismus 1917—1933.
Cologne: Pahl-Lugenstein (1973), 310 pp.
The first survey of "social liberalism" as a distinctive entity; contains a considerable amount of interesting information.

PORTNER, Ernst.
Die Verfassungspolitik der Liberalen 1919: ein Beitrag zur Deutung der Weimarer Reichsverfassung. Bonn: Röhrscheid (1973), 278 pp.
See section 2 for review.

PORTNER, Ernst.
"Der Ansatz zur demokratischen Massenpartei im deutschen Linksliberalismus". *Vierteljahrshefte für Zeitgeschichte*, vol. 13, pt. 2 (1965), p. 150—61.
Discusses DDP attempts in 1918—20 to utilize modern methods of propaganda and self-advertisement in a way which broke completely with German liberal tradition. The methods, partly influenced by American presidential methods, were colourful and noisy and designed to attract a wide audience. However, the DDP slumped badly at the polls in 1920 because its problems were far deeper and more complex than the question of what kind of propaganda it should employ. An interesting paper.

REIMANN, Joachim.
Ernst Müller-Meiningen senior und der Linksliberalismus in seiner Zeit. Munich: Wölfle (1968), 305 pp.
A readable biography of the Bavarian DDP leader (1866—1944), though it contains few insights into the weaknesses of the party itself.

SCHIEDER, Theodor.
"Das Verhältnis von politischer und gesellschaftlicher Verfassung und die Krise des bürgerlichen Liberalismus". *Historische Zeitschrift*, no. 177 (1954), p. 49—74.
See section 2 for review.

SCHUSTEREIT, Hartmut.
Linksliberalismus und Sozialdemokratie in der Weimarer Republik: eine vergleichende Betrachtung von DDP und SPD 1919—1930.
Düsseldorf: Schwann (1975), 296 pp.
See section 6B (i) for review.

SCHUSTEREIT, Hartmut.
"Unpolitisch — Überparteilich—Staatstreu: Wehrfragen aus der Sicht der Deutschen Demokratischen Partei 1919—1930". *Militärgeschichtliche Mitteilungen*, vol. 16 (1974).

The DDP did not pay much attention to problems of defence, which were left to *Reichswehr* minister Gessler. Nothing that happened either inside or outside the party caused it to change its mind about not formulating a defence policy of its own.

STEPHAN, Werner.
Aufstieg und Verfall des Linksliberalismus 1918—1933: Geschichte der Deutschen Demokratischen Partei. Göttingen: Vandenhoeck und Ruprecht (1973), 520 pp.
The author was formerly a high-ranking DDP official, and this is an important study of the party. Every major aspect of the party's development, its ideas, policies, membership and organization are discussed with a remarkable degree of detachment. The result is a comprehensive and judicious assessment of the party, but also of the many weaknesses of the DDP in Weimar.

(vi) The Centre Party and Bavarian Peoples' Party (BVP)

Section 10B (Catholicism) should be consulted in conjunction with this section.

BECKER, Josef.
"Das Ende der Zentrumspartei und die Problematik des politischen Katholizismus in Deutschland". *Die Welt als Geschichte*, vol. 23 (1963), p. 149—172.
An interesting reflection on the difficulties facing German Catholicism when its political representative, the Centre Party, was dissolved. The author refers also to pre-1933 trends in the Catholic political world.

BECKER, Josef.
"Joseph Wirth und die Krise des Zentrums während des IV Kabinetts Marx (1927 bis 1928): Darstellung und Dokumente". *Zeitschrift für die Geschichte des Oberrheins*, vol. 109 (1961), p. 361—482.
A good, incisive look at the internal development of the party; the author concludes that the Centre was already on a definite right-wing course in 1927, as opposed to 1928 when Ludwig Kaas became party chairman.

BECKER, Josef (ed.).
Heinrich Köhler: Lebenserinnerungen des Politikers und Staatsmänners 1878—1949.
Stuttgart: Kohlhammer (1964), 412 pp.
Memoirs of the Baden Centre politician and former *Reichsminister* of Finance (1927—28). He does not impart much new detail about either the Centre Party or the Republic.

BECKER, Josef.
"Heinrich Köhler, Lebensbild eines badischen Politikers". *Zeitschrift für die Geschichte des Oberrheins*, vol. 110 (1962), p. 434—51.
An appreciative biographical outline and sketch of the main stages of his political career.

BECKER, Josef.
"Brüning, Prälat Kaas und das Problem einer Regierungsbeteiligung der NSDAP 1930—1932". *Historische Zeitschrift*, no. 196 (1963), p. 74—111.

The negotiations between the Centre Party and the NSDAP in the summer of 1932 are a controversial subject, and the Centre Party has been criticized for even contemplating a coalition with Hitler. Becker seeks to clear the air about the Centre's approach to the issue, and the attitudes of Brüning and Kaas. He does not entirely succeed, however, in rationalizing the Centre's position.

DUNNE, Edward J.
The German Center Party in Empire and Republic: a Study in the Crisis of Democracy. Dissertation, University of Georgetown (USA) (1950).
Too general and based on too limited sources to be of much help in understanding how the party coped with the transition to a parliamentary system.

EPSTEIN, Klaus.
"The Zentrum Party in the Weimar Republic". *Journal of Modern History*, vol. 39, pt. 2 (1967), p. 160—3.
A critical but highly complimentary review of Rudolf Morsey's *Die deutsche Zentrumspartei 1917—1923* (see below). Epstein refers to it as "the single most important contribution to our understanding of the Weimar Republic since the publication of Bracher's classic, *Die Auflösung der Weimarer Republik*".

EVANS, Ellen L.
The Center Party in the Weimar Republic, 1924—1930. Dissertation, Columbia University (1956).
A useful study, though better on the internal development of the party than on its role in Weimar politics.

EVANS, Ellen L.
"The Center Wages Kulturpolitik: Conflict in the Marx-Keudell Cabinet of 1927". *Central European History*, vol. 2, pt. 2 (1969), p. 139—58.
Sets out to show that the area of disagreement between the Centre Party and the DVP/DDP was greater in matters such as education and cultural policy than the Centre's antagonism towards the SPD. By 1928, the Centre had concluded that coalition with the "middle parties" was as unacceptable as coalition with the SPD. The author argues that the decisive turning point in the growing Centre-DVP/DDP hostility was the collapse of the right-wing Marx-Keudell cabinet of 1927, mainly over educational and cultural policies. Within the limits necessarily imposed by exclusive reliance on secondary printed sources, the essay is not without importance.

GOTTWALD, Herbert.
"Franz von Papen und die Germania". *Jahrbuch für Geschichte*, vol. 6 (1972), p. 539—604.
See section 16A (vi) for review.

GREBING, Helga.
Zentrum und katholische Arbeiterschaft 1918—1933: ein Beitrag zur Geschichte des Zentrums in der Weimarer Republik. Dissertation, Free University of Berlin (1952).
An examination of the attitudes of the Catholic working class and a party whose common denomination was religion not class. The Centre did succeed in attracting most of the Catholic working class vote before 1933 and Grebing puts forward reasons why this was so.

GRUENTHAL, Günther.
Reichsschulgesetz und Zentrumspartei in der Weimarer Republik. Düsseldorf: Droste (1968), 324 pp.
An excellent study, well documented and perceptive, of one of the most controversial political issues of Weimar's middle years. Gruenthal has skilfully examined the major principles of Catholic educational policy in the republican period, and the ways in which the Centre Party sought to uphold them in this law.

JUNKER, Detlef.
Die deutsche Zentrumspartei und Hitler, 1932/33: ein Beitrag zur Problematik des politischen Katholizismus in Deutschland. Stuttgart: Klett (1969), 248 pp.
An important work which sees the negotiations between the Centre Party and the NSDAP in 1932, as well as their subsequent relations, as symptomatic of a deep crisis in political Catholicism that had been building up throughout the period of the Weimar Republic. Further work is needed, however, on the attitudes of the NSDAP to political Catholicism, for this aspect is not fully considered here.

KNAPP, Thomas A.
"The German Center Party and the Reichsbanner: a Case Study in Political and Social Consensus in the Weimar Republic". *International Review of Social History*, vol. 14, pt. 2 (1969), p. 159—79.
The major theme is the political ambivalence, opportunism and philosophy of the Centre Party 1924—30. The party's relationship with the *Reichsbanner* was usually suspicious and aloof and this, argues Knapp, is an indication of the deeper political problems the party faced, including its ambivalent attitude to the Republic itself, and its unceasing hostility towards the SPD (on ideological and religious grounds). The tone of the essay is sharply critical of the party.

KNAPP, Thomas A.
Joseph Wirth and the Democratic Left in the German Center Party 1918—1928. Dissertation, Catholic University of America (1967).
An interesting investigation of the Centre's left wing and its leadership. The main purpose of the dissertation is to present the first full-length critical biography of Joseph Wirth and his political career as party politician, Finance Minister (1920—21), and Chancellor (1921—22). His position in the Centre Party was one of increasing isolation as the party moved rightwards. The biographical sketch is useful but hardly definitive.

MORSEY, Rudolf.
"The Centre Party between the Fronts". In L. Wilson (translator). *The Road to Dictatorship: Germany 1918—33.* London: Oswald Wolff (1964), p. 75—92.
An analysis of the political repercussions of the Centre's support for the presidential cabinet system of government under Brüning after 1930, and for an increasingly authoritarian ideology. As it moved rightwards, the party lost contact with its previous coalition partners, but did not compensate for this loss by winning support from moderate right-wing groups. Hence, in 1930—33, the Centre fell between two fronts until it was dissolved in the summer of 1933.

MORSEY, Rudolf.
Die deutsche Zentrumspartei 1917—1923. Düsseldorf: Droste (1966), 651 pp.
A highly important, scholarly, and definitive examination of the early Centre Party. Based on a wealth of new pri-

mary material, the book is rich in ideas and information and besides providing a detailed history of the party, it throws much new light on the functioning of the parliamentary system and the nature of coalition politics.

MORSEY, Rudolf (ed.).
Die Protokolle der Reichstagsfraktion und des Fraktionsvorstands der deutschen Zentrumspartei 1926—1933. Mainz: Matthias-Grünewald-Verlag (1969), 690 pp.
An excellent edition of the minutes of the sessions held by the Centre parliamentary faction from 12 January 1926 to 24 March 1933, though the emphasis is on the 1926—30 period. A great deal of detailed information is thereby provided in a volume superbly annotated by Morsey.

SCHÄFFER, Fritz.
"Die Bayerische Volkspartei (BVP)". *Politische Studien*, no. 218, vol. 25 (1974), p. 616—33.
An outline of BVP attitudes to political developments in Weimar from the Eisner régime to Hitler, including the BVP split from the Centre Party in 1922, the different policies adopted by the BVP and Centre at the 1925 Reich presidential election, and the BVP's relations with the NSDAP.

SCHAUFF, Karin.
Erinnerung an Ludwig Kaas zum 20. Todestag am 25. April 1972. Pfullingen: Neske Verlag (1972), 31 pp.
A brief recollection of the political role and importance of the former Centre Party leader.

SCHMITT, Veit.
Die Stellungnahme der Deutschnationalen Volkspartei, des Zentrums, und der Sozialdemokratischen Partei im Reichstag zur Steuerreform von 1925. Dissertation, University of Erlangen (1951).
See section 3A for review.

SCHÖNHOVEN, Klaus.
Die Bayerische Volkspartei 1924—1932. Düsseldorf: Droste (1972), 305 pp.
A study of limited value. The author gives a clear narrative of the BVP's strengths and weaknesses, but the book is neither comprehensive nor profound. Hence, his treatment of BVP-Centre Party and BVP-Reich government relations is not exhaustive, and his analysis of BVP relations with the other two major Weimar parties is disappointing. This is not a full history of the BVP, and the crucial last year of the Republic, 1932, is not considered.

SPECKNER, Herbert.
Die Ordnungszelle Bayern: Studien zur Politik des bayerischen Bürgertums, insbesondere der Bayerischen Volkspartei. Dissertation, University of Erlangen (1955).
Not of particular help in understanding Bavarian politics 1918—23, but contains some details of the BVP.

STUMP, Wolfgang.
Geschichte und Organisation der Zentrumspartei in Düsseldorf 1917—1933. Düsseldorf: Droste (1971), 168 pp.
The author describes the response of the Düsseldorf Centre Party to important crises at a national level before 1933, but there is very little on the local social and political situation in which the party operated. Hence, we are not told whether Düsseldorf provides anything about the party we did not know before. The Düsseldorf Centre is related neither to the overall Centre Party nor to other parties in Düsseldorf. The book also lacks a theoretical framework.

WACHTLING, Oswald.
Joseph Loos, Journalist, Arbeiterführer, Zentrumspolitiker: politische Biographie 1878—1933. Mainz: Matthias-Grünewald-Verlag (1974), 179 pp.
A well written biography of Loos, a leading left-wing member of the Centre Party. Of working class origins, he was heavily involved in Catholic workers' organizations, and sat in the *Reichstag* 1918—33. The study also offers insights into the policies and ideas of the Centre's left wing.

ZEENDER, John K.
"A New Look at the German Center Party in a Period of Crisis". *Catholic Historical Review*, Vol. 54 (1968—69), p. 320—4.
A review of Morsey's monograph on the party (see above).

(vii) The German Communist Party (KPD)

(a) General

ANGRESS, Werner T.
"Pegasus and Insurrection: Die Linkskurve and its Heritage". *Central European History*, vol. 1, pt. 1 (1968), p. 35—55.
See section 15B (ii) for review.

BAHNE, Siegfried.
"Die KPD im Ruhrgebiet in der Weimarer Republik". In *Arbeiterbewegung an Rhein und Ruhr.* Edited by Jürgen Reulecke. Wuppertal: Hammer Verlag (1974), p. 315—53.
A valuable, detailed analysis of the party's organization, leadership and tactics in an area where it drew substantial support before 1933.

BUBER-NEUMANN, Margarete.
Von Potsdam nach Moskau: Stationen eines Irrweges. Stuttgart: Deutsche Verlagsanstalt (1957), 480 pp.
Autobiography of a former KPD member who was the wife of a prominent party leader, Heinz Neumann. The book contains many revealing notes on the organization and development of the party, and on party leaders like Thälmann, Ulbricht, and Münzenberg (her brother-in-law). Her own career as a party member is well documented and she also describes the existence of German Communist exiles in Russia in the 1930s. A controversial argument put forward by her is that Stalin had no desire to see the KPD being successful in Germany in case it might work against Russian interests.

COLLOTTI, Enzo.
Die Kommunistische Partei Deutschlands 1918—1933: ein bibliographischer Beitrag. Milan: Feltrinelli (1961), 217 pp.
A classified compilation of sources and writings on the KPD which serves as an extremely helpful guide. Citations are drawn from periodicals, monographs, pamphlets, general studies, records of party meetings and congresses, memoirs and autobiographies. A number of appendices contain useful information on members of the central party organization 1919—23, party membership statistics, and *Reichstag* election results. Collotti, in his preface, underlines the main stages of the party's development in Weimar.

DAVID, Fritz.
"Zur Geschichte der Zeitschrift 'Die Internationale' (1919—1933)". *Beiträge zur Geschichte der Deutschen Arbeiterbewegung,* vol. 15, pt. 6 (1973), p. 967—86.
See section 16A (v) for review.

DUHNKE, Horst.
Die KPD von 1933 bis 1945. Cologne: Kiepenheuer & Witsch (1972), 605 pp.
This excellent study is useful for the pre-1933 period in showing that the KPD was as unprepared as the SPD for the advent of a National Socialist régime. On the other hand, the author subscribes to the fallacious proposition that a KPD-SPD united front (he does not say how this could have come about in the first place) would have defeated the National Socialist bid for power.

FLECHTHEIM, Ossip K.
Die Kommunistische Partei Deutschlands in der Weimarer Republik. Frankfurt: Europäische Verlagsanstalt (1969), 360 pp. New ed.
A generally sound analysis by a democratic socialist. His main point is that KPD policy before 1933 was a major contribution to the collapse of the Republic and hence to the victory of Hitler. Indeed, he criticizes the policies of the party as alien to the needs of the German working class and as having been dictated to the KPD by Moscow. For Flechtheim, therefore, the KPD was a complete failure. The book is not a comprehensive party history, for its foreign policy, economic policies and parliamentary activities are overlooked.

FLECHTHEIM, Ossip K.
"The Role of the Communist Party". In L. Wilson (translator). *The Road to Dictatorship: Germany 1918—1933.* London: Oswald Wolff (1964), p. 93—109.
Repeats the major thesis of his book that the KPD must bear a heavy responsibility for the victory of National Socialism because of its negative and divisive policies.

GREBING, Helga.
"Die Linke in der Weimarer Republik: ein Literatur- und Forschungsbericht". *Politische Studien,* vol. 18 (1967), p. 334—40.
A brief look at a few new books on radical socialist and Communist splinter groups.

HEIDER, Paul.
"Die Stellung der Kommunistischen Partei Deutschlands zur Armee in der Zeit der Weimarer Republik und während der faschistischen Diktatur (I)". *Zeitschrift für Militärgeschichte,* vol. 10, pt. 1 (1971), p. 20—33.

Lays down the rigid party line (SED) that the KPD rejected militarism and the imperialistic *Reichswehr* in the Weimar Republic.

HEIDER, Paul.
"Der Internationalismus in der Militärpolitik der KPD im Kampf gegen Faschismus und Kriegsgefahr". *Zeitschrift für Geschichtswissenschaft,* vol. 21, pt. 11 (1973), p. 1342—51.
This piece is no more convincing than his aforementioned work.

JUNG, Franz.
Der Weg nach unten: Aufzeichnungen aus einer grossen Zeit. Neuwied: Luchterhand (1961), 482 pp.
The autobiography of a *déclassé* in Weimar who meddled in radical politics of the left. The book reveals something of the mindless radicalism and passion for left-wing extremism (he was a member of the *Spartakusbund* for a short period) of one element in Weimar's milieu.

KINNER, Klaus.
"Zum Kampf der KPD gegen die Verfälschung des revolutionären Vermächtnisses von Friedrich Engels in den Jahren der Weimarer Republik". *Beiträge zur Geschichte der Deutschen Arbeiterbewegung,* vol. 12, pt. 5 (1970), p. 773—87.
A description of the KPD's "heroic" fight to preserve the undiluted purity of Engels' works.

KINNER, Klaus.
"Die Lehren der Revolution von 1848/49 im Ringen der KPD um die schöpferische Aneignung des Leninismus in den Jahren der Weimarer Republik". *Jahrbuch für Geschichte,* vol. 8, special number (1973), p. 251—90.
Amounts to a contorted piece of political propaganda on lines similar to his aforementioned paper, only on this occasion the subject is Lenin himself.

LANGE, Karl-Heinz.
Die Stellung der kommunistischen Presse zum Nationalgedanken in Deutschland, untersucht an Hand der "Roten Fahne" 1918—1933. Dissertation, University of Munich (1947).
See section 16A (v) for review.

MARX-ENGELS-LENIN INSTITUT.
Zur Geschichte der Kommunistischen Partei Deutschlands. East Berlin: Dietz (1955), 473 pp.
A fairly useful collection of documents, memoranda, writings and speeches pertaining to party history from 1914 to 1946.

MEISEL, Gerhard.
"Zur Entwicklung der wissenschaftlichen Auffassung vom Sozialismus und Kommunismus in der Kommunistischen Partei Deutschlands während der Jahre der Weimarer Republik". *Jahrbuch für Geschichte,* vol. 9 (1973), p. 129—216.
A prolix discussion of the KPD's ideological development before 1933. The main point of this paper is to try to show

that the KPD did think for itself and was not totally dependent on Moscow, but the author does not succeed in this hopeless aim.

MEISEL, Gerhard.
"Das sowjetische Grundmodell und die Entwicklung der Sozialismusvorstellungen der KPD". *Beiträge zur Geschichte der Deutschen Arbeiterbewegung*, vol. 12, pt. 3 (1970), p. 355—71.
On how the KPD developed its socialist awareness by copying the Soviet example. Once again in this essay, the argumentative framework is historically fallacious.

OTTO, Karl.
Vom Anwaltsstift zum Hochverräter: Erinnerungen. East Berlin: Dietz (1961), 212 pp.
Memoirs of a lawyer who was a KPD member in the 1920s and 1930s. Offers some interesting insights into party development.

PALMON, J. E.
"Eine Judendebatte mit Kommunisten in den Tagen der Weimarer Republik". *Zeitschrift für die Geschichte der Juden*, vol. 4 (1967), p. 147—51.
See section 11 for review.

PLATO, Alexander von.
Zur Einschätzung der Klassenkämpfe in der Weimarer Republik: KPD und Comintern, Sozialdemokratie und Trotzkismus. Berlin: Oberbaumverlag (1973), 403 pp.
A discussion of how the Left approached the question of class struggle in theory and practice.

REULECKE, Jürgen (ed.).
Arbeiterbewegung an Rhein und Ruhr: Beiträge zur Geschichte der Arbeiterbewegung in Rheinland-Westfalen. Wuppertal: Hammer Verlag (1974), 468 pp.
A collection of fourteen essays, most of them valuable, on various aspects of the working class movement in the Rhineland and Westphalia during the nineteenth and twentieth centuries. Siegfried Bahne's paper on the KPD is already noted in this section.

RÜHLE, Jürgen.
Literatur und Revolution. Cologne: Kiepenheuer und Witsch (1960), 610 pp.
See section 15C for review.

SCHMIDT, Konrad (ed.).
Feuilleton der Roten Presse 1918—1933. East Berlin: Verlag des Ministeriums für Nationale Verteidigung (1960), 179 pp.
See section 16A (v) for review.

SMOTRICZ, Israel.
"Die Stellung der KPD zwischen beiden Weltkriegen zum Nationalismus und zur Judenfrage". *Zeitschrift für die Geschichte der Juden*, vol. 4 (1967), p. 37—9.
Simply contains a few thoughts on the subject. The piece is unimportant.

TOPPE, Hilmar.
Der Kommunismus in Deutschland. Munich: Günter Olzog Verlag (1961), 148 pp.
A general discussion of the development of German Communism from 1919 to 1961; there is a useful survey of the KPD in the Weimar era.

WEBER, Hermann.
"Kommunismus in der Weimarer Republik: revolutionäre Politik in nichtrevolutionärer Zeit". *Die Neue Gesellschaft*, vol. 17, pt. 2 (1970), p. 257—61.
Contains a few documents illustrating the irrelevance of KPD tactics.

WEBER, Hermann.
Demokratischer Kommunismus: zur Theorie, Geschichte und Politik der kommunistischen Bewegung. Hanover: Dietz (1969), 313 pp.
A collection of the author's essays on German Communism in the twentieth century. Many of these papers have been published before.

WEBER, Hermann (ed.).
Der deutsche Kommunismus: Dokumente. Cologne: Kiepenheuer und Witsch (1963), 679 pp.
Contains about 200 documents which illustrate the domestic and foreign policies and attitudes of the KPD, and the East German Communist Party (SED). A few of the items refer to the internal disputes in the KPD. The volume is a sound source of reference, enhanced by a good introduction, a substantial bibliography, and a series of appendices.

WEBER, Hermann.
Von Rosa Luxemburg zu Walter Ulbricht: Wandlungen des deutschen Kommunismus. Hanover: Verlag für Literatur und Zeitgeschehen (1961), 112 pp.
A general, clear, and concise narrative of the KPD from 1919 to 1946. The main stages of the party's development are ably outlined with the aid of quotes from a wide range of contemporary sources. The ideology of the party is hardly touched upon, and the author tends to romanticize the early days of the KPD.

WILLMANN, Heinz.
Geschichte der "Arbeiter-Illustrierten-Zeitung" 1921—1938. Berlin: Verlag das Europäische Buch (1974), 359 pp.
See section 16A (v) for review.

(b) Origins

BADIA, Gilbert.
Le Spartakisme: les dernières années de Rosa Luxemburg et de Karl Liebknecht 1914—1919.
Paris: L'Arche (1967), 438 pp.
A factual narrative of the daily activities of the left-wing opposition to the SPD, ending with the foundation of the KPD and the Berlin uprising in January 1919. The book's information contains no serious errors, but the author's interpretations, such as they are, reveal a lack of objectivity.

BASSLER, Gerhard P.
"The Communist Movement in the German Revolution, 1918—1919: a Problem of Historical Typology". *Central European History*, vol. 6, pt. 3 (1973), p. 233—77.
Posits the hypothesis that German Communism was shaped more by concrete experience in German politics and society than by sheer ideological motivation, that is, that German Communism represented a type *sui generis*. The essay also provides an excellent discussion of recent historiographical interpretations of the November Revolution, examining in particular the role, aims, and organization of the Communists.

CONZE, Werner.
"Die Befestigung der KPD-Tradition durch Mehring und Rosa Luxemburg". *Historische Zeitschrift*, no. 188 (1959), p. 76—82.
An assessment of the part played by Franz Mehring and Luxemburg in founding the KPD.

FIEBER, Hans-Joachim; WOHLGEMUTH, Heinz.
"Forschungen zur Novemberrevolution und zur Gründung der KPD". *Zeitschrift für Geschichtswissenschaft*, vol. 18, special number (1970), p. 508—14.
A note of available literature on these topics.

FRÖHLICH, Paul.
Rosa Luxemburg: Gedanke und Tat. Frankfurt: Europäische Verlagsanstalt (1967), 374 pp.
New ed.
A comprehensive but at times over-sympathetic study. Originally published in 1940, it is still important and readable.

HOWARD, Richard.
Rosa Luxemburg: Selected Political Writings. New York: Monthly Review Press (1971).
Not one of the better volumes of the genre, largely because the extracts from her writings are not representative of the entire spectrum of her political ideas.

IMIG, Werner; BUCHHOLZ, Bernhard; JANITZ, Gerhard.
"Zur Hilfe W. I. Lenins bei der Herausbildung der KPD". *Beiträge zur Geschichte der Deutschen Arbeiterbewegung*, vol. 12, pt. 3 (1970), p. 390—409.
A suitably sycophantic discussion of Lenin's 8-volume work *Geschichte der deutschen Arbeiterbewegung* and the

excellent advice it provided for the development of the KPD. The paper also outlines his "indispensable" practical help to the radical Left in Germany 1917—19.

KOLBE, Helmut.
"Das aussenpolitische Programm des Gründungsparteitages der KPD". *Deutsche Aussenpolitik*, vol. 3 (1958), p. 1033—41.
The foreign policy programme of the KPD was naturally enthusiastically pro-Russian and anti-Western.

KÜSTER, Heinz.
"Die Rolle der 'Roten Fahne' bei der Vorbereitung der Gründung der KPD". *Zeitschrift für Geschichtswissenschaft*, vol. 11, pt. 8 (1963), p. 1466—78.
Emphasizes the importance of the newspaper and later official organ of the party in spreading the message and stimulating proletarian self-consciousness.

LASCHITZA, Annelies; RADCZUN, Günter.
Rosa Luxemburg: ihr Wirken in der deutschen Arbeiterbewegung. Frankfurt: Verlag Marxistische Blätter (1971), 582 pp.
A detailed chronicle of Luxemburg's activities in the German working class movement. The last chapter deals with the period from the Bolshevik Revolution to Luxemburg's murder in January 1919. Unfortunately, her contribution to the founding of the KPD is glossed over — a reflection perhaps of the current SED party line. For example, the differences between Lenin and Luxemburg are not duly stressed.

LOOKER, Robert.
Rosa Luxemburg: Selected Political Writings.
London: Cape (1972).
Useful to a limited degree.

LOWENTHAL, Richard.
"The Bolshevisation of the Spartakus League".
In *International Communism*. (St. Antony's Papers, no. 9). London: Chatto & Windus (1960), p. 23—71.
A good, detailed discussion of the League's and the KPD's progressive trend towards acceptance of Bolshevism as its ideological and organizational mentor. Paul Levi is the central figure for discussion in the essay, but unfortunately his private papers were not used by the author.

LUBAN, Ottokar.
"Zwei Schreiben der Spartakus-zentrale an Rosa Luxemburg". *Archiv für Sozialgeschichte*, vol. 11 (1971), p. 225—40.
Publishes two letters of June 1917 and November 1918 from the *Spartakus* central committee to Rosa Luxemburg. Their theme is the radicalization of working class youth and their connections with the Spartacists.

MARX-ENGELS-LENIN INSTITUT.
Protokoll des Gründungsparteitages der Kommunistischen Partei Deutschlands (30 Dezember 1918—1 Januar 1919). East Berlin: Dietz (1972), 359 pp.
An invaluable documentary source — the full record of the minutes of the meetings held to establish the KPD.

MEYER, Karl W.
Karl Liebknecht: Man without a Country.
Washington, D.C.: Public Affairs Press (1957),
180 pp.
An important interpretative synthesis of his political career
as anti-militarist, youth movement member, anti-war
campaigner, and revolutionary. Meyer is scholarly and
objective throughout, seeing his subject as a utopian radical
who was not made for revolutionary leadership. His role in
the November Revolution is particularly criticized as ineffective and unrealistic.

MISHARK, John W.
**The Road to Revolution: German Marxism and
World War I, 1914—1919.** Detroit: Moira Books
(1967), 310 pp.
As a whole, this book compares unfavourably with
A. J. Ryder's study on the German Revolution (see section
4A(iii)) which covers more or less the same ground. Mishark
puts more stress on the development of Marxism in
Germany, and this theme is treated satisfactorily.

NAUMANN, Horst.
**"Ein neues Dokument des Gründungsparteitages
der KPD".** *Beiträge zur Geschichte der Deutschen
Arbeiterbewegung*, vol. 15, pt. 1 (1973),
p. 95—100.
Helps illustrate a footnote to the proceedings of the
founding conference.

NETTL, John P.
Rosa Luxemburg. 2 vols. London: Oxford
University Press (1966), 984 pp.
Perhaps the best biography available on Luxemburg. Not
only does the author give a lucid critical exposition of her
ideas and political importance, he provides the fullest assessment of her personality. The only flaw in this outstanding
and scholarly contribution is Nettl's failure to estimate the
long-term significance of her ideas in the socialist movement.

RETZLAW, Karl.
**Spartakus: Aufstieg und Niedergang; Erinnerungen
eines Parteiarbeiters.** Frankfurt: Verlag Neue Kritik
(1972), 510 pp.
Lively memoirs which contain interesting observations on
several prominent KPD members. The author was a one-
time head of the KPD's intelligence section in the 1920s,
but was expelled from the party before 1933. The book is
especially informative on the *Spartakus* League's activities
in 1918—19.

RICHARDS, Michael.
**Reform or Revolution: Rosa Luxemburg and the
Marxist Movement 1893—1919.** Dissertation, Duke
University (1969).
A brief work, mainly devoted to assessing Luxemburg's
thoughts and writings on the nature of revolution. This is
not intended to be a political biography.

SCHIEL, Ilse; **MILZ**, Erna (eds.).
**Karl und Rosa: Erinnerungen zum 100. Geburtstag
von Karl Liebknecht und Rosa Luxemburg.** East
Berlin: Dietz (1971), 299 pp.

A collection of reminiscences of friends and colleagues of
both; 34 authors make contributions, relating personal or
political experiences. An interesting volume which enhances
our knowledge of Luxemburg and Liebknecht as people
rather than as political leaders.

SCHMIDT, Giselher.
Spartakus: Rosa Luxemburg und Karl Liebknecht.
Frankfurt: Akademische Verlagsgesellschaft
(1971), 175 pp.
Mainly concerned with analysing the political ideas of both
Liebknecht and Luxemburg. But the author tends to
simplify many problems and does not bring out in full the
differences between Lenin and Luxemburg. On the other
hand, she is objective and impartial in what she does discuss.

SCHULZE-WILDE, Harry.
Rosa Luxemburg: eine Biographie. Munich:
Molden (1970), 264 pp.
A competent general account for those coming to the
subject for the first time.

TROTNOW, Helmut.
**"Karl Liebknecht und die russische Revolution:
ein unveröffentlichter Diskussionsbeitrag Karl
Liebknechts zu Karl Radeks Rede auf dem
Gründungsparteitag der KPD 1918/19".** *Archiv für
Sozialgeschichte*, vol. 13 (1973), p. 379—97.
Liebknecht's theme was the importance of the Bolshevik
model for the German revolutionary workers' movement.

VOLKMANN, Hans-Erich.
**"Die Gründung der KPD und ihr Verhältnis zum
Weimarer Staat im Jahre 1919".** *Geschichte in
Wissenschaft und Unterricht*, vol. 23, pt. 2 (1972),
p. 65—80.
Discusses the early hostility shown by the KPD towards the
"bourgeois" Republic.

WEBER, Hermann (ed.).
**Der Gründungsparteitag der KPD: Protokoll und
Materialien.** Frankfurt: Europäische Verlagsanstalt
(1969), 345 pp.
A most useful reference source, containing the text of the
minutes of the founding congress. These illuminate many
aspects of early KPD attitudes and policies, and the sociological composition of the party membership, and in
addition provide valuable biographical details on the leadership.

WEBER, Hermann.
**"Ein historisches Dokument im politischen
Zwielicht: zum Protokoll des Gründungsparteitages
der KPD".** *Geschichte in Wissenschaft und
Unterricht*, vol. 24, pt. 10 (1973), p. 594—7.
Sums up the reasons why the author believes the protocols
of the founding congress are an important historical source.

(c) Early Development (1920–1923)

ANGRESS, Werner T.
Stillborn Revolution: the Communist Bid for Power in Germany, 1921–1923. Princeton: Princeton University Press (1963), 513 pp.
A critical yet balanced, valuable account of the KPD, preceded by a discussion of the origins of the party. Angress has dealt in scholarly fashion with the most important problems facing the party in these years, when it was making a bid for power by revolutionary means; hence, he discusses relations with other left-wing groups, including the SPD; the nature and extent of Russian influence; intra-party conflicts, rivalries in the leadership, and the formulation of policy. The theme of the book is the increasing loss of independence by the KPD and its corresponding subservience to Moscow. The only major regret about this study is that the author did not have access to large and important KPD materials in East German archives. (N.B. In a new German edition, *Die Kampfzeit der KPD 1921–1923* (Düsseldorf: Droste (1973), 547 pp.), the early chapters have been revised.)

BETHGE, Werner; BRAMKE, Werner; FINKER, Kurt.
"Grundzüge der Militärpolitik der KPD in den Jahren 1919/20". *Zeitschrift für Militärgeschichte*, vol. 12, pt. 1 (1973), p. 41–62.
A good and informative paper which explains clearly the fundamental priorities on which the KPD acted in formulating its policy on military affairs. Sharp opposition to the *Reichswehr* was emphasized.

BLUMBERG, N. B.
The German Communist Movement 1918–1923. Dissertation, University of Oxford (1950).
Extremely limited.

ERSIL, Wilhelm.
Aktionseinheit stürzt Cuno: zur Geschichte des Massenkampfes gegen die Cuno-Regierung 1923 in Mitteldeutschland. East Berlin: Dietz (1962), 408 pp.
A study of KPD activity in Saxony and Thuringia during the period of the Ruhr occupation. The author grossly exaggerates the contribution of the Left to the fall of the Cuno government and in fact the tone of the book is overwhelmingly propagandistic.

GAST, Helmut.
"Die proletarischen Hundertschaften als Organe der Einheitsfront im Jahre 1923". *Zeitschrift für Geschichtswissenschaft*, vol. 4, pt. 3 (1956), p. 439–65.
Describes the activity of the paramilitary Communist formations within the context of the revolutionary situation in Saxony during 1923. The author certainly exaggerates their strength and influence, though they did pave the way for the notorious *Rotfrontkämpferbund*.

HABEDANK, Heinz.
Zur Geschichte des Hamburger Aufstandes 1923. East Berlin: Dietz (1958), 215 pp.
Adduces the highly questionable thesis that the rising was not in fact spontaneous but planned and organized by the KPD. The author discusses the event largely in terms of its significance for the internal direction of the party, arguing that the rising demonstrated the need for a tightly centralized party. The fall of Brandler is thus justified.

HANISCH, Wilfried.
Die Hundertschaften Arbeiterwehr: die proletarischen Hundertschaften 1923 in Sachsen. East Berlin: Verlag des Ministeriums für Nationale Verteidigung (1958), 110 pp.
A full account of the origins and development of the *Hundertschaften* as fighting formations of the proletariat, but the tone of the book is very propagandistic. Some of the details are undoubtedly erroneous, particularly regarding the size of the membership.

KIEFNER, Martin; MAUR, Hans; SIMON, Heinz.
"Das Ringen der Bezirksleitung Grossthüringen der KPD um die Durchsetzung der Leninschen Lösung 'Heran an die Massen!' (1921–22)". *Zeitschrift für Geschichtswissenschaft*, vol. 11, pt. 7 (1963), p. 1305–20.
Some useful details on the activity of a local (but powerful) branch of the party as it attempted to widen its support.

KINNER, Klaus.
"Zur Herausbildung und Rolle des marxistisch-leninistischen Geschichtsbildes in der KPD im Prozess der schöpferischen Aneignung des Leninismus 1918 bis 1923". *Jahrbuch für Geschichte*, vol. 9 (1973), p. 217–80.
A long-winded and dull paper on the general theme of the KPD's successful adaptation to the historical precepts of Marxist-Leninism. The article is unashamedly politically and ideologically slanted and is frankly worthless.

KÖLLER, Heinz.
Kampfbündnis an der Seine, Ruhr und Spree: der gemeinsame Aktion der KPF und KPD gegen die Ruhrbesatzung 1923. East Berlin: Rütten & Loening (1963), 348 pp.
Interesting in revealing the preparedness of the French Communists to work with the KPD against the Poincaré government. The author's aim is to show the extent of proletarian solidarity in the face of capitalist imperialism, but unfortunately, despite the useful details provided, the book is yet another exercise in glorifying the KPD's role.

KÖNNEMANN, Erwin.
"Zu den Hintergründen der Märzkämpfe 1921". *Zeitschrift für Militärgeschichte*, vol. 10, pt. 2 (1971), p. 207–22.
The "March Action" was the first concentrated attempt at armed revolution staged by the KPD. The author provides some useful background information on the military preparations for the rising.

MARX-ENGELS-LENIN INSTITUT.
Die Märzkämpfe 1921. Mit Dokumentenanhang. East Berlin: Dietz (1959), 188 pp.
The official Communist party version of the uprising; it is generally unreliable. The documentary appendix is the most useful part of the volume.

MAUR, Hans.
"Zur Einheitsfrontpolitik der KPD im Eisenbahner-streik 1922". *Beiträge zur Geschichte der Deutschen Arbeiterbewegung*, vol. 14, pt. 2 (1972), p. 237–59.
On the theme of how the railwaymen's strike afforded the KPD an opportunity to demonstrate the sincerity and effectiveness of its "united working class" policy.

MEISTER, Rudolf; VOIGT, Harry.
"Der Kampf der KPD für den Aufbau proletarischer Wehrorganisationen (Sommer 1921-Herbst 1923)". *Zeitschrift für Militärgeschichte*, vol. 12, pt. 5 (1973), p. 525—33.
Mainly concerns the (exaggerated) efforts of the KPD to set up the proletarian *Hundertschaften* in central Germany.

MÖLLER, Dietrich.
"Stalin und der 'deutsche Oktober' 1923". *Jahrbücher für Geschichte Osteuropas*, vol. 13 (1965), p. 212—25.
The author correctly emphasizes how the collapse of the Communist rising in central and northern Germany in 1923 dealt a decisive blow to the aims of international Communism.

OELSNER, Manfred.
Der Hamburger Aufstand im Jahre 1923. Leipzig: Urania Verlag (1957), 35 pp.
An unimportant pamphlet.

REICHMANN, R. S.
The German Communist Party in Rhineland-Westphalia 1918—25. Dissertation, University of Oxford (1974).
An informative and detailed local study.

REISBERG, Arnold.
"Um die Einheitsfront nach dem Rathenaumord". *Beiträge zur Geschichte der Deutschen Arbeiterbewegung*, vol. 5, pt. 6 (1963), p. 995—1017.
Describes the policies of the KPD aimed at uniting the working class against right-wing reaction, but the paper is clearly biased towards the KPD.

REISBERG, Arnold.
An den Quellen der Einheitsfrontpolitik: der Kampf der KPD um die Aktionseinheit in Deutschland 1921—1922. East Berlin: Dietz (1971), 843 pp.
A detailed study of KPD policy 1921—23, based on extensive documentation from East German and Soviet archives. Reisberg's interpretations, however, are open to dispute; he adheres rigidly to the political outlook of the SED, and he argues that before 1923 the KPD was not controlled by the Comintern, which is untrue. His assessment of the contributions to the party of certain personalities like Radek and Trotsky, however, is sound. He stresses the authoritative influence of Lenin and the Comintern on the party's strategic and tactical policies.

STERN, Leo.
Die Volksmassen, Gestalter der Geschichte: Festgabe für Professor Dr. Leo Stern zu seinem 60. Geburtstag. East Berlin: Rütten & Loening (1962), 576 pp.
A collection of 22 papers. The only one of interest for the Weimar period is Ernst Stern's general survey of the KPD in central Germany 1919—20.

UHLEMANN, Manfred.
Arbeiterjugend gegen Cuno und Poincaré: das Jahr 1923. East Berlin: Verlag Neues Leben (1960), 230 pp.
See section 6B(vii)(h) for review.

WAGNER, Raimund.
"Zur Frage der Massenkämpfe in Sachsen von Frühjahr bis zum Sommer 1923". *Zeitschrift für Geschichtswissenschaft*, vol. 4, pt. 2 (1956), p. 246—64.
Purports to show the growing influence of the KPD among the working class in Saxony as the revolutionary spirit of the state rose in 1923. The author argues unconvincingly that the common action of the KPD and many SPD workers brought the domination of the German bourgeoisie to the brink of collapse in autumn 1923. Clearly a piece of political propaganda.

WAGNER, Raimund.
"Über die Chemnitzer Konferenz und die Widerstandsaktionen der sächsischen Arbeitermassen gegen den Reichswehreinmarsch im Oktober 1923". *Beiträge zur Geschichte der Deutschen Arbeiterbewegung*, vol. 3 (1961), p. 188—208.
Stresses the importance of the conference in preparing the workers for the *Reichswehr* onslaught in Saxony in 1923.

ZEISSIG, Eberhard.
"Der Entwurf eines Aktionsprogramms für die Chemnitzer Konferenz vom 21. Oktober 1921". *Beiträge zur Geschichte der Deutschen Arbeiterbewegung*, vol. 6 (1964), p. 1060—5.
Discusses proposals for workers' resistance in Saxony in October 1923.

ZELT, Johannes.
"Kriegsgefangen in Deutschland: neue Forschungsergebnisse zur Geschichte der Russischen Sektion bei der KPD (1919—21)". *Zeitschrift für Geschichtswissenschaft*, vol. 15, pt. 4 (1967), p. 621—32.
Instructive in that it reveals something of the nature and activity of the party's obscure "Russian section".

(d) The "Stalinization" Era (1924—1928)

BAHNE, Siegfried.
" 'Sozialfaschismus' in Deutschland: zur Geschichte eines politischen Begriffs". *International Review of Social History*, vol. 10, pt. 2 (1965), p. 211—45.
This excellent article discusses the KPD-SPD relationship as well as the origins and significance of the derogatory term "social fascism" in Germany. The term was originally coined in 1926, was in wide use among German Communists in 1927, and became a favourite KPD catchword in 1928 after the adoption of the ultra-leftist tactics. The SPD became the main enemy of the KPD, especially following the infamous left-wing rioting in Berlin in 1929. The essay is well informed on KPD development and stresses the important influence of events outside Germany on the direction and policy of the KPD.

FIEBER, Hans-Joachim.
"Zur Bedeutung der Zentralausschusstagung der KPD vom 9. und 10. Mai 1925 für die Heraus-bildung einer marxistisch-leninistischen Führung". *Zeitschrift für Geschichtswissenschaft*, vol. 15, pt. 7 (1967), p. 1212—26.
Regards this Central Committee meeting as crucial to the new direction of the party. Valuable details of the meeting are provided, and the author makes his case convincingly.

FÖLSTER, Elfriede.
"Sozialpolitik der KPD in den Jahren 1927 und 1928: Dokumente". *Beiträge zur Geschichte der Deutschen Arbeiterbewegung*, vol. 16, pt. 6 (1974), p. 1015—32.
Contains five KPD documents of which two are most inter-esting; firstly, a programme of detailed social and welfare reform dated April 1927; and secondly, a proposal of June 1928 by the KPD *Reichstag* faction for a law to protect mothers and children. The author does not say whether these humanitarian proposals were representative of KPD social policy as a whole.

FRITSCH, Werner.
"Der Kampf der KPD 1926/27 in Thüringen". *Wissenschaftliche Zeitschrift der Friedrich-Schiller-Universität Jena*, vol. 23, pt. 6 (1974), p. 811—26.
A few useful details are given here.

HAFERKORN, Katja.
"Ein Dokument der deutschen Sektion der 'Internationalen Arbeiterhilfe' aus dem Jahre 1925". *Beiträge zur Geschichte der Deutschen Arbeiterbewegung*, vol. 15, pt. 6 (1973), p. 963—6.
Of little significance. The IAH was headed by Willi Münzenberg.

HAFERKORN, Katja.
"Demokratische Initiativen der KPD in den Jahren 1925 bis 1928 zur Herstellung der Aktionseinheit der Arbeiterklasse". *Beiträge zur Geschichte der Deutschen Arbeiterbewegung*, vol. 16, pt. 2 (1974), p. 260—74.
Publishes five documents composed by the party's Central Committee in October 1925 and distributed to editors of the KPD press. They were drawn up following the no confidence motion of the right-wing parties in the Prussian *Landtag*, and put forward suggestions for the KPD to co-operate with the SPD at forthcoming provincial elections in Prussia, and for co-operation in the Saxon *Landtag*; the question of the KPD supporting the SPD in Thuringia in 1927 and 1928 is also raised.

INSTITUT FÜR MARXISMUS-LENINISMUS.
Ernst Thälmann: Geschichte und Politik. East Berlin: Dietz (1973), 237 pp.
See Section 6B(vii)(i) for review.

KARL, Heinz.
Die deutsche Arbeiterklasse im Kampf um die Enteignung der Fürsten (1925/1926). East Berlin: Dietz (1957), 108 pp.
The campaign initiated and sustained by the Left to have the properties of the former German royal houses expro-priated by the state is the theme of this poor and tenden-tious study.

KINNER, Klaus.
"Die Lehren der frühbürgerlichen Revolution in der ideologischen Arbeit der KPD (1925 bis 1929)". *Beiträge zur Geschichte der Deutschen Arbeiterbewegung*, vol. 17, pt. 5 (1975), p. 873—85.
A scarcely intelligible piece of ideological obfuscation.

KÖLLING, Mirjam.
"Der Kampf der Kommunistischen Partei Deutschlands unter der Führung Ernst Thälmanns für die Einheitsfront in den ersten Jahren der relativen Stabilisierung (1924 bis 1927)". *Zeitschrift für Geschichtswissenschaft*, vol. 2, pt. 1 (1954), p. 3—36.
This essay is heavily critical of the SPD for not recipro-cating the KPD's advances for a united front of the Left. The author, however, in presenting this theme within a rigid SED party line, overlooks the fundamental difficulties in the way of such a union.

LABOOR, Ernst.
Der Kampf der deutschen Arbeiterklasse gegen Militarismus und Kriegsgefahr 1927 bis 1929. East Berlin: Dietz (1961), 363 pp.
Describes and exaggerates the role of the KPD in the struggle against remilitarization, and in particular, in the campaign against the proposal to build an armoured cruiser in 1928. The SPD is singled out for bitter criticism, and the book is yet another East German exercise in historical distortion.

MADLOCH, Norbert.
"Der Kampf der KPD 1925 gegen den Locarnopakt und für eine demokratische und friedliche Aussen-politik". *Zeitschrift für Geschichtswissenschaft*, vol. 12, pt. 2 (1964), p. 231—45.
Quotes from contemporary KPD propaganda against Germany entering into partnership with "Western imperi-alism". There the value of the paper ends, for the author's interpretation of the foreign policy situation facing Germany in 1925 is hopelessly biased.

OPPERMANN, Sigrid.
"Die marxistisch-leninistische Staatslehre in der Propagandaarbeit der KPD (November 1925 — bis Mai 1929)". *Beiträge zur Geschichte der Deutschen Arbeiterbewegung*, vol. 16, pt. 4 (1974), p. 565—86.
An informative look at the nature of KPD propaganda which reveals, perhaps unwittingly, the dominating influ-ence of the Soviets.

RÜSS, Kurt.
"Vom Kampf der Kommunistischen Partei Deutschlands in Thüringen gegen die Sammlung militaristischer und faschistischer Kräfte in den Jahren 1924 bis 1926". *Beiträge zur Geschichte der Deutschen Arbeiterbewegung*, vol. 6 (1964), p. 1081—7.
Provides a few details of the Thuringian political situation.

VERLAG ROTE FAHNE.
Die Bolschewisierung der KPD: Dokumente und
Analysen zur Geschichte der Kommunistischen
Arbeiterbewegung. Berlin: Verlag Rote
Fahne (1970), 360, 176 pp.
A collection of facsimile reprints of official articles from
the KPD organ *Internationale Pressekorrespondenz* of
1925—26. The theme of the articles is the need for a cen-
tralized and disciplined party loyal to Moscow. The collec-
tion is of limited value.

WEBER, Hermann.
"Die Stalinisierung der KPD 1924—1929".
Politische Vierteljahrsschrift, vol. 9, pt. 4 (1968),
p. 519—43.
A lucid discussion of a number of themes: the bolshevization
of the party 1924—25, the expulsion of the Left and ultra-
Left 1925—27, and the struggles against the "Right" and
the *Versöhnler* 1928—29.

WEBER, Hermann.
Die Wandlung des deutschen Kommunismus: die
Stalinisierung der KPD in der Weimarer Republik.
2 vols. Frankfurt: Europäische Verlagsanstalt
(1969), 465, 427 pp.
A heavily documented and comprehensive narrative and
analysis of an important phase of KPD development: the
transformation from a party of deep internal dissensions to
one that was tightly knit, centralized, hierarchical, and subservient to Moscow. Weber recounts this process from the
dismissal of the old leadership in December 1923 to the
12th party congress in June 1929. The second volume contains short biographies of over five hundred KPD officials.
An important work.

WEBER, Stefan.
"Zur Herausbildung des marxistisch-
leninistischen Zentralkomitees der KPD unter
Ernst Thälmanns Führung". *Beiträge zur
Geschichte der Deutschen Arbeiterbewegung*,
vol. 17, pt. 4 (1975), p. 615—35.
Treats an important stage in the bolshevization process of
the party and adds a few interesting details not found in
Hermann Weber's aforementioned study. The author
corrects the common view that the Central Committee met
on 20 August 1925; apparently it met on 1 September 1925.

(e) The "Ultra-Left" Era (1929—1933)

ARENDT, Hans-Jürgen.
"Eine demokratische Massenbewegung unter
Führung der KPD im Frühjahr 1931". *Zeitschrift
für Geschichtswissenschaft*, vol. 19, pt. 2 (1971),
p. 212—23.
Exaggerates the importance of the KPD as part of the
movement of popular feeling aroused by the promulgation
of the papal encyclical *Casti Connubii*. Presents the KPD as
the earliest advocate of women's liberation.

ARENDT, Hans-Jürgen.
"Der erste Reichskongress werktätiger Frauen
Deutschlands 1929". *Zeitschrift für Geschichts-
wissenschaft*, vol. 20, pt. 4 (1972), p. 467—79.
Some useful details of the Communist-dominated congress
are provided in this short paper.

BAHNE, Siegfried.
Der Trotzkismus in Deutschland 1931—1933: ein
Beitrag zur Geschichte der KPD und der
Komintern. Dissertation, University of Hamburg
(1959).
Most interesting, and a valuable detailed study of a neglected
aspect of German Communism.

BARCLAY, David E.
The Communist Response to the Rise of National
Socialism in Germany, September 1930 to
November 1932. Dissertation, University of
Florida (1970).
A promising theme, but it needs much wider research than
is evident here.

BERTHOLD, Lothar.
Das Programm der KPD zur nationalen und
sozialen Befreiung des deutschen Volkes vom
August 1930. East Berlin: Dietz (1956), 308 pp.
The event referred to is a proclamation of the party on
national and social liberation. The proclamation is published in full, which is useful; what is not useful is the
accompanying commentary, which is blatantly propagandistic.

BRAHM, H.
"Trockijs Aufrufe gegen Hitler 1930—1933".
Jahrbücher für Geschichte Osteuropas, vol. 11
(1963), p. 521—42.
Trotsky was more aware of the dangerous threat of German
fascism than the KPD; his warnings are given reasonably
detailed coverage in this paper.

BRAUN, Wilhelm.
See his work in section 6B(i).

HEYE, Harold H.
The Communist Party of Germany 1928—1930.
Dissertation, Yale University (1954).
Based on a narrow range of sources.

IRELAND, Waltraud.
The Lost Gamble: the Theory and Practice of the
Communist Party of Germany between Social
Democracy and National Socialism 1929—1931.
Dissertation, Johns Hopkins University (1971).
It is argued that the adoption of ultra-left tactics was indicative of the Comintern's concern with the revolutionary
perspective in Germany which had been blunted largely
because the SPD policies had integrated the working classes
into the capitalist system. Hence, the struggle against the
SPD must be seen as part of a larger strategy aimed at
undermining capitalism and increasing the political prospects of the KPD. This is an interesting challenge to the
conventional thesis that the post-1928 ultra-left tactics
were motivated by the requirements of Soviet foreign
policy.

KARL, Heinz; KÜCKLICH, Erika.
Die antifaschistische Aktion: Dokumentation und
Chronik. East Berlin: Dietz (1965), 423 pp.
The theme is the efforts of the KPD to mobilize working
class resistance to the upsurge of National Socialism
betwen May 1932 and January 1933. The documentation is
taken from a wide variety of sources, mostly KPD, and is
useful.

KÜCKLICH, Erika.
"Streik gegen Notverordnungen! Zur Gewerkschafts- und Streikpolitik der KPD gegen die staatsmonopolistische Offensive der Regierung Papen im Sommer und Herbst 1932". *Beiträge zur Geschichte der Deutschen Arbeiterbewegung*, vol. 13, pt. 4 (1971), p. 454—69.
On the same theme as the aforementioned·study. Once again, the role of the KPD is presented in exaggerated terms, and the author ignores many of the fundamental reasons why the SPD and trade unions were not prepared to go along with the Communists' plans.

KÜCKLICH, Erika; LIENING, Elfriede.
"Die anti-faschistische Aktion". *Beiträge zur Geschichte der Deutschen Arbeiterbewegung*, vol. 4, pt. 8 (1962), p. 872—97.
A general discussion of the role of "Anti-Fascist Action" in resistance to National Socialism in 1932. The authors also consider the place of this struggle in the overall strategy of the KPD.

KÜHN, Traudel.
"Über die Teilnahme der revolutionären Arbeiterkulturbewegung an den Klassenkämpfen des Proletariats in Deutschland 1928—1933". *Beiträge zur Geschichte der Deutschen Arbeiterbewegung*, vol. 2, pt. 3 (1960).
Among other aspects the author discusses the work and activity of the Willi Münzenberg-controlled *Internationale Arbeiterhilfe* in disseminating the Communist gospel.

LUDWIG, Kurt.
Die Arbeiterklasse in Thüringen im Kampf gegen das Vordringen des Faschismus. Dissertation, University of Jena (1960).
Mainly devoted to describing KPD resistance to the Thuringian state government, of which the National Socialist leader, Wilhelm Frick, was a member in 1929—30.

ROSSMANN, Gerhard.
Der Kampf der KPD um die Einheit aller Hitlergegner. East Berlin: Dietz (1963), 300 pp.
An absurd and historically inaccurate work which seeks to show that the KPD, despite all evidence to the contrary, was fully aware of the National Socialist danger. Even more ludicrous is the author's attempt to depict the KPD as the defender of democratic liberties against fascism.

WONNEBERGER, Günther.
Deutsche Arbeitersportler gegen Faschisten und Militaristen 1929—1933. East Berlin: Sportverlag (n.d.), 225 pp.
A description of the revolutionary working class sports movement and its opposition to fascism. The author vastly overestimates the importance of the movement and the extent of its political activities.

(f) International Communism and the Communist International.

BORKENAU, Frank.
World Communism: a History of the Communist International. Ann Arbor: University of Michigan Press (1962).
A general survey which is for the most part reliable.

BRAUNTHAL, Julius.
Geschichte der Internationale, Vol. 2. 2 parts. Hanover: Dietz (1963—71), 617 pp.
An impressive history of the Socialist and Communist Internationals. The second part of volume two deals with the period from 1917 to 1945. The origins and early development of the Comintern are treated skilfully, though he underplays the patriotism of German workers in the post-1918 situation. The account of the failings and errors of Comintern policy in Germany, 1929—33, is good.

BUBER-NEUMANN, Margarete.
Kriegsschauplätze der Weltrevolution: ein Bericht aus der Praxis der Komintern 1919—1943. Stuttgart: Seewald Verlag (1967), 522 pp.
A valuable book which provides an incisive critique of both KPD and Comintern policies.

DEGRAS, Jane (ed.).
The Communist International 1919—1943. Vol. I: 1919—1927. Vol. II: 1923—1928. Vol. III: 1929—1943. 3 vols. London: Oxford University Press (1955—65).
An indispensable collection of documents which vividly illustrates the changing face of the Comintern during the inter-war period. The volumes are well edited and organized.

GRUBER, Helmut.
International Communism in the Era of Lenin: a Documentary History. Ithaca (New York): Cornell University Press (1967), 512 pp.
Contains many useful extracts from original documents; for Germany, the period 1918—23 is covered more satisfactorily than any other phase of the Weimar Republic.

KARL, Heinz.
"Dokumente brüderlicher Unterstützung der KPD durch die Komintern". *Beiträge zur Geschichte der Deutschen Arbeiterbewegung*, vol. 12, pt. 3 (1970), p. 410—40.
A number of documents which in fact indicate not the Comintern's "fraternal support" for the KPD, but its domination of the German party.

KRUSCH, Hans-Joachim.
"Zum Zusammenwerken von K. I. und deutscher Sektion in der Frage der Arbeiter- und Bauernregierung im Jahre 1923". *Beiträge zur Geschichte der Deutschen Arbeiterbewegung*, vol. 15, pt. 5 (1973), p. 757—73.
A discussion of the considerable intervention of the Comintern in KPD affairs during the six months or so preceding the formation of the left-wing coalition government in Thuringia in the autumn of 1923.

LAZITCH, Branko; DRACHKOVITCH, Milorad M.
Lenin and the Comintern. Vol. I. Stanford: Hoover
Institution Press (1972), 683 pp.
The principal theme is the role of Lenin as founder and
leader of the Comintern, but there is a worthwhile discus-
sion of relations between both the KPD and the splinter
KAPD and the Comintern which throws light on the nature
of German Communism in 1919—21.

NOLLAU, Günther.
**Die Internationale: Wurzeln und Erscheinungs-
formen des proletarischen Internationalismus.**
Cologne (1959).
A general survey of limited value.

PIRKER, Theo (ed.).
**Utopie und Mythos der Weltrevolution: zur
Geschichte der Komintern 1920 bis 1940.** Munich:
Günter Olzog Verlag (1964).
A sound selection of documents which allow the changing
tactics and policies of the Comintern to be easily grasped.

PLAMENATZ, John.
German Marxism and Russian Communism.
London: Longman (1954), 379 pp.
A well written and clear analysis of the ideas of Marx,
Lenin, Trotsky, Engels and Stalin on the concept of class
struggle and world revolution.

REISBERG, Arnold.
**An den Quellen der Einheitsfrontpolitik: der
Kampf der KPD um die Aktionseinheit in
Deutschland 1921—1922.** East Berlin: Dietz
(1971), 843 pp.
See section 6B(vii)(c) for review.

RUGE, Wolfgang.
**"Die Hilfe der Sowjetunion im nationalen Kampf
des deutschen Volkes in den 20'er und 30'er
Jahren des 20. Jahrhunderts".** *Zeitschrift für
Geschichtswissenschaft*, vol. 10, special number
(1962).
Ruge naturally believes the Soviet Union played the most
significant role of all in developing German communism.
The article is one of the worst examples of Ruge's abject
servility to Russia, a characteristic that is to be discerned in
most of his writings to one degree or another.

WEBER, Hermann.
Die Kommunistische Internationale. Hanover:
Verlag für Literatur und Zeitgeschehen (1966).
A carefully compiled collection of relevant documents
which illustrates the main stages of the Comintern's
development since 1919.

WEBER, Hermann.
**"Zu den Beziehungen zwischen der KPD und der
Kommunistischen Internationale".** *Vierteljahrshefte für Zeitgeschichte*, vol. 16, pt. 2 (1968),
p. 177—208.

A collection of thirteen annotated documents from the
Nachlass of former KPD leader, Ernst Meyer. Most of them
cast interesting light on the KPD-Comintern relationship
1922—28, confirming the dominating influence of the latter.

WHEELER, Robert F.
See his article (*Central European History* 1975) in section
6B(ii).

(g) Paramilitary Groups

DÜNOW, Hermann.
**Der Rote Frontkämpferbund: die revolutionäre
Schutz- und Wehrorganisation des deutschen
Proletariats in der Weimarer Republik.** East Berlin:
Verlag des Ministeriums für Nationale Verteidigung
(1958), 101 pp.
A short, uncritical account of the organization which was
officially prohibited in 1929, but which continued under-
ground. There are a number of interesting details, however,
on organization, activities, and membership.

FINKER, Kurt.
**"Zur Auseinandersetzung des Roten Frontkämp-
ferbundes mit der Wehrpolitik der rechten SPD-
Führer in den Jahren der relativen Stabilisierung
des Kapitalismus".** *Zeitschrift für Geschichtswissenschaft*, vol. 7, pt. 4 (1959), p. 797—819.
Purports to illustrate the opposition of the RFB to the
alleged militaristic policies of the SPD, 1924—29. The lack
of objectivity in the discussion is all too obvious.

FINKER, Kurt.
**"Aufgaben und Rolle des Roten Frontkämp-
ferbundes in den Klassenschlachten der Weimarer
Republik".** *Zeitschrift für Militärgeschichte*,
vol. 13, pt. 2 (1974), p. 133—44.
The RFB was designed as the revolutionary spearhead of
the German proletariat against capitalism and fascism: this
is the author's definition of the main role of the organization.

GAST, Helmut.
See his article in section 6B(vii)(c).

HANISCH, Wilfried.
See his work in section 6B(vii)(c).

MEISTER, Rudolf; VOIGT, Harry.
See their article in section 6B(vii)(c).

SCHUSTER, Kurt G. P.
**Der Rotfrontkämpferbund 1924—1929: Beiträge
zur Geschichte und Organisationsstruktur eines
politischen Kampfbundes.** Düsseldorf: Droste
(1975), 290 pp.
The first objective account of this organization, based on a

thorough investigation of available sources. Most important aspects of its development are discussed in considerable detail and the author's conclusions are generally sound and convincing.

WIMMER, Walter.
"Der Rote Frontkämpferbund und die Rote Armee". *Zeitschrift für Militärgeschichte*, vol. 13, pt. 2 (1974), p. 167—73.
A brief review of material and moral links between the two organizations.

(h) Youth Groups

BRAMKE, Werner; FINKER, Kurt.
"Die Rote Jungfront: Verkörperung der Wehranhäftigkeit der revolutionären deutschen Arbeiterjugend (1924—1929)". *Zeitschrift für Militärgeschichte*, vol. 11 (1972), p. 72—9.
Die Rote Jungfront was the youth wing of the extremist *Rotfrontkämpferbund* and had a membership of around 25,000 at the end of the 1920s. This short paper has a few other facts on the group.

JAHNKE, Karl-Heinz, and others.
Geschichte der deutschen Arbeiterjugendbewegung 1904—1945. Dortmund: Weltkreis-Verlag (1973), 631 pp.
An excellent narrative, fully documented and reliable. The sections on Communist groups are especially informative.

KURELLA, Alfred.
Unterwegs zu Lenin: Erinnerungen. East Berlin: Verlag Neues Leben (1967), 160 pp.
Memoirs of a former minister of the German Democratic Republic who in his earlier days was a prominent member of the revolutionary wing of the *Freideutsche Jugend* movement, and who in 1918 founded the pro-Communist *Freie Sozialistische Jugend* group. He was also a KPD member from an early date. His book, however, is disappointingly dull.

SCHULT, Johannes.
Aufbruch einer Jugend: der Weg der deutschen Arbeiterjugendbewegung. East Berlin: Verlag Schaffende Jugend (1950), 249 pp.
The book's historical perspective is severely distorted, and its facts are not entirely reliable.

SCHWABE, Herbert.
"Zur wehrerzieherischen Arbeit der Roten Jungfront". *Zeitschrift für Militärgeschichte*, vol. 13, pt. 2 (1974), p. 181—9.
Presents some documentary material to illustrate the military preparedness of this youth group.

TRAMSEN, Eckhard.
Bibliographie zur geschichtlichen Entwicklung der Arbeiterjugendbewegung bis 1945. Frankfurt:

Verlag Roter Stern (1973), 141 pp.
An excellent reference source; comprehensive and intelligently organized.

UHLEMANN, Manfred.
Arbeiterjugend gegen Cuno und Poincaré: das Jahr 1923. East Berlin: Verlag Neues Leben (1960), 230 pp.
A somewhat romanticized account of the opposition offered by Communist youth in the Ruhr to the "bourgeois" Cuno government and the "imperialist" Poincaré regime.

VERLAG NEUES LEBEN.
Geschichte der deutschen Arbeiterjugendbewegung 1904—1945. East Berlin: Verlag Neues Leben (1973), 632 pp. (Originally published in 1956).
A useful documentary collection composed of extracts from proclamations, manifestoes and the like, illustrating the development of radical working class youth groups.

ZENTRALRAT DER FREIEN DEUTSCHEN JUGEND (ed.).
Deutschlands junge Garde: 50 Jahre Arbeiterjugendbewegung. East Berlin: Verlag Neues Leben (1954), 374 pp.
Originally devised as the companion volume of the aforementioned study, this book is highly propagandistic, especially where it deals with the Communist youth movement in the Weimar era (p. 161—232).

(i) Personalities (A—Z)

1. MAX HOLZ

HÖLZ, Max.
Vom "Weissen Kreuz" zur roten Fahne: Jugend-, Kampf- und Zuchthauserlebnisse. Frankfurt: Verlag Neue Politik (1969), 393 pp.
Originally published in 1929, the memoirs of swashbuckling revolutionary Hölz make fascinating reading. He was a "Robin Hood" figure in Saxony in the early 1920s, a bandit who robbed the rich to give to the poor, and he was heavily involved in the resistance to the Kapp Putsch in the same state in 1920. Later, he was expelled from the KPD and joined the oppositional KAPD. He spent some time in prison, and when released in 1929 emigrated to Russia where he met his death at the hands of the secret police. Although not a person of significant political interest, his colourful career provides an insight into the turbulent postwar era in Weimar.

2. WILHELM KOENEN

NAUMANN, Horst.
"Verkörperung des Kampfes dreier Generationen der revolutionären Arbeiterbewegung: Wilhelm Koenen". *Beiträge zur Geschichte der Deutschen Arbeiterbewegung*, vol. 13 (1971), p. 287—95.
Eulogizes Koenen as one of the grand old men of the Communist movement.

3. PAUL LEVI

BERADT, Charlotte.
Paul Levi: ein demokratischer Sozialist in der Weimarer Republik. Frankfurt: Europäische Verlagsanstalt (1969), 157 pp.
A sympathetic assessment of Levi's ideas, personality, and his role in the KPD and outside it. But the work is too general to be considered as anything other than a useful introduction to the life of an interesting but complex personality.

BERADT, Charlotte (ed.).
Paul Levi: zwischen Spartakus und Sozialdemokratie; Schriften, Aufsätze, Reden und Briefe. Frankfurt: Europäische Verlagsanstalt (1970), 335 pp.
The documentation, consisting of extracts from Levi's political writings and speeches, is taken from the Levi *Nachlass,* and is extremely helpful as an aid to comprehending his political and ideological orientation as a democratic-revolutionary socialist.

4. KARL LIEBKNECHT

See under authors Badia, Meyer, Schiel, Schmidt, and Trotnow in section 6B(vii)(b).

5. ROSA LUXEMBURG.

See under authors Badia, Conze, Fröhlich, Howard, Laschitza, Looker, Nettl, Richards, Schiel, Schmidt, and Schulze-Wilde in section 6B(vii)(b).

6. HERMANN MATERN

MATERN, Hermann.
Im Kampf für Frieden, Demokratie und Sozialismus: ausgewählte Reden und Schriften. Vol. I: 1926—1956. East Berlin: Dietz (1963), 582 pp.
Nothing very remarkable about this collection of Matern's speeches and writings, which for the period before 1933 include the popular Communist argument that the SPD bore a major responsibility for the advent of Hitler as Chancellor.

7. FRANZ MEHRING

See under Werner Conze in section 6B(vii)(b).

8. WILLI MÜNZENBERG

CAREW HUNT, Richard N.
"Willi Münzenberg". In *International Communism.* (St. Antony's Papers, no. 9). London: Chatto & Windus (1960), p. 72—87.
A brief but informative assessment.

GROSS, Babette.
Willi Münzenberg: eine politische Biographie. Stuttgart: Deutsche Verlagsanstalt (1967), 352 pp.
The best portrait available, written by his common law wife. The account is full, sympathetic, but also revealing and balanced.

GRUBER, Helmut.
"Willi Münzenberg's German Communist Propaganda Empire 1921—1933". *Journal of Modern History,* vol. 38, pt. 3 (1966), p. 278—97.
An informative essay on Münzenberg's life and political career as the KPD's leading propagandist. Gruber discusses his considerable ingenuity as a publicist, as well as outlining his activities as a party member and KPD *Reichstag* deputy. The author stresses Münzenberg's achievement in being able to associate Communism with humanitarianism and proletarian solidarity.

SCHULZ, Til (ed.).
Willi Münzenberg: Propaganda als Waffe. Frankfurt: März Verlag (1972), 363 pp.
A well edited volume of his writings 1919—40; as such it forms a useful companion to Gross's biography.

9. WILHELM PIECK

PIECK, Wilhelm.
Reden und Aufsätze. Vol. IV: Parlamentsreden: Auswahl aus den Jahren 1906—1933. East Berlin: Dietz (1955), 795 pp.
Pieck was the first President of the German Democratic Republic, and this volume contains a large number of his political speeches in the *Reichstag* during the periods 1906—10 and 1921—33, as well as speeches in the Prussian *Landtag* and the Prussian State Council. A good source for left-wing views on important issues before 1933.

PIECK, Wilhelm.
Gesammelte Reden und Schriften. Vol. III: Mai 1925—Januar 1927. East Berlin: Dietz (1961), 611 pp.
Also of interest because his speeches indicate KPD policy on a wide range of matters during the middle years of the Republic.

10. ARTHUR ROSENBERG

CARSTEN, Francis L.
"Arthur Rosenberg: Ancient Historian into Leading Communist". *Journal of Contemporary History,* vol. 8, pt. 1 (1973), p. 63—75.
An interesting sketch of Rosenberg, distinguished historian but also a Communist party member, KPD *Reichstag* deputy, and leading official of the Comintern. Before joining the KPD, he had been a member during the First World War of the extreme right-wing Fatherland Party, and in 1918 of the USPD. Rosenberg clearly deserves a full biography.

CARSTEN, Francis L.
"Arthur Rosenberg als Politiker". In *Geschichte und Gesellschaft: Festschrift für Karl R. Stadler zum 60. Geburtstag.* Vienna: Europa-Verlag (1974), p. 267—80.
Adds a few more details to the aforementioned paper.

11. ERNST SCHNELLER

KIESSING, Wolfgang.
Ernst Schneller: Lebensbild eines Revolutionärs.
East Berlin: Dietz (1972), 382 pp.
Schneller was one of the most important yet relatively unknown KPD leaders in the 1920s, who played a significant part in developing party organization. This is a comprehensive assessment, though presented within the framework of the party (SED) line.

12. WALTER STOECKER

STOECKER, Helmuth.
Walter Stoecker: die Frühzeit eines deutschen Arbeiterführers 1891—1920. East Berlin: Dietz (1970), 270 pp.
Contains some interesting details of his activities in 1919—20.

13. AUGUST THALHEIMER

KITCHEN, Martin.
"August Thalheimer's Theory of Fascism". *Journal of the History of Ideas*, vol. 33, pt. 1 (1973), p. 67—78.
Kitchen explains Thalheimer's politico-sociological thesis on National Socialism and fascism. As such the theory was the first and most successful attempt to apply a Marxist analysis to the problem of fascism, in contrast to the crude KPD official doctrine of social fascism (1928—33). Thalheimer, the intellectual leader of the KPD in the early 1920s, was expelled from the party in 1924 and later joined Brandler's oppositional group. This appraisal would have been more significant if Kitchen had dwelt longer on the shortcomings of Thalheimer's theory, for example, its naive view of class relationships.

14. ERNST THÄLMANN

BREDEL, Willi.
Ernst Thälmann: Beitrag zu einem politischen Lebensbild. East Berlin: Dietz (1961), 208 pp. 8th ed.
Can hardly be described as an objective appraisal, but furnishes details of his early life which are not generally known.

INSTITUT FÜR MARXISMUS-LENINISMUS.
Ernst Thälmann: Geschichte und Politik. East Berlin: Dietz (1973), 237 pp.
A volume containing a selection of writings and speeches from 1925 to 1933 which throws light on Thälmann's role as party leader, as well as on party policies.

THÄLMANN, Ernst.
Reden und Aufsätze zur Geschichte der deutschen Arbeiterbewegung. Vol. I: Auswahl aus den Jahren Juni 1919 bis November 1928. Vol. II: Auswahl aus den Jahren November 1928 bis September 1930. 2 vols. East Berlin: Dietz (1955—56), 655, 567 pp.

The first volume is useful for the insights it provides into the internal development of the KPD; the second volume contains many references to the economic crisis and to the fight against the "social fascist" SPD. Altogether, an important documentary source.

WIMMER, Walter.
"Ernst Thälmann-proletarische Internationalist".
Beiträge zur Geschichte der Deutschen Arbeiterbewegung, vol. 14, pt. 2 (1972), p. 193—221.
Predictably eulogistic, but among the ideological verbiage there is an element of noteworthy information.

15. CLARA ZETKIN

DORNEMANN, Luise.
Clara Zetkin: Leben und Wirken. East Berlin: Dietz (1973), 562 pp. New ed.
A very thorough but interpretatively unbalanced study.

HAFERKORN, Katja; KARL, Heinz. (eds.).
Clara Zetkin: zur Theorie und Taktik der kommunistischen Bewegung. Leipzig: Reclam (1974), 511 pp.
A carefully selected compilation of Zetkin's writings and speeches on theoretical Marxism and Communist party tactical policies.

WEBER, Hermann.
"Zwischen kritischen und bürokratischen Kommunismus: unbekannte Briefe von Clara Zetkin". *Archiv für Sozialgeschichte*, vol. 11 (1971), p. 417—48.
Presents eleven previously unpublished letters of Zetkin, written between 1918 and 1933, which help illuminate changing trends in the KPD.

ZETKIN, Clara.
Ausgewählte Reden und Schriften. Vol II: Auswahl aus den Jahren 1918—1923. Vol. III: Auswahl aus den Jahren 1924 bis 1933. East Berlin: Dietz (1960), 748, 640 pp.
Volume II reveals in particular Zetkin's keen interest in international affairs; volume III contains her ideas on the women's movement, on her anti-militarism, on her belief in the importance of the Soviet experience for the German working class, and, finally, her reminiscences of Lenin. An important collection.

(j) Splinter Groups and KPD-Opposition

BAHNE, Siegfried.
"Zwischen 'Luxemburgismus' und 'Stalinismus': die 'ultralinke' Opposition in der KPD". *Vierteljahrshefte für Zeitgeschichte*, vol. 9, pt. 4 (1961), p. 359—83.
An interesting and detailed analysis of the significant degree of internecine feuding among numerous factions within the

KPD during the mid-1920s as the party, in response to changes in the Comintern, underwent fundamental changes itself in tactics, strategy and leadership. After 1924 ultra-left oppositional groups arose, and their ideas, motives and leaders are discussed here.

BOCK, Hans M.
Syndikalismus und Linkskommunismus von 1918–1923: zur Geschichte und Soziologie der Freien Arbeiter-Union Deutschlands (Syndikalisten), der Allgemeinen Arbeiter-Union Deutschlands und der Kommunistischen Arbeiterpartei Deutschlands. Meisenheim: Hain (1969), 480 pp.

The author is somewhat indiscriminate in bringing together the groups he believes represent radical left-wing Communism. On the other hand, he has investigated an impressively wide range of sources to provide an excellent account. The various secessions from the KPD, and then from the KAPD, are treated in immense detail, as are their ideas, aims and leaders.

FISCHER, Ruth.
Stalin and German Communism: a Study in the Origins of the State Party. Cambridge (Mass.): Harvard University Press (1948), 687 pp.

Written by a former leading member of the KPD and its Left opposition, the book is mainly valuable as a source of information on the KPD opposition in the 1920s. The author discusses her own break with Thälmann in 1926, and rejects the charge that she was simply an opportunist. Her views and interpretations, however, are often and perhaps inevitably influenced by her own close involvement in the events she is describing.

GRUPPE ARBEITERPOLITIK (ed.).
Der Faschismus in Deutschland: Analysen der KPD-Opposition aus den Jahren 1928–1933. Frankfurt: Europäische Verlagsanstalt (1973), 219 pp.

A valuable collection of contributions on important aspects of the KPD oppositional movement; the ideas, objectives, and character of the different groups involved are discussed in a highly informative manner.

TJADEN, Karl H.
Struktur und Funktion der "KPD-Opposition" (KPO): eine organisationssoziologische Untersuchung zur "Rechts"-Opposition im deutschen Kommunismus zur Zeit der Weimarer Republik. Meisenheim: Hain (1964), 585 pp.

A difficult book to come to terms with, largely because of its unconventional methodological approach. Part I is a detailed chronological narrative of the ideological and organizational origins of the "Right" opposition (Brandler, Thalheimer, etc.) which was forced to leave the KPD in 1928. Part II consists of short but useful biographies of those involved as well as a number of documents illustrative of the split. A valuable contribution on the whole.

(viii) Other Parties

JONAS, Erasmus.
Die Volkskonservativen 1928–1933: Entwicklung, Struktur, Standort und staatspolitische Zielsetzung. Düsseldorf: Droste (1965), 199 pp.

The *Volkskonservative* element in the DNVP emerged at the end of the 1920s in clear form, and seceded to constitute the new *Konservative Volkspartei* (KVP) in 1929–30, led by Treviranus and Westarp. The party represented moderate conservative nationalist opinion, rejected extremism of the right and left, and supported Brüning's presidential cabinet style of government. This study is a thorough history of the group, its policies and leadership, and sources of support (which were never very significant).

OPITZ, Günter.
Der christlich-soziale Volksdienst: Versuch einer protestantischen Partei in der Weimarer Republik. Düsseldorf: Droste (1969), 371 pp.

A very good, detailed analysis and description of a party which sought to bring together the concepts of Protestantism and social concern. The party took part in its first national election in September 1930 and won a creditable fourteen seats, but it declined thereafter. The author rightly interprets the appearance of the party as another manifestation of the crisis in the Protestant middle classes that became so apparent in the late 1920s. He examines the origins, aims, membership, and leadership of the party ably and objectively.

PRILOP, Hans.
Die Vorabstimmung in Hannover: Untersuchungen zur Vorgeschichte und Geschichte der Deutsch-Hannoverschen Partei im preussisch-deutschen Kaiserreich und in der Weimarer Republik. Dissertation, University of Hamburg (1953).

A tentative look at the origins and development of the DHP, known to its opponents as the Guelphs; it represented the old Hanoverian aristocracy and especially the rural bourgeoisie, and strove to restore the Guelph dynasty and Hanoverian independence.

SCHUMACHER, Martin.
Mittelstandsfront und Republik: die Wirtschaftspartei - Reichspartei des deutschen Mittelstandes 1919–1933. Düsseldorf: Droste (1972), 271 pp.

The party was founded in 1921 to defend the interests of the *Mittelstand* and to find a third course between capitalism and socialism, though it was clearly right of centre. From the mid-1920s, the party (under a new name) attempted to rally the *Mittelstand* for corporative ideas, but in reality it remained an economic interest group of dwindling support. Because of the party's political failure, the author's main thesis is that the Republic broke down finally, not only due to pressure from the right and left, but also due to the ineffectiveness of the middle. This could have been an outstanding monograph on a most important theme; but although the author describes the party's organization well, he leaves too many other basic questions unanswered, among them, the reasons for the radicalization of the *Mittelstand*.

SCHUMACHER, Martin (ed.).
Johann Victor Bredt: Erinnerungen und Dokumente, 1914 bis 1933. Düsseldorf: Droste (1970), 425 pp.

Complements Schumacher's previous work on *Mittelstand* politics in Weimar. Bredt was the leading parliamentarian of the *Wirtschaftspartei* and was Minister of Justice in Brüning's government for a spell in 1930. These memoirs and documents pertain to the policies of the party and to the theme that the collapse of confidence in parliamentary government among the *Mittelstand* was a crucial factor in the demise of the Republic.

Political Movements

7

A. ANARCHISM

LANDAUER, Gustav.
See section 15C (ii).

LINSE, Ulrich.
"Die Transformation der Gesellschaft durch die anarchistische Weltanschauung". *Archiv für Sozialgeschichte*, vol. 11 (1971), p. 289—371.
A thoroughly detailed and richly documented examination of the anarchist ideology and the assortment of anarchist groups in Weimar Germany. The author sees anarchism as part of the revolutionary socialist-democratic impulse of the German working class, and as a factor which contributed to the collapse of the Republic. A previously neglected aspect of Weimar history is illuminated in decisive fashion.

LINSE, Ulrich.
Organisierter Anarchismus im deutschen Kaiserreich von 1871. Berlin: Duncker und Humblot (1969), 410 pp.
A most informative study which ably discusses the diversity of anarchist ideological and organizational development. It contains also a valuable exposition of the ideas of Carl Landauer and Erich Mühsam. The latter's political activity in the 1920s is related including his attempt to come to a *modus vivendi* with Otto Strasser's Black Front organization in 1930.

VALLANCE, Margaret.
"Rudolf Rocker — a Biographical Sketch". *Journal of Contemporary History*, vol. 8, pt. 3 (1973), p. 75—95.
A brief résumé of the career of the famous anarchist (1873—1958), including his close involvement with Jewish anarchist circles in Britain before 1914. During the Weimar era he was an important influence on anarchist development but had to flee the National Socialists in 1933. He settled in the United States, where he died.

B. MONARCHISM

KAUFMANN, Walter.
Monarchism in the Weimar Republic. New York: Bookman Associates (1953), 305 pp.
A concise, reliable study of the monarchist movement and of the attitudes of various political parties towards monarchism. The monarchist movement as a whole, the author shows, declined rapidly after 1924, and he argues that Hindenburg's election to the Reich Presidency in 1925 doomed monarchism to defeat because his personality and popularity overshadowed the former royal house of Hohenzollern.

SWEETMAN, Jack.
The Unforgotten Crowns: the German Monarchist Movements 1918—1945. Dissertation: Emory University (1973).
Stresses the Kapp Putsch as a turning point in monarchist thinking; most monarchists realized then that the Hohenzollerns could be restored only at the unacceptable price of a civil war. In any case, the working classes would never tolerate a return to the pre-1914 situation. But in Bavaria, he adds, the monarchist movement was powerful; after 1933, many Wittelsbach supporters joined the anti-Nazi resistance. The author's main contention, however, that the monarchist movement contributed to the rise of National Socialism, is not sufficiently documented.

C. NATIONAL BOLSHEVISM

See also section 15B (iii) (a) (Neo-Conservatism).

ASCHER, Abraham; LEWY, Guenter.
"National Bolshevism in Weimar Germany". *Social Research*, vol. 23 (1956), p. 450—80.
An analysis which aims to dispel the nebulosity which clouded discussion of National Bolshevism. Based entirely on secondary sources, the paper discusses the origins of the movement, the ideology of National Bolshevism, and the groups and personalities who associated themselves with it. A good introduction to the problem which concludes that the Communists saw National Bolshevism in largely strategic terms, while the nationalists had a definite commitment to it.

BRUNZEL, Hans P.
Die "Tat" 1918—1933: ein publizistischer Angriff auf die Verfassung von Weimar innerhalb der konservativen Revolution. Dissertation, University of Bonn (1952).
An examination of the orientation and ideas of the most celebrated of National Bolshevik magazines, Hans Zehrer's *Die Tat*, which made its own idiosyncratic contribution to the intellectual ferment on the Right in the late 1920s and early 1930s.

BUCHHEIM, Hans.
"Ernst Niekischs Ideologie des Widerstandes". *Vierteljahrshefte für Zeitgeschichte*, vol. 5, pt. 4 (1957), p. 334—61.
A scholarly and balanced consideration of Niekisch's place in the intellectual tradition of the Right.

CAREY, Ann T.
Ernst Niekisch and National Bolshevism in Weimar Germany. Dissertation, University of Rochester (1972).
An intellectual and political biography of Niekisch as Weimar's leading National Bolshevik, with a look at the National Bolshevik movement as background. The study is based largely on his writings, including his monthly journal, *Widerstand*. His relations with the NSDAP and KPD form part of an absorbing analysis, which concludes that by the late 1920s Niekisch's ideas were those of Prussian socialism rather than National Bolshevism.

DEMANT, Ebbo.
Von Schleicher zu Springer: Hans Zehrer als politischer Publizist. Mainz: Hase und Koehler (1971), 263 pp.
A most useful description of Zehrer's checkered political career; the author's tone is suitably critical but fair. Zehrer's activities in the 1920s are especially well treated.

DREXEL, Joseph E.
Der Fall Niekisch: eine Dokumentation. Cologne: Kiepenheuer und Witsch (1964), 208 pp.
A general survey of his pre- and post-1945 political and intellectual career based on selected documents.

ESCHENBURG, Theodor.
"Bilanz eines konservativen Revolutionärs". *Geschichte in Wissenschaft und Unterricht*, vol. 2 (1951), p. 617—20.
A review of E. von Salomon's book, *Der Fragebogen* (Hamburg: Rowohlt (1951), 808 pp.), and a brief discussion of Salomon's role in National Bolshevism.

FISCHER, Ruth.
"Wanderer ins Nichts: der National-Bolschewismus am Beispiel Ernst Niekischs". *Frankfurter Hefte*, vol. 14 (1959), p. 871—80.
A severely critical assessment.

JONES, D. C. K.
Ernst Jünger and the National Bolsheviks. Dissertation, University of Cambridge (1969).
A study of strictly limited value.

JÜNGER, Ernst.
See section 15 C(ii).

KABERMANN, Friedrich.
Widerstand und Entscheidung eines deutschen Revolutionärs: Leben und Denken von Ernst Niekisch. Cologne: Verlag Wissenschaft und Politik (1972), 420 pp.
A badly written, poorly organized, and unbalanced work of the life and thought of Niekisch. The author's predilection for extensive quotes from Niekisch's writings, followed by obscure analysis, contributes to the unsatisfactory nature of this book.

KLEMPERER, Klemens von.
"Towards a Fourth Reich? The History of National Bolshevism in Germany". *Review of Politics*, vol. 13, pt. 2 (1951), p. 191—210.
Discusses National Bolshevism in terms of *rapprochement* between German nationalism and Russian Communism, but also in a wider sense, as representing a chapter in German-Russian relations since 1918. The author discusses the origins and development of what he regards as a serious philosophy in its own right, emphasizing the early contribution of Karl Radek. Klemperer surely errs, however, in including Otto Strasser's Black Front group in his review of National Bolshevik groups: the Black Front was Social Revolutionary in character.

KUSSEROW, Hans U.
"Ernst Niekisch: ein Leben im Widerstand". *Politische Studien*, no. 192, vol. 21 (1970), p. 451—64.
A brief résumé of Niekisch's political activities: his involvement in the Munich Revolution in 1918—19, his period in the early 1920s as a USPD deputy in the Bavarian *Landtag*. Kusserow also looks at his ambivalent relationship with Hitler and his ideas of Prussian socialism. Informative.

NIEKISCH, Ernst.
Gewagtes Leben: Begegnungen und Begebnisse. Cologne: Kiepenheuer und Witsch (1958), 392 pp.
Fascinating memoirs which relate Niekisch's full range of political activities in Weimar. Niekisch himself comes across as a person of courage and resilience, and also as a perceptive observer of what might loosely be called the German character.

NIEKISCH, Ernst.
Politische Schriften. Cologne: Kiepenheuer und Witsch (1966), 347 pp.
A collection of Niekisch's own political writings which faithfully reflect his political ideas on a comprehensive range of subjects. Included is his famous pamphlet written in 1931 in which he describes Hitler as the Austrian "revenge for Sadowa".

PAETEL, Karl O.
Versuchung oder Chance? Zur Geschichte des deutschen Nationalbolschewismus. Göttingen: Musterschmidt (1965), 345 pp.
Paetel was himself a National Bolshevik and this interesting book draws partly on his own experiences. The book is packed with relevant facts and details, and notes on leading members of the movement. Paetel's interpretations, however, are not always sound.

PAETEL, Karl O.
"Der deutsche Nationalbolschewismus 1918—1932:
ein Bericht". *Aussenpolitik*, vol. 3, pt. 4 (1952),
p. 229—42.
A short preliminary report on the main trends of the
movement.

PAETEL, Karl O.
"Der 'Hamburger Nationalkommunismus' ".
Geschichte in Wissenschaft und Unterricht, vol. 10,
pt. 10 (1959), p. 734—43.
Examines an idiosyncratic form of National Bolshevism in
Hamburg which originated on 6 November 1918 when the
Hamburg workers' and soldiers' councils determined to
carry out the fight against Western imperialism under the
banner of socialism. Later, National Communist groups in
Hamburg discussed their animosities against the "capitalist"
and "imperialist" Treaty of Versailles. Fritz Wolffheim and
Heinrich Laufenberg were the leaders, but the group
remained isolated and unimportant, on the periphery of
National Bolshevism. An interesting paper.

SALOMON, Ernst von.
See section 15C (ii).

SCHÜDDEKOPF, Otto-Ernst.
Linke Leute von rechts: die national-
revolutionären Minderheiten und der
Kommunismus in der Weimarer Republik.
Stuttgart: Kohlhammer (1960), 547 pp.
A brilliant, scholarly and objective study of National
Bolshevism and attendant phenomena; a work of prodigious
and exacting research which is unlikely to be superseded.
The author examines in detail the National Bolshevik movement, its ideological origins, organizational development,
leadership, and ambitions. The documentation is rich and
the analysis incisive and judicious. Part I of the book
examines the preconditions for the growth of National
Bolshevism; part II describes the origins and early development of the movement 1918—24, national revolutionary
ideas in the youth movement and in the NSDAP, and the
second phase of National Bolshevism 1929—33.

SONTHEIMER, Kurt.
"Der Tatkreis". *Vierteljahrshefte für
Zeitgeschichte*, vol. 7, pt. 3 (1959), p. 229—60.
An excellent analysis and description of Hans Zehrer's
circle of National Bolshevik supporters. Sontheimer
examines in detail the considerable literary and intellectual
outpourings of the *Tat* Circle, its ideas and policies, and its
role within the National Bolshevik movement as a whole.

SPENCER, Arthur.
"National Bolshevism". In W. Laqueur (ed.). *Russia
and Germany: a Century of Conflict*. London:
Weidenfeld and Nicolson (1965).
A useful discussion; the author emphasizes the Russian
dimension of National Bolshevism and the extent to which
German-Soviet foreign relations affected the different
phases of the movement.

STRUVE, Walter.
"Hans Zehrer as a Neoconservative Elite Theorist".
American Historical Review, vol. 70, pt. 4 (1965),
p. 1035—57.
An able discussion of Zehrer's élitist ideas, which were
propagated by his journal, *Die Tat*. Zehrer advocated
authoritarian government in which the intellectual élite
would play a decisive role, and as such he was the most
prominent neo-conservative élitist thinker.

WARD, James J.
Between Left and Right: Ernst Niekisch and
National Bolshevism in Weimar Germany. Dissertation, State University of New York (1973).
The author examines Niekisch's political ideas and activities
in order to define the place of National Bolshevism in the
political spectrum of the Weimar Republic. Niekisch's
relationship with the NSDAP and KPD is also explored.
Ward has simply gone over well-trodden ground and has
nothing new to say about either Niekisch or National
Bolshevism.

D. PACIFISM

BARKELEY, Richard.
Die deutsche Friedensbewegung 1870—1933.
Hamburg: Hammerich und Lesser (1948), 147 pp.
A general survey of the German pacifist movement, but too
vague to be anything other than a tentative introduction to
the subject.

FIEDOR, Karol.
"Die deutsche pazifistische Bewegung und das
Problem der deutsch-polnischen Beziehungen in
der Zwischenkriegszeit". *Jahrbuch für die
Geschichte Mittel- und Ostdeutschlands*, vol. 24
(1975), p. 143—63.
A valuable discussion which makes use of original material
from Polish archives.

HALLGARTEN, Constanze.
Als Pazifistin in Deutschland: biographische
Skizze. Stuttgart: Conseil Verlag (1956), 112 pp.
An unimportant record of fragmentary notes by a former
member of the pacifist movement.

SCHOENAICH, Paul von.
Mein Finale. Mit dem geheimen Tagebuch
1933—1945. Flensburg: Wolff (1947), 515 pp.
Some general comments on the movement, but they are not
of much significance. Part I of these memoirs deals with the
1928—33 period.

SCHUMANN, Rosemarie.
See her article in section 19D (i).

E. RACIALISM[1]

BORST, Gert.
Die Ludendorff-Bewegung 1919—1961. Augsburg:
Blasaditsch-Verlag (1969), 357 pp.
A comprehensive and detailed narrative.

BREUCKER, Wilhelm.
Die Tragik Ludendorffs: eine kritische Studie auf
Grund persönlicher Erinnerungen an den General
und seine Zeit. Stollhamm: Rauschenbusch (1953),
198 pp.
Contains a few notable observations, but otherwise of little
value.

1. The author feels justified in including in this section
works by or on General Erich Ludendorff because if he was
of any significance after 1918 it was as a result of his involvement in racist politics.

CRONENBERG, Allen T.
See his work in section 19I.

FRENTZ, Hans.
Der unbekannte Ludendorff: der Feldherr in seiner Umwelt und Epoche. Wiesbaden: Limes-Verlag (1972), 318 pp.
Of interest for the light thrown on Ludendorff's personality.

GOODSPEED, Donald J.
Ludendorff: Soldier, Dictator, Revolutionary. London: Hart-Davis (1966), 271 pp.
A popular and unreliable work; only the last few chapters refer to his post-1918 career and then only in vague terms.

GRIMM, Hans.
See section 15C(ii).

HAMEL, Iris.
See her study in section 14.

KALTENBRUNNER, Gerd-Klaus.
See his article on H.S. Chamberlain in section 15C(ii).

KATER, Michael H.
See his article in section 18C(ii).

LEISEN, Adolf.
See his study in section 17B.

LOHALM, Uwe.
Völkischer Radikalismus: die Geschichte des deutschvölkischen Schutz- und Trutz Bundes 1919–1923. Hamburg: Leibniz-Verlag (1970), 492 pp.
A scholarly and objective account of the most important and influential right-wing and anti-semitic organizations in the early Weimar period; at the same time, the author gives coverage of the radical *völkisch* movement as a whole. In his examination of the *Schutz- und Trutz Bund*, he analyses its sources of guidance and membership, its aims, organization and propaganda. His thesis that the politicized racialism and anti-semitism of early Weimar was a direct outgrowth of similar trends in imperial Germany is impressively vindicated, and as such the study is also a significant contribution to the continuity debate in modern German history.

LUDENDORFF, Erich.
Vom Feldherrn zum Weltkriegsrevolutionär und Wegbereiter deutscher Volksschöpfung. Vol I: 1919–1925; Vol. II: 1926–1933. Stuttgart: Verlag Hohe Warte (1940–51).
The memoirs of Ludendorff are a mixture of the ridiculous and the sublimely incorrigible. They cannot be regarded as a valuable historical source.

LUTZHÖFT, Hans-Jürgen.
Der nordische Gedanke in Deutschland 1920–1940. Stuttgart: Klett (1971), 436 pp.
This is the first systematic study of the origins, development, and disappearance of Nordic racial ideology in Germany. The author has unearthed a considerable amount of relevant and absorbing material and he has organized this into a very good narrative. Among other points, he stresses that the NSDAP's interest in the Nordic cult was spasmodic and propagandistic.

MAHLBERG, Hartmuth.
Erich Ludendorff. Hanover: Pfeiffer (1965), 301 pp.
A very ordinary and unexciting narrative which says little of Ludendorff's political activities after 1918.

PETERS, Elke.
See her work in section 17C.

PHELPS, Reginald H.
" 'Before Hitler Came': Thule Society and Germanen Orden". *Journal of Modern History*, vol. 35, pt. 3 (1963), p. 245–61.
Considers the origins and history of the *völkisch* and anti-semitic Thule Society and *Germanen Orden*, and their connections with the early German Workers' Party, the NSDAP, the *Freikorps Oberland*, and the *Deutschsozialistische Partei*. It is Phelps' aim to show, on the basis of archival material, how erroneous is the account of these groups in Rudolf von Sebottendorff's book *Bevor Hitler kam* (1933). Phelps shows that contrary to Sebottendorff's views, these two groups had only tenuous links with the DAP and NSDAP. A valuable essay.

PIAZZA, Richard.
Ludendorff: the Totalitarian and völkisch Politics of a Military Specialist. Dissertation, Northwestern University (1969).
Unlike most biographical studies of Ludendorff, this dissertation concentrates on his revolutionary social and political activity after 1918. The author traces the general's adoption of racist ideas, his involvement with the NSDAP, and his establishment of the *Tannenbergbund*. Provides many useful details, though the author's discussion of Ludendorff's dealings with the NSDAP is weak and incomplete.

POLIAKOV, Leon.
The Aryan Myth: a History of Racist and Nationalist Ideas in Europe. London: Heinemann (1974).
A general but scholarly study of the origins of European nationalism and racialism, and of the role of the "myth" in the evolution of national consciousness in each major European power. Special emphasis is laid on the concept of Aryanism in Germany and its links with anti-semitism.

SILFEN, Paul H.
See his study in section 15C(ii).

WULFF, R.
Die Deutschvölkische Freiheitspartei 1922–1928. Dissertation, University of Marburg (1968).
A sound investigation of the origins, organization, and membership of the party which for a time was a serious competitor of the NSDAP for the leadership of the *völkisch* political camp. The party went into steep decline after 1924–25, finally collapsing in 1927–28.

8

Paramilitary Formations and Right-Wing Groups

A. GENERAL[1]

FIEDOR, Karol.
See his article in section 19D(i).

FINKER, Kurt.
"Die militaristischen Wehrverbände in der Weimarer Republik: ein Beitrag zur Strategie und Taktik der deutschen Grossbourgeoisie".
Zeitschrift für Geschichtswissenschaft, vol. 14, pt. 3 (1966), p. 357—77.
The article is couched in the stern language of Marxist-Leninism and its purpose is to prove that the "terroristic activity" of certain paramilitary groups like *Wehrwolf, Bund Oberland, Reichskriegsflagge*, etc. was an instrument employed by the "imperialistic bourgeoisie" to maintain their political hegemony. The author erroneously states that the uniform political objective of these groups was the establishment of a fascist dictatorship. Finker throws historical objectivity to the winds in this paper, which mostly concentrates on the 1918—25 period.

HOEPKE, Klaus-Peter.
Die deutsche Rechte und der italienische Faschismus: ein Beitrag zum Selbstverständnis und zur Politik von Gruppen und Verbänden der deutschen Rechten. Düsseldorf: Droste (1968), 348 pp.
An interesting examination of the impact of Italian Fascism on the German Right, and of the links between Italy and right-wing groups in Germany before 1933. The author looks at how the German groups, such as the neo-conservatives, the National Socialists, authoritarian Catholics and others, interpreted fascism in ideological terms, and shows how diverse their reactions were. Much research still needs to be done on this important subject, but Hoepke has made a start in the right direction.

ILLERT, Helmut.
Die deutsche Rechte der Weimarer Republik im Urteil der englischen Presse 1928—1932.
Dissertation, University of Cologne (1966).
There are no startlingly new conclusions made in this study.

---

1. See also section 6B(vii)(g) for Communist paramilitary organizations.

It confirms the well-known fact that the conservative press in Britain was often more than a little sympathetic towards the National Socialists and radical nationalist groups.

NUSSER, Horst G. W.
Konservative Wehrverbände in Bayern, Preussen und Österreich 1918—1933. Mit einer Biographie von Georg Escherich 1870—1941. 2 vols. Munich: Nusser (1973), 364, 64 pp.
A generally reliable reference book of right-wing paramilitary groups, containing details of their membership, organization, aims, policies and leaders. It also provides the first full-length biographical portrait of the notorious Georg Escherich. Volume II includes some documents and a bibliography of works relating to these groups.

B. FREIKORPS

BIDLINGMEIER, Gerhard.
"Die Entstehung der Freikorps im Baltikum 1918: eine Richtigstellung". *Wehrwissenschaftliche Rundschau*, vol. 15, pt. 8 (1965), p. 458—62.
The author's purpose is to take issue with an article by David E. Mercer entitled "The Baltic Sea Campaign 1918—1920" in the journal *US Naval Institute Proceedings* (Sept. 1962, p. 63—9), in which he discusses the origins of the Baltic *Freikorps*.

GORDON, Harold J.
"München, Böhmen und die bayerische Freikorpsbewegung". *Zeitschrift für Bayerische Landesgeschichte*, vol. 38, pt. 2 (1975), p. 749—59.
The article informatively describes the development of the first *Freikorps* to be set up in Bavaria (as late as April 1919), the social and political background (mixed) of its members, and its aims (one of which was to act as a defence force against Czechoslovakia).

KRÜGER, Gabriele.
Die Brigade Ehrhardt. Hamburg: Leibniz-Verlag (1971), 176 pp.
An objective study of the best known *Freikorps* unit. Apart from discussing its origins and brief history, Krüger shows

that during 1919 the unit was permeated by *völkisch* anti-semitism. In 1920, the brigade led the abortive Kapp Putsch, after which it was dissolved, but part of it was incorporated into the German navy, and other parts settled in Pomerania and Bavaria ready for action should the need arise. The author has skilfully examined the group's ethos, sources of membership and finance, objectives, and links with other extremist organizations, including the NSDAP.

KURON, Hans J.
Freikorps und Bund Oberland. Dissertation, University of Erlangen (1960).
A very detailed and absorbing study of another prominent *Freikorps* organization. The *Bund Oberland* played an important part in post-1918 Bavarian politics until the Hitler Putsch, and the author has ably investigated the major aspects of the group's organization and membership, and its relationship with the NSDAP.

MÜLLER, Kurt.
"Die 'Rossbacher' als Schutztruppe des mecklenburgischen Grossgrundbesitzes".
Wissenschaftliche Zeitschrift der Friedrich-Schiller-Universität Jena, no. 1 (1972).
A clumsy and unconvincing attempt to depict the *Freikorps* Rossbach as a class instrument.

PAULUS, Günter.
"Die soziale Struktur der Freikorps in den ersten Monaten nach der Novemberrevolution".
Zeitschrift für Geschichtswissenschaft, vol. 3, pt. 5 (1955), p. 685—704.
The author berates the *Freikorps* as the combat formations of the bourgeoisie, in league with the Prussian *Junker*, militarists, and the SPD, to defeat the Revolution. The units of the *Freikorps*, he adds, were composed exclusively of middle class elements.

SCHULZE, Hagen.
Freikorps und Republik 1918—20.
Boppard: Boldt (1969), 363 pp.
An excellently documented and judicious study. The only major regret is that the author halts his narrative in 1920. The membership, organization, and activities of the various *Freikorps* units are given in rich detail. The author's interpretations, however, will not find universal acceptance; he argues that the *Freikorps* are to be seen as a phenomenon of the troubled times, a kind of inevitable evil, and he is not too critical of their attitude to the Republic.

STERN, Howard.
"The Organisation Consul". *Journal of Modern History*, vol. 35, pt. 1 (1963), 20—32.
A brief investigation of the development and activities of this infamous murder squad which perpetrated many of the political crimes in early Weimar. Most of its members were drawn from the dissolved Ehrhardt Brigade in late 1920; it received financial aid for a time from the German government. Its organization and aims (the establishment of a racist dictatorship) are discussed, and Stern regards it as an important factor in helping to pave the way for National Socialism. The information provided in this paper is interesting but inconclusive and some of Stern's interpretations are difficult to accept.

TRADITIONSGEMEINSCHAFT DES FREIKORPS UND BUNDES OBERLAND (ed.).
Bildchronik zur Geschichte des Freikorps und des Bundes Oberland. Munich: Print Service (1974), 301 pp.
A pictorial history of the *Freikorps* with accompanying short commentary. The illustrations are generally good and of interest.

VENNER, Dominique.
Söldner ohne Sold: die deutschen Freikorps 1918—1923. Berlin: Neff (1974), 335 pp.
An updated book on the *Freikorps* has been needed for some time, but Venner's study, although adequate in many respects, still leaves considerable ground in need of further research. Moreover, the author's interpretations are not always as critical as his material would appear to require.

WAITE, Robert G. L.
Vanguard of Nazism: the Free Corps Movement in Postwar Germany 1918—1923. Cambridge (Mass.): Harvard University Press (1952), 344 pp.
A generally sound history of the more important *Freikorps* units and their activities; the author's main thesis is implicit in the book's title, that the *Freikorps* constituted a funda-mental and direct link with National Socialism. The *Freikorps'* relations with the *Reichswehr* and political parties are analysed also, but the question of how they were financed is not dealt with in a satisfactory manner.

WILLIAMS, Warren W.
"Die Politik der Allierten gegenüber den Freikorps im Baltikum 1918—1919". *Vierteljahrshefte für Zeitgeschichte*, vol. 12, pt. 2 (1964), p. 147—69.
This paper sheds interesting light on the chaotic situation in the Baltic states at the end of the war, and the development of Allied policy towards the *Freikorps*. Initially, the Allies encouraged the *Freikorps* to fight the Red Army in the Baltic, but when the *Freikorps* were seen to be highly successful, the Allies feared they might become the spear-head of German imperialist expansion in that area. The essay discusses the international diplomatic and political tangle that resulted. The *Freikorps* were finally ordered to leave and, feeling let down by the German government, they nurtured hostile attitudes towards the infant Weimar Republic.

C. EX-SERVICEMEN

ALBERTIN, Lothar.
"Stahlhelm und Reichsbanner: Bedrohung und Verteidigung der Weimarer Demokratie durch politische Kampfverbände". *Neue Politische Literatur*, vol. 13 (1968), p. 456—65.
A critical review of three scholarly monographs on the *Stahlhelm* (V. R. Berghahn and A. Klotzbücher) and on the *Reichsbanner* (K. Rohe). All contribute to a better under-standing of the political role of the major paramilitary organizations in the Weimar Republic.

BERGHAHN, Volker R.
Der Stahlhelm: Bund der Frontsoldaten 1918—1935. Düsseldorf: Droste (1966), 304 pp.
A diligently researched and scholarly monograph which, in

discussing the group's political profile, clearly underlines its progressive involvement in the politics of the radical Right: by 1928—29, this also came to mean direct contact with the NSDAP. Berghahn rightly stresses the delusions under which the *Stahlhelm* engaged in political campaigning 1930—33; for one thing, it was tolerated by the NSDAP only so long as it helped its propaganda and electoral prospects; otherwise it had no place in Hitler's future plans.

BRAMKE, Werner.
"Die Funktion des Kyffhäuserbundes im System der militaristischen Organisation in der Weimarer Republik". *Zeitschrift für Militärgeschichte*, vol. 10, pt. 1 (1971), p. 64—78.
The author characterizes its political attitude as being profascist, imperialistic and anti-republican; he also accuses the group of influencing millions of Germans to believe in militarism and imperialism. Bramke's study is more of a political polemic than an historical essay, and those wishing for an objective assessment of the *Kyffhäuserbund* (membership about 100,000 in 1930) will have to look elsewhere.

DIEHL, James M.
"The Organisation of German Veterans 1917—1919". *Archiv für Sozialgeschichte*, vol. 11 (1971), p. 141—84.
Left- and right-wing groups began to organize veterans as early as 1917 in response to the progressively more tense political and social situation; it was felt by both sides that the soldiers' support would be important in the postwar political struggle. The main protagonists were the long established conservative *Kriegervereine* and the social democrats, and this article discusses the efforts of both sides to establish veterans' organizations before the end of the war; hence the conservative *Kyffhäuserbund* and the social democratic *Reichsbund* arose as the leading groups in the respective camps, but they were joined by other groups in 1918 and 1919. The author's main conclusion is that these veterans' groups faithfully reflected the deep social and political divisions of German society.

DUESTERBERG, Theodor.
Der Stahlhelm und Hitler. Wolfenbüttel: Wolfenbütteler Verlag (1949), 157 pp.
A largely apologetic account from the former deputy chairman of the *Stahlhelm*. Duesterberg tries unconvincingly to exonerate the *Stahlhelm* from the stigma of association with Hitler and the victory of National Socialism in 1933. The author's comprehension of the nature of politics in 1930—33 is rather naive and, indeed, from this one can readily appreciate how easily the *Stahlhelm* allowed itself to be manipulated by Hitler for his own nefarious ends.

ELLIOT, Christopher J.
Ex-Servicemen's Organisations and the Weimar Republic. Dissertation, University of London (1971).
A sound study, extracts of which appear in the article listed below.

ELLIOT, Christopher J.
"The Kriegervereine and the Weimar Republic". *Journal of Contemporary History*, vol. 10, pt. 1 (1975), p. 109—29.
The *Kriegervereine* in Weimar adopted a position of uneasy and ambivalent political neutrality towards the Republic, and they never formed an active part of the radical Right campaign against the parliamentary system. The *Kyffhäuserbund*, the largest of the veterans' groups,

epitomized this political stance despite being overwhelmingly conservative and monarchist at heart, and its activities were confined to welfare work and military exercises. This useful essay evaluates the status and function of the veterans' organizations during the Weimar period.

KLOTZBÜCHER, Alois.
Der politische Weg des Stahlhelm, Bund der Frontsoldaten, in der Weimarer Republik: ein Beitrag zur Geschichte der "Nationalen Opposition" 1918—1933. Erlangen: Hogl-Verlag (1965), 349 pp.
A very competent analysis which does not differ fundamentally from the main conclusions presented by Berghahn (see above).

PIERSON, Ruth.
"Embattled Veterans: the Reichsbund jüdischer Frontsoldaten". *Yearbook of the Leo Baeck Institute*, vol. 19 (1974), p. 139—54.
An informative discussion of the cruel fate of those Jews who fought bravely for Germany in the First World War, and yet who found themselves more and more isolated and rejected as the Weimar Republic headed towards collapse.

D. REICHSBANNER SCHWARZ-ROT-GOLD

ALBERTIN, Lothar.
See his article in section 8C.

CHICKERING, Roger P.
"The Reichsbanner and the Weimar Republic 1924—26". *Journal of Modern History*, vol. 40, pt. 4 (1968), p. 524—34.
This brief and rather superficial paper traces the origins and early development of the *Reichsbanner*, which was established in February 1924. Within a year this group, which started life as a force to counter the paramilitary organizations of the Right, and which was designed to be representative of all elements loyal to the Republic, had lost its above-party image and become an SPD formation. The two other parties originally involved, the Centre and the DDP, lost faith in it. Although the *Reichsbanner* enjoyed immediate mass support, the author doubts its value to the image of democratic government.

KNAPP, Thomas A.
See his article in section 6B(vi).

ROHE, Karl.
Das Reichsbanner Schwarz-Rot-Gold: ein Beitrag zur Geschichte und Struktur der politischen Kampfverbände zur Zeit der Weimarer Republik. Düsseldorf: Droste (1966), 494 pp.
An outstanding monograph which is certainly definitive. The author has amassed a wide range of materials which he has used admirably to provide a detailed and scholarly assessment of the *Reichsbanner's* structure, ideology, development, leadership, political involvement, and in fact everything of importance relating to it. In addition, by employing a typological and comparative methodology, Rohe is able to increase our knowledge of the paramilitary situation generally, and of the political situation in the Weimar Republic.

E. PAN-GERMAN LEAGUE

CHAMBERLAIN, Brewster S.
The Enemy on the Right: the Alldeutsche Verband in the Weimar Republic 1918—1926. Dissertation, University of Maryland (1972).
Argues that the role of the League in Weimar politics has been either underestimated or distorted. The author believes it played an important part in undermining democracy because from the beginning it was actively engaged in plotting the Republic's downfall, sometimes alone, but usually in conjunction with right-wing groups. The author stresses the close links between the League and the NSDAP, especially before 1923, but his viewpoint needs to be more thoroughly documented. Also, he seems to contradict his major point by saying that the League was fast running out of steam by the late 1920s.

KRUCK, Alfred.
Geschichte des Alldeutschen Verbandes 1890—1939. Wiesbaden: Steiner (1954), 258 pp.
A critical and thorough appraisal which argues (as Chamberlain should note — see previous entry) that the League made a major contribution to the victory of National Socialism in 1933. The author stresses above all the League's role in post-1918 politics, its involvement with a range of right-wing groups, the army, big business, and the paramilitary associations. He also shows that many National Socialist leaders had contact with the League, but he is wrong in regarding the League as a forerunner of the NSDAP. Indeed, Kruck most certainly overestimates the League's political significance as a whole.

F. DEFENCE MILITIA (EINWOHNERWEHRVERBÄNDE)

BUCHER, Peter.
"Zur Geschichte der Einwohnerwehren in Preussen 1918—1921". *Militärgeschichtliche Mitteilungen*, vol. 10, pt. 1 (1971), p. 15—59.
A very good essay, rich in detail and convincing in analysis. The author traces the circumstances in which these Citizens' Defence Militia originated and their development as anti-revolutionary, and later, in many cases, as anti-republican organizations. As such, they often supplied recruits for extreme right-wing and paramilitary groups.

KÖNNEMANN, Erwin.
Einwohnerwehren und Zeitfreiwilligen-verbände: ihre Funktion beim Aufbau eines neuen imperialistischen Militärssystem (November 1918—1920). East Berlin: Deutscher Militärverlag (1971), 485 pp.
A comprehensive study whose obvious Marxist-Leninist framework does not seriously impair its usefulness. The author regards the Citizens' Defence Militia as agents of the counter-revolution, dominated by and serving the interests of the bourgeoisie. Aided by reactionary conservative and capitalist forces, the Militia, Könnemann affirms, were an important instrument in the recreation of a capitalist-imperialist-militarist system in Germany after 1918. One's interest in the book declines rapidly, however, once the author engages in blatant political propaganda; he describes uncritically the policy of the KPD 1919—20, but much worse, he attacks the present day SPD in the Federal Republic as being the lackey of Western and NATO imperialists, and denounces the *Bundeswehr* as the continuation of the *Einwohnerwehren*!

G. JUNGDEUTSCHE ORDEN

HORNUNG, Klaus.
Der Jungdeutsche Orden: Beiträge zur Geschichte des Parlamentarismus und der politischen Parteien. Düsseldorf: Droste (1958), 160 pp.
A scholarly but in places oversympathetic analysis of the nationalist organization which during the course of the 1920s abandoned its anti-democratic views and came round to the policy of working within the parliamentary system of the Weimar Republic. Hornung has read extensively through the voluminous literature produced by the *Orden* as well as through the considerable writings of its leader, Artur Mahraum. He discusses its origins in the *Freikorps* movement, its ideology and membership, and stresses its hostility to National Socialism.

KESSLER, Alexander.
Der Jungdeutsche Orden in den Jahren der Entscheidung, 1928—1930. Munich: Lohmüller (1974), 174 pp.
This is an extremely competent study of the group's close involvement in Weimar politics and its major contribution to the establishment of the German State Party in 1930. The author stresses the influence of the *Orden*'s leader, Mahraum, who believed in a socially progressive conservatism and moderate nationalism. Although this account does not challenge the basic conclusions of Hornung, Kessler has presented some new archival material and has successfully placed the *Orden*'s role within the wider political context of Weimar.

MASTE, Ernst.
See his work in section 2.

WOLF, Heinrich.
Die Entstehung des Jungdeutschen Ordens und seine frühen Jahre 1918—1922. Munich: Lohmüller (1970), 47 pp.
Does not add anything new or important to what we already know from previous studies.

WOLF, Heinrich.
Der Jungdeutsche Orden in seinen mittleren Jahren 1922—1925. Munich: Lohmüller (1972), 71 pp.
Same comment applies as for the previous entry.

Political Regional Studies

9

A. GENERAL

BEHREND, H.-K.
See his article in section 3B.

BENZ, Wolfgang.
Süddeutschland in der Weimarer Republik: ein Beitrag zur deutschen Innenpolitik 1918—1923. Berlin: Duncker & Humblot (1970), 371 pp.
A scholarly, detailed, and objective study of the constitutional difficulties plaguing relations between the Reich government and the South German states of Baden, Württemberg, and Bavaria in early Weimar; the essential problem was the clash between the powers of the central authority in Berlin, and the powers of federalism. Benz describes the opposition of the South German states to Berlin's plans for a centralized unitary state, and they were able to influence the final Weimar constitutional formula in a way that protected their particularist prerogatives. But South German solidarity *vis-à-vis* Berlin was consistently undermined by Bavaria's insistence on having a special position over and above her South German neighbours. Hence, a viable federalist alternative to Berlin's unitary concept failed to emerge, so that an uneasy constitutional stalemate ensued. Benz has concentrated almost entirely on the 1918—20 period; only the last chapter looks at 1920—23. This book, however, is undoubtedly an important contribution to the early constitutional history of the Republic.

BRECHT, Arnold.
Federalism and Regionalism in Germany: the Division of Prussia. New York: Oxford University Press (1945), 202 pp.
A useful general survey which outlines the main areas of difficulty between federalism and centralism. Serves as an introduction to the problem, and particularly to the often anomalous position of Prussia.

EISSNER, Albin.
"Die deutschen Ostgebiete zwischen den Kriegen". *Aussenpolitik*, vol. 13, pt. 2 (1962), p. 106—13.
Draws our attention to the economic poverty of the eastern provinces, which remained socially and politically backward.

JACOB, Herbert.
German Administration since Bismarck: Central Authority versus Local Autonomy. New Haven: Yale University Press (1963), 224 pp.
The problem confronting successive German governments since Bismarck, of how to cope with the administrative and constitutional problems of particularism *vis-à-vis* the powers of the national government, is the theme of this broad narrative. In Weimar the problem was complicated more than ever before by political considerations. Jacob does not dwell on details, nor has he anything essentially new to say, but his survey is a useful introduction.

B. PRUSSIA

(i) General

BECK, Earl R.
The Death of the Prussian Republic: a Study of Reich-Prussian Relations 1932—1934. Tallahassee: Florida State University Press (1959), 283 pp.
The central theme of this study is the political and legal relationships between Prussia and the Reich. The author provides a sound, if unoriginal, analysis of the complex constitutional issues involved and places this discussion in the wider political perspective of the last days of the Republic. As an account of the collapse of the Republic, the book is mediocre; as a study of the Prussian-Reich relationship, it is adequate. There is plenty of information but not nearly enough interpretation of that information and, as a whole, the book lacks a conceptual framework.

EHNI, Hans-Peter.
Bollwerk Preussen? Preussenregierung, Reich-Länder-Problem und Sozialdemokratie 1918—1932. Stuttgart: Verlag Neue Gesellschaft (1975), 252 pp.
A political and constitutional study of considerable merit on the Prussian-Reich dilemma. The author's analysis of the political relationships between the national government and the Prussian state government, which was controlled by the SPD 1918—32, is the best aspect of the book, because Ehni has not clearly disentangled the complex legal and constitutional difficulties of the relationship.

EHNI, Hans-Peter.
"Zum Parteienverhältnis in Preussen 1918—1932:
ein Beitrag zur Funktion und Arbeitsweise der
Weimarer Koalitionsparteien". *Archiv für
Sozialgeschichte*, vol. 11 (1971), p. 241—88.
A detailed examination of the parties involved in the coal-
ition government (1918—32) and of how they managed to
work together, in contrast to the situation at national level.
Most of the material presented here is included in the
author's book.

EIMERS, Enno.
Das Verhältnis von Preussen und Reich in den
ersten Jahren der Weimarer Republik (1918—1923).
Berlin: Duncker & Humblot (1969), 503 pp.
The author examines the problem of reestablishing Reich-
Prussian relations on a new basis following the collapse of
the old order in 1918. He analyses the bureaucracies in-
volved on both sides but he does not clearly mark out how
much they were affected by political and social changes.
His conclusion, after presenting a mass of detail, is that the
Reich-Prussian dualism continued after 1918 with the only
real change being a tilting of the balance in favour of the
Reich. But Prussia was still sufficiently strong to resist the
Berlin government in important matters, and this situation,
the author argues, contributed to the weakness of the
government and hence to the weakness of the Republic
itself. This latter contention is speculative in this book,
since the study ends in 1923.

FAUTH, Reinhold.
See his study in section 17C.

FEUCHTWANGER, E. J.
Prussia: Myth and Reality; the Role of Prussia in
German History. London: Oswald Wolff (1970),
262 pp.
A general and on the whole unsatisfactory book which fails
to analyse many basic and important issues while spending
too much time discussing trivialities. The author's principal
aim is to assess Prussia's contribution to German history, but
he has signally failed to do so, even if he does show that
Prussia should not be seen as a stereotyped phenomenon.
The post-1918 period, moreover, is dealt with only in a
brief epilogue.

GLEES, Anthony.
"Albert C. Grzesinski and the Politics of Prussia
1926—1930". *English Historical Review*, vol. 89,
pt. 4 (1974), p. 814—34.
An examination of the period when Grzesinski was Minister
of the Interior in Prussia (1926—30). The argument is that
he was typical of a younger generation of SPD politicians
who were alive to the anti-republican threat and who
sought to meet that threat by initiating imaginative policies,
in Grzesinski's case, in the areas of law enforcement and
civil service reform. This essay sympathetically reviews his
record on these two important issues.

GOLOMBEK, Dieter.
Die politische Vorgeschichte des Preussen-
konkordats (1929). Mainz: Matthias-Grünewald-
Verlag (1970), 135 pp.
A somewhat superficial outline of the political negotiations
and manoeuvrings involving the major parties and the
Church authorities prior to the signing of the concordat in
1929.

HOLBORN, Hajo.
"Prussia and the Weimar Republic". *Social
Research*, vol. 23, pt. 3 (1956), p. 331—42.
A sympathetic appreciation of the political achievements in
Prussia during Weimar of the SPD minister, Otto Braun,
whom Holborn regards as one of the men who had the
greatest personal influence on the development of democracy before 1933. The essay, however, ranges over Prussian
history from the nineteenth century onwards. Unimportant
paper which carries no footnotes or references to source
material.

HORNSCHU, Hans-Erich.
Die Entwicklung des Finanzausgleichs im
deutschen Reich und in Preussen von 1919 bis
1944. Kiel (1950), 198 pp.
The aim of this book is to demonstrate that taxation
arrangements between the new Bonn government and the
Länder can only be resolved by past experience. Hence, the
author examines the financial relationships between them
under the Weimar Republic and the Third Reich. For the
Weimar era, he discusses the complex fiscal arrangements
governing Reich-*Länder* relations, and financial arrangements within Prussia itself. As in other spheres, experience
eventually produced a *modus vivendi*. An interesting introduction to a highly complicated problem.

KOHLER, Eric D.
Otto Braun, Prussia and Democracy, 1872—1955.
Dissertation, Stanford University (1971).
A political biography of Braun, which seems an over-
ambitious assignment for a Ph.D. The approach is strictly
chronological and Kohler has not added important new
vistas to his subject.

KOKOT, Josef (ed.).
The Miseries of the Prussian Eastern Provinces.
Poznan: Western Press Agency (1958), 115 pp.
This is a translation of a memorandum submitted to
Hindenburg and the *Reichstag* in 1930, drawing their atten-
tion to the economic and cultural decline of the eastern
provinces, and calling for immediate remedial action. The
memorandum blames the territorial losses suffered by
Germany under the Versailles Treaty in the east as the root
cause of this decline.

MUNCY, Lysbeth S.
See her article in section 13A(iii)(c).

PIKART, Eberhard.
See his article in section 3B.

RUNGE, Wolfgang.
See his work in section 3B.

SCHLEIER, Hans.
"Linksliberale Kritik an der reaktionären
Preussenlegende zwischen 1871 und 1933".
Zeitschrift für Geschichtswissenschaft, vol. 18
(1970), p. 1047—53.
Very general and says little of value.

STEFFANI, Winifred.
Die Untersuchungsausschuss des Preussischen Landtages zur Zeit der Weimarer Republik: ein Beitrag zur Entwicklung, Funktion, und politischen Bedeutung parlamentarischer Untersuchungsausschüsse. Düsseldorf: Droste (1960), 378 pp.
A study of the competence and importance of the inquiry committees that were used fairly frequently by the Prussian *Landtag* 1918—33 to investigate uprisings, political and financial scandals, etc. The attitudes of the major parties in Prussia to the committees are also related.

TRUMPP, Thomas.
See his work in section 4G.

WIDDER, Erwin.
Reich und Preussen von Regierungsantritt Brünings bis zum Reichsstatthaltergesetz Hitlers: Beiträge zum Reich-Länder-Problem der Weimarer Republik. Dissertation, University of Frankfurt (1956).
A rather cursory review of some of the main areas of conflict between the Reich and Prussian governments; the constitutional and legal problems are not analysed clearly while the financial and institutional aspects are virtually ignored.

(ii) Berlin

BÜSCH, Otto.
See his articles in section 13A(ii)(d).

CASTONIER, Elizabeth.
Stürmisch bis Leiter: Memoiren einer Aussenseiterin. Munich: Nymphenburger Verlag (1964), 362 pp.
Memoirs of a Jewess which recapture quite vividly the atmosphere in Berlin during the 1920s and early 1930s. Very readable.

ENGELI, Christian.
Gustav Böss: Oberbürgermeister von Berlin 1921—1930. Stuttgart: Kohlhammer (1971), 288 pp.
This biography forms a useful supplement to the scholarly political studies of the period. The problems of Berlin, political, economic and social, are given good coverage here.

ERMAN, Hans.
Bei Kempinski: aus der Chronik einer Weltstadt. East Berlin: Argon Verlag (1956), 257 pp.
Interesting for its vivid, and so far as can be gathered, accurate description of social and economic conditions in a working class area of Berlin in the 1920s.

FRIEDRICH, Otto.
Weltstadt Berlin: Grösse und Untergang 1918—1933. Munich: Desch-Verlag (1973), 327 pp.
One of the best and most comprehensive narrative studies of Berlin in the Weimar period. Social, economic, political

and cultural activities are all covered in detail. There is also an interesting collection of illustrations from the period.

HERZFELD, Hans.
"Berlin als Kaiserstadt und Reichshauptstadt 1871—1945". In H. Herzfeld. *Ausgewählte Aufsätze.* Berlin: de Gruyter (1962), p. 281—313.
A useful piece, especially for its description of social and economic conditions in the Weimar period.

KARDORFF, Ursula von.
Berliner Aufzeichnungen. Munich: Oldenbourg (1962).
Interesting reminiscences.

KETTIG, Konrad.
"Hauptstadt der Weimarer Republik (1918—1933)". In Otto-Friedrich Gandert, and others. *Heimatchronik Berlin.* Cologne: Archiv für Deutsche Heimatpflege (1962).
A critical review of social and economic conditions in Berlin.

KIAULEHN, Walther.
Berlin: Schicksal einer Weltstadt. Munich: Biederstein (1958), 594 pp.
A general survey of Berlin in the nineteenth and twentieth centuries, including a description of social and economic life in the 1918—33 period.

LANGE, Friedrich C. A.
Gross-Berliner Tagebuch, 1920—1933. Berlin: Borkenhagen (1951), 190 pp.
Contains some informative accounts of everyday life in the capital.

MANN, Willy.
Berlin zur Zeit der Weimarer Republik. East Berlin: Verlag das Neue Berlin (1957), 182 pp.
A politically slanted but nonetheless worthwhile study of economic and political life in Berlin before 1933.

MAYER, E.
Skizzen aus dem Leben der Weimarer Republik: Berliner Erinnerungen. Berlin: Duncker & Humblot (1962), 165 pp.
A series of interesting observations on various facets of life in Berlin.

PLESCH, J.
Janos erzählt von Berlin. Munich: List (1958), 213 pp.
Contains a few details of note on Berlin's social and economic conditions during Weimar.

REUTER, Fritz (ed.).
Das Hauptstadtproblem in der Geschichte.
Tübingen: Niemeyer Verlag (1951).
Included in this collection of essays are six on Berlin at various stages in history up to post-1945 days. One essay discusses the turbulent political situation in Berlin before 1933, emphasizing that the National Socialists never did very well at elections there.

SCHMIEDER, Eberhard.
"Wirtschaftsgeschichte Berlins im 19/20 Jahrhundert: vom Ersten bis zum Zweiten Weltkrieg". In Otto-Friedrich Gandert, and others. *Heimatchronik Berlin.* Cologne: Archiv für Deutsche Heimatpflege (1962).
Berlin's economic life during Weimar is touched upon.

WEIDMÜLLER, Helmut.
Die Berliner Gesellschaft während der Weimarer Republik. Dissertation, Free University of Berlin (1956).
A full discussion of social life and conditions in Berlin, and of the pervasiveness of class consciousness.

WILLIAMS, Robert.
"'Changing Landmarks' in Russian Berlin, 1922–1924". *Slavic Review,* vol. 27, pt. 4 (1968), p. 581–93.
Political opinion in the Russian *émigré* colony in Berlin moved leftwards after 1922, when Mensheviks and intellectuals arrived from Russia. This essay reviews aspects of a movement of Russian intellectuals back to the Soviet Union in 1923–24 and the efforts of the Bolshevik régime to encourage this trend.

C. BAVARIA

BENZ, Wolfgang (ed.).
Politik in Bayern 1919–1933: Berichte des württembergischen Gesandten Carl Moser von Filseck. Stuttgart: Deutsche Verlagsanstalt (1971), 290 pp.
Moser von Filseck was Württemberg's ambassador to Bavaria 1906–33. This volume contains 253 reports from January 1919—March 1933 in which he describes political, economic and social developments in Bavaria and Munich. Included are his impressions of the early NSDAP, the Bavarian Revolution, and the Soviet Republic. For the 1930–33 period, his reports deal largely with *Reichstag* and *Landtag* election results in Bavaria. As a whole the volume is a useful documentary collection.

BENZ, Wolfgang.
"Bayerische Auslandsbeziehungen im 20. Jahrhundert". *Zeitschrift für Bayerische Landesgeschichte,* vol. 32 (1969), p. 962–94.
An examination of Bavaria's diplomatic connections abroad before 1918, and of their liquidation following the end of the First World War.

BIESINGER, Joseph.
The Presidential Elections in Bavaria in 1925 and 1932 in Relation to the Reich. Dissertation, Rutgers University (1972).
An analysis of the influence of Bavarian political forces on the Reich presidential elections, with some emphasis on the controversial attitudes (particularly in 1925) of the BVP. This work merely covers familiar ground.

DEUERLEIN, Ernst.
"Der Freistaat Bayern zwischen Räteherrschaft und Hitler-Putsch". *Das Parlament: Aus Politik und Zeitgeschichte,* B44 (28.10.1964).
A very informative review of major political trends in Bavaria 1919—23.

DONOHOE, James.
Hitler's Conservative Opponents in Bavaria 1930—1945: a Consideration of Catholic, Monarchist and Separatist Anti-Nazi Activities. Leiden: Brill (1961), 348 pp.
Although this book deals with the specifically Bavarian characteristics of the anti-Hitler resistance movement after 1933, there is a fairly useful introductory part on Bavarian conservative attitudes to the NSDAP before the *Machtergreifung.*

EHLERS, Carol J.
See her work in section 22D.

ERDMANN, Josef.
Coburg, Bayern und das Reich 1918—1923.
Coburg: Rossteutscher-Verlag (1969), 177 pp.
Coburg, a medium-sized town in Bavaria, developed as a nationalist stronghold in the 1920s and the NSDAP made a spectacular breakthrough there in local council elections before the party had begun to make progress in any other part of Germany. This somewhat unscholarly book provides a few details about the town in the early Weimar period.

FENSKE, Hans.
Konservatismus und Rechtsradikalismus in Bayern nach 1918. Bad Homburg: Verlag Gehlen (1969), 340 pp.
An ambitious work whose principal aim is to determine the organizational, traditional, ideological, and personal composition of the political Right in Bavaria after 1918. The author also attempts to place the activities and attitudes of the political Right within the context of the complex constitutional relationship between Bavaria and the Berlin government. He is not wholly successful in realizing both objectives. He has certainly provided much valuable detailed material on a host of right-wing groups, but he does not make his case that rightist radicalism was a direct outgrowth of the weaknesses of Bavarian conservatism. Hence, the connections between the extremist organizations and the elements of conservatism (big business, the army, etc.) are not thoroughly enough investigated.

FRANZ-WILLING, Georg.
Die bayerische Vatikangesandtschaft 1803—1934.
Munich: Ehrenwirth Verlag (1965), 284 pp.
A general study of diplomatic links between Bavaria and the Vatican. Of interest for the Weimar period is the material presented from the papers of Bavaria's last emissary to the Vatican, Freiherr von Ritter. A major theme of the

book is the struggle Bavaria had with the Berlin government over Catholic representation in Rome; Berlin wanted a national delegation, but Bavaria, true to her strong particularist tendencies, insisted on retaining her own. Hence, some new aspects of the federalist-centralist phenomenon are revealed here.

GOLLWITZER, Heinz.
"Bayern 1918—1933". *Vierteljahrshefte für Zeitgeschichte*, vol. 3, pt. 4 (1955), p. 363—87.
Contains a substantial amount of information on Bavarian political and social attitudes and developments.

GÖMMEL, R; HAERTEL, G.
Arbeitslosigkeit und Wählerentscheidungen in Nürnberg von 1928 bis 1933. Dissertation, University of Erlangen (1968).
Draws a useful correlation between the rising level of unemployment and the increase in support for the radical parties of the Left and Right in Nuremberg.

HABEL, Bernd.
Verfassungsrecht und Verfassungswirklichkeit: eine Untersuchung zum Problem Reich-Länder.
Munich: Reuther Verlag (1968), 265 pp.
A scholarly but heavy contribution to the constitutional entanglements between Berlin and Bavaria during the Held administration in Bavaria 1924—33.

HAUSHOFER, Heinz.
See his work in section 13A (iii)(a).

HELD, Joseph.
Heinrich Held, ein Leben für Bayern. Regensburg: "Zeit und Welt" Verlag (1958).
A brief biographical sketch of perhaps the most important politician of the BVP during the Weimar era, written by his son. However, the author finds it difficult to be objective, though there are a few worthwhile details on certain Bavarian political developments.

KESSLER, Richard.
Heinrich Held als Parlamentarier: eine Teilbiographie 1868—1924. Berlin: Duncker & Humblot (1971), 532 pp.
A very full, detailed, and on the whole satisfactory study which is also reasonably instructive about general political trends in Bavaria in early Weimar.

KRITZER, Peter.
Die bayerische Sozialdemokratie und die bayerische Politik in den Jahren 1918 bis 1923.
Munich: Wölfle (1969), 243 pp.
This study covers some important ground but leaves unanswered a number of fundamental questions. The extent to which the Bavarian SPD differed from the party as a whole is not made sufficiently clear, and the SPD's influence on Bavarian politics before 1923 is not always measured correctly. This is an interesting but limited work.

MENGES, Franz.
Reichsreform und Finanzpolitik: die Aushöhlung der Eigenständigkeit Bayerns auf finanzpolitischen Wege in der Zeit der Weimarer Republik. Berlin: Duncker & Humblot (1971), 467 pp.
A long, detailed, and sometimes confusing study of the financial and political relationship between Bavaria and the Reich. The author writes from a strongly federalist standpoint, and on the whole condemns the financial policy of the Berlin government as having been negative. Not everyone will agree.

MENNEKES, Friedhelm.
Die Republik als Herausforderung: konservatives Denken in Bayern zwischen Weimarer Republik und antidemokratischer Reaktion 1918—1925.
Berlin: Duncker & Humblot (1972), 275 pp.
This work has little of substantial importance to say about Bavarian politics, but it can be regarded as reliable for the purposes of background reading.

NUSSER, Horst.
"Militärischer Druck auf die Landesregierung Johannes Hoffmann vom Mai 1919 bis zum Kapp-Putsch". *Zeitschrift für Bayerische Landesgeschichte*, vol. 33 (1970), p. 818—50.
Concerned not so much with the threat from right-wing paramilitary groups to the Hoffmann government as with the militaristic preparations and activities of the radical Left, including the Independent Social Democrats and the Communists. The essay incorporates some new material which illuminates one of the most neglected periods in early Bavarian politics.

OSWALD, Josef.
"Bayerische Heimatbewegung und -forschung zwischen den zwei Weltkriegen". *Historisches Jahrbuch*, vol. 72 (1953), p. 606—14.
Looks at the phenomenon of local patriotism in Bavaria, which was considerably strengthened by the outcome of the First World War and the inflation period that followed. The first organized movement arose in 1920, embracing areas close to the Austrian border and a number of Austrian districts around Salzburg. Eduard Kriechbaum was the leading light. This article traces the modest development and aims of the movement; most of the information is taken from contemporary newspapers and journals.

SAGERER, G.; SCHULER, Emil.
See their work in section 3B.

SCHULER, Emil.
See his work in section 3B.

SCHWEND, Karl.
Bayern zwischen Monarchie und Diktatur: Beiträge zur bayerischen Frage 1918—1933. Munich: Pflaum Verlag (1954), 590 pp.
The principal theme is the development of the BVP, of which Schwend was a member. He is not uncritical of the BVP's role, arguing for example that it could have done more about the rise of right-wing extremism. But Schwend argues unconvincingly that Bavaria should have had more power *vis-à-vis* the Berlin government. The book's usefulness lies largely in its clear description of Bavarian politics in general.

SENDTNER, Karl.
Rupprecht von Wittelsbach, Kronprinz von Bayern. Munich: Pflaum Verlag (1954).
Bavarian monarchism was a substantial political force during the Weimar period, and the Crown Prince was very

much the focal point of it. He comes out well from this study, though the book as a whole does not provide a definitive or even a comprehensive account of the monarchist movement.

SPECKNER, Herbert.
See his work in section 6B(vi).

STEINBORN, Peter.
See his work in section 2.

THRÄNHARDT, Dietrich.
Wahlen und politische Strukturen in Bayern 1848—1953: historische-soziologische Untersuchungen zum Entstehen und zur Neuerrichtung eines Parteiensystems. Düsseldorf: Droste (1973), 360 pp.
A most interesting and scholarly work which furnishes a great deal of detailed information on political developments and their sociological background in Bavaria. The section on the Weimar Republic is as good as any in the book.

WIESEMANN, Falk.
Die Vorgeschichte der nationalsozialistischen Machtübernahme in Bayern 1932/33. Berlin: Duncker & Humblot (1975), 328 pp.
A detailed and wide-ranging look at the Bavarian political situation. An appreciable amount of original material is presented.

ZIMMERMANN, Werner G.
Bayern und das Reich 1918—1923: der bayerische Föderalismus zwischen Revolution und Reaktion. Munich: Pflaum Verlag (1953), 202 pp.
A study of the constitutional, legal, and economic relationships between Bavaria and Berlin, with emphasis on the peculiarities of Bavarian federalism. The author's viewpoint is that of a conservative monarchist and this tends too often to colour his judgement. The book is based entirely on secondary printed sources, but as a general introduction to Bavaria in this period, it has some value.

ZORN, Wolfgang.
Kleine Wirtschafts- und Sozialgeschichte Bayerns 1806—1933. Munich (1962).
Too brief and general to be of any use to specialists or advanced students, but this book provides an introduction to the economic background of Bavarian politics.

D. OTHERS (AACHEN—WÜRTTEMBERG)

1. AACHEN

PLUM, Günter.
Gesellschaftsstruktur und politisches Bewusstsein in einer katholischen Region 1928—1933: Untersuchung am Beispiel des Regierungsbezirks Aachen. Stuttgart: Deutsche Verlagsanstalt (1972), 319 pp.

A scholarly monograph of considerable merit; it provides an in-depth analysis of social, economic, political, ideological and confessional influences in the Aachen area, where the overwhelming bulk of the population was Catholic.

2. BADEN

REHBERGER, Horst.
Die Gleichschaltung des Landes Baden 1932/33. Heidelberg: Winter Verlag (1966), 162 pp.
A competent survey which is, however, only partially successful in explaining and accounting for the preconditions in the state before 1933 which made for the relative ease of the National Socialist takeover during the course of that same year.

3. DÜSSELDORF

FOERST, Walter.
Robert Lehr als Oberbürgermeister: ein Kapitel deutscher Kommunalpolitik. Düsseldorf: Econ-Verlag (1962), 310 pp.
A rather dull book concerning local government administration and politics. The author fails to draw the appropriate wider conclusions which would have made the study more meaningful.

4. EAST PRUSSIA

HERTZ-EICHENRODE, Dieter.
Politik und Landwirtschaft in Ostpreussen 1919—1930: Untersuchung eines Strukturproblems in der Weimarer Republik. Cologne: Westdeutscher Verlag (1969), 352 pp.
An informative and well researched study whose primary emphasis is on the economic problems resulting from the backwardness and inefficiency of agriculture. The author is less successful, however, in explicitly linking the problems of the economy to political and social attitudes. On the other hand, the political complications of the *Osthilfe* programme are competently discussed.

KLATT, Rudolph.
Ostpreussen unter dem Reichskommissariat 1919/1920. Heidelberg: Quelle und Meyer (1958), 271 pp.
Most useful for its discussion of the wide range of problems facing the province as a result of war and revolution.

MARZIAN, Herbert.
Selbstbestimmung für Ostdeutschland. Göttingen: Arbeitskreis (1970), 128 pp.
A commemorative documentary study of the plebiscite held in East Prussia and West Prussia in July 1920.

5. ESSEN

KÜHR, Herbert.
Parteien und Wahlen im Stadt- und Landkreis Essen in der Zeit der Weimarer Republik. Düsseldorf: Droste (1973), 309 pp.

Using a sophisticated methodology, this excellent analysis is a valuable contribution to local studies in the Weimar period. A number of interesting points to be noted here are: that the KPD was the strongest working class party in Essen; that Catholicism was a more important influence in politics than class; and that the NSDAP was very weak in Essen until 1930—33.

6. FRANKFURT

EMRICH, Willi.
Das Goldene Buch der Stadt Frankfurt am Main.
Frankfurt: Kramer (1958), 303 pp.
A general history of the city; the section on Weimar (p. 108*ff*) pays particular attention to social and economic conditions.

FRY, Joan M.
Zwischen zwei Weltkriegen in Deutschland: Erinnerungen einer Quäkerin. Bad Pyrmont: Friedrich Verlag (1947), 146 pp.
Included in these sparse memoirs are a few observations on social conditions in Frankfurt during the Weimar era. The rest of the book is entirely forgettable.

7. HAMBURG

DANNER, Lothar.
See his work in section 3B.

LIPPMANN, Leo.
Mein Leben und meine amtliche Tätigkeit: Erinnerungen und Beitrag zur Finanzgeschichte Hamburgs. Edited by Werner Jochmann. Hamburg: Christian Verlag (1964), 720 pp.
Chapters III and IV deal with the 1918—33 period. There is some useful information on Hamburg's economic and financial situation.

LÜTH, Erich.
Bürgermeister Carl Petersen 1868—1933. Hamburg: Christians (1971), 147 pp.
Petersen, a one-time chairman and *Reichstag* deputy of the DDP, was Mayor of Hamburg, 1924—27 and 1931—33. His political activities receive sympathetic but fair comment in this slim biography.

TIMKE, Henning (ed.).
Dokumente zur Gleichschaltung des Landes Hamburg 1933. Frankfurt: Europäische Verlagsanstalt (1964), 327 pp.
An excellent collection of documentary material of varying description, a small proportion of which refers to events before 1933.

8. HESSE

KAHLENBERG, Friedrich (ed.).
Die Berichte Eduard Davids als Reichsvertreter in Hessen 1921—1927. Wiesbaden: Steiner (1970), 262 pp.
David, a leading member of the SPD faction in the *Reichstag*, was the Berlin government's representative in the Hessian capital of Darmstadt, 1921—27. His 170 reports to Berlin constitute an important primary source for Reich-*Lander* relationships in Weimar. His reports cover a wide range of activities and developments and as such are a vivid exposition of what Hesse was like during that period. The collection is expertly edited.

ULRICH, C.
Erinnerungen des ersten hessischen Staatspräsidenten. Edited by Ludwig Bergsträsser. Offenbach: Bollwerk-Verlag (1953), 226 pp.
Complements Kahlenberg's study (see above) in that these memoirs record much of the political and constitutional history of Hesse in the 1920s as seen by an insider.

9. LIPPE

HÜLS, Hans.
Wähler und Wahlverhalten im Land Lippe während der Weimarer Republik. Detmold: Naturwissenschaftlicher und Historischer Verein für das Land Lippe (1965).
A concise and informative study of Lippe's electoral history and electorate, including the background to and details of the famous election there in January 1933 when the NSDAP scored a badly needed morale-boosting victory.

10. LOWER SAXONY

FRANZ, Günther.
Die politischen Wahlen in Niedersachsen 1867—1949. Bremen: Walter Dorn Verlag (1951), 303 pp.
A valuable reference work, consisting for the most part of tables indicating electoral results and trends in Lower Saxony. The results are broken down into local districts so that, for example, NSDAP strongholds are easy to consult. Lower Saxony as a whole, of course, was a bastion of the National Socialists.

FRANZ, Günther.
Die Entwicklung der politischen Parteien in Niedersachsen im Spiegel der Wahlen 1867—1949. Bremen: Walter Dorn Verlag (1951), 273 pp.
A companion volume to the above. Franz interprets the electoral results in terms of what they meant for individual political parties.

KAISER, Klaus.
Braunschweiger Presse und Nationalsozialismus: der Aufstieg der NSDAP im Lande Braunschweig im Spiegel der Braunschweiger Tageszeitungen 1930 bis 1933. Brunswick: Waisenhaus-Buchhandlung (1970), 196 pp.
An analysis of how the right-wing press regarded National Socialism in terms of an ideological, political, and governmental force 1930—33. Kaiser's findings confirm the well established fact that the NSDAP drew increasing support from the conservative nationalist and Protestant middle classes.

KÜHLING, Karl.
Osnabrück 1925--1933: von der Republik bis zum Dritten Reich. Osnabrück: Fromm-Verlag (1963), 164 pp.
Osnabrück's political history stands in vivid contrast to most other areas of Lower Saxony before 1933; it did not

register any notable support for the NSDAP. The main reason was that the city's population was predominantly Catholic, and voted in the main for the Centre Party. Kühling's study confirms, therefore, the fact that the NSDAP was invariably poorly supported in Catholic areas of Germany.

NOAKES, Jeremy.
See his work in section 22D(7).

PRILOP, Hans.
See his work in section 6B(viii).

ROLOFF, Ernst-August.
Bürgertum und Nationalsozialismus, 1930—1933: Braunschweigs Weg ins Dritte Reich. Hanover: Verlag für Literatur und Zeitgeschehen (1961), 176 pp.
Concerned with analysing the NSDAP's approach to and participation in coalition government in Brunswick with middle class parties. Roloff argues that the NSDAP used Brunswick as a test case on the question of how best to deal with this kind of coalition situation on a national scale. Much of the emphasis, however, is on the other parties in-volved. The study is thoroughly researched and well informed.

ROLOFF, Ernst-August.
Braunschweig und der Staat von Weimar.
Brunswick: Weisenhaus (1964), 230 pp.
A very useful survey of major political, economic and social developments in Brunswick 1918—33, and of the state's relationship with the Berlin government in its various institutional forms.

SALDERN, Adelheid von.
Vom Einwohner zum Bürger: zur Emanzipation der städtischen Unterschicht Göttingens 1890—1920; eine sozial- und kommunalhistorische Untersuchung. Berlin: Duncker & Humblot (1973), 508 pp.
A valuable and informative analysis of how the lower classes in Göttingen were affected by industrialization before 1914 and then by war and revolution from 1914—18. The theme is the changing social status of the working class, from inhabitant to citizen. The author directs much credit for this transformation to the trade union movement and the SPD.

VOGELSANG, Thilo.
Hinrich Wilhelm Kopf und Niedersachsen. Hanover: Verlag für Literatur und Zeitgeschehen (1963), 218 pp.
Kopf was the first Prime Minister of Lower Saxony, and became known as the "Red Guelph" because of his unusual *Weltanschauung* of socialism combined with Lower Saxon patriotism. This biography of him is sympathetic, but learned and clearly written.

11. OFFENBACH AM MAIN

BÖSCH, Hermann.
Politische Parteien und Gruppen in Offenbach am Main 1860—1960. Offenbach: Selbstverlag der Offenbacher Geschichtsverein (1973), 132 pp.
Useful for the details it provides on Offenbach's politics during Weimar.

12. SAXONY

HOHLFELD, Klaus.
Die Reichsexekution gegen Sachsen im Jahre 1923: ihre Vorgeschichte und politische Bedeutung. Erlangen: Hogl (1964), 152 pp.
Bears rather too many scars of a former doctoral thesis, but nonetheless has gathered together some interesting material. The author's interpretation of the importance of the Reich's action against the Saxon left-wing government in autumn 1923 is, however, open to dispute.

13. SCHLESWIG-HOLSTEIN

ERDMANN, Karl D.
"Die Frage des 14. März 1920: Rede in Flensburg zur 50. Wiederkehr des Abstimmungstages".
Geschichte in Wissenschaft und Unterricht, vol. 21, pt. 11 (1970), p. 645—60.
Reflections on the significance of the 1920 plebiscite in Schleswig-Holstein, by which the northern part of Schleswig reverted to Denmark. The foreign policy, diplomatic and domestic implications of the event are reviewed here, as well as the repercussions on the province itself.

HEBERLE, Rudolf.
Landbevölkerung und Nationalsozialismus: eine soziologische Untersuchung der politischen Willensbildung in Schleswig-Holstein 1918—1932. Stuttgart: Deutsche Verlagsanstalt (1963), 171 pp.
An excellent, concise study of the development of political attitudes in a province which before 1914 was a stronghold of the SPD and liberals, but which by 1932 had produced a majority for the NSDAP. Heberle analyses the reasons for this radical transformation: leading factors were the economic crisis, which devastated agriculture and radicalized the small farmers, and anti-semitic and racial ideas. Con-siderable attention is devoted to the evolution of the *Land-volk* movement and its collapse, and its exploitation by the NSDAP. In short, this is a valuable case study of the rise of right-wing political radicalism in an agricultural and Protestant region of Germany.

HEUER, Jürgen.
Zur politischen, sozialen und ökonomischen Problematik der Volksabstimmungen in Schleswig 1920. Kiel: Mühlau (1973), 238 pp.
A comprehensive investigation of the repercussions of the plebiscite for the German-speaking inhabitants of Danish Schleswig. The work is based entirely on secondary sources, but Heuer has produced a clear and balanced narrative.

LEHMANN, Hans.
Der "Deutsche Ausschuss" und die Abstimmung in Schleswig 1920. Neumünster: Wachholtz (1969), 322 pp.
A detailed exposition of the German effort to obtain a favourable result in the plebiscite, but, as the author points out, the odds were weighted heavily against the Germans, due partly to the policies of the Allies.

STOLTENBERG, Gerhard.
Politische Strömungen im schleswig-holsteinischen Landvolk 1919—1933: ein Beitrag zur politischen Meinungsbildung in der Weimarer Republik. Düsseldorf: Droste (1962), 219 pp.
A well documented account of the *Landvolk* movement, the problems in agriculture, the rapid radicalization of the peasantry, and the advance of the NSDAP.

WULF, Peter.
Die politische Haltung des schleswig-holsteinischen Handwerks 1928—1932. Cologne: Westdeutscher Verlag (1969), 160 pp.
Documents and confirms the established fact that the artisans of the province gave massive support to the NSDAP before 1933. Inflation, depression, and the competition of capitalism and big business all combined to make their social and economic situation desperate, and thus they turned to the radical promises of the National Socialists.

14. THURINGIA

TRACY, Donald R.
Thuringia under the Early Weimar Republic, 1919—1924: a Study in Reform and Reaction. Dissertation, University of Maryland (1967).
Thuringia was dominated by the political Left until 1924. In 1921—23 the state had a progressive socialist administration which attempted to achieve a wide range of important reforms. Right-wing resistance to the government increased steadily, reaching a climax in the autumn of 1923 when the *Reichswehr* was sent in to break up the SPD-KPD coalition. The socialist experience before 1924 was a major factor, the author argues, in pushing Thuringia rightwards after 1924. This is an interesting narrative of major political, social and economic developments in Thuringia.

TRACY, Donald R.
"Reform in the Early Weimar Republic: the Thuringian Example". *Journal of Modern History*, vol. 44, pt. 2 (1972), p. 195—212.
Presents extracts from the author's thesis: the early revolutionary enthusiasm, the persistent impetus towards reform of the state administration, the reform programme of the socialist government 1921—23, and the failure of these reforms in the long term because they were introduced prematurely.

WITZMANN, Georg.
Thüringen von 1918—1933: Erinnerungen eines Politikers. Meisenheim: Hain (1958), 184 pp.
The author was a former socialist member of the Thuringian *Landtag*, and his memoirs of the state in the Weimar era make fascinating reading. The atmosphere of those times is vividly recreated as he reviews political, economic and social developments, and the policies of the major parties.

15. TRIER

MICK, Guenter.
Politische Wahlen und Volksentscheide in der Stadt Trier zur Zeit der Weimarer Republik. Dissertation, University of Bonn (1969), 434 pp.
A detailed and sound analysis of the electorate and socio-economic and political conditions in a mainly Catholic city.

16. WÜRTTEMBERG

BESSON, Waldemar.
Württemberg und die deutsche Staatskrise 1928—1933: eine Studie zur Auflösung der Weimarer Republik. Stuttgart: Deutsche Verlagsanstalt (1959), 425 pp.
An outstanding scholarly monograph on the collapse of democratic government in a traditionally liberal Protestant state. Based on wide and thorough research, it opens up new perspectives on the fall of the Weimar Republic as a whole by analysing the institutional framework of Württemberg. The author's analysis of Württemberg politics and society is also of an exemplary standard. As a whole, the book throws new light on many important problems, including the questions of *Reichsreform*, federalism, finance, etc. The Brüning era is dealt with at length and Besson takes a more sympathetic view of it than many historians.

GADE, Warren.
Württemberg and the Reich, 1924—1928: a Study in the Relations between the Reich and Länder. Dissertation, Stanford University (1972).
Concentrates on an analysis of the rise and fall of the DNVP-led coalition in Württemberg 1924—28. Wilhelm Bazille, the local DNVP leader, became State President, but he and his government steadily lost ground. The thesis concentrates on his struggles with the Berlin government for more power to be given to Württemberg. A useful work.

KOHLHAAS, Wilhelm.
Chronik der Stadt Stuttgart 1918—1933. Stuttgart: Klett (1964), 379 pp.
Comprehensive, detailed, and immensely interesting local study. Politics, the local economy, the social classes, education, and other major aspects are all given adequate coverage.

10

The Churches

A. GENERAL

CONWAY, John S.
The Nazi Persecution of the Churches 1933—45.
London: Weidenfeld & Nicolson (1968), 474 pp.
A good analysis which contains a few useful introductory remarks on the position of the Churches in the pre-1933 period.

HELMREICH, Ernst C.
See his work in section 17C.

HOLL, Karl.
"Konfessionalität, Konfessionalismus und demokratische Republik — zu einigen Aspekten der Reichspräsidentenwahl von 1925". *Vierteljahrshefte für Zeitgeschichte*, vol. 17, pt. 3 (1969), p. 254—75.
An informative discussion of left-wing attacks on the fessional attitudes on the election of 1925 (in which a surprisingly large minority of Catholics voted for the Protestant Hindenburg), and also the wider relationship between religion and politics in Weimar.

SCHREIBER, Georg.
"Deutsche Kirchenpolitik nach dem Ersten Weltkrieg: Gestalten und Geschehnisse der Novemberrevolution 1918 und der Weimarer Republik". *Historisches Jahrbuch*, vol. 70 (1951), p. 296—333.
An informative discussion of left-wing attacks on the privileged status of the Churches during 1918—19. The Left insisted that religion should become a purely private affair, and that in consequence the institutional influence of the Churches in schools, certain professions, etc. must be abolished altogether. Such proposals constituted a fundamental threat to the whole position of the Churches as they had evolved since at least the early nineteenth century. This paper also examines the nature of the resistance to the Left's proposals, but the struggle continued unabated and largely unresolved into the Weimar Republic.

ZIPFEL, Friedrich.
Kirchenkampf in Deutschland 1933—1945: Religionsverfolgung und Selbstbehauptung der Kirchen in nationalsozialistischer Zeit. Berlin: de Gruyter (1965), 571 pp.
A standard work. Some background to the pre-1933 situation is provided.

B. CATHOLIC

ADOLPH, Walter.
Erich Klausener. Berlin: de Gruyter (1955).
An informative and sympathetic portrait of the distinguished Catholic lay leader, who was chairman of the Catholic Action organization.

ALTMANN, Wolfgang.
See his work in section 11.

BECKER, Josef.
See his article in section 6B(vi).

BIERBAUM, Max.
Nicht Lob nicht Furcht: das Leben des Kardinals von Galen nach unveröffentlichten Briefen und Dokumenten. Münster: Verlag Regensberg (1955), 222 pp.
A fairly reasonable biography of Clemens August von Galen (1878—1946), the somewhat unorthodox Bishop of Münster. Extracts referring to the pre-1933 era are of some interest because they reveal the attitude to the Weimar Republic (unrepresentative though it may be) of a leading churchman. He was a particularly outspoken critic of National Socialism before Hitler came to power.

BREUNING, Klaus.
Die Vision des Reiches: deutscher Katholizismus zwischen Demokratie und Diktatur, 1929—1934.
Munich: Hueber Verlag (1969), 403 pp.
A full and detailed study, which underlines the conservative-authoritarian trends in German Catholicism, and how these trends grew stronger after 1929. Thus in 1933 an accommodation of sorts between the National Socialist régime and the Catholic Church became a temporary possibility.

BUSSMANN, Walter.
"Der deutsche Katholizismus im Jahre 1933".
In Walter Bussmann. *Wandel und Kontinuität in Politik und Geschichte.* Boppard: Boldt (1973), p. 187—211.
Most of this essay discusses the response and adjustment of German Catholicism to the Hitler régime. The author also has a few instructive things to say about Catholic developments before 1933.

DEUERLEIN, Ernst.
Der deutsche Katholizismus 1933. Osnabrück:
Fromm Verlag (1963), 186 pp.
The first half of this book (p. 13—84) provides a scholarly
and informative assessment of the weaknesses and strengths
of German Catholicism.

DIRKS, Walter.
"Katholizismus und Nationalsozialismus".
Frankfurter Hefte, vol. 18 (1963), p. 515—22.
Reproduces an article written in 1932 on the subject,
drawing attention to elements of common ground between
the two.

DOETSCH, Wilhelm J.
Württembergs Katholiken unterm Hakenkreuz
1930—1935. Stuttgart: Kohlhammer (1969),
223 pp.
Mostly concerned with a description of the post-1933 situation of Catholics in Württemberg; what is said about their
position before Hitler is only mildly interesting.

DÜLMEN, Richard von.
See his article in section 16A(vi).

ESCHENBURG, Theodor.
"Carl Sonnenschein". *Vierteljahrshefte für*
Zeitgeschichte, vol. 11, pt. 4 (1963), p. 333—61.
A sympathetic review of the life and work of the outstanding Catholic apologist and propagandist who was also
one of the most active leaders of the left-wing, reformist/
social trend in German Catholicism. He went to considerable
lengths to bring Catholics out of their alleged "ghetto
mentality" and take a responsible part in public affairs.
Eschenburg argues that Sonnenschein (1876—1929) was the
only real charismatic Catholic personality of the 1890—1933
era.

FERBER, Martin.
"Der Weg Martin Spahns: zur Ideengeschichte des
politischen Rechtskatholizismus". *Hochland*,
vol. 62, pt. 2 (1970), p. 218—29.
A brief look at Spahn's ideas and political involvement
before and after 1918. He was the leading Catholic member
of the DNVP *Reichstag* faction, but in 1933 he joined the
NSDAP.

FRANZ-WILLING, Georg.
See his work in section 9C.

GOTTWALD, Herbert.
See his article in section 16A(vi).

GREIVE, Hermann.
Theologie und Ideologie: Katholizismus und
Judentum in Deutschland und Österreich
1918—1935. Heidelberg: Lambert Schneider
(1969), 320 pp.
A useful pioneering work in a controversial field. The
relationship between Catholics and Jews on a theological
and political level showed many similarities in Germany and
Austria. A great deal of uneasiness and even distrust was
mutually shared. Not all important aspects of the problem
are raised here, but Greive has produced a thought-provoking
study.

HEINE, Ludwig.
Geschichte des Kirchenkampfes in der Grenzmark
Posen-Westpreussen 1930—1940. Göttingen:
Vandenhoeck & Ruprecht (1961), 115 pp.
Rather sketchy, and not much use for the pre-1933 period.

LEWY, Guenter.
The Catholic Church and Nazi Germany. London:
Weidenfeld & Nicolson (1964), 416 pp.
Only the first chapter (p. 3—24) has anything to say about
the attitude of German Catholicism to National Socialism
before 1933. But here, as throughout the book as a whole,
the author is too critical of the Church's role, though he is
right to stress the anti-semitic and authoritarian tendencies
within the Church which made a compromise possible with
the National Socialists in 1933.

LUTZ, Heinrich.
Demokratie im Zwielicht: der Weg der deutschen
Katholiken aus dem Kaiserreich in die Republik
1914—1925. Munich: Kösel Verlag (1963), 143 pp.
Chapters IV and V relate to the Weimar era, and Lutz
argues that the Catholic Right after 1918 (represented by
persons such as Guardini and Carl Schmitt) helped prepare
the way for dictatorship. Only a minority of Catholics were
really democratic and pro-republican, he adds. His thesis,
however, needs more detailed documentation; and he does
not take full account of different phases in Catholic
attitudes after 1918.

MÜLLER, Hans.
"Der deutsche Katholizismus 1918/1919".
Geschichte in Wissenschaft und Unterricht, vol. 17,
pt. 9 (1966), p. 521—36.
A tentative discussion of the role played by Catholicism in
1918—19, and especially of the nature of the new relationship between Church and state, and Church and democracy.
As a whole, the Church rejected the November Revolution
and despaired of the advances made by atheism and
Bolshevism. Adjustment to such a situation was a painful
and uncomfortable process.

MÜLLER, Hans (ed.).
See his work in section 29.

NATTERER, Alois.
Der bayerische Klerus in der Zeit dreier
Revolutionen, 1918—1933—1945: 25 Jahre
Klerusverband, 1920—1945. Munich: Katholische
Kirche Bayerns (1946), 427 pp.
Overwhelmingly apologetic in tone in describing how the
Church coped with the November Revolution, the National
Socialist seizure of power, and the total collapse of 1945.

NITZSCHKE, Volker.
See his work in section 17C.

REPGEN, Konrad.
Hitlers Machtergreifung und der deutsche
Katholizismus. Saarbrücken (1967).
A useful general survey.

RHODES, Anthony.
The Vatican in the Age of the Dictators,
1922—1945. London: Hodder & Stoughton (1973),
383 pp.
A broad survey of the policies of the Vatican. For the pre-
1933 period in Germany, the author states that the Pope
was more or less satisfied with the Concordats in Bavaria
and Prussia, but adds incorrectly that the Pope did not want
a general Reich Concordat. Much of the rest of the book is
highly unsatisfactory in terms of factual accuracy and
sound interpretation.

RUST, Hendrik.
Die Rechtsnatur von Konkordaten und Kirchen-
verträgen unter besonderer Berücksichtigung der
bayerischen Verträge von 1924. Dissertation,
University of Munich (1964).
A rather heavy legalistic discussion with little historical
background.

SCHARNAGL, A.
"Das Reichskonkordat und die Länderkonkordate
als Konkordatssystem". *Historisches Jahrbuch*,
vol. 74 (1955), p. 584—607.
Discusses constitutional and legal implications of Concordat
arrangements, and the effectiveness of Concordats themselves.

SCHOELEN, Georg.
Der Volksverein für das katholische Deutschland
1890—1933: eine Bibliographie. Mönchengladbach:
Staatsbibliothek (1974), 110 pp.
A useful source of reference.

SPAEL, Wilhelm.
Das katholische Deutschland im 20. Jahrhundert:
seine Pionier- und Krisenzeiten 1890—1945.
Würzburg: Echter (1964), 376 pp.
A well written and informative general introduction,
though many complex problems are given somewhat simplified treatment. Pages 195—289 deal with the Weimar era.

STEGMANN, Franz J.
Der soziale Katholizismus und die Mitbestimmung
in Deutschland: von Beginn der Industrialisierung
bis zum Jahre 1933. Munich: Schöningh (1974),
230 pp.
This is a fairly good introduction to an important but
generally neglected theme. Stegmann stresses the existence
from the early phase of industrialization in Germany of
active Catholic concern for the employee. He discusses the
question of codetermination which came to the fore during
the Weimar Republic, and the positive attitude adopted
towards the concept by many Catholics.

VOLK, Ludwig.
Das Reichskonkordat vom 20. Juli 1933: von den
Ansätzen in der Weimarer Republik bis zur
Ratifizierung am 10. September 1933. Mainz:
Matthias-Grünewald-Verlag (1972), 265 pp.
It is Volk's discussion of the background to the 1933
Concordat which is useful for our purposes. In exploring
the motives of both sides in wanting an agreement, he goes
back into the Weimar period, analysing various attempts
made then to reach a formal understanding; the Prussian
(1929) and Bavarian (1924) Concordats are used as examples
of what could be achieved. He discusses why no agreement
emerged on a national level between the Catholic Church
and the Weimar Republic (largely political factors were
involved). A thorough and authoritative study.

VOLK, Ludwig.
Bayerns Episkopat und Klerus in der Auseinandersetzung mit dem Nationalsozialismus 1930—34.
Mainz: Matthias-Grünewald-Verlag (1965), 216 pp.
A too apologetic account of the relationship between the
Bavarian Catholic hierarchy and National Socialism. Volk is
right to underline the bishops' condemnation of Hitler's
extreme nationalism and racialism, but he does not give as
much emphasis as he should to the innate conservatism and
anti-democratic outlook of the same bishops, a factor
which in 1933 made the Church as a whole susceptible to
National Socialism. Volk pays much attention to the role of
Cardinal Faulhaber, the leading Catholic cleric in Bavaria.

VOLK, Ludwig (ed.).
Akten Kardinal Michael von Faulhabers
1917—1945. Vol I: 1917—34. Mainz: Matthias-
Grünewald-Verlag (1975), 1007 pp.
An indispensable documentary source not only for comprehending the outlook of this important churchman, but also
for gaining further insight into the political attitudes of the
Catholic Church during the Weimar era. Volume I contains
some 450 documents, most of them not published before,
taken from the Faulhaber papers.

ZEENDER, John K.
"The German Catholics and the Presidential
Election of 1925". *Journal of Modern History*,
vol. 35, pt. 4 (1963), p. 366—81.
The author discusses the importance of the dissident anti-
democratic Catholic vote in securing Hindenburg's election.
These Catholics hoped to exploit Hindenburg's victory to
disrupt the working relationship between the Centre Party
and the SPD. Zeender defines the nature of the sociological
composition and geographical location of the Catholic vote
for Hindenburg and the connection between that development and the orientation of the Centre Party after April
1925 (the date of the election). Despite a suspicion that
Zeender may have got his arithmetic wrong, the essay is
informative.

ZEENDER, John K.
"German Catholics and the Concept of an Interconfessional Party 1900—1922". *Journal of
Central European Affairs*, vol. 23, pt. 4 (1963—64),
p. 424—39.
An analysis of the reasons why some Catholics thought in
interconfessional terms and of how such ideas were thwarted
by the opposition of the conservative-minded Catholic
establishment. Stegerwald was, of course, a leading advocate of interconfessionalism.

C. PROTESTANT

ARNDT, Ino.
Die Judenfrage im Licht der evangelischen
Sonntagsblätter von 1918—1933. Dissertation,
University of Tübingen (1960).
An analysis of how Protestant Sunday newspapers and
magazines treated the Jewish question. It is highly questionable whether any one source of information can produce a
representative viewpoint, and Arndt's conclusions must be
regarded with considerable caution.

ALTMANN, Wolfgang.
See his work in section 11.

BRAMSTED, Ernst.
"The Position of the Protestant Church in
Germany, 1871—1933, Part II. The Church during
the Weimar Republic." *Journal of Religious
History*, vol. 3, pt. 1 (1964), p. 61—79.
Publishes in English translation six important documents
which reveal the changing attitude of the Protestant Church
leadership towards the Weimar Republic.

BREDENDICK, Walter.
Zwischen Revolution und Restauration: zur
Entwicklung im deutschen Protestantismus
während der Novemberrevolution und in der
Weimarer Republik. Berlin: Union-Verlag (1969),
54 pp.
A brief but concise and useful review of Protestantism's
response to the Revolution and the changes that marked
the establishment of a new form of state after 1919.

BÜHLER, Karl-Werner.
See his work in section 16A(vi).

CHRIST, Herbert.
Der politische Protestantismus in der Weimarer
Republik. Dissertation, University of Bonn (1966).
An extensively documented study of the formation of
Protestant political attitudes. However, too many sweeping
conclusions undermine the usefulness of the work.

DAHM, Karl-Wilhelm.
Pfarrer und Politik: soziale Position und politische
Mentalität des deutschen evangelischen
Pfarrerstandes zwischen 1918 und 1933. Cologne:
Westdeutscher Verlag (1965), 225 pp.
A very interesting study of considerable value. The author
shows that as the social status of the Protestant pastor
declined after 1918, so his political attitudes became more
radical, and by 1930–33, most pastors supported the
extreme Right (DNVP and NSDAP). He discusses the
reasons for the pastors' social decline — the falling influence
of religion generally in a liberal and more questioning kind
of society, lack of support for the Church from the
Republic, intellectual hostility, etc. Dahm sees the pastor's
flight into political extremism as a sign of his failure to
come to terms politically, ideologically, and psychologically
with the Republic.

DAIIM, Karl-Wilhelm.
"German Protestantism and Politics 1919–39".
Journal of Contemporary History, vol. 3, pt. 1
(1968), p. 29–49.
More or less based on material in his book. Dahm discusses
the failure of Protestantism to meet the challenges of the
Weimar era. The political mentality of Protestants is analysed
under four headings: Revolution (1918–19), the Republic,
Nation, and Hitler. Apart from the widespread conservative-
authoritarian attitudes among the Protestant clergy, Dahm
also stresses the existence of a powerful underlying anti-
semitism.

DIEPHOUSE, David.
The Protestant Church in Württemberg
1918–1925: Church, State and Society in the
Weimar Republic. Dissertation, Princeton
University (1974).
A case study of the Protestant Church's role in this liberal
and predominantly Protestant state. The Revolution of
1918 did not drastically disturb the pattern of Church-state
relations in the province, so by the mid-1920s a comfor-
table modus vivendi had been reached between them. But
nonetheless, the Church had lost a substantial degree of its
former status and moral authority, and in Weimar remained
an essentially middle class institution.

GAEDE, Reinhard.
Kirche, Christen, Krieg und Frieden: die
Diskussion im deutschen Protestantismus während
der Weimarer Zeit. Hamburg: Reich Verlag (1975),
129 pp.
A critical appraisal of the value of the discussion among
Protestants as they confronted complex problems and a
series of dilemmas during the republican period.

GRESCHAT, Martin.
Der deutsche Protestantismus im Revolutionsjahr
1918–19. Witten: Luther-Verlag (1974), 202 pp.
A valuable and clear study, mainly of the theological and
moral problems which the Protestant Church and laity had
to face up to as a result of the collapse of the monarchy and
all that that institution meant for them.

GUTTERIDGE, Richard.
Open Thy Mouth for the Dumb: the German
Evangelical Church and the Jews 1879–1950.
Oxford: Basil Blackwell (1975), 266 pp.
A comprehensive analysis of the attitudes of a cross-section
of German Protestants to the Jewish question. One important theme of continuity which the author stresses is
anti-semitism, and its wide prevalence among the ranks of
the Protestant clergy.

KINDER, Christian.
Neue Beiträge zur Geschichte der evangelischen
Kirche in Schleswig-Holstein und im Reich
1924–1945. Flensburg: Karfeld Verlag (1964),
238 pp.
The author is a former member of the notorious "German
Christians", the pro-National Socialist group that appeared
in the Evangelical Church even before 1933. His account of
the Church, its activities, policies, and aims, defends the
German Christian attitude, proving that he has in fact
learned nothing.

KÖHLER, Günter.
Die Auswirkungen der Novemberrevolution von
1918 auf die altpreussische evangelische
Landeskirche. Berlin: Ernst-Reuter-Gesellschaft
(1967), 219 pp.
A competent, clearly expressed work which, however,
comes to no startling conclusions.

KUPISCH, Karl.
Das Jahrhundert des Sozialismus und die Kirche.
Berlin: de Gruyter (1958).
A general survey of the often hostile relationship between
the SPD and the Protestant Church from the 1860s to the
post-Second World War period.

KUPISCH, Karl.
"Strömungen der evangelischen Kirche in der
Weimarer Republik". Archiv für Sozialgeschichte,
vol. 11 (1971), p. 373–415.
A good analysis of major trends in Protestant official
thought towards important political and social questions
in the Weimar Republic.

KUPISCH, Karl.
Zwischen Idealismus und Massendemokratie: eine
Geschichte der evangelischen Kirche in Deutschland
von 1815–1945. Berlin: Lettner-Verlag (1955),
296 pp.
Designed for the general reader, this book takes a very
broad look at how the Protestant Church has changed with
the times, and the limitations of such changes. Chapters
8–10 cover 1918–33.

MEHNERT, Gottfried.
Evangelische Kirche und Politik 1917–1919: die
politischen Strömungen im deutschen
Protestantismus von der Julikrise 1917 bis zum
Herbst 1919. Düsseldorf: Droste (1959), 254 pp.
A balanced and objective study of the political response of
the Protestant clergy to developments in German politics
1917–19. Most of the clergy were right-wing, of course,
and bitterly resented the consequences of the November
Revolution for their social and pastoral status. The involvement of the clergy in post-1918 political parties is discussed
only in cursory terms.

MOTSCHMANN, Klaus.
Evangelische Kirche und preussischer Staat in den Anfängen der Weimarer Republik: Möglichkeiten und Grenzen ihrer Zusammenarbeit. Lübeck: Matthiesen (1969), 148 pp.

Not a very informative study of Church-Prussian relations, despite the considerable factual material the author has presented. The material is not sufficiently interpreted and the reader is obliged to form most of his own conclusions. The author believes that relations between Church and state were not as hostile as is generally believed, and provides examples of their co-operation. To what extent such co-operation was typical of a wider atmosphere of mutual tolerance he does not say. Indeed, the author's own evidence would seem clearly to contradict his thesis about Church-state co-operation.

NORDEN, Günther van.
Kirche in der Krise: die Stellung der evangelischen Kirche zum nationalsozialistischen Staat im Jahre 1933. Düsseldorf: Presse der Evangelischen Kirche im Rheinland (1963), 211 pp.

Absurdly tendentious and apologetic in many instances.

SCHÄFER, Gerhard.
Die evangelische Landeskirche in Württemberg: eine Dokumentation zum Kirchenkampf. Vol. I: Um das politische Engagement der Kirche 1932/33. Stuttgart: Calwer-Verlag (1971), 607 pp.

An excellent documentary work which puts the right perspective on the political attitudes of the Church in Württemberg during the last days of Weimar and early Hitler period. The Protestant Church in Württemberg had not attracted the working classes after 1918, and as it was essentially an institution of the middle classes the Church's politics could not help but reflect the changing attitudes of the bourgeoisie.

SCHOLDER, Klaus.
"Die evangelische Kirche und das Jahr 1933". *Geschichte in Wissenschaft und Unterricht,* vol. 16, pt. 11 (1965), p. 700—14.

Says nothing that has not been said better or in more detail in other studies.

SCHOLDER, Klaus.
"Die evangelische Kirche in der Sicht der national-sozialistischen Führung bis zum Kriegsausbruch". *Vierteljahrshefte für Zeitgeschichte,* vol. 16, pt. 1 (1968), p. 15—35.

The author questions the commonly held belief that Hitler was from the beginning deeply hostile to the Protestant Church. He argues that there is enough evidence from the 1927—34 period to show that Hitler was serious about harnessing the Church to his régime in the form of a new evangelical *Reichskirche.* Scholder refers to conversations along these lines that Hitler had with Protestant Church leaders in 1927 and 1930. Also, before 1933 Hitler could not afford to pursue a destructive policy towards the Church because most of the NSDAP support came from Protestants. Scholder's argument is interesting but not entirely convincing because Hitler's moderate approach before 1933 was dictated by the requirements of political expediency.

TROELTSCH, Ernst.
See entries under his name in section 15C(ii).

WRIGHT, Jonathan.
"Above Parties": the Political Attitudes of the German Church Leadership 1918—1933. London: Oxford University Press (1974), 216 pp.

This book's central thesis is that the Protestant Church leadership was more accommodating towards the Weimar Republic than has been previously believed. But Wright seems to have made the same fatal error as Klaus Motschmann in his study (see earlier in this section). He has taken examples of toleration and co-operation to indicate something more fundamental and comprehensive than is warranted. Too often, he has ignored or skimmed over important evidence which conclusively substantiates the predominant conservative-nationalist-authoritarian outlook of the Church, and in the last analysis this had to mean the Church's deep hostility to the values the Republic represented.

The Jews and Anti-Semitism

11

ADLER, Hans G.
Die Juden in Deutschland: von der Aufklärung bis
zum Nationalsozialismus. Munich: Kösel-Verlag
(1960), 178 pp.
A broad survey of the position of Jews in German society
through the centuries. Adler strongly suggests that racial
anti-semitism of the type emerging during the 1920s and
1930s was the inevitable consequence of long established
anti-semitic feeling in Germany. The thesis is highly
questionable, of course; in addition, the full background to
the reasons for anti-semitism is not discussed. Only p. 139—
55 refer to the Weimar period.

ADLER-RUDEL, S.; BAECK, Leo.
Ostjuden in Deutschland 1880—1940: zugleich
eine Geschichte der Organisationen die sie
betreuten. Tübingen: Mohr (1959), 175 pp.
An interesting survey of the position of those Eastern Jews
who came into Germany, particularly following the First
World War. Their social, economic and political situation is
reviewed here in competent fashion, though the topic needs
more detailed study.

ALTMANN, Alexander.
"The German Rabbi: 1910—1939". *Yearbook of
the Leo Baeck Institute*, vol. 19 (1974), p. 31—50.
The author speaks admiringly of the new type of rabbi who
emerged in Germany between the wars, and provides a
characterization. Above all, the German rabbi was an intellectual and scholar. There is interesting data on the numbers and geographical location of rabbis.

ALTMANN, Wolfgang.
Die Judenfrage in evangelischen und katholischen
Zeitschriften zwischen 1918 und 1933. Disser-
tation, University of Munich (1971).
The author has gathered a great deal of material to illustrate
Catholic and Protestant attitudes towards the Jewish ques-
tion. The increasing emphasis during the course of the
Weimar era on anti-semitic themes by both confessional
publications is made clear.

ANGRESS, Werner T.
"Juden im politischen Leben der Revolutionszeit".
In Werner E. Mosse & Arnold Paucker (eds.).
*Deutsches Judentum in Krieg und Revolution
1916—1923: ein Sammelband.* Tübingen: Mohr
(1971).

A sober, scholarly analysis of the role of Jews in the
political upheavals of the revolutionary period 1918—19.
The author draws a contrast between the well publicized
radical politics of individual Jews such as Kurt Eisner or
Rosa Luxemburg, and the moderation of the mass of Jews.
The overwhelming proportion of Jews during the Revolution
and afterwards were essentially unpolitical and reticent in
political debate.

ARNDT, Ino.
See section 10C for review.

BEIN, Alex.
"The Jewish Parasite — Notes on the Semantics of
the Jewish Problem, with Special Reference to
Germany". *Yearbook of the Leo Baeck Institute*,
vol. 9 (1964), p. 3—40.
Included are a number of references to Hitler's and
Rosenberg's ideas on the Jews, with extracts from the
National Socialist leaders' works.

BEIN, Alex.
"Die Judenfrage in der Literatur des modernen
Antisemitismus als Vorbereitung zur 'Endlösung' ".
Bulletin des Leo Baeck Instituts, no. 21, vol. 6
(1963).
The works of various neo-conservative (Spengler) and
racialist (Hans Blüher) writers are included in this interesting
analysis.

BERNSTEIN, Reiner.
See his work in section 16A(vii).

BOLKOSKY, Sidney M.
The Distorted Image: German-Jewish Perceptions
of Germans and Germany 1918—1935. Dissertation, State University of New York (1973).
The author shows that Jewish responses to the rise of
National Socialism were relatively calm, largely because the
Jews underestimated the potential destructive capability of
the movement. Many Jews tried to demonstrate more
openly their Germanness, scores of Jewish publications
optimistically reported on the improving relations between
the two peoples over the centuries, and the Germans were
depicted as reasonable open-minded people. But all this
was, of course, an illusion which was generated despite
stark reality. A valuable study.

CHANOCH, Rinott.
See his work in section 18E.

COHN, Ernst T.
"Three Jewish Lawyers of Germany". *Yearbook of the Leo Baeck Institute*, vol. 17 (1972), p. 155—78.
Discusses the lives and works of Max Hachenburg of Mannheim, Max Pappenheim, a law professor at Kiel University before 1914, and Otto Opet. All three made a name for themselves in legal circles.

COHN, Norman.
Warrant for Genocide: the Myth of the Jewish World Conspiracy and the Protocols of the Elders of Zion. London: Eyre & Spottiswoode (1967), 303 pp.
The author's main concern is to describe how anti-semitism became an integral part of modern conspiracy theories despite the fact that the Protocols were a forgery of the Russian secret police. Cohn argues that National Socialism and anti-semitism drew considerable impetus from the Jewish conspiracy theory, though he underplays Hitler's notion of the Jews as bacilli fit only for extermination.

EDELHEIM-MUEHSAM, Margaret T.
See her articles in section 16A(vii).

EISNER, Ruth.
Nicht wir allein . . . . Aus dem Tagebuch einer Berliner Jüdin. Berlin: Arani-Verlag (1971), 296 pp.
Not especially interesting or relevant to Weimar.

FLITNER, Andreas (ed.).
Deutsches Geistesleben und Nationalsozialismus: eine Vortragsreihe der Universität Tübingen. Tübingen: Wunderlich (1965), 243 pp.
The major theme of this series of lectures is the trends in German intellectual and cultural life which gave rise to racial anti-semitism.

GREIVE, Hermann.
See his work in section 10B.

GRUENEWALD, Max.
See his article in section 16A(vii).

GUTTERIDGE, Richard.
See his work in section 10C.

HAAG, John.
See his article under Spann in section 15C(ii).

HAMBURGER, Ernst.
Jews, Democracy, and Weimar Germany. New York: Leo Baeck Institute (1973), 31 pp.
Originally delivered as a lecture in the Leo Baeck Memorial Series, this paper examines the political commitment of Jews to liberal and democratic ideas in the Weimar era.

HERZSTEIN, Robert E.
"Richard Wagner at the Crossroads of German Anti-Semitism, 1848—1933: a Reinterpretation". *Zeitschrift für die Geschichte der Juden*, vol. 4 (1967), p. 119—40.
Argues that Wagner's anti-semitism is a key for understanding the transformation from a pre-industrial type of cultural and religious anti-semitism to the racial anti-semitism that led to the extermination of Jews under Hitler.

HEUSS, Theodor.
An und über Juden. Düsseldorf: Econ-Verlag (1964), 231 pp.
A collection of the author's writings and speeches 1906—63 which discuss the position of Jews in German society, and also the nature of the Jewish question. Most interesting.

HIRSCHBERG, Alfred.
"Ludwig Hollaender, Director of the C.V.". *Yearbook of the Leo Baeck Institute*, vol. 7 (1962), p. 39—74.
A biographical sketch of Hollaender (1877—1936), former director of the Central-Verein of German Citizens of the Jewish Faith.

HUSS, Hermann; **SCHRÖDER**, Andreas (eds.).
Antisemitismus. Frankfurt: Lang (1965).
A valuable collection of essays by various hands.

JOSPE, Alfred.
"A Profession in Transition — the German Rabbinate 1910—1939". *Yearbook of the Leo Baeck Institute*, vol. 19 (1974), p. 51—62.
Examines certain important factors which affected the role and functions of the rabbi, including the rapid urbanization of the Jewish community, the adoption of the system of district rabbinates in Prussia in the mid-1920s, and the attempts of younger rabbis to become better acquainted with the people.

KNUETTER, Hans-Helmuth.
Die Juden und die deutsche Linke in der Weimarer Republik 1918—1933. Düsseldorf: Droste (1971), 259 pp.
An examination of the relationship between Jews and the left-wing parties. The author shows that the majority of Jews were not radical revolutionaries or even socialists, but solid democrats whose support went to the DDP rather than the SPD or KPD. The socialist parties struggled against anti-semitism as a factor in political debate, but there was some evidence of anti-semitic feeling in certain trade unions and even in the KPD leadership. The book as a whole is a disappointment: it provides no new interpretations or conclusions, is repetitious, does not satisfactorily define the term "Jew", and fails to make a proper assessment of the Jewish relationship to the DDP.

LAQUEUR, Walter.
See his article in section 18B.

MEHRMANN, W.
See his work in section 18B.

MOSSE, George L.
See his work in section 15C(i).

MOSSE, George L.
See his article in section 6B(i).

MOSSE, Werner E; **PAUCKER**, Arnold (eds.).
Deutsches Judentum in Krieg und Revolution 1916—1923: ein Sammelband. Tübingen: Mohr (1971), 704 pp.
An important contribution to our understanding of German-Jewish relations in this period. The essays are all very good and of note for students of Weimar is Werner Angress's paper (see earlier in this section).

116

MOSSE, Werner E. (ed.).
Entscheidungsjahr 1932: zur Judenfrage in der Endphase der Weimarer Republik. Tübingen: Mohr (1966), 608 pp. 2nd and enlarged ed.
Admirably complements the aforementioned volume. All fourteen papers are interesting and scholarly. The most important can be briefly summarized as follows. George L. Mosse discusses the widespread desire among Germans to escape from modern industrial society and their tendency to blame the Jews for creating this unwanted modernity. Werner E. Mosse writes on the decline of the Weimar Republic and the Jews, and contributes a second piece on the attitudes of the German Right towards Jews. Arnold Paucker describes the attempts of patriotic Jews to demonstrate their loyalty and Germanness, but also how Jewish organizations helped the struggle against anti-republican forces in 1931—32. Eva Reichmann's paper is concerned with debates on the Jewish question 1930—32.

NIEWYK, Donald L.
"Jews and the Courts in Weimar Germany". *Jewish Social Studies*, vol. 37 (Spring 1975), p. 99—113.
An interesting but rather tentative survey.

NIEWYK, Donald L.
"The Economic and Cultural Role of the Jews in the Weimar Republic". *Yearbook of the Leo Baeck Institute*, vol. 16 (1971), p. 163—73.
Attempts a balanced view of the significance of the Jewish contribution to the German economy and culture by presenting interesting data regarding their pattern of occupation and their cultural achievements: the author concludes that while Jews were useful rather than essential to the economy, their role in culture was much more important and without them Weimar culture would have lost a great deal of its richness and diversity.

PALMON, J. E.
"Eine Judendebatte mit Kommunisten in den Tagen der Weimarer Republik". *Zeitschrift für die Geschichte der Juden*, vol. 4 (1967), p. 147—151.
A few words on the KPD campaign led by Otto Heller to attract revolutionary-inclined Jewish youth to the party. The author notes the contradictions in the Communist appeal, and a famous debate on the KPD-Jewish relationship in Berlin in 1931.

PAUCKER, Arnold.
Der jüdische Abwehrkampf gegen Anti-Semitismus und Nationalsozialismus in den letzten Jahren der Weimarer Republik. Hamburg: Leibniz-Verlag (1968), 311 pp.
An important work which analyses the various ways in which German Jewry responded to the increasing anti-semitism of the last years of the Republic. The author focuses attention on the activities of the assimilationist Central-Verein of German Citizens of the Jewish Faith; he documents the CV's political commitment to the DDP (later the SPD) and the Republic. The major conclusion of the book is that the Jews were too fragmented to offer any worthwhile resistance to National Socialism, and, in any case, too many of them did not take Hitler seriously enough.

PIERSON, Ruth.
See her article in section 8C.

PINSON, Kippel S. (ed.).
Essays on Antisemitism. New York: Conference in Jewish Relations (1946), 269 pp.
A rather uneven collection of papers which discuss anti-semitism from the early centuries to the twentieth century. The essay to note is that by Waldemar Gurian, "Anti-Semitism in Modern Germany", a broad but instructive survey.

PULZER, Peter G.
The Rise of Political Anti-Semitism in Germany and Austria: 1867—1918. New York: John Wiley (1964), 364 pp.
For students of Weimar a valuable, detailed introduction to racial anti-semitism in twentieth century Germany.

REICHMANN, Eva.
"Die Lage der Juden in der Weimarer Republik". In *Die Reichskristallnacht: der Antisemitismus in der deutschen Geschichte.* Bonn: Friedrich-Ebert-Stiftung (1959), p. 19—31.
A short but scholarly overall view of the Jewish situation.

SAUER, Paul.
Die jüdischen Gemeinden in Württemberg und Hohenzollern: zur Geschichte der Juden in Württemberg 1924—1939. Stuttgart: Kohlhammer (1966), 230 pp.
A well documented and objective description of the Jewish community, its size, economic and social status, and political attitudes.

SCHOEPS, Hans-Joachim.
Bereit für Deutschland. Der Patriotismus deutscher Juden und der Nationalsozialismus. Frühe Schriften 1930—1939: eine historische Dokumentation. Berlin: Haude & Spener (1970), 320 pp.
A collection of the author's articles written during 1930—39 which testify to the patriotism of many German Jews (including the author), but also to the despair and bewilderment into which the same Jews were plunged in 1930 with the virtual collapse of German liberalism (the DDP, to which the majority of Jews had given allegiance 1919—30, broke up in early 1930).

SCHWARZ, Stefan.
Die Juden in Bayern im Wandel der Zeiten. Munich: Kösel-Verlag (1963).
A general and rather unsatisfactory narrative of the Jewish population in Bavaria over the centuries.

SMOTRICZ, Israel.
See his article in section 6B(vii)(a).

STRAUS, Rahel.
Wir lebten in Deutschland: Erinnerungen einer deutschen Jüdin 1880—1933. Stuttgart: Deutsche Verlagsanstalt (1961), 307 pp.
The author was one of the first female medical doctors in Germany, a pioneer of women's liberation, and a convinced Zionist. The book's value lies in the insight it provides into the character of German intellectual Jewry before 1933.

TOURY, Jacob.
"Organizational Problems of German Jewry — Steps towards the Establishment of a Central Organization (1893—1920)". *Yearbook of the Leo Baeck Institute*, vol. 13 (1968), p. 57—88.
As regards the post-1918 period, such efforts included the "Congress Movement" 1918—19, but efforts proved abortive in 1920. A central organization did not in fact appear until the Third Reich era.

TOURY, Jacob.
Die politischen Orientierungen der Juden in Deutschland, von Jena bis Weimar. Tübingen: Mohr (1966), 387 pp.
Outline of Jewish political attitudes from the early nineteenth century to 1933; contains no new conclusions. In Weimar, certain individual Jews became prominent in radical left-wing politics, but most Jews preferred a moderate approach to parliamentary democracy.

WELTSCH, Robert (ed.).
Deutsches Judentum: Aufstieg und Krise. Gestalten, Ideen, Werke: 14 Monographien. Stuttgart: Deutsche Verlagsanstalt (1963), 426 pp.
A collection of fourteen well written essays on various aspects of German Jewry in the nineteenth and twentieth centuries.

The Armed Forces

A. THE ARMY (REICHSWEHR)

(i) General

BREDOW, Wilfried von.
"Die Demokratie und ihre Wächter: zum Problem
der Integration von Streitkräften in die Gesellschaft". *Das Parlament: Aus Politik und
Zeitgeschichte*, B50 (11.12.1971).
A discussion of the problem of militarism in general and the
army's position in state and society. Also has something to
say about the social composition of the officer corps in the
Reichswehr.

BURDICK, Charles B.
"German Military Planning and France 1930—
1938". *World Affairs Quarterly*, vol. 30 (1959—60),
p. 299—313.
A brief review of the consideration given to France in the
German army's war contingency plans.

CASTELLAN, Georges.
Le Réarmament clandestin du Reich 1930—1935.
Paris: Plon (1954), 550 pp.
An informative study based to a large extent on material
from the files of the French *Deuxième Bureau.* The first
part of the book deals with the organization and equipment
of the army, finance, the structure of the High Command,
and the *Reichswehr's* relations with the Red Army. The
second half discusses Germany's war potential, strategy, and
other aspects. The author sees decisive developments in the
army as having taken place in the autumn of 1931, as the
army believed a war against Poland would be necessary to
redress the injustices of Versailles. The value of the book
is not its hypothesis, which is familiar, but the interesting
primary material it presents from French sources.

DEMETER, Karl.
The German Officer Corps in Society and State:
1650—1945. London: Weidenfeld and Nicolson
(1965), 414 pp. English ed.
The book is arranged in five sections, within each of which
different aspects of the officer corps are analysed:
provenance, education, code of honour, relation to state
and to society. A reliable discussion, on the whole, of the
evolution of the officer corps.

ECKHARDT, Andreas.
"Die Militärmusik in der Reichswehr". *Wehrwissenschaftliche Rundschau*, vol. 19, pt. 1 (1969),
p. 41—56.
An interesting footnote.

FABER DU FAUR, Moriz von.
Macht und Ohnmacht: Erinnerungen eines alten
Offiziers. Stuttgart: Günther (1953), 296 pp.
Moderately useful.

GAERTNER, Franz von.
Die Reichswehr in der Weimarer Republik:
erlebte Geschichte. Darmstadt: Fundus-Verlag
(1969), 158 pp.
A chronicle of personal experiences which provides a few
insights into the *esprit de corps* in the *Reichswehr.*

GERSDORFF, Ursula von.
"Frauen in der Nachrichtentruppe 1918—1920".
Wehrwissenschaftliche Rundschau, vol. 17, pt. 4
(1967), p. 229—36.
Useful in pointing out the generally neglected fact that
women were employed in reasonably important army posts.

GEYER, Michael.
"Die Wehrmacht der deutschen Republik ist die
Reichswehr: Bemerkungen zur neueren Literatur".
Militärgeschichtliche Mitteilungen, vol. 14, pt. 2
(1973), p. 152—99.
An excellent objective review of recent literature on the
Reichswehr.

GEYER, Michael.
"Das zweite Rüstungsprogramm (1930—1934)".
Militärgeschichtliche Mitteilungen, vol. 16, pt. 1
(1975), p. 125—72
Provides important documents pertaining to the armaments
programme.

HERZFELD, Hans.
**"Zur neueren Literatur über das Heeresproblem in
der deutschen Geschichte".** *Vierteljahrshefte für
Zeitgeschichte*, vol. 4, pt. 4 (1956), p. 361—86.
Balanced and scholarly appraisal of some recent publications on the history of the army and the problem of
militarism in Germany.

HERZFELD, Hans.
Das Problem des deutschen Heeres 1919—1945.
Laupheim: Steiner (1952), 24 pp.
Generalized observations on the fateful historical role of
the German army.

HEUSINGER, Adolf.
**Befehl im Widerstreit: Schicksalsstunden der
deutschen Armee, 1923—45.** Tübingen: Leins
Verlag (1950).
Of dubious value to serious students. Heusinger's treatment
of key problems facing the army is embellished with a
considerable degree of fantasy.

HILLGRUBER, Andreas.
**Grossmachtpolitik und Militarismus im 20.
Jahrhundert: 3 Beiträge zum Kontinuitätsproblem.**
Düsseldorf: Droste (1974), 67 pp.
A brief but important contribution to the debate on the
degree of continuity in modern German history, seen from
the perspective of the military's involvement.

HOSSBACH, Friedrich.
**Die Entwicklung des Oberbefehls über das Heer in
Brandenburg, Preussen und im deutschen Reich
von 1655—1945.** Würzburg: Holzner (1957).
The evolution of the army High Command structure is the
subject of this somewhat superficial study. The coverage of
the Weimar era in particular is not nearly deep enough.

HOWARD, Michael (ed.).
Soldiers and Government. London: Eyre and
Spottiswoode (1957), 192 pp.
Of the essays presented in this volume, the most notable is
that by F. L. Carsten (see under Carsten in Section 12A(ii)).

HÜRTEN, Heinz.
**"Das Wehrkreiskommando VI in den Wirren des
Frühjahrs 1920".** *Militärgeschichtliche Mitteil-
ungen*, vol. 15, pt. 2 (1974), p. 127—56.
An in-depth description of the reaction of the military
district in which the disorders emanating from the Kapp
Putsch took place.

KEHRIG, Manfred.
**Die Wiedereinrichtung des deutschen militärischen
Attachédienstes nach dem Ersten Weltkrieg
(1919—1933).** Boppard: Boldt (1966), 254 pp.
A useful consideration of the military/diplomatic role of
the attachés and their function within the limited army
organization of the Weimar period.

KERN, Wolfgang; SPERLING, Heinz.
**"Der deutsche Militarismus vom Ende des Ersten
Weltkrieges bis zur Zerschlagung der faschistischen
Diktatur".** *Zeitschrift für Militärgeschichte*, vol.
13, pt. 5 (1974), p. 562—71.
Quite unimportant.

KULBAKIN, Wilhelm D.
Die Militarisierung Deutschlands. East Berlin:
Dietz (1956), 227 pp.
The author concentrates on developments in the military
sphere and the role of government during 1928—30. The
SPD receives its usual Marxist-Leninist castigation.

MANSTEIN, Eric von.
Aus einem Soldatenleben 1887—1939. Bonn:
Athenäum (1958), 359 pp.
Extremely disappointing memoirs of one of Germany's
most venerable soldiers.

MEIER-WELCKER, Hans.
**"Die Stellung des Chefs der Heersleitung in den
Anfängen der Republik".** *Vierteljahrshefte für
Zeitgeschichte*, vol. 4, pt. 2 (1956), p. 145—60.
Assesses the theoretical and practical importance of this
top position, occupied from 1920—26 by Hans von Seeckt.

MEINCK, Gerhard.
Hitler und die deutsche Aufrüstung, 1933—1937.
Wiesbaden: Steiner (1959), 246 pp.
The early sections of this solid study analyse the status and
organization of the army during the Weimar era, and
include an interesting exposition of the 1930 "A-Plan"
and of the second armaments plan of 1932.

MILITÄRGESCHICHTLICHE
FORSCHUNGSAMT (ed.).
Die Generalstäbe in Deutschland 1871—1945.
By Wiegand Schmidt-Richberg. **Die Entwicklung
der militärischen Luftfahrt in Deutschland 1920—
1933.** By Karl-Heinz Völker. Stuttgart: Deutsche
Verlagsanstalt (1962), 292 pp.
This volume contains two separate essays. In the first,
Schmidt-Richberg provides a clear narrative (without
presenting any new material) of the relationship of the
General Staff to the state. He does not sufficiently stress
the political importance of the army, nor does he really
face up to the fundamental problems relating to the army's
historical development. Völker's work is a different proposition altogether. Based on much previously unpublished
material, his study of the development of the German air
force in Weimar is extremely interesting. He reveals the
extent of government connivance at violating the Versailles
Treaty, which forbade the development of a military air
force, and he argues convincingly that solid foundations
were laid before 1933 for the later expansion of Goering's
Luftwaffe.

MORGAN, J. H.
Assize of Arms: the Disarmament of Germany
and her Rearmament 1919—1939. London:
Methuen (1945), 291 pp.
An extremely poor book which ultimately tells us virtually
nothing of significance about the development of the
German army. The author was formerly attached to the
Inter-Allied Commission but he has clearly been unable
to acquire any real understanding of the problem of Ger-
man militarism and the army.

OBERMANN, Emil.
Soldaten, Bürger, Militaristen: Militär und
Demokratie in Deutschland. Stuttgart: Cotta'sche
Buchhandlung (1958), 327 pp.
A broad but very helpful history of German militarism
from the eighteenth century to 1945. The tone is appro-
priately critical, particularly in Part 3 of the book, entitled
"Militaristen", which refers to the 1918—45 era.

PRERADOVICH, Nikolaus von.
"Die soziale Herkunft der Reichswehr-Generalität
1930". *Vierteljahrsschrift für Sozial- und*
Wirtschaftsgeschichte, vol. 54 (1967—68),
p. 481—6.
Analyses the social origins of *Reichswehr* generals in 1930
(this date is chosen because many scholars, especially those
in East Germany, believe that after 1930 the *Reichswehr*
became a dominating influence in politics, and that their
attitudes reflected their aristocratic background). Only 11
out of 42 generals were true aristocrats.

RAU, Friedrich.
Personalpolitik und Organisation in der vorläufigen
Reichswehr. Dissertation, University of Munich
(1972).
A discussion of the expansion potential of the *Reichswehr*.
Not particularly edifying.

REYNOLDS, N. E.
The Career and Thought of General Ludwig Beck,
1880—1944. Dissertation, University of Oxford
(1974).
An ambitious attempt at a full-scale biographical study.

RITTER, Gerhard.
The Sword and the Sceptre: the Problem of
Militarism in Germany. Vol. IV: The Reign of
Militarism and the Disaster of 1918. London:
Allen Lane (1973), 496 pp.
This volume concludes Ritter's monumental survey of
the nature and role of militarism in German society and
politics. He describes the steady decline in civilian control
during the war and the corresponding increase in military
influence, culminating in the Hindenburg-Ludendorff
military dictatorship in 1917. The last year of the war and
the defeat of 1918 is handled with outstanding skill.
Ritter's overall interpretation of German militarism has
been challenged by the works of Fritz Fischer, and indeed
most scholars would now accept the main findings of the
latter.

ROSINSKI, Herbert.
Die deutsche Armee: eine Analyse. Düsseldorf:
Econ-Verlag (1970), 335 pp. New ed.
Despite a certain effort to update this work which was
originally published in 1940, it still remains too superficial and unreliable a chronicle of the German army
from the early nineteenth century to 1945.

SALEWSKI, Michael.
Entwaffnung und Militärkontrolle in Deutschland
1919—1927. Munich: Oldenbourg (1966), 421 pp.
An extensively documented and absorbing study of the
political, military, and diplomatic problems connected with
German disarmament and Allied military administration.
A considerable amount of new material is presented.

SCHRAMM, Wiegand R. von.
Staatskunst und bewaffnete Macht. Munich:
Isar Verlag (1957), 154 pp.
On the general theme of the position of the army in the
state, this volume has no original interpretations to offer;
it may be reasonably helpful for the general reader. Chapter
III of Part 2 is entitled "Hitler, Weimarer Republik und
Reichswehr".

TESKE, Hermann.
"Analyse eines Reichswehr-Regiments".
Wehrwissenschaftliche Rundschau, vol. 12, pt. 5
(1962), p. 252—69.
The regiment analysed is the 9th Prussian Infantry Regi-
ment between 1921 and 1934.

TESSIN, Georg.
Deutsche Verbände und Truppen 1918—1939.
Osnabrück: Biblio-Verlag (1974), 468 pp.
A review and bibliographical survey of the *Reichswehr*,
but also of other military and paramilitary organizations,
including the *Luftwaffe* and *Landespolizei*.

TRAMPE, Gustav.
See his work in section 16A(iii)(a).

WALSH, Billie K.
"The German Military Mission in China 1928—38".
Journal of Modern History, vol. 46, pt. 3 (1974),
p. 502—13.
Uses new material to reassess the activities of the German
military mission in China and to analyse the extent of its
influence on the military development of nationalist
China. General von Seeckt was head of the mission 1934—
35.

WATZDORF, Bernhard.
"Die getarnte Ausbildung von General-
stabsoffizieren der Reichswehr von 1932 bis
1935". *Zeitschrift für Militärgeschichte*, vol. 2
(1963), p. 78—87.
Adds a few details to the debate on Germany's clandestine
rearmament.

WOHLFEIL, Rainer; DOLLINGER, Hans (eds.).
Die deutsche Reichswehr: Bilder, Dokumente,
Texte. Zur Geschichte des Hunderttausend-Mann-
Heeres 1919—1933. Frankfurt: Bernard & Graefe
(1972), 258 pp.
A somewhat popularized work with nothing new to say
about the army, but on the other hand it does reproduce
some illustrations of interest, and provides a number of
extracts from important documentary sources.

(ii) The Army in Politics[1]

BETHGE, Werner, and others.
See their collective work in section 6B(vii)(c).

BOYLE, Hugh C.
Weimar Defense Minister: Between Government and Reichswehr. Dissertation, University of Wisconsin (1961).
Deals with the success with which the military resisted civilian interference in army affairs, even when the Weimar constitution specifically laid down the principles of lay supervision. Noske did little to assert his control over the army, while Otto Gessler even allowed certain generals to influence civilian policy. Thus by 1928 when Groener replaced Gessler, all opportunity for subordinating the military to government control was lost. All this, of course, is standard knowledge to which the dissertation has nothing substantial to add.

BRACHER, Karl D.
"Die deutsche Armee zwischen Republik und Diktatur (1918—1945)". In *Schicksalsfragen der Gegenwart: Handbuch politisch-historischer Bildung. Vol. III.* Ed. by Bundesministerium für Verteidigung. Tübingen: Niemeyer (1958), p. 95—120.
A general appraisal of the army's position *vis-à-vis* the Weimar Republic and Third Reich.

BUCHER, Peter.
Der Reichswehrprozess: der Hochverrat der Ulmer Reichswehr-offiziere 1929/30. Boppard: Boldt (1967), 524 pp.
An in-depth and richly detailed analysis of this most famous of army trials in the Weimar Republic. However, the author's interpretations and conclusions about the important issues raised at the trial are often dubious, while his sympathetic treatment of the *Reichswehr* is quite unwarranted.

CARSTEN, Francis L.
"Germany from Scharnhorst to Schleicher: the Prussian Officer Corps in Politics, 1806—1932". In Michael Howard (ed.). *Soldiers and Governments.* London: Eyre & Spottiswoode (1957), p. 75—98.
A general discussion of how the army successfully strove to maintain its privileged position free from parliamentary control. For the Weimar period, the efforts of Seeckt, Groener, and Schleicher in this direction are related.

CARSTEN, Francis L.
The Reichswehr and Politics: 1918—1933.
London: Oxford University Press (1966), 427 pp.
A thoroughly documented and objective study of the army's political involvement in the Weimar Republic. Carsten has provided clear and convincing arguments on a host of important issues relating to the army's attitude to the Republic; he discusses its evasion of the Versailles Treaty, its political ambitions, its role in the rise of National Socialism, and its contacts with the Red Army. In brief, this is a standard and indispensable work of high scholarship.

1. See also relevant titles in sections (iv), (v) and (vi) following.

CASPER, Gustav A.
See his article in section 6B(i).

CRAIG, Gordon A.
The Politics of the Prussian Army 1640—1945.
Oxford: Clarendon Press (1955), 536 pp.
A comprehensive and detailed study, though based to a large extent on printed secondary sources. The author's major hypothesis, that the army was the institution in Germany which primarily bears responsibility for the stunted growth of liberalism and parliamentary democracy, is contentious. The army, it may be said, was a product and not the major cause of the ultra-conservative nature of Germany's social, economic, and political conditions. Moreover, the book lacks a common theme. Despite these reservations, however, Craig has much to offer in each of his twelve chapters, including that on Weimar, which includes material from the papers of Groener and Seeckt.

ERFURTH, Waldemar.
Die Geschichte des deutschen Generalstabes von 1918 bis 1945. Göttingen: Musterschmidt (1957), 326 pp.
A valuable contribution by a former top-ranking army officer, despite the fact that most of his material is drawn from secondary sources, supplemented by his own "inside" information and extracts from the Blomberg papers. The narrative is clear and smooth and he covers many important aspects of the army problem: the organization of the General Staff, army influence on Weimar politics, its attitude to National Socialism, and clandestine rearmament. Having discussed all this, however, he then defies his own evidence to argue that the army's role was essentially non-political.

ERNST, Fritz.
"Aus dem Nachlass des Generals Walther Reinhardt". 2 pts. *Die Welt als Geschichte*, vol. 18, pt. 1 (1958), p. 39—65; pt. 2—3, p. 67—121.
An important and revealing article which presents letters and documents from the papers of General Reinhardt, the last Prussian Minister of War and first chief of the Army Command in the Weimar Republic. Much light is shed on the army's adjustment to the post-1918 situation, its attitude to the Versailles Peace Treaty, and to the Kapp Putsch.

ERNST, Fritz.
Aus dem Nachlass Walther Reinhardt. Stuttgart: Kohlhammer (1958), 81 pp.
This is simply the aforementioned two-part article presented as one text.

FOERSTER, Wolfgang.
"Zur geschichtlichen Rolle des preussisch-deutschen Generalstabes: Kommentare zu Werk von Walter Görlitz". *Wehrwissenschaftliche Rundschau*, vol. 1, pt. 8 (1951), p. 7—20.
A review of Görlitz's book (see below); only p. 18—20 discuss the Weimar era and Third Reich.

GESSLER, Otto.
Reichswehrpolitik in der Weimarer Zeit. Edited by Karl Sendtner. Stuttgart: Deutsche Verlagsanstalt (1958), 582 pp.
Most of this book concentrates on the period 1920—28,

when Gessler was *Reichswehr* Minister; it is supplemented by a biography of him by Sendtner. Gessler's account is clear and interesting and covers crucial topics such as deliberations of the cabinet on the army problem, the Army Command structure, the political parties, and above all, the position of the army in the Weimar Republic. In addition, he judiciously assesses leading personalities of the period, including Seeckt. These memoirs are an important source.

GESSNER, Manfred.
See his work in section 14.

GORDON, Harold J.
"Reichswehr und Politik in der Weimarer Republik". *Politische Studien*, no. 195, vol. 22 (1971), p. 34—45.
Argues that any assessment of the army's politics must take account of the four basic questions of the integrity of the army leadership, the loyalty of the army, the legality of the army's politics, and the success of those politics. Affirmative answers can be given on the first three questions, but not on the last. Schleicher, he adds, finally became less of a military man and more of a civilian politician. The conclusions are unremarkable.

GORDON, Harold J.
The Reichswehr and the German Republic 1919—1926. Princeton: Princeton University Press (1957), 478 pp.
A monograph of first-rate significance. The author provides a thorough and on the whole balanced view of the difficult problems facing the army in the early Weimar period. The army is given a fair hearing, for he regards its role as having been more constructive in many respects than most scholars have previously considered. He has much to say on the organization and structure of the army, its relations with the *Freikorps*, and its attitude to political questions.

GORDON, Harold J.
"Die Reichswehr und Sachsen, 1923". *Wehrwissenschaftliche Rundschau*, vol. 11, pt. 12 (1961), p. 677—92.
A careful analysis of this controversial episode when in October 1923 the SPD-KPD coalition government in Saxony was finally broken by the *Reichswehr*, which had been sent in by Chancellor Stresemann. Gordon tries to present a balanced view of the *Reichswehr's* involvement in the affair.

GORDON, Harold J.
"Ritter von Epp und Berlin 1919—1923". *Wehrwissenschaftliche Rundschau*, vol. 9, pt. 6 (1959), p. 329—41.
A useful and informative paper which discusses the significance of Epp's position in the complicated and disturbed relationship between Berlin and Munich in *Reichswehr* matters. The question of who controlled the army and what kind of army should develop constituted the military dimension of the wider federalist-centralist controversy between the Berlin and Bavarian governments.

GÖRLITZ, Walter.
Der deutsche Generalstab: Geschichte und Gestalt 1657—1945. Frankfurt: Verlag der Frankfurter Hefte (1950), 708 pp.
Useful only as a general introduction to a highly specialized field. There is a distinct lack of depth, not least in the second half of the book which covers 1918—45. The author's thesis is the steady decline of the General Staff as an institutional force largely because of its active or passive collaboration with National Socialism.

GÖRLITZ, Walter.
"Wallensteins Lager 1920—38: das Verhältnis der deutschen Generalität zur Republik und zum Nationalsozialismus". *Frankfurter Hefte*, vol. 3, pt. 5 (1948), p. 414—24.
The author castigates the *Reichswehr* leadership for forsaking its high ideals and becoming involved in politics, a development which eventually led to the army's own destruction under Hitler.

HEIDER, Paul.
See his work in section 6B(vii)(a).

HERZFELD, Hans.
"Politik, Heer, und Rüstung in der Zwischenkriegszeit: ein Versuch". In H. Herzfeld. *Ausgewählte Aufsätze. Dargebracht als Festgabe zum siebzigsten Geburtstage.* Berlin: de Gruyter (1962), p. 255—77.
A general but mature interpretative essay on the army's standing in politics and the question of armaments.

JACOBSEN, Hans A.
"Zum Verhältnis von Heer und Staat in der Weimarer Republik". *Das Parlament: Aus Politik und Zeitgeschichte*, B41 (12.10.1966).
A useful brief résumé of some of the main points of the army-Republic relationship.

MEIER-WELCKER, Hans.
"Zur politischen Haltung des Reichswehr-Offizierkorps". *Wehrwissenschaftliche Rundschau*, vol. 12, pt. 7 (1962), p. 407—17.
Publishes a number of revealing documents on the subject.

MEIER-WELCKER, Hans.
"Aus dem Briefwechsel zweier junger Offiziere des Reichsheeres 1930—1938". *Militärgeschichtliche Mitteilungen*, vol. 14, pt. 1 (1973), p. 57—100.
Valuable for the Weimar era in that it allows a full insight into the radical political attitudes of young army officers.

O'NEILL, Robert J.
The German Army and the Nazi Party 1933—1939. London: Cassell (1966), 286 pp.
The first chapter provides an accurate summary of the army's relationship to politics and National Socialism before 1933.

POLLMÜLLER, I.
"Die Rolle der Reichswehr von 1918 bis 1933". *Frankfurter Hefte*, vol. 4, pt. 8 (1949), p. 745—53; pt. 9, p. 833—43.
Contains what must be regarded only as a few preliminary remarks.

POST, Gaines.
The Civil-Military Fabric of Weimar Foreign Policy. Princeton: Princeton University Press (1973), 398 pp.
The theme is the relationship between the *Reichswehr* and the German Foreign Office 1918—33. In this well-documented account, Post shows that the army was keenly aware of the importance of politics and foreign policy, and that in the latter its aims often corresponded to those of the foreign office. Hence, despite certain periods of strain and personal bitterness, the army did co-operate with the government in many areas of mutual concern.

REHM, Walter.
"Reichswehr und politische Parteien der Weimarer Republik". *Wehrwissenschaftliche Rundschau*, vol. 8, pt. 12 (1958), p. 692—708.
A general review of the different factors which influenced relations between the army and the parties during various phases of the Weimar Republic. There is nothing original in this paper, which takes account only of secondary sources.

SCHERINGER, Richard.
Das grosse Los unter Soldaten, Bauern und Rebellen. Hamburg: Rowohlt (1959), 518 pp.
Memoirs of one of the central figures in the 1930 *Reichswehr* trial. Contains some interesting observations on the development of political attitudes in the army before 1933.

SCHMÄDEKE, Jürgen.
Militärische Kommandogewalt und parlamentarische Demokratie. Lübeck: Matthiesen (1967), 216 pp.
An interesting discussion of the limits of military power in a democratic system of government and of the difficult position of the *Reichswehr* Minister as the link man between the civilian and military authorities.

SCHÜDDEKOPF, Otto-Ernst.
Heer und Republik — Quellen zur Politik der Reichswehrführung 1918—1933. Frankfurt: Norddeutsche Verlagsanstalt (1955), 400 pp.
A stimulating and detailed study which clearly explains the complex role of the army in the Republic. Schüddekopf does this by presenting well-chosen extracts from documentary sources with an accompanying commentary. The theme is the endeavour of the army to re-establish its position after 1918; there were a number of phases in this process, for the Seeckt policy of strict neutrality gave way later to one of association with right-wing politics.

SCHÜTZLE, Kurt.
Reichswehr wider die Nation: zur Rolle der Reichswehr bei der Vorbereitung und Errichtung der faschistischen Diktatur in Deutschland (1929—1933). East Berlin: Deutscher Militärverlag (1963), 243 pp.
The book presents a familiar Marxist-Leninist thesis, that the *Reichswehr* made a major contribution to the rise of National Socialism, and that this was linked to the class interests of the aristocracy, big business, and the landowners.

SPERLING, Heinz.
"Dokumente über den Unterdrückungs-feldzug der Reichswehr 1923 in Sachsen". *Zeitschrift für Militärgeschichte*, vol. 12, pt. 5 (1973), p. 567—81.
The documents indicate the anti-communist and anti-revolutionary attitudes of the Army Command. Sperling's added commentary is too politically orientated to be of any value.

VOGELSANG, Thilo.
Reichswehr, Staat und NSDAP: Beiträge zur deutschen Geschichte 1930—1932. Stuttgart: Deutsche Verlagsanstalt (1962), 507 pp.
A splendid, scholarly and objective analysis of the army's role in the politics of the Republic and of its relationship with the National Socialists. His theme is the steady political involvement of the army, largely due to the activities of Schleicher. The book's documentation is wide and impressive. Essential reading.

VOGELSANG, Thilo.
"Die Reichswehr in Bayern und der Münchener Putsch 1923". *Vierteljahrshefte für Zeitgeschichte*, vol. 5, pt. 1 (1957), p. 91—104.
Includes important documents illustrative of the army's somewhat ambiguous position in late 1923.

VOGELSANG, Thilo.
Die Reichswehr und die Politik 1918—1934. Bad Gandersheim: Niedersächsische Landeszentrale für Heimatdienst (1959), 31 pp.
A generalized review of the army's politicalization.

VOGELSANG, Thilo.
"Neue Dokumente zur Geschichte der Reichswehr 1930—1933". *Vierteljahrshefte für Zeitgeschichte*, vol. 2, pt. 4 (1954), p. 397—436.
A large number of significant documents which relate to the army's political attitudes and general involvement in Weimar politics.

WHEELER-BENNETT, John W.
Nemesis of Power: the German Army in Politics 1918—1945. London: Macmillan (1953), 702 pp.
An outstanding work of scholarship which amounts to a bitter indictment of the army's role in Weimar and Third Reich politics. The author's thesis is that the army played a dominating role in politics before 1933 but paid the price in loss of status and independence, culminating in its control by Hitler. Indeed, he sees the army as having made a major contribution to the rise of National Socialism. The author also discusses at length other vital aspects of the army's development before 1933, such as rearmament and *Reichswehr*-Red Army relations. The book's perspectives and interpretations are not all correct or acceptable, but its principal conclusions remain valid.

ZBORALSKI, Dietrich.
"Zur Stellung der Reichswehr-Generalität in den letzten Jahren der Weimarer Republik". *Zeitschrift für Geschichtswissenschaft*, vol. 3, pt. 6 (1955), p. 934—1030.
Comments on documents published by Thilo Vogelsang

in the *Vierteljahrshefte für Zeitgeschichte*, vol. 2, pt. 4 (1954) (see earlier in this section). Zboralski attacks alleged West German efforts to whitewash the army. He argues that 52% of army generals in May 1932 were from the aristocracy or upper bourgeoisie and that as a result the army was in league with big business to prepare the advent to power of Hitler. Familiar arguments, familiar limitations.

(iii) Reichswehr—Red Army Relations

CARSTEN, Francis L.
"Reports by Two German Officers on the Red Army". *Slavonic & East European Review*, no. 96, vol. 41 (1962), p. 217—44.
The reports made by two German generals, Werner von Blomberg and Hans Halm, on their visits to Russia in 1928 and 1930, are reproduced here. Both naively accepted the Soviet line on domestic conditions in Russia, but more importantly both advocated closer collaboration between the *Reichswehr* and the Red Army.

CARSTEN, Francis L.
"The Reichswehr and the Red Army". In Walter Laqueur (ed.). *Russia and Germany: a Century of Conflict.* London: Weidenfeld & Nicolson (1965).
A very useful, objective account of their relations between 1920 and 1933.

ERICKSON, John.
The Soviet High Command 1918—1941. London: Macmillan (1962), 889 pp.
Included in this masterful study is a very full and accurate description of Red Army-*Reichswehr* relations in the Weimar era.

GATZKE, Hans W.
"Russo-German Military Collaboration during the Weimar Republic". *American Historical Review*, vol. 62, pt. 3 (1958), p. 565—97.
In reviewing the extent of Red Army-*Reichswehr* collaboration, the author pays particular attention to the theme of Germany's secret rearmament. Gatzke makes use for the first time of important material from the Seeckt papers and from the files of the German Foreign Ministry. For one thing, the complicity of the German government in the *Reichswehr's* evasion of the disarmament clauses of Versailles is fully revealed. An important essay.

HALLGARTEN, George W. F.
"General Hans von Seeckt and Russia, 1920—22". *Journal of Modern History*, vol. 21, pt. 1 (1949), p. 28—34.
Seeckt is depicted as the main figure in promoting Russo-German reconciliation. He was consistently pro-Russian after 1919 and desired the military advantages of a pact with Russia. The article discusses the nature of the negotiations and the German personnel involved in secret Red Army-*Reichswehr* talks which contributed to Rapallo. Chancellor Josef Wirth was one of the persons who took part. This essay has made good use of material from Seeckt's private papers.

SMITH, Arthur L.
"The German General Staff and Russia 1919—1926". *Soviet Studies*, vol. 8, pt. 2 (1956), p. 125—33.
Examines Seeckt's efforts to promote Russo-German military collaboration. Seeckt set down his reasons for

wanting this co-operation in an undated letter of late 1919 or early 1920, in which he stated that the Russian link would strengthen the *Reichswehr* and in the long term lead to the disintegration of the country he hated most — Poland. Seeckt drew a distinction between political Russia, which he unequivocally rejected, and military Russia, which would strengthen Germany.

SPALCKE, Karl.
"Begegnungen zwischen Reichswehr und Roter Armee: ein Rückblick". *Aussenpolitik*, vol. 9, pt. 8 (1958), p. 506—13.
A brief and unimportant review.

SPEIDEL, Helm.
"Reichswehr und Rote Armee". *Vierteljahrshefte für Zeitgeschichte*, vol. 1, pt. 1 (1953), p. 9—45.
This essay has been superseded to a certain extent by more recent publications which have had access to wider sources.

STEIN, George H.
"Russo-German Military Collaboration: the Last Phase, 1933". *Political Science Quarterly*, vol. 77 (1962—63), p. 54—71.
Discusses the end put to such collaboration by Hitler.

(iv) General Hans von Seeckt

GERSDORFF, Ursula von.
"Zum Nachlass Seeckt". *Wehrwissenschaftliche Rundschau*, vol. 10 (1960), p. 336—40.
A few observations on this important historical source.

GORDON, Harold J.
"Hans von Seeckt als Mensch". *Wehrwissenschaftliche Rundschau*, vol. 7, pt. 10 (1957), p. 575—84.
A sympathetic portrait of Seeckt's personality and character, although it does not show a deep understanding of him.

GUSKE, Klaus.
Das politische Denken des Generals von Seeckt: ein Beitrag zur Diskussion des Verhältnisses Seeckt-Reichswehr-Republik. Lübeck: Matthiesen (1971), 283 pp.
An excellent study, richly documented and presenting original interpretations. However, it extends only as far as 1923.

HALLGARTEN, George W. F.
See his article in section 12A(iii).

KAULBACH, Eberhard.
"Generaloberst Hans von Seeckt — zur Persönlichkeit und zur Leistung". *Wehrwissenschaftliche Rundschau*, vol. 16, pt. 12 (1966), p. 666—81.
A full assessment of Seeckt's career and importance. Generally sympathetic, but strangely inconclusive.

KESSEL, Eberhard.
"Seeckts politisches Programm von 1923".
In Konrad Repgen & Stephan Skalweit (eds.).
Spiegel der Geschichte: Festgabe für Max Braubach. Münster: Aschendorff (1964), p. 887—914.
A good discussion of Seeckt's anti-democratic political conceptions.

MEIER-WELCKER, Hans.
Seeckt. Frankfurt: Bernard & Graefe (1967), 744 pp.
A definitive biography; detailed, balanced and scholarly. The author discusses Seeckt's effectiveness as head of the *Reichswehr*, his attitude towards the Republic and politics, his view of Russia and the Red Army, and his own political and military outlook. At the same time, he has got closer than anyone else to explaining Seeckt's obscure and ostensibly contradictory personality.

MEIER-WELCKER, Hans.
"Seeckt in der Kritik". *Wehrwissenschaftliche Rundschau,* vol. 19, pt. 5 (1969), p. 265—84.
An excellent review article.

MEIER-WELCKER, Hans.
"Seeckt über die Chefstellung im Generalstab". *Wehrwissenschaftliche Rundschau,* vol. 17, pt. 1 (1967), p. 15—21.
Considers Seeckt's stated views on the nature and importance of his own high office.

SCHERMANN, Bernard.
General Hans von Seeckt: Architect of the Wehrmacht. Dissertation, University of Maryland (1975), 442 pp.
Concentrates on his military career, with special emphasis on his period as Chief of the Army Command. The work says little that is original.

SEIZ, Wolfgang.
"Zum Ursprung einiger Seeckt-'Zitate'". *Wehrwissenschaftliche Rundschau,* vol. 8, pt. 6 (1958), p. 319—24.
Discusses the origins of famous phrases attributed to Seeckt such as, "Die Reichswehr steht hinter mir" and ". . . in Deutschland kann niemand einen Putsch machen als ich", and how they have been handled in secondary works.

SMITH, Arthur L.
General Hans von Seeckt and German Secret Rearmament 1919—1926. Dissertation, University of Southern California (1956).
A competent assessment of Seeckt's role in this sphere, though the author has apparently not had access to all available important sources, such as the Seeckt papers.

SMITH, Arthur L.
"Le Désarmement de l'Allemagne en 1919: les vues du Général von Seeckt". *Revue Historique,* vol. 86, pt. 1 (1962), p. 17—34.
Describes Seeckt's endeavours to delay and frustrate German disarmament in 1919 and afterwards.

SMITH, Arthur L.
"Le Général von Seeckt et l'armée allemande après la défaite (1919—1926)". *Revue d'Histoire Moderne et Contemporaine,* vol. 10 (1963), p. 271—88.
An inconclusive revisionist reassessment of Seeckt's contribution to the reorganization of the *Reichswehr.*

SMITH, Arthur L.
See also his article in section 12A(iii).

(v) General Wilhelm Groener

BREUCKER, Wilhelm.
"Die Erinnerungen des Generals Groener". *Wehrwissenschaftliche Rundschau,* vol. 5, pt. 7 (1955), p. 315—22.
An informative assessment of the study of Groener by his daughter (see below).

CRAIG, Gordon A.
"The Reichswehr and National Socialism; the Policy of Wilhelm Groener, 1928—32". *Political Science Quarterly,* vol. 63, pt. 2 (1948), p. 194—229.
A reasonably useful assessment of Groener's political attitudes and policies, but much new and important material has come to light since this essay was published, with the result that Craig's conclusions require revision.

FENSCH, Dorothea; GROEHLER, Olaf.
"Imperialistische Ökonomie und militärische Strategie: eine Denkschrift Wilhelm Groeners". *Zeitschrift für Geschichtswissenschaft,* vol. 19, pt. 9 (1971), p. 1167—77.
Reproduces a memorandum written by Groener sometime in 1927—28 entitled "The Importance of the Modern Economy for Strategy". The authors have interpreted this (or perhaps "distorted" would be a more appropriate term) as indicative of the close collaboration between the armaments industry and militarists as they prepared for a war of revenge against the victor powers of the First World War.

HILLER von GAERTRINGEN, Friedrich
"Zur 'Odyssee der Groener-Papiere'". *Die Welt als Geschichte,* vol. 19 (1959), p. 244—54.
Gaertringen adds his comments to the problems raised by Groener's daughter as she tried to obtain access to her father's personal papers (see below).

GROENER, Wilhelm.
Lebenserinnerungen: Jugend, Generalstab, Weltkrieg. Edited by F. H. von Gaertringen. Göttingen: Vandenhoeck & Ruprecht (1957), 584 pp.
The memoirs stop at 1920. Of interest for our purposes is the author's account of his co-operation with Ebert and the SPD in 1918—19.

GROENER-GEYER, Dorothea.
General Groener, Soldat und Staatsmann.
Frankfurt: Societäts-Verlag (1955), 406 pp.
Groener's daughter has written an admirably clear and sound account of her father's military and political career, though her evaluation of his perspicacity and political awareness as Minister of Defence 1928—32 and Minister of the Interior 1931—32 tends to be perhaps a little too generous. She has made extensive use of her father's private papers.

GROENER-GEYER, Dorothea.
"Die Odyssee der Groener-Papiere". *Die Welt als Geschichte*, vol. 19 (1959), p. 75—95.
The author recounts the difficulties encountered in securing free access to General Groener's papers.

PHELPS, Reginald.
"Aus den Groenerdokumenten". *Deutsche Rundschau*, vol. 76 (1950), p. 915—22, 1013—22; vol. 77 (1951), p. 19—31.
A revealing insight into Groener's ideas and actions in late 1932.

REED, Edward A.
Wilhelm Groener and the SPD, January 1928 to May 1932. Dissertation, University of Pennsylvania (1972).
Describes Groener's efforts at improving the traditionally bad army-SPD relations on coming into office in 1928, and analyses why this attempted *rapprochement* failed. In 1928-30 the SPD's negative attitude to military matters precluded any agreement, while in 1930—32 it was an embittered High Command which would not countenance a deal.

(vi) General Kurt von Schleicher

BARBER, Charles M.
Wehrmachts-Abteilung and Ministeramt: the Political and Social Ambit of Kurt von Schleicher 1926—1932. Dissertation, University of Wisconsin (1971).
Examines Schleicher's role as the creator and holder of these two offices in the *Reichswehr* Ministry, which were established in 1926 and which he controlled until he became *Reichswehr* Minister in June 1932. On the basis of both offices, Schleicher made himself the leading political advisor to the army. As a direct result, the office of Chief of the Army Command lost a good deal of its significance. However, Barber states that Schleicher never acquired too much political sagacity, so he was easily outmanoeuvred by opponents, including Hitler and Papen, in the last phase of Weimar.

BECKER, Josef.
"Zur Politik der Wehrmachtabteilung in der Regierungskrise 1926/27". *Vierteljahrshefte für Zeitgeschichte*, vol. 14, pt. 1 (1966), p. 69—78.
Publishes two important documents from the Schleicher *Nachlass* which provide a clear insight into the political objectives of the Schleicher clique during the government crisis of December 1926 when the Marx cabinet collapsed. The first document is a report compiled by the *Wehrmacht-abteilung* of the *Reichswehr* Ministry on the prevailing political situation. The second document, compiled by the same department, weighs up the prospects for different cabinet formations to succeed the Marx administration.

BERNDORFF, Hans R.
General zwischen Ost und West: aus den Geheimnissen der Weimarer Republik. Hamburg: Hoffmann & Campe (1951), 320 pp.
A somewhat sparse and unsatisfactory biography of Schleicher. The author did not have access to many important sources, and his account is impressionistic to a large extent.

CRAIG, Gordon A.
"Briefe Schleichers an Groener". *Die Welt als Geschichte*, vol. 11 (1951), p. 122—33.
A selection of 22 letters, dating from March 1926 to May 1934, written by Schleicher to Groener. They do not tell us very much about political events, or even of army affairs; indeed, the letters mainly serve to cast some light on Schleicher's personality. Unfortunately, Craig has not provided a commentary.

GELLERMANN, J. E.
Generals as Statesmen. New York (1959).
A poor, ill informed and superficial study which attempts to say something about Schleicher among others.

HAMMERSTEIN, Kunrat von.
"Schleicher, Hammerstein und die Machtübernahme 1933". *Frankfurter Hefte*, vol. 11 (1956), p. 11—18, 117—28, 163—76.
Very interesting discussion based on the papers of General von Hammerstein, Schleicher's aide and confidant in the political intrigue of 1932—33.

OTT, Eugen.
"Ein Bild des Generals Kurt von Schleicher". *Politische Studien*, vol. 10 (1959), p. 360—71.
A portrait of Schleicher which carries no penetration.

SALL, Larry D.
See his work in section 16A(i).

STEELY, Melvin T.
Kurt von Schleicher and the Political Activities of the Reichswehr 1918—1926. Dissertation. Vanderbilt University (1971).
An examination of the political struggle within the army High Command and Schleicher's role in that struggle. In one of the most interesting chapters Steely discusses Schleicher's involvement with the political parties 1923—26. The Schleicher who emerges from these pages is not only the political intriguer, but also the diligent and conscientious officer who worked his way through the ranks.

TREVIRANUS, Gottfried R.
"Zur Rolle und zur Person Kurt von Schleichers". In F. A. Hermens & T. Schieder (eds.). *Staat, Wirtschaft und Politik in der Weimarer Republik: Festschrift für Heinrich Brüning.* Berlin: Duncker & Humblot (1967), p. 363—82.
A not unsympathetic portrait of Schleicher by one who knew him privately and in politics. Schleicher's promising early career in the army is outlined, but the focus is on the 1930—33 period. Although adding nothing new to our knowledge of these years, Treviranus does provide some interesting minor details and makes a few perceptive remarks about Schleicher who, he stresses, was a passionate enemy of Hitler.

VOGELSANG, Thilo.
Kurt von Schleicher: ein General als Politiker.
Göttingen: Musterschmidt (1965), 112 pp.
A scholarly and objective interpretative essay on the nature and extent of Schleicher's political significance. This work can be highly recommended.

VOGELSANG, Thilo.
"Zur Politik Schleichers gegenüber der NSDAP".
Vierteljahrshefte für Zeitgeschichte, vol. 6, pt. 1 (1958), p. 86—118.
Publishes a number of important documents which illustrate Schleicher's motives and objectives in his dealings with the National Socialists.

B. THE NAVY (REICHSMARINE)

BIRD, Keith W.
Officers and Republic: the German Navy and Politics. Dissertation, Duke University (1972).
Based on an impressive range of primary material, Bird's study stresses the anti-republican outlook of the navy from 1918—19. Most naval officers were former members of the Imperial Navy and their outlook was decisively settled by the experience of defeat in 1918, the November Revolution, and the right-wing backlash. In Weimar, the political Left hated the navy, but Erich Raeder, who became Chief of the Navy in 1928, tried to reach a *modus vivendi* with the government.

DUELFFER, Jost.
Weimar, Hitler und die Marine: Reichspolitik und Flottenbau 1920—1939. Düsseldorf: Droste (1973), 615 pp.
A massive and important study which is a significant contribution not only to our knowledge of the development of naval policy 1920—39, but also to the whole controversy on the nature of Hitler's foreign policy after 1933. The author shows that the hatred of the Weimar governments for the navy made the latter responsive to the NSDAP well before 1933. This situation in fact served to increase the navy's latent expansionist aims (a legacy of the Tirpitz era).

GEMZELL, Carl-Axel.
Organisation, Conflict and Innovation: a Study of German Naval Strategic Planning 1888—1940.
Lund: Berlinska Boktryckeriet (1973), 448 pp.
Utilizing sociological techniques of enquiry, this study of German strategic thinking and planning is disappointing, largely because Gemzell adduces an ambitious theoretical framework which he does not substantiate with convincing empirical evidence.

GIESE, Fritz.
Die deutsche Marine 1920 bis 1945: Aufbau und Untergang. Frankfurt: Verlag für Wehrwesen (1956), 150 pp.
Useful as a general introduction to the history of the navy, but has now been overtaken, of course, by more recent specialized studies.

GÜTH, Rolf.
Die Marine des deutschen Reiches, 1919—1939.
Frankfurt: Bernard & Graefe (1972), 263 pp.
A clear, thoughtful general narrative.

HERWIG, Holger H.
"From Kaiser to Führer: the Political Road of a German Admiral, 1923—33". *Journal of Contemporary History*, vol. 9, pt. 2 (1974), p. 107—20.
An interesting discussion of the political ideas of Rear-Admiral Magnus von Levetzow who was forced into premature retirement in 1920 due to his support of the Kapp

Putsch. Levetzow really aimed at a monarchist restoration, but was prepared to work with many right-wing groups which might serve his ultimate cause. By 1931 he had become an important link man between Hitler and the conservative nationalists and by the following year had come to accept Hitler as the man most likely to restore the Hohenzollerns by dictatorial methods.

HUBATSCH, Walter.
Der Admiralstab und die obersten Marinebehörden in Deutschland 1848—1945. Frankfurt: Verlag für Wehrwesen (1956), 317 pp.
A very useful general survey of the structure, organization and composition of the naval High Command.

RAEDER, Erich.
Mein Leben: bis zum Flottenabkommen mit England 1935. Tübingen: Schlichtenmayer (1956), 317 pp.
Mildly interesting memoirs by the former German navy chief. There is not a great deal that is significant for the pre-1933 period.

SALEWSKI, Michael.
"Marineleitung und politische Führung 1931—1935". *Militärgeschichtliche Mitteilungen*, vol. 10, pt. 2 (1971), p. 113—58.
Publishes a large selection of important documents concerning the political orientation of the navy.

SANDHOFER, Gert.
"Das Panzerschiff 'A' und die Vorentwürfe von 1920 bis 1928". *Militärgeschichtliche Mitteilungen*, vol. 7, pt. 1 (1968), p. 35—62.
The proposal for a battleship caused a great deal of political uproar in 1928; this essay traces the prehistory of the issue and the politics involved from 1920.

WACKER, Wolfgang.
Der Bau des Panzerschiffs "A" und der Reichstag.
Tübingen: Mohr (1959), 180 pp.
A careful analysis of the motives of the political forces involved in the *Reichstag* debate on the construction of the battleship, and of the important political and constitutional issues raised. At the centre of the controversy was the ambivalent attitude of the SPD; its government ministers were in favour of the battleship, but the SPD parliamentary faction was not. The damage inflicted on the SPD is fully explained, as is the debate in general, but the author has signally failed to place his theme in the wider context of Weimar politics.

C. THE AIR FORCE (LUFTWAFFE)

IRVING, David.
The Rise and Fall of the Luftwaffe: the Life of Luftwaffe Marshal Erhard Milch. London: Weidenfeld and Nicolson (1974), 451 pp.
This revealing book is based overwhelmingly on the Third Reich era. The first chapter describes Milch's early career and also contains a few references to Göring's involvement with Lufthansa before 1933.

MASON, Herbert M.
The Rise of the Luftwaffe: Forging the Secret German Air Weapon 1918—1940. New York: Dial Press (1973), 402 pp.
Contains some interesting information, but is unreliable in general interpretation.

VÖLKER, Karl-Heinz.
"Die geheime Luftrüstung der Reichswehr und ihre Auswirkung auf den Flugzeugbestand der Luftwaffe bis zum Beginn des Zweiten Weltkrieges". *Wehrwissenschaftliche Rundschau*, vol. 12, pt. 9 (1962), p. 540—9.
This is merely a brief extract from Völker's book on the subject (see section 12A(i)).

Economic and Social Development 13

A. THE ECONOMY

(i) General

BRUCK, Werner F.
Social and Economic History of Germany from William II to Hitler, 1888—1938: a Comparative Study. New York: Russell & Russell (1962), 292 pp.
A solid general survey; chapter III deals with the Weimar era.

FACIUS, Friedrich.
Wirtschaft und Staat: die Entwicklung der staatlichen Wirtschaftsverwaltung in Deutschland vom 17. Jahrhundert bis 1945. Boppard: Boldt (1959), 271 pp.
Contains an interesting chapter (IV) on the efforts of the Reich Ministry of the Economy to promote greater economic integration in Germany during 1919—33.

FISCHER, Wolfram.
Die wirtschaftspolitische Situation der Weimarer Republik. Celle: Pohl (1960), 68 pp.
A brief but instructive discussion of the general relationship between the economy and politics.

FISCHER, Wolfram.
Deutsche Wirtschaftspolitik von 1918 bis 1945. Opladen: Leske Verlag (1968), 125 pp.
A good reliable introduction to economic developments.

KAFTAN, Kurt.
Der Kampf um die Autobahnen: Geschichte und Entwicklung des Autobahnengedankens in Deutschland von 1907—1935. Berlin: Wigankow (1955), 192 pp.
A useful contribution to German transport history. The author compares German plans for motorways with similar plans in other European countries.

KOCKA, Jürgen.
"Recent Historiography of Germany and Austria. Theoretical Approaches to Social and Economic History of Modern Germany: Some Recent Trends, Concepts, and Problems in Western and Eastern Germany". *Journal of Modern History*, vol. 47, pt. 1 (1975), p. 101—19.
A stimulating discussion of the changing methodology of German historians from 1900 onwards. Until 1945 they clung to basically nineteenth century principles of historiography, neglecting typologies and in particular the methods and theories of the social sciences. This changed after 1945 in the latter respect. Kocka goes on to discuss some of the problems and deficiencies of present-day German historiography.

PETZINA, Dieter.
Grundriss der deutschen Wirtschaftsgeschichte 1918—1945. Stuttgart: Deutsche Verlagsanstalt (1973), 792 pp.
An excellent work, balanced and highly informative, and clearly a standard reference work for students and specialists alike.

STOLPER, Gustav.
Deutsche Wirtschaft seit 1870. Tübingen: Mohr (1964), 375 pp. New ed.
First published in 1940, this remains a good concise general history, and is brought up to date in the new edition.

(ii) Industry

(a) Capitalism

BECK, Earl R.
Verdict on Schacht: a Study in the Problem of Political Guilt. Tallahassee: Florida State University Press (1955), 183 pp.
A short but moderately useful study of Schacht's economic and political career. For the pre-1933 period, the book's usefulness lies in its presentation of some facts pertaining to his activities as an economic expert and President of the *Reichsbank*. The book, however, is written on the basis of printed secondary sources.

BÖHRET, Carl.
Aktionen gegen die "kalte Sozialisierung" 1926–1930: ein Beitrag zum Wirken ökonomischer Einflüssverbände in der Weimarer Republik. Berlin: Duncker & Humblot (1966), 279 pp.
"Cold nationalization" in Weimar meant the growth of public enterprise. This book provides a solid narrative of the campaign waged by the employers' organizations against this development, which they obviously regarded as inimical to their interests. Much new material is incorporated into this study.

CROON, Helmuth.
"Die wirtschaftlichen Führungsschichten des Ruhrgebietes in der Zeit von 1890 bis 1933". *Blätter für Deutsche Landesgeschichte*, vol. 108 (1972), p. 143–59.
The author stresses above all the continuity of the social composition of the economic leadership in the Ruhr. The great families of the coal and steel barons were relatively undisturbed by war, defeat, or revolution from 1890 to 1933.

FELDMAN, Gerald D.
"The Social and Economic Policies of German Big Business, 1918–1929". *American Historical Review*, vol. 75, pt. 1 (1969), p. 47–55.
A discussion of the relationship between, on the one hand, the socio-economic concerns of big business and, on the other, the political activity of big business. Feldman shows that businessmen put economic above political considerations, while their political activity was usually a function of their socio-economic concerns. Hence, they were prepared to tolerate the Republic politically as long as it served and protected their economic priorities. Their resentments grew as government extended state control over industry and initiated costly social welfare programmes.

FELDMAN, Gerald D.
"Der deutsche organisierte Kapitalismus während der Kriegs- und Inflationsjahre 1914–1923". In Heinrich Winkler (ed.). *Organisierter Kapitalismus: Voraussetzungen und Anfänge.* Göttingen: Vandenhoeck und Ruprecht (1974), p. 150–71.
A valuable paper on the conservative and conventional economic outlook and priorities of most German businessmen.

FELDMAN, Gerald D.
"German Business between War and Revolution: the Origins of the Stinnes-Legien Agreement". In G.A. Ritter (ed.). *Entstehung und Wandel der modernen Gesellschaft: Festschrift für Hans Rosenberg.* Berlin: de Gruyter (1970), p. 312–41.
A stimulating contribution to a comparatively neglected aspect of the 1917–19 period in Germany. The author examines the policies of the employers' organizations and the trade unions, which came together on 15 November 1918 to make the agreement governing labour-business disputes (specifically, they agreed to keep politics out of such disputes).

FELDMAN, Gerald D.
Army, Industry and Labor in Germany 1914–1918. Princeton: Princeton University Press (1966), 572 pp.
A searching and thoroughly documented study of the complex relationship between these three important organizations. Feldman shows that between them, the army and big business gained ascendancy in government

and the economy as the war dragged on, and that consequently the workers were in a more vulnerable position in 1918 than they had been four years earlier. Also, Feldman has lucidly examined the origins of fundamental social conflicts which were carried over into the Weimar period. Only in the attempt to establish links between wartime developments and the post-1918 situation does the book show real weaknesses.

FLECHTNER, Hans-Joachim.
Carl Duisberg: vom Chemiker zum Wirtschaftsführer. Düsseldorf: Econ-Verlag (1959), 413 pp.
This biography of the leading industrialist contains some very useful information concerning certain aspects of big business practice in the Weimar era, including his own company, I. G. Farben, the chemical giant.

GOSSWEILER, Kurt.
See his work in section 13A (iv).

HENDERSON, Wilhelm O.
"Walther Rathenau: a Pioneer of the Planned Economy". *Economic History Review*, vol. 4, pt. 1 (1951), p. 98–108.
A brief examination of Rathenau's ideas on a planned economy as expressed in his writings 1917–20. He, of course, was a brilliant critic of early twentieth century capitalism and wanted to recast the organization of capitalism without recourse to socialism. His ideas on the planned economy, however, were not influential.

KLASS, Gert von.
Die drei Ringe: Lebensgeschichte eines Industrieunternehmens. Tübingen: Wunderlich (1953), 479 pp.
A full and competent general history of the Krupp empire.

KLASS, Gert von.
Hugo Stinnes. Tübingen: Wunderlich (1958), 355 pp.
Very informative, especially on Stinnes' economic and political activities in the Weimar period.

KLEIN, Fritz.
"Neue Dokumente zur Rolle Schachts bei der Vorbereitung der Hitler-Diktatur". *Zeitschrift für Geschichtswissenschaft*, vol. 5, pt. 4 (1957), p. 818–22.
A selection of letters from files of the *Deutsches Zentralarchiv* in Potsdam. They were written by Schacht in 1932 to Hitler (12.4.32), to Hindenburg (25.10.32), and to Hess (17.10.32). Collectively, the letters purport to reveal Schacht's active role in bringing together the NSDAP and big business, and to demonstrate further Hitler's relationship with big business. The documents are certainly interesting but Klein makes too much of them.

KOLKO, Gabriel.
"American Business and Germany, 1930–1941". *Western Political Quarterly*, vol. 15, pt. 4 (1962), p. 713–28.
Useful for providing a description of the various links between major American companies and German industry. The author also shows that the American business press was opposed to National Socialism.

KÖNIG, Harold.
Entstehung und Wirkungsweise von Fachverbänden der Nahrungs- und Genussmittelindustrie. Berlin: Duncker & Humblot (1966), 279 pp.
An investigation of the origins and pre-1933 history of various industrial associations in the brewing, distillery,

confectionery, sugar, and tobacco industries. König explains the self-protective measures taken by the associations, including schemes for taxation concessions, and also their overall role in the national economy.

KOSZYK, Kurt.
See his work in section 16B.

LASER, Kurt.
"Der Russlandsausschuss der deutschen Wirtschaft 1928—1941". *Zeitschrift für Geschichtswissenschaft*, vol. 20, pt. 11 (1972), p. 1382—1400.
The "Russian Committee" was set up in September 1928 as "an instrument of German monopoly capitalism", as Laser alleges. He argues that it pursued an aggressive and imperialistic policy towards Russia on behalf of the *Reichsverband der deutschen Industrie*, the employers' association.

MANCHESTER, William.
The Arms of Krupp 1587—1968. Boston: Little, Brown (1968), 1068 pp.
Although this massive work provides a detailed narrative of the Krupps, the author has overlooked important archival sources as well as certain valuable printed sources. Manchester's knowledge of Germany outside the specialized theme he has chosen is generally dismal and causes him to make a whole series of factual errors. Politics are not given much careful consideration and the book is primarily a narrow family history, albeit an incomplete one.

MÜHLEN, Norbert.
The Incredible Krupps: the Rise, Fall, and Comeback of Germany's Industrial Family. New York: Holt (1959), 308 pp.
As the title may suggest, this book is written for the popular market and has no scholarly pretensions whatever. Indeed, it is even more ill informed and misleading than Manchester's work.

MÜLLER, Helmut.
See his work in section 13A (iv).

NUSSMANN, Manfred.
"Unternehmenskonzentration und Investstrategie nach dem Ersten Weltkrieg". *Jahrbuch für Wirtschaftsgeschichte*, vol. 15, pt. 2 (1974), p. 51—75.
A detailed but hardly balanced examination of the investment patterns of heavy industry after 1918, but particularly during the period of acute inflation in the early 1920s. The author discusses a pronounced tendency towards capital concentration in times of economic stress.

PARKER, William N.
"Entreprencurship, Industrial Organisation and Economic Growth: a German Example". *Journal of Economic History*, vol. 14, pt. 4 (1954), p. 380—400.
Attempts to show how the organization of the German coal mining industry represented a good example of the connection between industrial initiative and national economic growth. Setting up a series of economic models, the author uses case examples to substantiate his hypothesis that industrial organization is an important link between entrepreneurship and economic growth.

PETERSON, Edward Norman.
Hjalmar Schacht. For and Against Hitler: a Political-Economic Study of Germany 1923—1945. Boston: Christopher (1954), 416 pp.
Gives a thorough description of social and economic

changes in Germany after 1918, as well as charting the economic career of Schacht. Peterson certainly tends to overstate Schacht's influence and achievements, but the book's main value is its sensible discussion of major economic problems.

RAUMER, Hans von.
See his article in section 14.

REISHAUS-ETZOLD, Heike.
"Die Herausbildung von monopolkapitalistischen Lenkungsorganen der Wissenschaft während der Weimarer Republik unter dem Einfluss der Chemiemonopole". *Jahrbuch für Wirtschaftsgeschichte*, vol. 13, pt. 3 (1972), p. 13—35.
A detailed analysis of how the chemical industry took the lead in establishing various research and educational bodies which gave that industry a decisive influence in German academic administration. For example, the chemical industry was able to dominate the important *Notgemeinschaft der deutschen Wissenschaft*. The purpose of the essay is, of course, to underline the comprehensive influence of monopoly capitalism in society at large.

REISHAUS-ETZOLD, Heike.
"Die Einflussnahme der Chemiemonopole auf die 'Kaiser-Wilhelm-Gesellschaft zur Förderung der Wissenschaften e.V' während der Weimarer Republik". *Jahrbuch für Wirtschaftsgeschichte*, vol. 14, pt. 1 (1973), p. 37—61.
Again, an essay on the theme of the extensive influence of the chemical industry on an important research organization. By dint of using its vast financial resources, the chemical industry was by the end of the Weimar era in dominant control of the *Kaiser-Wilhelm-Gesellschaft* which, in turn, meant that the state monopoly of research was considerably consolidated. In essence, therefore, the argument is that the state of Weimar and the chemical industry as a representative of big business had identical interests. The political motivation of this paper is all too obvious.

RICHTER, Werner.
See his work in section 14.

SCHIECK, Hans.
Der Kampf um die deutsche Wirtschaftspolitik nach dem Novemberumsturz 1918. Dissertation, University of Heidelberg (1959).
An excellent study, with interesting data, though Schieck does not follow through all the lines of possible investigation raised in his narrative.

SCHWARZBACH, Helmut.
"Die Differenzen zwischen dem Verband sächsischer Industrieller und dem Reichsverband der deutschen Industrie 1931". *Jahrbuch für Wirtschaftsgeschichte*, vol. 12, pt. 3 (1971), p. 75—93.
Includes eight useful tables of the unemployed in Germany 1930—31, and data relating to the types of factory in Saxony, and production figures. The remainder of the paper is obtuse.

SIEMENS, Georg.
Geschichte des Hauses Siemens. 3 vols. Freiburg im Breisgau: Alber-Verlag (1947—52).
A "house history" which is only moderately informative on the whole, but unhelpful as regards economic/political questions. Volume II is devoted to 1903—22, and volume III to 1922—45.

SIMPSON, Amos E.
Hjalmar Schacht in Perspective. The Hague:
Mouton (1969), 202 pp.
It is difficult to know why so many historians find Schacht
an interesting subject to write about. This latest effort
sets out to define his economic and political significance,
yet essentially all we have is another competent but dull
narrative about a thorough bore.

STEGMANN, Dirk.
"Die Silverberg-Kontroverse 1926: Unternehmer-
politik zwischen Reform und Restauration".
In *Sozialgeschichte Heute: Festschrift für Hans
Rosenberg zum 70. Geburtstag.* Göttingen:
Vandenhoeck und Ruprecht (1974), p. 341—71.
An excellent analysis of a major dilemma in German
industrial circles, involving a clash of priorities between
progressive and conservative elements of big business.

THOMAS, Georg.
Geschichte der deutschen Wehr- und
Rüstungswirtschaft (1918—1945). Boppard: Boldt
(1966), 552 pp.
Must be considered a standard work on the organization,
size, policies and relationships of the armaments industry.
The political dimensions of the subject are also adequately
covered.

TREUE, Wilhelm.
"Die deutschen Unternehmer in der Welt-
wirtschaftskrise, 1928—33". In W. Conze & H.
Raupach (eds.). *Die Staats- und Wirtschaftskrise
des deutschen Reiches 1929/33.* Stuttgart: Klett
(1967), p. 82—125.
A balanced and detailed review of the employers and their
policies.

WINKLER, Hans-Joachim.
Preussen als Unternehmer 1923—1932. Berlin:
de Gruyter (1965), 223 pp.
A compact examination of the record of the Prussian state
as an industrial employer and of the political factors
intervening. Winkler bases his survey on three firms:
Preussag, Hibernia and Veba.

(b) Big Business and Politics

HALLGARTEN, George W. F.; RADKAU,
Joachim.
Deutsche Industrie und Politik: von Bismarck bis
heute. Frankfurt: Europäische Verlagsanstalt
(1974), 576 pp.
A comprehensive and detailed investigation of the influence of industry and industrialists on the political
development of Germany 1870—1970.

HEINRICHSBAUER, August.
Schwerindustrie und Politik. Essen: Kettwig
(1948).
A tendentious and generally unreliable account of relations
between big business and the political parties in Weimar.
The author was himself involved as an intermediary, and he
had close links with certain members of the NSDAP,
including Gregor Strasser.

HENNIG, Eike.
"Industrie und Faschismus: Anmerkungen zur
sowjetmarxistischen Interpretationen". *Neue
Politische Literatur*, vol. 15 (1970), p. 432—44.
A brief but useful review of the industry-fascism problem
with reference to some secondary works on the subject
published by Russian authors.

KÁŇA, Otakar.
"Aktionen der deutschen Nationalisten im
Industrierevier Ostrau-Oberschlesien im Interesse
des deutschen Imperialismus 1918 bis 1939".
Jahrbuch für Wirtschaftsgeschichte, vol. 14, pt. 3
(1973), p. 69—86.
Without foundation, the author interprets the nationalist
organizational activity in Upper Silesia as controlled by
and serving the interests of the capitalist system. The
author's material is new and interesting, but his thesis is a
distorted version of the same.

LOCHNER, Louis P.
Tycoons and Tyrants: German Industry from
Hitler to Adenauer. Chicago: Regney (1954),
312 pp.
Impressionistic and unscholarly, this book tries to whitewash big business involvement in politics, especially *vis-
à-vis* National Socialism.

MOMMSEN, Hans; PETZINA, Dieter;
WEISBROD, Bernd (eds.).
Industrielles System und politische Entwicklung
in der Weimarer Republik. Düsseldorf: Droste
(1974), 1017 pp.
A volume of papers originally delivered to an international
symposium in Bochum in June 1973. The papers reach a
very high standard and include: Wolfram Fischer's discussion of the impact of the international economy on the
social relationships, politics and economy of the Weimar
Republic; Kurt Koszyk's piece on the relationship between
industry and the press; Henry A. Turner's essay on entre-
preneurial views of National Socialism; and R. A. Gates's
essay on the policies of the SPD in the depression 1929—
33. Some of these papers have already been published
in academic journals.

MÜLLER, Werner; STOCKFISCH, Jürgen.
"Die 'Veltenbriefe': eine neue Quelle über die
Rolle des Monopolkapitals bei der Zerstörung der
Weimarer Republik". *Zeitschrift für
Geschichtswissenschaft*, vol. 17, pt. 12 (1969),
p. 1565—89.
The so-called *Veltenbriefe* were a series of highly confidential reports on current political, economic and social
events in Germany during the early 1930s, which were
read by only a small group of influential industrialists who
were pledged to secrecy about the contents of the reports.
Paul Silverberg, a leading coal baron, and I. G. Farben
exerted most influence on the reports. The authors contend that the reports further illustrate the complicity
of big business in the downfall of the Weimar Republic
and the advent of dictatorship in 1933. Eleven such reports
dating from November 1930 to October 1932 are reproduced here.

NOLTE, Ernst.
"Big Business and German Politics: a Comment".
American Historical Review, vol. 75, pt. 1 (1969),
p. 71—8.
Nolte is mainly concerned here with reviewing H.A.
Turner's findings on the relationship between heavy industry and the rise of Nazism (see section 26A). He concludes that the whole question of the relations between
big business and politics in general needs more examination.

POHL, Karl H.
"Die Finanzkrise bei Krupp und die Sicherheits-politik Stresemanns: ein Beitrag zum Verhältnis von Wirtschaft und Aussenpolitik in der Weimarer Republik". *Vierteljahrsschrift für Sozial- und Wirtschaftsgeschichte*, vol. 61, pt. 4 (1974), p. 505—25.
An interesting essay on the entanglements of Krupps with the government and Stresemann's foreign policy and dealings with the West in 1925. Krupps faced a severe financial crisis in 1925 and was on the point of collapse; this occurred during a delicate phase of Stresemann's negotiations with the Allies, and the paper discusses how Krupps managed to use Stresemann's political problems to solve its financial crisis. The paper's conclusion is that the action of the government in finally coming to the aid of Krupps, in late summer 1925, clearly shows that politically uncontrolled powers from the economy could have a decisive influence on what were ostensibly purely foreign policy matters.

SCHÄFER, D.
Der deutsche Industrie- und Handelstag als politisches Forum der Weimarer Republik: eine historische Studie zum Verhältnis von Politik und Wirtschaft. Hamburg: Verlag Weltarchiv (1966), 76 pp.
A short but very informative analysis of the considerable influence of this powerful organization on Weimar politics.

SÖRGEL, Werner.
Metallindustrie und Nationalsozialismus: eine Untersuchung über Struktur und Funktion industrieller Organisationen in Deutschland 1929—1933. Frankfurt: Europäische Verlagsanstalt (1965), 96 pp.
Very useful in outlining the political interests of the metal industry and its increasingly close relationship with the NSDAP.

TURNER, Henry A.
"The Ruhrlade, Secret Cabinet of Heavy Industry in the Weimar Republic". *Central European History*, vol. 3, pt. 3 (1970), p. 195—228.
A detailed look at the organization and political activities of the *Ruhrlade*, an exclusive group of Rhenish-Westphalian industrialists set up under Paul Reusch in early 1928. Its political involvement extended to financing conservative organizations and parties, although it remained largely aloof from the NSDAP. As a whole, however, the *Ruhrlade* was politically ineffective.

WINKLER, Heinrich A.
"Unternehmerverbände zwischen Ständeideologie und Nationalsozialismus". *Vierteljahrshefte für Zeitgeschichte*, vol. 17, pt. 4 (1969), p. 341—71.
Winkler shows that the links between the employers and National Socialism before 1933 were concerned with more than party finance. He examines the attitude of the economic associations of big business to parties and the institutions of the Republic, as well as the ideologies of "pressure groups", particularly the concept of corporatism. A detailed and scholarly paper.

(c) Labour Conditions and Employment[1]

BENZ, Wolfgang.
"Vom Freiwilligen Arbeitsdienst zum Arbeits-dienstpflicht". *Vierteljahrshefte für Zeitgeschichte*, vol. 16, pt. 4 (1968), p. 317—46.
This detailed paper centres on the development of ideas of voluntary labour service (FAD) from 1918—33, of the National Socialist idea after 1933 of a national labour

1. Consult relevant titles in section 14.

service (RAD), and then of compulsory labour service (ADP). Benz discusses the wide range of people and organizations advocating FAD before 1933, but no concrete plans were forthcoming until 1929 when the depression forced the government to take the initiative. In 1931, Brüning introduced FAD as a means of relieving unemployment. The NSDAP did not take the idea of labour service seriously until 1932—33.

BERG, Volker von.
"Die Arbeitszeitfrage im Ruhrbergbau als politisches Problem der frühen Weimarer Republik". *Geschichte in Wissenschaft und Unterricht*, vol. 26, pt. 3 (1975), p. 360—80.
Contains some interesting remarks and details.

BRY, Gerhard.
Wages in Germany, 1871—1945. Princeton: Princeton University Press (1960), 486 pp.
A collection and analysis of statistics relating to price and wage levels. Many tables and graphs are provided showing the course of German economic development in *per capita* income, wages, unemployment, cost of living and other variables. The author is able to show wage differentials from industry to industry, and he makes clear the considerable change in incomes during the 1918—33 period due to inflation and depression. Altogether, this is a solid and illuminating work.

DEUERLEIN, Ernst.
"Heinrich Brauns — Schattenriss eines Sozial-politikers". In F.A. Hermens & T. Schieder (eds.). *Staat, Wirtschaft, und Politik in der Weimarer Republik: Festschrift für Heinrich Brüning.* Berlin: Duncker & Humblot (1967), p. 41—96.
A detailed assessment of Brauns' period of office as Reich Labour Minister (June 1920—June 1928), his achievements and failures. On the whole, Deuerlein is impressed by his subject.

HARTWICH, Hans-Hermann.
Arbeitsmarkt, Verbände und Staat, 1918—1933: die öffentliche Bindung unternehmerischer Funktionen in der Weimarer Republik. Berlin: de Gruyter (1967), 488 pp.
A scholarly treatment of the labour market in the Berlin metal industry. The documentation is impressive and well organized. The author discusses the central role of arbitration procedures in wage disputes, which generally benefited the workers, and the contribution in this respect of Rudolf Wissell. The book is an important contribution to Weimar social history.

KÖHLER, Henning.
"Sozialpolitik von Brüning bis Schleicher". *Vierteljahrshefte für Zeitgeschichte*, vol. 21, pt. 2 (1973), p. 146—50.
Deals with government efforts to create employment in a period of exceptionally high unemployment. The associated problem of unemployment insurance relief is also outlined. Government policies as a whole failed to make an impression on unemployment.

KÖHLER, Henning.
Arbeitsdienst in Deutschland: Pläne und Verwirklichungsformen bis zur Einführung der Arbeitsdienstpflicht im Jahre 1935. Berlin: Duncker & Humblot (1967), 281 pp.
Discusses the origins of labour service ideas in right-wing nationalist quarters after 1918—19 and their development during the Weimar period until they were taken over by the National Socialist régime. This study is sound and well informed.

KÖHLER, Henning.
"Arbeitsbeschaffung, Siedlung und Reparationen in der Schlussphase der Regierung Brüning".
Vierteljahrshefte für Zeitgeschichte, vol. 17, pt. 3 (1969), p. 276—307.
A very good analysis of the voluntary labour service introduced by Brüning in 1931—32, as well as of government encouragement of other employment and reclamation programmes. Köhler also cleverly ties in these endeavours with the reparations issue, which was the lynchpin of Brüning's domestic policy.

KUCZYNSKI, Jürgen.
A Short History of Labour Conditions under Industrial Capitalism. Volume 3, Part I: Germany, 1800 to the Present Day. London: Muller (1945), 268 pp.
Useful for background reading.

MARCON, Helmut.
Arbeitsbeschaffungspolitik der Regierungen von Papen und Schleicher: Grundsteinlegung für die Beschäftigungspolitik im Dritten Reich. Frankfurt: Lang (1974), 520 pp.
A massively documented and important study of government efforts to stimulate employment during the last six months of Weimar. Marcon's thesis is that these endeavours facilitated the consolidation of the Hitler régime because by 1933 there already existed a solid foundation on which, aided by the upswing of the economy in general, the National Socialists were able to build for their own advantage. In the short term, Papen and Schleicher did not improve the unemployment situation.

PRELLER, Ludwig.
Sozialpolitik in der Weimarer Republik. Stuttgart: Deutsche Verlags-Union (1949).
A very general and not very informative summary.

RADANT, Hans.
"Unternehmerschaft — Arbeiterschaft: Berlin 1919—39". *Jahrbuch für Wirtschaftsgeschichte*, vol. 1 (1962).
On the basis of the records and files of *Rote Fahne*, Radant examines relations between management and workers in the Treptow electrical works in Berlin 1919—39. He also argues that the *Allgemeine Elektrizitäts-Gesellschaft* was more heavily involved in war material production than is usually claimed. Some interesting documents are appended.

SCHLICKER, Wolfgang.
"Arbeitsdienstbestrebungen des deutschen Monopolkapitals in der Weimarer Republik".
Jahrbuch für Wirtschaftsgeschichte, vol. 12, pt. 3 (1971), p. 95—122.
The author considers that the whole labour service concept was part and parcel of monopolistic capitalism and imperialism, and the first step towards the National Socialist compulsory system. He concludes therefore, that labour service fulfilled a political and not an economic function. The whole question is hopelessly distorted by Schlicker within Marxist-Leninist terms of reference.

(d) Kommunalpolitik

BLAICH, Fritz.
"Möglichkeiten und Grenzen kommunaler Wirtschaftspolitik während der Wirtschaftskrise 1929—1932" *Archiv für Kommunalwissenschaften*, vol. 9, pt. 1 (1970), p. 92—108.

Analyses the activity of municipal economic policy during the depression, using as an example the town of Ludwigshafen, a centre of the chemical industry. Here, the unemployment insurance system paralysed the employment policy of the town council. The council got round the problem for a short time by operating a compensatory fiscal policy.

BÜSCH, Otto.
"Die kommunale Wirtschaft in der Berliner Geschichte der Weimarer Zeit". *Jahrbuch für die Geschichte Mittel- und Ostdeutschlands*, vol. 8 (1959), p. 223—64.
A summary of the main conclusions in the author's book (see below).

BÜSCH, Otto.
Geschichte der Berliner Kommunalwirtschaft in der Weimarer Epoche. Berlin: de Gruyter (1960), 230 pp.
A readable and well researched study which presents a good deal of interesting data on the major aspects of the city's economic administration. Büsch very ably discusses the political implications of the subject.

HERZFELD, Hans.
See his work in section 2.

RIBHEGGE, Wilhelm.
See his work in section 2.

STEINBORN, Peter.
See his work in section 2.

(e) Inflation and Stabilization (1919—1928)[1]

BIECHELE, Ernst.
Der Kampf um die Gemeinwirtschaftskonzeption des Reichswirtschaftsministeriums im Jahre 1919.
Dissertation, Free University of Berlin (1972).
A brief investigation of the economic policies pursued by Reich Economics Minister Rudolf Wissell.

CZADA, Peter.
"Ursachen und Folgen der grossen Inflation".
In Harald Winkel (ed.). *Finanz- und Wirtschaftspolitische Fragen der Zwischenkriegszeit*. Berlin: de Gruyter (1973), p. 9—43.
A balanced assessment of the debate among economists on the advantages and disadvantages of Germany's inflationary policy before 1924.

FELDMAN, Gerald D., and others.
See their collective work in section 14.

FELDMAN, Gerald D.
"Economic and Social Problems of the German Demobilisation 1918—19". *Journal of Modern History*, vol. 47, pt. 1 (1975), p. 1—47.
A stimulating paper on a much neglected aspect of the postwar German situation which adds considerably to our awareness of the problems of that time. The author argues that the decisions taken in Germany in 1918—19 formed part of a more general restorative development of the pre-1914 status quo. The second half of the paper (p. 24—47) contains critical comments on its contents from a number of leading scholars. Feldman agrees with his critics that the paper, however interesting, raises more questions than it answers.

1. Consult relevant titles in sections 4C and 4D.

HOMBURG, Heidrun.
Gewerkschaften, Unternehmer und Staat in der Demobilmachungsphasen (November 1918-Mai 1919). Dissertation, University of Freiburg (1973).
The social and economic problems associated with demobilization, and the attitudes and policies of the trade unions, entrepreneurs and government are discussed in this informative study. The author shows that industrialists in the Ruhr could bypass the official demobilization office in Berlin and have their problems sorted out by the very influential Colonel Josef Koeth, head of the Raw Material Section of the War Office.

HONHART, Michael W.
See his work in section 6B(i).

KEESE, Dietmar.
"Die volkswirtschaftlichen Gesamtgrössen für das deutsche Reich in den Jahren 1925—1936". In W. Conze and H. Raupach (eds.). *Die Staats- und Wirtschaftskrise des deutschen Reiches 1929—33.* Stuttgart: Klett (1967), p. 35—81.
A full discussion of the factors involved in the business cycle of 1925—26.

KROHN, Claus-Dieter.
See his article in section 13A(iv).

LAURSEN, Karsten; **PEDERSEN**, Jørgen.
The German Inflation 1918—23. Amsterdam: North-Holland (1964), 138 pp.
A useful description of the main causes and manifestations of the inflation, though the political side of it is not adequately discussed.

LINK, Werner.
See his article in section 19A(iv).

MUTHESIUS, Volkmar.
Augenzeuge von drei Inflationen: Erinnerungen und Gedanken eines Wirtschaftspublizisten. Frankfurt: Knapp (1973), 239 pp.
Some remarks on the 1923 situation are mildly interesting.

PEDERSEN, Jørgen.
"Einige Bemerkungen zur deutschen Inflation von 1919—1923". *Zeitschrift für die Gesamte Staatswissenschaft*, vol. 122 (1966), p. 418—30.
Argues that the currency depreciation had by itself no decisive effect on production, contrary to common assumption. The author's main purpose, however, is to rationalize the social consequences of the inflation and put them in proper perspective; thus he examines the causes of the inflation and its effects above all on production and income distribution. An interesting paper, but his arguments seem sophistical.

RINGER, Fritz K. (ed.).
The German Inflation of 1923. London: Oxford University Press (1969), 228 pp.
This sound work comprises extracts from the writings of prominent historians which shed light on the economic causes and the political and social consequences of the 1923 inflation. The editor provides a competent linking commentary, and the book as a whole will be welcomed by undergraduates in particular.

SCHMIDT, Günter.
"Zur Staats- und Machtfrage in der November-revolution". *Jahrbuch für Geschichte*, vol. 2 (1967), p. 249—82.
Apart from the ideological framework within which the paper is presented, this is an interesting and detailed description of the activities and initiatives of the government's demobilization office in 1918—19.

WITT, Peter-Christian.
See his article ("Finanzpolitik und sozialer Wandel") in section 13A(iv).

(f) Depression (1929—1933)[1]

BENNECKE, Heinrich.
Wirtschaftliche Depression und politisches Radikalismus 1918—1938. Munich: Olzog (1970), 408 pp.
Says nothing that is new. The author concentrates on the 1930—33 period, stating that the depression led to a radicalization of the far Left and Right, and that the NSDAP drew its support in the main from the *Mittelstand*. He does not examine the origins and development of the economic crisis and does not attempt to investigate the connection between crisis-torn capitalism and fascism. A poor book.

BLAICH, Fritz.
See his article in section 13A(ii)(d).

GROTKOPP, Wilhelm.
Die grosse Krise: Lehren aus der Überwindung der Wirtschaftskrise 1929/32. Düsseldorf: Econ-Verlag (1954), 408 pp.
A solid assessment of the depression's origins, development, consequences, and long-term lessons.

HANAU, Klaus.
See his work in section 13A(iii)(a).

HEYL, John D.
Economic Policy and Political Leadership in the German Depression 1930—1936. Dissertation, Washington University (1971).
A sound discussion of the deficiencies of the economic programmes of the Weimar government 1930—33 and the corresponding failures of political leaders to provide a lead.

HOCK, Wilhelm.
Deutscher Antikapitalismus: der ideologische Kampf gegen die freie Wirtschaft im Zeichen der grossen Krise. Frankfurt: Knapp Verlag (1960).
Anti-capitalist feeling was strong on the political Left and also in many sections of the political Right in the late 1920s and early 1930s. This study examines the ideological opposition offered, though it does not really succeed in assessing the fundamental causes of anti-capitalism.

KINDLEBERGER, Charles P.
The World Depression 1929—1939. London: Allen Lane (1973), 336 pp.
The author argues in this well written and scholarly book that the major reason why the impact of the depression was so drastic was that the capitalist system itself was basically unstable. He adds that the international economy

---

1. Consult relevant titles in sections 4E, 4F, 4G, and 4H.

was unstable from 1918, thus making the economy more susceptible to crises. Kindleberger does not give adequate consideration, however, to the efforts of Western European governments to promote recovery.

KROLL, Gerhard.
Von der Weltwirtschaftskrise zur Staatskonjunktur. Berlin: Duncker & Humblot (1958).
A very good work, covering the 1919—36 period. Kroll discusses the origins and development of the depression with skill, though his information is not new for the most part. His major conclusions are sound.

LÜKE, Rolf E.
Von der Stabilisierung zur Krise. Zürich: Polygraphischer Verlag (1958), 363 pp.
A good economic history of Germany 1924—33. The author underlines the fundamental relationship between Germany's reparations problem and her economic difficulties during the depression — a thesis which needs to be modified in the light of more recent research.

PETZINA, Dieter.
"Germany and the Great Depression". *Journal of Contemporary History*, vol. 4, pt. 4 (1969), p. 59—74.
Argues that the great depression was very different in its social, economic, and political consequences in Germany as compared with other countries. In Germany, the economic and political crises were much worse than elsewhere because of the First World War and its aftermath, which made the German economy more susceptible to profound crisis. The main value of an otherwise lacklustre paper lies in its presentation of points of detail about the economic situation.

PETZINA, Dieter.
"Elemente der Wirtschaftspolitik in der Spätphase der Weimarer Republik". *Vierteljahrshefte für Zeitgeschichte*, vol. 21, pt. 2 (1973), p. 127—33.
Mainly concerned with a critical look at Brüning's financial and economic policy, but the author begins by usefully outlining the special features of the Weimar economy, and the international restrictions which weighed down on any national policy designed to combat crisis. He rightly reminds us that, anyway, most politicians incorrectly diagnosed the causes of depression.

PETZINA, Dieter.
"Hauptprobleme der deutschen Wirtschaftspolitik 1932—33". *Vierteljahrshefte für Zeitgeschichte*, vol. 15, pt. 1 (1967), p. 18—55.
A thorough and important study of the significance of economic policy in national politics, especially from the time of Brüning's fall in May 1932 to Hugenberg's resignation as Minister of the Economy and Agriculture in the summer of 1933. Petzina focuses his discussion on the two aspects which lay at the heart of economic policy: the creation of employment and agrarian policies. He examines the ideas and policies adopted towards these issues by Papen, Schleicher and Hitler. The paper is essential reading for a deeper understanding of the 1932—33 economic and political situation.

PREDÖHL, Andreas.
"Die Epochenbedeutung der Weltwirtschaftskrise von 1929 bis 1931". *Vierteljahrshefte für Zeitgeschichte*, vol. 1, pt. 2 (1953), p. 97—118.
A valuable interpretative essay on the wider significance of the depression.

TEMIN, Peter.
"The Beginning of the Depression in Germany". *Economic History Review*, vol. 24, pt. 2 (1971), p. 240—8.
Presents a challenging argument that the fall in American capital exports in 1929 did not initiate the German depression in that year. The main difficulty, the author argues, was a substantial fall-off in inventory investment, but this fall in investment was not due to American credit drying up.

TREUE, Wilhelm (ed.).
Deutschland in der Weltwirtschaftskrise in Augenzeugenberichten. Düsseldorf: Rauch (1967), 439 pp.
A most useful documentary source which above all permits a valuable insight into the social response to and social consequences of the depression.

VIERHAUS, Rudolf.
"Auswirkungen der Krise um 1930 in Deutschland: Beiträge zu einer historisch-psychologischen Analyse". In W. Conze and H. Raupach (eds.). *Die Staats- und Wirtschaftskrise des deutschen Reiches 1929—33.* Stuttgart: Klett (1967), p. 155—75.
A perceptive and highly interesting look at the social and psychological effects of the depression on the millions of unemployed and despairing Germans.

(iii) Agriculture

(a) General

BARMEYER, Heide.
Andreas Hermes und die Organisation der deutschen Landwirtschaft: Christliche Bauernvereine, Reichslandbund, Grüne Front, Reichsnährstand 1928 bis 1933. Stuttgart: Fischer Verlag (1971), 176 pp.
An assessment of the contribution to the fall of the Republic of agrarian interest politics. Using a biographical basis (Hermes was a leading agrarian organization politician), Barmeyer concentrates on the organizational and political aspects of Hermes' activity as President of the German Christian Peasants' Leagues. But the book is too superficial on the whole, evades too many important questions, and lacks a critical approach. As a result, a comprehensive assessment of the extent of agrarian political influence 1928—33 still has to be written.

BERTHOLD, Rudolf.
"Zur Entwicklung der deutschen Agrarproduktion und der Ernährungswirtschaft zwischen 1907 und 1925". *Jahrbuch für Wirtschaftsgeschichte*, pt. 4 (1974) p. 83—111.
Contains extremely useful statistical data and graphs on the development of German agrarian and food production.

BERTHOLD, Rudolf.
"Zur sozialökonomischen Struktur des kapitalistischen Systems der deutschen Landwirtschaft zwischen 1907 und 1925". *Jahrbuch für Wirtschaftsgeschichte*, pt. 3 (1974), p. 105—26.
The author's conclusion that the socio-economic structure of German agriculture was fundamentally capitalist comes as no surprise. But of note is the considerable amount of important statistical information in the essay.

BORCKE-STARGORDT, Henning.
Der ostdeutsche Landbau zwischen Fortschritt, Krise und Politik: ein Beitrag zur Agrar- und Zeitgeschichte. Würzburg: Holzner (1957), 200 pp.
Provides a satisfactory survey of the development of German agriculture during the Weimar period, and in particular analyses in competent fashion the problem of *Osthilfe*. What is not so impressive is the author's attempt to prove that Hindenburg was his own man and not unduly influenced by any social group.

GERSCHENKRON, Alexander.
Bread and Democracy in Germany. Berkeley: University of California Press (1945), 238 pp.
Provides an excellent analysis of Prussian agriculture from the 1890s to 1933. But the book is quite unreliable when discussing political developments, such as the importance of the *Junker* to the rise of National Socialism.

HANAU, Klaus.
Landwirtschaft und allgemeine Wirtschaftskrise 1929—1932. Dissertation, University of Freiburg im Breisgau (1959).
A brief examination of how far the fall in prices in the world agrarian market was a cause, and how far a result, of the economic depression.

HAUSHOFER, Heinz.
Ein halbes Jahrhundert im Dienste der bayerischen Landwirtschaft: zur Geschichte des Bayerischen Staatsministeriums für Ernährung, Landwirtschaft und Forsten. Munich: Oldenbourg (1969).
Not particularly interesting unless one has a passionate interest in Bavarian agriculture. To be noted, however, are the useful data on the peasant movement in Bavaria in 1918—19 and the activities of the peasant councils (*Bauernräte*).

MUTH, Heinrich.
"Agrarpolitik und Parteipolitik im Frühjahr 1932". In F.A. Hermens & T. Schieder (eds.). *Staat, Wirtschaft und Politik in der Weimarer Republik: Festschrift für Heinrich Brüning.* Berlin: Duncker und Humblot (1967), p. 317—60.
An informative narrative concerning the development of *Osthilfe* measures by the Brüning government in 1930—31, with emphasis on the political implications of the measures. Muth assesses the contribution of agrarian problems to the fall of Brüning as Chancellor, in particular analysing the so-called *Siedlungsverordnung* of May 1932 which was designed to help the large estates in East Prussia. The considerable importance of agrarian interests in Weimar politics is made abundantly clear in this essay.

PANZER, Arno.
Das Ringen um die deutsche Agrarpolitik von der Währungsstabilisierung bis zur Agrardebatte im Reichstag in Dezember 1928. Kiel: Mühlau (1970), 198 pp.
A most useful and able description and analysis of the agrarian problem during the "quiet" years of the Weimar Republic (1924—28). The attitudes of the major political parties to the problem are clearly illustrated.

RAUPACH, Hans.
"Der interregionale Wohlfahrtsausgleich als Problem der Politik des Deutschen Reiches". In W. Conze and H. Raupach (eds.). *Die Staats- und Wirtschaftskrise des deutschen Reiches 1929—33.* Stuttgart: Klett (1967), p. 13—34.
A detailed and objective assessment of the many problems confronting East Prussian agriculture.

SCHLICKER, Wolfgang.
"Die Artamanen-bewegung, eine Frühform des Arbeitsdienstes und Kaderzelle des Faschismus auf dem Lande". *Zeitschrift für Geschichtswissenschaft*, vol. 18, pt. 1 (1970), p. 66—75.
Provides some useful details, but its political bias makes the essay boring to read.

SCHULZ, Gerhard.
"Staatliche Stützungsmassnahmen in den deutschen Ostgebieten: zur Vorgeschichte der 'Osthilfe' der Regierung Brüning." In F.A. Hermens and T. Schieder (eds.). *Staat, Wirtschaft und Politik in der Weimarer Republik: Festschrift für Heinrich Brüning.* Berlin: Duncker & Humblot (1967), p. 141—204.
An extremely valuable paper on the social and economic situation in East German farming areas prior to the assistance programme of the Brüning government. A declining agriculture in an age of industrialization and the existence of semi-feudal attitudes on the part of landowners and small farmers constituted the heart of the economic and social problem, which became worse after 1918. Schulz criticizes the parties for not taking measures to break up the estates and lay the foundations for a profitable agriculture. Instead, piecemeal financial aid was given out (*Ostpreussenhilfe*) until the onset of the depression demanded an even greater injection of capital to keep the large estates going. This was the overture to the notorious *Osthilfe*.

(b) The Small Farmers

ANGRESS, Werner T.
"The Political Role of the Peasantry in the Weimar Republic". *Review of Politics*, vol. 21, pt. 4 (1959), p. 530—49.
The peasantry played no significant role in the November Revolution, except perhaps in Bavaria for a short time. Afterwards, they remained politically passive, nurtured fond memories of the monarchy, and spent their time working the farms. However, the agricultural crisis and depression of the late 1920s brought the peasantry over to the side of right-wing political extremism. The essay is a competent summary of well-known political developments among the German peasantry, and is based entirely on secondary sources.

BURKHARDT, Jürgen.
Bauern gegen Junker und Pastoren: Feudalreste in der mecklenburgischen Landwirtschaft nach 1918. East Berlin: Akademie-Verlag (1963), 192 pp.
Provides interesting detail on surviving feudal relics in the backward province of Mecklenburg.

FLEMMING, Jens.
"Landarbeiter zwischen Gewerkschaften und 'Werksgemeinschaft': zum Verhältnis von Agrarunternehmer und Landarbeiterbewegung im Übergang vom Kaiserreich zur Weimarer Republik". *Archiv für Sozialgeschichte*, vol. 14 (1974), p. 351—418.
Analyses the relationship between agricultural concerns and farm workers 1900—33 and in so doing presents a good deal of new and important material. The author stresses the continuity of anti-socialist and anti-trade union attitudes in this relationship during 1919—33. The landowners founded "yellow" workers' associations which were meant to integrate rural workers into their economic and political interests. This policy was largely successful, so the SPD did not make much of an impression on the rural peasants, and democracy itself remained an alien creed on the land. Thus, in 1929—33, the agricultural areas of Germany became bastions of National Socialism.

KASPER, Martin.
Der Lausitzer Bauernbund: ein Beitrag zur Geschichte der demokratischen Bauernbewegung in der Oberlausitz 1924—32. Bautzen: Domowina Verlag (1967), 151 pp.
A tendentious and unreliable account, both factually and interpretatively.

SCHUMACHER, Martin.
"Agrarische Interessenpolitik: Andreas Hermes". *Neue Politische Literatur*, vol. 18, pt. 1 (1973), p. 96—101.
A brief portrait of this important figure in peasant politics.

WUNDERLICH, Frieda.
Farm Labor in Germany 1810—1945. Princeton: Princeton University Press (1961), 390 pp.
The problem of farm labour is complex, since in Germany agrarian conditions varied significantly from one area to another. But there were three important developments during the Weimar period: the farm worker was given full legal rights for the first time, rural depopulation made farm labour scarce, and foreign workers declined drastically in number. This book, which concentrates heavily on the 1919—45 period, is very well documented and convincing in argument.

(c) The Landowners

BUCHTA, Bruno.
Die Junker und die Weimarer Republik: Charakter und Bedeutung der Osthilfe in den Jahren 1928—1933. East Berlin: Deutscher Verlag der Wissenschaften (1959), 176 pp.
The author adds very little to what was already known about the *Junker*, their estates, and *Osthilfe*, despite having access to archives in East Germany. His main concern, in fact, is to praise the policy of the KPD, and to denounce that of the SPD, and indeed the obvious political bias robs the work of any worth.

DENECKE, Horst.
Die agrarpolitischen Konzeptionen des deutschen Imperialismus beim Übergang vom bürgerlich-parlamentarischen System zur faschistischen Diktatur (Frühjahr 1930 bis Herbst 1934). Dissertation, Humboldt University, East Berlin (1972).
Almost unreadable because of the heavy Marxist-Leninist jargon used by the author in place of rational argument.

GÖRLITZ, Walter.
Die Junker: Adel und Bauer im deutschen Osten. Geschichtsbilanz von 7 Jahrhunderten. Glücksburg: Verlag Starke (1956), 462 pp.
A sympathetic general chronicle of the economic and political role of the *Junker* through the centuries. The author's discussion of the situation in the Weimar Republic is superficial.

HERTZ-EICHENRÖDE, Dieter.
See his work in section 9D.

LABUDA, G.
"Bruno Buchta, die Junker und die Weimarer Republik". *Polish Western Affairs*, vol. 2, pt. 1 (1962), p. 156—61.
A critical review of Buchta's book (see above).

MUNCY, Lysbeth S.
"The Junkers and the Prussian Administration from 1918 to 1939". *Review of Politics*, vol. 9, pt. 4 (1947), p. 482—501.
Examines how the *Junker* retained a substantial measure of political influence in Weimar through their domination of their estates, the agrarian organizations, and Hindenburg. But the author overestimates the extent of their say in politics. On the other hand, he provides very useful data on the *Junker*.

NORDEN, Albert.
See his work in section 13A(iv).

PUHLE, Hans-Jürgen.
Agrarische Interessenpolitik und preussischer Konservatismus im wilhelminischen Reich (1893—1914): ein Beitrag zur Analyse des Nationalismus in Deutschland am Beispiel des Bundes der Landwirte und der Deutsch-Konservativen Partei. Hanover: Verlag für Literatur und Zeitgeschehen (1966), 365 pp.
This important and scholarly study has as its theme the reasons for the radicalization of agrarian politics before 1914, and the development of the *Bund der Landwirte* as a powerful pressure group. More relevant for students of Weimar is Puhle's full history of the *Bund* (1893—1921) and of its successors before 1933.

ROSENBERG, Hans.
Probleme der deutschen Sozialgeschichte. Frankfurt: Suhrkampf (1969), 149 pp.
Consists of three readable studies of German agrarian history, including one on the historical role of the *Junker*.

SCHREINER, Albert.
See his work in section 13A(iv).

VETTER, Klaus.
"Bodo von der Marwitz: der Beitrag eines preussischen Junkers zur ideologischen Verbreitung des Faschismus auf dem Lande". *Zeitschrift für Geschichtswissenschaft*, vol. 23, pt. 5 (1975), p. 552—68.
Provides some documentary evidence to illustrate the extreme right-wing views of von der Marwitz.

(iv) Finance and Banks

BAUMGARTEN, Dieter.
Deutsche Finanzpolitik 1924—1928. Berlin: Ernst-Reuter-Gesellschaft (1965), 223 pp.
A solid contribution to the economic and financial aspects of Weimar's middle years. The approach to financial matters and policies of government and the political parties is clearly outlined.

BORN, Karl-Erich.
Die deutsche Bankenkrise 1931: Finanzen und Politik. Munich: Piper (1967), 286 pp.
An excellent analysis of the weaknesses of the German banking system which caused the collapse of 1931. The failure of bankers and governments to solve these problems is particularly well handled.

DIECKMANN, Hildemarie.
See her book and article in section 3B.

GOSSWEILER, Kurt.
Grossbanken, Industriemonopole, Staat: Ökonomie und Politik des staatsmonopolistischen Kapitalismus in Deutschland 1914—1932. East Berlin: Deutscher Verlag der Wissenschaften (1971), 428 pp.
Contains some valuable details of the organization and activities of big banks, but the author's arguments and conclusions adhere strictly to the party line.

HÖFLER, Gustav.
Erzbergers Finanzreform und ihre Rückwirkungen auf die bundesstaatliche Struktur des Reiches. Dissertation, University of Freiburg (1955).
A competent review of the theoretical and practical nature of Erzberger's ideas on financial reform, but the book offers little original interpretation.

HORNSCHU, Hans-Erich.
See his work in section 9B(i).

KROHN, Claus-Dieter.
"Helfferich contra Hilferding: konservative Geldpolitik und die sozialen Folgen der deutschen Inflation 1918—1923". *Vierteljahrsschrift für Sozial- und Wirtschaftsgeschichte*, vol. 62, pt. 1 (1975), p. 62—92.
A searching examination of the inflation and financial crisis in early Weimar, especially in autumn 1923. The debate over monetary and currency policy at that time was led by Helfferich and Hilferding, whose views were completely opposite. This paper discusses their theories in order to clarify the question of what was the essential cause of the 1923 inflation. Krohn lays considerable emphasis on the policies of certain interest groups in big business as a major factor in the crisis, and from this he attempts to rehabilitate the arguments of Hilferding against his conservative critics.

KROHN, Claus-Dieter.
Stabilisierung und ökonomische Interessen: die Finanzpolitik des deutschen Reiches 1923—1927. Düsseldorf: Bertelsmann (1974), 287 pp.
A provocative study which, by using much primary material from the Potsdam archives, argues that during the 1924—27 period the government promoted the economic interests of big business at the expense of the middle classes and the workers, who were forced to bear the brunt of reparations payments. In brief, the author states that the Weimar Republic in these years helped to boost the power of monopoly capitalism.

LEIDEL, Herbert.
Die Begründung der Reichsfinanzverwaltung. Dissertation, University of Münster (1964).
A brief study of the problems associated with setting up Weimar's financial administration after 1918. Competent but dull.

LUTHER, Hans.
Vor den Abgrund, 1930—1933: Reichsbankpräsident in Krisenzeiten. Berlin: Propyläen (1964), 316 pp.
Only partially useful recollections of Luther's time as President of the *Reichsbank*. The data on financial and currency problems is informative, but political aspects are rather poorly treated.

MENGES, Franz.
See his work in section 9C.

MÖLLER, Alex.
Im Gedanken an Reichsfinanzminister Rudolf Hilferding. Bonn: Seidl (1971), 42 pp.
A fresh look at the controversy over financial and currency problems which forced Hilferding's resignation as Reich Finance Minister in 1923.

MÖLLER, Alex.
See also his work in section 5B.

MORSEY, Rudolf.
"Brünings Kritik an der Reichsfinanzpolitik 1919—1929". In *Geschichte, Wirtschaft, Gesellschaft: Festschrift für Clemens Bauer zum 75. Geburtstag.* Berlin: Duncker & Humblot (1974), p. 359—74.
A most informative analysis.

MÜLLER, Helmut.
Die Zentralbank — eine Nebenregierung: Reichsbankpräsident Hjalmar Schacht als Politiker der Weimarer Republik. Opladen: Westdeutscher Verlag (1973), 139 pp.
Underlines the central importance of the *Reichsbank*, whose influence stretched far beyond purely banking affairs. Schacht is the main figure in the book and his image as a vain, grasping and thoroughly unpleasant person is not changed by anything Müller writes.

NETZBAND, Karl-Bernhard; WIDMAIER, Hans P.
Währungs- und Finanzpolitik der Ära Luther 1923—1925. Tübingen: Mohr (1964), 286 pp.
Contains a good deal of technical data on financial matters which the ordinary reader may find difficult to digest. Otherwise, the book is a solid contribution.

NORDEN, Albert.
Lehren deutscher Geschichte: zur politischen Rolle des Finanzkapitals und der Junker. East Berlin: Dietz (1947), 279 pp.
A distorted Marxist view of German history 1914—47. The familiar theme of the wickedness of militarists and industrialists in plunging Germany into war in 1914 and 1939 is regurgitated with little sophistication. The author asserts that the main cause of the collapse of Weimar was the failure to break up the big banks, estates and monopolies. The book is blatantly propagandistic and characterized by an overweening subservience to Russia.

SCHMITT, Veit.
See his work in section 3A.

SCHREINER, Albert.
"Die Eingabe deutscher Finanzmagnaten, Monopolisten und Junker an Hindenburg für die Berufung Hitlers zum Reichskanzler (November 1932)". *Zeitschrift für Geschichtswissenschaft*, vol. 4, pt. 2 (1956), p. 366—69.
Tries to illustrate further the complicity of high finance in the victory of National Socialism by stressing the initiatives displayed by Kurt von Schröder and Schacht. Published here is a letter from Schacht to Hindenburg of November 1932 calling on him to appoint Hitler as Chancellor. The letter is signed by many leading names in the financial and business world.

SCHWERIN von KROSIGK, Lutz G.
Staatsbankrott: die Geschichte des deutschen
Reiches 1920—1945. Geschrieben vom letzten
Reichsfinanzminister. Göttingen: Musterschmidt
(1974), 412 pp.
Written by a former Reich Minister of Finance, this is an
accurate, detailed, and comprehensive history of state
finances in Germany 1920—45.

STUCKEN, R.
Die deutsche Geld- und Kreditpolitik 1914—1963.
Tübingen: Mohr (1964).
A good general survey of the main developments in German
monetary and credit policy.

THIERAUF, Hans.
Der Finanzausgleich in der Weimarer Republik.
Dissertation, University of Würzburg (1961).
Moderately useful.

WEISS, Otto.
"Die Münzen der Weimarer Republik". *Geschichte*
in Wissenschaft und Unterricht, vol. 11, pt. 1
(1960), p. 37—9.
A note on the coins in use during the Weimar period.

WILHELMY, Rudolf.
Geschichte des deutschen wertbeständigen
Notgeldes von 1923—1924. Berlin: Selbstverlag
(1962), 172 pp.
Includes a number of interesting details, but otherwise a
rather unpolished description.

WILLIAMSON, John G.
Karl Helfferich 1872—1924: Economist, Financier,
Politician. Princeton: Princeton University Press
(1971), 439 pp.
A full and on the whole useful biography of the right-wing
politician perhaps best known as the man who reformed the
inflated currency. His ideas are clearly analysed and the
book's conclusions are sound.

WITT, Peter-Christian.
"Reichsfinanzminister und Reichs-
finanzverwaltung: zum Problem des Verhältnisses
von politischer Führung und bürokratischer
Herrschaft in den Anfangsjahren der Weimarer
Republik (1918/19—1924)". *Vierteljahrshefte für*
Zeitgeschichte, vol. 23, pt. 1 (1975), p. 1—61.
An important article on a neglected aspect of the Weimar
Republic's administrative structure. Witt is concerned with
the general problem of the relationship between government and administration in a modern state, and he illustrates the problem by analysing financial administration in
early Weimar. He concentrates on a detailed examination
of the personnel structure and selection of personnel in
leading positions of the central and regional financial
bureaucracy. The problems of the leadership structure of
the Reich government, the position of the Reich Finance
Minister, as well as the role of the financial bureaucracy in
the formulation of political decisions, are investigated.

WITT, Peter-Christian.
"Finanzpolitik und sozialer Wandel in Krieg und
Inflation 1914—1924". In H. Mommsen (ed.).
Industrielles System und politische Entwicklung
in der Weimarer Republik. Düsseldorf: Droste,
(1974), p. 395—420.
An illuminating analysis of the elements of continuity and
discontinuity in German financial and economic development during these years, and the important role of financial
policy.

WITT, Peter-Christian.
"Finanzpolitik und sozialer Wandel: Wachstum
und Funktionswandel der Staatsausgaben in
Deutschland 1871—1933". In *Sozialgeschichte*
heute: Festschrift für Hans Rosenberg zum 70.
Geburtstag. Göttingen: Vandenhoeck und
Ruprecht (1974), p. 565—74.
On basically the same theme as the aforementioned article,
only in a wider perspective.

B. SOCIAL GROUPS AND DEVELOPMENT

(i) General

DAHRENDORF, Ralf.
Society and Democracy in Germany. New York:
Doubleday (1967), 482 pp.
A brilliant and absorbing study which tackles the problem
of why a strong enough liberal ideology conducive to the
acceptance of modernization within a democratic political
framework did not emerge. Dahrendorf's methodology
comprises historical and sociological techniques of analysis.

GEIGER, Theodor.
Die soziale Schichtung des deutschen Volkes:
soziographischer Versuch auf statistischer
Grundlage. Stuttgart: Enke Verlag (1967). New ed.
An excellent and detailed statistical analysis of the entire
German social structure, based on the 1925 occupational
census.

ZAPF, Wolfgang.
Wandlungen der deutschen Elite 1919—1961.
Munich: Kösel (1965).
A systematic analysis of the development, nature and
function of social élites and social mobility. Combines
historical and social scientific techniques.

(ii) Social Legislation

ERDMANN, Gerhard.
Die Entwicklung der deutschen Sozial-
gesetzgebung. Göttingen: Musterschmidt (1957),
405 pp.
A broad discussion of social legislation development in
Germany 1839—1956, covering subjects such as social
security, unemployment welfare, and apprenticeship.
A very good introductory study.

FÖLSTER, Elfriede.
See her work in section 6B(vii)(d).

MIELKE, Friedrich.
"Studie über den Berliner Wohnungsbau 1914—
1933". *Jahrbuch für die Geschichte Mittel- und*
Ostdeutschlands, vol. 21 (1972), p. 227—58.
A detailed and informative examination of the gross failings
of the housing situation and housing administration in
Berlin.

RICHTER, Peter.
"Wohlfahrtspflege, Caritas, Medizinalpolitik nach
dem Ersten Weltkrieg". *Historisches Jahrbuch*,
vol. 72 (1953), p. 549—62.
A brief review of the activities of charitable bodies in the
social welfare field after 1918.

SCHRAEPLER, Ernst.
Quellen zur Geschichte der sozialen Frage in Deutschland. Vol. 2: 1871 bis zur Gegenwart.
Göttingen: Musterschmidt (1957), 246 pp.
A rather vague consideration of the evolution of social conceptions in Germany.

SILVERMAN, Dan P.
"A Pledge Unredeemed: the Housing Crisis in Weimar Germany". *Central European History*, vol. 3, pt. 1—2 (1970), p. 112—39.
An analysis of the poor record of successive Weimar governments on the acute housing problem, which amounted to a social scandal. The inflation, depression, lack of capital, etc., were the principal drawbacks, but nevertheless national and local government agencies, as well as private enterprise, did not display nearly enough urgency. The result was a virtual paralysis in the sector of the building industry concerned with housing.

(iii) The Middle Classes

COYNER, Sandra.
Class Patterns of Family Income and Expenditure during the Weimar Republic: German White-Collar Employees as Harbingers of Modern Society.
Dissertation, Rutgers University (1975).
A study of important aspects of social stratification and class attitudes, with emphasis on the white-collar employee (*Angestellte*). By examining income and consumption patterns, Coyner identifies the values and life style of the *Angestellte*. Wide differences among this class in terms of income, expenditure on housing, education, food, etc., are revealed; taken as a whole, the life style of the *Angestellte* shows marked dissimilarities from that of workers and government officials. The final conclusion is that white-collar families anticipated the consumption behaviour patterns characteristic of modern mass society.

CRONER, Fritz.
Die Angestellten in der modernen Gesellschaft: eine sozialhistorische und soziologische Studie.
Frankfurt (1954).
Produces useful statistical data on social mobility in Germany during the late nineteenth and twentieth centuries.

GINSBERG, Lev I.
"Auf dem Wege zur Hitlerdiktatur: der Kurs der Monopolbourgeoisie auf die offene Diktatur im Jahre 1931". *Zeitschrift für Geschichtswissenschaft*, vol. 17, pt. 7 (1969), p. 825—43.
The author challenges the popular notion that National Socialism was primarily a movement of the petty bourgeoisie. By examining the composition of right-wing forces in the Harzburg Front in autumn 1931, he states that the "monopolistic bourgeoisie" and their militaristic and imperialist allies were the main contributors to the victory of National Socialism.

HABEDANK, Heinz.
Der Feind steht rechts: bürgerliche Linke im Kampf gegen den deutschen Militarismus (1925— 1933). East Berlin: Buchverlag Der Morgen (1965), 232 pp.
A polemical work of no real historical value.

KLEIN, Fritz.
"Zur Vorbereitung der faschistischen Diktatur durch die deutsche Grossbourgeoisie (1929— 1932)". *Zeitschrift für Geschichtswissenschaft*, vol. 1, pt. 6 (1953), p. 872—904.
Sets out to discover which social groups actively overthrew democracy in favour of Hitler. Not surprisingly, the author blames big industrialists and their capitalist allies above all; hence, he examines evidence of direct financial links between Hitler and heavy industry, the activity of the *Reichsverband der deutschen Industrie* (the powerful employers' association), and preparations for the reorganization of the Brüning government in late 1931. Altogether, the essay is quite unconvincing in pointing the accusing finger at the upper bourgeoisie.

KOCKA, Jürgen.
"Zur Problematik der Angestellten 1914—33".
In H. Mommsen (ed.). *Industrielles System und politische Entwicklung in der Weimarer Republik.*
Düsseldorf: Droste (1974), p. 792—811.
A commendable paper which provides a thorough analysis of the problems of identification, status, economic standing and political outlook of this amorphous social class.

KRACAUER, Siegfried.
Die Angestellten: eine Schrift vom Ende der Weimarer Republik. Bonn: Verlag für Demoskopie (1959), 111 pp.
An interesting and valuable contribution.

LEBOVICS, Herman.
Social Conservatism and the Middle Classes in Germany 1914—1933. Princeton: Princeton University Press (1969), 248 pp.
An important study of the *Mittelstand*, relating their socio-economic circumstances to neo-conservative ideas (as conceived by Spengler, Niekisch, Spann, etc.). The author stresses the contradictory economic interests of the various groups comprising the *Mittelstand*, though their political conceptions were uniformly right-wing. Caught between capitalism and socialism, and ruined by inflation, the *Mittelstand* became susceptible to the neo-conservative ideology.

RUGE, Wolfgang.
"Die 'Deutsche Allgemeine Zeitung' und die Brüning-Regierung". *Zeitschrift für Geschichts-wissenschaft*, vol. 16, pt. 1 (1968), p. 19—53.
Following on from Klein's article (see above), Ruge makes yet another rather clumsy and unscholarly effort to prove the culpability of the upper bourgeoisie (a class not precisely defined by him) for the success of National Socialism.

SCHWEITZER, Arthur.
Die Nazifizierung des Mittelstandes. Stuttgart: Enke Verlag (1970), 208 pp.
This is simply a German translation of some early chapters of the author's comprehensive study, *Big Business and the Third Reich* (London: Eyre and Spottiswoode (1964), 739 pp.). He shows how extensive was the support given to the NSDAP by small businessmen threatened by the department stores, the craftsmen menaced by big business, the farmers facing ruin, and the white collar workers placed on the verge of proletarianization.

UHLIG, Heinrich.
Die Warenhäuser im Dritten Reich. Cologne: Westdeutscher Verlag (1954), 230 pp.
Although devoted largely to the post-1933 period, this book offers a useful introduction to middle class thinking regarding small businesses and shops before 1933. The author discusses the receptivity of these classes to National Socialist economic ideas, including "German Socialism", and considers the theme of middle class socialism through Weimar into the Third Reich. Subjects such as the crisis of the small retail business in the depression and the repressive taxation system after 1930 are convincingly covered.

WINKLER, Heinrich A.
Mittelstand, Demokratie und Nationalsozialismus: die politische Entwicklung von Handwerk und Kleinhandel in der Weimarer Republik. Cologne: Kiepenheuer und Witsch (1972), 307 pp.

A good study of the political attitudes of the groups that made up the "old" *Mittelstand*, small businessmen, independent craftsmen, and others. The author argues that a basic continuity can be discerned in the politics of these groups from before 1914 to 1933 because they were most threatened by industrialism and modernization. In Weimar, additional factors such as the inflation and depression turned them into ardent supporters of the NSDAP. This part of the book is well documented and powerfully argued. The part which examines the relationship between the *Mittelstand* and National Socialism, however, is thin and unsatisfactory.

(iv) Women

ARENDT, Hans-Jürgen.
See his work in section 6B(vii)(e).

BREMME, Gabrielle.
Die politische Rolle der Frau in Deutschland: eine Untersuchung über den Einfluss der Frauen bei Wahlen und ihre Teilnahme in Partei und Parlament. Göttingen: Vandenhoeck und Ruprecht (1956), 288 pp.

A general but illuminating and pioneering study.

BRIDENTHAL, Renate.
"Beyond Kinder, Küche, Kirche: Weimar Women at Work". *Central European History*, vol. 6, pt. 2 (1973), p. 148—66.

Tries to demonstrate that in Weimar, the notion of women's economic emancipation had no substance in reality. Economic modernization, rather than being a liberating force for women, was a retrogressive phenomenon. The author proceeds to examine the statistical and practical situation of women in various sectors of the economy including agriculture and industry.

KATER, Michael H.
"Krisis des Frauenstudiums in der Weimarer Republik". *Vierteljahrsschrift für Sozial- und Wirtschaftsgeschichte*, vol. 59 (1972), p. 207—55.

An excellent paper, with detailed information on the economic and financial crisis affecting women in higher education.

McINTYRE, Jill.
"Women and the Professions in Germany 1930—1940". In A.J. Nicholls and E. Matthias (eds.). *German Democracy and the Triumph of Hitler*. London: Allen and Unwin (1971), p. 175—213.

A stimulating paper which examines the role of women in professional life during the Third Reich, with a survey of the pre-1933 situation.

STEPHENSON, Jill (née McINTYRE).
See above under McINTYRE and see also her article in section 17B.

THÖNESSEN, Werner.
See his work in section 6B(i).

WHEELER, Robert F.
See his article (*Central European History*, 1975) in section 6B(ii).

(v) Sociological Research [1]

DUBIEL, Helmut.
See his article in section 15B(i).

EISERMANN, Gottfried.
"Die deutsche Soziologie im Zeitraum von 1918 bis 1933". *Kölner Zeitschrift für Soziologie- und Sozialpsychologie*, vol. 11, pt. 1 (1959), p. 54—71.

An informative and critical survey of developments in this field.

KÖNIG, René.
"Zur Soziologie der zwangiger Jahre". In Leonhard Reinisch. *Die Zeit ohne Eigenschaften: eine Bilanz der zwanziger Jahre*. Stuttgart: Kohlhammer (1961), p. 82—118.

A maturely written paper, which discusses among other things the subject of social reality in Weimar.

LENK, Kurt.
"Das tragische Bewusstsein in der deutschen Soziologie der zwanziger Jahre". *Frankfurter Hefte*, vol. 18 (1963), p. 313—20.

A discussion of the methodology of German sociological studies in Weimar.

SCHAD, Susanne P.
Empirical Social Research in Weimar Germany. The Hague: Mouton (1972), 155 pp.

Empirical research, we are informed, was not taken seriously by German sociologists during Weimar. Statistical analysis, for one thing, was regarded as much more important.

SCHLEIER, Hans.
"Die Stellung der bürgerlichen deutschen Geschichtsforschung zur Soziologie in der Zeit der Weimarer Republik". *Jahrbuch für Geschichte*, vol. 5 (1971), p. 209—62.

The author criticizes bourgeois (i.e. non-Marxist) historians in Weimar for neglecting sociology and sociological analytical techniques in their history writing. He concludes, therefore, that these historians had only a superficial awareness of political and economic developments. Schleier has a point.

1. Consult relevant titles in sections 15B(i) and 15C.

The Labour Movement and Trade Unions[1]

14

ABENDROTH, Wolfgang.
"Das Problem der Beziehungen zwischen
politischer Theorie und politischer Praxis in
Geschichte und Gegenwart der deutschen
Arbeiterbewegung". *Die Neue Gesellschaft*, vol. 5
(1958), p. 466—77.
A general discussion, written from a Marxist standpoint,
of the dilemma of accommodating political practice to
political theory, which constantly faced the German
working class movement from 1848 onwards.

ABENDROTH, Wolfgang.
**Die deutschen Gewerkschaften: Wege
demokratischer Integration.** Heidelberg: Meyer
(1955). 2nd ed.
Contains some noteworthy reflections on the nature of
German trade union development.

ALTENHÖFER, Ludwig.
**Stegerwald: ein Leben für den kleinen Mann; die
Adam-Stegerwald-Story.** Bad Kissingen: Verlag
für Politische Schriften (1965), 131 pp.
A short, appreciative, but unscholarly biography of the
Catholic trade union leader.

ANDERSON, Evelyn.
**Hammer or Anvil: the Story of the German
Working Class Movement.** London: Victor
Gollancz (1945), 207 pp.
A concise and reliable narrative and analysis of the labour
movement since 1871, written from a left-wing social
democratic viewpoint. Most of the book is devoted to the
1918—33 period.

BECKER, Josef.
**"'Der Deutsche' und die Regierungsbildung des 30.
Januar 1933".** *Publizistik*, vol. 6, pt. 4 (1961),
p. 195—202.
Der Deutsche was the leading organ of the German Trade
Union Association (DGB). Becker discusses the paper's
editorial policy towards the important political events of
late 1932 and early 1933.

BRANTZ, Rennie W.
See his work in section 6B(v).

BRAUNTHAL, Gerald.
**The Politics of the German Free Trade Unions
during the Weimar Period.** Dissertation, Columbia
University (1954).
The author's principal conclusions are summarized in his
article (see below).

BRAUNTHAL, Gerald.
**"The German Free Trade Unions during the Rise
of Nazism".** *Journal of Central European Affairs*,
vol. 15, pt. 4 (1956), p. 339—53.
Analyses the main policies of the free unions from July
1932 to January 1933 in order to determine why they
offered no resistance to Hitler. The author shows that, by
the latter date, the rank and file had lost faith in their
leadership because they lacked imaginative policies, and as a
result widespread apathy characterized the attitudes of
union members to politics. Overall, the demoralizing effect
of the depression, the growth of nationalism, and weak
leadership reduced the will of the unions to resist the
NSDAP. The essay is reasonably competent but suffers
from a string of ill considered interpretations.

BRUMME, Wolfgang.
**Untersuchungen zur Kulturarbeit der freien
Gewerkschaften Deutschlands in der Zeit der
relativen Stabilisierung des Kapitalismus.**
Dissertation, University of Leipzig (1972).[2]

BUCHSBAUM, Ewald.
**Die Linkentwicklung der Gothaer Arbeiter-
bewegung von 1914 bis 1920.** Dissertation,
University of Halle (1965).
Tries to show that the working class movement in Gotha
was from 1914 more or less pro-Communist.

COMFORT, Richard A.
**Revolutionary Hamburg: Labor Politics in the
Early Weimar Republic.** California: Stanford
University Press (1966), 226 pp.
The main stress of this valuable study is on the November
Revolution and the period immediately afterwards. Com-

1. See relevant titles in section 13A(ii)(c).

2. I was unable to obtain a copy for review.

fort provides a detailed analysis of the issues affecting the labour movement, especially the trade unions and their concern for jobs. The trade union-SPD relationship is also treated with skill. A major fault is that he does not discuss these problems within the wider context of the local Hamburg economy.

COMFORT, Richard A.
"The Political Role of the Free Unions and the Failure of Council Government in Hamburg, November 1918 to March 1919". *International Review of Social History*, vol. 9, pt. I (1964), p. 47—64.
An analysis of the development and failure of the council movement in Hamburg; crucial factors affecting the council's collapse in January 1919 were the hostile standpoints taken up to then by the SPD and the trade unions. However, the author is guilty of contradicting himself on occasion, and a number of statements are speculative.

DEUTZ, Josef.
Adam Stegerwald: Gewerkschaftler, Politiker, Minister 1874—1945: ein Beitrag zur Geschichte der christlichen Gewerkschaften in Deutschland. Cologne: Bund-Verlag (1952), 172 pp.
Reads too much like a badly revised dissertation, which this work is. Deutz does not do full justice to his subject in this rather superficial work.

DILL, George M.
The Christian Trade Unions and Catholic Corporatism in Germany 1916—1924. Dissertation, Harvard University (1949).[1]

DÖRNEMANN, Manfred.
Die Politik des Verbandes der Bergarbeiter Deutschlands von der Novemberrevolution 1918 bis zum Osterputsch 1921. Bochum: Berg Verlag (1966), 271 pp.
A detailed look at not only the coal miners' association but also at the state of industrial relations in the Ruhr area in general. The author pays particular attention to the clash between the trade union and the radical Left.

EVANS, Ellen L.
"Adam Stegerwald and the Role of the Christian Trade Unions in the Weimar Republic". *Catholic Historical Review*, vol. 59 (1973—74), p. 602—26.
Argues that Stegerwald's right-wing influence in the Christian trade unions helped to discredit parliamentary democracy in Weimar. His political principles, the author adds, proved divisive and dangerous for the programme of the Centre Party. Her claims seem somewhat exaggerated.

FELDMAN, Gerald D; KOLB, Eberhard; RÜRUP, Reinhard.
"Die Massenbewegungen der Arbeiterschaft in Deutschland am Ende des Ersten Weltkrieges (1917—1920)". *Politische Vierteljahresschrift*, vol. 13, pt. 2 (1972), p. 84—105.
An excellent and detailed examination of demobilization, social unrest, and the policies of businessmen, the government and the trade unions in 1918—19.

FLEMMING, Jens.
See his article in section 13A(iii)(b).

1. I was unable to obtain a copy for review.

FRAENKEL, Ernst.
"Der Ruhreisenstreit 1928—1929 in historisch-politischer Sicht". In F.A. Hermens and T. Schieder (eds.). *Staat, Wirtschaft, und Politik in der Weimarer Republik: Festschrift für Heinrich Brüning.* Berlin: Duncker & Humblot (1967), p. 97—118.
The author takes this event as evidence of the deep tension in the Republic during the so-called "calm middle years". The coal strike in the Ruhr revealed as much class bitterness as any other period during 1918—33. The cause was the dispute over the Social Labour Law, with the employers on one side and the trade unions on the other. Fraenkel discusses the full political, economic and social implications of the confrontation, which resulted in an uneasy compromise. The incident was a symptom of serious crisis in the Republic which threatened the democratic order.

GATES, Robert A.
The Economic Policies of the German Free Trade Unions and the German Social Democratic Party, 1930—1933. Dissertation, University of Oregon (1970).
A study of the differences between the unions and the SPD over economic policy. The SPD had no plans to combat unemployment and its other economic policies lacked imagination. The unions were alienated by this sterile approach, but Gates argues that their differences originated fundamentally in the 1890s, when the SPD came to regard social legislation as the best means of relieving hardship caused by capitalism. The unions wanted more than social legislation. Their disagreement came into the open in 1932 and thus contributed to the failure of both sides to come together to defend democracy.

GÄTSCH, Helmut.
Die freien Gewerkschaften in Bremen 1919—1933. Bremen: Schünemann (1969), 180 pp.
An interesting examination of how the KPD tried to gain control of the unions by constructing a cell system within the organization, and by establishing rival associations outside. Neither method was successful. The union leadership retained the loyalty of the rank and file by concentrating on obtaining material benefits and rejecting ideological warfare.

GEMKOW, Heinrich.
"Gemeinsame Traditionen der revolutionären deutschen und polnischen Arbeiterbewegung 1917/18 bis 1945". *Beiträge zur Geschichte der Deutschen Arbeiterbewegung*, vol. 16, pt. 1 (1974), p. 15—30.
A spurious piece of historical analysis.

GERLACH, Erich (ed.).
Karl Korsch: Arbeitsrecht für Betriebsräte (1922). Frankfurt: Europäische Verlagsanstalt (1968), 153 pp.
Korsch was a prominent member of the labour movement's extreme left wing and was a firm advocate of the council system of government. This study discusses his efforts to further his beliefs in the immediate post-1918 situation in Germany. The book's tone is too polemical.

GESSNER, Manfred.
Wehrfrage und freie Gewerkschaftsbewegung in den Jahren 1918 bis 1923 in Deutschland. Berlin: Ernst-Reuter-Gesellschaft (1962), 183 pp.
An analysis of the attitudes adopted towards defence and military affairs by the German trade unions. The conclusions are fairly predictable.

GREBING, Helga.
Geschichte der deutschen Arbeiterbewegung.
Munich: Nymphenburger Verlagsanstalt (1966),
334 pp.
The narrative of this general but useful survey revolves
around the SPD, but the role of the trade unions is given
adequate coverage.

HAMEL, Iris.
**Völkischer Verband und nationale Gewerkschaft:
der Deutschnationale Handlungsgehilfen-Verband,
1893—1933.** Frankfurt: Europäische Verlagsanstalt
(1967), 289 pp.
This white collar association was founded in 1893 in
Hamburg to protect the interests of the sorely pressed
Mittelstand. Links were established with a variety of
right-wing nationalist and *völkisch* groups and after 1918
the association developed a powerful antisemitism. This
solid monograph discusses the development, activities and
political orientation of the association, relating the discussion to the wider crisis of the *Mittelstand* in the Republic.

HEER, Hannes.
**Burgfrieden oder Klassenkampf: zur Politik der
sozialdemokratischen Gewerkschaften 1930—1933.**
Neuwied: Luchterhand (1971), 240 pp.
The author's main contention is that the German trade
union movement capitulated to National Socialism not so
much because of bad leadership, but because of the reformist traditions that had become entrenched in the
unions since around 1900. In this well researched study,
the unions' relations with big business are outlined, as well
as their increasingly bad relations with the SPD. The final
result was the unions' failure to resist in 1933.

HIRSCH-WEBER, Wolfgang.
**Gewerkschaften in der Politik, von der Massen-
streikdebatte zum Kampf um das Mitbestimmungs-
recht.** Cologne: Westdeutscher Verlag (1959),
170 pp.
Aims to demonstrate that the trade unions were as much
concerned about political issues as they were about
economic affairs, by analysing their attitudes to the mass
strike debate in 1905—06, the general strike against the
Kapp Putsch, the threat of National Socialism, and other
case examples. But the author's own evidence refutes his
thesis because, except for the Kapp Putsch episode, the
unions were politically disinterested and ineffective. The
second half of the book, which looks at the transformation
of the West German union movement after 1945, is more
convincing than the first part.

HOMBURG, Heidrun.
See his work in section 13A(ii)(e).

HÜLLBÜSCH, Ursula.
**Gewerkschaften und Staat: ein Beitrag zur
Geschichte der Gewerkschaften zu Anfang und
zu Ende der Weimarer Republik.** Dissertation,
University of Heidelberg (1958).
A useful discussion of trade union attitudes to the Weimar
Republic, showing how in the early years the unions were
enthusiastic defenders of the state, but apathetic onlookers
by 1932—33. A familiar theme.

HÜLLBÜSCH, Ursula.
**"Die deutschen Gewerkschaften in der Welt-
wirtschaftskrise".** In W. Conze and H. Raupach
(eds.). *Die Staats- und Wirtschaftskrise des
deutschen Reiches 1929—33.* Stuttgart: Klett
(1967), p. 126—54.
A summary of the main conclusions presented in the
author's dissertation.

INSTITUT FÜR MARXISMUS-LENINISMUS
(ed.).
**Dokumente und Materialien zur Geschichte der
deutschen Arbeiterbewegung. Vol. 2: November
1917-Dezember 1918. Vol. 3: Januar 1919-Mai
1919.** East Berlin: Dietz (1957—58), 770, 499 pp.
A valuable documentary source covering all major aspects
of the working class movement.

KLEIN, Jürgen.
**Vereint sind sie alles? Untersuchungen zur
Entstehung von Einheitsgewerkschaften in
Deutschland. Von der Weimarer Republik bis
1946—47.** Hamburg: Fundament-Verlag (1972),
436 pp.
Provides in its early chapters a competent review of trade
union development in Germany before 1933, the causes of
its weaknesses and divisions, and its failure to resist Hitler.
The remainder of the book discusses trade unionists in exile
and the trade union resistance to Hitler.

KLOTZBACH, Kurt.
**Bibliographie zur Geschichte der deutschen
Arbeiterbewegung, 1914—1945.** Stuttgart: Verlag
Neue Gesellschaft (1975), 278 pp.
An excellent source of reference; comprehensive and well
organized.

KOSTHORST, Erich.
Jacob Kaiser: der Arbeiterführer. Stuttgart:
Kohlhammer (1967), 286 pp.
A balanced, lively and informative biography of the promi-
nent trade union leader and former secretary-general of
the Christian trade unions.

KRAFT, Emil.
**80 Jahre Arbeiterbewegung zwischen Meer und
Moor: ein Beitrag zur Geschichte der politischen
Bewegungen in Weser-Ems.** Bremen: Schünemann
(1952).
A general narrative which does not alter anything of what
we know already about the trade union movement as a
whole.

KRUSCH, Hans-Joachim.
**Um die Einheitsfront und eine Arbeiterregierung:
zur Geschichte der Arbeiterbewegung im Bezirke
Erzgebirge-Vogtland unter besonderer
Berücksichtigung des Klassenkampfes in Zwickau-
Oelsnitzer Steinkohlenrevier von Januar bis August
1923.** East Berlin: Verlag Tribüne (1966), 399 pp.
A discussion of the formation of the coalition SPD-KPD
government in Saxony in October 1923, interpreted as a
victory for the working class movement as a whole. The
usual Marxist-Leninist propagandistic jargon is much to
the fore.

KRUSCH, Hans-Joachim.
**"Zur Bewegung der revolutionären Betriebsräte
in den Jahren 1922-23".** *Zeitschrift für
Geschichtswissenschaft*, vol. 11, pt. 2 (1963),
p. 360—78.
Contains interesting details of the working class organization in 1922—23.

LEBER, Julius.
**Ein Mann geht seinen Weg: Schriften, Reden,
und Briefe.** Berlin: Mosaik Verlag (1952), 296 pp.
A useful but not very revealing collection of his writings,
etc.

MARTINY, Martin.
"Arbeiterbewegung an Rhein und Ruhr von Scheitern der Räte- und Sozialisierungsbewegung bis zum Ende der letzten parlamentarischen Regierung der Weimarer Republik 1920—1930".
In *Arbeiterbewegung an Rhein und Ruhr*.
Wuppertal: Hammer Verlag (1974), p. 241—73.
A very clear and informative description and analysis of the working class and trade union movements in one of the most heavily industrialized areas of Germany. Incorporates new and interesting material.

MERKER, Paul.
"Erinnerungen an den gewerkschaftlichen Kampf des Berliner Gaststättenproletariats (1920/21)".
Beiträge zur Geschichte der Deutschen Arbeiterbewegung, vol. 15, pt. 3 (1973), p. 466—71.
A short narrative of the struggle for trade union recognition.

MERKER, Paul.
See also his work in section 6B(i).

MOMMSEN, Hans.
"Die Bergarbeiterbewegung an der Ruhr 1918—1933". In *Arbeiterbewegung an Rhein und Ruhr*.
Wuppertal: Hammer Verlag (1974), p. 275—314.
A comprehensive and informative account of major political and economic developments in the coal mining industry.

MOMMSEN, Hans.
"Der Ruhrbergbau im Spannungsfeld von Politik und Wirtschaft in der Zeit der Weimarer Republik". *Blätter für Deutsche Landesgeschichte*, vol. 108 (1972), p. 160—75.
Spotlights the tension between capital and labour in the coal industry; increased militancy on the part of the miners resulted.

MORSEY, Rudolf.
"Zur Gründung der Tageszeitung 'Der Deutsche' (1921)". *Publizistik*, vol. 17, pt. 4 (1972), p. 351—8.
Adam Stegerwald, chairman of the German Trade Union Association, was the leading influence behind the launching of this paper as the daily organ of the DGB. He saw it as part of his political aim to make the DGB the core of an interconfessional, national, Christian peoples' party. Documents are appended relating to the character and aims of the newspaper.

OERTZEN, Peter von.
"Die grossen Streiks der Ruhrbergarbeiterschaft im Frühjahr 1919: ein Beitrag zur Diskussion über die revolutionäre Entstehungsphase der Weimarer Republik". *Vierteljahrshefte für Zeitgeschichte*, vol. 6, pt. 2 (1958), p. 231—62.
An excellent discussion of the origins, development and outcome of the coal miners' strike, with fresh material and soundly argued conclusions.

OPEL, Fritz.
Der Deutsche Metallarbeiter-Verband während des Ersten Weltkrieges und der Revolution. Hanover: Norddeutsche Verlagsanstalt (1957), 144 pp.
Shows that the November Revolution created a significant gulf between the radically minded ordinary members and the conservative leadership of the one million strong union.

Opel, however, does not tell us anything new about this important union; the book is altogether too brief and sketchy.

RAASE, Werner.
Die Entwicklung der deutschen Gewerkschaftsbewegung in der Zeit der revolutionären Nachkriegskrise. East Berlin: Verlag Tribüne (1967), 166 pp.
Contains a good deal of extremely useful information taken from reports and publications of the General Commission and a number of individual unions. Raase is critical of the unions for not fully understanding what the November Revolution was all about, but qualifies this later when he accuses the SPD of having betrayed the revolutionary zeal of the unions. Much of the book's argumentation is propagandistic and does not come near to challenging the views of Western historians such as Gerald Feldman.

RAUMER, Hans von.
"Unternehmer und Gewerkschaften in der Weimarer Zeit". *Deutsche Rundschau*, vol. 80 (May 1954), p. 425—34.
A competent general survey (without footnotes) of employer-trade union relations. It reiterates the theme that the trade unions were "destroyed" by the great depression, so that by the end of 1933 one-third of trade unionists were Communist, and one-third were National Socialist. The latter contention, however, is undoubtedly erroneous.

REMER, Claus.
Deutsche Arbeiterdelegation in der Sowjetunion: die Bedeutung der Delegationsreisen für die deutsche Arbeiterbewegung in den Jahren 1925/26. East Berlin: Rütten & Loening (1963), 339 pp.
As could be anticipated, this is a highly propagandistic narrative of the visits made by a group of German workers to Russia (Leningrad) in 1925. Remer interprets the trip as having had a powerful influence on the "delegation movement" within the German working class movement. Above all, however, the trip demonstrated the historic solidarity of the German and Soviet proletariats. A study empty of historical value and marked by a distasteful obsequiousness towards the Soviet Union.

REMER, Claus.
"Die drei grossen deutschen Arbeiterdelegationen nach der Sowjetunion (1925—27)". *Zeitschrift für Geschichtswissenschaft*, vol. 4, pt. 2 (1956), p. 343—65.
A report of the three trips of German workers to Russia in July-August 1925, July-October 1926 and October-November 1927. The essay in effect summarizes the main points of the author's book.

RICHTER, Werner.
Gewerkschaften, Monopolkapital, und Staat im Ersten Weltkrieg und in der Novemberrevolution, 1914—1919. East Berlin: Verlag Tribüne (1959), 403 pp.
Richter is severely critical of the trade union movement for allegedly opposing Communism among its membership and for acting therefore at the behest of big business against the interests of the proletariat during the Revolution. This biased book is an unhelpful contribution.

RITTER, Gerhard; SCHRAEPLER, Ernst; DÜBBER, Ulrich (eds.).
Hundert Jahre deutsche Arbeiterbewegung. Hamburg: Girardet (1963), 64 pp.
A short booklet, put out by the West German government's Political Education Department, containing an overview of working class and trade union movement history.

SCHIEFFER, Jack.
Geschichte der deutschen Gewerkschaften. Vol. I:
Geschichte der deutschen freien Gewerkschaften.
Aachen: Grenzland Verlag (1947), 190 pp.
A poorly informed and unreliable general account.

SCHMITT, Heinz.
Entstehung und Wandlungen der Zielsetzungen,
der Struktur, und der Wirkungen der
Berufsverbände. Berlin: Duncker & Humblot
(1966), 275 pp.
An interesting general survey of the origins and development of professional organizations, with the emphasis on
the 1871—1933 period.

SCHNEIDER, Michael.
Das Arbeitsbeschaffungsprogramm des ADGB:
zur gewerkschaftlichen Politik in der Endphase der
Weimarer Republik. Bad Godesberg: Verlag Neue
Gesellschaft (1975), 271 pp.
A thoroughly detailed and worthy exposition of the work
creation plans of the trade union leadership, and of the
political complications that arose.

SCHNEIDER, Michael.
Unternehmer und Demokratie: die freien
Gewerkschaften in der unternehmerischen
Ideologie der Jahre 1918—1933. Stuttgart: Verlag
Neue Gesellschaft (1975), 220 pp.
A well documented, objective assessment of the extent to
which the conservative-orientated employers distrusted the
"democratic" unions, and of the political and economic
repercussions.

SCHORR, Helmut J.
Adam Stegerwald: Gewerkschafter und Politiker
in der ersten deutschen Republik. Ein Beitrag zur
Geschichte der christlichsozialen Bewegung in
Deutschland. Recklinghausen: Kommunalverlag
(1966), 350 pp.
A full and informative biography which makes extensive
use of the Stegerwald papers, discovered in 1963. There is
considerable stress on the Weimar period and Stegerwald's
activities as Centre Party politician, trade unionist, and
Reich Minister.

STEIN, Alexander.
Rudolf Hilferding und die deutsche Arbeiter-
bewegung: Gedenkblätter. Hanover: SPD-Verlag
(1946), 44 pp.
Unimportant.

ŠULPLJAK, P.
"Die revolutionäre Gewerkschaftsopposition . . .
1930/31". *Wissenschaftliche Zeitschrift der*
Friedrich-Schiller-Universität Jena, vol. 23, pt. 6
(1974), p. 827—40.
Somewhat unreliable in detail and even more so in interpretation.

THIERINGER, Rolf.
Das Verhältnis der Gewerkschaften zu Staat und
Parteien in der Weimarer Republik. Dissertation,
University of Tübingen (1954).
A rather vague study which has not investigated all possible
sources of material. The stress is on the ideological dif-
ferences within the trade union movement.

UEBERHORST, Horst.
"Bildungsgedanke und Solidaritätsbewusstsein in
der deutschen Arbeitersportbewegung zur Zeit
der Weimarer Republik". *Archiv für Sozial-*
geschichte, vol. 14 (1974), p. 275—92.
An informative analysis of two important aspects of the
workers' sport movement. Educational work in the sphere
of physical culture involved not only care of the body,
but also intellectual and political training; its main purpose was to strengthen solidarity consciousness. The
centre for such training was the Federation School in
Leipzig, which was opened in 1926.

UEBERHORST, Horst.
Frisch, frei, stark und treu: die Arbeitersport-
bewegung in Deutschland. Düsseldorf (1973).
The first scholarly and comprehensive examination of the
workers' sport movement not only as a physical culture
phenomenon but also as a political and intellectual organization aligned to the principles of democratic socialism.
The organization, objectives and ethos of this movement
are explored with admirable clarity.

VARAIN, Heinz J.
Freie Gewerkschaften, Sozialdemokratie und
Staat: die Politik der Generalkommission unter
der Führung Carl Legiens (1890—1920).
Düsseldorf: Droste (1956), 207 pp.
A thorough study of the relationship between the unions
and the SPD. The focus is on the policies of Legien who
wanted to integrate the labour movement into state and
society where it would be encouraged to perform a responsible and constructive role. For this reason, the unions
moved closer to the Majority Socialist position after 1917
and this resulted in the unions playing a moderating role in
the November Revolution and in early Weimar.

VIETZKE, Siegfried; WOHLGEMUTH, Heinz.
Deutschland und die deutsche Arbeiterbewegung
in der Zeit der Weimarer Republik 1919—1933.
East Berlin: Dietz Verlag (1966), 524 pp.
The argumentation of this book is strictly Marxist-Leninist
in orientation, but much of the information is undoubtedly
of value.

VRING, T. von der
See his article in section 4G.

WHEELER, Robert F.
"German Labor and the Comintern: a Question of
Generations?" *Journal of Social History*, vol. 7,
pt. 3 (1973—74), p. 304—21.
A stimulating and novel look at the nature of the relationship and disagreements between the German labour movement and the Comintern.

15

Culture and Literature

A. GENERAL

BONN, Moritz J.
Wandering Scholar. New York: John Day (1948), 403 pp.

The author provides shrewd portraits of leading political and intellectual personalities of the Weimar era, and the memoir as a whole effectively recaptures the cultural atmosphere of the period.

BOSSENBROOK, William J.
The German Mind. Detroit: Wayne State University Press (1961).

A competent, readable survey of intellectual and cultural trends in modern Germany.

CRAIG, Gordon A.
"Engagement and Neutrality in Weimar Germany".
Journal of Contemporary History, vol. 2, pt. 2 (1967), p. 49—63.

This essay discusses the difficulties encountered by German literary men during Weimar in trying to break out of the isolation of their intellectual and artistic pursuits into the "real" world of political engagement. Craig shows that where men of letters did become involved in politics, invariably on the side of left-wing radicalism, their ventures were unsuccessful, so that by the late 1920s most of them returned to intellectual neutrality.

DÜWELL, Kurt.
"Staat und Wissenschaft in der Weimarer Epoche".
Historische Zeitschrift. Supplement I: Beiträge zur Geschichte der Weimarer Epoche (1971), p. 31—74.

An informed and well written analysis of the cultural policies adopted by Minister C. H. Becker.

FÄHANDERS, Walter; **RECTOR**, Martin (eds.).
Literatur im Klassenkampf: zur proletarisch-revolutionären Literaturtheorie 1919—1923; eine Dokumentation. Munich: Hanser Verlag (1971), 238 pp.

An introduction tries to establish the essential links between literature and proletarian consciousness, and the KPD emerges as the shining example for all to follow. There is reference to the *Bund für proletarische Kultur* (1919—20) and its contribution to the emergence later of the *Arbeiter-korrespondentenbewegung* and the *Bund proletarisch-revolutionärer Schriftsteller*. An anthology of excerpts from the writings of Franz Jung, Oskar Kanehl and Rudolf Leonhard is provided.

FÄHANDERS, Walter; **RECTOR**, Martin (eds.).
Linksradikalismus und Literatur: Untersuchungen zur Geschichte der sozialistischen Literatur in der Weimarer Republik. 2 vols. Reinbek/Hamburg: Rowohlt (1974), 380, 335 pp.

Despite the somewhat dogmatic Marxist introduction, this work is an important contribution to the study of radical left-wing literature in Weimar. Included are many examples of socialist writers whose work also had a political connotation.

FRENZEL, Ivo.
"Utopia and Apocalyse in German Literature".
Social Research, vol. 39, pt. 2 (1972), p. 306—21.

A general and unsatisfactory survey of some aspects of Weimar literature. There are a number of references to the West German political scene in the 1960s which do not help the essay to be scholarly in tone. In asking the basic question, what role did the intellectuals play in the Weimar Republic, the author considers the main works of Spengler, Karl Jasper, and Ernst Bloch, and concludes that the motifs of utopia and apocalyse are the outstanding hallmarks of the literature of the period.

GAY, Peter.
Weimar Culture: the Outsider as Insider. New York: Harper & Row (1968), 197 pp.

A brilliant, concise and highly readable study whose thesis is that intellectuals, alienated from the state during the Second Empire, were transformed into "insiders" in the Weimar era, enjoying enhanced status and influence. However, they retained the old fault of being too utopian and irresponsible.

HEYNEN, Walter (ed.).
Deutsche Briefe des 20. Jahrhunderts. Stuttgart: Deutscher Taschenbuch Verlag (1962), 203 pp.

Part of this volume adds to our general knowledge of Weimar's cultural scene.

KOHN, Hans.
The Mind of Germany: the Education of a Nation. London: Macmillan (1969), 370 pp. Revised ed.

The theme of this valuable study is the cynical and deliberate destruction of the German intellectual tradition by writers who rejected the democratic and humanitarian ethos originally established by the French Revolution. *Völkisch* and anti-semitic ideas, chauvinism and authoritarianism emerged as dominant trends, thus laying the foundations for the triumph of National Socialism.

KUHN, Helmut.
"Das geistige Gesicht der Weimarer Zeit". *Zeit-schrift für Politik*, vol. 8, pt. 1 (1961), p. 1—10.
A well written reflection on the inadequacies and failings of the cultural/intellectual scene in Weimar.

KÜHN, Traudel.
See her work in section 6B(vii) (e).

LAQUEUR, Walter Z.
"America and the Weimar Analogy". *Encounter*, vol. 38, pt. 5 (1972), p. 19—25.
A few brief but interesting notes about Weimar's intellectual climate.

LAQUEUR, Walter Z.
Weimar: a Cultural History 1918—33. London: Weidenfeld & Nicolson (1974), 308 pp.
A balanced, informative and smooth description and analysis of Weimar's brilliant and progressive culture, seen against the political background. The author is sympathetic towards most of what he narrates.

LEED, Eric J.
From Experience to Ideology: an Analysis of the Images of War in German War Literature 1914—1930. Dissertation, University of Rochester (1972).
Attempts to ascertain the extent and nature of the psychological impact of the First World War on the combatants by analysing the experiences of veterans who recorded their thoughts in letters, novels and journals. In particular, the author is interested to know how far the *Fronterlebnis* affected later political and psychological attitudes. He concludes that the front-soldier nationalism of the 1920s was not an important factor in the formulation of political attitudes.

LETHEN, Helmut.
Neue Sachlichkeit 1924—1932: Studien zur Literatur des "Weissen Sozialismus". Stuttgart: Metzler (1970), 214 pp.
Readable and edifying.

MÖBIUS, Hanno.
"Der Rote Eine-Mark-Roman". *Archiv für Sozialgeschichte*, vol. 14 (1974), p. 157—211.
The "Red One-Mark Series" (1930—32) represented an important breakthrough in the German Communist concept of mass literature. The series was influenced to a large extent by the Soviet writers' association and the author has much to say about the development of worker correspondence as an important form of proletarian literature.

OSBORN, Max.
Der bunte Spiegel: Erinnerungen aus dem Kunst-Kultur- und Geistesleben der Jahre 1890—1933. New York: Krause (1945), 280 pp.
A not very interesting or reliable guide to German literary and cultural developments.

PRÜMM, Karl.
Die Literatur des soldatischen Nationalismus der 20'er Jahre 1918—1933: Gruppenideologie und Epochenproblematik. 2 vols. Kronberg/Taunus: Scriptor-Verlag (1974).
A valuable work which traces the origins, influences and development of militaristic nationalism in Weimar.

REINISCH, Leonhard (ed.).
Die Zeit ohne Eigenschaften: eine Bilanz der zwanziger Jahre. Stuttgart: Kohlhammer (1961), 243 pp.
A collection of five essays by different historians on aspects of Weimar's literary and cultural life, followed by informative observations about each paper by a discussion group. See under Siegfried Giedion (section 15B (vi)), Bruno Werner (section 15E), René König (section 13B (v)), and Emil Dovifat (section 16A (i)).

ROTHE, Wolfgang (ed.).
Die deutsche Literatur in der Weimarer Republik. Stuttgart: Reclam (1974), 486 pp.
An excellent volume of articles which deal with selected aspects of Weimar literature. The emphasis is very much on the social and political context of literature.

SAUER, Wolfgang.
"Weimar Culture: Experiments in Modernism". *Social Research*, vol. 39, pt. 2 (1972) p. 254—84.
A stimulating though at times somewhat obtuse essay which evaluates the cultural achievements of the Weimar era, seeing the work of intellectuals in terms of their aesthetic and cultural value rather than in their political implications. The author suggests that most cultural forms in Weimar can be truly appreciated only if we conceptualize them in terms of modernism.

SCHRÖTER, Klaus.
Literatur und Zeitgeschichte. Mainz: Hase & Koehler (1970), 153 pp.
Comprises five brief essays on Weimar literary themes.

STERNBERGER, Dolf (ed.).
Hoppla, wir leben! Die 14 Jahre der Weimarer Republik in Bilden von Karl Arnold. Hanover: Fackelträger-Verlag (1956), 156 pp.
Karl Arnold was one of Weimar's most famous political satirists, and many of his best cartoons are reproduced in this very interesting volume. The theme of his work is the fight against the political Right, including the NSDAP.

WENDE, Erich.
C.H. Becker: Mensch und Politiker. Ein biographischer Beitrag zur Kulturgeschichte der Weimarer Republik. Stuttgart: Deutsche Verlagsanstalt (1959), 336 pp.
This book examines in particular Becker's important influence on the development of pedagogical ideas and educational reforms during the Weimar Republic. The author's analysis in this respect is both solid and clear. Becker's period as Minister of Culture (1925—30) is also given detailed coverage.

WITTENBERG, Erich.
Bismarcks politische Persönlichkeit im Bilde der Weimarer Republik: eine ideengeschichtliche Beleuchtung einer politischen Tradition. Vol. I: Geschichte und Tradition von 1918—1933 im Bismarckbild der deutschen Weimarer Republik. Lund: Gleerup Bokförlag (1969), 319 pp.
Much of this book does not touch upon the Weimar Republic at all and indeed is meant only to serve as background to two later planned volumes. These will discuss historical interpretations of Bismarck during Weimar as a way of illustrating the intellectual atmosphere and flavour of the period. The present volume is very disappointing; the material is badly organized and Wittenberg spends most of the time theorizing in a meaningless pseudo-philosophical manner.

WURGAFT, Lewis.
The Activist Movement: Cultural Politics on the German Left, 1914—1933. Dissertation, Harvard University (1971)[1].

Zur Geschichte der sozialistischen Literatur 1918—1933: elf Vorträge gehalten auf einer internationalen Konferenz in Leipzig vom 23. bis 25. Januar 1962. East Berlin: Aufbau-Verlag (1963), 361 pp.
The eleven papers discuss in an informative manner the development of Communist literature during the Weimar era. The influence of Russian literature is naturally stressed.

B. (i) Groups[2]

DUBIEL, Helmut.
"Theorie- und Organisationsstruktur des Frankfurter Instituts für Sozialforschung". *Kölner Zeitschrift für Soziologie- und Sozialpsychologie*, vol. 26, pt. 2 (1974), p. 237—66.
An informative and detailed examination of this leading institute from 1930 onwards.

ENSELING, Alf.
"Die Weltbühne": Organ der "intellektuellen Linken". Münster: Verlag Fahle (1962), 191 pp.
In contrast to Deak's study — see below in section B (ii) — Enseling has examined not only the magazine *Die Weltbuhne*, but also the motives and background of those who constituted the intellectual Left. It is in the latter respect that the book is absorbing and penetrating.

JACOBY, Russell.
Marxism and the Politics of Subjectivity: Towards a History of the Frankfurt School. Dissertation, University of Rochester (1974).
This is a study of subjectivity as a political and philosophical concept, as treated and developed by Western Marxism and the Frankfurt School. Among the theorists examined are Max Horkheimer, Theodor Adorno, Henryk Grossman, and Herbert Marcuse. The work helps to explain part of the leftist intellectual activity in Weimar.

JAY, Martin.
"The Frankfurt School's Critique of Marxist Humanism". *Social Research*, vol. 39, pt. 2 (1972), p. 285—305.
The School is usually depicted as belonging to the camp of Marxist Humanism, but Jay questions this, arguing that it was Marxist-Humanist only in the loose sense that it consistently opposed Stalinism. Otherwise, it provided a trenchant critique of both traditional and humanist Marxism, so that its position must lie somewhere between the two. This paper therefore examines how valid it is to categorize the School as a variant of Marxist-Humanism.

JAY, Martin.
The Dialectical Imagination: a History of the Frankfurt School and the Institute of Social Research 1923—1950. Boston: Little, Brown (1973), 382 pp.
A comprehensive and detailed history of the School and its dialectical critical theory, and of the host of brilliant Marxist thinkers it attracted. Jay's research has been thorough and valuable.

1. I was unable to obtain a copy for review.
2. See relevant titles in section 13B (v).

REICHMANN, Eva G.
"Max Horkheimer the Jew — Critical Theory and Beyond". *Yearbook of the Leo Baeck Institute*, vol. 19, (1974), p. 181—96.
A brief, sympathetic review of Horkheimer's career as head of the Institute of Social Research (Frankfurt School), as an exile, and as a scholar in post-war West Germany. Throughout, he maintained his Jewishness in a very real sense.

(ii) Literary Journals

ANGRESS, Werner T.
"Pegasus and Insurrection: "Die Linkskurve" and its Heritage". *Central European History*, vol. I, pt. 1 (1968), p. 35—55
An interesting piece on the only journal of the political Left in Weimar which advocated the revolutionary overthrow of the Republic, *Die Linkskurve*, a Communist publication of the closing years of the period. It was a journal of revolutionary political dissent under the editorship of Johannes R. Becher, a prominent German expressionist and KPD member. The journal was founded in 1929 on the initiative of the League of German Proletarian Revolutionary Writers, and Angress discusses the journal's attitudes.

DEAK, Istvan.
Weimar Germany's Left-Wing Intellectuals: a Political History of the "Weltbühne" and its Circle. Berkeley: University of California Press (1968), 346 pp.
The book is concerned only with *Die Weltbuhne* and its supporters, and not Weimar intellectuals as a whole. The content and policies of the small circulation but highly influential intellectual left-wing journal are clearly described; it specialized in acid political satire and attracted many brilliant radically minded writers and intellectuals including Ossietsky and Tucholsky. The journal became more and more radical and settled eventually into a pro-KPD line.

NASARSKI, Gerlind.
Osteuropavorstellungen in der konservativ-revolutionären Publizistik: Analyse der Zeitschrift "Deutsches Volkstum" 1917—1941. Frankfurt: Lang (1974), 241 pp.
This journal was the main intellectual spearhead and disseminator of *völkisch* ideas in Eastern Europe. Nasarski traces its origins and development, ideas and policies, and effectiveness.

PETER, Lothar.
Literarische Intelligenz und Klassenkampf. Cologne: Pahl-Rugenstein (1972), 221 pp.
An analysis of the left-wing journal *Die Aktion* 1911—32. An interesting and well written account.

PROSS, Harry E.
Literatur und Politik: Geschichte und Programm der politisch-literarischen Zeitschriften im deutschen Sprachgebiet seit 1870. Olten: Walter-Verlag (1963), 376 pp.
A general review of modern German periodicals, including for the Weimar period *Die Weltbuhne*, *Das Tagebuch*, and others.

SCHOENBERNER, Franz.
Confessions of a European Intellectual. New York: Macmillan (1946), 315 pp.
The autobiography of a former editor of the humorous weekly magazine *Simplicissimus*. Contains interesting notes on Weimar literary and bohemian life.

STERN, Guy.
"Efraim Frisch and the 'Neue Merkur'". *Yearbook of the Leo Baeck Institute*, vol. 6 (1961), p. 125—51.
Neue Merkur, a political journal with an intellectual readership, was edited by Frisch. Stern evaluates Frisch's contribution to the journal's development and orientation.

STERN, Guy.
War, Weimar and Literature: the Story of the "Neue Merkur", 1914—1925. Pittsburgh: Pennsylvania State University Press (1972), 281 pp.
A full discussion of the journal's origins and development and contribution to the literary world of early Weimar. The journal, though initially influential, became stodgy and unimaginative.

(iii) Intellectual Movements

(a) Neo-Conservatism[1]

BUSSMANN, Walter.
"Politische Ideologien zwischen Monarchie und Weimarer Republik: ein Beitrag zur Ideengeschichte der Weimarer Republik". *Historische Zeitschrift*, no. 190 (1960), p. 55—77.
A good discussion of neo-conservative thought is included (Ernst Jünger and Moeller van den Bruck).

EDMONDSON, Nelson.
"The Fichte Society: a Chapter in Germany's Conservative Revolution". *Journal of Modern History*, vol. 38, pt. 2 (1966), p. 161—80.
An absorbing paper on a neglected part of the conservative revolution; the Fichte Society, founded in Hamburg in 1916, stressed cultural and educational rather than political aims. Its idiosyncratic brand of neo-conservatism is analysed as, unsatisfactorily, are its relations with the NSDAP.

GERSTENBERGER, Heide.
Der revolutionäre Konservatismus: ein Beitrag zur Analyse des Liberalismus. Berlin: Duncker & Humblot (1969), 171 pp.
A thoughtful analysis, with the accent on new interpretations rather than new information.

KELLER, Ernst.
Nationalismus und Literatur: Langemarck, Weimar, Stalingrad. Munich: Francke (1970), 289 pp.
An unsatisfactory study of nationalist influence and motivation in literary work.

KLEMPERER, Klemens von.
Germany's New Conservatism: Its History and Its Dilemma in the Twentieth Century. Princeton: Princeton University Press (1957), 250 pp.
A scholarly appraisal of intellectual neo-conservatism in Weimar, with discussion of major writers like Niekisch, Spengler and Jünger, and groups such as the *Tatkreis*. The thesis, that neo-conservatism must be seen essentially as one force, does not enjoy unanimous support.

1. Cross-refer this sub-section to 7C.

MOHLER, Armin.
Die konservative Revolution in Deutschland 1918—1932: Grundriss ihrer Weltanschauungen. Stuttgart: Vorwerk Verlag (1950), 287 pp.
Useful in providing an outline of the intellectual motivation behind the conservative revolution; there is a good deal of information, but not nearly enough analysis and interpretation. There is, however, a very good bibliography attached.

ORR, J. M.
The Fighter in Bondage: Revolutionary Nationalism in Germany 1914—33. Dissertation, University of Edinburgh (1972).
Adds little that is new or significant.

SCHWEDHELM, Karl (ed.).
Propheten des Nationalismus. Munich: List (1969), 319 pp.
A discussion of various writers of the early twentieth century in Germany and their nationalist and racialist views.

SONTHEIMER, Kurt.
Antidemokratisches Denken in der Weimarer Republik: die politischen Ideen des deutschen Nationalismus zwischen 1918 und 1933. Munich: Nymphenburger Verlagshandlung (1962), 413 pp.
An excellent, informative and authoritative study of the ideas of the radical Right. Sontheimer has read extensively in contemporary sources to produce a work that is absorbing and convincing. He concludes that the ideas of the far Right did much to destroy the credibility of the Republic, but he does not believe they were the intellectual forerunners of National Socialism.

SONTHEIMER, Kurt.
"Antidemokratisches Denken in der Weimarer Republik". *Vierteljahrshefte für Zeitgeschichte*, vol. 5, pt. 1 (1957), p. 42—62.
A summary of the findings of the author's book.

STERN, Fritz.
The Politics of Cultural Despair: a Study in the Rise of the Germanic Ideology. Berkeley: University of California Press (1961), 367 pp.
An outstanding book, thought-provoking, perceptive and fluent. The author analyses the ideas and writings of Lagarde, Langbehn and Moeller van den Bruck and discerns in them a fundamental element of cultural crisis. Stern's thesis is that the cultural despair of 1890—1914 in Germany was an essential precondition for the triumph of National Socialism in 1933.

STERN, Fritz.
The Failure of Illiberalism: Essays on the Political Culture of Modern Germany. New York: Knopf (1972), 233 pp.
Very good for background reading to the intellectual developments on the Right in 1918—33.

STRUVE, Walter.
Elites Against Democracy: Leadership Ideals in Bourgeois Political Thought in Germany 1890—1933. Princeton: Princeton University Press (1973), 486 pp.
A significant and scholarly monograph which, in examining the character of Germany's political culture, emphasizes the demand for an authoritarian leadership élite in right-wing circles; in particular, the author analyses the thought of élitist theorists such as Hans Zehrer, Ernst Jünger, Max Weber and others. This kind of thought, Struve argues, contributed importantly to the rise of National Socialism.

WHITE, A. D.
"Kolbenheyer's Use of the Term 'Volk' 1910—
1933: a Study in Nationalist Ideology". *German
Life and Letters*, vol. 23, pt. 4 (1969—70),
p. 355—62.
Erwin G. Kolbenheyer's (1875—1962) development towards
National Socialism is traced together with his important
contribution to the twentieth century historical novel. His
use of the term *Volk* in his works tells us about his ideas as
a writer and political theorist.

(b) Expressionism

EDSCHMID, Kasimir.
Lebendiger Expressionismus: Auseinandersetz-
ungen, Gestalten, Erinnerungen. Munich: Desch
(1961), 408 pp.
Tries to capture the essence of expressionism with the help
of about thirty portraits of intellectuals and writers associated with the movement. But the volume is no more than
moderately useful or interesting.

GRUBER, Helmut.
The Politics of German Literature, 1914 to 1933: a
Study of the Expressionist and Objectivist Movements. Dissertation, Columbia University (1962).
Examines the ideas of the expressionist (1914—23) and
objectivist (1927—33) movements, particularly their concept of the writer's role and function in society. The author
also points out the severe limitations of their methods and
the profound disillusionment experienced by followers of
both movements.

MUSCHG, Walter.
Von Trakl zu Brecht: Dichter des Expressionismus.
Munich: Piper (1961), 379 pp.
A useful discussion of some of the personalities involved in
the expressionist movement, and of their hopes and ideas.

PINTHUS, Kurt (ed.).
Menschheitsdämmerung: ein Dokument des
Expressionismus, mit Biographien und Biblio-
graphien. Hamburg: Rowohlt (1960), 282 pp.
A selection of documents illustrative of expressionist
thought.

(iv) Songs

LIDTKE, Vernon L.
"Songs and Politics: an Explanatory Essay on
Arbeiterlieder in the Weimar Republic". *Archiv
für Sozialgeschichte*, vol. 14 (1974), p. 253—73.
The author first of all makes a distinction between songs
that have been "folklorized" (*Arbeitervolkslieder*) and the
ordinary workers' songs (*Arbeiterlieder*). He discusses the
function of both genres, and compares their use in both the
KPD and SPD. He shows that the points of contrast between the two organizations' approaches to the songs
clearly outnumbered their similarities.

(v) Poetry

RÜLCKER, Christoph.
Ideologie der Arbeiterdichtung 1914—1933: eine
wissenssoziologische Untersuchung. Stuttgart:
Metzlersche Verlagsbuchhandlung (1970), 160 pp.
The author's definition of *Arbeiterdichtung* is very limited,
for he completely excludes consideration of Communist

contributions in this field. Most poets of this kind were of
bourgeois origin and stressed a traditional value system, as
exemplified in the works of Karl Bröger, Heinrich Lersch,
and Alfons Petzold.

(vi) Architecture

FRANCISCONO, Marcel.
Walter Gropius and the Creation of the Bauhaus in
Weimar: the Ideals and Artistic Theories of its
Founding Years. Chicago: University of Illinois
Press (1971), 336 pp.
A scholarly and detailed work which is a valuable contrib-
ution to architectural studies. The author discusses the
problems of German art and architecture in early Weimar
with commanding authority and his analysis and character-
ization of Gropius is very convincing.

GIEDION, Siegfried.
"Das Bauhaus und seine Zeit". In L. Reinisch (ed.).
*Die Zeit ohne Eigenschaften: eine Bilanz der
zwanziger Jahre*. Stuttgart: Kohlhammer (1961), p.
15—31.
The author sets the Bauhaus experiment in the wider context of the development of architectural taste, and assesses
what he considers to have been the practical achievements
of the Bauhaus.

GREENBERG, Alan C.
Artists and the Weimar Republic: Dada and the
Bauhaus 1917—1925. Dissertation, University of
Illinois (1967).
Analyses the involvement of Weimar artists in social and
political affairs, with emphasis on the Dadaist group and
the Bauhaus; the latter is shown to have exerted little
practical influence on society and politics, largely because
its followers were too idealistic and utopian.

MILLER LANE, Barbara.
Architecture and Politics in Germany 1918—1945.
Cambridge (Mass.): Harvard University Press
(1968), 278 pp.
A serious, thoughtful work which examines the ideas of
leading architects of the modern movement in Germany
and describes the political difficulties which afflicted the
Bauhaus movement. The author shows how much architecture was viewed in political and ideological terms, with
the Bauhaus seen as a representative of extreme leftist
politics.

C. WRITERS, ARTISTS AND INTELLECTUALS

(i) General

ALBRECHT, Friedrich.
Deutsche Schriftsteller in der Entscheidung: Wege
zur Arbeiterklasse 1918—1933. East Berlin:
Aufbau Verlag (1970), 699 pp.
This is an interesting and worthwhile study which examines
the different stages in the development of "bourgeois" literature in Germany since 1900. The author also spotlights
the conversion to Marxism of bourgeois intellectuals such as
Johannes Becher and Erich Weinert. As a whole, the book
ably explores the connection between literature and radical
left-wing politics in Weimar.

JENS, Walter.
Zueignungen: 11 literarische Porträts. Munich:
Piper (1962), 95 pp.
Includes short and superficial sketches of writers such as
Brecht, Tucholsky and Döblin.

KAISER, Helmut (ed.).
Die Dichter des sozialistischen Humanismus:
Porträts. Munich: Dobbeck (1960), 106 pp.
Short portraits of leading writers including Becher, Toller and Brecht.

KESTON, Hermann.
Lauter Literaten: Porträts — Erinnerungen. Munich: Desch (1963), 455 pp.
Another selection of literary portraits, of a higher calibre than the two aforementioned efforts.

KLEIN, Alfred.
Im Auftrag ihrer Klasse: Weg und Leistung der deutschen Arbeiterschriftsteller 1918—1933. East Berlin: Aufbau Verlag (1972), 854 pp.
The theme is Weimar working class (Communist) literature and its position within the context of socialist (Communist) literature in general. There is also considerable emphasis on the work of selected left-wing revolutionary writers, such as Willi Bredel and Adam Scharrer.

LAQUEUR, Walter Z.
"The Role of the Intelligentsia in the Weimar Republic". *Social Research*, vol. 39, pt. 2 (1972), p. 213—27.
A valuable discussion of the political role of the intelligentsia. The author argues that the German intelligentsia consisted of disparate groups holding conflicting views about almost everything. Their political influence, moreover, was very small and they were powerless to prevent the collapse of the Weimar Republic, even if they had wanted to.

LAQUEUR, Walter Z.; MOSSE, George L. (eds.).
The Left-Wing Intellectuals Between the Wars 1919—1939. New York: Harper & Row (1966).
A series of most interesting and informative articles, originally published in the *Journal of Contemporary History;* among the authors are James Joll and Stuart Woolf.

MOSSE, George L.
Germans and Jews: the Right, the Left, and the Search for a "Third Force" in pre-Nazi Germany. New York: Grosset & Dunlap (1970), 260 pp.
The search for a third force was made by those intellectuals who rejected capitalism and Marxism between roughly 1890 and 1939. The third force took various forms, including *völkisch* nationalism. The Jewish contribution in the search is also discussed in detail, as is that of non-Marxist left-wing intellectuals. This volume, which consists of a number of previously published articles now revised by the author, is scholarly and incisive.

NATAN, Alex (ed.).
German Men of Letters: Twelve Literary Essays. London: Oswald Wolff (1963), 298 pp.
Among the writers discussed are Heinrich Mann and Stefan Zweig.

PACHTER, Henry M.
"The Intellectuals and the State of Weimar". *Social Research*, vol. 39, pt. 2 (1972), p. 228—53.
A brilliant essay, balanced, highly informative, and written with style and vigour. In adducing his main thesis that Weimar intellectuals were neither as influential nor as leftist as is often thought, and that in any case Weimar culture was heavily influenced by foreign developments, the author provides an excellent analysis of ideas, intellectuals, their writings, and cultural and aesthetic trends in the Weimar Republic. He concludes that intellectuals had outmoded ideas on politics which rendered them not only uninfluential but also irrelevant in Weimar's political life.

ROLLING, Vance W.
Artists on the Left: Four Examples from the Weimar Republic. Dissertation, University of Indiana (1972).
The four examples are Käthe Kollwitz, Ernst Barlach, Georg Grosz and Otto Nagel. Their ideas and views on a wide range of political and other topics are discussed, and in general the study throws some light on Weimar's political and intellectual Left.

RUARK, Lawrence B.
Admiration for Mussolini among German Intellectuals, 1922—1932. Dissertation, Boston University (1970).
Certain right-wing intellectuals, motivated by their hatred of the Republic and their belief in the great man in history theory, found much to admire in the *Duce*. The same writers, however, did not regard National Socialism as the German equivalent of Fascism and they rejected Hitler. Most of them were traditional conservative nationalists and pro-monarchist, and few supported the NSDAP before 1933.

RÜHLE, Jürgen.
Literatur und Revolution: die Schriftsteller und der Kommunismus. Cologne: Kiepenheuer & Witsch (1960), 610 pp.
A massive and thoroughly documented volume illustrating the links between intellectuals and writers on the one hand, and Communism on the other.

SCHUMACHER, Martin.
"Autoren und Verleger in der deutschen Inflationszeit". *Vierteljahrsschrift für Sozial- und Wirtschaftsgeschichte*, vol. 58 (1971), p. 88—94.
A brief note on the financial and economic plight of authors and publishers during 1923 and 1924.

SCHWARZ, Egon (ed.).
Nation im Widerspruch: Deutsche über Deutschland. Hamburg: Wegner (1963), 284 pp.
Includes excerpts from the writings of Spengler, Hesse and others to illustrate the development of two often contradictory intellectual traditions in Germany.

SCHWÄRZLER, Gertrud (ed.).
Dichter des humanistischen Aufbruchs: Porträts. Munich: Dobbeck (1960), 103 pp.
Portraits, brief and not very informative, of Arnold Zweig, Georg Kaiser and Heinrich Mann among others.

WASSERMANN, Jacob.
Bekenntnisse und Begegnungen: Porträts und Skizzen zur Literatur- und Geistesgeschichte. Zürich: Posen (1950), 159 pp.
A series of sketches of literary and intellectual figures.

(ii) Individual (Chamberlain—Winnig)[1]

1. HOUSTON STEWART CHAMBERLAIN

KALTENBRUNNER, Gerd-Klaus.
"Houston Stewart Chamberlains germanischer Mythos". *Politische Studien*, vol. 18 (1967), p. 568—83
Outlines Chamberlain's career, his friendships, his ideas, his correspondence with Kaiser Wilhelm II, and his relationship with Hitler.

1. This section is arranged alphabetically by author.

2. HANS GRIMM

See also section 7E for relevant titles.

CARSTEN, Francis L.
"'Volk ohne Raum': a Note on Hans Grimm".
Journal of Contemporary History, vol. 2, pt. 2
(1967), p. 221—7.
A discussion of Grimm's most famous novel, published in
1926, which was an immediate best-seller, largely because
it appealed to the political prejudices of masses of non-
political Germans. Carsten contends that by arousing the
feelings of so many, especially among the middle classes,
the book helped prepare the ground for Hitler's rise to
power.

FREUND, Michael.
"Hans Grimm und Adolf Hitler". *Geschichte in*
Wissenschaft und Unterricht, vol. 7 (1956), p. 131
—40.
A short review of their relationship, direct and indirect.

GRIMM, Hans.
Suchen und Hoffen: aus meinem Leben 1928—
1934. Lippoldsberg: Klosterhaus-Verlag (1960),
338 pp.
The famous *volkisch* writer's memoirs are very disappointing from the point of view of political developments in late
Weimar.

3. GEORG GROSZ

LEWIS, Beth I.
George Grosz: Art and Politics in the Weimar
Republic. Madison: University of Wisconsin Press
(1971), 328 pp.
A scholarly and revealing analysis of the life and work of
one of the most outstanding left-wing artists of Weimar.
The author traces his increasing political involvement. His
best work emerged when he was attacking political reaction
on the Right. Nonetheless, the quality of his work declined
once he lost faith in the KPD during the mid-1920s.

4. EDGAR JULIUS JUNG

JENSCHKE, Bernhard.
Zur Kritik der konservativ-revolutionären Ideol-
ogie in der Weimarer Republik: Weltanschauung und
Politik bei Edgar Julius Jung. Munich: Beck (1971),
200 pp.
An unsatisfactory work on the whole. Much of what
Jenschke has to say is ill considered and tendentious and
the book does not provide a critique of national revolutionary ideas, which should have been its primary objective. Instead, the reader is often treated to long and unexplained
extracts from Jung's main work, *Die Herrschaft der*
Minderwertigen, and Jenschke does not attempt to explain
just how worthless his subject's ideas were.

PETZOLD, Joachim.
"Konservative Revolutionsdemagogie. Edgar Julius
Jungs Verhältnis zur Weimarer Republik und zur
faschistischen Diktatur". *Zeitschrift für Geschichts-*
wissenschaft, vol. 23, pt. 3 (1975), p. 284—94.
A brief burst of polemics which virtually denounces Jung as
a fascist stooge.

5. ERNST JÜNGER

See also section 7C for relevant titles.

GUDER, G.
"Ernst Jünger". *German Life and Letters*, vol. 2,
pt. 1 (1948—49), p. 62—71.
A few observations about Junger's ideas and career.

HAFKESBRINK, Hanna.
"Ernst Jünger's Quest for a New Faith". *The*
Germanic Review, vol. 26, pt. 4 (1951), p. 289—
300.
A discussion of Junger's nationalist revolutionary ideology.

JÜNGER, Ernst.
Strahlungen. Tübingen (1949).
Absorbing diaries in which Junger throws much interesting light on Weimar politics and in particular the anti-democratic Right.

JÜNGER, Ernst.
Werke: Essays I. Betrachtungen zur Zeit. Stuttgart:
Klett (1960), 538 pp.
A collection of nine essays written between 1922—34 and
1941—60, in which Junger makes a special plea for the
assertion of "Germanic" as opposed to "European" values.

KAISER, Helmut.
Mythos, Rausch und Reaktion: der Weg Gottfried
Benns und Ernst Jüngers. East Berlin: Aufbau
Verlag (1962) 371 pp.
Too tendentious and politically weighted to be considered
as a serious academic study.

MOHLER, Armin.
Die Schleife: Dokumente zum Weg von Ernst
Jünger. Zürich: Verlag Die Arche (1955), 153 pp.
Superficial and uninformative for the most part.

SCHOERS, Rolf.
"Der kontemplative Aktivist: Versuch über Ernst
Jünger". *Merkur*, vol. 19 (1965), p. 211—25.
A useful review of Junger's career which Schoers sees as
essentially representing that of a contemplative activist.

SCHWARZ, Hans-Peter.
Der konservative Anarchist: Politik und Zeitkritik
Ernst Jüngers. Freiburg: Verlag Rombach (1962),
320 pp.
This is a well balanced interpretation of Junger's ideas, in
which Schwarz stresses the continuity of what he prefers
to call Junger's conservative Neo-Platonism. As such, however, the author sees his subject as more of an apolitical
romanticist than a political theorist, and also as a complete
outsider. Schwarz has unearthed a considerable number of
Junger's most obscure writings to substantiate his thesis,
which is certainly stimulating. Additionally, Junger's
relations with National Socialism are fully documented in
admirable fashion.

STERN, J. P.
Ernst Jünger: a Writer of Our Time. Cambridge:
Bowes (1953), 63 pp.
A short biography which emphasizes the relevance of
Junger's ideas for understanding the nature of modern
society. But Schwarz's study (see above) has clearly demon-
strated that Junger was too much of a "loner" to be re-
garded as typical or as representative of an idea or an epoch.

6. PAUL DE LAGARDE

LOUGEE, Robert W.
**Paul de Lagarde 1827—1891: a Study of Radical
Conservatism in Germany.** Cambridge (Mass.):
Harvard University Press (1962), 357 pp.
Lougee tries to see his subject as an independent writer and
not as a mere forerunner of National Socialism. The result
is an intellectual biography which makes an honest attempt
at a balanced appraisal of Lagarde's ideas, but the author
has neglected Lagarde's more important role as a link man
between the cultural crisis of pre-1914 Germany and the
rise of Hitler.

LOUGEE, Robert W.
**"Paul de Lagarde as Critic: a Romantic Protest in
an Age of Realism".** *Journal of Central European
Affairs*, vol. 13, pt. 3 (1953), p. 232—45.
A look at the pattern of thought in Lagarde's ideas; the
essay would have been better if Lougee had expatiated on
the influence of Lagarde on people like Alfred Rosenberg
and Ernst Troeltsch (p. 236).

7. GUSTAV LANDAUER

See also section 7A for relevant titles.

KALZ, Wolf.
Gustav Landauer: Kultursozialist und Anarchist.
Meisenheim: Hain (1967), 161 pp.
A solid narration of Landauer's political career, including
his involvement in the Bavarian Revolution in 1918—19,
and of his ideas, which are described but not systematically
analysed. A political biography, therefore, of limited value.

LUNN, Eugene.
**Prophet of Community: the Romantic Socialism
of Gustav Landauer.** Berkeley: University of California Press (1973), 434 pp.
Well researched and smoothly written, this sympathetic
but objective appraisal of Landauer's career and ideas fills
a significant gap. Lunn effectively conveys the romantic-
mystical quality of the anarchist's outlook.

PROSS, Harry E.
"Die Aktualität des Gustav Landauer". *Hochland*,
vol. 66, pt. 4 (1974), p. 517—33.
An account of Landauer's life which, interestingly, in-
cludes a letter he wrote on 16 April 1919 to the Action
Committee of the Bavarian Soviet Republic.

8. HEINRICH MANN

GROSS, David.
**Heinrich Mann: the Writer and Society
1890—1920. A Study of Literary Politics in
Germany.** Dissertation, University of Wisconsin
(1969).
Most of this thesis discusses Mann's social and political
ideas and his development from a neo-conservative to a
democratic socialist standpoint. The last part of the study
describes his activities in Munich in 1918—19, his attitude
to the Republic, and his commitment to socialism. Competent rather than innovative.

GROSS, David.
"Heinrich Mann and the Politics of Reaction".
Journal of Contemporary History, vol. 8, pt. 1
(1973), p. 125—45.
Discusses how Mann has become a model for liberal democrats and East German Communists. This is despite the fact
that prior to 1914 he was an ultra-right-wing reactionary.

HERDEN, Werner.
**Geist und Macht: Heinrich Manns Weg an der Seite
der Arbeiterklasse.** East Berlin: Aufbau-Verlag
(1971), 342 pp.
Discusses in considerable detail Mann's transformation from
a right-wing extremist to a democratic socialist who tried to
organize resistance to Hitler during the 1930s. For this
reason, and also for his later anti-militarist and anti-chauvin-
ist outlook, he is seen as something of a folk hero in East
Germany. This account sustains that image.

HERDEN, Werner (ed.).
**Heinrich Mann: Verteidigung der Kultur. Anti-
faschistische Streitschriften und Essays.** East
Berlin: Aufbau-Verlag (1971), 527 pp.
A selection of Mann's writings illustrative of his later
socialist and anti-Nazi commitment.

KÖNIG, Hanno.
Heinrich Mann: Dichter und Moralist. Tübingen:
Niemeyer (1972), 470 pp.
A full, comprehensive and balanced biography, but it does
not say anything essentially new.

PLESSNER, Monika.
**"Identifikation und Utopie: Versuch über Heinrich
und Thomas Mann als politische Schriftsteller".**
Frankfurter Hefte, vol. 16 (1961), p. 812—26.
A useful comparative study.

9. THOMAS MANN

BITTERLI, Urs.
**Thomas Manns politische Schriften zum National-
sozialismus 1918—1939.** Aarau: Keller Verlag
(1964), 108 pp.
A brief and none too helpful examination of what Mann
had to say about National Socialism.

GARLEFF, Michael.
**"Ein unbekannter Brief Thomas Manns an Paul
Schiemann aus dem Jahre 1932".** *Vierteljahrshefte
für Zeitgeschichte*, vol. 17, pt. 4 (1969), p. 450—3.
Publishes a letter written by Mann to the liberal Baltic
German lawyer and journalist Paul Schiemann on the
problem of nationalism in Europe.

KRAUSNICK, Helmut.
See his article in section 4H.

MANN, Erika (ed.).
Thomas Mann: Briefe 1889—1936. Frankfurt:
Fischer (1961), 581 pp.
A well edited collection of Mann's writings which is cer-
tainly to be regarded as a standard reference work. His
social and political conceptions are fully illustrated.

MANN, Thomas.
**Thomas Mann an Ernst Bertram: Briefe aus den
Jahren 1910—1955.** Pfullingen: Neske (1960),
316 pp.
A most useful collection.

PROSS, Harry E.
"On Thomas Mann's Political Career". *Journal of
Contemporary History*, vol. 2, pt. 2 (1967), p. 65—
80.
A good summary of the main highlights of his career, men-
tioning his wholehearted support for the war in 1914, his

defence of the Weimar Republic, and his exile in 1933. However, Mann never exerted much political influence on others.

SONTHEIMER, Kurt.
"Thomas Mann als politischer Schriftsteller".
Vierteljahrshefte für Zeitgeschichte, vol. 6, pt. 1 (1958), p. 1—44.
An excellent, detailed paper which effectively strikes the right balance in assessing the importance of Mann's political role.

10. ARTHUR MOELLER VAN DEN BRUCK

KALTENBRUNNER, Gerd-Klaus.
"Von Dostojewski zum Dritten Reich: Arthur van den Bruck und die 'Konservative Revolution'".
Politische Studien, vol. 20 (1969), p. 184—200.
An adequate commentary on the significance of some of Moeller's ideas in a European context. He was not only the advocate of a "third way", but was also representative of a type of latent political romanticism which was not confined simply to Germany.

PETZOLD, Joachim.
"Zur Funktion des Nationalismus: Moeller van den Brucks Beitrag zur faschistischen Ideologie".
Zeitschrift für Geschichtswissenschaft, vol. 21, pt. 11 (1973), p. 1285—1300.
A somewhat unsophisticated paper; the author has no doubt that Moeller was a proto-fascist.

SCHWIERSKOTT, Hans-Joachim.
Arthur Moeller van den Bruck und der revolutionäre Nationalismus in der Weimarer Republik.
Göttingen: Musterschmidt (1962), 202 pp.
A thorough and detailed study of Moeller's life, career and ideas and of the circle which he frequented and influenced. The development of his political attitudes to the Weimar Republic is clearly outlined, and so also is Moeller's standing *vis-à-vis* National Socialism. But the book does not discuss sufficiently the impact made by Moeller and the Young Conservatives on contemporary political figures or on the mass of Germans.

SILFEN, Paul H.
The völkisch Ideology and the Roots of Nazism: the Early Writings of Arthur Moeller van den Bruck. New York: Exposition Press (1973), 85 pp.
A short, unscholarly work which tries unsuccessfully to establish the precise links between Moeller in his pre-1914 period and National Socialism. The theme is old, and Silfen does not tell us anything we did not know previously.

11. CARL VON OSSIETSKY

FREI, Bruno.
Carl von Ossietsky: Ritter ohne Furcht und Tadel.
East Berlin: Aufbau-Verlag (1966), 335 pp.
A reasonable biography, but it does suffer from major weaknesses. There is far too much gratuitous invective against the Federal Republic, and the author considerably underestimates Ossietsky's criticism of the KPD and its leadership during Weimar.

FREI, Bruno (ed.).
Carl von Ossietsky: Rechenschaft. Publizistik aus den Jahren 1913—1933. Frankfurt: Fischer (1972), 330 pp.
A very interesting and useful collection of his writings over a range of political and social topics.

GREUNER, Ruth; GREUNER, Reinhard.
Ich stehe links . . . . Carl von Ossietsky über Geist und Ungeist der Weimarer Republik. East Berlin: Buchverlag Der Morgen (1963), 211 pp.
A close examination of Ossietsky's political outlook during the Weimar period.

GROSSMANN, Kurt R.
Ossietsky: ein deutscher Patriot. Munich: Kindler Verlag (1963), 580 pp.
This first full biography by a former close associate is informative and well written, though Grossmann's thesis, that Ossietsky is best understood as a genuine German patriot, is open to dispute.

GROSSMANN, Kurt R.
"Ein Mensch allein. Zum 25. Todestag von Carl von Ossietsky". *Blätter für Deutsch- und Internationale Politik*, vol. 8, pt. 5 (1963), p. 369—76.
A résumé of the principal conclusions reached by the author in his biography of Ossietsky.

HARTMANN, Heinz E.
Carl von Ossietsky: 3. Oktober 1889—4. Mai 1938.
Fürstenfeldbruck: Steinklopfer (1960), 36 pp.
A summary of Ossietsky's career.

KOPLIN, Raimund.
Carl von Ossietsky als politischer Publizist. Frankfurt: Leber (1964), 248 pp.
A competent and generally informative study.

MEHRING, Walter.
"Carl von Ossietsky: 3.10.1889—4.5.1938".
Deutsche Rundschau, vol. 85 (1959), p. 900—6.
An unimportant summary of Ossietsky's life.

PRITCHARD, Jean F.
The Political Journalism of Carl von Ossietsky.
Dissertation, University of Cambridge (1970).
Says little that is original.

12 ERNST VON SALOMON

See also relevant titles in section 7C.

SALOMON, Ernst von.
Die Geächteten. Reinbek/Hamburg: Rowohlt (1962), 481 pp. Revised ed.
A novel-cum-memoir which contains many interesting observations on nationalist and right-wing politics in Weimar; it is particularly reliable on the development of the *Freikorps* movement.

SALOMON, Ernst von.
Der Fragebogen. Hamburg: Rowohlt (1951).
An autobiography based on an elaborate questionnaire presented to Salomon by the post-1945 Allies. The book amounts to a cynical apologia for his pro-nationalist and militaristic beliefs, and he reaffirms his support for German nationalism and his rejection of democracy.

13. MAX SCHELER

STAUDE, John.
Max Scheler 1874—1928: a Historical Portrait.
Glencoe (Illinois): The Free Press (1967).
A valuable work on Scheler and the pre-1933 intellectual and academic community in Germany.

14. OTHMAR SPANN

HAAG, John.
"The Spann Circle and the Jewish Question".
Yearbook of the Leo Baeck Institute, vol. 18
(1973), p. 95—126.
An outline of the racialist and anti-semitic ideas of this
Austrian writer (1878—1950).

SCHNELLER, Martin.
**Zwischen Romantik und Faschismus: der Beitrag
Othmar Spanns zum Konservativismus in der
Weimarer Republik.** Stuttgart: Klett (1970),
225 pp.
A critical evaluation of Spann's influence and ideas, espec-
ially his doctrine of the "true" corporate state. Schneller
argues that Spann's conservative and neo-romantic ideas
contributed to the intellectual undermining of the Weimar
Republic.

SIEGFRIED, Klaus-Jörg.
**Universalismus und Faschismus: das Gesellschafts-
bild Othmar Spanns. Zur politischen Funktion
seiner Gesellschaftslehre und Ständestaatskonzep-
tion.** Vienna: Europa-Verlag (1974), 289 pp.
An objective study of Spann's social and political ideas and
his political activities (which never reached any great
heights). Siegfried's interpretation lays stress on Spann's
middle class background and the essentially bourgeois
function of his ideological outlook.

15. OSWALD SPENGLER

KOKTANEK, Anton M. (ed.).
Oswald Spengler: Briefe 1913—1936. Munich: Beck
(1963), 818 pp.
For students of Weimar, this large collection of Spengler
letters provides some clear insights into the anti-democratic
right-wing movement. Moreover, the letters largely recapture
the atmosphere of the pre-1933 period. Available in a
rather unsatisfactory, abbreviated English edition edited by
Arthur Helps (London: Allen & Unwin (1966), 320 pp.).

KOKTANEK, Anton M.
**"Spenglers Verhältnis zum Nationalsozialismus in
geschichtlicher Entwicklung".** *Zeitschrift für
Politik*, vol. 13, pt. 1 (1966), p. 32—55.
A good analysis which brings out Spengler's dislike of Hitler
and National Socialism as a whole, and his disappointment
at the form of the Third Reich which emerged after 1933.

PETZOLD, Joachim.
**"Das politische Programm Oswald Spenglers im
System der imperialistischen Ideologie".** *Jahrbuch
für Geschichte*, vol. 5 (1971), p. 175—207.
A biased appraisal whose inevitable verdict is that Spengler
ranks as an agent of imperialism and militarism.

STUTZ, Ernst.
Oswald Spengler als politischer Denker. Berne:
Francke Verlag (1958), 279 pp.
A critical assessment of Spengler's political writings which
attempts to show a line of unity between his political and
philosophical works. Among Stutz's challenging conclusions
is that the differences between Spengler and National
Socialism were tactical rather than fundamental. Spengler
himself comes across as a romantic Pan-German and an
authoritarian Prussian nationalist, an intellectual who was
essentially anti-intellectual.

16. ERNST TOLLER

ELSASSER, Robert.
**Ernst Toller and German Society: the Role of the
Intellectual as Critic 1914—1939.** Dissertation,
Rutgers University (1973)
The involvement of one of Weimar's most gifted and radical
playwrights in politics forms the theme of this interesting
study. Elsasser sees Toller's work against the background of
left-wing intellectual activity during the 1918—33 period.

17. ERNST TROELTSCH.

See also relevant titles in Section 10C.

BORRIES, Achim von.
"Wiedergelesen: Ernst Troeltsch". *Hochland*, vol.
66, pt. 2 (1974), p. 282—8.
A report on the life and work of this important writer and
Protestant theologian.

KASCH, Wilhelm F.
Die Sozialphilosophie von Ernst Troeltsch.
Tübingen: Mohr (1963), 283 pp.
A critical, well researched evaluation of this aspect of
Troeltsch's outlook.

KOLLMANN, Eric C.
**"Eine Diagnose der Weimarer Republik: Ernst
Troeltschs politische Anschauungen".** *Historische
Zeitschrift*, no. 182 (1956), p. 291—320.
A scholarly consideration of Troeltsch's diagnosis of the
Republic as given in his famous "Spectator's Letters".

18. KURT TUCHOLSKY

DOERFEL, Marianne.
**"The Origins of the Left Intellectual: Kurt
Tucholsky, the Romantic Conservative".** *Oxford
German Studies*, vol. 7 (1972—73), p. 119—42.
Doerfel ably analyses the significance of Tucholsky's earlier
career.

POOR, Harold L.
**Kurt Tucholsky: a Leftist Intellectual Views the
Weimar Republic.** New York: Scribners (1968),
285 pp.
An interesting and detailed biography which examines the
range of Tucholsky's political and cultural views, his biting
satirical wit, his disillusionment with the Republic, and his
involvement with *Die Weltbühne*.

TUCHOLSKY, Kurt.
Briefe an eine Katholikin 1929—1931. Hamburg:
Rowohlt (1970), 88 pp.
Conveys something of political developments during the
early depression years.

TUCHOLSKY, Kurt.
Ausgewählte Briefe 1913—1935. Edited by Mary
G. Tucholsky and Fritz J. Raddatz. Hamburg:
Rowohlt (1962), 567 pp.
An excellent and absorbing collection of his letters.

19. AUGUST WINNIG

LANDGREBE, Wilhelm.
August Winnig: Arbeiterführer, Oberpräsident,
Christ. Dinglingen: Schweickhardt (1961), 95 pp.
A brief and too vague biographical sketch.

RIBHEGGE, Wilhelm.
August Winnig: eine historische Persönlichkeits-
analyse. Bad Godesberg: Verlag Neue Gesellschaft
(1973), 315 pp.
A good, detailed and objective biography which traces his
chequered political career: a member of the revisionist
faction in the SPD before 1914, a social imperialist, a
fellow traveller of the NSDAP, a Third Reich official. His
writings also receive adequate treatment.

WINNIG, August.
Aus zwanzig Jahren: 1925 bis 1945. Hamburg:
Wittig Verlag (1951), 296 pp.
Moderately interesting autobiography. Contains a few
points about his political involvement with the left-wing
group in the NSDAP and his association with the Old Social
Democratic Party (ASP), which he co-founded in 1926.

D. HISTORIANS

BESSON, Waldemar.
"Friedrich Meinecke und die Weimarer Republik".
Vierteljahrshefte für Zeitgeschichte, vol. 7, pt. 2
(1959), p. 113—29.
A scholarly appraisal of this liberal historian's support for
the Republic.

CARSTEN, Francis L.
See his articles on Arthur Rosenberg in section 6B (vii) (i).

SCHLEIER, Hans.
Die bürgerliche deutsche Geschichtsschreibung der
Weimarer Republik. 2 vols. Cologne: Pahl-Rugenstein (1975), 593 pp.
A stimulating and critical study. Volume I examines schools
of thought and intellectual attitudes of bourgeois Weimar
historians, while volume II looks at left-liberal historians.

TOBLER, Douglas F.
German Historians and the Weimar Republic.
Dissertation, University of Kansas (1967).
An examination of the relationship of German historians to
the Republic, and of their attitudes to it. Most historians
rejected it, but some lent their support. Among those con-
sidered are Georg von Below, Friedrich Meinecke, Walter
Goetz and Adolf von Harnack.

WEISZ, Christoph.
Geschichtsauffassung und politisches Denken:
Münchener Historiker der Weimarer Zeit. Berlin:
Duncker & Humblot (1970), 309 pp.
The views of six historians, including Erich Marcks, Karl
Alexander von Müller and Hermann Oncken, on a range of
historical events from 1848 to 1945, are examined. But
Weisz's discussion is somewhat banal and lacking in sound
judgement.

E. THEATRE AND DRAMA[1]

BRUMME, Wolfgang.
See his work in section 14.

HOFFMANN, Ludwig; HOFFMANN-OSTWALD,
Daniel.
Deutsches Arbeitertheater 1918—1933. 2 vols.
East Berlin: Henschelverlag (1972), 399, 475 pp.

1. See also the sub-section on the KPD (6B(vii)).

These volumes provide a wealth of detailed and valuable
information on working class theatrical groups, or rather
Communist-orientated groups of this type. The social
and political background of Weimar is ably set into the
narrative. Volume I covers 1918—29, and volume II 1929—
33.

KÄNDLER, Klaus.
Drama und Klassenkampf: Beziehungen zwischen
Epochenproblematik und dramatischen Konflikt in
der sozialistischen Dramatik der Weimarer
Republic. East Berlin: Aufbau-Verlag (1970), 466
pp.
An ideologically orientated book, but nonetheless interesting. Socialist art and literature are placed within a political
context and are seen as part of the process towards the
achievement of "socialist realism" of the East German
variety.

KNELLESSEN, Friedrich W.
Agitation auf der Bühne: das politische Theater
der Weimarer Republik. Emsdetten: Lechte (1970),
348 pp.
A detailed and very useful discussion of how the theatre
was employed by the radical Left as an effective tool in
the political struggle.

MARCUSE, Ludwig.
Obszön: Geschichte einer Entrüstung. Munich: List
(1962), 407 pp.
Some parts of this book throw fresh light on events in the
theatrical world during the 1920s. For example, p. 207—63
discuss the theme, "Berlin 1920: Sex, Politik, und Kunst —
im Reigen", a reference to a scandal associated with the
performance of Schnitzler's *Der Reigen*.

PISCATOR, Erwin.
Das politische Theater. Hamburg: Rowohlt (1963),
253 pp.
A semi-autobiographical description of the development of
political theatre in Weimar, by the former leader of the
Berlin Proletarian Theatre, one of the most outstanding
working class theatrical groups.

RÜHLE, Günther.
Theater für die Republik 1917—1933: im Spiegel
der Kritik. Frankfurt: Fischer (1967), 1263 pp.
An authoritative and indispensable work.

RÜHLE, Jürgen.
Das gefesselte Theater: vom Revolutionstheater
zum Sozialistischen Realismus. Cologne: Kiepenheuer & Witsch (1957), 457 pp.
A thorough and well documented study of the political
theatre and its development as an entity in radical left-
wing politics.

SCHERER, Herbert.
"Die Volksbühnenbewegung und ihre interne
Opposition in der Weimarer Republik". *Archiv für*
Sozialgeschichte, vol. 14 (1974), p. 213—51.
A detailed look at the different stages of the relationship
between the Popular Theatre movement and the SPD.
After 1918, the movement developed as an instrument of
state cultural policy to encourage all sections of the pop-
ulation to attend the theatre regularly. Later in Weimar, the
SPD and KPD fought for control of the movement.

WERNER, Bruno E.
"Literatur und Theater in den zwanziger Jahren".
In Leonhard Reinisch (ed.). *Die Zeit ohne*
Eigenschaften: eine Bilanz der zwanziger Jahre.
Stuttgart: Kohlhammer (1961), p. 50—81.
An informed, impressionistic review of some of the literary
and theatrical highlights of the Weimar era, related with a
heavy sense of nostalgia. The theatre is dealt with from
p. 66 onwards.

The Media

16

A. THE PRESS

(i) General

BAUER, Peter.
Die Organisation der amtlichen Pressepolitik in der Weimarer Zeit. Dissertation, Free University of Berlin (1962).
A short and superficial examination of the press departments of the Reich government and Foreign Office before 1933.

DOVIFAT, Emil.
"Die Publizistik der Weimarer Zeit: Presse, Rundfunk, Film". In Leonhard Reinisch (ed.). *Die Zeit ohne Eigenschaften: eine Bilanz der zwanziger Jahre.* Stuttgart: Kohlhammer (1961), p. 119—38.
A general but informative survey of the main developments and problems of the press, film and broadcasting industries and their place in the cultural life of Weimar.

DOVIFAT, Emil.
"Journalistische Kämpfe um die Freiheit der Presse in der Weimarer Republik: tragischer Rückblick eines Beteiligten". *Publizistik*, vol. 8, pt. 4 (1963), p. 216—21.
The *Spartakusbund* was the first to raise the question of press freedom in 1919, a call subsequently taken up by the *Reichsverband der deutschen Presse.* Some of the leading figures involved in the struggle are discussed, such as Georg Bernhard of the *Vössische Zeitung* and Heinrich Rippler of the *Tagliche Rundschau.*

FISCHER, Heinz-Dietrich (ed.).
Deutsche Zeitungen des 17. bis 20. Jahrhunderts. Pullach/Munich: Verlag Dokumentation (1972), 145 pp.
Contains histories of over two dozen German daily papers and provides useful factual data on the development of the newspaper industry in Germany. But analysis of the influence of papers, individually and collectively, is sadly lacking.

FLEISS, Peter J.
Freedom of the Press in the German Republic 1918—1933. Baton Rouge: Louisiana State University Press (1955), 147 pp.
A general but hardly exhaustive examination of the prob-

lem. However, at least the factual outline of the struggle for press freedom is accurate.

GÖTTE, Karl-Heinz.
"Die Glaubensbewegung 'Deutsche Christen' in der publizistischen Auseinandersetzung". *Publizistik,* vol. 6, pt. 1 (1961), p. 12—25.
Considers the attitudes of the German press towards the German Christians as well as the propaganda methods of the latter during the late Weimar period.

GÖTTE, Karl-Heinz.
Die Propaganda der Glaubensbewegung "Deutsche Christen" und ihre Beurteilung in der deutschen Tagespresse: ein Beitrag zur Publizistik im Dritten Reich. Dissertation, University of Münster (1957).
The very early part of this study looks at the impact of the German Christians on the contemporary German press.

HALE, Oron J.
The Captive Press in the Third Reich. Princeton: Princeton University Press (1964), 353 pp.
The early chapters of this pioneering and scholarly monograph outline the development of the German press before 1933. Most of the book examines how the press was "co-ordinated" after 1933 by the National Socialists.

KAISER, Klaus.
See his work in section 9D.

KOSZYK, Kurt.
Deutsche Presse 1914—1945. Berlin: Colloquium Verlag (1972), 588 pp.
This is the third volume in the author's authoritative history of the German press. Using a mass of new material, he provides here a comprehensive and detailed survey of press developments during Weimar and the Third Reich. He lays some emphasis on the question of press freedom, which he argues was constantly threatened before 1933 by a number of institutions, including the government.

MATTHIES, Marie.
Journalisten in eigener Sache: zur Geschichte des Reichsverbandes der deutschen Presse. Berlin: Verlag des Journalisten-Verbands (1969), 248 pp.
A competent and fairly objective description of the main representative of Weimar press interests and the kind of work it performed. But the political side of the *Reichsverband's* activities is glossed over.

MENDELSSOHN, Peter de.
Zeitungsstadt Berlin: Menschen und Mächte in der Geschichte der deutschen Presse. Berlin: Ullstein (1959), 522 pp.
A very interesting narrative of the personalities involved in the German press in modern times. Stalwarts of the Weimar era receive due attention.

PIEPENSTOCK, Klaus.
Die Münchener Tagespresse 1918—1933. Dissertation, University of Munich (1955).
Describes the aims, interests and readership of the major Munich newspapers, including the *Münchener Neueste Nachrichten* on the one hand, and the *Völkischer Beobachter* on the other.

SALL, Larry D.
The German Press and Kurt von Schleicher, May 1932-February 1933. Dissertation, Wayne State University (1973).
Examines what sort of press Schleicher enjoyed and his efforts to control what was written about himself. Initially, he was soundly criticized for involving the army in politics, but there was a major shift in press opinion when Schleicher was challenging for the chancellorship. Most of the liberal and conservative papers supported him against Hitler.

SCHOLAND, Hildegard.
"Die Diskussion um ein Journalistengesetz: Dokumentation zum Gesetzentwurf von 1924". *Publizistik*, vol. 13, pt. 3 (1968), p. 316—29.
Outlines the main arguments in favour of a press law during the early 1920s, and some relevant documents illustrative of the debate are appended. However, most of the paper is simply a bibliography of secondary literature dealing with the subject.

STARKULLA, Heinz.
Organisation und Technik der Pressepolitik des Staatsmannes Gustav Stresemann: ein Beitrag zur Pressegeschichte der Weimarer Republik. Dissertation, University of Munich (1951).
Does not say anything of great moment.

ZAHN, Manfred.
See his work in section 4G.

(ii) Social Democratic

KOSZYK, Kurt.
Die Presse der deutschen Sozialdemokratie: eine Bibliographie. Hanover: Verlag für Literatur und Zeitgeschehen (1966), 404 pp.
An important reference source, containing a list of over two thousand publications on the development of the SPD press.

KOSZYK, Kurt.
Zwischen Kaiserreich und Diktatur: die sozialdemokratische Presse von 1914 bis 1933. Heidelberg: Quelle & Meyer (1958), 276 pp.
An excellent historical study of the SPD press, particularly of the Weimar period, during which the party press expanded prodigiously. The years 1924—25 witnessed the changeover of the socialist press from a party political instrument to a modern popularly orientated press. Organizational rationalization complemented this development. Koszyk has been careful to relate the press history of the SPD to the background of party and national developments. Altogether, a sound and thoroughly documented work.

RÜLCKER, Christoph.
"Arbeiterkultur und Kulturpolitik im Blickwinkel des 'Vorwärts' 1918—1928". *Archiv für Sozialgeschichte*, vol. 14 (1974), p. 115—55.
The author of this detailed paper argues that the attitude of *Vorwärts*, the leading SPD organ, to cultural policy was uncritical and emotionally coloured. Consequently, its attitudes did not involve anything other than passive defence of the Weimar constitution, and even encouraged the growth of bourgeois thinking among the working class. The policy of *Vorwärts* led directly to the embourgeoisement of workers' culture. The most unsatisfactory aspect of the essay is the author's stereotyped definitions of "worker" and "bourgeoisie", and as a result the essay's argumentation lacks clarity.

(iii) Liberal[1]

(a) The Frankfurter Zeitung

BECKER, Werner.
Demokratie des sozialen Rechts: die politische Haltung der "Frankfurter Zeitung", der "Vössischen Zeitung" und des "Berliner Tageblatts" 1918—1924. Göttingen: Musterschmidt (1971), 320 pp.
A detailed and convincing comparative analysis of the political outlook of Weimar's great left-liberal papers; their attitudes to the major political events of the period are carefully scrutinized.

BOVARI, Margret.
"Joseph Roth und die 'Frankfurter Zeitung'". *Merkur*, vol. 25 (1971), p. 786—98.
Assesses Roth's contribution as editor on the basis of an examination of his papers.

EDGAR, James H.
The "Frankfurter Zeitung" and the Political Parties of the Radical Right in the Weimar Republic, 1918—1933. Dissertation, University of Virginia (1972).
An examination of the paper's untiring efforts to defend the Republic against its right-wing enemies. But the paper mistakenly believed that the NSDAP would not come to power, and even if it did, that it would not last long. This study covers a lot of familiar ground and does not tell us all we want to know about the paper.

EKSTEINS, Modris.
"The 'Frankfurter Zeitung': Mirror of Weimar Democracy". *Journal of Contemporary History*, vol. 6, pt. 4 (1971), p. 3—28.
The author traces the gradual weakening of liberal democracy in late Weimar, using the FZ for purposes of illustration. He shows how the paper reacted with resignation to the *Machtergreifung* and how quickly it adopted an accommodating editorial policy towards the régime. He contrasts this with the positive and valuable role of the paper in supporting the Republic before 1933, though its commitment to democratic institutions slackened perceptibly. An informative essay.

KREJEI, Michael.
Die "Frankfurter Zeitung" und der Nationalsozialismus, 1923—1933. Dissertation, University of Würzburg (1965).
Explains the paper's consistent opposition to the NSDAP.

1. See also sub-section 6B(v).

REIFENBERG, Bruno (ed.).
Hundert Jahre "Frankfurter Zeitung", 1856–1956. Frankfurt (1956).
A history of the paper's main developments on its one hundredth birthday.

TRAMPE, Gustav.
Reichswehr und Presse. Dissertation, University of Munich (1960).
A brief and shallow analysis of the attitude to military matters adopted by several leading left-wing and liberal papers, including the FZ.

WERBER, Rudolf.
Die "Frankfurter Zeitung" und ihr Verhältnis zum Nationalsozialismus. Dissertation, University of Bonn (1964).
In fact this study is almost entirely concerned with the relationship as it developed during the Third Reich. Only the first chapter reviews the last year of Weimar.

(b) Others

KOSZYK, Kurt.
"Jacob Stöcker und der Dortmunder 'General-Anzeiger' 1929–1933". *Publizistik*, vol. 8, pt. 4 (1963), p. 282–95.
The 'G-A' was a pacifist-republican paper in Dortmund with a circulation of 250,000 in 1929 when Stöcker became editor. He took a hostile stand against National Socialism and was inevitably taken over in 1933.

LOWENTHAL-HENSEL, Cécile; PAUCKER, Arnold (eds.).
Ernst Feder: heute sprach ich mit . . . . Tagebücher eines Berliner Publizisten 1926–1932. Stuttgart: Deutsche Verlagsanstalt (1971), 431 pp.
Feder, a Jewish lawyer and journalist, was political editor of the *Berliner Tageblatt* 1919–31. These extracts from his diaries record his impressions of Weimar politics and personalities, of the DDP, and also of the affairs of the newspaper for which he worked. An absorbing chronicle.

PAUCKER, Arnold.
"Searchlight on the Decline of the Weimar Republic: the Diaries of Ernst Feder". *Yearbook of the Leo Baeck Institute*, vol. 13 (1968), p. 161–234.
After a helpful summary of Feder's career, Paucker provides extracts from Feder's diaries relating to the 1930–33 period (p. 171–234).

SCHWARZ, Gotthart.
Theodor Wolff und das "Berliner Tageblatt": eine liberale Stimme in der deutschen Politik 1906–1933. Tübingen: Mohr (1968), 311 pp.
Wolff was the long-serving editor-in-chief of the *Berliner Tageblatt* who, according to Schwarz, epitomized better than most the strengths and weaknesses of German liberalism during the Weimar era. Wolff retained an unquenchable optimism in the ability of the middle classes in Germany to accept democracy, but he was blind to the power of National Socialism. This is a solid and readable study of Wolff, his paper, and the cause of liberalism.

(iv) Conservative

DOESER, Ute.
See her work in section 19C(i).

GNICHWITZ, S.
Die Presse der bürgerlichen Rechte in der Ära Brüning. Dissertation, University of Münster (1956).
A modest review of the conservative press.

GURATZSCH, Dankwart.
Macht durch Organisation: die Grundlagen des Hugenbergschen Presseimperiums. Düsseldorf: Bertelsmann (1974), 486 pp.
An extremely detailed examination of the structure and extent of the Hugenberg press empire which became a factor of fundamental political importance, especially during the last years of Weimar.

HAMMERSCHMIDT, Rudolf.
"Die Politik der Schlagworte: der Kampf der bürgerlichen Rechtspresse gegen die Weimarer Republik". *Die Neue Gesellschaft*, vol. 17, pt. 2 (1970), p. 160–9.
A superficial look at some of the major themes of the right-wing press campaign against the Republic; for example, the "policy of fulfilment" and the *Dolchstoss* myth.

PFEIFER, Eva.
Das Hitlerbild im Spiegel einiger konservativer Zeitungen in den Jahren 1929–33. Munich: Piper (1968), 190 pp.
An unsatisfactory, superficial study whose methodology is weak.

RUGE, Wolfgang.
See his work in section 13B(iii).

TREUDE, Burkhard.
Konservative Presse und Nationalsozialismus. Bochum: Brockmeyer (1975), 195 pp.
An analysis of the contents of the *Neue Preussische (Kreuz-) Zeitung*, particularly its response to the rise of the NSDAP during the last years of Weimar.

(v) Radical Leftist

DAVID, Fritz.
"Zur Geschichte der Zeitschrift 'Die Internationale' (1919–1933)". *Beiträge zur Geschichte der Deutschen Arbeiterbewegung*, vol. 15, pt. 6 (1973), p. 967–86.
An assessment of the paper's policies and contribution to the cause of the KPD.

KÜSTER, Heinz.
See his article in section 6B(vii)(b).

LANGE, Karl-Heinz.
Die Stellung der kommunistischen Presse zum Nationalgedanken in Deutschland. Dissertation, University of Munich (1947).
Based on the attitude of *Rote Fahne* to the national idea, 1918–33.

SCHMIDT, Konrad (ed.).
Feuilleton der Roten Presse 1918–1933.
East Berlin: Verlag des Ministeriums für Nationale Verteidigung (1960), 179 pp.
Contains informative but biased discussions of leading KPD journals and newspapers, including *Rote Fahne*.

WILLMANN, Heinz.
Geschichte der "Arbeiter-Illustrierten-Zeitung"
1921—1938. Berlin: Verlag das Europäische Buch
(1974), 359 pp.
A full, detailed explanation of the origins, development and
objectives of this major Communist publication.

(vi) Confessional

BÜHLER, Karl-Werner.
Presse und Protestantismus in der Weimarer
Republik: Kräfte und Krisen evangelischer
Publizistik. Witten: Luther-Verlag (1970),
182 pp.
This is a solid piece of research on the development of the
Protestant press 1918—33, although written with little
flair.

DÜLMEN, Richard von.
"Katholischer Konservativismus oder die 'sozialog-
ische' Neuorientierung: das 'Hochland' in der
Weimarer Zeit". *Zeitschrift für Bayerische*
Landesgeschichte, vol. 36, pt. 1 (1973), p. 254—
303.
Hochland, the most widely distributed Catholic periodical
in Germany, preached Christian socialism and democracy
after 1918, but at the same time it had also a strong component of nationalist, racialist, and Pan-German ideas.
Dülmen further shows that the periodical, though it did not
support the Republic, rejected National Socialism and other
extreme right-wing movements.

GOTTWALD, Herbert.
"Franz von Papen und die 'Germania': ein Beitrag
zur Geschichte des politischen Katholizismus
und der Zentrumspresse in der Weimarer
Republik". *Jahrbuch für Geschichte*, vol. 6 (1972),
p. 539—604.
Delineates the uneasy and at times hostile relations between
Papen and the leading German Catholic newspaper.

KOEHLER, Henning.
Autonomiebewegung oder Separatismus? Die
Politik der "Kölnischen Volkszeitung" 1918—19.
Berlin: Colloquium Verlag (1974), 114 pp.
A well researched examination of this Catholic paper's
attitude to the question of a breakaway Rhineland during
the immediate postwar period.

WALZEL, Richard E.
Die "Augsburger Postzeitung" und der National-
sozialismus: ein Beitrag zur Geschichte der
katholischen Presse 1920—1933. Dissertation,
University of Munich (1956).
Demonstrates the sometimes ambivalent attitude of this
provincial Catholic newspaper to the NSDAP.

(vii) Jewish[1]

BERNSTEIN, Reiner.
Zwischen Emanzipation und Antisemitismus: die
Publizistik der deutschen Juden am Beispiel der
"C.V. Zeitung", Organ des Centralvereins
deutscher Staatsbürger jüdischen Glaubens 1924—
1933. Dissertation, Free University of Berlin
(1969).
Recounts the assimilationist philosophy of the leading
Jewish newspaper in Weimar and its approach to political
events of the period.

1. See also section 11.

EDELHEIM-MUEHSAM, Margaret T.
"Reactions of the Jewish Press to the Nazi
Challenge". *Yearbook of the Leo Baeck Institute*,
vol. 5 (1960), p. 308—29.
Very informative paper which underlines how much the
Jewish community as a whole tended to underestimate the
threat of National Socialism.

EDELHEIM-MUEHSAM, Margaret T.
"The Jewish Press in Germany". *Yearbook of the*
Leo Baeck Institute, vol. 1 (1956), p. 163—76.
Contains a list of Jewish periodicals and newspapers of the
Weimar era, with foundation dates, circulation figures and
names of editors.

GRÜNEWALD, Max.
"Critic of German Jewry: Ludwig Feuchtwanger
and his 'Gemeindezeitung'". *Yearbook of the Leo*
Baeck Institute, vol. 17 (1972), p. 75—92.
Feuchtwanger was a member of a well established South
German Jewish family, and editor of the *Bayerische*
Israelitische Gemeindezeitung, organ of Bavarian Jewry.
Grünewald analyses his articles, many of which, in re-
viewing German-Jewish relations, could be critical of
Jewish attitudes.

POPPEL, Stephan M.
"Salmon Schocken and the Schocken Verlag".
Yearbook of the Leo Baeck Institute, vol. 17
(1972), p. 93—113.
Sketches Schocken's career as prosperous businessman,
publisher and active Zionist in the 1920s and 1930s. The
latter part of the essay examines post-1933 developments
in his publishing business.

SICHEL, Frieda H.
"The Rise and Fall of the 'Kasseler Tageblatt'".
Yearbook of the Leo Baeck Institute, vol. 19
(1974), p. 237—43.
Outlines the history of the paper through the German-
Jewish family which owned it from the nineteenth century
to September 1932 when it ceased publication; the family
was the Gotthelfts of Kassel.

B. PUBLICISTS

BERGLAR, Peter.
"Harden und Rathenau: zur Problematik ihrer
Freundschaft". *Historische Zeitschrift*, no. 209
(1969), p. 75—94.
Berglar has written a scholarly and shrewd essay which
explains the importance of Harden's friendship for a
better understanding of Rathenau's work and personality.
The paper is based on correspondence between the two
men and a very good characterization of both is provided.

BIEBER, Horst.
Paul Rohrbach — ein konservativer Publizist und
Kritiker der Weimarer Republik. Berlin: Verlag
Dokumentation (1972), 270 pp.
A thorough and detailed biography of the leading Weimar
conservative publicist who remained a consistent enemy
of democratic institutions.

GOTTGETREU, Erich.
"Maximilian Harden: Ways and Errors of a
Publicist". *Yearbook of the Leo Baeck Institute*,
vol. 7 (1962), p. 215—46.
A competent biographical outline of the colourful and
somewhat extraordinary Jewish publicist and journalist.

KESSLER, Heinrich.
Wilhelm Stapel als politischer Publizist.
Nuremberg: Spindler Verlag (1967), 326 pp.
Stapel was active in the cause of the conservative Right during Weimar and this well documented biography has presented his political career in clear and objective terms.

KOSZYK, Kurt.
"Paul Reusch und die 'Münchener Neuesten Nachrichten': zum Problem Industrie und Presse in der Endphase der Weimarer Republik".
Vierteljahrshefte für Zeitgeschichte, vol. 20, pt. 1 (1972), p. 75—103.
An examination of connections between industrial circles and newspaper publishers during Weimar. Reusch, a right-wing publicist and leading industrialist, tried in 1930 to make the *Münchener Neueste Nachrichten* an instrument of industrial interests. The documentation appended to this paper illustrates Reusch's efforts to control the newspaper and also reveals the outlook of an industrialist of a conservative-nationalist stamp. His plan ultimately failed in late 1932.

KOSZYK, Kurt.
"Das abenteuerliche Leben des sozial-revolutionären Agitators Carl Minster (1873—1942)". *Archiv für Sozialgeschichte*, vol. 5 (1965), p. 193—225.
Traces the career of Carl Minster, active before 1914 in the SPD press and after 1918 as a Communist within and without the KPD. During the early 1920s, he edited the *Freiheit*, organ of the Independent Social Democractic Party (USPD), and later the same party's *Weckruf*. During the last years of the Republic, he was a member of the radical *Sozialistische Arbeiterpartei* (SAP) and became involved in its publishing ventures. The paper does not make clear why Minster is worth bothering about, for the man was of no political importance and his career in publishing was spasmodic and unsuccessful.

LERG, Winfried B.
"Der preussische Pressechef 1919—1932: ein biobibliographischer Hinweis auf Hans Goslar".
Publizistik, vol. 14, pt. 2 (1969), p. 223—7.
Goslar, as head of the Prussian Ministry of State's Press Office, was intimately tied up with the publishing world of Weimar, and earned a reputation as the most publicized civil servant of Prussia. A Jew, he was a stout defender of the Republic, and died in a concentration camp.

MAUERSBERGER, Volker.
Rudolf Pechel und die "Deutsche Rundschau": eine Studie zur konservativ-revolutionären Publizistik in der Weimarer Republik (1918—1933). Bremen: Schünemann (1971), 344 pp.
An incisive and detailed work which has brought together material from a wide range of sources.

ROGGE, Helmuth.
"Aus Maximilian Hardens politischer Publizistik 1912—1922". *Publizistik*, vol. 6, pt. 5 (1961), p. 301—32.
The second part of this essay discusses Harden's publicist activities in early Weimar, particularly his involvement with his periodical *Die Zukunft*. Rogge analyses his ideas and outlook, and his fierce rejection of both the political Right and the Republic. Harden, it is made clear, was an individualist *par excellence*.

SCHWARZSCHILD, Valerie (ed.).
Leopold Schwarzschild: die letzten Jahre vor Hitler. Hamburg: Wegner (1966), 294 pp.
Contains interesting excerpts from his diaries, 1929—33.

STERN, Guy.
"Hanns Braun, Kritiker der zwanziger Jahre".
Publizistik, vol. 8, pt. 5 (1963), p. 572—5.
Looks at this essayist's and poet's contributions to the periodical *Neue Merkur* in the early 1920s. Braun was modest in his role as critic *vis-à-vis* the creative artist.

WELLER, Uwe B.
Maximilian Harden und die "Zukunft". Bremen: Schünemann (1970), 485 pp.
A thoroughly detailed and informative biography of the Jewish publicist; sympathetic yet fair in assessment, and concentrating on the postwar era.

YOUNG, Harry F.
Maximilian Harden: ein Publizist im Widerstreit von 1892—1927. Münster: Regensberg (1971), 291 pp.
A scholarly study at its best and most detailed when discussing the 1892—1914 period, emphasizing Harden's role as the most incisive critic of the Kaiser and his entourage. The sections of the book on the Weimar era are sparse and disappointing.

C. THE RADIO

BAUSCH, Hans.
Der Rundfunk im politischen Kräftespiel der Weimarer Republik, 1923—1933. Tübingen: Mohr (1956), 224 pp.
An examination of the organization and control of radio broadcasting in Weimar, and as such a valuable contribution to the institutional history of the Republic. Using a good deal of previously unpublished data, the author shows how the political possibilities of radio were being fully exploited by the Reich government in particular by 1932. This degree of state control paved the way for the National Socialist monopoly of the radio after 1933.

FESSMANN, Ingo.
Rundfunk und Rundfunksrecht in der Weimarer Republik. Frankfurt: Knecht (1973), 261 pp.
Concerned more with the technical organization of the radio than anything else.

LERG, Winfried B.
"Die Anfänge der Rundfunkwerbung in Deutschland". *Publizistik*, vol. 8, pt. 4 (1963), p. 296—314.
Radio advertising began in 1925, but this paper does not investigate political advertising by the Weimar parties.

POHLE, Heinz.
Der Rundfunk als Instrument der Politik: zur Geschichte des deutschen Rundfunks von 1923—1938. Hamburg: Verlag Hans-Bredow-Institut (1955), 480 pp.
A useful history, but not as well researched or as perceptive on the whole as Bausch's study (see earlier in this section). The main emphasis, moreover, is on the Third Reich era.

SCHÜTTE, Wolfgang.
Regionalität und Föderalismus im Rundfunk: die geschichtliche Entwicklung in Deutschland 1923—1945. Frankfurt: Knecht (1971), 260 pp.
Analyses the development of radio in different parts of Germany.

D. THE CINEMA

KRACAUER, Siegfried.
From Caligari to Hitler: a Psychological History of the German Film. Princeton: Princeton University Press (1947), 361 pp.
Tries to show, through an analysis of films made in Germany 1918—33, certain psychological trends in the German public. But the author talks rather aimlessly about the "German national character" and the "bourgeois" organization of the German cinema. The second half of this unsatisfactory work discusses post-1933 National Socialist war films.

LÜDECKE, Willi.
Der Film in Agitation und Propaganda der revolutionären deutschen Arbeiterbewegung.
Berlin: Oberbaumverlag (1973), 111 pp.
An interesting theme, but Lüdecke does not do full justice to it in this rather superficial study.

MONACO, Paul M.
Cinema and Society in France and Germany 1919—1929. Dissertation, Brandeis University (1974).
Considers the cinema as an aspect of popular culture in France and Germany. The most noteworthy parts are chapters 2—5 which deal with the role of the film industry in both countries in terms of the sociology of cinemagoers and relations with government. During 1919—29 German films revealed an obsession with the defeat of 1918 and the November Revolution, and in so doing helped perpetuate the myth that Germany had been stabbed in the back.

SPIKER, Jürgen.
Film und Kapital: der Weg der deutschen Filmwirtschaft zum nationalsozialistischen Einheitskonzern. Berlin: Verlag Volker Spiess (1975), 297 pp.
The author's thesis is that since the German film industry was always dominated by capitalist interests, the monopoly set up by Hitler after 1933 was a logical development. Spiker subscribes to the theory which sees National Socialism as a phenomenon of decaying capitalism. As a result, the intellectual framework of the book is naive and unconvincing.

Education

17

A. GENERAL

FISCHER, Kurt G. (ed.).
Politische Bildung in der Weimarer Republik: Grundsatzreferate der "Staatsbürgerlichen Woche" 1923. Frankfurt: Europäische Verlagsanstalt (1970), 190 pp.
Contains informative and relevant documents on an interesting educational experiment in Weimar which eventually proved unsuccessful.

HOHENDORF, Gerd.
Die pädagogische Bewegung in den ersten Jahren der Weimarer Republik. East Berlin: Volk und Wissen Verlag (1954), 192 pp.
Informative and critical even if the work is heavily conditioned by Marxist-Leninist doctrinal constraints.

KURUEZ, Jenφ.
Struktur und Funktion der Intelligenz während der Weimarer Republik. Cologne: Grote (1967), 188 pp.
An interesting but incomplete sociological study of the role of the intelligentsia in a pluralistic society such as existed in Weimar.

SCHLICKER, Wolfgang.
"Zu Max Plancks Bedeutung für die Leitung der Wissenschaft und Organisation der Forschung: unter besonderer Berücksichtigung seines Wirkens in der Weimarer Republik". *Jahrbuch für Wirtschaftsgeschichte*, pt. 2 (1975), p. 161—85.
Usefully discusses Planck's contribution to new research organizations and his reform plans for, among others, the Berliner Akademie.

SEILER, Alois.
"Die Behandlung des Völkerbundes im Unterricht während der Weimarer Zeit". *Geschichte in Wissenschaft und Unterricht*, vol. 22, pt. 4 (1971), p. 193—211.
The educational treatment of the League of Nations issue reveals divergencies which were partly the result of political factors.

SÜLE, Tibor.
Bücherei und Ideologie: politische Aspekte im "Richtungsstreit" deutscher Volksbibliothekäre 1910—1930. Cologne: Greven Verlag (1972), 87 pp.
A discussion of the struggle for political control of German public libraries. Walter Hofmann took the lead in advocating a popular orientation as opposed to a bureaucratic-bourgeois system. During the late 1920s, however, neo-romantic ideas held sway and the author argues weakly that this development weakened resistance to National Socialism.

B. UNIVERSITIES, ACADEMICS, AND STUDENTS

BARKIN, Kenneth D.
"Fritz K. Ringer's 'The Decline of the Mandarins'". Journal of Modern History, vol. 43, pt. 2 (June 1971), p. 276—86.
A review of Ringer's book (see below). While commending the book as important and "indispensable reading", Barkin expresses his misgivings about many of the assumptions and conclusions that are central to Ringer's argument.

BEATUS, Morris.
Academic Proletariat: the Problem of Overcrowding in the Learned Professions and Universities during the Weimar Republic 1918—1933. Dissertation, University of Wisconsin (1975), 321 pp.
An investigation of the salient features of academic middle class insecurity arising from fears of proletarianization and overcrowding in the professions, and the political consequences. Much of this is well trodden territory.

BLEUEL, Hans Peter.
Deutschlands Bekenner: Professoren zwischen Kaiserreich und Diktatur. Munich: Scherz (1968), 255 pp.
A study, patchy in quality, of the German academic community, its structure, gradation and politics; there is some reasonably useful information but the book's conclusions are weakly argued. As a whole, the book is unscholarly and has been apparently designed to appeal to the popular market.

BLEUEL, Hans Peter; KLINNERT, Ernst.
Deutsche Studenten auf dem Weg ins Dritte
Reich: Ideologien-Programm-Aktionen 1918–
1935. Gütersloh: Mohn (1967), 295 pp.
Useful only as a general introduction to the topic because
it is shallow and treats in cavalier fashion many complex
problems while it ignores others. The book's theme is the
conservative and nationalist orientation of Weimar university students.

CARMON, Arye Z.
The University of Heidelberg and National Socialism
1930–1935. Dissertation, University of Wisconsin
(1974).
Heidelberg is taken as a case study to indicate how the
universities lost their traditional aloofness and tranquillity
under the impact of national political and economic
developments during the last years of Weimar. Increased
friction within the university over several matters allowed
the National Socialist Student League (NSDStB) to make
substantial headway, so that by 1933 the university had
lost much of its strength to resist the National Socialist
Gleichschaltung programme. This is an interesting and
valuable study.

DÖRING, Herbert.
Der Weimarer Kreis. Meisenheim: Hain (1975),
336 pp.
A solid monograph which treats the political attitudes of
pro-republican and democratic university teachers 1918–33.
Because they were such a small minority, their commitment was all the more definite.

DÖRING, Herbert.
"Deutsche Professoren zwischen Kaiserreich und
Dritten Reich". *Neue Politische Literatur*, vol. 19
(1974), p. 340–52.
Discusses some recent publications in the field and in
particular the radical political outlook of most professors
before 1933.

FLIESS, Gerhard.
Die politische Entwicklung der Jenaer Studenten-
schaft von November 1918 bis zum Januar 1933.
2 vols. Dissertation, University of Jena (1959),
377, 390 pp.
A thorough and detailed study which has made use of a
wide range of sources, though, perhaps inevitably, the
author exaggerates the left-wing and Communist influence
among the student body.

FORMAN, Paul.
"The Financial Support and Political Alignment of
Physicists in Weimar Germany", *Minerva*, vol. 12,
pt. 1 (1974), p. 39–66.
The author examines new forms of financing academic
scientific research which arose in Germany as a result of
inflation during the early 1920s, basing his analysis on the
two leading fund-raising institutions of the period, the
Notgemeinschaft der deutschen Wissenschaft and the
Helmholtz-Gesellschaft. He investigates the reasons why
funds were made available on a comparatively generous
scale, and concludes that political factors played a large
part in the distribution of research grants.

FRANZE, Manfred.
Die Erlanger Studentenschaft 1918–1945. Würzburg: Schöningh (1972), 440 pp.
An excellent scholarly monograph which has produced a
mass of interesting and important detail on major aspects
of the student fraternity at Erlangen University. The
political side of student activities before 1933 is very well
covered.

FRANZ, Ludwig.
Der politische Kampf an den Münchener
Hochschulen von 1929 bis 1933 im Spiegel der
Presse. Dissertation, University of Munich (1949).
A mediocre work; the author is reluctant to draw the
appropriate conclusions from his material, scanty though
it may be.

HIRCHE, Walter.
Quellenlage und Forschungsstand zur Geschichte
der Studentenschaft in der Weimarer Republik.
Heidelberg: Quelle & Meyer (1969).
A useful review of materials suitable for studies of university
students, as well as a few notes on what has been achieved
so far in scholarly research on the subject.

KAHLE, Paul E.
Bonn University in Pre-Nazi and Nazi Times.
London (1945).
Disappointing; does not bear comparison with more up-to-
date studies of other universities.

KARL, Willibald.
"Students and the Youth Movement in Germany:
Attempt at a Structural Comparison". *Journal of*
Contemporary History, vol. 5, pt. 1 (1970), p. 113
–27.
The author compares the student movement of West
Germany of the 1960s with the pre-1933 youth movement.
The comparison, however, is superficial and far-fetched,
and his conclusions are quite unconvincing.

KATER, Michael H.
"The Work Student: a Socio-Economic Phenom-
enon of Early Weimar Germany". *Journal of*
Contemporary History, vol. 10, pt. 1 (1975),
p. 71–94.
Work students in German universities during the 1920s
had to work in vacations to earn enough money to get
through their studies. Kater discusses the social and political
consequences of the phenomenon, including the gravitation
of work students to National Socialism in the later 1920s.
He therefore spotlights in this interesting paper a further
example of social alienation in Weimar.

KATER, Michael H.
Studentenschaft und Rechtsradikalismus in
Deutschland 1918–1933: eine sozialgeschichtliche
Studie zur Bildungskrise in der Weimarer Republik.
Hamburg: Hoffmann & Campe (1975), 361 pp.
This is a highly competent, solidly detailed monograph
which, by employing a socio-historical methodology, brings
new and important perspectives to bear on a well-worked
theme. As a result, our understanding of right-wing
student politics after 1918 is significantly deepened.

KATER, Michael H.
See also his article in section 13B (iv)

KLUKE, Paul.
Die Stiftungsuniversität Frankfurt a. M. 1914–
1932. Frankfurt: Kramer (1972), 593 pp.
A painstakingly detailed and diligently researched history
of the university.

KREUTZBERGER, Wolfgang.
Studenten und Politik 1918–1933: der Fall
Freiburg im Breisgau. Göttingen: Vandenhoeck &
Ruprecht (1972), 230 pp.

The author's methodology utilizes the principles of Marxist social analysis of the Frankfurt School of Sociology. He examines in this way the most important aspects of student life and their politics at the University of Freiburg, emphasizing the favourable response of the students after 1930 to National Socialism. A provocative but on the whole convincing work.

KUHN, Helmut.
"Die deutsche Universität am Vorabend der Machtergreifung". *Zeitschrift für Politik*, vol. 13 (1966), p. 235—50.
A general survey of the development of German universities after 1918 and their susceptibility in the end to the advances of National Socialism.

LEISEN, Adolf.
Die Ausbreitung des völkischen Gedankens in der Studentenschaft der Weimarer Republik. Dissertation, University of Heidelberg (1964).
An interesting discussion of the extent of *völkisch* ideological influence among students, though the author does not explain satisfactorily the reasons for this development.

LINSE, Ulrich.
See his work in section 4A (iii)

MARSHALL, Elizabeth R.
The Political Development of German University Towns in the Weimar Republic. Dissertation, University of London (1973).
A useful study of the universities of Göttingen and Münster.

MEHRMANN, W.
See his work in section 18B.

NIPPERDEY, Thomas.
"Die deutsche Studentenschaft in den ersten Jahren der Weimarer Republik". In Adolf Grimm (ed.). *Kulturverwaltung der zwanziger Jahre: alte Dokumente und neue Beiträge.* Stuttgart: Deutsche Verlagsanstalt (1961), p. 19—48.
A very good analysis which stresses the fact that despite the war and Revolution, the student body, retaining its predominantly bourgeois social composition, continued to espouse right-wing and nationalist ideas.

RINGER, Fritz K.
The Decline of the German Mandarins: the German Academic Community 1890—1933. Cambridge (Mass): Harvard University Press (1969), 528 pp.
A perceptive and far-ranging study whose theme is the fundamental failure of university professors and students to accept modern trends in society such as industrialization and democracy, and their consequent withdrawal into radical right-wing politics as a way of protecting their threatened social and economic status. After 1918, this latter trend was intensified by their rejection of the Republic and its value system and their propensity for National Socialism. Ringer's use of sociological methods in his analysis adds an original dimension to the book.

SAUERBACH, Ferdinand.
Das war mein Leben. Munich: Kindler (1960).
The autobiography of a professional surgeon provides some interesting insights into the mood of German university students during the Weimar period.

SCHAIRER, Reinhold.
"Das erste Jahrzehnt des Deutschen Studentenwerkes (1921—1932)". In *Deutsches Studentenwerk 1921—1961.* Bonn: Röhrscheid (1961).
Outlines the functions and activities of this student body.

SCHWARZ, Jürgen.
Studenten in der Weimarer Republik: die deutsche Studentenschaft in der Zeit von 1918 bis 1923 und ihre Stellung zur Politik. Berlin: Duncker & Humblot (1971), 488 pp.
A detailed and objective analysis of the political attitudes of university students during the early Weimar period. Schwarz argues with considerable vigour that it is a myth to suggest that the vast majority of students were radical right-wingers and anti-republican before 1923. The older students were more patient with the new governmental system, while it was the younger ones who rejected the Republic and democracy from the beginning.

SCHWARZ, Jürgen.
"Arnold Bergsträsser und die Studentenschaft der frühen zwanziger Jahre". *Zeitschrift für Politik*, vol. 15 (1968), p. 300—11.
An examination of the nature and extent of Bergsträsser's influence on students.

SPITZNAGEL, Peter.
Studentenschaft und Nationalsozialismus in Würzburg 1927—1933. Dissertation, University of Würzburg (1974), 434 pp.
Convincingly discusses the reasons why an increasing number of Würzburg students (30% by 1930) were attracted to National Socialism.

STEINBERG, Michael S.
Sabres, Books and Brown Shirts: the Radicalization of the German Student 1918—1935. Dissertation, Johns Hopkins University (1971).
A massive thesis which looks at the radicalization of students' political attitudes through various student organizations, including the *Deutscher Hochschulring* and the Nazi Student League. The *Gleichschaltung* of these groups in 1933—35 is also examined in detail. The thesis as a whole, however, does not add much of importance to our knowledge.

STEPHENSON, Jill.
"Girls' Higher Education in Germany in the 1930s". *Journal of Contemporary History*, vol. 10, pt. 1 (1975), p. 41—69.
The first part of an interesting essay outlines the difficulties faced by women who wanted to enter university during the Weimar era. However, women made progress thanks to the liberal educational policies of the Republic, so that by 1932 they constituted almost one-fifth of the university student population. The NSDAP was one of the groups most hostile to higher education for women.

STITZ, Peter.
Der Cartell-Verband 1919—1938. Munich: Seitz & Höfling (1970), 419 pp.
A detailed chronicle of the organization's political development. A rather dull book.

WARLOSKI, Ronald.
Neudeutschland: German Catholic Students 1919—1939. The Hague: Nijhoff (1970), 220 pp.
A useful, informative analysis. Catholic students in the main were conservative and loyal to Catholic principles

both during the Weimar Republic and the Third Reich. Warloski ably discusses the organization and aims of the principal association representing Catholic students.

WARLOSKI, Ronald.
"Catholic Students and Revolutionary Germany: the Establishment of 'Neudeutschland' in 1918—1919". *Catholic Historical Review*, vol. 53 (1967—68), p. 600—20.
Argues that the main reason for the formation of the Catholic student organization was the negative Catholic reaction to the November Revolution. Initially, the leadership of *Neudeutschland* was divided over aims, but the conservative wing prevailed.

WIPPERMANN, Klaus W.
"Die Hochschulpolitik in der Weimarer Republik". *Politische Studien*, vol. 20 (1969), p. 143—57.
This review of university politics adds nothing original to the debate.

ZORN, Wolfgang.
"Die politische Entwicklung des deutschen Studententums 1924—1931". In *Festschrift für Ulrich Noack*. Göttingen: Vandenhoeck & Ruprecht (1961), p. 296—330.
Comprehensive and detailed essay, showing the progressive gravitation of students towards the Right.

ZORN, Wolfgang.
"Die politische Entwicklung des deutschen Studententums 1918—1931". In Kurt Stephenson and others (eds.). *Darstellungen und Quellen zur Geschichte der deutschen Einheitsbewegung im neunzehnten und zwanzigsten Jahrhundert, vol. 5.* Heidelberg: Quelle & Meyer (1965), p. 223—307.
Very much on the same lines as the previously mentioned article, with the developments of the early Weimar period added.

ZORN, Wolfgang.
"Student Politics in the Weimar Republic". *Journal of Contemporary History*, vol. 5, pt. 1 (1970), p. 128—43.
A résumé of his previous work, but the author's attempts at linking up the pre-1933 student movement with post-1945 students are not very convincing.

C. SCHOOLS

DEUERLEIN, Ernst (ed.).
Das Ringen um das sogenannte Reichsschulgesetz. Cologne: Bachem Verlag (1956), 190 pp.
A well edited collection of documents taken from the protocols of the parliamentary debates on the controversial issue of the Reich School Law, 1919—27.

DIERE, Horst.
Rechtssozialdemokratische Schulpolitik im Dienste des deutschen Imperialismus: der Geschichtsunterricht an den höheren Schulen Preussens zwischen 1918 und 1923 im Zeichen des Klassenverrats der rechten SPD-Führung. East Berlin: Volk und Wissen Verlag (1964), 222 pp.
The abrasive title of this book sums up the author's tendentious and politically motivated argument.

DÜWELL, Kurt.
"Probleme des deutschen Auslandschulwesens in der Weimarer Republik". *Geschichte in Wissenschaft und Unterricht*, vol. 26, pt. 3 (1975), p. 142—54.
An able discussion of a peripheral aspect of Weimar school education.

FAUTH, Reinhold.
Der Kampf um die Schule in der verfassunggebenden preussischen Landesversammlung (1919—1921). Dissertation, Humboldt University, East Berlin (1948).
The theme is important but this dissertation fails completely to do it justice. Fauth founds his study on an inadequate basis — mostly official reports of meetings of the Prussian *Landesversammlung*.

FÜHR, Christoph.
Zur Schulpolitik der Weimarer Republik: die Zusammenarbeit von Reich und Ländern im Reichsschulausschuss (1919—1923) und im Ausschuss für Unterrichtswesen (1924—1933); Darstellung und Quellen. Weinheim: Beltz Verlag (1970), 371 pp.
Concentrates on one specific aspect of educational policy in Weimar — the activities of national and state governments regarding the establishment of a nationwide educational system. Despite early optimism, educational reform became bogged down because of conflicting party interests and sheer apathy. Later episodes of dispute over school policy are not well treated in this otherwise methodical study.

GIESECKE, Hermann.
"Zur Schulpolitik der Sozialdemokraten in Preussen und im Reich 1918/19". *Vierteljahrshefte für Zeitgeschichte*, vol. 13, pt. 2 (1965), p. 164—77.
The debate on school reform was extremely important in 1918—19 and here the SPD attitude to the issue is analysed, in particular the policies of two SPD members, Konrad Haenisch and Adolf Hoffmann, in the Prussian Ministry of Education. The political controversy raised by their plans for radical school reform is detailed, including the resistance offered by the Centre Party. A compromise was eventually agreed.

GÜNTHER, Karl-Heinz (ed.).
Quellen zur Geschichte der Erziehung. East Berlin: Dietz (1959).
A documentary collection which includes some interesting pieces on the question of school reform in 1918—19.

GRUENTHAL, Günther.
See his work in section 6B (vi)

HAGENER, Dirk.
Radikale Schulreform zwischen Programmatik und Realität: die schulpolitischen Kämpfe in Bremen vor dem Ersten Weltkrieg und in der Entstehungsphase der Weimarer Republik. Bremen: Schünemann (1973), 255 pp.
An examination of the conflict over the place of the Churches and religion in the Bremen *Volksschule* before and after the war. This specific problem acted as a catalyst for the other problems besetting elementary education. The conflict developed into a situation where more and more teachers began to question the traditional assumptions of

schools and their role in society. Reform attempts were defeated before 1918, and again after the war. The book is at its best when dealing with the situation pre-1918; the Weimar section is disappointing and lacking in analysis.

HELMREICH, Ernst C.
Religious Education in German Schools: an Historical Approach. Cambridge (Mass.): Harvard University Press (1959), 365 pp.
Only a small proportion of this general survey refers to the Weimar period (Part 3: Chapter IX).

HENDERSON, James L.
Adolf Reichwein, eine politisch-pädagogische Biographie. Stuttgart: Deutsche Verlagsanstalt (1958), 223 pp.
A competent biography of one of Germany's most famous educationalists.

LOTT, Jürgen.
Religionsunterricht in der Berufsschule seit der Weimarer Republik. Dissertation, University of Mainz (1971).[1]

NITZSCHKE, Volker.
Die Auseinandersetzung um die Bekenntnisschule in der Weimarer Republik in Zusammenhang mit dem bayerischen Konkordat. Würzburg: Selbstverlag (1965), 275 pp.
A solid work of research and explanation of one of the thorniest school questions of the early Weimar era. The author shows how the issue of confessional schools, how they were financed and organized, became part of the wider centralist-federalist conflict as far as Bavaria was concerned.

PETERS, Elke.
Nationalistisch-völkische Bildungspolitik in der Weimarer Republik: Deutschkunde und höhere Schule in Preussen. Weinheim: Beltz-Verlag (1972), 224 pp.
An examination of the extent to which nationalist and racist ideas were disseminated in Prussian educational establishments. Some surprising evidence is presented here.

RADDE, Gerd.
Fritz Karsen: ein Berliner Schulreformer der Weimarer Zeit. Berlin: Colloquium Verlag (1973), 364 pp.
Radde has written a very sound, sympathetic biography of a distinguished man of ideas whose radical school reform projects, however, met with considerable opposition and hostility.

1. I was unable to obtain a copy in time for review.

ROEMHELD, Regine.
Demokratie ohne Chance: Möglichkeiten und Grenzen politischer Sozialisatoren am Beispiel der Pädagogen der Weimarer Republik. Ratingen: Henn Verlag (1974), 183 pp.
Laments on the few openings for a thoroughgoing reform of education in Weimar. The failure to achieve reform was, it is argued here, a serious handicap for democracy. The case, however, is not well presented.

SCHALLENBERGER, Horst.
Untersuchungen zum Geschichtsbild der Wilhelminischen Ära und der Weimarer Zeit. Ratingen: Henn Verlag (1964), 262 pp.
An interesting comparative analysis of how school history textbooks treated historical themes during the later Second Empire and the Weimar Republic.

URBACH, Dietrich.
Die Volkshochschule Gross-Berlin 1920—1933. Stuttgart: Klett (1971), 214 pp.
A dull, rather boring book.

D. ADULT EDUCATION

HENNINGSEN, Jürgen.
Die neue Richtung in der Weimarer Zeit: Dokumente und Texte. Stuttgart: Klett (1960), 174 pp.
A useful documentary compilation illustrative of experimental developments in adult education.

HENNINGSEN, Jürgen.
Der Hohenrodter Bund: zur Erwachsenenbildung in der Weimarer Zeit. Heidelberg: Quelle & Meyer (1958).[2]

HENNINGSEN, Jürgen.
Zur Theorie der Volksbildung: historisch-kritische Studien zur Weimarer Zeit. Cologne: Heymann (1959), 99 pp.
A brief, interpretative essay which has a few noteworthy things to say about popular education.

MEYER, Klaus.
Arbeiterbildung in der Volkshochschule: die "Leipziger Richtung"; ein Beitrag zur Geschichte der deutschen Volksbildung in den Jahren 1922—1933. Stuttgart: Klett (1969), 292 pp.
The author stresses that in Leipzig during the Weimar era adult education had a pronounced working class orientation. He ably describes its development.

2. I was unable to obtain a copy in time for review.

18

The Youth Movement and Organizations

A. GENERAL

EDELMANN, M. (ed.).
Die deutsche Jugendbewegung. Nuremberg:
Weidner (1960), 183 pp.
A bibliography of literature on the youth movement; a very useful reference source.

GREIFF, Walter; JENTSCH, Rudolf; RICHTER, Hans.
Gespräch und Aktion in Gruppe und Gesellschaft 1919—1969: Freundesgabe für Hans Dehmel.
Frankfurt: Dipa-Verlag (1970), 490 pp.
A collection of generally interesting articles on aspects of the German youth culture, presented to Hans Dehmel, a former leader in the pre-1933 youth group, *Silesien Jung-mannschaft.*

JANTZEN, Hinrich (ed.).
Namen und Werke: Biographien und Beiträge zur Soziologie der Jugendbewegung. Vol. 2, vol. 3.
Frankfurt: Dipa-Verlag (1974—75), 379, 350 pp.
Both tomes, part of a planned 10-volume series, provide a significant amount of detailed material on the membership of the youth movement and as such they constitute a most useful source of reference. However, the editor's criteria for selecting names is not made clear in his introduction, so there are notable omissions. Moreover the biographical information is by no means complete, particularly in relation to activities during the Third Reich era. Finally, some attempt at a collective interpretation of the careers examined would have enhanced both works.

KARL, Willibald.
See his article in section 17B.

KNEIP, Rudolf (ed.).
Jugend der Weimarer Zeit: Handbuch der Jugend-verbände 1919—1938. Frankfurt: Dipa-Verlag (1974), 383 pp.
A valuable reference book, arranged alphabetically. Kneip has included the names of hundreds of youth groups of the Weimar period, independent, political, confessional and so on, with brief accounts of their origins, aims, development, membership and leaders.

NASARSKI, Peter (ed.).
Deutsche Jugendbewegung in Europa: Versuch einer Bilanz. Cologne: Verlag Wissenschaft und Politik (1967), 415 pp.
A number of authors describe interesting examples of youth activity among German (*volksdeutsche*) communities in Europe during the twentieth century.

NÖLDECHEN, Waldemar.
Die deutsche Jugendbewegung: Versuch einer Wesensdeutung. Osnabrück (1953).
A brief and rather unsatisfactory general survey of the youth movement's development.

PAETEL, Karl O.
"Jugend von gestern und heute". *Neue Politische Literatur,* vol. 9 (1964).
Reflects briefly on the difference between the present and former generations of youth.

PAETEL, Karl O.
Das Bild von Menschen in der deutschen Jugend-führung. Bad Godesberg: Voggenreiter (1954), 59 pp.
A general but perceptive survey of youth groups and their members to 1945.

PAETEL, Karl O.
"Die deutsche Jugendbewegung als politisches Phänomen". *Politische Studien,* no. 86, vol. 8 (1957), p. 1—14.
Evaluates the political influence of the youth movement.

PAETEL, Karl O.
Jugendbewegung und Politik: Randbemerkungen.
Bad Godesberg: Voggenreiter (1961), 189 pp.
On the same theme as the previously cited article, only in more detail. The book makes interesting reading, and contains a substantial amount of useful information about the youth movement.

PAETEL, Karl O.
Jugend in der Entscheidung 1913, 1933, 1945. Bad
Godesberg: Voggenreiter (1963), 308 pp.
This is the enlarged second edition of his *Jugendbewegung
und Politik*, continuing the story in 1945.

PROSS, Harry E.
**Jugend, Eros, Politik: die Geschichte der deutschen
Jugendverbände.** Berne: Scherz (1964), 524 pp.
A very good comprehensive history of the youth movement in Germany, though better for its detailed information on youth groups and their leaders than analysis. The
author also usefully provides an appendix listing the major
groups he has discussed, a biography of youth leaders, and
a full bibliography.

RÖSSLER, Wilhelm.
**Jugend im Erziehungsfeld: Haltung und Verhalten
der deutschen Jugend in der ersten Hälfte des 20.
Jahrhunderts.** Düsseldorf: Diederichs (1957).
A wide-ranging discussion of the constitution and attitude
of youth to education over the last half century or so. The
youth movement of the Weimar era receives a mention.

SCHNEIDER, B.
Daten zur Geschichte der Jugendbewegung. Bad
Godesberg: Voggenreiter (1965).
A detailed chronology of the youth movement's history. A
good reference source.

SEIDELMANN, Karl.
**Bund und Gruppe als Lebensformen deutscher
Jugend.** Munich: Wiking-Verlag (1955), 382 pp.
A tortuous and dull description of the different organiz-
ational forms adopted by German youth and youth groups.

STREBIN, Friedrich.
Jugendbewegung und politische Erziehung. Dissert-
ation, University of Heidelberg (1958).
An unhelpful analysis of the youth movement's influence
on educational development. The topic is important, but
Strebin has not faced up to fundamental problems.

B. THE INDEPENDENT YOUTH MOVEMENT

AHLBORN, Knud.
**Kurze Chronik der Freideutschen Jugendbewegung
1913 bis 1953.** Bad Godesberg: Voggenreiter
(1953).
Very vague; there is little useful information or analysis in
this work.

BECKER, Howard.
German Youth: Bond or Free. London: Routledge
& Kegan Paul (1946), 286 pp.
As a general history, this book, though providing a reasonable amount of information, is too prone to factual error
and dubious interpretations. It must therefore be read with
considerable caution.

BORINSKI, Fritz; **MILCH**, Werner.
**Jugendbewegung: the Story of German Youth
1896—1933.** London: James Clarke (1945), 46 pp.
(Enlarged version, Frankfurt: Dipa-Verlag (1967),
139 pp.)
Serves only as an introductory survey of the youth movement. The book was designed in fact to aid educational
rehabilitation in Germany after 1945.

BRANDENBURG, Hans-Christian; **DAUR**, Rudolf.
**Die Brücke zu Köngen: 50 Jahre Bund der
Köngener 1919—1969.** Stuttgart: Steinkopf (1969),
235 pp.
A detailed chronicle of this right-wing group of the independent youth movement which, under leader Jacob Wilhelm Hauer, voluntarily joined the NSDAP in 1933.

BRANDENBURG, Hans-Christian.
"Zur Geschichte des Bundes der Köngener".
*Jahrbuch des Archivs der Deutschen Jugend-
bewegung*, vol. 4 (1972), p. 122—7.
A brief outline of the group's history, compressed from the
above-mentioned book.

COPALLE, Siegfried; **AHRENS**, Heinrich.
Chronik der Freien Deutschen Jugendbewegung.
Bad Godesberg: Voggenreiter (1954).
An unremarkable, semi-autobiographical history by two
former youth movement members. Their interpretations
are clearly influenced by their own past experiences.

CROON, Helmuth.
"Jugendbewegung und Arbeitsdienst". *Jahrbuch
des Archivs der Deutschen Jugendbewegung*, vol.
5 (1973), p. 66—84.
A discussion of how the idea of voluntary labour service
developed in the youth movement during the mid-1920s.
But the author does not sustain his case that labour service
in the youth movement was fundamentally different in
practice and concept from the later National Socialist
version.

DOMANDI, Mario.
The German Youth Movement. Dissertation,
Columbia University (1960).
Mostly concerned with an account of the *Wandervogel*, but
the latter sections of the thesis look at the effects of war
and revolution on German youth, and how this experience
shaped the latter's opinion of the Weimar Republic. The
survey is competent enough, though it does not open up
new perspectives on the character of the youth movement.

GEISSLER, Wilhelm.
Kunst und Künstler in der Jugendbewegung.
(Schriftenreihe des Archivs, I). Burg Ludwigstein: Archiv der Deutschen Jugendbewegung
(1975), 64 pp.
Some of the most important names and dates in the cultural life of the youth movement are briefly discussed. There
is a considerable number of interesting illustrations.

HELD, Joseph.
**Embattled Youth: the Independent German Youth
Movements in the 20th Century.** Dissertation,
Rutgers State University (1968).
An examination of the character of the *Wandervogel* and
the Free German Youth (1913—24) movements, as well
as *Bündische* Youth (1923—33). The author stresses the
absence of a consistent ideology in the independent youth
movement, a point that has been made by many previous
writers. His conclusion that the youth movement must not
be regarded as a forerunner of National Socialism is also
unoriginal.

HÖCKNER, Hilmar.
Die Musik in der deutschen Jugendbewegung.
Wolfenbüttel (1957).
The youth movement produced a rich musical literature,
much of which was later taken over by the *Hitlerjugend*.
Höckner writes informatively about this theme.

JANTZEN, Walter.
"Die soziologische Herkunft der Führerschicht in der deutschen Jugendbewegung: 1900 bis 1933".
In *Führungsschicht und Eliteproblem: Konferenz der Ranke-Gesellschaft* .Frankfurt (1957), p. 127—37.
Concludes that the leadership of the youth movement was overwhelmingly middle class in origin.

JOVY, E. Michael.
Jugendbewegung und Nationalsozialismus: Versuch einer Klärung ihrer Zusammenhänge und Gegensätze. Dissertation, University of Cologne (1952).
A very solid and informative analysis of the similarities, differences, and connections between the youth movement and National Socialism. The author clearly shows that behind apparent similarities in organization and ideology, there were fundamental differences.

KINDT, Werner (ed.).
Grundschriften der deutschen Jugendbewegung. Düsseldorf: Diederichs (1963), 596 pp.
An excellent documentary collection of carefully chosen extracts from the programmatic statements, memoranda and so on of the youth organizations. The character, ethos and objectives of the groups are fully illustrated.

KINDT, Werner (ed.).
Die deutsche Jugendbewegung, 1920 bis 1933: die Bündische Zeit. Quellenschriften. Düsseldorf: Diederichs (1974), 1840 pp.
This massive collection of documents must rank as the most complete record available on the *Bundische* phase of the youth movement. The editor has searched extensively for the material gathered here, and the volume is without doubt indispensable.

KNEIP, Rudolf.
Wandervogel — Bündische Jugend, 1909—1943: der Weg der sächsischen Jugendschaft zum grossen Bund. Frankfurt: Dipa-Verlag (1967), 264 pp.
A detailed and reliable account.

KNEIP, Rudolf and others.
Jugend zwischen den Kriegen: eine Sammlung von Aussagen und Dokumenten über den Sachsenkreis im Freideutschen Konvent. Heidenheim: Südmarkverlag Fritsch (1967).
A documentary collection which usefully complements his aforementioned book.

KORN, Elizabeth; SUPPERT, Otto; VOGT, Karl (eds.).
Die Jugendbewegung: Welt und Wirkung. Zur 50. Wiederkehr der Freideutschen Jugendtages auf den Hohen Meissner. Düsseldorf: Diederichs (1963), 254 pp.
An extremely useful and well edited collection of extracts from documents, pamphlets, songs, etc. from the youth movement, illustrating its rich culture.

LAQUEUR, Walter Z.
Young Germany: a History of the German Youth Movement. London: Routledge & Kegan Paul (1962), 253 pp.
A concise chronicle of the youth movement from the late nineteenth century to beyond 1945, though the emphasis is very much on the development and character of the independent youth movement to 1933. As such, this is the best account available in English; it is succinct, informative, reliable, and fluently written. The major weakness of the book lies in the cursory treatment of the *Hitlerjugend*, which is regrettable since the author demonstrates that the youth movement and the *Hitlerjugend* had certain characteristics in common.

LAQUEUR, Walter Z.
"The German Youth Movement and the 'Jewish Question': a Preliminary Survey". *Yearbook of the Leo Baeck Institute*, vol. 6 (1961), p 193—205.
An interesting discussion of the place of Jews in the youth movement and the attitude of the *Wandervogel* and post-1918 groups to their Jewish members.

LINSE, Ulrich.
Die Kommune der deutschen Jugendbewegung: ein Versuch der Überwindung des Klassenkampfes aus dem Geiste der bürgerlichen Utopie. Munich: Becksche Verlag (1973), 185 pp.
Chronicles an unprecedented experiment to establish a model of social harmony at Blankenburg (Donauwörth) in 1919—20. The endeavour unhappily failed, for much the same reason that the independent youth movement in general was unable to solve major problems besetting it during the Weimar era: clash of personalities, lack of realism, etc.

MAU, Hermann.
Die deutsche Jugendbewegung von 1901—1933: Rückblick und Ausblick. Munich (1949).
A short, rather too general survey which only mentions the major events of the youth movement's development.

MEHRMANN, W.
Der Antisemitismus in der bürgerlichen Jugendbewegung und an den Universitäten. East Berlin (1972).
Superficial and polemical for the most part.

MÜLLER, Jacob.
"Der Jungdeutsche Bund 1921—1924". *Jahrbuch des Archivs der Deutschen Jugendbewegung*, vol. 2 (1970), p. 33—43.
An analysis of the role of Frank Glatzel in the group. He more than anyone else shaped its ideas, and also helped to make it pro-DNVP.

MÜLLER, Jacob.
Die Jugendbewegung als deutsche Hauptrichtung neukonservativer Reform. Frankfurt: Europa-Verlag (1971), 411 pp.
An outstanding, scholarly monograph, which concentrates in particular on the 1914—24 period when the independent German youth movement went through a major crisis. Müller opens up many new perspectives and ideas on the development and function of the youth movement, revealing that many previous theories have been too simplistic.

PLUTA, Hans.
"Muck Lamberty und die 'Neue Schar' im Jahre 1920 in Thüringen: Erinnerungen eines Teilnehmers". *Jahrbuch des Archivs der Deutschen Jugendbewegung*, vol. 2 (1970), p. 103—7.
A former associate reflects on an extraordinary character who is hailed by East German historians as a courageous anti-fascist. Lamberty's exploits have been recounted in several histories of the youth movement (see, for example, H. Pross, *Jugend, Eros, Politik*, cited in section 18A).

PROSS, Harry E.
Nationale und soziale Prinzipien in der Bündischen Jugend. Dissertation, University of Heidelberg (1949).
A useful but limited study.

RAABE, Felix.
Die Bündische Jugend: ein Beitrag zur Geschichte der Weimarer Republik. Stuttgart: Brentanoverlag (1961), 256 pp.
Probably the most authoritative contribution to the history of *Bündische* Youth. Raabe has gathered material from a wide variety of sources and is particularly good when analysing the movement's political outlook and its links with National Socialism.

RAABE, Felix.
"Bündische Jugend in der Weimarer Republik". *Politische Studien*, no. 141, vol. 12 (1962), p. 34—42.
A summary of the conclusions reached in the author's book.

ROSENBUSCH, Heinz.
Die deutsche Jugendbewegung in ihren pädagogischen Formen und Wirkungen. Frankfurt: Dipa-Verlag (1973), 202 pp.
In this analysis of the important contribution made by the youth movement to education and educational theories, Rosenbusch has a lot more to offer in terms of information, but especially in terms of analysis and interpretation, than previous writers on the topic.

RUEGG, Walter (ed.).
Kulturkritik und Jugendkult. Frankfurt: Klostermann (1974), 157 pp.
Various authors discuss, somewhat oversympathetically, the cultural pretensions of the youth movement.

SCHMIDT, Ulrike.
Die Jugendbewegung und ihre Nachwirkungen in die Hitler-Jugend. Dissertation, Hochschule Bielefeld (1960).
The interaction between the youth movement and the Hitler Youth in respect of organizational forms and ideology is a subject which requires more research and consideration than is presented in this weak contribution.

SCHMIDT, Ulrike.
"Über das Verhältnis von Jugendbewegung und Hitlerjugend". *Geschichte in Wissenschaft und Unterricht*, vol. 16, pt. 1 (1965), p. 19—37.
Presents the incomplete conclusions of her above-cited dissertation.

SCHULZ, Ursula (ed.).
Adolf Reichwein: ein Lebensbild aus Briefen und Dokumenten. Munich: Gottfried Müller-Verlag (1974), 371 pp.
Moderately revelatory of the influential free youth movement (*Wandervogel*) leader and, later, opposition figure in the Third Reich.

SEIDELMANN, Karl.
Die deutsche Jugendbewegung. (Pädagogische Quellentexte). Bad Heilbrunn: Klinkhardt Verlag (1966), 165 pp.
A reference work.

SEIDELMANN, Karl.
"Die Pfadfinder in der deutschen Jugendbewegung der zwanziger Jahre". *Jahrbuch des Archivs der Deutschen Jugendbewegung*, vol. 6 (1974), p. 107—26.
A sound analysis of the strengths and failings of the numerically small boy scout movement.

SIEFERT, Hermann.
Der Bündische Aufbruch 1919—1923. Bad Godesberg: Voggenreiter (1963), 199 pp.
Siefert ably traces the disintegration of the traditional forms of the independent youth movement after the First World War, and the emergence of the *Bündische* Youth as the authentic heir of the *Wandervogel* ethos.

ZIEMER, Gerhard.
"Die Übergangszeit zwischen Wandervogel und Bündische Jugend". *Jahrbuch des Archivs der Deutschen Jugendbewegung*, vol. 4 (1972), p. 54—62.
A subjective and unsatisfactory note on the major developments in the youth movement 1919—23.

ZIEMER, Gerhard.
"Die deutsche Jugendbewegung und der Staat". *Jahrbuch des Archivs der Deutschen Jugendbewegung*, vol. 5 (1973), p. 42—51.
Emphasizes the cultural and educational function of the youth movement in Weimar.

ZIEMER, Gerhard; WOLF, Hans.
Wandervogel und Freideutsche Jugend. Bad Godesberg: Voggenreiter (1961).
The latter stages of this general and unoriginal account focus on the early years of the Weimar Republic and the impact of the lost war on the *Freideutsche Jugend*.

C. POLITICAL

(i) Left-Wing[1]

LINK, Werner.
Die Geschichte des Internationalen Jugend-Bundes (IJG) und des Internationalen Sozialistischen Kampf-Bundes (ISK). Meisenheim: Hain (1964), 381 pp.
Although this is the first full history of both these organizations, the author's obvious Marxist bias robs the study of any critical, objective quality. Within his narrow ideological terms of reference, he is mainly concerned with discussing the views of Leonard Nelson, who provided the groups with their ideological orientation.

(ii) Right-Wing

KATER, Michael H.
"Die Artamanen - Völkische Jugend in der Weimarer Republik". *Historische Zeitschrift*, no. 213 (1971), p. 577—638.
Kater has presented a good deal of new archival material in this thorough and important essay. The *Artamanen* group was established in the early 1920s with the immediate aim of replacing Polish with German labour on East German estates, but the group's ideology and ambitions were on a grander scale and corresponded closely to National

1. Cross refer to section 6B (vii)(h) for Communist Youth.

Socialism and later SS ideology. Indeed, several leaders of the NSDAP, including Himmler and Darré, were one-time *Artamanen* members. Kater discusses at length the group's organization, leadership and ethos in admirable fashion.

SCHLICKER, Wolfgang.
See his work in section 13A (iii)(a).

D. CONFESSIONAL

(i) Catholic

HASTENTEUFEL, Paul.
Jugendbewegung und Jugendseelsorge: Geschichte und Probleme der katholischen Jugendarbeit im 20. Jahrhundert. Munich: Kösel (1962), 116 pp.
Discusses the problem of combining conventional youth work with pastoral care, as faced by Catholic youth organizations. The historical background into which the author tries to place his theme is, however, very superficially treated.

MESSERSCHMID, Felix.
"Bilanz einer Jugendbewegung: Quickborn und Rothenfels von den Anfängen bis 1939".
Frankfurter Hefte, vol. 24 (1969), p. 786—97.
A general description of *Quickborn*, a Catholic youth group led from 1924 by Romano Guardini and numbering some 6,000 youths in 1929.

(ii) Protestant

BLUM, Emil.
Die Neuwerk-Bewegung 1922—1933: Kirche zwischen Planen und Hoffen. Kassel: Johannes Stauda-Verlag (1973), 48 pp.
The *Neuwerk* movement was in many ways an experimental type of youth organization founded in 1919 as a religious-social renewal movement. It was organized according to occupational categories and was led from 1923 by Hermann Schafft. This pamphlet adequately describes the group's development.

KUPISCH, Karl.
Der deutsche CVJM: aus der Geschichte der Christlichen Vereine Jünger Männer Deutschlands.
Kassel: Pflugschar-Verlag (1958), 143 pp.
The CVJM was established in 1883 and grew into one of the largest and most influential Protestant groups. This study provides an adequate summary of the principal milestones in its history.

PRIEPKE, Manfred.
Die evangelische Jugend im Dritten Reich 1933—1936. Hanover: Norddeutsche Verlagsanstalt (1960), 244pp.
This scholarly monograph shows that before 1933 large sections of the Protestant youth movement were susceptible to National Socialist ideas. In 1933, therefore, many Protestant youths enthusiastically acclaimed the advent to power of Adolf Hitler.

SMIDT, Udo (ed.).
Dokumente evangelischer Jugendbünde: Wandlungen zwischen zwei Weltkriegen. Stuttgart: Evangelisches Verlagswerk (1975), 223 pp.
This collection of documents, for which the editor has written a rather perfunctory introduction, is simply a separate publication of those items relating to the Protestant youth movement contained in Werner Kindt's volume *Die deutsche Jugendbewegung, 1920 bis 1933.* (See section 18B).

VOLLMER, Antje.
Die Neuwerkbewegung 1919—1935: ein Beitrag zur Geschichte der Jugendbewegung, des religiösen Sozialismus und der Arbeiterbildung. Augsburg (1973).[1]

E. JEWISH[2]

MERLIN, Rafael W.
Wandervogel und Blau-Weiss: über die jüdische Jugendbewegung im Vor-Hitler-Deutschland. Manuscript, Hessischer Rundfunk, Frankfurt (30 July 1968).[3]

RINOTT, Chanoch.
"Major Trends in Jewish Youth Movements in Germany". *Yearbook of the Leo Baeck Institute*, vol. 19 (1974), p. 77—96.
A detailed description of the variegated Jewish youth movement in Germany from the foundation of the *Blau-Weiss Wanderbund* in 1912 to the prohibition of the groups in 1933. The author reveals that despite historical, ideological, and typological differences, there were certain fundamental common traits and patterns in the development of the Jewish youth movement. The influence on it of the German youth movement is stressed.

ROSENSTOCK, Werner.
"The Jewish Youth Movement". *Yearbook of the Leo Baeck Institute*, vol. 19 (1974), p. 97—106.
The author describes his experience as a member of a German-Jewish youth group, the *Deutsch-Jüdische Jugend-Gemeinschaft* (DJJG), small but influential, and led by Ludwig Tietz. The history and character of the group is outlined, the author arguing that it was typical of other Jewish *Bunde*.

STRAUSS, Herbert.
"The Jugendverband: a Social and Intellectual History". *Yearbook of the Leo Baeck Institute*, vol. 6 (1961), p. 206—235.
An outline history of the *Verband der Jüdischen Jugendvereine Deutschlands*, the first organized Jewish youth group in Germany, which in 1930 had about 12,000 members. Its official policy was to maintain political neutrality.

F. SPORTS

DIECKERT, Jürgen.
Edmund Neuendorff und die Turnerjugendbewegung: ein Beitrag zur Erziehungsgeschichte der ausserschulischen Jugenderziehung während der Weimarer Republik. Dissertation, University of Saarbrücken (1968).
Neuendorff was a well established figure in youth movement circles even before 1914. From 1912 to 1919 he was leader of a *Wandervogel* group, and was involved after 1919 in many others of the independent type. But he made his mark in Weimar as leader of the German sports youth movement. Dieckert outlines his contribution, but more than two-thirds of the dissertation is composed of a documentary appendix.

1. I was unable to obtain a copy for review.
2. See also section 11.
3. I was unable to obtain a copy for review.

Foreign Policy

19

A. THE WESTERN POWERS

(i) General

BRETTON, Henry L.
Stresemann and the Revision of Versailles: a Fight for Reason. Stanford: Stanford University Press (1953), 199 pp.
A well argued study, mainly useful for its clear exposition of Stresemann's foreign policy techniques. However, the author did not have access to important primary sources, including the Stresemann papers and the records of the German Foreign Ministry, so in consequence the book's value is strictly limited.

BREUNING, Eleonore C.M.
German Foreign Policy between East and West 1921—6. Dissertation, University of Oxford (1966).
An unremarkable survey.

CAMPBELL, F. Gregory.
"Goals and Methods of German Diplomacy". *Review of Politics*, vol. 35, pt. 2 (1973), p. 272—3.
Unimportant.

CONZE, Werner.
"Deutschlands weltpolitische Sonderstellung in den zwanziger Jahren". *Vierteljahrshefte für Zeitgeschichte*, vol. 9, pt. 2 (1961), p. 166—77.
A thoughtful interpretative essay (without footnotes) on the renewed importance of the German question after 1918.

CORMIER, Thomas.
German Foreign Policy, 1923—1926: the Illusion of Western versus Eastern Orientation. Dissertation, The American University, Washington, D.C. (1968).
Aims to show how Germany was able to achieve by dint of skilful diplomacy a remarkable recovery from the debacle of 1923 to become once again a leading European power by 1926. Between these dates, German policy abandoned its former pro-Eastern orientation for a more flexible approach. Generally competent work, but the author undoubtedly overstates his case on occasion.

CRAIG, Gordon A.
From Bismarck to Adenauer: Aspects of German Statecraft. Baltimore: Johns Hopkins Press (1958), 156 pp.
Consists of five essays, originally delivered as the Albert Shaw Lectures at Johns Hopkins University, and amounts to a sound interpretation of German statecraft in the modern era. Stresemann and Brüning are the major Weimar statesmen considered; Craig admires the former's courage, but disapproves of the latter's lack of proportion.

CRAIG, Gordon A; **GILBERT**, Felix (eds.).
The Diplomats, 1919—1939. Princeton: Princeton University Press (1953), 720 pp.
A collection of essays by seventeen established scholars on aspects of European diplomatic affairs. The quality is unevenly distributed and the book is discursive; there is also little original material presented. For the purposes of our study, the essay to note is by Hajo Holborn (see later in this section under Holborn).

DEHIO, Ludwig.
Deutschland und die Weltpolitik im 20. Jahrhundert. Munich: Oldenbourg (1955), 155 pp.
This volume consists of six previously published papers which examine Germany's role in twentieth century world history. As such, Dehio's arguments are clear, objective and relevant, and his book forms an extremely able introduction to modern German diplomatic development.

DIRKSEN, Herbert von.
Moskau, Tokyo, London: Erinnerungen und Betrachtungen zu 20 Jahren deutscher Aussenpolitik 1919—1939. Stuttgart: Deutsche Verlags-Union (1949).
A disappointing memoir which offers few insights into the motives of German foreign policy.

DOCKHORN, Robert B.
The Wilhelmstrasse and the Search for a New Diplomatic Order. Dissertation, University of Wisconsin (1972).
Explores the aims of German foreign policy after Locarno, emphasizing German attitudes towards revisionism and reconciliation — in essence Germany's implementation after 1926 of a "new diplomacy". The study is too chronological and does not provide nearly enough analysis.

EULER, Heinrich.
Die Aussenpolitik der Weimarer Republik 1919—1923: vom Waffenstillstand bis zum Ruhrkonflikt. Aschaffenburg: Pattloch-Verlag (1957), 471 pp.
A somewhat shapeless study which concentrates on giving a straightforward narrative of domestic and international political events 1919—23. There is precious little by way of analysis or interpretation and even his factual information contains nothing new. The book is therefore of no consequence.

EWALD, Josef.
Die deutsche Aussenpolitik und der Europaplan Briands. Dissertation, University of Marburg (1961).
Helps to a limited degree in clarifying some of the western aspects of German foreign policy.

FRANZIUS, Enno.
German Foreign Policy, 1923—1926: Stresemann and Press Opinion. Dissertation, Columbia University (1954).
Based on few sources, this study is extremely tentative.

GÄRTNER, Margarete.
Botschafterin des guten Willens: aussenpolitische Arbeit, 1914—1950. Bonn: Athenäum Verlag (1955), 622 pp.
Disappointing memoirs, over-long and boring.

GATZKE, Hans W. (ed.).
European Diplomacy Between Two Worlds 1919—1939. Chicago: Quadrangle Books (1972), 277 pp.
A collection of previously published articles or extracts from books relating to international diplomacy. All relevant papers are cited elsewhere in this bibliography: see under A.J. Mayer; H.W. Gatzke; A. Thimme; and F.G. Stambrook.

GRATHWOL, Robert.
"Gustav Stresemann: Reflections on his Foreign Policy". *Journal of Modern History*, vol. 45, pt. 1 (1973), p. 52—70.
An attempted revisionist interpretation of Stresemann's aims and policies in foreign policy during the mid-1920s which is interesting and vigorously presented; however, the paper is too sympathetic towards Stresemann and is not entirely convincing. A main theme of the essay is a reassessment of the charges of duplicity levelled against Stresemann, which Grathwol finds insupportable.

HEINEMAN, John L.
Constantin Freiherr von Neurath as Foreign Minister, 1932—1935: a Study of a Conservative Civil Servant and Germany's Foreign Policy. Dissertation, Cornell University (1965).
Partly an examination of a wide spectrum of German conservatism and partly a biography of a representative conservative figure. Concludes that both the conservative establishment and Neurath lacked vision and a political programme, which is not new. The book is useful insofar as it furnishes a character sketch of Neurath; otherwise, it is mundane.

HILLGRUBER, Andreas.
Kontinuität und Diskontinuität in der deutschen Aussenpolitik von Bismarck bis Hitler. Düsseldorf: Droste (1969), 28 pp.
A valuable interpretative essay on a current major debate in modern German history. Hillgruber's views are well considered and scholarly.

HOLBORN, Hajo.
"Diplomats and Diplomacy in the Early Weimar Republic". In G.A. Craig & F. Gilbert (eds.). *The Diplomats 1919—1939.* Princeton: Princeton University Press (1953), p. 123—71.
Discusses German efforts to convince the Allies that Germany's political system changed fundamentally in 1918—19. The Allies remained unhelpfully sceptical in the main.

KLÖSS, Erhard.
Von Versailles zum Zweiten Weltkrieg: Verträge zur Zeitgeschichte 1918—1939. Munich: Deutscher Taschenbuch Verlag (1965), 277 pp.
A general discussion of international treaties and their significance.

KNAUSS, Bernhard.
"Politik ohne Waffen; dargestellt an der Politik Stresemanns". *Zeitschrift für Politik*, vol. 10 (1963), p. 249—56.
A few notes on the problems of conducting foreign affairs from a position of fundamental weakness — as Stresemann did.

KOCHAN, Lionel.
"Stresemann and the Historians". *Wiener Library Bulletin*, vol. 7 (Sept.-Dec. 1953).
Argues that Stresemann's position in foreign policy was fundamentally the same as that adopted by Hitler; only the methods differed.

KORDT, Erich.
Nicht aus den Akten: die Wilhelmstrasse in Frieden und Krieg; Erlebnisse, Begegnungen und Eindrücke 1928—1945. Stuttgart: Union Deutsche Verlagsgesellschaft (1950).
Better for its observations on the Hitler era and the diplomatic methods of the Third Reich. Kordt has nothing of importance to say on Weimar diplomacy.

KRÜGER, Peter.
"Friedenssicherung und deutsche Revisionspolitik; die deutsche Aussenpolitik und die Verhandlungen über den Kellogg-Pakt". *Vierteljahrshefte für Zeitgeschichte*, vol. 22, pt. 3 (1974), p. 227—57.
Argues that as far as German foreign policy in the 1920s was concerned, there was no fundamental contradiction between the aim of revising the Versailles Treaty and contributing to general quests for peace in Europe, which culminated in the signing of the Kellogg Pact in August 1928. In this article, a solid contribution to German foreign policy in Weimar, Krüger examines in detail German motives, and the negotiations leading to the Pact.

LIPGENS, Walter.
"Europäische Einigungsidee 1923—1930 und Briands Europaplan im Urteil der deutschen Akten". *Historische Zeitschrift*, no. 203 (1966), p. 46—89, 316—63.
Lipgens argues a powerful case for attaching more importance to Briand's plans for European union than is customary, and takes Brüning to task for his negative attitude to them.

MALANOWSKI, Wolfgang.
Der Widerspruch von Tradition und Doktrin in der deutschen Aussenpolitik. Dissertation, University of Hamburg (1956).
A competent review of foreign policy trends and the dilemmas confronting German statesmen, mainly from 1924 to 1933.

PUTLITZ, Wolfgang G. E. von.
Unterwegs nach Deutschland: Erinnerungen eines ehemaligen Diplomaten. Berlin: Verlag der Nation (1956), 378 pp.
Memoirs of a former member of the German diplomatic corps covering 1918—52. Putlitz is scathingly critical of just about everyone and everything, but he has little of note to say about the Weimar era.

RHEINBABEN, Werner von.
Viermal Deutschland: aus dem Erleben eines Seemannes, Diplomaten, Politikers 1895—1954. Berlin: Argon Verlag (1954), 454 pp.
Informative to an extent on aspects of Stresemann's conduct of foreign affairs.

RIESSER, Hans A.
Von Versailles zu UNO: aus den Erinnerungen eines Diplomaten. Bonn: Bouvier (1962), 284 pp.
Part of this diplomat's memoirs (p. 35—179) deal with the Weimar era, but little of substance is said.

ROSEN, Friedrich.
Aus einem diplomatischen Wanderleben. 4 vols. Wiesbaden: Limes (1959), 441 pp.
Volume IV deals uninterestingly with the Weimar era.

ROTHFELS, Hans, and others (eds.).
Akten zur deutschen auswärtigen Politik 1918—1945, Series B: 1925—1933. (Vol. II, 1: Dezember 1925—Juni 1926. Vol. II, 2: Juni bis Dezember 1926. Vol. III: Dezember 1925 bis Dezember 1926. Vol. IV, 1: 1. Januar 1927—16. März 1927. Vol. IV, 2: 1. Juli bis 30. September 1927. Vol. V: 1. Oktober bis 31. Dezember 1927.) Göttingen: Vandenhoeck & Ruprecht (1967—74), 543, 555, 560, 583, 567, 659 pp.
An excellently edited documentary reference work of prime importance.

RUGE, Wolfgang.
"Die Aussenpolitik der Weimarer Republik und das Problem der europäischen Sicherheit 1925—1932". *Zeitschrift für Geschichtswissenschaft*, vol. 22, pt. 3 (1974), p. 273—90.
A typically vitriolic and unhistorical article from Ruge who is more of a Marxist-Leninist propagandist than a scholar.

RUGE, Wolfgang; SCHUMANN, Wolfgang.
"Die Reaktion des deutschen Imperialismus auf Briands Paneuropaplan 1930". *Zeitschrift für Geschichtswissenschaft*, vol. 20, pt. 1 (1972), p. 40—70.
A scathing attack on the forces of militarism and imperialism in Germany for cold-shouldering Briand's plans for union. The essay's tone is, as usual, intemperate.

SCHIEDER, Theodor.
"Das Dokumentarwerk zur deutschen auswärtigen Politik 1918—1945". *Historische Zeitschrift*, no. 218 (1974), p. 85—95.
Reviews the latest volumes in the outstanding series of German Foreign Ministry documents (see under Hans Rothfels above).

SCHMACKE, Ernst.
Die Aussenpolitik der Weimarer Republik, 1922—1925. Dissertation, University of Hamburg (1951).
Now almost entirely out of date.

SCHMIDT, Paul.
Statist auf diplomatischer Bühne 1923—1945: Erlebnisse des Chef-dolmetschers im Auswärtigen Amt mit den Staatsmännern Europas. Bonn: Athenäum (1949), 604 pp.
The former chief interpreter in the German Foreign Ministry has written an interesting and in some parts revealing memoir. He makes shrewd comments about the work of Stresemann and Hitler in particular and he is well informed and readable on other matters.

SEABURY, Paul.
The Wilhelmstrasse: a Study of German Diplomats under the Nazi Regime. Berkeley: University of California Press (1954), 330 pp.
A rather disappointing study; it is not a full history of German diplomats between 1933 and 1945 and it contains very little specialized material. Seabury does not have a great deal to say about the pre-1933 period, except a few comments on the work and methods of the Ministry of Foreign Affairs.

USCHAKOW, Vladimir B.
Deutschlands Aussenpolitik 1917—1945. East Berlin: Deutscher Verlag der Wissenschaften (1964), 471 pp.
This is the German translation of an original Russian work and is obviously designed for East German consumption. Many of the interpretations are hopelessly distorted and evidence which does not fit easily into the Marxist-Leninist terms of reference has been conveniently ignored. In other words, a good example of how not to write history.

VIETSCH, Eberhard von.
Arnold Reisberg und das Problem der politischen West-Orientierung Deutschlands nach dem Ersten Weltkrieg. Koblenz: Bundesarchiv (1958), 270 pp.
An interesting study.

WEIDENFELD, Werner.
"Gustav Stresemann — der Mythos vom engagierten Europäer". *Geschichte in Wissenschaft und Unterricht*, vol. 24, pt. 12 (1973), p. 740—50.
Draws attention to Stresemann's essentially nationalist motivation in conducting foreign affairs.

WEINBERG, Gerhard L.
"The Defeat of Germany in 1918 and the European Balance of Power". *Central European History*, vol. 2, pt. 3 (1969), p. 248—60.
A reassessment of the long-term implications of Germany's defeat in the First World War. Weinberg concludes that unlike Austria, certain factors worked to consolidate and even strengthen Germany's position as a great power in Europe. A refreshing interpretative essay, but one which appears too fond of facile generalization.

WIRTH, Joseph.
"Die deutsche Neutralitätspolitik der Jahre 1922—1932". *Blätter für Deutsch- und Internationale Politik*, vol. 5 (1960), p. 1013—20.
The former Reich Chancellor discusses the general principles of Weimar foreign policy as he understands them.

WOLLSTEIN, G.
Vom Weimarer Revisionismus zu Hitler: das deutsche Reich und die europäische Grossmächte in der Anfangsphase der nationalsozialistischen Herrschaft. Bonn: Athenäum (1974).
A solid contribution which effectively examines the direction of Weimar foreign policy before concentrating on the post-1933 period.

ZIMMERMANN, Ludwig.
Deutsche Aussenpolitik in der Ära der Weimarer Republik. Göttingen: Musterschmidt (1958), 486 pp.
When published, this was the only book to offer a comprehensive survey of Weimar foreign policy. But its use of archival material was largely restricted to the Stresemann papers, and has been subsequently superseded by a number of specialist works. Thus, the study serves now as no more than a general introduction to foreign policy developments 1918—33. Even so, Zimmermann's main conclusions have to be treated with circumspection because they lack supporting evidence (e.g., the assertion that military weakness was the principal reason for the failures of Weimar foreign policy).

ZIMMERMANN, Ludwig.
Deutschland und die grossen Mächte 1918—1932. Stuttgart: Klett (1964), 65 pp.
A general review of Germany's external relations.

ZWOCH, Gerhard.
Die Erfüllungs- und Verständigungspolitik der Weimarer Republik und die deutsche öffentliche Meinung. Dissertation, University of Kiel (1950).
Out of date.

(ii) Anglo-German Relations

BERTRAM-LIBAL, Gisela.
Aspekte der britischen Deutschlandspolitik 1919—1922. Dissertation, University of Tübingen (1970).
An outstanding analysis and discussion of the motives of British policy.

BERTRAM-LIBAL, Gisela.
See also her article in section 19D(iii).

BOADLE, Donald G.
Winston Churchill and the German Question in British Foreign Policy, 1918—1922. The Hague: Martinus Nijhoff (1974), 193 pp.
A penetrating and worthwhile monograph which convincingly analyses Churchill's aims in foreign policy and his methods of prosecuting them. However, Lloyd George always thwarted him.

CHAPPIUS, Charles W.
Anglo-German Relations 1929—1933: a Study of the Role of Great Britain in the Achievement of the Aims of German Foreign Policy. Dissertation, University of Notre Dame (1966).
A narrative of the main events in Anglo-German relations 1929—33, the Austro-German Customs Union, reparations, and armaments. There is little analysis or interpretation of the motives of either country in their approach to these problems.

D'ABERNON, Viscountess.
Red Cross and Berlin Embassy 1915—1926. London: John Murray (1946), 152 pp.
Contains extracts from the diary of the wife of the British Ambassador to Berlin (1920—26). Interesting to note are her impressions of Berlin and its diplomatic crowd, as well as leading German personalities such as Stresemann and Ebert.

DONALDSON, Robert C.
British Policy toward Germany, 1932—1933. Dissertation, University of Michigan (1954).
An incomplete and ill informed study.

GAJDA, Patricia A.
See her work in section 19D(ii).

GILBERT, Martin.
The Roots of Appeasement. London: Weidenfeld & Nicolson (1966).
In his attempt to rehabilitate to a degree the concept of appeasement, the author usefully discusses its origins and development before 1933, and the people who supported it. The term usually meant removing Germany's grievances over Versailles.

GILBERT, Martin.
Britain and Germany between the Wars. London: Longmans (1964), 179 pp.
Various aspects of Anglo-German relations are touched upon here; the volume consists of short extracts from a wide range of documentary sources which illustrate the main development of British policy and opinion towards Germany and the major issues affecting relations between both countries. Designed for the undergraduate, the book serves a useful purpose in seminar teaching.

JORDAN, W. M.
Great Britain, France and the German Problem 1918—1939. London: Frank Cass (1971).
Reprinted from the 1943 edition, this book offers a general survey of the tripartite relationship. But it is hopelessly out of date and it is difficult to see why the publishers decided to reissue the work.

KADZIK, Konrad.
England und Deutschland 1930—1932. Dissertation, Free University of Berlin (1959).
A competent review of the attitudes adopted by Britain towards disarmament and reparations during the Brüning era.

LOUIS, William R.
Das Ende des deutschen Kolonialreiches: britischer Imperialismus und die deutschen Kolonien 1914—1919. Stuttgart: Bertelsmann (1973), 120 pp. (English ed.: **Great Britain and Germany's Lost Colonies, 1914—1919.** New York: Oxford University Press (1967).)
A brief but very good analysis of the diplomatic history relating to the end of Germany's colonial empire at the conclusion of the First World War.

MOSS, Ronald J.
Gustav Stresemann and the Development of Anglo-German Relations: Perceptions, Illusions, and Realities 1921—1924. Dissertation, Rutgers University (1975).
Examines the achievement of Stresemann in recreating a trusting working relationship with Britain in international affairs. Moss analyses his motives in seeking such an under-

standing, and the reasons why it failed to produce the results Stresemann wanted. In consequence, he was obliged to establish a new method for dealing with the French. Moss sees these changes taking place as Stresemann himself matured as a statesman. A clear and helpful study.

NELSON, Keith L.
See his work in section 19A(iv).

PFEIFFER, R.
Die deutsch-britischen Beziehungen unter den Reichskanzlern von Papen und von Schleicher.
Würzburg: Holzner (1971).
The author shows that both Papen and Schleicher benefited from the work done by Brüning in Anglo-German relations, which were probably during that time more amicable than at any other period after the end of the war.

RHEINBABEN, Werner von.
"Deutschland und England". *Das Parlament: Aus Politik und Zeitgeschichte* (19.5.65).
A sound comparative study.

RYAN, Marie J.
Lord D'Abernon and Britain's Policy toward Germany, 1920–1926. Dissertation, Catholic University of America (1975).
A study of D'Abernon's ambassadorship to Berlin and of his major contribution to improving Anglo-German relations. The author demonstrates that D'Abernon wanted a powerful Germany to form a bulwark against Bolshevism and to restore the balance of power on the continent. In these endeavours, his aims were entirely consistent with official British government policy.

WEIDENFELD, Werner.
Die Englandspolitik Gustav Stresemanns: theoretische und praktische Aspekte der Aussenpolitik. Mainz: Hase & Koehler (1972), 382 pp.
The latest and by far the most satisfying analysis of Stresemann's attitude and policies towards Britain. Weidenfeld has brought together a considerable amount of new material to illustrate the motives, development and consequences of Stresemann's approach, and he also tries to place the British dimension within the wider context of Stresemann's overall foreign policy ambitions — a difficult task which the author has carried out with scholarly skill.

(iii) Franco-German Relations[1]

BARIÉTY, Jacques; BLOCH, Charles.
"Une Tentative de réconciliation franco-allemande et son échec (1932–1933)". *Revue d'Histoire Moderne et Contemporaine*, vol. 15 (1968), p. 433–65.
An essay on the private discussions of French, German, and Belgian personalities before and after the Lausanne Conference. Their aim was to satisfy German demands, which they ultimately failed to do. At the same time, this attempted reconciliation only created further diplomatic problems for France *vis-à-vis* Poland, and for Germany *vis-à-vis* Russia.

HÜTTENBERGER, Peter.
"Methoden und Ziele der französischen Besatzungspolitik nach dem Ersten Weltkrieg in der Pfalz". *Blätter für Deutsche Landesgeschichte*, vol. 108 (1972), p. 105–21.
A clear exposition of the principal elements of French policy in the occupied Pfalz region.

1. Cross-refer to sections 19B(i) and 19B(ii) for relevant titles.

JACOBSON, Jon; WALKER, John T.
"The Impulse for a Franco-German *entente*: the Origins of the Thoiry Conference, 1926". *Journal of Contemporary History*, vol. 10, pt. 1 (1975), p. 157–81.
A detailed and authoritative analysis of the abortive attempt at a Franco-German *entente* at the Thoiry Conference in September 1926, when Briand and Stresemann sought to reach agreement on a number of important problems then disturbing relations between the two countries.

JORDAN, W. M.
See his work in section 19A(ii).

LEONHARDT, Fritz.
Aristide Briands Deutschlandpolitik. Dissertation, University of Heidelberg (1951).
Based on a narrow range of sources but otherwise a useful narrative.

MAXELON, Michael O.
Stresemann und Frankreich, 1914–1929: deutsche Politik in der Ost-West Balance.
Düsseldorf: Droste (1972), 309 pp.
The best and most complete study available of Stresemann's French policy. The author establishes the right perspective for Stresemann's dealings with France during 1924–29 by examining his earlier associations with that country. Presenting new archival material, Maxelon's book is scholarly and satisfying on most major counts.

McDOUGALL, Walter A.
French Rhineland Policy and the Struggle for European Stabilization: Reparations, Security, and Rhenish Separatism, 1918–1924. Dissertation, University of Chicago (1974).
Using new primary material, particularly from French sources, this is a refreshing re-examination of French motivation in the Rhineland. It was a policy dictated not only by security considerations, but also by an ambition which envisaged an independent Rhineland as the key to future peace and prosperity for France. This well organized and deftly handled work links up the complex problems of security, reparations, separatism, etc., into a compact whole.

MIDDLETON, James R.
The Embassy of William Mayer: a Case Study in Weimar Diplomacy. Dissertation, Columbia University (1969).
Mayer was the first post-1918 German representative to France, and this study discusses the main problems he faced in trying to recreate normal diplomatic ties between the two countries. Not very interesting, and a study whose terms of reference are much too narrow.

NELSON, Keith L.
"The Black Horror on the Rhine". *Journal of Modern History*, vol. 42, pt. 4 (1970), p. 606–27.
Examines the factor of race in Franco-German relations during the early 1920s, specifically the use of black troops by France in their occupation of the Rhineland, and the concerted German propaganda campaign against this "Black Shame". The Germans, whom the French knew to be humiliated on this account, won sympathy from all over Europe and the German government employed this as part of its diplomatic effort to terminate the Allied military occupation of Germany. The essay ignores important aspects of the issue, for example, the attitudes of the German political parties and *völkisch* groups, but nonetheless is worthwhile.

NELSON, Keith L.
See also his work in section 19A(iv).

REINDERS, Robert C.
"Racialism on the Left: E. D. Morel and the 'Black Horror on the Rhine'". *International Review of Social History*, vol. 13, pt. 1 (1968), p. 1—28.
Looks at the controversy aroused in Britain and other parts of Europe on account of reports in the left-wing *Daily Herald* by its correspondent Edmund Morel concerning alleged sexual atrocities committed by black French troops in the Rhineland in early 1920. Morel's accounts were taken up by the British Left and developed into a general criticism of imperialism and militarism as well as the Treaty of Versailles. The British Left feared that French militarism would destroy the Weimar Republic, which would be a severe blow to the cause of international socialism. A stimulating paper.

SAUNDERS, Donald B.
Stresemann vs. Poincaré: the Conduct of Germany's Western Policy during Gustav Stresemann's Chancellorship, August-November 1923. Dissertation, University of North Carolina (1974).
Examines how Stresemann failed in his aim to obtain concessions from France before terminating the policy of passive resistance, a policy urged on him by powerful economic and political interest groups in Germany. But Stresemann did succeed in arousing British and American sympathy for Germany, which produced important post-occupation advantages. The author, however, automatically assumes that all favourable results for Germany can be traced back to Stresemann. This was not so.

SIEBURG, Heinz-Otto.
"Das Gespräch zu Thoiry". In Ernst Schulin (ed.). *Gedenkschrift Martin Göhring: Studien zur europäischen Geschichte*. Wiesbaden: Steiner (1968), p. 317—37.
Offers a scholarly reinterpretation of the overall historical significance of this famous Conference on the basis of some new or underworked primary material. The Thoiry Conference achieved no concrete results.

(iv) American-German Relations

ADLER, Selig.
"The War-Guilt Question and American Disillusionment 1918—1928". *Journal of Modern History*, vol. 23, pt. 1 (1951), p. 1—28.
A critical look at the impact of revisionist writing on the First World War, particularly writing on the war-guilt question and its effect on American public thinking. Among other points, the essay underlines how this question dulled American reaction to the rise of National Socialism.

AMBROSIUS, Lloyd E.
The United States and the Weimar Republic 1918—1923: from the Armistice to the Ruhr Occupation. Dissertation, University of Illinois (1967).
Covers a good deal of familiar ground in orthodox fashion.

BERBUSSE, Edward J.
Diplomatic Relations between the United States and Weimar Germany 1919—1929. Dissertation, University of Georgetown (1952).
Far too vague and general.

BERG, Peter.
Deutschland und Amerika 1918—1929: über das deutsche Amerikabild der zwanziger Jahre.
Lübeck: Matthiesen (1963), 163 pp.
An interesting examination of the German view and image of the U.S.A. in the postwar decade. Feelings were mixed; there was admiration for American economic and technological power, but disdain and even hatred for her materialism and culture. On balance, most Germans, regardless of political leanings, did not care very much for the United States. Berg does not discuss all important aspects of the German-American relationship, however, so that his book must be regarded as only an introduction to the topic.

BURKE, Bernard V.
American Diplomats and Hitler's Rise to Power, 1930—1933: the Mission of Ambassador Sackett. Dissertation, University of Washington (1966).
Frederic M. Sackett was appointed U.S. Ambassador to Germany in 1930, and he immediately saw Hitler as the main threat to the Weimar Republic. He therefore did as much as he could to lend support to the Brüning government, even arranging financial aid. This is a good account of a very pro-German envoy.

BURNHAM, Walter D.
"Political Immunization and Political Confessionalism: the United States and Weimar Germany". *Journal of Interdisciplinary History*, vol. 3, pt. 1 (1972), p. 1—30.
Analyses voting patterns in Weimar and in recent U.S. national elections to determine whether there exists potential in the United States for the emergence of an extreme right-wing political movement of the bourgeoisie. Drawing parallels between the National Socialist vote in Weimar and the Wallace vote in the 1968 presidential elections, he concludes that the mass of floating non-voters was the crucial factor in the process of political radicalization.

GIRARD, Jolyon P.
Bridge on the Rhine: American Diplomacy and the Rhineland, 1919—1923. Dissertation, University of Maryland (1973).
Examines the problems arising from the lack of a definite direction in American foreign policy; on the one hand, the powerful isolationist sentiment, and on the other, the commitment to maintaining an army of occupation in Germany. The result of this ambivalence was increasing American unease in Germany. A useful study, but one which does not fully extend its own arguments.

GOTTWALD, Robert.
Die deutsch-amerikanischen Beziehungen in der Ära Stresemann. Berlin: Colloquium Verlag (1965), 167 pp.
An adequate survey of the 1924—29 period.

HESTER, J. M.
America and the Weimar Republic. Dissertation, University of Oxford (1956).
An analysis of the impact of American politics on Germany 1918—25; more of an introduction to the topic than anything else.

HIRSCH, Felix.
"Stresemann, Ballin, und die Vereinigten Staaten". *Vierteljahrshefte für Zeitgeschichte*, vol. 3, pt. 1 (1955), p. 20—35.
An important study of Stresemann's relations with and ideas on the United States before and after the First World War. Among the sources used are the papers of Alanson B. Houghton, U.S. Ambassador to Germany in the 1920s.

LINK, Werner.
Die amerikanische Stabilisierungspolitik in Deutschland 1921—32: die Vereinigten Staaten von Amerika und der Wiederaufstieg Deutschlands nach dem Ersten Weltkrieg. Düsseldorf: Droste (1970).
An important contribution, which in presenting a mass of new archival material has further clarified the motives and significance of the United States' role in Europe after 1918. The author stresses the identity of interests, political and economic, which drew Berlin and Washington closer together from the early 1920s onwards.

LINK, Werner.
"Der amerikanische Einfluss auf die Weimarer Republik in der Dawesplanphase: Elemente eines 'penetrierten Systems'". *Das Parlament: Aus Politik und Zeitgeschichte*, B45 (10.11.73).
A mass of data is used in this thorough assessment. The author argues that during 1924—29 the internal and external condition of the Republic was heavily influenced by America, politically, economically, financially, and in terms of personnel. Thus, the 1924—29 period forms a perfect example of a "penetrated economy".

LINK, Werner.
See also his article in section 19B(i).

LOCHNER, Louis P.
Herbert Hoover and Germany. New York: Macmillan (1960), 244 pp.
A rather imprecise and superficial work.

NELSON, Keith L.
The First American Military Occupation in Germany 1919—1923. Dissertation, University of California (1965).
Analyses American aims in occupying Germany and her efforts to make that occupation as moderate as possible. She was reluctant to withdraw too soon in case a full-scale international crisis ensued, particularly from the French side.

NELSON, Keith L.
Victors Divided: America and the Allies in Germany 1918—1923. Berkeley: University of California Press (1975), 441 pp.
Usefully examines the most important sources of inter-Allied disputes over German policy, but there are still certain aspects which need further study — for example, German attitudes and responses, which are not discussed in sufficient depth here.

OBERMANN, Karl.
Die Beziehungen des amerikanischen Imperialismus zum deutschen Imperialismus in der Zeit der Weimarer Republik (1918—1925). East Berlin: Rütten & Loening (1952), 167 pp.
A study which has all the hallmarks of a product of the cold war. The tone is, of course, bitterly hostile to the United States and West German "revanchists", and the argumentation totally lacks objectivity.

SCHOENTHAL, Klaus F.
American Attitudes toward Germany 1918—1932. Dissertation, University of Ohio (1959).
A very broad review whose conclusions are far from convincing.

SCHWABE, Klaus.
See his article in section 19B(iv).

SPENCER, Frank.
"The United States and Germany in the Aftermath of War: I — 1918 to 1929". *International Affairs*, vol. 43, pt. 4 (1967), p. 693—703.
Most of this essay is devoted to a consideration of American attitudes towards reparations during the 1919—23 period. Spencer comes to some ridiculous conclusions, such as: the United States bears a major responsibility for the Second World War because her loans to Germany in 1924—29 enabled the latter to reorganize her heavy industry and thus to prepare the groundwork for an armaments industry.

B. THEMES OF GERMAN-WESTERN RELATIONS

(i) The Ruhr

ARTAUD, Denise.
"A Propos de l'occupation de la Ruhr". *Revue d'Histoire Moderne et Contemporaine*, vol. 17 (1970), p. 1—21.
A stimulating essay which puts a different interpretation on France's motives in occupying the Ruhr. The argument here is that France was not so much concerned to obtain reparations payments as to initiate a policy that was ultimately aimed at extending her influence in Eastern Europe at the expense of Britain.

CORNEBISE, Alfred E.
Some Aspects of the German Response to the Ruhr Occupation, January-September 1923. Dissertation, University of North Carolina (1965).
Examines aspects of Germany's passive resistance to the occupation forces, and the background in Germany against which this policy was undertaken. A study of modest stature.

CORNEBISE, Alfred E.
"Gustav Stresemann and the Ruhr Occupation: the Making of a Statesman". *European Studies Review*, vol. 2, pt. 1 (1972), p. 43—67.
Argues the case for regarding the Ruhr occupation and its consequences as the decisive event in transforming Stresemann from an ordinary German politician into a statesman of European rank. This idea was in fact put forward by Baron Rochus von Rheinbaben, one of Stresemann's earliest biographers, in 1929.[1]

FAVEZ, Jean-Claude.
Le Reich devant l'occupation franco-belge de la Ruhr en 1923. Geneva (1969).
An informative and detailed account of the period preceding the Ruhr occupation, with particular stress on the German situation.

HORTZSCHANSKY, Günter.
Der nationale Verrat der deutschen Monopolherren während des Ruhrkampfes 1923. East Berlin: Dietz (1961), 327 pp.
Adduces the extravagant hypothesis that the occupation was provoked by German capitalists so as to aid them somehow in their fight against the proletariat. Hence, they were working against German national interests. This rigidly Marxist-Leninist study need not be taken very seriously. The KPD emerges *de rigueur* as the hero of the hour.

1. Rochus von Rheinbaben. *Stresemann: the Man and the Statesman.* New York: Brooks & Herzl (1929), 225 pp.

JONES, Kenneth P.
Stresemann and the Diplomacy of the Ruhr Crisis 1923—1924. Dissertation, University of Wisconsin (1970).
A full study of Stresemann's diplomacy during the crisis, from January 1923 to August 1924. The thesis is that the Dawes Plan was the foundation for all that Stresemann achieved in foreign affairs before 1929, and that he was delighted with the Plan as a solution to the Ruhr crisis.

LENOIR, Nancy R.
The Ruhr in Anglo-French Diplomacy: from the Beginning of the Occupation until the End of Passive Resistance. Dissertation, University of Oklahoma (1972).
Explains why the crisis alienated Britain from France, but also explains Britain's reasons for not hindering the occupation. Lenoir agrees with previous scholars that France got virtually nothing out of her action and that subsequently she tended to become subservient to Britain's diplomatic leadership. The dissertation contains no surprises.

LINK, Werner.
"Die Ruhrbesatzung und die wirtschaftspolitischen Interessen der USA". *Vierteljahrshefte für Zeitgeschichte*, vol. 17, pt. 4 (1969), p. 372—82.
An analysis of an important dimension of the crisis and the whole question of reparations payments from the American point of view. The essay considers the reaction of American big business to the occupation and its later political and diplomatic moves to secure its own interests in the Ruhr.

ROMAN, Eric.
The Ruhrkampf in History. Dissertation, State University of New York (1965).
A brief study which argues that the occupation only served to weaken German democracy. The author does not follow through with this viewpoint and as a whole the dissertation adds nothing to our knowledge.

RUGE, Wolfgang.
See his work in section 19C(iii).

SCHMIDT, Royal J.
Versailles and the Ruhr, Seedbed of World War II. The Hague: Martinus Nijhoff (1968), 310 pp.
The author sees the French action in the Ruhr as an attempt to obtain what Versailles had not given France — security. As a consequence of the failure of this policy, he continues, German nationalism and National Socialism were considerably boosted. But he fails to make his case; after all, the Ruhr was but one of a series of international incidents between 1919 and 1939. His description of the Ruhr crisis itself is incomplete and pedestrian and in general the book is a failure.

(ii) Separatism

BISCHOF, Erwin.
Rhenischer Separatismus 1918—1924: Hans Adam Dorstens Rheinstaatsbestrebungen. Frankfurt: Lang (1969), 151 pp.
By no means an exhaustive history of the separatist movement in the Rhineland. Nor is the book a definitive account of the role of H.A. Dorsten, the separatist leader. There is some useful information here, but the book is no more than an adequate introduction to the complexities of the problem.

BOIS, Jean-Pierre.
"L'Opinion catholique rhénane devant le séparatisme en 1923". *Revue d'Histoire Moderne et Contemporaine*, vol. 21, pt. 2 (1974), p. 221—51.
A detailed examination of Catholic attitudes towards separatism which also throws some fresh light on the nature of the Rhenish separatist movement.

DORSTEN, Hans A.
La Tragédie rhénane. Paris: Libraire Robert Laffont (1945), 259 pp. 15th ed.
An apologetic and extremely limited account of the Rhenish separatist movement by its former leader and one-time provisional head of the Rhenish Republic.

EPSTEIN, Klaus.
"Adenauer 1918—1924". *Geschichte in Wissenschaft und Unterricht*, vol. 19, pt. 9 (1968), p. 553—61.
The author examines the frequently made accusation that Adenauer was involved in the separatist movement and had wanted to work with France against German national interests. He shows that Adenauer in 1923 already had the idea for a West German Republic, something which he was able to implement in 1949.

ERDMANN, Karl D.
Adenauer in der Rheinlandpolitik nach dem Ersten Weltkrieg. Stuttgart: Klett (1966), 386 pp.
A comprehensive study which presents a good deal of new material on Adenauer's political activities and ambitions in early Weimar. It is the most detailed account available of his involvement in the separatist movement, though it is unlikely to have cleared up all the controversies surrounding this much disputed period of Adenauer's life.

KAHLENBERG, Friedrich P.
"Grosshessenpläne und Separatismus: das Problem der Zukunftsorientierung des Rhein-Main-Gebietes nach dem Ersten Weltkrieg (1919—1923)". In *Festschrift Ludwig Petry*. Wiesbaden: Steiner (1969), p. 355—95.
The author produces much new material on neglected areas of the separatist phenomenon in this detailed and scholarly study. He demonstrates for one thing that separatist plans were not simply confined to the Rhineland.

KLEIN, Peter.
"Zur separatistischen Bewegung der deutschen Bourgeoisie nach dem Ersten Weltkrieg". *Deutsche Aussenpolitik*, vol. 6 (1961), p. 572—83.
A superficial class definition of the character of the separatist movement.

KLEIN, Peter.
Separatisten an Rhein und Ruhr: die konterrevolutionäre separatistische Bewegung der deutschen Bourgeoisie in der Rheinprovinz und in Westfalen, November 1918 bis Juli 1919. East Berlin: Rütten & Loening (1961), 196 pp.
Highly propagandistic, and hopelessly tendentious in interpretation.

KOEHLER, Henning.
See his work in section 16A(vi).

McDOUGALL, Walter A.
See his work in section 19A(iii).

MEINHARDT, Günther.
Adenauer und der rheinische Separatismus.
Recklinghausen: Kommunal-Verlag (1962), 96 pp.
Adds little to Erdmann's study (see above).

MOWEN, Howard A.
Rhenish Separatism 1919—1923: a Study in the Franco-German Problem. Dissertation, Western Reserve University (1955).
A tentative examination of the diplomatic aspects of the separatist issue.

(iii) The Locarno Era

ALEXANDER, Manfred.
See his work in section 19F.

DICHTL, Klaus; **RUGE**, Wolfgang.
"Zu der Auseinandersetzung innerhalb der Reichsregierung über den Locarnopakt 1925".
Zeitschrift für Geschichtswissenschaft, vol. 22, pt. 1 (1974), p. 64—88.
A short introduction leads into a fully printed record of the minutes of cabinet meetings held in June, July and September 1925 which discussed the Locarno problem. The differences of opinion within the government over the issue are clearly revealed.

GRÜN, George A.
"Locarno: Idea and Reality". *International Affairs*, vol. 21, pt. 4 (1955), p. 477—85.
A critical examination of the degree of importance we should give the Locarno agreement. The ideas and principles behind Locarno are intelligently discussed and the author concludes that in practice the Pact amounted to very little; its real significance lay exclusively in the psychological and emotional effect it had on a Europe desperate to be rid of conflict.

JACOBSON, Jon.
Locarno Diplomacy: Germany and the West 1925—29. Princeton: Princeton University Press (1972), 420 pp.
An excellently documented and soundly argued study which examines the policies and aims of the major powers involved. The author asks why the goodwill of 1925 was ephemeral and answers that the interests of the major powers were essentially incompatible and bound to lead to international conflict. Locarno, he argues, dealt only with immediate and not long standing, fundamental problems.

JACOBSON, Jon.
"The Conduct of Locarno Diplomacy". *Review of Politics*, vol. 34, pt. 1 (1972), p. 67—81.
Discusses the mechanics of the negotiations before and during the Locarno Conference, particularly the series of conferences and private meetings characteristic of the "old diplomacy". The author also summarizes some of the main conclusions of his book regarding the reasons for the failure of Locarno.

LUTHER, Hans.
"Luther und Stresemann in Locarno: historisches Material, beigetragen aus eigener Erinnerung".
Politische Studien, vol. 8, pt. 1 (1957), p. 1—15.

A personal recollection of Locarno by the former Reich Chancellor which adds nothing of substance to the Conference, or for that matter to Stresemann.

MADLOCH, Norbert.
See his work in section 6B(viii)(d).

MEGERLE, Klaus.
Deutsche Aussenpolitik 1925: Ansatz zu aktivem Revisionismus. Frankfurt: Lang (1974), 307 pp.
The author's thesis is that the Locarno Pact initiated a new era in German diplomacy which saw the offensive being taken at last against the Versailles system. But, in essence, the book simply dresses up old interpretations in new clothing and presents them as original.

MINISTERIUM FÜR AUSWÄRTIGE ANGELEGENHEITEN DER DDR.
Locarno-Konferenz 1925: eine Dokumentensammlung. East Berlin: Dietz (1962).
A disappointing documentary collection which fails to provide fresh light on any important aspect of the Conference. In an introduction, Wolfgang Ruge once again displays his skill as a political polemicist, this time blaming Stresemann for being an accomplice in causing the Second World War.

RÖSSLER, Hellmuth (ed.).
Locarno und die Weltpolitik 1924—1932.
Göttingen: Musterschmidt (1969), 213 pp.
A collection of essays by various authors. Of particular note is Jacques Bariéty's piece on Locarno; he sees it as essentially the result of a universal quest for peace in Western Europe after 1919.

STAMBROOK, F. G.
"'Das Kind' — Lord D'Abernon and the Origins of the Locarno Pact". *Central European History*, vol. 1, pt. 3 (1968), p. 233—63.
An examination of the close identification of D'Abernon with the origins and final signing of the Pact, which he referred to in its initial stages as "Das Kind". The paper reveals the significant role played by him in the drafting of the proposals which were incorporated in the Pact.

THAYER, Philip.
Locarno and its Aftermath: a Study of the Foreign Policy of Aristide Briand and Gustav Stresemann 1925—1928. Dissertation, University of North Carolina (1956).
A competent but dull comparative study.

THIMME, Annelise.
"Die Locarnopolitik im Lichte des Stresemann-Nachlasses". *Zeitschrift für Politik*, vol. 3, pt. 1 (1956), p. 42—63.
An unsatisfactory paper in several important respects: firstly, the author has not fully appreciated the intrinsically political nature of Stresemann's acceptance of the Dawes Plan; and secondly, she does not bring out the political nature of the connection between the Plan and Locarno.

TURNER, Henry A.
"Eine Rede Stresemanns über seine Locarno-Politik". *Vierteljahrshefte für Zeitgeschichte*, vol. 15, pt. 4 (1967), p. 412—36.
A speech delivered by Stresemann at a meeting of the DVP's Central Committee in Berlin on 22 November 1925 is reproduced here in full. It throws light on his attitude to Locarno, and is important because he was speaking freely

and confidentially to a small group of party officials. The speech reveals Stresemann's interpretation of events leading up to Locarno and provides his analysis of the Treaty's worth to Germany and to Europe as a whole. The image which emerges of Stresemann himself is one of a tough-minded master of *Realpolitik*.

URBANITSCH, Peter.
Grossbritannien und die Verträge von Locarno.
Vienna: Verlag Notring (1968).
Deals with the diplomatic preparations for the Conference and adequately outlines the British and German positions. But a great deal of archival material has been ignored by the author, including the files of the British Foreign Office and Cabinet Office.

WEHN, Paul B.
Germany and the Treaty of Locarno — 1925.
Dissertation, Columbia University (1968).
Presents a mass of detailed material relating to Germany's motives, her negotiations with the West, and the problems involved in making the Treaty acceptable to the German public. Locarno is depicted as an outstanding diplomatic triumph for Stresemann and Germany. Overall, the quality of analysis does not match the quantity of data in this study.

ZIMMERMANN, Ludwig.
"Die Locarnoverträge als Versuch einer Lösung der Sicherheitsfragen". In L. Zimmermann (ed.). *Studien zur Geschichte der Weimarer Republik.* Erlangen (1956), p. 48—68.
Shows that Stresemann was not responsible for initiating the diplomatic developments which culminated in Locarno, but that once they were in motion he took charge of the German side.

(iv) The League of Nations

BROSZAT, Martin.
"Aussen- und innenpolitische Aspekte der preussisch-deutschen Minderheiten in der Ära Stresemann". In *Politische Ideologien und nationalstaatliche Ordnung: Studien zur Geschichte des 19. und 20. Jahrhunderts. Festschrift für Theodor Schieder.* Munich: Piper (1968), p. 393—445.
A detailed and scholarly analysis of the minorities problem which is especially interesting when discussing its international complications.

DEXTER, Byron.
The Years of Opportunity: the League of Nations, 1920—26. New York (1967).
A sympathetic treatment of the League's early years, but the author tends to gloss over or even ignore some fundamental deficiencies of the League as an effective force in international affairs.

FINK, Carole.
The Weimar Republic as the Defender of Minorities, 1919—1933. Dissertation, University of Yale (1968).
A well researched and interesting study.

FINK, Carole.
"Defender of Minorities: Germany in the League of Nations, 1926—1933". *Central European History*, vol. 5, pt. 4 (1972), p. 330—57.
An informative excerpt from her dissertation which re-

counts Germany's controversial policies on the minorities problem, thus providing a further insight into how Weimar diplomacy actually functioned. It is shown that many of Germany's achievements in the minorities sphere were lost by inept statesmanship during the early 1930s.

FRAENKEL, Ernst.
"Idee und Realität des Völkerbundes im deutschen politischen Denken". *Vierteljahrshefte für Zeitgeschichte*, vol. 16, pt. 1 (1968), p. 1—14.
Contrasts the almost universal rejection by Germans in the Weimar period of the League (because it was seen as a tool of the victorious powers and also because it was organizationally connected with the Versailles Treaty) with the acceptance by some German groups, 1916—19, of progressive ideas relating to the scope of a League of Nations. The USPD in particular looked favourably on the concept. But the postwar League did not in German eyes correspond to these earlier ideals and was therefore rejected. An interesting and detailed paper.

HENIG, Ruth B. (ed.).
The League of Nations. Edinburgh: Oliver & Boyd (1973), 203 pp.
Designed for undergraduates, this volume comprises a series of extracts from contemporary speeches and writings relating to the League and its functions; the editor supplies a brief commentary and a useful résumé of the main reasons why the League failed.

JAECKH, R.; SCHWARZ, Wilhelm.
Die Politik Deutschlands im Völkerbund. Paris: Droz (1957), 96 pp.
A too brief and general survey.

LEE, Marshall M.
Failure in Geneva: the German Foreign Ministry and the League of Nations 1926—1933.
Dissertation, University of Wisconsin (1974).
Based on wide sources, this study examines the guiding principles of the Foreign Ministry's policy at the League, including German reform proposals. The author shows that essentially the Foreign Office, as part of its overall aim of revising Versailles, wanted to neutralize the League, but that this had too many innate contradictions to bring success. Indeed, Germany's position in the League grew weaker after 1930, a fact which the author attributes to the deficiencies of the German policies. An informative and valuable study.

MAROTTE, Paul.
Germany at the League of Nations Council: the Defence of German Minority Groups in Poland, Memel and Yugoslavia. Dissertation, University of North Carolina (1954).
Useful in supplying information about the complex minorities problem, though clearly the author left much work undone.

PIEPER, Helmut.
Die Minderheitenfrage und das deutsche Reich 1919—1933/4. Hamburg: Metzner (1974), 348 pp.
A thoroughly documented and sober analysis which effectively dispels most of the obscurity surrounding this topic. Pieper has amassed an impressive amount of interesting material which has been presented clearly and cogently. The role of the League of Nations is discussed with authority.

RUSSELL, Frank M.
The Saar: Battleground and Pawn. Stanford: Stanford University Press (1951), 204 pp.
The Saar was administered by the League of Nations after

1919; part of this very general work (p. 7—91) fills in some detail about the province during the Weimar period.

SCHWABE, Klaus.
"Woodrow Wilson and Germany's Membership in the League of Nations 1918—19". *Central European History*, vol. 8, pt. 1 (1975), p. 3—22.
Considers the development of Wilson's original hope of including a democratic Germany in the League. Wilson changed his mind several times on the matter and by the autumn of 1918 he had given up his initial universalist concept of the League, which meant the exclusion of Germany, due to opposition from France and the Republican Party in the United States.

SCOTT, George.
The Rise and Fall of the League of Nations.
New York: Macmillan (1974), 432 pp.
A prolix, poorly argued, and popular book which is based on a limited selection of secondary sources. The author has completely ignored the vast amount of primary documentation that is available. As a serious study, therefore, the book is without value.

SEILER, Alois.
See his article in section 17 A.

SHERDAN, Vincent.
See his work in section 6B(i).

SPENZ, Jürgen.
Die diplomatische Vorgeschichte des Beitritts Deutschlands zum Völkerbund 1924—1926: ein Beitrag zur Aussenpolitik der Weimarer Republik.
Göttingen: Musterschmidt (1966), 216 pp.
A competent narrative of the negotiations leading up to Germany's admittance to the League and of the domestic problems Stresemann had to contend with at the same time, including the efforts of Brockdorff-Rantzau to sabotage his plans. It is demonstrated that Stresemann himself was primarily motivated in his approach to the League by German national considerations.

STROMBERG, Roland N.
"Uncertainties and Obscurities about the League of Nations." *Journal of the History of Ideas*, vol. 33, pt. 1 (1972), p. 139—54.
A good discussion of the dilemmas afflicting the concept and practice of the League from the American point of view. The League, the author states, never had a clearly defined role or objective; by combining a number of conflicting ideas it sowed confusion in the minds of politicians and the general public and thereby "contributed to the collapse of international order in the 1930s" — a contentious conclusion.

WALTERS, Francis P.
A History of the League of Nations. 2 vols.
London: Oxford University Press (1951), 864 pp.
A very competent narrative, but it is based almost exclusively on published secondary sources. Until such time as the voluminous primary data on the League is tapped, however, this book is likely to remain the best available on the subject.

WELISCH, Sophie A.
See her work in section 19F.

ZENNER, Maria.
Parteien und Politik im Saargebiet unter dem Völkerbundsregime 1920—1935. Saarbrücken: Minerva Verlag (1966), 434 pp.
Although the emphasis is on the internal development of the Saar, there is adequate coverage given of the policies of the League of Nations in the region. The author is by and large fair and balanced in her analysis.

(v) Reparations

BENNETT, Edward W.
Germany and the Diplomacy of the Financial Crisis, 1931. Cambridge (Mass.): Harvard University Press (1962), 345 pp.
This is a detailed and scholarly treatment of a complex international problem, judiciously set against the background of German domestic policy 1930—32. As a diplomatic history of negotiations revolving around reparations, the book is very good, and the author also marks out clearly the influence of high finance circles on the conduct of international affairs. Interwoven into the study is a critical assessment of Brüning's foreign policy, and he argues that the Brüning government could not have been saved by timely concessions from the West in 1932.

BICKERT, Hans G.
"Die Vermittlerrolle Grossbritanniens während der Reparationskonferenz von Lausanne 1932". *Das Parlament: Aus Politik und Zeitgeschichte*, B23 (1973), p. 13—22.
Shows the essentially sympathetic attitude towards Germany's reparations problems displayed by Britain at the Lausanne Conference.

CARROLL, John M.
The Making of the Dawes Plan 1919—1924.
Dissertation, University of Kentucky (1972).
Mainly concerned with an assessment of American diplomacy after 1919. The author tries to show that the United States worked for a new order in the 1920s of which the Dawes Plan was but one element. The German side of the events which culminated in the adoption of the Plan, however, is not dealt with at all, though the international problems arising from the Ruhr crisis of 1923 are given some attention.

CASTILLON, Richard.
Les Réparations allemands: deux expériences 1919—1932, 1945—1952. Paris: Presses Universitaires (1953), 198 pp.
A comparative study of limited value. There are a few interesting details on the 1919—32 period, but otherwise there is little here to arouse interest.

CURTIUS, Julius.
Der Young-Plan: Entstellung und Wahrheit.
Stuttgart: Mittelbach Verlag (1950), 122 pp.
A brief account, written largely from memory, of the diplomatic and political negotiations leading to the Plan in 1929. The author's purpose is to take Hjalmar Schacht to task for distorting the meaning of the Plan in his writings, but since much of the author's evidence is circumstantial his case is not convincing. From what we know of Schacht from other studies, however, Curtius is correct to describe him as a petty, ambitious, and deceitful bore.

FELIX, David.
"Reparations Reconsidered with a Vengeance".
Central European History, vol. 4, pt. 2 (1971),
p. 171—9.
The author takes issue with Sally Marks (see her articles in
this section). He agrees with her that the reparations issue
was misunderstood but argues that the reasons for this
are quite different from those adduced by Marks. Felix
criticizes her for formulating arguments without using
economic data to back them up; he disagrees that the
1921 London Schedule of Payments was "a tremendous
German victory" as Marks states, and argues that it was instead "a terribly damaging problem in the German
economy". On balance, Felix's arguments are more substantive, though his tone is unnecessarily polemical.

FELIX, David.
See also his work and article in section 5D.

GESCHER, Dieter B.
**Die Vereinigten Staaten von Nordamerika und die
Reparationen 1920—1924: eine Untersuchung der
Reparationsfrage auf der Grundlage amerikanischer
Akten.** Bonn: Röhrscheid (1956), 226 pp.
A reasonably clear but oversimplified review of the major
developments leading up to the adoption of the Dawes
Plan. The study is mainly useful for showing how far the
reparations question dominated relations between Germany
and the United States 1920—24.

KRÜGER, Peter.
**Deutschland und die Reparationen 1918/19:
die Genesis des Reparationsproblems in
Deutschland zwischen Waffenstillstand und
Versailler Friedensschluss.** Stuttgart: Deutsche
Verlagsanstalt (1973), 224 pp.
This is a very significant study of the German position on
reparations before the Versailles Treaty was adopted. A
considerable amount of fresh documentary material is
presented, backed up by clear and persuasive analysis
and sound interpretations. Indeed, this may be regarded as
the definitive study of the problem. At the same time,
Krüger has provided an excellent account of German
diplomatic preparations for the Peace Conference as well
as a notable contribution to understanding the difficult
relationship between foreign policy and domestic affairs in
early Weimar.

LINK, Werner.
See his article in section 19A(iv).

MARKS, Sally.
"Reparations Reconsidered: a Reminder". *Central
European History*, vol. 2, pt. 4 (1969), p. 356—65.
Takes a fresh look at a controversial aspect of the repar-
ations debate — how much did Germany actually pay?
The author argues that Germany never paid anything like
the much quoted figure of 132 billion marks, and that the
London Schedule of Payments of May 1921 was a major
German victory. The treatment accorded this problem here,
however, is far too brief.

MARKS, Sally.
"Reparations Reconsidered: a Rejoinder". *Central
European History*, vol. 5, pt. 4 (1972), p. 358—61.
Marks replies to David Felix's points (see his article in this
section).

McDOUGALL, Walter A.
See his work in section 19A(iii).

RONDE, Hans.
**Von Versailles bis Lausanne: der Verlauf der
Reparationsverhandlungen nach dem Ersten
Weltkrieg.** Stuttgart: Kohlhammer (1950), 211 pp.
Ronde was an advisor to the Weimar government on reparations and he attended the major international conferences on the subject 1920—32. He has produced a
competent narrative of reparations which is at its best
when discussing the Dawes and Young Plans.

RUPIEPER, Hermann-Josef.
**Politics and Economics: the Cuno Government and
Reparations 1922—1923.** Dissertation, Stanford
University (1974).
An analysis of the political and economic forces which
influenced the reparations policy of the Allies and Germany
before and after the 1923 Ruhr crisis. The author shows
how Cuno's room for manoeuvre in reparations was severely limited due to French intransigence and previous commitments entered into by his predecessors. The Ruhr
crisis is also given extensive coverage in a useful but unexciting study.

SHARP, A. J.
See his work in section 4B(ii).

SHEPARD, Carl E.
Germany and the Hague Conferences 1929—1930.
Dissertation, Indiana University (1964).
Examines German policy at these Conferences in terms of
Germany's new concern for political rather than economic
concessions. Stresemann's role is discussed, as is Curtius's,
which is seen as a continuation of the former's aims. The
dissertation covers old and well-worn ground in the main.

SMILEY, Ralph.
**The Lausanne Conference, 1932: the Diplomacy of
the End of Reparations.** Dissertation, Rutgers
University (1971).
The Conference is depicted as representing the culmination
of revisionist thinking on reparations. Of note, however, is
the analysis of Papen's policy, which was aiming at a
Franco-German *entente* and European reconstruction based
on military parity. Smiley concludes that since Papen did
not obtain all he wanted for Germany at Lausanne, the
Weimar Republic suffered yet another resounding blow.
Conclusions such as this need to be treated with considerable caution.

STRAUSBAUGH, Melvin R.
**Great Britain and the Diplomacy of Reparation:
1919—1921.** Dissertation, Case Western Reserve
University (1974).
Concentrates on the 1920—21 period and on the questions
of how much Germany should pay in reparations, how long
she should be allowed to pay, and how much payment each
ally should receive. British policy on these matters is
detailed, but the dissertation as a whole adds relatively
little to our understanding of reparations in general.

TRACHTENBERG, Marc.
French Reparation Policy, 1918—1921.
Dissertation, University of California (1974).
A generally sound and informative study which has made
use of French documentary sources.

UNITED KINGDOM GOVERNMENT.
**Documents on British Foreign Policy 1919—1939.
Series 1A: 1925—1929, vol. 6: The Young Report
and the Hague Conference: Security Questions
1928—1929.** London: H.M.S.O. (1975), 880 pp.
An important documentary source.

VOGELSANG, Thilo.
"Papen und das aussenpolitische Erbe Brünings: die Lausanner Konferenz 1932". In *Neue Perspektiven aus Wirtschaft und Recht: Festschrift für Hans Schäffer.* Stuttgart: (1966), p. 487—507.
An objective assessment of Papen's aims at the Conference.

WANDEL, Eckhard.
Die Bedeutung der Vereinigten Staaten von Amerika für das deutsche Reparationsproblem 1924—1929. Tübingen: Mohr (1971), 332 pp.
A well researched contribution. The Dawes Plan is discussed in detail and shown to have conferred substantial benefits on Germany. Indeed, Wandel argues convincingly that since the United States, who held the key to reparations, never really believed in the policy, the whole matter was rather futile from the start.

(vi) Disarmament

BOYLE, Thomas E.
France, Great Britain and German Disarmament: 1919—1927. Dissertation: State University of New York (1972).
Examines the disarmament policies of the three countries and tries to relate disarmament to the broader context of European diplomacy during the 1920s. The author focuses attention on the various disarmament commissions which operated in Germany 1919—27 and he concludes that most of the disarmament clauses of the Versailles Treaty were in fact carried out by Germany.

DEIERHOI, Tyler.
The Conduct of German Policy at the Disarmament Conference of 1932. Dissertation, Duke University (1964).
Analyses German disarmament policy, in particular her quest for equality of rights (*Gleichberechtigung*), and its implications for her foreign policy. Her objectives remained constant, but the methods used varied from one German government to another. The aggressiveness with which the Germans pursued their aims only stiffened French resistance and in the end contributed significantly to the failure of German policy.

DEIST, Wilhelm.
"Brüning, Herriot, und die Abrüstungsgespräche von Bessinge 1932". *Vierteljahrshefte für Zeitgeschichte*, vol. 5, pt. 3 (1957), p. 265—72.
Spotlights an interesting but abortive episode in the disarmament debate between France and Germany.

DEIST, Wilhelm.
"Schleicher und die deutsche Abrüstungspolitik im Juni/Juli 1932". *Vierteljahrshefte für Zeitgeschichte*, vol. 7, pt. 2 (1959), p. 163—76.
A scholarly and informative assessment.

GATZKE, Hans W.
Stresemann and the Rearmament of Germany. Baltimore: Johns Hopkins University Press (1954), 132 pp.
A brief but penetrating study based upon diligent research into Stresemann's papers. The author shows conclusively that Stresemann was fully aware of German army violations of the disarmament clauses of the Treaty of Versailles, and that Stresemann was a nationalist first and foremost; he was neither the "good European" nor the honest idealist seen by his contemporaries.

GORDON, Harold J.
See his article in section 1.

KINSLEY, Samuel D.
German Diplomacy and the Preparatory Commission for the Disarmament Conference.
Dissertation, University of North Carolina (1972).
Describes the work of the German delegation in the League of Nations Preparatory Commission. The author argues that during the later 1920s, Germany worked in good faith to achieve a general disarmament agreement for Europe as a whole. But by 1929, the Germans themselves had become disillusioned by their own policy. An unremarkable study.

MALANOWSKI, Wolfgang.
"Die deutsche Politik der militärischen Gleichberechtigung von Brüning bis Hitler". *Wehrwissenschaftliche Rundschau*, vol. 5, pt. 1 (1955), p. 351—64.
A moderately interesting review of German efforts to achieve military equality, especially 1930—33. The author stresses that despite Locarno and all other endeavours to establish peace and reconciliation, the European powers, especially France, were simply not prepared to alter the *status quo*.

RAUTENBERG, H. J.
Deutsche Rüstungspolitik vom Beginn der Genfer Abrüstungskonferenz bis zur Wiedereinführung der allgemeinen Wehrpflicht. Dissertation, University of Bonn (1973).
A competent survey.

RICHTER, Rolf.
"Der Abrüstungsgedanke in Theorie und Praxis und die deutsche Politik (1920—1929)". *Wehrwissenschaftliche Rundschau*, vol. 18, pt. 8 (1968), p. 442—66.
The paper examines the concept and practice of demilitarization and disarmament in Germany in the 1920s, and the accompanying problem of security; all three became intertwined. The author notes different phases in the disarmament efforts of the League of Nations. Most of what Richter has to say, however, has been said in one form or another by previous writers, and besides he does not fulfil the promise of exploring the internal political implications of either disarmament or demilitarization.

SALEWSKI, Michael.
See his work in section 12A(i)

SALEWSKI, Michael.
"Zur deutschen Sicherheitspolitik in der Spätzeit der Weimarer Republik". *Vierteljahrshefte für Zeitgeschichte*, vol. 22, pt. 2 (1974), p. 121—47.
This paper sets out to explain the German approach to and interpretation of the fundamental diplomatic problem of "security" 1930—33. German security policy was a fundamental part of the general policy of German revisionism so that the German "security" policy was a dynamic one from the very beginning. This is contrasted with the more static security policies of the other major powers. A thorough study.

SHARP, A. J.
See his work in section 4B(ii).

C. RUSSO-GERMAN RELATIONS

(i) General

CARR, Edward H.
German-Soviet Relations between the Two World Wars, 1919—1939. Baltimore: Johns Hopkins University Press (1951), 146 pp.
This book consists of six papers originally delivered under the auspices of Johns Hopkins University's Albert Shaw Lectures in 1951. The theme is the *rapprochement* in German-Soviet relations during the 1920s, and the gradual cooling of those relations in the early 1930s. The book is certainly scholarly in tone and appraisal, but has since been entirely superseded by other more up-to-date studies.

DOESER, Ute.
Das bolschewistische Russland in der deutschen Rechtspresse 1918—1925: eine Studie zum publizistischen Kampf in der Weimarer Republik. Dissertation, Free University of Berlin (1961).
The author has diligently combed through much unpromising right-wing press material to show how negatively the German Right viewed Russia during the early 1920s. The dissertation, however, arrives at no startling conclusions and generally suffers from the limitations of most studies of this genre; for example, she has not investigated sources other than those directly associated with the press.

DYCK, Harvey L.
Weimar Germany and Soviet Russia 1926—1933: a Study in Diplomatic Instability. London: Chatto & Windus (1966), 279 pp.
This is a detailed but limited account of relations between both countries. The author has not fully utilized all available documentary materials (especially from the Russian side) and his understanding of Russian motives *vis-à-vis* Germany is inadequate. Moreover, the recent availability of additional archival sources has rendered some parts of his chronicle out of date.

FREUND, Gerald.
Unholy Alliance: Russian-German Relations from the Treaty of Brest-Litovsk to the Treaty of Berlin. London: Chatto & Windus (1957), 283 pp.
A solid work of research whose value, however, is undermined by the findings of more up-to-date studies. Also, as in so many studies in this field, the Russian side of the relationship with Germany is treated rather superficially. However, the book still serves as a reasonably sound introduction to the theme, for Freund has written on the political, economic and military aspects of the relationship.

GRIESER, H.
Die Sowjetpresse über Deutschland in Europa, 1922—1932. Stuttgart: Metzlar (1970).
An interesting book which reveals in particular Soviet attitudes to the themes of revision of the Versailles Treaty and Rapallo.

HELBIG, Herbert.
"Die Moskauer Mission des Grafen Brockdorff-Rantzau". *Forschungen zur Osteuropäischen Geschichte*, vol. 2 (1955), p. 286—344.
A valuable assessment of the efforts of Brockdorff-Rantzau (he was the German Ambassador to Moscow during the first half of the Weimar era) to promote German-Soviet relations despite many obstacles, and his reasons for doing so.

HILGER, Gustav; MEYER, Alfred.
The Incompatible Allies: German-Soviet Relations 1918—41. New York: Macmillan (1953), 350 pp.
Hilger was a former member of the German embassy in Moscow, and this somewhat thin and unsatisfactory book is semi-autobiographical. Too many of his observations are fragmentary and unenlightening, and he does not touch upon most major aspects of German-Soviet relations during the interwar era.

KLEIN, Fritz.
Die diplomatischen Beziehungen Deutschlands zur Sowjetunion 1917—32. East Berlin: Rütten & Loening (1952), 190 pp.
Written from a rigidly Marxist-Leninist viewpoint, Klein sees only bad on the German side and good on the Russian. He concentrates on explaining the nefarious motivation of German big business in the relationship, though most of his interpretations are distorted. As an exercise in scholarly objectivity, the book is, to put it mildly, worthless.

KLUKE, Paul.
"Deutschland und Russland zwischen den Weltkriegen". *Historische Zeitschrift*, no. 171 (1951), p. 519—52.
A cautious but preliminary evaluation of the more important factors involved in the relationship. The author competently summarizes the principal conclusions reached so far by specialists in the field.

KOCHAN, Lionel.
Russia and the Weimar Republic. Cambridge: Bowes & Bowes (1954), 190 pp.
In its day, this was a clear and reliable survey of German-Soviet relations from 1918 to 1934. Obviously, it has since been superseded by other works which have been able to make use of wider sources of material. However, unlike most studies, the strength of this book is its emphasis on the Russian side.

KRUMMACHER, Friedrich A.; LANGE, Helmut.
Krieg und Frieden: Geschichte der deutsch-sowjetischen Beziehungen, von Brest-Litowsk zum Unternehmen Barbarossa. Munich: Bechtle (1970), 564 pp.
A general history, competent in most ways, but in essence a synthesis of previously published material in the field.

LAQUEUR, Walter Z. (ed.).
Russia and Germany: a Century of Conflict. London: Weidenfeld & Nicolson (1965), 197 pp.
A volume which consists of papers originally presented in the journal *Survey* (no. 44—45, October 1962). One of the best papers is by the editor himself and entitled "Hitler and Russia 1919—1923"; it is a detailed analysis of the importance of Russian *émigrés* on the early development of the NSDAP. In addition, Golo Mann writes on "Rapallo: the Vanishing Dream", and Francis L. Carsten assesses relations between the *Reichswehr* and the Red Army.

LASER, Kurt.
See his work in section 13A(ii)(a).

MARKERT, Werner (ed.).
Deutsch-russische Beziehungen von Bismarck bis zur Gegenwart. Stuttgart: Deutsche Verlagsanstalt (1964).
Not a particularly interesting collection of articles by various authors. The paper to note is by Richard Lowenthal, and entitled "Russland und die Bolschewisierung der deutschen Kommunisten".

MIELCKE, Karl.
Deutschland und Russland 1918—1941. Bad Gandersheim: Hertel Verlag (1960), 47 pp.
A brief interpretative essay of little importance.

NOACK, Paul.
"Deutsch-russische Beziehungen von 1922—1933".
Politische Studien, vol. 11 (1960), p. 77—88.
Too general a survey to be of much use.

NORDEN, Albert.
**Zwischen Berlin und Moskau: zur Geschichte
der deutsch-sowjetischen Beziehungen.** East
Berlin: Dietz (1954), 387 pp.
Unobjective, biased and quite useless.

PUCHERT, Berthold.
**"Die Entwicklung der deutsch-sowjetischen
Handelsbeziehungen von 1918 bis 1939".** *Jahrbuch
für Wirtschaftsgeschichte*, vol. 14, pt. 4 (1973),
p. 11—36.
Deals mainly with commercial relations during the Weimar
era (p. 11—31) and produces some interesting and relevant
data, for example, on the amount of credit provided by
German industry. The author notes that commercial links
between the two countries were strengthened even during
periods of cool political relations, as during the early 1930s.

STEPANOV, Andrej I.
**"Die deutsch-sowjetischen Beziehungen 1917 bis
1927 im Lichte der diplomatischen Akten".**
Zeitschrift für Geschichtswissenschaft, vol. 14,
pt. 2 (1966), p. 255—65.[1]
An interesting discussion of relations in the light of recently
published foreign policy documents of the Soviet Union
(Vols. I-XIV). The documents clearly constitute an important source.

STRUGER, Marlane.
**Nikolai Nikolaievich Krestinsky and Soviet-German
Relations 1921—1930.** Dissertation, University of
Wisconsin (1973).
Krestinsky (1883—1938) was Soviet Ambassador to Germany 1921—30; he consistently tried to promote German-
Russian understanding and was involved in the preparation
for the Rapallo and Berlin Treaties of 1922 and 1926
respectively. This is an interesting examination of the
temporary success and ultimate failure of his ambassadorship.

TESKE, Hermann (ed.).
**General Ernst Köstring: der militärische Mittler
zwischen dem deutschen Reich und der Sowjetunion 1921—1941.** Frankfurt: Mittler (1965),
334 pp.
Reproduces some interesting documentation relating to
military links between Germany and Russia, and to
Köstring's apparently central role in them.

WHEELER-BENNETT, John W.
**"Twenty Years of Russo-German Relations:
1919—1939".** *Foreign Affairs*, vol. 25, pt. 1
(1946), p. 23—43.
A now completely out-of-date and misleading general
survey.

1. The same article is reproduced in the West German
journal *Blätter für Deutsch- und Internationale Politik*,
vol. 14, pt. 9 (1969), p. 980—9.

WHEELER-BENNETT, John W.
**A Wreath to Clio: Studies in British, American and
German Affairs.** New York: St. Martin's Press
(1967), 225 pp.
In this disappointing volume of essays, many of them
previously published by the author, his aforementioned
paper on German-Soviet relations is reproduced in largely
unrevised form.

(ii) Brest-Litovsk to Rapallo (1918—1922)

ALTER, Peter.
**"Rapallo — Gleichgewichtspolitik und
Revisionismus".** *Neue Politische Literatur*, vol. 19
(1974), p. 509—17.
Discusses the motives behind the German approach to
Rapallo.

ANDERLE, Alfred.
**"Der Vertrag von Rapallo — eine nationale
Chance".** *Zeitschrift für Geschichtswissenschaft*,
vol. 10, pt. 2 (1962), p. 336—70.
A political polemic whose real purpose is to criticize the
policy of the Federal Republic towards the Soviet Union.
As background, the author muses on the missed oppor-
tunity for lasting peace in Europe in 1922; Germany, he
states, should have built further on the foundations laid by
Rapallo. A piece of trite propaganda.

BAUMGART, Winfried.
See her work in section 4B(ii).

ERDMANN, Karl D.
"Deutschland, Rapallo und der Westen".
Vierteljahrshefte für Zeitgeschichte, vol. 11, pt. 2
(1963), p. 105—65.
A thoroughly detailed and important essay which asks in
what ways Rapallo affected Germany's relations with the
West. The author bases his answer on an analysis of the
Geneva Conference (April-May 1922) and the Paris meeting
of the Allies (May-June 1922). He concludes that tempor-
arily Rapallo produced a strong political reaction on the
part of the West against Germany; but this was an emotional response and did not materially affect the negotiations at
Geneva. Also, he argues that strategically Rapallo was a
success for Germany because it considerably helped to
normalize relations between the two sides. Finally, he
asserts that Rapallo laid the groundwork for Locarno.

FISHER, Ernest F.
**Road to Rapallo: a Study of Walther Rathenau
and German Foreign Policy, 1919—1922.**
Dissertation, University of Wisconsin (1952).
A useful but preliminary survey.

GATZKE, Hans W.
**"Zu den deutsch-russischen Beziehungen im
Sommer 1918".** *Vierteljahrshefte für Zeit-
geschichte*, vol. 3, pt. 1 (1955), p. 67—98.
Refers to an interesting episode in Stresemann's wartime
activities.

GOLDBACH, Marie-Luise.
**Karl Radek und die deutsch-sowjetischen
Beziehungen 1918—1923.** Bad Godesberg: Verlag
Neue Gesellschaft (1973), 163 pp.
A disappointing and superficial work which, although
outlining Radek's activities clearly enough, does not adequately analyse the motives behind them. Nor does the
author place her theme well enough in the wider context
of German-Soviet relations.

GRAML, Hermann.
"Die Rapallo-Politik im Urteil der westdeutschen Forschung". *Vierteljahrshefte für Zeitgeschichte,* vol. 18, pt. 4 (1970), p. 366—91.
An excellent and judiciously assessed review article which sums up the importance of Rapallo in German foreign policy after 1918.

GROTTIAN, Walter.
"Genua und Rapallo 1922: Entstehung und Wirkung eines Vertrages". *Das Parlament: Aus Politik und Zeitgeschichte* (20/27.6.1962).
A very useful review of the origins of Rapallo.

HAHLWEG, Werner.
Der Diktatfrieden von Brest-Litowsk 1918 und die Bolschewistische Weltrevolution. Münster: Aschendorff (1960), 87 pp.
This small work is essentially a bibliographical survey and review of scholarly verdicts on the Treaty. A brief outline of German and Soviet motives and of the negotiations is given, and finally a summary of the Treaty's significance.

HAHLWEG, Werner (ed.).
Der Friede von Brest-Litowsk: ein unveröffentlichter Band aus dem Werk des Untersuchungsausschusses der deutschen Verfassunggebenden Nationalversammlung und des deutschen Reichstages. Düsseldorf: Droste (1971), 737 pp.
A full documentary collection containing the evidence gathered by a sub-commission of the National Assembly and *Reichstag* on the attitudes and motives towards the Treaty of German politicians and army officers.

HELBIG, Herbert.
Die Träger der Rapallo Politik. Göttingen: Vandenhoeck und Ruprecht (1958), 214 pp.
This volume deals mainly with the efforts of Count Brockdorff-Rantzau and Moritz Schlesinger to promote and defend the Rapallo Treaty in Germany. In fact, much of the book is based on the Brockdorff papers. A number of Helbig's arguments are contradictory and on the whole the book does not clarify important aspects of German-Soviet relations. He rejects the idea, without providing sufficient evidence, that Rapallo was a conspiracy of the "outsiders", Germany and Russia, against the Versailles Treaty and the West.

HIMMER, George R.
Soviet Russia's Economic Relations with Germany 1918—22. Dissertation, Johns Hopkins University (1972).
In a study based on wide sources, Himmer analyses the nature and extent of economic factors in German-Soviet relations. After 1918, Germany saw Russia as a market for her industrial goods, and the various trade agreements which resulted are examined. But he argues interestingly that Rapallo was concluded despite the conflicting economic interests of the two countries.

KLEIN, Fritz.
"Zur Beurteilung des Rapallo-Vertrages durch die westdeutschen bürgerlichen Historiker". *Zeitschrift für Geschichtswissenschaft,* vol. 10, pt. 5 (1962), p. 1077—94.
The author reproves West German historians for failing in their "national duty" to learn from history, as shown in their "unenlightened" attitude to Rapallo. He provides a thoroughly biased review of secondary literature on the theme of Rapallo.

KOBLJAKOW, I. K.
Von Brest bis Rapallo: geschichtlicher Abriss der sowjetisch-deutschen Beziehungen von 1918 bis 1922. East Berlin: Dietz (1956).
Presents a one-sided Soviet view of relations 1918—22.

KOCHAN, Lionel.
"The Russian Road to Rapallo". *Soviet Studies,* vol. 2, pt. 2 (1950), p. 109—22.
Examines how Russian policy towards Germany developed from the 1919 idea of supporting Germany's struggle against Versailles to the 1921—22 position of alliance with Germany. This was above all else a matter of practical politics as far as the Russians were concerned.

LADEMACHER, Horst.
"Der Friede von Brest-Litowsk 1918". *Blätter für Deutsch- und Internationale Politik,* vol. 6 (1961), p. 856—68.
A brief consideration of the Treaty's subsequent importance in German-Soviet relations.

LADEMACHER, Horst.
"Von Brest-Litowsk nach Rapallo". *Blätter für Deutsch- und Internationale Politik,* vol. 6 (1961), p. 1037—54.
Discusses the concepts involved in German-Soviet relations — a combination of ideology, power politics, but especially of *Realpolitik.* An interesting and helpful paper.

LINKE, Horst G.
Deutsch-sowjetische Beziehungen bis Rapallo. Cologne: Verlag Wissenschaft und Politik (1970), 295 pp.
A well documented and comprehensive narrative which, however, does not offer any new interpretations of Rapallo or indeed of any other aspect of German-Soviet relations. The emphasis is almost exclusively on political, economic and military links.

LINKE, Horst G.
"Deutschland und die Sowjetunion von Brest-Litowsk bis Rapallo". *Das Parlament: Aus Politik und Zeitgeschichte,* B16 (15.4.1972).
A summary of the main conclusions of the author's book regarding the motives behind Russian and German policy before Rapallo. He includes, however, some new material from unpublished British sources.

MANN, Golo.
"Rapallo: the Vanishing Dream". In W.Z. Laqueur (ed.). *Russia and Germany: a Century of Conflict.* London: Weidenfeld & Nicolson (1965).
An interesting reflection on the significance of the Treaty.

MEYER, Klaus.
"Sowjetrussland und die Anfänge der Weimarer Republik". *Forschungen zur Osteuropäischen Geschichte,* vol. 20 (1973), p. 77—91.
A scholarly discussion of the complex relationship between Germany and Russia from November 1918 to January 1919; this period witnessed a particularly active Russian interest in German domestic affairs.

NOACK, Paul.
"Rapallo — Wunsch und Wirklichkeit". *Politische Studien*, vol. 117 (1960), p. 31—44.
Draws attention to the discrepancy between what was hoped for from Rapallo by both sides and the somewhat disappointing consequences of the Treaty. But Noack's assessment is not very convincing.

ORTH, Wilhelm.
Walther Rathenau und der Geist von Rapallo: Grösse und Grenzen eines deutschen Bürgers. East Berlin: Buchverlag Der Morgen (1962), 166 pp.
A not unsympathetic assessment of Rathenau's motives and actual role in the negotiations leading up to Rapallo.

ROSENFELD, Günter.
Sowjetrussland und Deutschland 1917—1922. East Berlin: Akademie-Verlag (1960), 423 pp.
Written and interpreted within a rigid Marxist-Leninist framework, this is too unobjective to be taken seriously despite the fact that a mass of material drawn mostly from East German sources is presented. This is history examined in black and white terms, with Soviet Russia depicted as the epitome of all that is good and holy, and German capitalists cast as the incorrigible villains.

ROSENFELD, Günter.
"Das Zustandekommen des Rapallo-Vertrages". *Zeilschrift für Geschichlswissenschaft*, vol. 4, pt. 4 (1956), p. 678—97.
In discussing the circumstances leading to Rapallo the author argues that for Germany economic factors were the primary motive force; all other factors are ignored. An unreliable paper.

SCHIEDER, Theodor.
"Die Entstehungsgeschichle des Rapallo-Vertrages". *Historische Zeitschrifl*, no. 204 (1967), p. 545—609.
The best analysis available on the origins of the Treaty. The author expertly weighs up the results of previous research, and fills the gaps with new and convincing material (especially from the Russian side). An outstanding paper.

SCHÜDDEKOPF, Otto-Ernst.
"Deutschland zwischen Ost und West: Karl Moor und die deutsch-russischen Beziehungen". *Archiv für Sozialgeschichte*, vol. 3 (1963), p. 223—63.
A detailed and scholarly appraisal of Moor's role during the first half of 1919.

STAATSVERLAG DER DDR.
Deutsch-sowjetische Beziehungen von den Verhandlungen in Brest-Litovsk bis zum Abschluss des Rapallovertrages: Dokumentensammlung. Vol. I: 1917—1918; vol. II: 1919—1922. East Berlin: Staatsverlag der DDR (1967—71), 886, 698 pp.
A generally important documentary collection, published jointly by East Germany and the Soviet Union, which specialists in German-Russian relations will find very useful for the early Weimar period.

WENGST, Udo.
Graf Brockdorff-Rantzau und die aussenpolitischen Anfänge der Weimarer Republik. Frankfurt: Lang (1973), 163 pp.
A well written study which forms a useful introduction to an understanding of Brockdorff's later prominent contribution to German-Soviet relations.

WHEELER-BENNETT, John W.
Brest-Litovsk: the Forgotten Peace, March 1918. London: Macmillan (1956), 478 pp.
Originally published in 1938, this large study still retains much of its usefulness as an overall survey of the last six months of the war in the east.

WINZER, Otto.
Der Rapallo-Vertrag und seine nationale Bedeutung für Deutschland. East Berlin: Dietz (1952), 42 pp.
A wholly propagandistic and pro-Soviet essay of no significance.

ZELT, Johannes.
"Die deutsch-sowjetischen Beziehungen in den Jahren 1917 bis 1921 und das Problem der Kriegsgefangenen und Internierten". *Zeitschrift für Geschichtswissenschaft*, vol. 15 (1967), p. 1015—32.
Adds some useful material on the problem of prisoners of war at the end of the war.

(iii) Rapallo to Stalin (1923—1928)

ANDERLE, Alfred.
Die deutsche Rapallo-Politik: deutsch-sowjetische Beziehungen 1922—1929. East Berlin: Rütten & Loening (1962), 248 pp.
Hopelessly tendentious piece of political propaganda in which the material has been clearly manipulated to conform to the Marxist-Leninist line. The author's general conclusion is that Rapallo shows how Russia and Germany can co-operate — an obvious reference to the present-day East German-Soviet relationship.

ANDERLE, Alfred.
"Die deutsch-sowjetischen Verträge von 1925—1926". *Zeitschrift für Geschichtswissenschaft*, vol. 5, pt. 3 (1957), p. 470—501.
Examines the practical economic consequences of the legal and economic treaty of 12 October 1925 and of the Berlin Treaty of 24 April 1926, concluding that both were important for the two countries. However, the real purpose of the essay is revealed in his conclusion, when he writes a flowery eulogy of Soviet foreign policy.

BLÜCHER, Wipert von.
Deutschlands Weg nach Rapallo. Wiesbaden: Limes (1951), 180 pp.
Unhelpful and dated memoirs of a former diplomat.

CECIL, Lamar.
"The Kindermann-Wolscht Incident: an Impasse in Russo-German Relations 1924—26". *Journal of Central European Affairs*, vol. 21, pt. 2 (1961), p. 188—99.
A discussion of one of the most notorious incidents in Russo-German relations during the 1920s, when two German Jewish students, Kindermann and Wolscht, were arrested during a trip to Russia in 1924 and accused of anti-Soviet terrorist activity. The affair threatened at one stage the diplomatic *rapprochement* between the two countries. The Russians used the students as a bargaining counter in the famous *Cheka* case in Germany in which Soviet agents were on trial for plotting revolution in Germany. Eventually, the Russians demonstrated that their policy of *Geiselpolitik* ("hostage diplomacy") could pay dividends when they persuaded the German government to exchange the *Cheka* leader for the two students.

DYCK, Harvey L.
"German-Soviet Relations and the Anglo-Soviet Break, 1927". *Slavic Review*, vol. 25, pt. 1 (1966), p. 67—83.
Based on material incorporated in his book (see section 19C(i)).

GASIOROWSKI, Zygmunt J.
"The Russian Overture to Germany of December 1924". *Journal of Modern History*, vol. 30, pt. 2 (1958), p. 99—117.
Spotlights an ostensibly unimportant diplomatic incident of 4 December 1924 when Russia made an approach to Germany, suggesting that their relations be concretized on the basis of recognition of each other's interests *vis-à-vis* Poland. Stresemann reacted coolly and by the time both countries got together Russia was more concerned about the repercussions of Locarno than anything else. The article is an example of old-fashioned writing on diplomatic matters, but it is solidly documented.

GATZKE, Hans W.
"Von Rapallo nach Berlin: Stresemann und die deutsche Russlandpolitik". *Vierteljahrshefte für Zeitgeschichte*, vol. 4, pt. 1 (1956), p. 1—29.
Based on material from the Stresemann *Nachlass*. Gatzke argues that there was no contradiction in the Foreign Minister's policies towards the West and East and that he was not trying to play one side off against the other.

GATZKE, Hans W.
"Stresemann and Russia". *World Affairs Quarterly*, vol. 27, pt. 1 (1957), p. 344—55.
A condensed version of his aforementioned article.

KLEPSCH, Egon.
Die deutsche Russlandpolitik unter dem Reichsminister des Auswärtigen Amts Gustav Stresemann. Dissertation, University of Marburg (1954).
Now out of date; for one thing, he did not use the Stresemann papers.

MORGAN, Roger P.
"The Political Significance of German-Soviet Trade Negotiations, 1922—5". *Historical Journal*, vol. 6, pt. 2 (1963), p. 253—71.
Treats the economic aspects of German-Soviet relations and in particular the complex bargaining conducted by both between Rapallo and the legal and economic treaties of October 1925. Throughout the 1920s Russian trade was not an important element in the German economy and on this basis Morgan states that the 1925 treaties were motivated mainly by political rather than economic factors. He also shows that Stresemann regarded these treaties as a way of reassuring Russia that Germany was not abandoning her after Locarno. A well argued and informative paper.

ROSENBAUM, Kurt.
Community of Fate: German-Soviet Diplomatic Relations 1922—1928. Syracuse: Syracuse University Press (1965), 325 pp.
Although designed as a general survey, this book is essentially a biography of Count Brockdorff-Rantzau, the German Ambassador to Moscow (1922—28). His efforts towards promoting German-Soviet understanding are fully recorded, as are military connections between both countries. The relationship between Brockdorff and Stresemann, however, is not adequately assessed. The study as a whole is careful and competent.

RUGE, Wolfgang.
"Zur Problematik und Entstehungsgeschichte des Berliner Vertrages von 1926". *Zeitschrift für Geschichtswissenschaft*, vol. 9, pt. 4 (1961), p. 809—48.
The author states that Germany did not take the Treaty seriously as a means of attaining peace, but as a temporary breathing space for her imperialistic designs. He contrasts this with the "peace-loving socialist power" (Russia). The essay follows the pattern of Ruge's other writings: propagandistic and servile towards Russia. He ends this piece with a totally irrelevant eulogy of the KPD.

RUGE, Wolfgang.
Die Stellungnahme der Sowjetunion gegen die Besetzung des Ruhrgebietes: zur Geschichte der deutsch-sowjetischen Beziehungen von Januar bis September 1923. East Berlin: Akademie-Verlag (1962), 198 pp.
Neither in interpretation nor in documentation does this uncritical work add to our knowledge of anything. In his subservience to the Soviet Union, Ruge surpasses even his own previous impeccable standards, and his line of argument that the KPD and Russia were the real defenders of the German people in 1923 is sheer nonsense.

SCHIEDER, Theodor.
Die Probleme des Rapallo-Vertrages: eine Studie über die deutsch-russischen Beziehungen 1922—1926. Cologne: Westdeutscher Verlag (1956), 100 pp.
A sound, scholarly and thoughtful survey, although it was written before important documentary material became available. Essentially a work of synthesis which evaluates the important problems associated with Rapallo.

WALSDORFF, Martin.
Westorientierung und Ostpolitik: Stresemanns Russlandpolitik in der Locarno-Ära. Bremen: Schünemann (1971), 325 pp.
A detailed, thoroughly researched monograph which analyses Stresemann's delicate handling of a difficult segment of German foreign policy. Germany's inclusion in the Locarno Pact caused concern and unease in Russia over the future of her relations with Germany. Stresemann's task was to reassure her that Germany still put considerable store by the alliances previously concluded between the two countries.

(iv) Stalin to Hitler (1928—1933)

ALLARD, Sven.
Stalin und Hitler: die sowjetrussische Aussenpolitik 1930—1941. Munich: Francke (1974), 314 pp.
The earlier sections of the book give a good summary and analysis of Soviet attitudes towards the Weimar Republic before 1933.

MILLIKAN, Gordon W.
Soviet and Comintern Policy towards Germany, 1928—1933: a Case Study of Strategy and Tactics. Dissertation, University of Columbia (1970).
An examination of how Soviet foreign policy became increasingly subjected to Stalin's personal authority, and of the motives and characteristics of the dictator's attitude to Germany.

NICLAUSS, Karl-Heinz.
Die Sowjetunion und Hitlers Machtergreifung: eine Studie über die deutsch-russischen Beziehungen der Jahre 1929 bis 1935. Bonn: Röhrscheid (1966), 208 pp.

A most capable and soundly documented study which clearly details the diplomatic, economic, military and political connections between the countries. Niclauss shows that the main aim of Soviet foreign policy under Stalin was to prevent an alliance between Germany and the Western powers. It is interesting to note that Stalin hoped Schleicher's advent as Chancellor would lead to more intensive Red Army-*Reichswehr* collaboration.

RAUCH, Georg von.
"Stalin und die Machtergreifung Hitlers". *Das Parlament: Aus Politik und Zeitgeschichte* (4.3.1964).

A brief consideration of the implications of Hitler's advent to power for German-Soviet relations, and for the position of the KPD.

WEINGARTNER, Thomas.
Stalin und der Aufstieg Hitlers: die Deutschland-politik der Sowjetunion und der Kommunistischen Internationale 1929—1934. Berlin: de Gruyter (1970), 302 pp.

This study presents a rather unflattering interpretation of Stalin's understanding of and reaction to the rise of National Socialism. Indeed, Weingartner argues fairly convincingly that Stalin contributed, albeit unwittingly, to Hitler's triumph. In addition, the book puts forward a new interpretation of the KPD's "social fascist" tactics. Overall, a stimulating and provocative study.

D. POLISH—GERMAN RELATIONS

(i) General

BORRIES, Kurt.
"Deutschland und Polen zwischen Diktatur und Verständigung". *Die Welt als Geschichte*, vol. 18 (1958), p. 222—55.

A wide-ranging survey of the German-Polish problem and the different forms it has assumed in modern times. For the Weimar period (p. 240*ff*), Borries criticizes the Polish policy of de-germanization in Upper Silesia, West Prussia and Poznań. The foreign policy of the Weimar Republic in the east is also briefly sketched. The paper is based entirely on printed secondary sources.

BREYER, Richard.
Das deutsche Reich und Polen 1932—1937: Aussenpolitik und Volksgruppenfragen. Würzburg: Holzner (1955), 372 pp.

The ill concealed pro-German bias of the author mars an otherwise sound diplomatic study. The major issues affecting relations between the two countries before 1933, the German minority in Poland, and German revisionism, are discussed very much from the German point of view. The book is better when analysing the changes that took place in relations after Hitler assumed power.

BROSZAT, Martin.
Zweihundert Jahre deutsche Polenpolitik. Munich: Ehrenwirth Verlag (1963), 269 pp.

A very sound, scholarly narrative which forms an excellent introduction to the problem of German-Polish relations.

CZUBINSKI, Antoni.
"Traditionen der polnisch-deutschen revolutionären Zusammenarbeit in den Jahren 1918—1945". *Beiträge zur Geschichte der Deutschen Arbeiterbewegung*, vol. 16, pt. 1 (1974), p. 31—43.

Attempts unconvincingly to show that despite national rivalries, the working classes of both countries sought to establish and sustain common aims. The paper is a rather unintelligent piece of propaganda.

EPSTEIN, Fritz T.
See his work in section 4B(ii).

ERDMANN, Karl D.
"Das Problem der Ost- oder Westorientierung in der Locarno-Politik Stresemanns". *Geschichte in Wissenschaft und Unterricht*, vol. 6 (1955), p. 133—62.

Stresemann's Polish policy, as revealed in his *Nachlass*, is discussed here for the first time. Erdmann affirms that Stresemann never lost hope that the German-Polish frontiers would be revised in Germany's favour, but this was to be achieved by peaceful diplomatic and economic means, not by war. Erdmann's points are generally acceptable, but he undoubtedly plays down Stresemann's hostility to Poland; in this, the Foreign Minister shared the prejudice of the vast majority of Germans of the Weimar period.

FIEDOR, Karol.
"The Attitude of German Right-Wing Organisations to Poland in the Years 1918—1933". *Polish Western Affairs*, vol. 14, pt. 2 (1973), p. 247—69.

The author has presented a good deal of new material from Polish and East German archives to document the large number of anti-Polish civilian and paramilitary organizations in the Weimar Republic. They all rejected the territorial settlement of the Versailles Treaty and the more extremist of them advocated a war of revenge and reconquest against Poland. What Fiedor tries but fails to do, however, is to show the extent to which many of these groups were supported by reactionary elements in German big business and *Junker* circles.

FIEDOR, Karol.
See also his article in section 7D.

GASIOROWSKI, Zygmunt J.
"Stresemann and Poland Before Locarno". *Journal of Central European Affairs*, vol. 18, pt. 1 (1958), p. 25—47.

Using material from the Stresemann *Nachlass* and the files of the German Foreign Ministry, the author writes that Stresemann, though sharing the traditional German hatred and contempt of Poland, believed that revision of the German-Polish frontier could be achieved only by peaceful measures. But the author questions whether a peaceful solution was in fact feasible. The various methods employed by Stresemann to pressure Poland into accepting revision are discussed within the wider context of the Minister's foreign policy. Though in many respects a solid contribution, this paper adopts an old-fashioned approach to the writing of diplomatic history, where domestic influences on foreign policy are largely ignored. Also, the main theme of the essay, German-Polish relations, too often becomes lost in the general discussion.

GASIOROWSKI, Zygmunt J.
"Stresemann and Poland After Locarno". *Journal of Central European Affairs*, vol. 18, pt. 3 (1958), p. 292—317.
Another piece of competent but dull diplomatic history of the old type. There is a mass of detail on meetings, ambassadorial despatches and so on, so the aims of the paper are sometimes difficult to ascertain and follow. The author works his way through German-Polish relations until October 1929 when Stresemann died, underlining the lack of success which the German Foreign Minister met in all his approaches to the Polish problem. The author adds that even if Poland had lost the diplomatic battle with Germany, she would have fought first rather than accede to German demands.

GEMKOW, Heinrich.
See his article in section 14.

GOLCZEWSKI, Frank.
Das Deutschlandbild der Polen 1918—1939: eine Untersuchung der Historiographie und der Publizistik. Düsseldorf: Droste (1974), 316 pp.
A well researched, detailed and informative study which examines how one side regarded the other; the author successfully illustrates in particular the large degree of ignorance on both sides which unfortunately bred even more hatred and distrust.

GÖTTINGER ARBEITSKREIS.
Das östliche Deutschland: ein Handbuch. Edited by the Göttinger Arbeitskreis. Würzburg: Holzner (1959), 1014 pp.
This large volume is unfortunately designed to serve an all too obvious propaganda aim: to establish the justness of Germany's claims to the lost eastern territories which nowadays constitute part of Poland. The propaganda is couched in impeccable scholarly paraphernalia. The paper worth noting is Richard Breyer's on the position of German *Volkstum* in Poland between the wars.

HEIKE, Otto.
Das Deutschtum in Polen 1918—39. Bonn: Selbstverlag (1955), 296 pp.
Contains some useful information relating to the organization and activities of the German minority in Poland, but lacks objectivity in interpretation.

HÖLZLE, Erwin, and others.
Die deutschen Ostgebiete zur Zeit der Weimarer Republik. Cologne: Böhlau (1966), 232 pp.
An informative survey of the eastern territories, with facts on population, economy, etc.

KELLERMANN, Volkmar.
Schwarzer Adler, weisser Adler: die Polenpolitik der Weimarer Republik. Cologne: Markus-Verlag (1970), 196 pp.
A rather too general and vague review of Polish-German relations, written from an ill concealed German standpoint.

KORBEL, Josef.
Poland between East and West: Soviet and German Diplomacy toward Poland 1919—1933. Princeton: Princeton University Press (1963), 321 pp.
A useful contribution which provides a sound narrative and analysis of the theme, but there are many important gaps still to be filled. For instance, an assessment of Polish attitudes towards Russia and Germany is needed here to underline the terrible dilemma confronting Poland, flanked on west and east by two bitterly hostile nations. Korbel tends to underestimate Germany's hatred of Poland.

KREKELER, Norbert.
Revisionsanspruch und geheime Ostpolitik der Weimarer Republik: die Subventionierung der deutschen Minderheit in Polen 1919—1933. Stuttgart: Deutsche Verlagsanstalt (1973), 158 pp.
This book offers a very good discussion of the German minority's position in Poland and the extent to which it was secretly supported by the Reich government, especially the Foreign Office. But the author does not clarify the overall role of this policy within the wider context of Weimar's eastern policy.

LIPPELT, Helmut.
"'Politische Sanierung': zur deutschen Politik gegenüber Polen 1925/26". *Vierteljahrshefte für Zeitgeschichte*, vol. 19, pt. 4 (1971), p. 323—73.
The general theme of this detailed paper is Germany's policy of territorial revision after 1918 in the east, and Stresemann's efforts to tie in his Polish with his western policy after Locarno. A good outline of German-Polish relations since 1918 is provided as background.

LUDAT, Herbert (ed.).
Polen und Deutschland: wissenschaftliche Konferenz polnischer Historiker über die polnisch-deutschen Beziehungen in der Vergangenheit. Cologne: Böhlau (1963), 206 pp.
Part of a series sponsored by the Johann Gottfried Herder-*Forschungsrat*, Marburg, which aims to present information on the development of East European historiography since 1945. This volume contains translations of papers delivered at an historical conference in Breslau (Wroclaw) on the history of Polish-German relations. As such, this is an excellent introduction to the theme.

PUCHERT, Berthold.
Der Wirtschaftskrieg des deutschen Imperialismus gegen Polen 1925—1934. East Berlin: Akademie-Verlag (1963), 210 pp.
German big business and Poland's pre-war landowning élite are the villains of this blatantly tendentious and propagandistic work. However, amidst the prejudiced argumentation, there are some interesting factual data on economic ties between Germany and Poland.

REILE, Oskar.
Geheime Ostfront: die deutsche Abwehr im Osten 1921—1945. Munich: Verlag Welsermühl (1963), 475 pp.
An unsatisfactory and unobjective account of the German position in Poland both before and after 1933.

RHODE, Gotthold (ed.).
Die Ostgebiete des deutschen Reiches: ein Taschenbuch. Würzburg: Holzner (1955), 288 pp.
A number of authors have contributed a series of informative and balanced essays on political, economic, and social aspects of German-Polish relations from the early nineteenth century to the present. The former German eastern territories receive special attention.

RICHTHOFEN, Bolko von.
Deutschland und Polen: Schicksal einer nationalen Nachbarschaft. Weener: Risius Verlag (1959), 72 pp.
Unimportant; adds nothing new.

RIEKHOFF, Harald von.
German-Polish Relations, 1918—1933. Baltimore: Johns Hopkins University Press (1971), 421 pp.
This is probably the fullest and most accomplished account available on the theme, though it is far from being a definitive study. The author devotes a good deal of attention to criticizing the lack of feasibility in Stresemann's policy of peaceful revisionism in view of Polish intransigence. Other main aspects of German-Polish relations are also competently covered. The book is fundamentally unbalanced, however, because the Polish side of the relationship is not explained or appreciated. As a result, the author commits an above-average number of factual errors for a scholarly monograph.

ROOS, Hans.
Polen und Europa: Studien zur polnischen Aussenpolitik 1931—1939. Tübingen: Mohr (1957), 421 pp.
An important study of Polish foreign policy; the major theme is the development of relations with Germany. The narrative is solid and well documented, though the book as a whole is written from a German standpoint.

SCHUMANN, Rosemarie.
"Initiativen deutscher Pazifisten gegen die reaktionäre Polenpolitik in der Weimarer Republik". *Zeitschrift für Geschichtswissenschaft*, vol. 22, pt. 11 (1974), p. 1223—32.
An interesting but partial account of the futile efforts of German pacifists to introduce a degree of realism and perspective into official policy towards Poland.

SZYMANSKI, Antoni.
"Als polnischer Militärattaché in Berlin (1932—1939)". *Politische Studien*, vol. 13 (1962), p. 42—51.
Not particularly useful.

(ii) Danzig

DENNE, Ludwig.
Das Danzig-Problem in der deutschen Aussenpolitik 1934—39. Bonn: Röhrscheid (1959), 322 pp.
The early parts of this good survey outline the development of Danzig from 1920, when it became a Free City, to the advent of Hitler. The author shows how the city enjoyed a fair degree of economic prosperity and how Reich German influence was powerful. The depression created a new climate, however, in which the NSDAP began making an impact for the first time.

GAJDA, Patricia A.
British Policy Respecting Danzig and Upper Silesia 1919—1925. Dissertation, Case Western Reserve University (1972).
Clearly shows how Britain's economic and political interests made her support for Germany in both Danzig and Upper Silesia inevitable. This made for strained Anglo-Polish relations, which only began to improve once Lloyd George was out of office. The Polish side of the relationship, however, is completely ignored.

KIMMICH, Christoph M.
The Free City: Danzig and German Foreign Policy 1919—1934. New Haven: Yale University Press (1968), 196 pp.
Kimmich argues that the city was used by the German government as part of its revisionist policy in the east. Using much previously unpublished material, he offers a clear account of a complex problem. There is also an informative discussion of political, economic and social aspects of Danzig's development, emphasizing its intrinsic instability and growing dependence on Germany. The major weakness of the book is its failure to take into consideration the Polish view of the whole situation.

MASON, John B.
The Danzig Dilemma. Stanford: Stanford University Press (1945), 377 pp.
Presents a considerable amount of detailed information on Danzig's development as a Free City from 1919—20 to 1939. The author concentrates on a discussion of Danzig as a legal problem, outlining Poland's rights of access and intervention, and in consequence the political aspects of the problem do not receive the attention they deserve.

SAHM, Heinrich.
Erinnerungen aus meinen Danziger Jahren 1919—1930. Marburg: Herder-Institut (1955), 242 pp.
Very readable, often absorbing reminiscences of a *Danziger*.

ZIEHM, Ernst.
Aus meiner politischen Arbeit in Danzig 1914—1939. Marburg: Herder-Institut (1960), 200 pp.
Helps fill in some of the gaps in our understanding of Danzig's internal political development.

(iii) Upper Silesia

BERTRAM-LIBAL, Gisela.
"Die britische Politik in der Oberschlesienfrage 1919—1922". *Vierteljahrshefte für Zeitgeschichte*, vol. 20, pt. 2 (1972), p. 105—32.
A good analysis of the differences, both practical and of principle, between Britain and France *vis-à-vis* the complex Upper Silesia issue. Britain's economic and political interests predisposed her to support Germany, while France's sympathies undoubtedly lay with Poland.

CAMPBELL, F. Gregory.
"The Struggle for Upper Silesia 1919—1922". *Journal of Modern History*, vol. 42, pt. 3 (1970), p. 361—85.
A clear narrative and analysis of the problem. The division of the province in 1922, following a plebiscite, he interprets as a defeat for Germany. Particular stress is laid on the vital role of the Catholic Church in the conflict.

HARRINGTON, Joseph F.
The International Problem of Upper Silesia 1919—1922. Dissertation, University of Georgetown (1971).
Examines the problem from the point of view of Anglo-French relations, stressing the unwillingness of both sides to compromise. A competent survey which, however, only treads familiar ground.

KROLL, Vincent.
Die Genfer Konvention, betreffend Oberschlesien vom 15. Mai 1922. Dissertation, University of Cologne (1959).
Provides details on the proceedings of the Geneva Convention which met to work out the future of the province.

ROSENTHAL, Harry K.
"National Self-Determination: Upper Silesia".
Journal of Contemporary History, vol. 7, pts.
3—4 (1972), p. 231—41.
Argues that the multi-racial population of Upper Silesia defied the concept of national self-determination since no complete sense of nationality developed there. The author illustrates the difficulty of applying the usual criteria of nationality to the efforts of Polish and German extremists to claim Upper Silesia as their own. In the middle were whole groups of the population who considered themselves neither exclusively Polish nor German. This uncertain situation persists even to the present day, he concludes in this stimulating essay.

SCHUMANN, Wolfgang.
Oberschlesien 1918—19: vom gemeinsamen Kampf deutscher und polnischer Arbeiter. East Berlin: Rütten und Loening (1961), 314 pp.
A discussion of the alleged solidarity of the German and Polish working classes against reactionary chauvinists and capitalists in both countries. The national conflict takes second place to the class conflict. The work is clearly designed to prove the virtues of Marxist-Leninism and passes as yet another example of falsified history from East Germany.

SOBCZAK, Janusz.
"The Weimar Republic's Propaganda Concerning the Plebiscites in Warmia and Mazuria". *Polish Western Affairs*, vol. 13, pt. 2 (1972), p. 334—55.
A critical and detailed examination of the wide range of propaganda activities undertaken by the *Reichszentrale für Heimatdienst* in preparation for plebiscites provided for by the Treaty of Versailles in the strongly germanized districts of Warmia and Mazuria. The basis of German propaganda in these districts themselves was the *Ostdeutscher Heimatdienst.*

SONTAG, Ernst.
Adalbert (Wojciech) Korfanty: ein Beitrag zur Geschichte der polnischen Ansprüche auf Oberschlesien. Würzburg: Holzner (1954), 213 pp.
A biased and over-critical biography of the Polish revolutionary leader who led the Polish risings in Upper Silesia during 1919—22. The author totally fails to free himself from the prejudice which poisoned German-Polish relations at that time.

WITT, Peter-Christian.
"Zur Finanzierung des Abstimmungskampfes und der Selbstschutzorganisationen in Oberschlesien 1920—1922". *Militärgeschichtliche Mitteilungen*, vol. 13, pt. 1 (1973), p. 59—76.
A detailed breakdown of the official sources of financial aid provided from within Germany for the Upper Silesian struggles.

(iv) Frontier Revision[1]

ALBEE, Parker B.
See his work in section 4B(i).

BOURRET, Mary L.
The German-Polish Frontier of 1919, and Self-Determination. Dissertation, Stanford University (1946).
Based on narrow sources, and clearly out of date now.

1. Many of the works cited in section 19D(i) refer to one extent or another to the question of frontier revision.

HÖLTJE, Christian.
Die Weimarer Republik und das Ostlocarno-Problem 1919—1934: Revision oder Garantie der deutschen Ostgrenze von 1919. Würzburg: Holzner (1958), 306 pp.
The author shows that there was no support in Germany for an eastern Locarno that would recognize or guarantee Germany's eastern frontier with Poland (and Czechoslovakia); there was a broad consensus of opinion in favour of revision of the frontier. Differences arose only over how this revision was to be achieved. This is a substantial work, but the Polish and Czechoslovakian sides of the matter are hardly considered.

NITSCHE, Peter.
"Der Reichstag und die Festlegung der deutsch-polnischen Grenze nach dem Ersten Weltkrieg". *Historische Zeitschrift*, no. 216 (1973), p. 335—61.
A very good analysis of the different attitudes adopted by the German political parties towards the Versailles Treaty's settlement of the German-Polish frontier.

E. AUSTRO-GERMAN RELATIONS

(i) Anschluss

BERNSTEIN, Richard H.
The Anschluss Question in Weimar Politics. Dissertation, University of Princeton (1969).
A somewhat diffuse work which examines not only the *Anschluss* question in terms of domestic and foreign politics, but also the 1931 Customs Union project, and Brüning's foreign policy. What conclusions he has on *Anschluss* are lost in the welter of discussion of other themes.

BRANCATO, Albert L.
German Social Democrats and the Question of Austro-German Anschluss, 1918 to 1945. Dissertation, Bryn Mawr College (1975), 204 pp.
A limp discussion of the attitudes of different factions within the SPD towards *Anschluss.*

DUMIN, Frederick.
Background of the Austro-German Anschluss Movement 1918—1919. Dissertation, University of Wisconsin (1963).
Examines not only the German and Austrian motives, but also whether *Anschluss* was in fact a realistic possibility in 1918—19. There was a distinct lack of enthusiasm for the idea in Germany, whereas in Austria it was the socialists and nationalists who were making the running. However, a clear definition of what form *Anschluss* should take never materialized. A solid contribution.

GEYL, Jürgen.
Austria, Germany and the Anschluss, 1931—38. London: Oxford University Press (1963), 212 pp.
A good book, thoroughly researched and presenting new interpretations and perspectives on the theme. The sections on the pre-1933 period, however, are almost wholly concerned with the Customs Union project.

GOULD, S. W.
"Austrian Attitudes toward Anschluss, October 1918—September 1919". *Journal of Modern History*, vol. 22, pt. 3 (1950), p. 220—31.
Austrian agitation for *Anschluss* was at once tactical and shortlived, and confined mainly to the socialists and nationalists. However, there was much active opposition within Austria to the idea. These are the major conclusions of a disappointingly superficial essay.

KOGAN, Arthur G.
"Genesis of the Anschluss Problem: Germany and the Germans of the Habsburg Monarchy in the Autumn of 1918". *Journal of Central European Affairs*, vol. 20, pt. 1 (1960), p. 24—50.
Provides a clear and detailed account of the origins of Germany's *Anschluss* policy.

KÖLLING, Mirjam.
"Die Annexionsbestrebungen des deutschen Imperialismus gegenüber Österreich im Frühjahr 1919". *Jahrbuch für Geschichte*, vol. 1 (1967), p. 282—306.
The author has ignored a good deal of evidence in arguing that the *Anschluss* movement in Germany was promoted by capitalist imperialists and their allies. This is a travesty of the truth.

KOZEŃSKI, Jerzy.
"The Problem of an Austro-German Union in 1918—1919". *Polish Western Affairs*, vol. 8, pt. 1 (1967), p. 96—133.
A good, informative discussion of the historical and practical obstacles to be surmounted by those in favour of *Anschluss*.

LOW, Alfred D.
"Austria between East and West: Budapest and Berlin, 1918—1919". *Austrian History Yearbook*, vol. 4—5 (1968—69), p. 44—62.
Discusses alternative avenues of practical co-operation open to the Austrian government in 1918—19.

LOW, Alfred D.
The Anschluss Movement 1918—1919 and the Paris Peace Conference. Philadelphia: American Philosophical Society (1974), 495 pp.
A far-ranging and informatively judicious study which presents much new material on the subject.

MILLER, Susanne.
"Das Ringen um 'die einzige grossdeutsche Republik': die Sozialdemokratie in Österreich und im deutschen Reich zur Anschlussfrage 1918—19". *Archiv für Sozialgeschichte*, vol. 11 (1971), p. 1—67.
A long, detailed and definitive article which analyses the attitudes adopted by the Austrian and German social democrats towards *Anschluss*. The author shows that the German SPD gave only half-hearted support to the idea, while their Austrian *confrères* saw it as the best way of ensuring that the Habsburgs would never return.

MYERS, Duane P.
"Berlin versus Vienna: Disagreement about Anschluss in the Winter of 1918—19". *Central European History*, vol. 5, pt. 2 (1972), p. 150—75.
Examines the nature of the Austrian and German governments' disagreement over which procedures to adopt in pursuit of *Anschluss*, and also over the degree of importance each attached to the concept itself. However, in the face of Western opposition to *Anschluss*, differences of opinion between Germany and Austria substantially decreased.

PRERADOVICH, Nikolaus von.
Die Wilhelmstrasse und der Anschluss Österreichs 1918—1933. Frankfurt: Lang (1971), 327 pp.
A rather disappointing study which in fact concentrates heavily on Austrian internal developments before 1933;

only passing reference is given to German government policies. The author has failed to digest his large amount of material, however, and the narrative lacks organization and coherence. We still await a solid diplomatic history of the pre-history and development of the *Anschluss* concept.

SUVAL, Stanley.
"Overcoming Kleindeutschland: the Politics of Historical Myth-Making in the Weimar Republic". *Central European History*, vol. 2, pt. 4 (1969), p. 312—30.
This paper traces the undermining of the traditional *kleindeutsch* concept in the German historical profession after 1918 and the concurrent promotion of the *Anschluss* idea. In this, Austria was allotted for the first time a new political importance, caused largely by Germany's defeat and isolation after 1919. The whole *kleindeutsch* historiography had to be scrapped after 1919, while historians such as Friedrich Meinecke, Hermann Oncken, Willy Andreas and others took the lead in propagating the new orthodoxy.

SUVAL, Stanley.
The Anschluss Question in the Weimar Era: a Study of Nationalism in Germany and Austria 1918—1932. Baltimore: Johns Hopkins University Press (1974), 240 pp.
An interesting study of how the concept of *Anschluss* developed in both countries before the advent to power of Hitler. The author argues that *Anschluss* became an important constituent of German nationalism and revisionist foreign policy, and that it had significant domestic repercussions, many of which created confusion and ambiguity.

(ii) Customs Union 1931

CURTIUS, Julius.
Bemühung um Österreich: das Scheitern des Zollunionsplans von 1931. Heidelberg: Winter Verlag (1947), 106 pp.
Argues contrary to all other evidence that the Union was meant, not as a first step towards *Anschluss*, but as a measure to strengthen Austria. Curtius, who succeeded Stresemann as Foreign Minister, seems to have believed in 1931 that the Allies would raise no serious objections to the project, which says something for his competence as Foreign Minister.

GEIGENMÜLLER, Ernst.
"Botschaften von Hoesch und der deutsch-österreichische Zollunionsplan von 1931". *Historische Zeitschrift*, no. 195 (1962), p. 581—95.
This essay is based largely on the private papers of von Hoesch, the German Ambassador to Paris in the early 1930s, and severely criticizes Brüning's handling of the issue.

HAUSER, Oswald.
"Der Plan einer deutsch-österreichischen Zollunion von 1931 und die europäische Föderation". *Historische Zeitschrift*, no. 179 (1955), p. 45—92.
A very good and well argued paper which puts forward the reasons why Germany wanted a customs union in 1931.

JOHNSON, Norman M.
The Austro-German Customs Union Project in German Diplomacy. Dissertation, University of North Carolina (1974).
Traces the origins and development of the idea for such a union within the wider framework of German diplomacy after 1918. The German Foreign Ministry was especially

keen on the idea but seriously underestimated France's opposition; the project was designed as a first step towards *Anschluss*, and would also stimulate Germany's foreign policy in a way favourable to its longer term aims in Europe (revision of Versailles, etc.). Domestic considerations also played a part. This is a full and satisfactory study.

KRULIS-RANDA, J.
Das deutsch-österreichische Zollunionsprojekt von 1931. Zürich (1955).
Useful in trying to place the 1931 project within the wider context of German-Austrian economic development since the nineteenth century.

STAMBROOK, F. G.
"The German-Austrian Customs Union Project of 1931: a Study of German Methods and Motives". *Journal of Central European Affairs*, vol. 21, pt. 1 (1961), p. 15—44.
A thought-provoking and scholarly paper which discusses Germany's motives and methods. The author sees the methods used to have been in stark contrast to Stresemann's careful diplomacy. He examines all possible German motives, and concludes that the project was not designed as a step towards European union, nor was it meant to aid the Austrian economy. It was a long-planned affair designed to achieve Curtius's aim of attaching Austria irrevocably to Germany, and ensuring for Germany a dominant position of influence in South-East Europe. In consequence, the so-called "Little Entente" would be disrupted, and ultimately a situation would be created in which Poland would be forced by economic pressure to make territorial concessions to Germany in the east. Clearly, therefore, German motivation was complex and exceedingly ambitious, but Stambrook does not believe there was ever much chance of success.

F. CZECHOSLOVAK-GERMAN RELATIONS

ALEXANDER, Manfred.
Der deutsch-tschechoslowakische Schiedsvertrag von 1925 im Rahmen der Locarno-Verträge. Munich: Oldenbourg (1970), 212 pp.
This work provides a competent and full discussion of German and Czech efforts to achieve an agreement which would help normalize relations between both countries. An impressive range of documentary material has been worked into the narrative, though the author has failed to examine adequately certain basic issues such as security and German revisionism.

BRÜGEL, Johann W.
Czechoslovakia before Munich: the German Minority Problem and British Appeasement Policy.[1] London: Cambridge University Press (1973), 334 pp.
Essentially a work of diplomatic history centring on the international problem of Czechoslovakia and appeasement in the 1930s. As such, the author's interpretations are too often dogmatic and tendentious. However, he does provide a clear summary of German-Czech relations and German-Sudeten relations before 1933 (though he ignores Hitler's attitudes to Czechoslovakia).

BURIAN, Peter.
"Tschechoslowakischer Verzicht auf die Sudetengebiete? Ein Vorschlag František Modráčeks aus dem Juni 1919". *Zeitschrift für Ostforschung*, vol. 23, pt. 3 (1974), p. 468—74.
Publishes an article which appeared on 21 June 1919 in *Socialistické Listy*, a weekly newspaper edited by Modráček; it forms an interesting footnote to German-Czech relations in Czechoslovakia in 1919.

1. This is an adapted version of his earlier book *Tschechen und Deutsche 1918—1938*. Munich: Nymphenburger Verlag (1967), 662 pp.

CAMPBELL, F. Gregory.
Czechoslovak-German Relations during the Weimar Republic, 1919—1933. Dissertation, Yale University (1967).
A brief review of a complex question. Campbell does say interesting things about Czech fears of a resurgent Germany, while adding that before 1933 Germany made no attempt to incorporate the Sudetenland into the Reich. Diplomatic relations between the two countries 1918—33 were therefore correct, and only with the onset of the depression did the Sudeten question begin to assume disturbing proportions.

CAMPBELL, F. Gregory.
Confrontation in Central Europe: Weimar Germany and Czechoslovakia. Chicago: University of Chicago Press (1975), 352 pp.
An enlarged version of his doctoral dissertation, though the same main lines of investigation are maintained. A substantial and competent survey.

FUCHS, Gerhard.
"Aggressive Planungen des deutschen Imperialismus gegenüber der Tschechoslowakei in der Zeit der Weimarer Republik". *Zeitschrift für Geschichtswissenschaft*, vol. 16, pt. 10 (1968), p. 1309—21.
What some might describe as ordinary commercial enterprise, Fuchs calls "aggressive plans". The title tells all there is to know about this biased essay.

FUCHS, Gerhard.
"Die Haltung des deutschen Imperialismus zur Gründung der tschechoslowakischen Republik 1918/19". *Jahrbuch für Geschichte*, vol. 6 (1972), p. 263—308.
Argues absurdly that German capitalists and imperialists had rapacious designs on Czechoslovakia from 1918. Ignores a mass of evidence which proves the contrary.

FUCHS, Gerhard.
"Die politischen Beziehungen der Weimarer Republik zur tschechoslowakischen Republik Frieden bis zum Ende der revolutionären Nachkriegskrise". *Jahrbuch für Geschichte*, vol. 9 (1973), p. 281—337.
Contains some useful and interesting information but again the author's rigid Marxist-Leninist outlook precludes an objective assessment.

GAJA, Koloman; KVACEK, Robert.
Germany and Czechoslovakia 1918—1945. Prgaue: Orbis (1965), 171 pp.
A highly selective compilation of documents designed to show German policy in the worst possible light.

GASIOROWSKI, Zygmunt J.
"Beneš and Locarno: Some Unpublished Documents". *Review of Politics*, vol. 20, pt. 2 (1958), p. 209—24.
Records the calm and positive reaction of Foreign Minister Beneš to Stresemann's offer to the West on 20 January 1925 for Germany to guarantee the territorial *status quo* on the Rhine, without being willing to give assurances about the territorial situation in eastern Europe. In private, however, Beneš expressed fears about the permanence of the Polish frontiers, as extracts from several documents listed here reveal.

RABL, Kurt (ed.).
Das Ringen um das sudetendeutsche Selbstbestimmungsrecht 1918/19. Munich: Lersche (1958), 245 pp.
Presents relevant documents illustrating the struggle over this issue.

RASCHHOFER, Hermann.
Die Sudetenfrage: ihre völkerrechtliche Entwicklung vom Ersten Weltkrieg bis zur Gegenwart. Munich (1953).
An unscholarly and superficial work.

SEIBT, Ferdinand.
Deutschland und die Tschechen: Geschichte einer Nachbarschaft in der Mitte Europas. Munich: List (1974), 356 pp.
A reliable and informative general survey.

WELISCH, Sophie A.
The Sudeten German Question in the League of Nations. Dissertation, Fordham University (1968).
Examines the rather uneasy position of the Sudeten Germans in Czechoslovakia, the Sudeten-Weimar Republic relationship, and the Sudeten question as an international problem. Particular emphasis is put on Sudeten efforts to call world diplomatic attention to their alleged plight; such efforts met with no success. All these themes, however, are not effectively brought together in a badly organized study.

WISKEMANN, Elizabeth.
Czechs and Germans. London: Oxford University Press (1967). New ed.
An adequate introductory review of the Czech-German *Gegensatz.*

G. ITALO-GERMAN RELATIONS

CASSELS, Alan.
"Mussolini and German Nationalism 1922–1925". *Journal of Modern History*, vol. 35, pt. 2 (1963), p. 137–57.
A revisionist analysis of Mussolini's early foreign policy which shows that as regards Germany, his policy was anything but moderate as was formerly believed. He promoted intrigues with German nationalist parties and *Reichswehr* generals in an attempt to exploit German nationalism for Italy's own ends. His main concern throughout was to protect Italian interests in the Alto Adige. Cassels also investigates the nature and extent of Mussolini's contact with the NSDAP. The author, however, does not quantify the extent of Fascist aid to German nationalists as a whole, nor does he specify which German groups (apart from the NSDAP) were approached. Too much of what he says is speculative and based on fragmentary sources.

CASSELS, Alan.
Mussolini's Early Diplomacy. Princeton: Princeton University Press (1970).
A study of Mussolini's diplomacy 1922–27, showing how he employed a variety of conventional and unconventional diplomatic methods; for example, the use of agents, force, threats, outrageous bluff. On Germany, the author has not made good the fundamental deficiencies already noted in his earlier article (see above).

EISMANN, Christian H.
Weimar Germany and Fascist Italy: Diplomatic Relations 1922–1933. Dissertation, University of Idaho (1973).
Despite ideological differences, democratic Germany and Fascist Italy developed a limited understanding during the pre-1933 period. Conservative elements in the German Foreign Office admired what Mussolini had done for Italy. Nonetheless, a close political association did not emerge for several reasons, including profound differences over the problem of South Tyrol, and the *Anschluss* issue. This is an informative and helpful survey.

ROSEN, Edgar R.
"Mussolini und Deutschland 1922–1923".
Vierteljahrshefte für Zeitgeschichte, vol. 5, pt. 1 (1957), p. 17–41.
Rosen argues that as a result of Mussolini's low opinion of Stresemann as a tool of France, the dictator lost interest in Germany. That this argument is erroneous is shown, however unsatisfactorily, by Alan Cassels' article (see earlier this section).

ROSEN, Edgar R.
"Die deutsche Rechte und das faschistische Italien". *Zeitschrift für Politik*, vol. 8 (1961), p. 334–8.
Relates a curious incident in German-Italian relations in 1923–24 in which the Italians, having lost confidence in Stresemann, sought to strengthen their friendly links with the DNVP in the expectation that this would somehow produce favourable results when Germany once again had a nationalist government.

STAMBROOK, F. G.
German Relations with Italy 1920–32, with Special Reference to the Danubian Region. Dissertation, University of London (1960).
Useful.

H. BALTIC-GERMAN RELATIONS

HIDEN, J. W.
German Policy towards the Baltic States of Estonia and Latvia. Dissertation, University of London (1970).
An instructive account.

HIDEN, J. W.
"The Baltic Germans and German Policy towards Latvia after 1918". *Historical Journal*, vol. 13, pt. 2 (1970), p. 295–317.
Germany was anxious for good relations with the Baltic states since they provided a means of indirect access to Russia. The German government was therefore compelled to change its attitude towards the Baltic Germans, encouraging those in Latvia to renounce their annexionist aims and to settle down and work constructively for Latvia, notwithstanding the loss of their former pre-eminent economic position as a result of Latvian reforms. Paul Schiemann, the most important German leader in Latvia, agreed with the policy of reconciliation, and consequently the Weimar Republic did manage to establish friendly relations with Latvia.

PLIEG, Ernst-Albrecht.
Das Memelland 1920–1939. Würzburg: Holzner (1962), 268 pp.
A discussion of the German minority's efforts for autonomous rights within the state of Lithuania. The study is written very much from a German point of view.

I. MISCELLANEOUS

CRONENBERG, Allen T.
The Volksbund für das Deutschtum im Ausland: völkisch Ideology and German Foreign Policy, 1881—1939. Dissertation, Stanford University (1970).
In the 1920s and 1930s the VDA was the largest organization concerned with the affairs of ethnic Germans outside the boundaries of the Reich; it also emerged as a powerful instrument of German propaganda against the Versailles Treaty, particularly after 1933. This is a brief study of the organization's origins and development, many aspects of which still require further research.

FIEBER, Hans-Joachim.
"Die Kolonialgesellschaft — ein Instrument der deutschen Kolonialpolitik in Afrika während der Weimarer Republik". *Zeitschrift für Geschichtswissenschaft*, vol. 9, special number (1961).
Treats the Colonial Society as a relic of the Second Empire, which in many respects it was, and as an agent of aggressive imperialism during the Weimar era, which it was not.

FIEDERLEIN, Friedrich M.
Der deutsche Osten und die Regierungen Brüning, Papen, Schleicher. Dissertation, University of Würzburg (1967).
A large, well documented but somewhat uneven work.

GLAIM, Lorne E.
Sino-German Relations 1919—1925: German Diplomatic, Economic and Cultural Re-Entry into China after World War I. Dissertation, Washington State University (1973).
Traces how Germany picked up the threads again in China following the collapse of her imperialist involvement there in 1917—18. Commercial and diplomatic motives predominated and by 1925 trade between the two countries had surpassed pre-1914 levels. German military personnel arrived only later. A useful introduction to the topic.

MAHRAD, Ahmad.
Die deutsch-persischen Beziehungen von 1918— 1933. Frankfurt: Lang (1974), 478 pp.
The author has researched his topic exhaustively and come up with a thorough and richly detailed study of the major aspects of Germany's connections with Persia. These links were not insignificant. But the study as a whole mainly serves to underline the fact that despite all its complex and burdensome domestic and foreign problems, the Weimar Republic was resourceful enough to develop interests in distant and relatively obscure parts of the globe.

PADE, Werner.
"Die Expansionspolitik des deutschen Imperialismus gegenüber Lateinamerika 1918— 1933". *Zeitschrift für Geschichtswissenschaft*, vol. 22, pt. 6 (1974), p. 578—90.
Was German commercial activity in Latin America motivated by the desire to extend Germany's capitalist-imperialistic ethos, or simply by the idea of making a profit? Pade, true to his stridently proclaimed Marxist-Leninist principles, has no doubt that the former motive prevailed. Others might differ.

SCHMOKEL, Wolf W.
Dream of Empire: German Colonialism 1919— 1945. New Haven: Yale University Press (1964), 204 pp.
A limited, somewhat fragmentary work whose principal objective is to show that, contrary to common belief, Hitler was after all deeply interested in colonies *per se.* Unfortunately, the author's case remains unproved; National Socialism never developed a systematic colonial policy as Schmokel seems to think. This interesting theme requires further and more careful research by someone with a better understanding of the dynamics of the Third Reich (see the work by Klaus Hildebrand in section 27).

PART **2**

The Rise of National Socialism

Documentary Sources

20

ALLIED GOVERNMENTS.
The Trial of the Major War Criminals before the International Military Tribunal. Proceedings: vols. 1—23; Documents in Evidence: vols. 24—42.
Nuremberg: The Allied Governments (1947—49).
This is a most important collection, containing the complete version of the main trials' proceedings as well as the full text of the documents used in evidence. For the pre-1933 period, however, the information provided therein is rather sketchy and low in quality.

ASKEN, William C.
"The Nuremberg Documents". *Journal of Central European Affairs*, vol. 11, pt. 3 (1951), p. 302—11.
A review article which assesses the importance of the documentation assembled at the major Nuremberg trial. A full description of the documents is provided. While stressing their incompleteness, and the need for historians to supplement them with other sources, the author concludes that this is "the most important single collection of documents on the Nazi régime".

UNITED KINGDOM GOVERNMENT.
The Trial of German Major War Criminals. 22 vols.
London: H.M.S.O. (1946—50).
A useful verbatim record of proceedings at the trial.

UNITED KINGDOM GOVERNMENT.
Law Reports of Trials of War Criminals. 15 vols.
London: H.M.S.O. (1947—49).
A record of subsequent trials held at Nuremberg.

UNITED STATES GOVERNMENT.
Nazi Conspiracy and Aggression. 8 vols. plus 2 supplementary vols. Washington, D.C.: U.S. Government Printing Office (1946—48).
Contains translations of most of the documents presented at the trial by the United Kingdom and United States prosecutions. There are also translated versions of a selection of important documents presented by defence attorneys, as well as translations of certain statements made by the accused.

UNITED STATES GOVERNMENT.
Trials of War Criminals before the Nuremberg Military Tribunals. 14 vols. Washington, D.C.: U.S. Government Printing Office (1951—53).
The United States government's record of subsequent trials held at Nuremberg.

21

Totalitarianism, Fascism, and Authoritarianism

ADORNO, Theodor W., and others.
The Authoritarian Personality. (Studies in
Prejudice). New York: Harper (1950), 990 pp.
A most interesting, comprehensive assessment of the many
facets of authoritarianism.

ALBRECHT, Dieter.
"Zum Begriff des Totalitarismus". *Geschichte in
Wissenschaft und Unterricht*, vol. 26, pt. 3 (1975),
p. 135—41.
A few not very helpful remarks on the meaning of total-
itarianism.

ALLARDYCE, G. (ed.).
The Place of Fascism in European History. Englewood Cliffs: Prentice-Hall (1971).
Not a particularly instructive volume; says little that has
not been said before.

ANDERSON, Eugene N.
**"Freedom and Authoritarianism in German
History".** In Gabriel A. Almond (ed.). *The Struggle
for Democracy in Germany*. New ed. New York:
Russell and Russell (1965), p. 3—32.
Anderson seeks to determine whether the German people
are congenitally authoritarian on the basis of a review of
general trends in modern Germany before 1933. The last
part of the essay provides an interesting overall synopsis of
developments in the Weimar Republic. He concludes that
the idea of authority in Germany was distorted by the
peculiar conditions prevailing during the 1918—33 period,
and that this became the basis for the rise of National
Socialism, which in turn abused the idea of authority for
its own totalitarian ends.

ARENDT, Hannah.
The Origins of Totalitarianism. New York:
Harcourt Brace Jovanovich (1973), 527 pp.
New ed.
A major theoretical analysis of the socio-psychological
background of National Socialism and totalitarianism in the
twentieth century. Scholarly and insightful, the book provides excellent treatment of the themes (anti-semitism,
völkisch nationalism, and imperialism) which paved the way
for the later emergence of right-wing totalitarianism.

ARON, Raymond.
Democracy and Totalitarianism. London: Weidenfeld & Nicolson (1968), 262 pp.
A work of theoretical sociology which examines the nature
of political organization in an industrial society. The book
is badly written, however, and is of only limited value in
helping one comprehend the elements of totalitarianism.

BAUER, Otto; **MARCUSE**, Herbert; **ROSENBERG**
Arthur, and others.
**Faschismus und Kapitalismus: Theorien über die
sozialen Ursprünge und die Funktion des Faschis-
mus.** Edited by Wolfgang Abendroth. Frankfurt:
Europäische Verlagsanstalt (1967), 187 pp.
A reader presenting different Marxist interpretations of the
origins of fascism from Otto Bauer, Herbert Marcuse,
Arthur Rosenberg, Angelo Tasca and August Thalheimer.
There is of course unanimous agreement that fascism orig-
inated in and represented the interests of capitalism.

BARBU, Zevedei.
Democracy and Dictatorship. New York: Grove
Press (1956), 275 pp.
An interesting and cogently argued study which emphasizes
above all the psychological impetus behind modern total-
itarian movements.

BLANK, A. S.
**"Der deutsche Faschismus in der sowjetischen
Historiographie".** *Zeitschrift für Geschichtswissen-
schaft*, vol. 23, pt. 4 (1975), p. 433—52.
A review article of more than usual interest from East
Germany.

BURROWES, Robert.
"Totalitarianism: the Revised Standard Version".
World Politics, vol. 21, pt. 2 (1969—70), p. 272—
94.
A critique of the theories of totalitarianism which held
sway from 1945 until the 1960s.

BUCHHEIM, Hans.
Totalitäre Herrschaft: Wesen und Merkmale.
Munich: Kösel (1962), 138 pp.

A thoughtful discussion of the mass psychological motivation of totalitarian movements, particularly of the fascist and Communist versions. The author offers a very good analysis and comparison of right-wing and left-wing totalitarianism.

CASSINELLI, C. W.
"Totalitarianism, Ideology and Propaganda".
Journal of Politics, vol. 22, pt. 1 (1960), p. 68—95.
A useful examination of some aspects of totalitarianism in practice.

CASSINELLI, C. W.
"The Totalitarian Party". *Journal of Politics*, vol. 24, pt. 2 (1962), p. 111—41.
Discusses the composition and nature of practical totalitarianism, but overemphasizes the influence and significance of the leader figure in totalitarian movements.

CHRISTIE, Richard; JAHODA, Marie (eds.).
Studies in the Scope and Method of "The Authoritarian Personality". Glencoe (Illinois): The Free Press (1954).
Not an especially distinguished collection of essays by various hands, though Edward A. Shils' piece on "Authoritarianism, 'Right' and 'Left'" (p. 24—49) is worth noting.

COLLOTTI, Enzo.
"International Fascism as a Historical Phenomenon". *Wiener Library Bulletin*, vol. 19, pt. 4 (1965), p. 3—5.
Discusses the problem of defining fascism and refers to a recent Italian publication on the topic by Angelo del Boca and Mario Giovana: *I 'Figli del Sole': Mezzo Secolo di Nazifascismo nel Mondo* (Milan: Feltrinelli (1965), 610 pp).

FETSCHER, Iring.
"Faschismus und Nationalsozialismus". *Politische Vierteljahrsschrift*, vol. 3, pt. 1 (1962), p. 42—63.
A critical and edifying evaluation of Soviet and Marxist interpretations of fascism which reveals the extent to which the term "fascist" has been abused for political purposes.

FRIEDRICH, Carl J. (ed.).
Totalitarianism. Cambridge (Mass.): Harvard University Press (1954), 386 pp.
Contains nineteen papers originally delivered at a conference at the American Academy of Arts and Sciences. As such, the volume constitutes one of the best introductions to the topic. Aspects such as political theory, psychology and sociology are brought into the discussion about the nature of totalitarianism. Friedrich himself sees totalitarianism as an historically unique force.

FRIEDRICH, Carl J.
"Fascism versus Totalitarianism: Ernst Nolte's Views Re-examined". *Central European History*, vol. 4, pt. 3 (1971), p. 271—84.
A critical but generous appraisal of Nolte's major works (see below). Nolte's concept of the "phenomenology" of fascism receives particular attention.

FRIEDRICH, Carl J.; BRZEZINSKI, Zbigniew K.
Totalitarian Dictatorship and Autocracy.
Cambridge (Mass.): Harvard University Press (1956), 346 pp.
An excellent and deep analysis of the typology of modern totalitarianism. In the authors' view, totalitarian dictatorship is completely different from autocracy; they explain this in clear, unequivocal terms.

GILBERT, G. M.
The Psychology of Dictatorship. New York: Ronald Press (1950), 327 pp.
A discussion of the nature of totalitarianism, and National Socialism in particular, from a psychological standpoint. Useful only as an introduction to the theme because many fundamental aspects of the problem are treated too lightly.

GREBING, Helga.
Aktuelle Theorien über Faschismus und Konservatismus. Mainz: Kohlhammer (1974), 117 pp.
A succinct, critical consideration of recent interpretations of fascism. Most useful as an introduction to the debate.

GREENE, N. (ed.).
Fascism: an Anthology. New York (1968).
Of no especial value.

GREGOR, A. James.
The Ideology of Fascism: the Rationale of Totalitarianism. New York: Free Press (1969), 493 pp.
The author's description of Italian Fascist ideology is very sound, but he then uses his description as an example to suggest a typology for all totalitarian movements, which is far-fetched and unconvincing.

GREGOR, A. James.
"Fascism and Modernization: Some Addenda".
World Politics, vol. 26, pt. 3 (1974), p. 370—84.
The author takes issue with H.A. Turner's article (see below in this section), arguing that fascism did not impede modern developments. He rejects Turner's allegedly ill-developed definition of "modernization".

GREIFFENHAGEN, Martin; KÜHNL, Reinhard; MÜLLER, Johann B.
Zur Problematik eines politischen Begriffs. Munich: List (1972), 156 pp.
A stimulating discussion of the nature, interpretation, and definition of fascism.

HAYES, Paul.
Fascism. London: Allen & Unwin (1973), 260 pp.
A quite uninspiring description of the origins of fascist ideology and its later development. Hayes hardly does credit to the complexity of the debate on this theme.

HILDEBRAND, Klaus.
"Stufen des Totalitarismus-Forschung". *Politische Vierteljahrsschrift*, vol. 9 (Sept 1968), p. 397—422.
A compelling critique of theories on totalitarianism prevailing since 1945. The author discusses how such theories became less convincing as a result of the thaw in the cold war.

HURST, Michael.
"What is Fascism?" *Historical Journal*, vol. 11 (1968), p. 165—85.
A critical and erudite review of a few notable recent books on fascism. The author offers a careful analysis of the difficulties involved in defining fascism and concludes that while fascist parties had a more or less uniform doctrine (if varying social compositions), fascist régimes were composed of diverse elements in which the original fascist doctrine was diluted. There are one or two minor blemishes in the essay, for example, where Hurst refers to Hitler as "a fundamentally crazy man" (p. 184). Such statements are tasteless as well as erroneous.

JÄNICKE, Martin.
Totalitäre Herrschaft: Anatomie eines politischen Begriffes. Berlin: Duncker & Humblot (1971), 282 pp.
An important appraisal of the concept of totalitarianism on the basis of a complex theoretical model. Indeed, the discussion is perhaps too theoretical; the introduction of a good deal more empirical data would have been more than welcome, and would have given the book a better balance.

KEDWARD, H. R.
Fascism in Western Europe 1900—45. Glasgow: Blackie (1969), 260 pp.
Although meant for non-specialists and the general reader, this volume is still too superficial and simplistic to be of much use. Incredibly, only English and French sources have been consulted despite the fact that Germany is included in the discussion. The book is characterized by sloppy thinking and unacceptable generalizations.

KITCHEN, Martin.
See his article in section 6B(vii)(i).

KUHN, Axel.
Das faschistische Herrschaftssystem und die moderne Gesellschaft. Hamburg: Hoffmann & Campe (1973), 157 pp.
A disappointingly thin and weakly argued examination of fascism. Rejecting the reductionist thesis of orthodox Marxism, he adduces a materialist theory within which he discusses the reasons for the success of National Socialism. In essence, however, Kuhn merely restates well-worn ideas which link Hitler to Germany's disturbed economic conditions during 1918—33.

KÜHNL, Reinhard.
Deutschland zwischen Demokratie und Faschismus. Munich: Carl Hanser (1969), 187 pp.
An unscholarly and frankly propagandistic work which only reiterates with minor adjustments the conventional Marxist view that fascism is an outgrowth and instrument of decaying capitalism. The discussion essentially amounts to an attack on the present political and social make-up of the Federal Republic. In short, the kind of work one normally associates with dogmatic East German historians.

KÜHNL, Reinhard.
Formen bürgerlicher Herrschaft: Liberalismus — Faschismus. Reinbek bei Hamburg: Rowohlt (1971), 189 pp.
Another ideologically slanted work which seems to have been designed for the popular market.

KÜHNL, Reinhard.
"Probleme einer Theorie über den internationalen Faschismus". *Politische Vierteljahrsschrift*, vol. 16, pt. 1 (1975), p. 89—121.
A useful review of the topic with reference to more recent scholarly publications and interpretations. Kühnl's own views on fascism, however, are highly debatable.

LAQUEUR, Walter Z.; MOSSE, George L. (eds.).
International Fascism, 1920—1945. London: Weidenfeld & Nicolson (1966), 201 pp.
Comprises a series of essays by a number of scholars on the development and characteristics of fascism in Europe. The papers, originally published in the *Journal of Contemporary History*, vol. I (1966), form a very good introduction to the subject.

LIPSET, Seymour M.
Political Man: the Social Bases of Politics. New York: Doubleday (1960), 432 pp.
An immensely sound and thoughtful sociological-political analysis of behavioural patterns in modern political development, especially where the latter relates to the function of democracy in advanced industrial societies. The author also discusses in stimulating fashion a number of governmental systems under the general label of "fascism"; he provides a penetrating appraisal of the traditional categories of "left", "right", and "centre".

LIPSET, Seymour M.
"Der 'Faschismus', die Linke, die Rechte, und die Mitte". *Kölner Zeitschrift für Soziologie- und Sozialpsychologie*, vol. 11 (1959), p. 401—44.
The theme of the different varieties of fascism is discussed in expert fashion.

NEUMANN, Friedrich L.
The Democratic and the Authoritarian State: Essays in Political and Legal Theory. Edited by Herbert Marcuse. Glencoe (Illinois): The Free Press (1957).
A rather heavy but useful theoretical work.

NEUMANN, Sigmund.
Permanent Revolution. New York: Praeger (1965). New ed.
Although originally published in 1942, this study has some interesting observations to make about modern totalitarianism. However, too much emphasis is put on the role of the leader figure in totalitarian movements.

NIPPERDEY, Thomas.
"Der Faschismus in seiner Epoche: zu den Werken von Ernst Nolte zum Faschismus". *Historische Zeitschrift*, no. 210 (1970), p. 620—38.
An instructive critical review of Nolte's theories.

NOLTE, Ernst.
"Zur Phänomenologie des Faschismus". *Vierteljahrshefte für Zeitgeschichte*, vol. 10, pt. 4 (1962), p. 373—407.
The author's thesis is that fascism is not simply to be associated with the Italian brand, but constitutes an historical phenomenon in its own right which must be assessed as such. He constructs a typological model by stressing the elements common to all varieties of post-1918 European fascism which in turn justifies, in his view, the application of the concept "phenomenology of fascism". The thesis is certainly challenging and forcefully prosecuted, but suffers from an over-philosophical approach and a distinct reluctance to acknowledge the importance of the many diverse ingredients that went into the make-up of fascism.

NOLTE, Ernst.
"Konservativismus und Nationalismus". *Zeitschrift für Politik*, vol. 11, pt. 1 (1964), p. 5—20.
A discussion of the relevance of conservatism and nationalism to the development of a climate conducive to fascism.

NOLTE, Ernst.
The Three Faces of Fascism: Action française, Italian Fascism, and National Socialism. London: Weidenfeld & Nicolson (1965), 561 pp.
An abstract, theoretical, and learned contribution which argues that fascism cannot be understood simply in political terms, but as part of a more general movement directed

against bourgeois civilization. The author seeks to justify his thesis on the basis of empirical data gathered on the three examples of fascism indicated in the book's subtitle. However, Nolte over-intellectualizes about a movement that was intrinsically anti-intellectual, pragmatic, and activist; he puts too much stress on the ideological and philosophical aspects of fascism, erroneously taking these as representative of the nature and character of the movement. Fascism is to be comprehended first and foremost by its actions and performance and not by the garbled writings of its principal advocates. Nolte's hypothesis, therefore, is unconvincing.

NOLTE, Ernst (ed.).
Theorien über den Faschismus. Cologne: Kiepenheuer & Witsch (1967), 513 pp.
A collection of papers by a number of different historians who have attempted to come to terms with fascism as an historical phenomenon. The volume reveals the wide diversity of opinion and interpretation of the subject from 1919 to 1960. In a good introduction, Nolte reviews the changing nature of this opinion.

NOLTE, Ernst.
"Zeitgenössische Theorien über den Faschismus". *Vierteljahrshefte für Zeitgeschichte*, vol. 15, pt. 3 (1967), p. 247—68.
A condensed version of a section of Nolte's introduction to the book mentioned above. He discusses the large number of different theories of fascism which arose between 1925—33, mentioning the ideas and writings of Ernst Bloch, Franz Bockenau, Ernst Niekisch and others.

NOLTE, Ernst.
Der Faschismus: von Mussolini zu Hitler; Texte, Bilder, und Dokumente. Munich: Verlag Desch (1968), 403 pp.
Designed for popular consumption, this volume has a large number of illustrations on various aspects of European fascism. Such comment as there is restates Nolte's well-known views on fascism.

NOLTE, Ernst.
Die Krise des liberalen Systems und die faschistischen Bewegungen. Munich: Piper (1968), 475 pp. New ed.
A broad survey of European fascist movements which does not come near to matching the scholarly standard of his previous works on fascism. Badly organized and hastily written, it also contains a surprisingly high number of factual errors.

NOLTE, Ernst.
"Kapitalismus, Marxismus, Faschismus". *Merkur*, vol. 27 (1973), p. 111—26.
A somewhat mundane consideration of Marxist views of the relationship between capitalism and fascism.

PIRKER, Theo (ed.).
Komintern und Faschismus 1920—1940: Dokumente zur Geschichte und Theorie des Faschismus. Stuttgart: Deutsche Verlagsanstalt (1965), 203 pp.
An illuminating and extremely useful documentary collection.

ROSNER, Jacob.
Der Faschismus: seine Wurzeln, sein Wesen, seine Ziele; fragmentarische Versüche. Vienna: Selbstverlag (1966), 255 pp.
An undistinguished work which adds little to our understanding of either the origins or nature of fascism.

SAUER, Wolfgang.
"National Socialism: Totalitarianism or Fascism?" *American Historical Review*, vol. 73, pt. 5 (1967), p. 404—24.
A significant paper dealing with the typology of classifying totalitarian and fascist institutions and movements. The author attempts to prove that as a typological label, the term "totalitarian" is less useful than the term "fascist".

SCHLANGEN, Walter.
Theorie und Ideologie des Totalitarismus. Bonn: Bundeszentrale für Politische Bildung (1972), 192 pp.
A clear but at times rather simplistic analysis and description of totalitarianism written from a liberal standpoint.

SCHÜDDEKOPF, Otto-Ernst.
Fascism. London: Weidenfeld & Nicolson (1973), 224 pp.
A brief, broad survey of the development of fascism in Europe, based on secondary sources. There is little that is original in fact or interpretation, but the book is a reliable synthesis for the general reader.

SCHULZ, Gerhard.
Faschismus-Nationalsozialismus: Versionen und theoretische Kontroversen 1922—1972. Berlin: Propyläen Verlag (1974), 222 pp.
An interesting review of contemporary interpretations of fascism and National Socialism. The author is especially critical of Marxist hypotheses of both phenomena.

SEIDEL, Bruno; **JENKNER**, Siegfried (eds.).
Wege der Totalitarismus-Forschung. Darmstadt: Wissenschaftliche Buchgesellschaft (1968), 638 pp.
A collection of articles and extracts from monographs designed to illustrate the various phases in scholarly research of totalitarianism. However, the 24 contributions presented in this volume are not fully representative of the debate on this topic, and the value of the book is reduced further by the failure of the editors to provide in their introduction an overall interpretation of the papers and extracts they have chosen. Altogether, an untidy work.

SHAPIRO, Leonard.
Totalitarianism. London: Pall Mall (1972), 144 pp.
This book might have been very useful some twenty years ago; it certainly does not offer much to either the specialist or the general reader of the mid-1970s because it is simply out of date. The author's comprehension of the meaning of "totalitarianism" is conceptually backward. Also, he ignores the entire range of recent research and debate on the theme, electing instead to summarize arguments which held sway a generation ago.

SHAPIRO, Leonard.
"The Concept of Totalitarianism". *Survey*, no. 73 (1969).
Like his book, Shapiro's paper has nothing new to say about the subject.

STRASSER, Otto.
Der Faschismus: Geschichte und Gefahr. Munich: Olzog (1965), 109 pp.
Typically idiosyncratic and predictably useless.

TALMON, Jacob L.
The Origins of Totalitarian Democracy. London: Secker & Warburg (1955), 366 pp.
In discussing the origins of totalitarian democracy, Talmon examines the ideas of a large number of writers and philos-

ophers from the point of view of their messianic and totalitarian propensities, and their relevance to twentieth century
forms of totalitarianism. Useful and interesting background
reading.

TUCKER, Robert C.
"The Dictator and Totalitarianism". *World Politics*,
vol. 17 (1964—65), p. 555—83.
An interesting discussion of the place of the leader figure
in totalitarian movements.

TURNER, Henry A.
"Fascism and Modernization". *World Politics*,
vol. 24, pt. 4 (1971—72), p. 547—64.
Seeks to establish a new conceptual framework for
characterizing fascism because the traditional theories of
totalitarianism are no longer satisfactory. This new framework may be provided, Turner argues, by a theory of
modernization. He examines the relationship between
fascism and the process of modernization and concludes
that despite the existence of some progressive elements in
Italian Fascism and National Socialism both phenomena
were essentially forms of utopian anti-modernism. A
stimulating paper, but one which overplays the game of
semantics; moreover, Turner's thesis is unlikely to gain wide
acceptance in its present embryonic form.

VIERHAUS, Rudolf.
"Faschistisches Führertum: ein Beitrag zur
Phänomenologie des europäischen Faschismus".
Historische Zeitschrift, no. 198 (1964), p. 614—39.
An important paper which tries to establish a typological
model within which the nature and meaning of fascism may
be characterized. His analysis is thoughtful and instructive.

WEBER, Eugene J.
Varieties of Fascism: Doctrines of Revolution in
the 20th Century. Princeton: Van Nostrand
(1964), 191 pp.

Designed for the general reader, this book offers a brief
description of fascist movements and extracts from the
writings and pronouncements of fascist spokesmen.

WIPPERMANN, Wolfgang.
Faschismus-Theorien: zum Stand der gegenwärtigen
Diskussion. Darmstadt: Wissenschaftliche
Buchgesellschaft (1972), 158 pp.
A competent and reliable summary and synthesis of the
more recent debate on the nature of fascism.

WOOLF, Stuart J. (ed.).
European Fascism. London: Weidenfeld & Nicolson (1968), 386 pp.
A collection of essays, three on European fascism in general,
and twelve on fascist movements in individual countries.
(A. J. Nicholls writes on National Socialism). As a whole,
however, the volume does not tackle many basic questions
relating to the nature and characteristics of fascism. This
may be because the majority of papers lack a decent
conceptual framework.

WOOLF, Stuart J (ed.).
The Nature of Fascism. London: Weidenfeld &
Nicolson (1968), 261 pp.
A collection of ten essays originally delivered as lectures
at Reading University's Graduate School of Contemporary
European Studies. The nature of fascism is examined
comparatively from the viewpoint of historians and social
scientists. Fascism's impact on class structure, the economy
and intellectuals are the major themes treated. The volume
is uneven in terms of quality and interest but provides a
useful starting point for further inquiry into the phenomenon of fascism.

The National Socialist Movement

22

A. GENERAL (1919–1933)[1]

ABEL, Theodore.
The Nazi Movement: Why Hitler Came to Power.
New York: Prentice-Hall (1965). New ed.
A study based on autobiographical data supplied by six
hundred NSDAP and SA members who joined the movement before 1933. Abel analyses on this basis the motivation
for joining, background of party members, and other
interesting aspects.

BECKER, Josef.
See his article in section 6B(vi).

BESSON, Wolfgang.
**"Neuere Literatur zur Geschichte des National-
sozialismus".** *Vierteljahrshefte für Zeitgeschichte,*
vol. 9, pt. 3 (1961), p. 314—30.
An informative review of recent literature on National
Socialism, including Martin Broszat's *Nationalsozialismus*
(reviewed in section 25) and Hanns Hofmann's book on
the Hitler Putsch (see section 22C).

BITTERLI, Urs.
See his work in section 15C(ii).

BLOOMBERG, Paula.
Hermann Rauschning and the German Emigration.
Dissertation, University of New Mexico (1967).
A very brief biography of Rauschning's life and career as
an illustration of German neo-conservative support for
National Socialism before 1933. However, the study is too
sketchy.

BORRIES, Archim von.
"William L. Shirer und seine Kritiker". *Blätter
für Deutsch- und Internationale Politik,* vol. 7,
pt. 10 (1962), p. 769—79.
A useful discussion of the controversy engendered by
Shirer's best-seller (see below).

1. See also section 23B for the many works on Hitler
which also provide an account and analysis of the National
Socialist movement as a whole (e.g. A. Bullock, K. Heiden,
etc.).

BRACHER, Karl Dietrich.
**Der Aufstieg des Nationalsozialismus als Problem
der Zeitgeschichte.** Bad Homburg: Gehlen (1957),
24 pp.
The published version of a paper originally delivered as a
lecture in which the author discusses the problem of placing
National Socialism in a wider European context.

BRACHER, Karl Dietrich.
**The German Dictatorship: the Origins, Structure,
and Consequences of National Socialism.** London:
Weidenfeld & Nicolson (1971). (Original German
ed. published in 1969).
A brilliant work of interpretative synthesis and analysis
which provides a comprehensive account of the rise and fall
of National Socialism. Detailed, balanced, and judicious, it
is clearly the best general survey of the phenomenon available.

BRACHER, Karl Dietrich; SAUER, Wolfgang;
SCHULZ, Gerhard.
**Die Nationalsozialistische Machtergreifung:
Studien zur Errichtung des totalitären Herrschafts-
systems in Deutschland 1933/34.** Cologne:
Westdeutscher Verlag (1960), 1034 pp.
A massive, richly documented, and standard work of the
crucial 1932—34 period. Based on extensive primary and
secondary sources, this paramount piece of scholarship
offers an objective, accurate, and painstakingly detailed
account and analysis of these years.

BRAUBACH, Max.
**"Von Hitler und seinen Gegnern: ein Bericht über
neue Veröffentlichungen zur Zeitgeschichte".**
Historisches Jahrbuch, vol. 88 (1968), p. 102—57.
An excellent and comprehensive book review.

BRONDER, Dietrich.
Bevor Hitler kam: eine historische Studie. Hanover: Pfeiffer (1964), 446 pp.
A broad survey, not particularly inspiring, but containing
a few interesting footnotes on party developments during
the 1920s.

BROSZAT, Martin.
"William Shirer und die Geschichte des Dritten Reiches". *Historische Zeitschrift*, no. 196 (1963), p. 112—23.
A bitterly critical assessment of Shirer's book.

BROSZAT, Martin.
Der Staat Hitlers: Grundlegung und Entwicklung seiner inneren Verfassung. Munich: Deutscher Taschenbuch Verlag (1969), 473 pp.
The early chapters of this scholarly and important study analyse the political and social factors that helped Hitler to power, as well as significant features of the National Socialist movement itself.

BROSZAT, Martin.
"Soziale Motivation und Führer-Bindung des Nationalsozialismus". *Vierteljahrshefte für Zeitgeschichte*, vol. 18, pt. 4 (1970), p. 392—409.
A valuable discussion of the problem of mass social mobilization and its relationship to the concept and practice of Hitler's absolute leadership in the NSDAP. The author depicts Hitler as an unprincipled opportunist of a Machiavellian type (as A. Bullock has done).

BROSZAT, Martin.
See also his work in section 25.

BROWNE, Harry.
Hitler and the Rise of Nazism. London: Methuen (1969), 93 pp.
An unimportant contribution.

BRUHN, Wolfgang.
Die NSDAP im Reichstag 1930—33. Dissertation, Free University of Berlin (1952).
Assesses the parliamentary role and contribution of the NSDAP. But this is only a tentative analysis, based on a narrow range of sources.

CARSTEN, Francis L.
The Rise of Fascism. London: Batsford (1967), 256 pp.
A brief, descriptive, comparative study of fascist movements. The book is competent but unoriginal, providing a summary of research on the topic. The chapter on National Socialism is more interesting than most others, but still limited.

CONWAY, John S.
"'Machtergreifung' or 'Due Process of History': the Historiography of Hitler's Rise to Power". *Historical Journal*, vol. 7, pt. 3 (1965), p. 399—413.
An intelligent and fair review of more notable studies on the rise of the NSDAP. The author discusses scholarly opinions on the reasons for the Republic's collapse and on the reasons why National Socialism was able to fill the gap. He is right to stress that the advent to power of Hitler was not inevitable.

CONWAY, John S.
"Hermann Rauschning as Historian and Opponent of Nazism". *Canadian Journal of History*, vol. 8, pt. 1 (1973), p. 67—78.
A brief but informative review of recent reprints of some books by Rauschning.

CONZE, Werner.
Der Nationalsozialismus: Hitlers Kampf gegen den demokratischen Staat (1919—1934). Stuttgart: Klett (1959), 80 pp.
A general survey, now needing considerable revision, but useful as an introduction to the subject.

DEUERLEIN, Ernst (ed.).
Der Aufstieg der NSDAP 1919—1933 in Augenzeugenberichten. Düsseldorf: Rauch Verlag (1968), 462 pp.
An important and illuminating documentary collection consisting of extracts from speeches, newspapers, official reports, etc., on the rise of the NSDAP. Every major feature of the National Socialist movement, its origins, early development in Bavaria, propaganda, ideology, struggle for power, etc., is dealt with.

DIEHL-THIELE, Peter.
Partei und Staat im Dritten Reich: Untersuchungen zum Verhältnis von NSDAP und allgemeiner innerer Staatsverwaltung. Munich: Oldenbourg (1969).
For the pre-1933 period, the book provides a good description of the NSDAP immediately following the resignation of Gregor Strasser in early December 1932.

DUESTERBERG, Theodor.
See his work in section 8C.

EPSTEIN, Klaus P.
"Shirer's History of Nazi Germany". *Review of Politics*, vol. 23 (1961), p. 230—45.
A brilliant work of demolition on Shirer's book, particularly as regards his major thesis.

EPSTEIN, Klaus P.
"Der Nationalsozialismus in amerikanischer und englischer Sicht". *Das Parlament: Aus Politik und Zeitgeschichte* (30.1.1963).
A brief review of Anglo-Saxon attitudes towards National Socialism.

FALLADA, Hans.
Bauern, Bonzen und Bomben. Hamburg: Rowohlt (1964), 565 pp. New ed.
A fictional novel originally published in 1931, which nonetheless contains interesting if not always reliable notes on the bitter controversy in the NSDAP concerning Hitler's right-wing policy after 1928.

FIGGE, Reinhard.
Die Opposition der NSDAP im Reichstag. Dissertation, University of Cologne (1963).
A disappointing work which spends a good deal of time uselessly criticizing the proportional representation system. The author's consideration of the parliamentary role of the NSDAP, 1924—33, leaves many important gaps.

FRANK, Hans.
Im Angesicht des Galgens: Deutung Hitlers und seiner Zeit auf Grund eigener Erlebnisse und Erkenntnisse. Gräfelfing: Beck Verlag (1953), 479 pp.
These memoirs of the notorious National Socialist lawyer and former Governor of occupied Poland provide surprisingly interesting details of internal party developments and intrigues during the pre-1933 period.

FRANK, Robert H.
Hitler and the National Socialist Coalition, 1924–1932. Dissertation, Johns Hopkins University (1969).
Discusses the fundamental changes in political strategy adopted by Hitler in the NSDAP and SA following the failure of the 1923 Putsch. On this score, the study simply repeats what has previously been established by earlier works. Frank's idea, that only when Röhm became SA Chief of Staff in 1931 did Hitler assert his complete control of the movement, is untenable. In all, an over-long and rather tedious dissertation.

FRANZEL, Emil.
Das Reich der brauen Jakobiner: der National-sozialismus als geschichtliche Erscheinung. Munich: Pfeiffer (1964), 230 pp.
A somewhat vapid and unhelpful interpretative essay on National Socialism as an historical phenomenon.

GAMM, Hans-Jochen.
"Politisches Fehlverhalten als Problem des Geschichtsunterrichts". *Frankfurter Hefte*, vol. 23, (1968), p. 390–402.
Discusses the widespread hopes in Weimar society for a "leader" who would guide Germany out of her depression to new heights of greatness (*Fuhrererwartung*).

GLUM, Friedrich.
Der Nationalsozialismus: Werden und Vergehen. Munich: Verlag Beck (1962), 474 pp.
Designed for the general reader, this book provides a broad interpretation of National Socialism and a reasonably sound description of some features of the movement before 1933.

GRANZOW, Brigitte.
A Mirror of Nazism: British Opinion and the Emergence of Hitler 1929–1933. London: Gollancz (1964), 248 pp.
A competent survey of British newspaper reaction to the National Socialist breakthrough.

GROSSER, Alfred (ed.).
Hitler, la presse et la naissance d'une dictature. Paris: Libraire Armand Colin (1959), 263 pp.
A series of extracts, arranged chronologically, from leading Western newspapers, dealing with the last months of the Weimar Republic and early days of Hitler's régime. It is noteworthy how many were prepared to write Hitler off altogether following the NSDAP setback at the November 1932 *Reichstag* election. This collection has its uses, but should be treated with some caution.

GRUNFELD, Frederick V.
The Hitler File: a Social History of Germany and the Nazis 1918–1945. London: Weidenfeld & Nicolson (1974).
The commentary on the reasons for the success of the NSDAP before 1933 is very ordinary and says nothing new, but the enormous number of illustrations presented are absorbing. However, the book's title is misleading for this is not a serious study of social conditions in either Weimar or the Third Reich.

HACKETT, David A.
The Nazi Party in the Reichstag Election of 1930. Dissertation, University of Wisconsin (1971).
Contains several serious ambiguities; for example, it is argued that the election was a turning point in NSDAP development because it brought conservative and nationalist support to Hitler, yet later we are told that the electoral campaign waged by the NSDAP was heavily slanted towards the workers. In any case, the first proposition is erroneous because the NSDAP's turn to the right had taken place in 1928, while there is plenty of evidence to show that the NSDAP's appeal to the workers, though not discontinued after 1928, was increasingly toned down.

HANFSTAENGL, Ernst.
Hitler: the Missing Years. London: Eyre & Spottiswoode (1957), 299 pp.
These memoirs, written in popular vein, contain some interesting details about Hitler and his entourage before 1933, but as a whole the book is apologetic, impressionistic and unreliable. Hanfstaengl, as friend and favourite piano player of the *Fuhrer*, was party to many of the incidents described but clearly his memory is not what it was.

HANFSTAENGL, Ernst.
Zwischen weissen und braunen Haus: Erinnerungen eines politischen Aussenseiters. Munich: Piper (1970), 402 pp.
These enlarged memoirs add little of substance to his earlier piece. There is no deep analysis of Hitler and the party as might have been reasonably expected from one who was so closely involved himself in the National Socialist movement.

HEFFTER, Heinrich.
"Forschungsprobleme der Geschichte des National-sozialismus". *Geschichte in Wissenschaft und Unterricht*, vol. 3, pt. 4 (1952), p. 197–215.
A report on the present state of research on National Socialism and an outline of the tasks ahead in this field of study.

HEUSS, Theodor.
Hitlers Weg: eine historischpolitische Studie über den Nationalsozialismus. Tübingen: Wunderlich (1968), 167 pp. New ed.
Originally published in 1932, this updated version of the book is very valuable in presenting a penetrating analysis of the factors which helped promote the rapid ascent of the NSDAP before 1933.

HIERL, Konstantin.
Im Dienst für Deutschland, 1918–1945. Heidelberg: Vorwinckel (1954), 208 pp.
Apologetic and disappointing memoirs of the former head of the *Reichsarbeitsdienst*. The description of his resignation from the army and his joining the NSDAP in the 1920s is the only mildly interesting section of the book.

HILDEBRAND, Klaus.
"Der 'Fall Hitler': Bilanz und Wege der Hitler-Forschung". *Neue Politische Literatur*, vol. 14, pt. 3 (1969), p. 375–86.
An incisive review of recent studies on Hitler and National Socialism.

HINDELS, Josef.
Hitler war kein Zufall: ein Beitrag zur Soziologie der Nazibarbarei. Vienna: Europa-Verlag (1962), 198 pp.
A fairly orthodox Marxist interpretation of the reasons for the victory of National Socialism. Political and constitutional factors are ignored; the stress is entirely on social and economic points. The author sees Hitler as the product of the decadent bourgeois society before 1914, and of industrialist and capitalist support after 1918. The limitations of the study are obvious.

HOESS, Rudolf.
Commandant of Auschwitz. London: Weidenfeld & Nicolson (1959), 204 pp.
Memoirs of the former concentration camp chief; in general, they are uninteresting, though there are a few noteworthy details given about his association with the NSDAP and extreme right-wing groups in the 1920s.

HOFER, Walther (ed.).
Der Nationalsozialismus: Dokumente, 1933—1945. Frankfurt: Fischer (1957), 398 pp.
Chapter I contains one or two useful documentary extracts on the early NSDAP, but there is also an interesting statistical table relating to the social composition of NSDAP members before 1933.

HOLBORN, Hajo (ed.).
Republic to Reich: the Making of the Nazi Revolution. New York: Random House (1972), 491 pp.
A collection of ten essays all previously published in the German scholarly journal *Vierteljahrshefte für Zeitgeschichte.*

HORN, Wolfgang.
"Hitler und die NSDAP: neue Untersuchungen zur Geschichte des Nationalsozialismus". *Neue Politische Literatur*, vol. 13 (1968), p. 466—84.
A good critical review of more recent literature.

HORN, Wolfgang.
Führerideologie und Parteiorganisation in der NSDAP (1919—1933). Düsseldorf: Droste (1972), 451 pp.
An interesting and well documented analysis of the interrelationship between rigid bureaucracy and the charismatic *Führer* cult in the NSDAP. Horn has no doubts that Hitler was the fundamental and necessary focal point of the movement, the leader figure *par excellence* whose power of control was unhampered by any organizational restraints. In essence, however, Horn merely confirms well-established hypotheses relating to Hitler's role as leader, using a slightly different approach. Also, this work brings together between two covers most of the important results of scholarly research on the pre-1933 NSDAP without adding very much that is really new.

HORN, Wolfgang.
"Zur Geschichte und Struktur des Nationalsozialismus und der NSDAP". *Neue Politische Literatur*, vol. 18 (1973), p. 194—209.
A review of some important recent books.

HÜTTENBERGER, Peter.
Die Gauleiter: Studie zum Wandel des Machtgefüges in der NSDAP. Stuttgart: Deutsche Verlagsanstalt (1969), 239 pp.
The first scholarly analysis of the *Gauleiter* as a composite entity within the structure of the NSDAP. The author investigates the role and functions of the *Gauleiter,* noting the significant changes in these as the NSDAP responded to different political circumstances between 1919 and 1945. The *Gauleiter* had a key role to play in promoting National Socialism before 1933 and his power base was extensive, though ultimately subject to Hitler's authority. As a body, however, the *Gauleiter* were anything but homogeneous. There is a good deal of solid information here, and altogether the author has fulfilled his pioneering task in this field with considerable credit.

ILSEMANN, Sigurd von.
Der Kaiser in Holland: Aufzeichnungen des letzten Flügeladjutanten Kaiser Wilhelms II. Vol. 2: Monarchie und Nationalsozialismus, 1924—1941. Munich: Biederstein (1968), 365 pp.
Contains a few notable observations on monarchist-National Socialist relations.

INTERNATIONAL COUNCIL FOR PHILOSOPHY AND HUMANISTIC STUDIES, and UNESCO.
The Third Reich. Edited by Edmond Vermeil and others. London: Weidenfeld & Nicolson (1955), 899 pp.
Published version of 28 papers delivered to an international symposium on National Socialism. Many important aspects are covered: ideology, propaganda, the phenomenon of Hitler, and so on, but many of the contributions now need to be revised in the light of updated research. There are a number of surprising omissions; for example, NSDAP-big business relations, and indeed the NSDAP as an organization itself, are ignored. Still, the volume is useful as an introduction to the topic.

JARMAN, Thomas L.
The Rise and Fall of Nazi Germany. London: The Cresset Press (1956), 388 pp.
Can no longer be regarded as a competent general history because so much new material and different interpretations have materialized since the book was written. The straightforward narrative style of the book's content conveys only a superficial impression of what National Socialism was all about.

JOLL, James.
"The Conquest of the Past: Some Recent German Books on the Third Reich". *International Affairs*, vol. 40, pt. 3 (1964), p. 481—91.
A judicious review of recent important works on the rise of the NSDAP and the collapse of the Weimar Republic.

JORDAN, Rudolf.
Erlebt und erlitten: Weg eines Gauleiters von München bis Moskau. Leoni am Starnberger See: Drüffel (1971), 368 pp.
Autobiography of the former *Gauleiter* of Halle-Merseburg (1930—37) and of Magdeburg-Anhalt (1937—45) who spent some ten years in Russian captivity after 1945. His account is readable and useful details of his early NSDAP activities are supplied.

JUNKER, Detlef
See his work in section 6B(vi).

KATZ, Henryk.
"Arbeiter, Mittelklasse und die NSDAP". *Internationale Wissenschaftliche Korrespondenz zur Geschichte der Deutschen Arbeiterbewegung*, vol. 10, pt. 3 (1974), p. 300—13.
A disappointingly unperceptive review article.

KELE, Max H.
Nazis and Workers: National Socialist Appeals to German Labor 1919—1933. Chapel Hill: University of North Carolina Press (1972), 243 pp.
The author's purpose is to show that the NSDAP's appeal to the working class, far from being a propandistic façade, was genuine and sustained throughout the pre-1933 period. Hence, he rejects the notion that there was a funda-

mental turning point in the orientation of the NSDAP in the late 1920s when the party allegedly "turned to the right". This work is therefore partly revisionist and it undoubtedly makes interesting reading. But Kele's thesis is not convincing. For a start, no one has ever disputed that the party continued to make an appeal to the working class, even when it had become obvious by 1928 that the NSDAP would never come to power with predominantly working class support. Kele exaggerates the importance of NSDAP worker propaganda after the late 1920s, and he fails to take into account the pro-middle class direction of most of the party's propaganda after that time. It will not do to pass off "socialistic" propaganda emanating from "Nazi Left" sources as representative of the NSDAP as a whole from 1929—33. What we know about NSDAP members' and workers' social backgrounds also contradicts Kele's arguments which, in any case, utilize the term "worker" too loosely.

KESSEL, Eberhard.
"Zur Geschichte und Deutung des Nationalsozial-ismus". *Archiv für Kulturgeschichte*, pt. 3 (1963), p. 357—94.
An extensive and balanced review of literature on National Socialism 1919—45.

KIELMANSEGG, Peter G.
"Hitler und die deutsche Revolution". *Merkur* vol. 28 (1974), p. 922—36.
Re-examines the proposition (most recently put forward by Joachim Fest in his biography of Hitler — see section 23B) that National Socialism constituted the German revolution of the twentieth century. Interesting.

KIMMEL, Adolf.
Der Aufstieg des Nationalsozialismus im Spiegel der französischen Presse 1930—1933. Bonn: Bouvier (1969), 218 pp.
A competent but unexciting study.

KLUKE, Paul.
"Der Fall Potempa". *Vierteljahrshefte für Zeitges-chichte*, vol. 5, pt. 3 (1957), p. 279—97.
Provides revealing documentation on this notorious incident in a small Silesian village in August 1932 when the SA brutally murdered a young Communist.

KLUKE, Paul (ed.).
Gutachten des Instituts für Zeitgeschichte. 2 vols. Munich, Stuttgart: Deutsche Verlagsanstalt (1958—66), 439, 479 pp.
Contains the *Gutachten* (Opinions) which the Institute for Contemporary History in Munich has rendered on matters of legal and historical importance arising from the National Socialist era, and which have been used by the government and courts of the Federal Republic to settle restitution claims by persons and institutions persecuted by Hitler. The vast bulk of the information therein relates to the 1933—45 period, but the NSDAP's relationships and activities during the *Kampfzeit* are also touched upon.

KNAUERHASE, Ramon.
An Introduction to National Socialism 1920 to 1939. Columbus (Ohio): Merrill (1972), 143 pp.
Unreliable and unhelpful even as a general introduction to the topic.

KRAMER, David R.
Fascism and Communism in Germany: Historical Anatomy of a Relationship. Dissertation, Tulane University (1973).
Investigates the ideological and practical relationship between National Socialism and German Communism 1930—

49. Kramer shows what leading National Socialists thought of the Communists, but lamely concludes that "anti-semitic anti-Communism" was a principal feature of National Socialist ideology. The Berlin transport workers' strike of November 1932 is discussed within the context of the practical co-operation between both sides. Generally, the work offers nothing original.

KREBS, Albert.
Tendenzen und Gestalten der NSDAP: Erinner-ungen an die Frühzeit der Partei. Stuttgart: Deutsche Verlagsanstalt (1959), 245 pp.
The memoirs of a former NSDAP *Gauleiter* of Hamburg make fascinating and instructive reading because they provide a deep insight into the workings, rivalries, and ambitions of the National Socialist movement before 1933. Vivid character sketches are given of party leaders, including Hitler, Goebbels, and Gregor Strasser. Krebs also has many valuable observations to make of the party's relations with other right-wing organizations, including the influential *Deutscher Handlungsgehilfenverband* (DHV), of which he was a one-time member.

KUHN, Axel.
"Die Unterredung zwischen Hitler und Papen im Hause des Barons von Schröder". *Geschichte in Wissenschaft und Unterricht*, vol. 24, pt. 12 (1973), p. 709—20.
Underlines the limitations of documentary sources for this famous interview in January 1933.

KÜHNL, Reinhard.
Die nationalsozialistische Linke 1925—1930: eine Untersuchung über Geschichte, Struktur und Ideologie der Strasser-Gruppe. Meisenheim: Hain (1966), 378 pp.
A partial scholarly history of the so-called "Nazi Left", examining the ideological and organizational basis of the informal group whose spiritual leader was Gregor Strasser. The author presents considerable documentary material, but his interpretations of it are unconvincing for the most part, and he is guilty of many factual errors in his narrative. In short, this is no more than a moderately useful introduction to the problem of the NSDAP's left wing as well as to the position of Gregor Strasser in the party. Much research remains to be done and more balanced considerations brought to bear.

KÜHNL, Reinhard.
"Zur Programmatik der nationalsozialistischen Linken: das Strasser-Programm von 1925/26". *Vierteljahrshefte für Zeitgeschichte*, vol. 14, pt. 3 (1966), p. 317—33.
This paper discusses the present state of research on the problem of the "Nazi Left", though Kuhnl tends to over-stress the differences between the socialist and nationalist wings of the NSDAP. The draft alternative programme drawn up by Gregor Strasser and others in 1925, which arose out of this conflict, is published in full.

KÜHNL, Reinhard.
"Zum Funktionswandel der NSDAP von ihrer Gründung bis zur 'Machtergreifung'", *Blätter für Deutsch- und Internationale Politik*, vol. 12, pt. 8 (1967), p. 802—11.
The author contrasts the early socialist aspirations of the NSDAP with the failure of the party to implement them after 1933. He argues that the emergence of a basically middle class leadership in the NSDAP made this rejection of former demands possible. Some of these points, interesting as they are, need to be expanded upon.

KÜHNL, Reinhard.
"Der deutsche Faschismus: Nationalsozialismus und 'Drittes Reich' in Einzeluntersuchungen und Gesamtdarstellungen". *Neue Politische Literatur*, vol. 15 (1970), p. 13—43.
A review of some recent publications. Kühnl argues for more research on the social history of National Socialism.

LEISER, Erwin.
"Mein Kampf": eine Dokumentation. Frankfurt: Fischer (1961).
A photographic record of National Socialism.

LEPSIUS, Mario R.
Extremer Nationalismus: Strukturbedingungen vor der nationalsozialistischen Machtergreifung. Stuttgart: Kohlhammer Verlag (1966), 40 pp.
Dwells lightly on nationalism as a crucial factor in preparing the way for the rise of National Socialism.

LEUSCHNER, Joachim.
"Der Nationalsozialismus". *Neue Politische Literatur*, vol. 6 (1961), p. 850—70.
A critical survey of recent biographies and documentary works relating to National Socialism and its leadership.

LOEWENBERG, Peter.
"The Psychohistorical Origins of the Nazi Youth Cohort". *American Historical Review*, vol. 76, pt. 5 (1971), p. 1457—1502.
An important and powerfully argued article with a challenging hypothesis. By combining the sociological concept of the age cohort with the methodology of psychoanalysis in relation to adolescence, the author establishes a definite causal relationship between the generation of German youth who grew up in the era of the First World War and its unsettled aftermath, and the successful rise of Hitlerism. He sees the problem as one of generational behaviour and response to contemporary political, social, and economic stimuli. The generation thus affected contributed substantially to the victory of National Socialism.

LOEWENBERG, Peter.
"Psychohistorical Perspectives on Modern German History". *Journal of Modern History*, vol. 47, pt. 2 (1975), p. 229—79.
In this original and thought-provoking paper, the author discusses among other things the application of psychohistorical perspectives as a way of understanding the ideas and personalities of various National Socialist leaders, and National Socialism itself.

LÜKEMANN, Ulf.
Der Reichsschatzmeister der NSDAP: ein Beitrag zur inneren Parteistruktur. Berlin: Ernst-Reuter-Gesellschaft (1963), 248 pp.

An important and informative contribution to the history of the NSDAP's internal organizational structure. Most of the study concentrates on the post-1933 period but the position and influence of Reich Treasurer Franz Xaver Schwarz in the early party hierarchy is well enough outlined. It is no fault of the author that the documentation does not exist for a deeper investigation of Schwarz's office during the *Kampfzeit*.

LUTZ, Hermann.
"Fälschungen zur Auslandsfinanzierung Hitlers". *Vierteljahrshefte für Zeitgeschichte*, vol. 2, pt. 4 (1954), p. 386—96.
Concentrates on the Third Reich era, but provides a few details about Hitler's financial sources abroad for the earlier period. Lutz has not succeeded in tying up all the loose ends of this theme.

MALITZ, Horst von.
The Evolution of Hitler's Germany: the Ideology, the Personality, the Movement. New York: McGraw-Hill (1973), 479 pp.
A disappointing attempt at a comprehensive synthesis of the National Socialist phenomenon; it is superficial and unoriginal. The author concentrates on a review of the origins of National Socialist ideology, which predictably takes him on a tour of Germany's intellectual and cultural past; his conclusions are to be found in many previous studies. Likewise, his analysis of Hitler is naive and often misleading. In all, a book to avoid.

MASON, Timothy W.
"The Legacy of 1918 for National Socialism".
In A.J. Nicholls & E. Matthias (eds.). *German Democracy and the Triumph of Hitler*. London: Allen & Unwin (1971), p. 215—39.
An intelligently argued paper which examines Hitler's and the general National Socialist view of the November Revolution, the conclusions they drew from it, and how after 1933 the Third Reich dealt with the practical implications of the event. The National Socialist interpretation of the Revolution is discussed within the context of Hitler's policy towards the working class after 1933.

MASON, Timothy W.
National Socialist Policies towards the German Working Classes 1925—39. 2 vols. Dissertation, University of Oxford (1971).
A massive and impressively documented work which is without doubt a major and significant contribution to our knowledge of the Third Reich's policy towards the working class. However, Mason's discussion of the NSDAP's policy in this field before 1933 is comparatively thin.

MAYER, Milton.
They Thought They Were Free: the Germans 1933—1945.
Chicago: University of Chicago Press (1955), 346 pp.
Thoroughly undistinguished but serves to remind us of the role of anti-semitism and anti-Marxism in the rise of the NSDAP.

McKALE, Donald M.
The Nazi Party Courts: Hitler's Management of Conflict in his Movement, 1921—1945. Lawrence: University of Kansas Press (1974), 252 pp.
A soundly researched history of the party's Investigation and Settlement Committee (shortened in German to *Uschla*) and of its role in and contribution to the development of the NSDAP bureaucracy. *Uschla* was designed to deal with intra-party disputes, but before 1933 it also served to assert and sustain Hitler's control of the movement. The author fails, however, to place his theme within the wider context of NSDAP development. Indeed, his knowledge of the party as a whole, and of the Weimar and Third Reich periods, is noticeably poor.

McKIBBON, R.J.
"The Myth of the Unemployed: Who Did Vote for the Nazis?" *Australian Journal of Politics and History*, vol. 15, pt. 2 (1969), p. 25—40.
A rather pointless essay. The author's purpose is to tell us what we have known for some considerable time, that the NSDAP did not attract significant numbers of the unemployed before 1933. He also throws in a few mundane and unoriginal remarks about why people voted for the party, and finishes up with a clumsy attempt to place National Socialism in some kind of general historical perspective.

MEINECKE, Friedrich.
Die deutsche Katastrophe: Betrachtungen und Erinnerungen. Wiesbaden: Brockhaus Verlag (1947), 177 pp.
A blunt, honest attempt to come to terms with National Socialism and its meaning for Germany. But Meinecke's explanation of what gave rise to Hitler (he lays emphasis on Versailles and reparations) is quite inadequate.

NICHOLLS, Antony J.
See his work in section 1.

NICHOLLS, Antony J.; MATTHIAS, Erich (eds.).
See their work in section 1.

NIEKISCH, Ernst.
Politische Schriften. Cologne, 1965.
Originally published in 1932 under the title *Hitler — ein deutsches Verhängnis*, this remarkably prophetic book is still worth consulting. Niekisch is highly critical of the NSDAP and his pessimistic fears about what Hitler would bring to Germany were largely realized.

NILSON, Sten A.
"Wahlsoziologische Probleme des Nationalsozialismus". *Zeitschrift für die Gesamte Staatswissenschaft*, vol. 110 (1954), p. 279—311.
A critical review of the works by Rudolf Heberle[1] and F.A. Hermens[2] on the theme of the electoral/sociological background to the rise of National Socialism: Nilson is impressed by Heberle's findings, which he applies to political conditions in Scandinavia in the early 1930s, but singularly unmoved by Hermens' conclusions.

NOAKES, Jeremy.
"Conflict and Development in the NSDAP 1924—1927". *Journal of Contemporary History*, vol. 1, pt. 4 (1966), p. 3—36.
An important and detailed paper on the main points of dispute in the NSDAP during the critical period following the failure of the 1923 Putsch. These disputes involved ideology, organization and tactics, and the party's relations with other extreme right-wing and *völkisch* groups. The essay includes a good discussion of the conflict between the northern "socialist" faction and the southern "petty bourgeois-nationalist" group in 1925—26. In this, Hitler's assertion of his authority, the author concludes, allowed him to go on and establish his autocratic rule over the whole party by 1927. However, this conclusion is debatable.

NOAKES, Jeremy; PRIDHAM, Geoffrey (eds.).
Documents on Nazism, 1919—1945. London: Jonathan Cape (1974), 704 pp.
The editors have translated many documents which will already be familiar to specialists, and added a few more which have hitherto remained unpublished. In this respect, the work will be of use primarily to the advanced undergraduate and the serious general reader. The editors have also written a commentary to each topic under which the documents are arranged. There is more cause here for the specialist to feel dissatisfied because Noakes and Pridham mainly summarize the fruits of previous scholarship without contributing anything significantly original. Indeed, the standard of commentary is uneven. In brief, a book of limited value.

1. *From Democracy to Nazism: a Regional Case Study on Political Parties in Germany.* Baton Rouge: Louisiana State Univ. Press (1945).
2. *Demokratie oder Anarchie? Untersuchung über die Verhältniswahl.* Frankfurt: Metzner (1951).

NYOMARKAY, Joseph.
"Factionalism in the National Socialist German Workers' Party, 1925—1926: the Myth and Reality of the 'Northern Faction'". *Political Science Quarterly*, vol. 80, pt. 1 (1965), p. 22—47.
A thorough and informative analysis of this important party crisis which is traced as far as the famous Bamberg meeting. This version is incorporated without basic alteration in the author's book (listed below).

NYOMARKAY, Joseph.
Charisma and Factionalism in the Nazi Party. Minneapolis: University of Minnesota Press (1967), 161 pp.
An absorbing and penetrating study of intra-party conflict and its relationship to Hitler's charismatic leadership. Indeed, the author argues that the strength of Hitler's charisma effectively doomed party factions of whatever colour to impotence and oblivion. Nyomarkay has many interesting observations to make about the "Nazi Left" and in general he makes a substantial contribution to our understanding of the internal development of the NSDAP.

O'LESSKER, Karl.
"Who Voted for Hitler? A New Look at the Class Basis of Nazism". *American Journal of Sociology*, vol. 74, pt. 1 (1968—69), p. 63—9.
Argues that electoral support for the NSDAP in 1930 came from a combination of former non-voters and traditional conservative nationalists, and that the bulk of the middle class vote went to the party only after 1930 when it was already established as the largest non-Marxist party in Germany.

ORLOW, Dietrich.
"The Conversion of Myths into Political Power: the Case of the Nazi Party 1925—1926". *American Historical Review*, vol. 72, pt. 3 (1967), p. 906—24.
A valuable discussion of the theoretical prerequisites for a successful totalitarian party in the twentieth century precedes a detailed examination of the steps taken by Hitler in 1925—26 to re-establish his absolute control over the NSDAP. He had to bring reality to the myth of him being the *völkisch* super-hero that had grown up after the 1923 Putsch. However, Orlow overstates the case relating to the propagation and acceptance of the *Führer* Myth in the NSDAP at this early date (1925—26) and he also exaggerates the extent of Hitler's power over the party by 1926. Most of the material in this paper is also to be found in his monograph (see below).

ORLOW, Dietrich.
The History of the Nazi Party, 1919—1933. Vol. I. Pittsburgh: University of Pittsburgh Press (1969), 338 pp.
This is the first comprehensive and thoroughly documented organizational history of the NSDAP. As such, the book is important and essential reading. But it also suffers from a number of fundamental weaknesses: Orlow fails to relate the development of its organizational structure to the development of the party as a whole — hence the book lacks a crucial sense of perspective; his analysis of the sociological composition of the NSDAP is ill-informed and indeed erroneous; his observations on the relationship between the party and big business are hopelessly outdated. Finally, the author's style of writing is turgid and unattractive.

PICARD, Max.
Hitler in uns selbst. Zürich (1946).
A superficial look at the conditions which gave rise to Hitler.

PLUM, Günter.
Bibliographie der Gauleiter der NSDAP. Munich:
Institut für Zeitgeschichte (1970), 46 pp. New ed.
Useful reference work.

PRATT, Samuel A.
See his work in section 3A.

PROSS, Harry.
**Vor und nach Hitler: zur deutschen Sozialpath-
ologie.** Olten: Walter-Verlag (1962), 267 pp.
Contains interesting notes on the German character.

RAUSCHNING, Hermann.
"Im Schatten des Nationalsozialismus (II)".
Blätter für Deutsch- und Internationale Politik, vol.
6, pt. 7 (1961), p. 611—23.
This essay usefully goes over some of the pre-1933 developments that led to Hitler's appointment as Chancellor, with
stress on the role of Hugenberg and the army.

RECKTENWALD, Johann.
**Woran hat Adolf Hitler gelitten? Eine neuro-
psychiatrische Deutung.** Munich: Reinhardt (1963),
122 pp.
Worthless piece of speculative hocus-pocus.

REMAK, Joachim (ed.).
The Nazi Years: a Documentary History. Englewood Cliffs, New Jersey: Prentice-Hall (1969),
178 pp.
A collection of documentary extracts from the writings of
NSDAP supporters designed to illuminate the principal
aspects of the National Socialist *Weltanschauung*. Only
undergraduates are likely to find anything worthwhile in
this work.

RIBBE, Wolfgang.
**"Flaggenstreit und heiliger Hain: Bemerkungen zur
nationalsozialistischen Symbolik in der Weimarer
Republik".** In *Aus Theorie und Praxis der
Geschichtswissenschaft: Festchrift für Hans
Herzfeld.* Berlin: de Gruyter (1972), p. 175—88.
Brings out the significance attached to means of party
identification by the NSDAP.

ROGGER, Hans; WEBER, Eugen J. (eds.).
The European Right: a Historical Profile. Berkeley:
University of California Press (1965), 589 pp.
The general theme is the origins and development of the
extreme Right in eleven European countries from the late
nineteenth century onwards. The volume lacks an overall
unity of approach, but offers a readable introduction to the
problems of fascism and National Socialism.

ROLOFF, Ernst-August.
**"Wer wählte Hitler? Thesen zur Sozial- und
Wirtschaftsgeschichte der Weimarer Republik".**
Politische Studien, vol. 15 (1964), p. 293—300.
Draws attention to the inadequate treatment of the source
of Hitler's pre-1933 support offered by most books. Reaffirms that it was above all the economically and socially
depressed middle classes and small farmers who flocked to
the NSDAP, and not the unemployed workers.

RÖHL, John C. G.
See his work in section 1.

ROSSBACH, Gerhard.
**Mein Weg durch die Zeit: Erinnerungen und
Bekenntnisse.** Weilburg: Vereinigte Weilburger
Buchdruckerei (1950), 240 pp.
Recaptures the atmosphere of the 1920s quite vividly. The
former leading *Freikorps* commander also recounts his
dealings with the NSDAP and Hitler, though he is not con-
sistently reliable on points of fact.

RUMPF, Maria R.
**Die lebensalterliche Verteilung des Mitglieder-
zuganges zur NSDAP vor 1933.** Dissertation,
University of Heidelberg (1951).
Offers statistical data to support the hypothesis that the
NSDAP was the party with the youngest officials and mem-
bers in Weimar politics.

SAAGE, Richard.
**"Antisozialismus, Mittelstand und NSDAP in der
Weimarer Republik".** *Internationale Wissenschaft-
liche Korrespondenz zur Geschichte der Deutschen
Arbeiterbewegung*, vol. 11, pt. 2 (1975), p. 146—
77.
A detailed and thoughtful probe of the nature of middle
class support for the NSDAP.

SCHÄFER, Wolfgang.
**NSDAP: Entwicklung und Struktur der Staatspartei
des Dritten Reiches.** Hanover: Norddeutsche
Verlagsanstalt (1956), 100 pp.
A pioneering study whose early sections provide a synopsis
of the main features of NSDAP development before 1933.

SCHILDT, Gerhard.
**Die Arbeitsgemeinschaft Nord-West:
Untersuchungen zur Geschichte der NSDAP 1925/
26.** Dissertation, University of Freiburg im
Breisgau (1964).
A thoroughly documented and important study which
deserves to be published.

SCHMIDT, Klaus F.
**"Die 'Nationalsozialistischen Briefe' (1925—30):
Programm, Anschauungen, Tendenzen, Anmer-
kungen zu innerparteilichen Diskussionen und
Richtungskämpfen der NSDAP".** In *Paul Kluke
zum 60. Geburtstag.* Frankfurt: Europäische
Verlagsanstalt (1968), p. 111—26.
A good analysis of the influential role played by the leftist
NS-Briefe in the internal party debate over ideology and
tactics 1925—30.

SCHIRACH, Baldur von.
Ich glaubte an Hitler. Hamburg: Mosaik-Verlag
(1967), 367 pp.
Extremely disappointing and unrevealing memoirs of the
former leader of the Hitler Youth. He tells us little we
did not know about either Hitler or the NSDAP, while his
remarks on the National Socialist youth movement seek
to perpetuate a fair number of myths and distortions.

SCHNAIBERG, Allan.
**"A Critique of Karl O'Lessker's 'Who Voted for
Hitler?'".** *American Journal of Sociology*, vol. 74
(1968—69), p. 732—5.
O'Lessker's views withstand this challenge.

SCHOENBAUM, David.
Hitler's Social Revolution: Class and Status in Nazi Germany 1933—1939. London: Weidenfeld & Nicolson (1967), 336 pp.
The first chapter of this interesting, provocative, but conceptually weak monograph discusses the social composition of the National Socialist movement and its early formulation of social and economic attitudes which later in practice were non-revolutionary.

SCHORSKE, Carl E.
"A New Look at the Nazi Movement". *World Politics*, vol. 9, pt. 1 (1956), p. 88—97.
A review of *The Third Reich*, sponsored by the International Council for Philosophy and Humanistic Studies and UNESCO (see earlier in this section).

SCHULZ, Gerhard.
Der Aufstieg des Nationalsozialismus: Krise und Revolution in Deutschland. Berlin: Propyläen Verlag (1975), 921 pp.
A comprehensive, richly detailed study which is likely to become a standard source of reference. But for the most part this is an integrated narrative without frills; although the author's discussion of ideological and intellectual trends in Weimar is very good, there is overall no innovative methodological framework or much by way of original interpretation. Important single events in the rise of the NSDAP (for example, the Strasser crisis of 1932) still require fuller and more convincing explanation.

SCHUMANN, Hans-Gerd.
Nationalsozialismus und Gewerkschaftsbewegung: die Vernichtung der deutschen Gewerkschaften und der Aufbau der "Deutschen Arbeitsfront". Hanover: Norddeutsche Verlagsanstalt (1958), 219 pp.
Although the bulk of this book is devoted to the development of the DAF after 1933, it provides one of the best available analyses of the National Socialist Factory Cell Organization (NSBO), of which Schumann was a former high-ranking official. Gregor Strasser's position in the NSDAP is also usefully outlined.

SHIRER, William L.
The Rise and Fall of the Third Reich. London: Heinemann, Secker & Warburg (1960), 1245 pp.
Shirer's best-seller is designed for the popular market and he gives a virtuoso performance for the gallery. There is undoubtedly plenty of useful information in the volume, though there are a large number of factual errors. But it is his interpretations and judgements which have aroused so much hostile criticism, and rightly so, for they are invariably ill-considered, tendentious, and subjective. His main thesis, that National Socialism was the inevitable outcome of certain long-term trends in Germany's historical evolution, is no longer taken seriously.

SHIRER, William L.
"Zur deutschen Kritik an 'Aufstieg und Fall des Dritten Reiches'". *Blätter für Deutsch- und Internationale Politik*, vol. 7, pt. 9 (1961), p. 707—8.
Shirer replies ineffectually to his critics.

SIMPSON, Amos E.; CAIN NEITZEL, Sarah (eds.).
Why Hitler? New Perspectives in History. Boston: Houghton Mifflin (1971), 170 pp.
Designed for use by undergraduates as an introduction to the reasons for the rise of National Socialism.

SMITH, Bradley F.
Hitler and the Strasser Challenge. Dissertation, University of California (1957).
A competent but by no means exhaustive work on the 1925—26 crisis. The exact nature and importance of Gregor Strasser's role in the NSDAP still needs a fundamental analysis.

SNELL, John L. (ed.).
The Nazi Revolution — Germany's Guilt or Fate? Boston: Heath (1959), 97 pp.
A volume in the extremely useful Problems in European Civilization series which presents brief extracts from the writings of reputable scholars on various aspects of the collapse of the Weimar Republic and the rise of Hitler. Thus different interpretations are presented succinctly and effectively.

SONTHEIMER, Kurt.
"Die grosse Lähmung: die demokratischen Kräfte und die nationalsozialistische Bewegung 1932". *Neue Gesellschaft*, vol. 9 (1962), p. 466—73.
Spotlights the weakness of democratic forces.

SPEER, Albert.
Inside the Third Reich: Memoirs. London: Weidenfeld & Nicolson (1970), 787 pp.
These extremely interesting memoirs of Hitler's former armaments minister deal overwhelmingly with the 1933—45 era, but the initial chapters record Speer's early impressions and contact with the NSDAP, including a report of a speech given by Hitler to the students of Berlin University in 1931.

SPECHT, Gustav.
Die Nationalsozialistische Deutsche Arbeiterpartei als organisiertes soziales Gebilde. Dissertation, University of Cologne (1948).
Discusses the social composition of the NSDAP.

STRASSER, Otto.
Mein Kampf. Frankfurt: Heinrich-Heine-Verlag (1969), 234 pp.
A superficial autobiography which contains no substantial revelations.

THORNTON, M. J.
Nazism 1918—45. London (1966).
A poor and outdated narrative.

TROTSKY, Leon.
The Struggle against Fascism in Germany. New York: Pathfinder Press (1971), 479 pp.
A selection of Trotsky's writings on the rise of National Socialism before 1933. Mildly interesting.

TURNER, Henry A. (ed.).
Nazism and the Third Reich. New York: Quadrangle Books (1972), 262 pp.
A collection of nine essays by various scholars which have been published previously in German and Anglo-Saxon academic journals. (All papers relevant to the pre-1933 era are reviewed individually and in their original form in this bibliography).

TYRELL, Albrecht.
Führer befiehl . . . . Selbstzeugnisse aus der Kampf-zeit der NSDAP: Dokumentation und Analyse.
Düsseldorf: Droste (1969), 403 pp.
A well organized and important documentary collection dealing with the organizational and political development of the NSDAP. The material, which is drawn from a wide range of sources, is arranged chronologically, and Tyrell has added an extensive and sound commentary. A final chapter provides statistical data on NSDAP membership, party officeholders, organization, and local and national elections.

UHSE, Bodo.
Söldner und Soldat. East Berlin: Dietz (1956).
New ed.
Despite a fictional format, this book has something to say about the conflict within the NSDAP in 1928—30 over Hitler's "turn to the right". Uhse was himself involved in the controversy as a fringe member of the "Nazi Left".

VIEFHAUS, Erwin.
"Der Nationalsozialismus". *Neue Politische Literatur*, vol. 6 (1961), p. 946—74.
A book review.

VOGT, Martin.
"Zur Finanzierung der NSDAP zwischen 1924 und 1928". *Geschichte in Wissenschaft und Unterricht*, vol. 21, pt. 4 (1970), p. 234—43.
Argues that the NSDAP in 1924—28 was overwhelmingly self-financing, and that industrial and big business support came only after the May 1928 *Reichstag* election. The election, Vogt implausibly maintains, was really a victory for the NSDAP.

WAGNER, G. S.
"Left Nazism". *Bulletin of the Society for the Study of Labour History*, vol. 18 (Spring 1969), p. 10—12.
A poor attempt at a résumé of "left-wing" developments in the NSDAP 1919—34. The author assumes what is "left-wing" but in any case his remarks betray deep ignorance of the topic.

WAHL, Karl.
. . . Es ist das deutsche Herz: Erlebnisse und Erkenntnisse eines ehemaligen Gauleiters. Augsburg (1954).
Memoirs, largely apologetic in tone, of the former *Gauleiter* of Swabia (1928—45).

WAHL, Karl.
Patrioten oder Verbrecher: aus fünfzigjähriger Praxis, davon 17 Jahre als Gauleiter. Heusenstamm: Orion-Heimreiter-Verlag (1973), 243 pp.
Enlarged version of the aforementioned work.

WEBER, Alexander.
Soziale Merkmale der NSDAP Wähler. Dissertation, University of Freiburg im Breisgau (1969).
An empirical investigation of the social status of NSDAP voters, based on data relating to certain districts in Baden and Hesse.

WERNER, Karl F.
Das NS-Geschichtsbild und die deutsche Gesch-ichtswissenschaft. Stuttgart: Kohlhammer (1967), 123 pp.
A factual rather than an analytical consideration of the historical profession during the Third Reich. The author ascribes the failure of scholars and universities to stand up to Hitler to the similarity of their political outlooks from 1919—33. Before 1933, he adds, romantic and racialist criteria already coloured history writing and many scholars venerated the concept of the *Machtstaat*.

WINKLER, Heinrich A.
"Extremismus der Mitte: sozialgeschichtliche Aspekte der nationalsozialistischen Machtergreifung". *Vierteljahrshefte für Zeitgeschichte*, vol. 20, pt. 2 (1972), p. 175—91.
A scholarly analysis of the kind of people who voted for Hitler before 1933, and of the character of the NSDAP itself. Winkler examines Weimar election returns, the NSDAP programme, etc., and finally rejects Lipset's thesis that the party represented the "extremists of the middle" in the electorate; the party did not stand somewhere between the Left and Right as Lipset believed, it came to power in association with the traditional Right. Winkler's conclusion is of course undeniable.

WINKLER, Heinrich A.
See also his work in section 13B(iii).

WITT, Thomas E. de.
The Nazi Party and Social Welfare 1919—1939.
Dissertation, University of Virginia (1972).
Argues that the success of the NSDAP's social welfare pro-gramme helps to account for the régime's popularity after 1933; traces NSDAP ideas on social welfare to Imperial and Weimar antecedents. This is a thesis which abounds in dangerous and unwarranted assumptions.

WÖRTZ, Ulrich.
Programmatik und Führerprinzip: das Problem des Strasser-Kreises in der NSDAP. Dissertation, University of Erlangen (1966).
A thoroughly documented and balanced study which has established a firm foundation for further research of this topic.

B. ORIGINS AND EARLY DEVELOPMENT (1919–1923)[1]

AUER, Johann.
See his article in section 23 B.

CAHILL, John J.
The NSDAP and May Day, 1923: Confrontation and Aftermath, 1923—1927. Dissertation, University of Cincinnati (1973).
Discusses the May Day rally of the Left in Munich in 1923 and how the right-wing reaction to the event was utilized by Hitler to assert his authority over the Working Associat-ion of Patriotic Combat Leagues (*Arbeitsgemeinschaft der Vaterländischen Kampfverbände*). In this way, Hitler re-placed Röhm as the leading figure in this movement and later, Cahill adds, in the confrontation with the "socialistic" northern wing of the NSDAP in 1925—26, the episode helped Hitler to defeat the Gregor Strasser initiative.

DEUERLEIN, Ernst.
See his article in section 30.

_____

1. Cross-refer to relevant titles in sections 22A, 22D, 23B, and 25.

DOUGLAS, Donald M.
The Early Ortsgruppen: the Development of National Socialist Local Groups 1919—1923.
Dissertation, University of Kansas (1968).
An examination of the proliferation and development of NSDAP local branches and their relations with Munich. The author's conclusions are unremarkable, namely, that the growth pattern was haphazard and for the most part free of centralized direction from Munich.

EHLERS, Carol J.
See her work in section 22D.

ENGELMANN, Ralph M.
See his work in section 23C.

FERBER, Walter.
Die Vorgeschichte der NSDAP in Österreich: ein Beitrag zur Geschichtsrevision. Konstanz: Verlagsanstalt Merk (1954), 40 pp.
Supplies a few useful details about extreme nationalist developments in pre-1918 Austria.

FERBER, Walter.
"Georg Ritter von Schönerer: zur Vorgeschichte des Nationalsozialismus". *Hochland*, vol. 63 (1971), p. 326—32.
An assessment of Schönerer's political views.

FRANZ-WILLING, Georg.
Die Hitlerbewegung, I: Der Ursprung 1919—1922.
Hamburg: Verlag G. Schenck (1962), 256 pp.
A curious book. The author has carried out considerable research and has presented a good deal of important material. Yet the scholarly merit of the work is severely undermined by his blatantly pro-Nazi sympathies. This uncritical approach mars his treatment of most themes considered: NSDAP organization, ideology, relations with other *völkisch* and nationalist groups, etc. Hence, although one is well advised to read this piece, one must beware of the pitfalls.

FUCHS, Albert.
Geistige Strömüngen in Österreich 1867—1918.
Vienna (1949).
A competent description of ideological and intellectual trends.

HALE, Oron J.
"Gottfried Feder Calls Hitler to Order: an Unpublished Letter on Nazi Party Affairs". *Journal of Modern History*, vol. 30, pt. 4 (1958), p. 358—62.
A letter (published here in full and in German) from Feder to Hitler on 10 August 1923 in which he criticizes the *Führer*'s failings as a party leader. Feder's criticisms were designed to reassert the influence in the party of "left-wing" members following Hitler's takeover of the NSDAP in July 1921.

HANSER, Richard.
Prelude to Terror: the Rise of Hitler, 1919—1923.
London: Hart-Davis (1971), 409 pp.
A weak, superficial and popular work which will hardly satisfy even the casual general reader.

KATER, Michael H.
"Zur Soziographie der frühen NSDAP". *Vierteljahrshefte für Zeitgeschichte*, vol. 19, pt. 2 (1971), p. 124—59.
A fresh and detailed analysis of the sociological composition of the NSDAP during the early 1920s. The author seeks to ascertain whether it was a class party, whether young or old members predominated, whether it was mainly confined to Bavaria, whether it was largely urban-based, and whether it attracted many women supporters. Kater's answers to these questions constitute the most definitive statement to date on the sociographic basis of the early NSDAP.

KUEHNELT-LEDDIHN, Erik R. von.
"The Bohemian Background of German National Socialism: the DAP, DNSAP, and NSDAP".
Journal of the History of Ideas, vol. 9, pt. 3 (1948), p. 339—71.
The author challenges what he regards as the simplistic theory that National Socialism was nothing but a combination of "Kaiserdom", feudalism, and medievalism, by tracing its immediate predecessors in Bohemia. He stresses the similarity in programme and ideas between the Bohemian parties (DAP, DNSAP) and the NSDAP. Based exclusively on secondary sources, this is nevertheless a stimulating article.

LAQUEUR, Walter Z.
See his article in section 19C(i).

MASER, Werner.
Die Frühgeschichte der NSDAP: Hitlers Weg bis 1924. Bonn: Athenäum (1965), 524 pp.
A minutely detailed chronicle of the NSDAP's internal development, emphasizing Hitler's struggle for control of the party machine. Yet Maser's obsession for petty and insignificant detail means that he fails to place his theme in a wider perspective. For example, the party's dealings with other right-wing organizations are more or less ignored. In all, a work of limited value.

McGRATH, William J.
Wagnerianism in Austria. Dissertation, University of California (1965).
A sound study.

ORLOW, Dietrich.
"The Organisation, History and Structure of the NSDAP, 1919—1923". *Journal of Modern History*, vol. 37, pt. 2 (1965), p. 208—26.
An informative article which tries to account for the rapid transformation of the obscure German Workers' Party (DAP) into the powerful NSDAP 1919—23. Stresses above all the crucial contribution by Hitler as party organizer, propagandist and tactician. Developments in 1923, however, are dealt with only in the concluding paragraphs of the essay.

PHELPS, Reginald H.
"Hitler and the Deutsche Arbeiterpartei".
American Historical Review, vol. 68, pt. 3 (1963), p. 974—86.
The author effectively demonstrates how false and incomplete a picture of the DAP Hitler presented in *Mein Kampf*. Hitler was concerned to create a myth of his own dramatic role. Phelps has instead provided an objective and accurate account of the origins, leadership, and activities of the DAP, and Hitler's role therein, which explodes the myths Hitler sought to foster.

PHELPS, Reginald H.
See also his articles in sections 7E, 23B and 23C.

PLEWNIA, Margarete.
See her work in section 23C.

SCHORSKE, Carl E.
"Politics in a New Key: an Austrian Triptych".
Journal of Modern History, vol. 39, pt. 4
(1967), p. 343—86.
A superb analysis of social movements which challenged the
liberal ethic in Austria during the late nineteenth century,
concentrating on the ideas and activities of Schönerer,
Karl Lueger, and Theodor Herzl. The author sees all three
movements as part of the cultural revolution which characterized the turn of the century; they all represented a certain type of reaction against liberalism.

SIDMAN, Charles F.
See his article in section 28.

TYRELL, Albrecht.
Vom "Trommler" zum "Führer": der Wandel von
Hitlers Selbstverständnis zwischen 1919 und 1924
und die Entwicklung der NSDAP. Munich: Fink
(1975), 296 pp.
A compelling and scholarly study of the development of
the power complex within the NSDAP. There is hardly any
new material here, but the author's original and stimulating
interpretations merit wide attention.

WHITESIDE, Andrew G.
"Nationaler Sozialismus in Österreich vor 1918".
Vierteljahrshefte für Zeitgeschichte, vol. 9, pt. 4
(1961), p. 333—59.
A stimulating paper on the political radicalization of German workers in the Habsburg Empire before 1918. The
paper is mainly concerned with a detailed survey of the
development, ideology and leadership of the German
Workers' Party, founded in 1904. Mentioned also are
various personalities of the DAP who were later active in
Austrian or Sudeten National Socialism.

WHITESIDE, Andrew G.
Austrian National Socialism before 1918. The
Hague: Martinus Nijhoff (1962), 143 pp.
A scholarly and balanced narrative of the nature, growth
and political orientation of German nationalism in Bohemia.
The work unequivocally establishes that herein lay the
immediate origins of German National Socialism. The DAP
and its successor, the DNSAP, receive detailed analysis.

WHITESIDE, Andrew G.
"The Deutsche Arbeiterpartei 1904—1918: a
Contribution to the Origins of Fascism". *Austrian
Historical Newsletter*, vol. 4 (1963), p. 3—14.
A condensed version of Whiteside's previous publications
on the DAP.

C. THE HITLER PUTSCH

BENNECKE, Heinrich.
"Die Bedeutung des Hitlerputsches für Hitler".
Politische Studien, vol. 13 (1962), p. 685—92.
A summary of the effect of the Putsch on Hitler's sub-
sequent political strategy and on his relations with estab-
lished bodies such as the *Reichswehr*.

BONNIN, Georges.
Le Putsch de Hitler à Munich en 1923. Paris: Les
Sables D'Olonne (1966), 230 pp.
By presenting a small number of significant documents not
included in their works by Ernst Deuerlein and Hanns
Hofmann, this book's main value lies in the way it supple-
ments the more comprehensive and definitive studies of the
Putsch.

DEUERLEIN, Ernst (ed.).
Der Hitler-Putsch: bayerische Dokumente zum 8.
und 9. November 1923. Stuttgart: Deutsche
Verlagsanstalt (1962), 759 pp.
An extremely valuable and standard documentary collection
to which all students of the Putsch must inevitably turn. In
places, Deuerlein tends to assume a fairly high standard of
knowledge on the part of his readers and does not therefore
provide as full an annotation of some documents as one
might want. However, this is a minor criticism of a superbly
edited volume.

FAVEZ, Jean-Claude
See his article in section 30.

GORDON, Harold J.
Hitler and the Beer Hall Putsch. Princeton: Princeton University Press (1972), 666 pp.
An immensely detailed and thorough investigation of the
Putsch, and as a narrative it will probably remain unsur-
passed. Gordon's analyses and interpretations, however, are
much less impressive. He is not convincing in his argument
that Kahr and his colleagues were forced by Hitler to fall in
with his wild schemes rather than being willing participants.
Also, the author's attempt to saddle the Left with considerable responsibility for the short-lived link-up between the
Bavarian political élite and Hitler is even less plausible.
Apart from these criticisms, there must remain a suspicion
that Gordon has not fully mastered or understood his vast
amount of information; a final chapter summarizing his
arguments and conclusions would have helped dispel this
feeling.

HOFMANN, Hanns H.
Der Hitlerputsch: Krisenjahre deutscher Geschichte
1920 bis 1924. Munich: Nymphenburger Verlag
(1961), 335 pp.
Hofmann's interpretations often differ sharply from those
in Gordon's book, largely because he has generally accepted
at face value the National Socialist narrative of events leading up to and during the Putsch. Moreover, Hofmann has
not made use of the full range of sources available to him
and he is prone to making elementary factual errors. The
book is certainly useful, but limited.

JÜNGER, Ernst.
Jahre der Okkupation. Stuttgart: Klett (1958).
Contains a vivid and interesting description of the Putsch.

PHELPS, Reginald H.
"Dokumente aus der 'Kampfzeit' der NSDAP —
1923". *Deutsche Rundschau*, vol. 84 (1958),
p. 459—68, 1034—44.
A report on documentary sources for the Putsch.

SCHÖNER, Hellmuth (ed.).
Hitler-Putsch im Spiegel der Presse. Munich:
Hornung-Verlag (1974), 184 pp.
Reproduces the original reports of the Putsch that appeared
in leading German and foreign newspapers at that time. The
value of these often ill-informed reports as an historical
source, however, is dubious.

STENZL, Otto.
"Der Hitlerputsch: Literatur zur Frühgeschichte
des Nationalsozialismus". *Politische Meinung*, no.
77, vol. 7 (1962), p. 83—7.
An unimportant literary review.

D. REGIONAL AND LOCAL STUDIES

1. BADEN

FARIS, Ellsworth.
"Take-off Point for the National Socialist Party:
the Landtag Election in Baden, 1929". *Central*
European History, vol. 8, pt. 2 (1975), p. 140—71.
A detailed and convincing analysis of the nature and extent
of the National Socialist voter appeal as revealed during the
campaign and election in 1929. The author shows that
support came from areas with a predominantly Protestant
population, a rural character and a white collar work force.
Much of this support was formerly given to other non-
Catholic middle class parties. The importance of the
women's vote is also considered to have been a factor
favouring the NSDAP. In short, this paper confirms and
also partly modifies previous research on the NSDAP at a
local level.

GRILL, Johnpeter H.
The Nazi Party in Baden 1920—1945. 2 vols.
Dissertation, University of Michigan (1975),
906 pp.
Richly documented, but merely endorsing the point that
the NSDAP only began to make a serious impact when its
principal efforts were directed towards the Protestant
middle classes and peasantry in the period after 1928.

2. BAVARIA

BOONE, Jasper C.
The Obersalzberg: a Case Study in National
Socialism. Dissertation, Middle Tennessee State
University (1972).
An examination of National Socialism in this area from
1923—45. However, the only new detail to emerge for the
pre-1933 era is that many prominent National Socialists
acquired homes in the region in the late 1920s. This is a
poor, unsophisticated study for which the author has not
even bothered to visit archives.

EHLERS, Carol J.
Nuremberg, Julius Streicher and the Bourgeois
Transition to Nazism, 1918—1924. Dissertation,
University of Colorado (1975), 820 pp.
A sound study which emphasizes the effective leadership of
Streicher in persuading the Nuremberg middle class to
support the NSDAP at an earlier date (1918—24) than their
counterparts in other areas of Germany. The reasons for
their conversion are detailed and there is also much material
on Streicher's political career, including his bitter struggle
against Hermann Luppe, the pro-Weimar mayor of Nuremberg.

FRANZ, Georg.
"Munich: Birthplace and Center of the National
Socialist German Workers' Party". *Journal of*
Modern History, vol. 29, pt. 4 (1957), p. 319—
34.
Stresses that the revolutionary era in Munich in 1918—19
holds the key to the role of the city in the history of the
NSDAP, though according to Franz, Munich was not finally
established as the "capital of the movement" until 1933.
There is in fact very little on the NSDAP in this superficial
essay, and he does not fully explain the reasons why
Munich did become the party's "capital".

HAMBRECHT, Rainer.
Der Aufstieg der NSDAP in Franken von 1928 bis
1933. Dissertation, University of Würzburg (1968).

Contains much informative detail but has not satisfactorily
related Franconia's National Socialist exprience to the
history of the party as a whole.

LENMAN, Robin.
"Julius Streicher and the Origins of the NSDAP in
Nuremberg, 1918—1923". In A.J. Nicholls & E.
Matthias (eds.). *German Democracy and the*
Triumph of Hitler. London: Allen & Unwin (1971),
p. 129—59.
Presents a good deal of new and interesting material from
archival sources.

MEMMING, Rolf B.
The Bavarian Governmental District Unterfranken
and the City Burgstadt 1922—1939: a Study of the
National Socialist Movement and Party-State
Affairs. Dissertation, University of Nebraska
(1974).
Stresses the haphazard manner in which local party business
was conducted before 1933 in Lower Franconia. The
nature of tension between the party and the SA is also discussed, but the author had added nothing new to our
understanding of how the NSDAP functioned or of the
rivalries within it.

NICHOLLS, Antony J.
"Hitler and the Bavarian Background to National
Socialism". In A.J. Nicholls & E. Matthias (eds.).
German Democracy and The Triumph of Hitler.
London: Allen & Unwin (1971), p. 99—128.
A soundly documented paper which argues that the
Bavarian background was of fundamental importance to
the later success of the NSDAP. However, to suggest that
Bavaria was the only region in which the NSDAP could
have laid such successful foundations is unacceptable. After
all, after 1928 the party made its largest gains in northern,
central and eastern Germany, and there had been from the
early 1920s a powerful party base in Saxony, Thuringia,
and other districts.

PRIDHAM, Geoffrey.
Hitler's Rise to Power: the History of the NSDAP
in Bavaria 1923—1933. London: Hart-Davis
MacGibbon (1973), 380 pp.
A well researched, detailed, and carefully organized study
which ultimately, however, merely confirms much of what
is already known about the NSDAP: its tight centralization,
Hitler's key role, and the weakness of the party in Catholic
areas. Pridham elevates the last point to the status of his
main hypothesis, so there could be no surprising revelations
on this account.

REICHE, Eric G.
See his work in section 22E(i).

WIESEMANN, Falk.
See his work in section 9C.

3. BERLIN

BROSZAT, Martin.
"Die Anfänge der NSDAP in Berlin 1926/27".
Vierteljahrshefte für Zeitgeschichte, vol. 8, pt. 1
(1960), p. 85—118.
An excellent scholarly treatment, supplemented by relevant
documentation. Only with the arrival of Goebbels as
Gauleiter in late 1926 did the Berlin NSDAP begin to make
a noteworthy political impact.

4. DANZIG

LEVINE, Herbert S.
Hitler's Free City: a History of the Nazi Party in Danzig 1925—1939. Chicago: University of Chicago Press (1973), 223 pp.
A perceptive study, based on considerable research, which analyses the special problems confronting the NSDAP in the city. These are discussed more interestingly for the post-1933 than for the earlier period. The book does not basically alter the picture we had previously about the pre-1933 NSDAP in Danzig.

5. HAMBURG

ANSCHÜTZ, Helga.
Die Nationalsozialistische Deutsche Arbeiterpartei in Hamburg: ihre Anfänge bis zur Reichstagswahl vom 14. September 1930. Dissertation, University of Hamburg (1956).
A highly competent account which clearly explains the rivalries and tensions retarding NSDAP development in the city until the late 1920s.

JOCHMANN, Werner (ed.).
Nationalsozialismus und Revolution: Ursprung und Geschichte der NSDAP in Hamburg 1922—1933; Dokumente. Frankfurt: Europäische Verlagsanstalt (1963), 451 pp.
An extremely well edited and valuable documentary collection (122 documents in all). The material throws light not only on the NSDAP but also on the scores of radical right-wing and *völkisch* groups which abounded in northern Germany at this time.

6. HESSE

MANN, Rosemarie.
"Entstehung und Entwicklung der NSDAP in Marburg bis 1933". *Hessisches Jahrbuch für Landesgeschichte*, vol. 22 (1972), p. 254—342.
There are a few noticeable gaps, but generally this is a useful account.

SCHÖN, Eberhard.
Die Entstehung des Nationalsozialismus in Hessen. Meisenheim: Hain (1972), 227 pp.
A most disappointing work, containing for the most part notes on trivial and unconnected items. There is no conceptual framework and a distinct paucity of worthwhile analysis.

7. LOWER SAXONY

ALLEN, William S.
The Nazi Seizure of Power: the Experience of a Single German Town 1930—1935. London: Eyre & Spottiswoode (1966), 345 pp.
An excellent account of the rise of the NSDAP in a small town (described fictitiously as "Thalburg") in Lower Saxony. The author pinpoints the nature of underlying social tensions and how the NSDAP was able to exploit this state of affairs for its own political advantage. The study confirms the view that most NSDAP support after 1930 came from small town or rural-based middle class Protestants.

FARQUHARSON, John.
"The NSDAP in Hanover and Lower Saxony 1921—26". *Journal of Contemporary History*, vol. 8, pt. 4 (1973), p. 103—20.
This examination of the origins of the NSDAP in Lower Saxony adds little of importance to Noakes's account (see below). Indeed, the author seems unaware of Noakes's work, which is not listed once in his footnotes.

KAISER, Klaus.
See his work in section 9D.

NOAKES, Jeremy.
The Nazi Party in Lower Saxony, 1921—1933. London: Oxford University Press (1971), 276 pp.
A thoroughly detailed and solid contribution which confirms that in predominantly agrarian-rural regions most of the NSDAP support came from the Protestant *Mittelstand* and peasantry. The author's description of the party's development and of the reasons for its success in Lower Saxony is full and satisfying, though his treatment of ancillary groups of the party is cursory.

ROLOFF, Ernst-August.
See his work in section 9D.

SCHWARZWÄLDER, Herbert.
Die Machtergreifung der NSDAP in Bremen 1933. Bremen: Schünemann (1966), 158 pp.
Has little of interest to say about the development of the NSDAP in Bremen before 1933 except to point out that the party was not particularly strong there. Most of the book describes political events in the city from January to March 1933.

8. PRUSSIA

TRUMPP, Thomas.
See his work in section 4G.

9. RHINELAND

HEYEN, Franz J. (ed.).
Nationalsozialismus im Alltag: Quellen zur Geschichte des Nationalsozialismus vornehmlich im Raum Mainz-Koblenz-Trier. Boppard: Boldt (1967), 373 pp.
Part of this useful collection of assorted documents throws a little light on NSDAP progress (or rather the lack of it) in the Rhineland before 1933. Reports of party meetings and rallies in Koblenz are included.

10. THE RUHR

BOEHNKE, Wilfried.
Die NSDAP im Ruhrgebiet 1920—1933. Bad Godesberg: Verlag Neue Gesellschaft (1974), 239 pp.
A carefully researched organizational history of the party in the Ruhr which confirms the previous opinion that the NSDAP did not make much headway among the working class population in this heavily industrialized region. More interestingly, Boehnke tries to show that big business kept its distance also.

GÖRGEN, Peter.
Düsseldorf und der Nationalsozialismus. Cologne: Gouder & Hansen (1968), 276 pp.
This study provides a large amount of detailed information but Görgen has not followed it up with sufficient analysis. The pre-1933 era receives only scanty attention.

KLOTZBACH, Kurt.
Gegen den Nationalsozialismus: Widerstand und Verfolgung in Dortmund 1930—1945; eine historisch-politische Studie. Hanover: Verlag für Literatur und Zeitgeschehen (1969), 316 pp.
Sketches in some background for the pre-1933 period.

MUHLBERGER, D. W.
The Rise of National Socialism in Westphalia 1920—33. Dissertation, University of London (1975).
A competent study which although furnishing considerable detail merely confirms the view that in heavily industrialized Westphalia, the NSDAP found it difficult to make substantial headway against the entrenched left-wing parties and the powerful force of Catholicism. Methodologically, the work is disappointing.

11. SCHLESWIG-HOLSTEIN

HEBERLE, Rudolf.
See his work in section 9D.

12. THURINGIA

DICKMANN, Fritz.
"Die Regierungsbildung in Thüringen als Modell der Machtergreifung: ein Brief Hitlers aus dem Jahre 1930". *Vierteljahrshefte für Zeitgeschichte,* vol. 14, pt. 4 (1966), p. 454—64.
The letter referred to was written by Hitler on 2 February 1930 to an old, unnamed friend then living abroad. The letter is a rarity in that it is warm, personal and confidential — Hitler's letters were invariably about politics. The letter is revealing of Hitler's hopes for the future and of his tactics regarding the formation of a government in Thuringia in 1930, tactics which served as an example for his bargaining in January 1933 when he was forming a national government.

TRACY, Donald R.
"The Development of the National Socialist Party in Thuringia 1924—30". *Central European History,* vol. 8, pt. 1 (1975), p. 23—50.
A detailed examination of an important NSDAP *Gau.* Tracy analyses the reasons for the party's success here, including the strength of *völkisch* traditions and the legacy of socialist rule 1921—23. The NSDAP participation in state government in 1930 is also explained.

13. WETZLAR

MAYER, Ulrich.
Das Eindringen des Nationalsozialismus in die Stadt Wetzlar. Wetzlar: Wetzlarer Geschichtsverein (1970), 124 pp.[1]

14. WÜRTTEMBERG

DOETSCH, Wilhelm J.
See his work in section 10B.

15. FOREIGN COUNTRIES (EXCLUDING AUSTRIA)

DIAMOND, S. A.
The Nazi Movement in the U.S.A. 1924—1941. Ithaca: Cornell University Press (1974), 380 pp.
Interesting for its account of links between the American party and the NSDAP.

1. I was unable to procure a copy for review.

LACHMANN, Günter.
Der Nationalsozialismus in der Schweiz 1931—1945: ein Beitrag zur Geschichte des Auslands-organisation der NSDAP. Dissertation, Free University of Berlin (1962).
Based on limited sources.

SCHMIDT, H. D.
"The Nazi Party in Palestine and the Levant 1932—9". *International Affairs (London),* vol. 28, pt. 4 (1952), p. 460—7.

E. ANCILLARY ORGANIZATIONS

(i) Storm Troopers (SA)

BENNECKE, Heinrich.
Hitler und die SA. Munich: Olzog (1962), 264 pp.
Written by a former high-ranking SA leader, this study's apologetic tone gravely undermines its value. He certainly has some interesting detail to provide, but important aspects of the SA's development are treated in cavalier fashion; for example, difficulties with the party, and leadership struggles.

BLOCH, Charles.
Die SA und die Krise des NS-Regimes 1934. Frankfurt: Suhrkamp Verlag (1970), 177 pp.
An early chapter gives a competent résumé of major events in the SA's history before 1933.

MITCHELL, Otis C.
An Institutional History of the National Socialist SA: a Study of the SA as a Functioning Organization within the Party Structure (1931—1934). Dissertation, University of Kansas (1964).
A short and not very enlightening examination of Röhm's period as Chief of Staff (1931—34); Mitchell's treatment of organization, leadership, activities and NSDAP-SA relations adds nothing new or original.

REICHE, Eric G.
The Development of the SA in Nuremberg 1922—1934. Dissertation, University of Delaware (1972).
Outlines the origins and history of the SA, emphasizing the mainly bourgeois social composition of its membership, and its increasingly stormy relations with the local NSDAP. It is not surprising to learn that Streicher was loathed by Nuremberg's SA commanders.

WERNER, Andreas.
SA: "Wehrverband", "Parteitruppe", oder "Revolutionsarmee"? Studien zur Geschichte der SA und der NSDAP 1920—33. Dissertation, University of Erlangen (1964).
By far the best study available on the SA. Werner has gathered an impressive amount of accurate information which he perceptively analyses. He stresses the independent ethos and socialistic orientation of the organization and rightly considers it to have played a major part in the final victory of National Socialism.

(ii) Protection Squads (SS)

HÖHNE, Heinz.
Der Orden unter dem Totenkopf: die Geschichte der SS. Gütersloh: Mohn (1967).
A very readable but somewhat popularly orientated work. There is a considerable amount of detailed information, and for the pre-1933 period there are interesting notes on the kind of recruits the SS attracted.

NEUSÜSS-HUNKEL, Ermenhild.
Die SS. Hanover: Norddeutsche Verlagsanstalt (1966), 143 pp.
An objective and highly competent analysis, but it concentrates exclusively on the post-1933 period.

REITLINGER, Gerald.
The SS: Alibi of a Nation, 1922—1945. London: Heinemann (1956), 513 pp.
Only a very small section of the book refers to the pre-1933 period, and in it the origins and early history of the SS are given only cursory treatment. The book as a whole lacks sober detachment and in-depth analysis.

(iii) Hitler Youth (HJ)

BRANDENBURG, Hans-Christian.
Die Geschichte der HJ: Wege und Irrwege einer Generation. Cologne: Verlag Wissenschaft und Politik (1968), 347 pp.
An attempted comprehensive history of the HJ which, however, leaves too many fundamental questions relating to its organization, leadership, ideology and political orientation unanswered. Brandenburg has not used all of the widely scattered sources of material that are available for this topic, and the result is an unsatisfactory, fragmentary study.

JOVY, E. M.
See his work in section 18B.

KLÖNNE, Arno.
Hitlerjugend: die Jugend und ihre Organization im Dritten Reich. Hanover: Norddeutsche Verlagsanstalt (1956), 108 pp.
A good synopsis of the ideology and organization of the HJ from 1933—45, with only a passing reference to pre-1933 developments.

KLOSE, Werner.
Generation im Gleichschritt: eine Dokumentation. Oldenburg: Stalling (1964), 296 pp.
Deals exclusively and badly with the Third Reich era.

KOCH, Hansjoachim W.
The Hitler Youth: Origins and Development 1922—45. London: MacDonald & Jane's (1975), 340 pp.
Written by a former member of the Hitler Youth, this book does more than any other to perpetuate the myths and distortions surrounding the history of the HJ. The work is lacking in objective analysis and reliable narrative, and specialists and general readers alike should beware. Koch seldom acknowledges the sources on which his material appears to be based.

POTEET, David C.
The Nazi Youth Movement 1920—1927. Dissertation, University of Georgia (1972).
A superficial glance at the various groups which constituted the National Socialist youth movement until 1927. The author mistakenly describes the *Schilljugend* as a party affiliate: in fact it was never officially recognized as the NSDAP's youth group.

SCHMIDT, Ulrike.
See her work in section 18B.

SCHROEDER, Richard E.
The Hitler Youth as a Paramilitary Organization. Dissertation, University of Chicago (1975).
Takes a rather simplistic and misleading view of the HJ's role before 1933. The HJ's individuality within the National Socialist movement is barely appreciated.

STACHURA, Peter D.
"The Ideology of the Hitler Youth in the Kampfzeit". *Journal of Contemporary History*, vol. 7, pt. 3 (1973), p. 155—67.
Argues that because of the HJ's basically socialistic ideology, it is valid to speak of the group possessing a distinctive ethos within not only the early National Socialist movement but also the German youth movement as a whole.

STACHURA, Peter D.
Nazi Youth in the Weimar Republic. Santa Barbara; Oxford: ABC-Clio Press (1975), 301 pp.
An in-depth analysis of the genesis, nature and development of the early HJ. The group emerged as a distinctive entity in the National Socialist movement and as a recognizable part of the so-called "Nazi Left", but came into serious political conflict with Hitler on this account following the NSDAP's adoption of conservative policies in 1928—29. An examination of the wide repercussions of this conflict provides additional insights into the character of Hitler's movement before 1933.

WALKER, Lawrence D.
Hitler Youth and Catholic Youth 1933—1936. Washington, D.C.: Catholic University of America Press (1971), 203 pp.
The early chapters give a thoroughly unsatisfactory and in places factually erroneous résumé of HJ development. The rest of the book maintains this abysmal standard.

(iv) Students' League (NSDStB)

BLEUEL, Hans P.; KLINNERT, Ernst.
See their joint work in section 17B.

CARMON, Arye Z.
See his work in section 17B.

DIBNERS, Ursula R. B.
The History of the National Socialist German Student League. Dissertation, University of Michigan (1969).[1]

1. I failed to obtain a copy in time for review.

FAUST, Anseln.
Der Nationalsozialistische Deutsche Studentenbund: Studenten und Nationalsozialismus in der Weimarer Republik. 2 vols. Düsseldorf: Verlag Schwann (1973), 178, 192 pp.
A partially satisfactory organizational history of the NSDStB 1925—33, tracing its rise under Baldur von Schirach (its leader from 1928) to a commanding position in student associations at German universities. The character of the NSDStB and the reasons for its success are not explained in entirely convincing fashion.

KATER, Michael H.
"Der NS-Studentenbund von 1926 bis 1928: Randgruppe zwischen Hitler und Strasser".
Vierteljahrshefte für Zeitgeschichte, vol. 22, pt. 2 (1974), p. 148—90.
This is a quite outstanding, richly detailed and powerfully argued analysis of the NSDStB during the period when Wilhelm Tempel was *Reichsführer*. The author has made extensive use of hitherto unpublished material from the former archives of the *Reichsstudentenführung* and NSDStB located at the University of Würzburg. The NSDStB tried unsuccessfully in 1926—28 to attract less affluent students by a vaguely "socialist" programme and the group remained insignificant until after Tempel had been replaced by Schirach who adopted a more nationalist approach.

SPITZNAGEL, Peter.
See his work in section 17B

STEINBERG, Michael S.
See his work in section 17B.

23

Biographies and Studies of National Socialist Leaders[1]

A. GENERAL

DAVIDSON, Eugene.
The Trial of the Germans — an Account of the Twenty-two Defendants Before the International Military Tribunal at Nuremberg. New York: Macmillan (1966), 636 pp.
The main focus is on a discussion of the careers and personalities of the twenty-two major defendants at the Nuremberg trial. There are many factual errors and the scholarship is generally poor, but some of the sketches (e.g. of Streicher) are useful.

FEST, Joachim C.
The Face of the Third Reich: Portraits of the Nazi Leadership. London: Weidenfeld & Nicolson (1970), 402 pp. (Original German ed. published in 1963).
A competent overall description of important NSDAP leaders, but it adds little by way of new facts or novel interpretation. Indeed, it is above all the general reader who will find the work useful.

GILBERT, Gustave M.
Nuremberg Diary. New York: Farner, Straus (1947), 471 pp.
Studies of some of the leading National Socialist defendants at the Nuremberg war crimes trial. The author, a psychiatrist, was officially assigned to the court. The book is interesting but needs to be read with caution because some of his value judgements are grossly misleading.

KEMPNER, Robert M. W.
Das Dritte Reich im Kreuzverhör — aus den unveröffentlichten Vernehmungsprotokollen des Anklägers. Munich (1969).
Useful for biographical sketches of Third Reich luminaries.

LERNER, Daniel.
The Nazi Elite. Stanford (Hoover Institute): Stanford University Press (1951), 112 pp.
A statistical analysis of National Socialist leader types, 1918—33, which substantiates previous notions about them. The method of material selection (from the *Deutsche Führerlexikon* of 1934, published by the NSDAP) is, however, open to criticism.

SCHWERIN von KROSIGK, Lutz G.
Es geschah in Deutschland: Menschenbilder unseres Jahrhunderts. Tübingen: Verlag Hermann Leins (1951), 384 pp.
The memoirs of the former Reich Minister of Finance, presented in a series of vignettes of various National Socialist leaders. Moderately useful.

STOCKHORST, Erich.
Fünftausend Köpfe: wer war was im Dritten Reich. Kettwig: Velbert (1967).
By far the most comprehensive collection of biographical data (arranged alphabetically) on leading National Socialists, yet the surprisingly high number of important omissions reveals that the book is far from complete.

B. ADOLF HITLER[2]

AUER, Johann:
"Zwei Aufenthalte Hitlers in Wien". *Vierteljahrshefte für Zeitgeschichte*, vol. 14, pt. 2 (1966), p. 207—8.
The two sojourns referred to are as follows: firstly, Hitler was in Vienna for a meeting on 28 December 1921 organized by the Austrian NSDAP against the recently concluded Treaty of Prague/Lana between Austria and Czechoslovakia. Secondly, Hitler was in Vienna on 17 June 1922 as guest speaker at an Austrian NSDAP rally. On both occasions, Hitler fulminated against the Jews, revealing his obsession with anti-semitism.

AUERBACH, Hellmuth.
"Hitlers Handschrift und Masers Lesefehler: eine notwendige Berichtigung". *Vierteljahrshefte für Zeitgeschichte*, vol. 21, pt. 3 (1973), p. 334—6.
A devastating critique of the many errors which Werner Maser (see below) has made in reading Hitler's letters. He has misread a large number of words and this must cast further doubt on the value of his biography of the *Führer*.

---

1. Cross-reference should be made to relevant parts of section 24.
2. See also section 24A.

BANULS, André.
"Das völkische Blatt 'Der Scherer': ein Beitrag zu Hitlers Schulzeit". *Vierteljahrshefte für Zeitgeschichte*, vol. 18, pt. 2 (1970), p. 196—203.
Disputes Daim's thesis (see below) that Lanz von Liebenfels was the person who first gave Hitler his anti-semitic racialist ideas. Banuls contends that before he went to Vienna, Hitler had already been susceptible to anti-semitic notions at his Linz school. He is certain that Hitler came into contact with a series of racialist journals, particularly *Der Scherer*.

BAYNES, Norman H. (ed.).
The Speeches of Adolf Hitler, 1922—1939. 2 vols. London: Oxford University Press (1968). New ed.[1]
A standard source of reference, though not without notable deficiencies: this is not a complete collection of Hitler's speeches and the translation is too often faulty.

BINION, Rudolph.
"Foam on the Hitler Wave". *Journal of Modern History*, vol. 46, pt. 3 (1974), p. 522—8.
The tone of this review article of recent Hitler biographies is exceedingly critical and scornful. Maser and Joachim Fest (see below) come in for particularly rough treatment.

BRACHER, Karl Dietrich.
"Das 'Phänomen' Adolf Hitler". *(Neue) Politische Literatur*, vol. 2 (1952), p. 207—12.
A review of some biographies of Hitler dating from the period before 1945.

BRACHER, Karl Dietrich.
Adolf Hitler. Munich: Scherz (1964), 77 pp.
A thoughtful essay.

BUCHHEIT, Gert (ed.).
Der Führer ins Nichts: eine Diagnose Adolf Hitlers. Rastatt: Grote (1960), 88 pp.
Contains four short appraisals of Hitler as a politician, ideologue, soldier, and personality. Written by Hans Buchheim and Edith Eucken-Erdsieck, the essays were originally presented on West German radio.

BULLOCK, Alan.
Hitler: a Study in Tyranny. London: Odhams Books (1964), 848 pp. Revised ed.
Still regarded as one of the best biographies of Hitler. The book is written clearly and fluently, yet several aspects of the narrative require revision. These include the assessment of the early part of Hitler's career, and of the internal development of the NSDAP 1925—30.

CALIC, Edouard.
Unmasked: Two Confidential Interviews with Hitler in 1931. London: Chatto & Windus (1971), 192 pp.
Records the meetings Hitler had with Richard Breiting, editor of the newspaper *Leipziger Neueste Nachrichten*, in 1931. They give a vivid picture of Hitler's thoughts and plans in politics, and an accurate forecast of developments involving the NSDAP during the next few years.

CHURCHILL, Winston S.
Great Contemporaries. Chicago: University of Chicago Press (1974), 388 pp. New ed.
Of note for Churchill's favourable remarks about Hitler.

1. Included in this bibliography, despite being originally published before 1945, because of its importance.

CROSS, Colin.
Adolf Hitler. London: Hodder & Stoughton (1973), 348 pp.
Unoriginal, superficial and clearly meant for popular consumption.

DAIM, Wilfried.
Der Mann, der Hitler die Ideen gab: von den religiösen Verirrungen eines Sektierers zum Rassenwahn des Diktators. Munich: Isar-Verlag (1958), 286 pp.
Argues not wholly convincingly that the source of Hitler's anti-semitic ideas was Dr. Georg Lanz von Liebenfels (real name Adolf Josef Lanz) of Vienna, a self-proclaimed prophet of Aryanism. Hitler apparently read Liebenfels' journal *Ostara*, but whether this was his first contact with anti-semitic literature is open to doubt.

DAIM, Wilfried.
"Der Mann, der Hitler die Ideen gab". *Politische Studien*, vol. 9 (1958), p. 341—50.
A summary of the main points of his book.

DEUERLEIN, Ernst.
Hitler: eine politische Biographie. Munich: List (1969), 87 pp.
An excellent, concise and perceptive study which deserves wider publicity among the reading public. Depicts Hitler as the personification of the fears and hopes of a Germany unable or unwilling to come to terms with the 1918 defeat.

DIETRICH, Otto.
12 Jahre mit Hitler. Munich: Isar-Verlag (1955), 285 pp.
Written by Hitler's former press chief. The second half of this rather ponderous and dull book records Dietrich's impressions of Hitler's character and attitudes. Nothing of importance emerges.

DOMARUS, Max (ed.).
Hitler: Reden und Proklamationen 1932—1945. Kommentiert von einem deutschen Zeitgenosse. 2 vols. Neustadt a.d. Aisch: Verlag Schmidt (1962) 987, 1347 pp.
The best and most exhaustive collection of Hitler's speeches available. A monumental and indispensable work of scholarship, brilliantly edited and annotated.

DORPALEN, Andreas.
"Hitler — Twelve Years After". *Review of Politics*, vol. 19 (1957), p. 486—506.
A critical and helpful review of recent biographical and memoir studies relating to Hitler.

ESH, Shaul.
"Eine neue literarische Quelle Hitlers: eine methodologische Überlegung". *Geschichte in Wissenschaft und Unterricht*, vol. 15, pt. 8 (1964), p. 487—93.
A comment on Ernst Nolte's essay "Eine frühe Quelle zu Hitlers Antisemitismus" (see later in this section), calling into question Nolte's views on the Hitler-Eckart relationship.

FABRY, Philipp W.
Mutmassungen über Hitler; Urteile um Zeitgenossen. Düsseldorf: Droste (1969), 265 pp.
A study which clearly reveals the lack of awareness and naivety towards Hitler and his aims shown by most prom-

inent political and civil leaders. Among those whose views are narrated are Stalin, Schleicher, Brüning, Churchill and Pope Pius XII.

FAUL, Erwin.
"Hitlers Über-Machiavellismus". *Vierteljahrshefte für Zeitgeschichte*, vol. 2, pt. 4 (1954), p. 344—72.
Examines the nature of Hitler's political cunning.

FEST, Joachim C.
Adolf Hitler: Gesichter eines Diktators. Hamburg (1968).
A very good essay, brief, to the point, and incisive.

FEST, Joachim C.
Hitler: eine Biographie. Berlin: Propyläen Verlag (1973), 1190 pp.
A massively detailed, serious biography which, however, is far from being definitive. The narrative is fluent and extremely readable yet the book has a large number of fundamental faults: it contains many factual errors, it presents no new material, it does not come near to solving the enigma of Hitler, and is too full of contradictions. In short, a book for the general reader, not for the specialist.

FEST, Joachim C.
"On Remembering Adolf Hitler". *Encounter*, vol. 41, pt. 4 (1973), p. 19--35.
Examines the various roles and moods of Hitler — dreamer, actor, propagandist, politician, tactician and so on. The material is condensed, of course, from his biography.

FISHMAN, Sterling.
"The Rise of Hitler as a Beer Hall Orator". *Review of Politics*, vol. 26 (1964), p. 244—56.
A tentative enquiry into the sources of Hitler's understanding of mass techniques which enabled him to become a uniquely successful demagogue.

FREUND, Michael.
See his article in section 15C (ii).

GATZKE, Hans.
"Hitler and Psychohistory". *American Historical Review*, vol. 78, pt. 2 (1973), p. 394—401.
A review article of Walter C. Langer's book (see below).

GISEVIUS, Hans B.
Adolf Hitler: Versuch einer Deutung. Munich: Rütten & Loening (1963), 465 pp.
A long, rather tortuous book of which only the initial chapters refer to the pre-1933 period. But Gisevius is objective in his assessment of Hitler, stressing the man's curious combination of evil brutality and political sagacity. For the advent to power of someone like this, the author concludes, the German people must accept most of the responsibility.

GÖRLITZ, Walter.
Adolf Hitler. Göttingen: Musterschmidt (1960), 145 pp.
Popularly orientated, and an adequate general summary of the main stages of Hitler's life, but no more. The breadth of Hitler's personality eludes the author, though he is right to underline the nihilist streak in the *Führer*'s make-up.

GÖRLITZ, Walter; QUINT, Herbert.
Adolf Hitler: eine Biographie. Stuttgart: Steingrüben Verlag (1952), 656 pp.

Unsatisfactory in the main because it perpetuates too many legends about Hitler. However, the book contains some interesting details. (Chapters IV-IX deal with the Weimar era.)

GRAML, Hermann.
"Probleme einer Hitler-Biographie: kritische Bemerkungen zu Joachim C. Fest". *Vierteljahrshefte für Zeitgeschichte*, vol. 22, pt. 1 (1974), p. 76—92.
A learned article on the special problems confronting any prospective biographer of Hitler, for example, the problem of bringing together the results and techniques of many different academic disciplines. There is also the problem of ploughing through a veritable mountain of secondary literature, as well as primary sources. Graml illustrates his argument by making critical references to parts of Fest's biography, though he believes that Fest has come as close as anyone to writing a definitive biography.

GREINER, Josef.
Das Ende des Hitler-Mythos. Vienna: Amalthea Verlag (1947), 343 pp.
Greiner befriended Hitler during the latter's stay in Vienna before 1914. In this book, he recollects that friendship with a touch of bitter irony. Greiner's reliability on points of fact is suspect, however, and not a few of his explanations are implausible.

GRIESWELLE, Detlev.
Propaganda der Friedlosigkeit: eine Studie zu Hitlers Rhetorik 1920—1933. Stuttgart: Ferdinand Emke Verlag (1972), 233 pp.
A scholarly and incisive analysis of the elements and techniques of Hitler's successful rhetorical powers. But the author also stresses that many Germans wanted to believe in Hitler, *faute de mieux*, because of their disillusionment with democracy and the Republic. Hence, it was not merely the techniques of rhetoric which brought success to Hitler: they were applied in an *ambience* conducive to rhetoric.

GÜNTHER, Hans F.
Mein Eindruck von Adolf Hitler. Pähl: Bebenburg (1969), 158 pp.
The author was a prolific and well-known *völkisch* propagandist and writer during the Weimar and Third Reich periods. His brief memoir recalls his view of Hitler and, if nothing else, has a certain curiosity value.

HALE, Oron J.
"Adolf Hitler: Taxpayer". *American Historical Review*, vol. 60, pt. 4 (1955), p. 830—42.
Based on Hitler's tax files for the years 1925—35, this paper adds a small footnote to our understanding of Hitler and the early NSDAP. The files allow only a partial assessment of Hitler's financial status and do not deal with the source of his income apart from book royalties. The *Führer* fell into considerable debt from 1925—28 but once his writings became more widely known, following the party's climb to national prominence in September 1930, his financial position was assured.

HAMMER, Wolfgang.
Adolf Hitler — ein deutscher Messias? Dialog mit dem Führer. Munich: Delp (1970), 250 pp.
Not to be taken seriously on any account.

HEER, Friedrich.
Der Glaube des Adolf Hitler: Anatomie einer politischen Religiosität. Munich: Bechtle (1968), 751 pp.
An analysis of Hitler's ideas and personality from a psychohistorical standpoint. Heer argues that Hitler really did see himself as a saviour given by the Almighty to the German people — an interesting but unconvincing hypothesis.

HEIBER, Helmut.
Adolf Hitler: eine Biographie. Berlin: Colloquium
Verlag (1960), 159 pp.
Pleasantly written, but aimed at the general and undiscern-
ing reader. Offers nothing new.

HEIDEN, Konrad.
Der Führer: Hitler's Rise to Power. London:
Pordes (1967), 614 pp. New ed.[1]
Still reasonably worthwhile, although now superseded by
other studies, and despite a series of glaring factual and
interpretative aberrations. Heiden's analysis of Hitler's
character, however, has stood the test of time and is very
good.

HEISIG, Klaus.
**Die politischen Grundlagen in Hitlers Schriften,
Reden und Gesprächen im Hinblick auf seine
Auffassung von Staat und Recht.** Dissertation,
University of Cologne (1965).
A scholarly, legalistic analysis of Hitler's views on the
state and the law during 1933—45; concludes that the
Third Reich was a state of illegality and even anarchy.

HEYL, John D.
See his article in section 27.

HILDEBRAND, Klaus.
**"Hitlers Ort in der Geschichte des preussisch-
deutschen Nationalstaates".** *Historische Zeitschrift*,
no. 217 (1973), p. 584—632.
An important and substantial paper which, in reviewing all
the significant literature written on Hitler since 1945, tries
to place him in the context of the "brown" and "white"
revolutions.

HOFFMANN, Heinrich.
Hitler Was My Friend. London: Burke (1955),
256 pp.
Hoffmann was Hitler's personal photographer for many
years and according to this book his fondness for his
former master remains largely undiminished. There is not
much information here, and what there is must be viewed
as unreliable for the most part.

HORN, Wolfgang.
**"Ein unbekannter Aufsatz Hitlers aus dem
Frühjahr 1924".** *Vierteljahrshefte für
Zeitgeschichte*, vol. 16, pt. 3 (1968), p. 280—94.
Horn refers to a previously unknown letter written by
Hitler in spring 1924 which was published as an article in
the April number of *Deutschlands Erneuerung*, a Pan-
German monthly periodical. The article throws fresh light
on the genesis of Hitler's foreign policy plans, especially
those concerning *Lebensraum*.

JÄCKEL, Eberhard.
Hitlers Weltanschauung: Entwurf einer Herrschaft.
Tübingen: Verlag Hermann Leins (1969), 159 pp.
A brilliant, concise, interpretative essay showing that
Hitler developed a coherent programme in the 1920s —
characterized by *völkisch* anti-semitism and the concept
of *Lebensraum* — to which he remained faithful to the very
end. This view therefore challenges the hitherto accepted
hypothesis among most scholars that Hitler's ideas were
unsystematic and empirical. A valuable and major contribution.

1. Heiden's other works on National Socialism have not
been included in this bibliography because they were published before 1945 and have not been reprinted.

JENKS, William A.
Vienna and the Young Hitler. New York: Columbia
University Press (1960), 252 pp.
Tells us quite a lot about pre-1914 Vienna but very little
that is new about Hitler's stay there. Otherwise a compe-
tent, clear narrative.

JETZINGER, Franz.
**Hitlers Jugend: Phantasien, Lügen und die
Wahrheit.** Vienna: Europa-Verlag (1956), 308 pp.
Perhaps the most reliable general study available on Hitler's
early years. The difficulties of accurate research in this
sphere are enormous but Jetzinger's approach is painstaking
and objective in the main.

JOCHMANN, Werner E. (ed.).
**Im Kampf um die Macht: Hitlers Rede vor dem
Hamburger Nationalklub von 1919.** Frankfurt:
Europäische Verlagsanstalt (1960), 121 pp.
In a very good introduction, the editor informatively
surveys relations between the NSDAP and the nationalist
Right in northern Germany during the 1920s. Hitler made
this speech in 1926 and it is an excellent example of how
easily and skilfully he could adapt his message to suit
different audiences. Here, he refrained from any anti-
semitic remarks in case his conservative/nationalist and
middle class listeners would be offended, and concentrated
instead on providing a distorted version of the November
Revolution.

JOCHMANN, Werner E.; **NELLESSEN**, Bernd.
Adolf Hitler: Persönlichkeit, Ideologie, Taktik.
Paderborn: Schöningh (1960), 64 pp.
A scholarly but unoriginal appraisal.

KLOSE, Werner.
Hitler: ein Bericht für junge Staatsbürger.
Tübingen: Heliopolis-Verlag (1961), 304 pp.
Designed to serve an educational purpose for young
Germans, this book is in fact a rather poor narrative.

KLÖSS, Erhard (ed.).
**Reden des Führers: Politik und Propaganda Adolf
Hitlers 1922—45.** Munich: Deutscher Taschenbuch
Verlag (1967).
The documentary extracts from Hitler's speeches which are
presented here are all well-known. The linking commentary
is competent.

KOENIGSBERG, Richard A.
**Hitler's Ideology: a Study in Psychoanalytic
Sociology.** New York: The Library of Social
Science (1975), 105 pp.
An original and provocative work which by analysing the
psychological sources of Hitler's ideology (although the
author is not always convincing on what constitutes
"psychological sources") develops a psychoanalytic theory
of nationalism. Much of what Koenigsberg has to say, however, seems frankly to be rather far-fetched.

KOTZE, Hildegard von; **KRAUSNICK**, Helmut;
and others.
**Es spricht der Führer: 7 exemplarische Hitler-
Reden.** Gütersloh: Mohn (1966), 378 pp.
This book provides an excellent analysis of Hitler's style
of public speaking and includes the text of some of the
Führer's speeches (made in 1937, 1938, 1942 and 1944)
not listed in Domarus's documentary collection (reviewed
above).

KUBIZEK, August.
Adolf Hitler, mein Jugendfreund. Graz: Stocker Verlag (1953), 352 pp.
This account of Hitler's early years needs to be used with considerable caution as there are many inaccuracies on points of detail. The tone is not nearly critical enough, but otherwise the book is a generally useful narrative.

KURTH, Gertrud M.
"The Jew and Adolf Hitler". *Psychoanalytic Quarterly*, vol. 16 (1947), p. 11—32.
Many of Kurth's facts are wrong, but she has some interesting comments on the consequences of Hitler's sexual repression in adolescence.

LANG, Jochen von (ed.).
Adolf Hitler: Gesichter eines Diktators. Hamburg: Wegner (1968), 16 pp.
An absorbing collection of pictures of Hitler, capturing his many different moods.

LANGER, Walter C.
The Mind of Adolf Hitler. London: Secker & Warburg (1973), 269 pp.
A fascinating psychological analysis of Hitler's ideas and personality originally written in 1943 for the American government's Office of Strategic Services (OSS). The book adds a much needed psychiatric dimension to an understanding of the Hitler enigma, though its findings and conclusions are controversial and likely to be rejected by some scholars in the field.

MASER, Werner.
Adolf Hitler: Legende, Mythos, Wirklichkeit. Munich: Bechtle Verlag (1971), 530 pp.
A book to be avoided by everyone. This over-long study purports to have filled important gaps in Hitler's biography, but in fact it merely adds confusion. Maser has a passion for minute but often erroneous detail; his conclusions are misleading and based on unwarranted assumptions; he claims to have discovered new material when this is demonstrably not so; his narrative is fragmentary and disjointed; and he repeats himself time and again. Amidst all this, the ostensible objective of the book, to dispel the legends around Hitler, is lost; we are left bemused and none the wiser about the Hitler phenomenon.

MASER, Werner (ed.).
Hitlers Briefe und Notizen: sein Weltbild in handschriftlichen Dokumenten. Düsseldorf: Econ-Verlag (1973), 399 pp.
A collection of Hitler's letters and notes gathered from private sources and archives. It is a pity that they have not been treated with proper editorial skill. Maser's editing is careless and his analysis of the material is very superficial. Indeed, he has misread many words in these letters so that his translation gives an incorrect version of what Hitler actually wrote. For these reasons, there must be grave doubts about this collection's value as an historical source.

MASER, Werner (ed.).
Mein Schüler Hitler: das Tagebuch seines Lehrers Paul Devrient. Pfaffenhofen: Ilmgau Verlag (1975), 303 pp.
In the 1920s and 1930s, Devrient (real name Walter Stieber) was a highly successful German opera singer of international repute. From 1929—33 he gave instruction in acting and techniques of public speaking, and his most famous and successful pupil was Hitler. Devrient accompanied the *Führer* on his speaking tours throughout Germany, particularly in 1932. This is his diary, which recalls this strange dimension of Hitler's political career and makes absorbing reading. Maser provides an unhelpful introduction.

McRANDLE, James H.
The Track of the Wolf: Essays on National Socialism and its Leader, Adolf Hitler. Evanston (Illinois): North Western University Press (1965), 261 pp.
The author believes that the wolf symbol is fundamental to an understanding of Hitler (who sometimes used the alias "Herr Wolf" in the early 1920s). The book consists of five separate essays, all of which unsuccessfully examine the *Führer's* personality. The author demonstrates his capacity for extravagant theorizing, which is rather amusing, but this is not what scholarship is about.

MOMMSEN, Hans.
"Nationalsozialismus". In *Sowjetsystem und demokratische Gesellschaft.* Edited by Claus D. Kernig. Freiburg (1971).
Mommsen merely restates the well-known theory that Hitler was an unprincipled opportunist who worked on an empirical basis. This applies, he adds, to both foreign and domestic policy.

MORSEY, Rudolf.
"Hitler als Braunschweiger Regierungsrat". *Vierteljahrshefte für Zeitgeschichte*, vol. 8, pt. 4 (1960), p. 419—48.
A full and learned explanation of the circumstances and subsequent results of Hitler's controversial appointment to the Brunswick state government's service in early 1932, which thus conferred German citizenship on him and enabled him to stand as a candidate in the presidential election of spring 1932. Morsey appends interesting and relevant documentation of the affair.

NEEDLER, Martin.
"Hitler's Anti-Semitism: a Political Appraisal". *Public Opinion Quarterly*, vol. 24 (Winter 1960), p. 665—9.
Short and uninformative.

NOLTE, Ernst.
"Eine frühe Quelle zu Hitlers Antisemitismus". *Historische Zeitschrift*, no. 192 (1961), p. 584—606.
Covers extreme right-wing politics in Bavaria before the emergence of Hitler, but the main point of the essay is to examine the influence on Hitler's anti-semitism of Dietrich Eckart's brochure, *Der Bolschewismus von Moses bis Lenin — Zweigespräch zwischen Adolf Hitler und mir*, published in 1924.

PAYNE, Robert.
The Life and Death of Adolf Hitler. London: Jonathan Cape (1973), 623 pp.
Does not contain anything for the specialist. Payne goes over well-trodden ground, though he writes coherently. The narrative is discursive, pedestrian and often factually inaccurate. There is not an original idea to be found anywhere, so the book in no way enhances our understanding of Hitler.

PESE, Walter W.
Hitler's Ideology, with Special Emphasis on Race, Nation, and Party. Dissertation, New School for Social Research (1952).
An ambitious project for a Ph.D. dissertation; well written, but suggestive rather than conclusive.

PHELPS, Reginald H.
"Hitler als Parteiredner im Jahre 1920". *Viertel-*
jahrshefte für Zeitgeschichte, vol. 11, pt. 3 (1963),
p. 274—330.
The author contrasts a description of the early NSDAP
given by Hitler in *Mein Kampf* with the reality of the
matter, which is provided by twenty documents from the
Hauptarchiv der NSDAP collection (now in the *Bundes-*
archiv, Koblenz). In his book, Hitler gives a glowing
account of how the party went from triumph to triumph
until the promulgation of the   NSDAP programme in
February 1920. The documentation provided paints a
rather more sombre picture and indeed constitutes an important source for the early NSDAP and Hitler's methods
and capabilities as a propagandist.

PHELPS, Reginald H.
"Hitlers 'Grundlegende' Rede über den Antisemit-
ismus". *Vierteljahrsefte für Zeitgeschichte*, vol.
16, pt. 4 (1968), p. 390—420.
Referred to is a typewritten 33-page document from
archival sources concerning a definitive statement on the
NSDAP's attitude to Jews and anti-semitism given by Hitler
in a carefully prepared speech in Munich on 13 August
1920. The title of the speech was "Warum sind wir Anti-
semiten?" Phelps provides a résumé of some of the speech's
main features and outlines the main influences which
shaped Hitler's anti-semitism. The text of the speech is
reproduced in full.

PICKER, Henry (ed.).
Hitlers Tischgespräche im Führerhauptquartier
1941—1942. Stuttgart: Seewald Verlag (1963),
546 pp. 2nd ed.
This new edition is a decided improvement on the first. The
material is organized much better, Hitler's conversations are
now arranged in chronological sequence, and factual inaccuracies which marred the original have been eliminated.
Moreover, Andreas Hillgruber has supplied a valuable commentary at the foot of each page. The long introduction
written by P.E. Schramm is the only major disappointment:
his discussion of Hitler's personality leaves something to be
desired. As a whole, the volume is an important source for
Hitler's ideas on a wide range of topics.

PICKER, Henry (ed.).
The Hitler Phenomenon. Newton Abbot: David &
Charles (1974), 223pp.
Contains some 350 photographs of Hitler taken over the
years by Heinrich Hoffmann with a poor explanatory text
by the editor. Perusing this misleading book, one might
easily get the impression that the *Führer* was really quite
a nice fellow, for in many of the illustrations he appears as
the kindly father figure or upright statesman. Nothing
could be further from the truth, of course, and this volume
should have been evened up with more pictures revealing the
brutality and evil of National Socialism and its leader.

RAUSCHNING, Hermann.[1]
Gespräche mit Hitler. Frankfurt: Europa-Verlag
(1973), 278 pp. New ed.
One of the earliest published (1939) collections of Hitler's
private conversations. Rauschning, a former NSDAP
member and President of the Senate of the Free City of
Danzig, hoped that the revelations in the book would alert
the world at large to the danger of Hitler. The authenticity
of the book was doubted in many scholarly circles but
more and more it has come to be accepted as a valid historical source for Hitler's ideas and motives.

1. Readers may wish to note a volume of Hitler speeches
published before 1945: Gordon W. Prange (ed.). *Hitler's*
Words: Two Decades of National Socialism, 1923—1943.
Washington: American Council on Public Affairs (1944),
400 pp.

RÖHRS, Hans-Dietrich.
Hitlers Krankheit: Tatsachen und Legenden.
Neckargemünd: Vowinckel (1966), 203 pp.
Purports to be a conclusive analysis of Hitler's medical
history, but in fact the book contains more speculative
nonsense than anything else and should not be taken
seriously.

SCHIEDER, Theodor.
Hermann Rauschnings "Gespräche mit Hitler" als
Geschichtsquelle. Opladen: Westdeutscher Verlag
(1972), 91 pp.
A critical assessment of the book which probes its origins
and authenticity. Schieder dispels some of the doubts
surrounding it, while suggesting that other points must still
be open to debate. A judicious and fair essay.

SCHRAMM, Percy Ernst.
Hitler: the Man and the Military Leader. London:
Allen Lane (1971), 214 pp. (Original German ed.
published in 1965).
Not a conventional biographical study but a volume consisting of previously published writings on Hitler by the
author, and two appendices: one of extracts from
Schramm's previous work on Hitler-army relations, and
the second a memorandum written in 1946 by General
Jodl on Hitler's capability as a military leader. The volume
is worth reading, though it offers no startling insights.

SMITH, Bradley F.
Adolf Hitler: His Family, Childhood and Youth
Stanford: Stanford University Press (1967), 180 pp.
Smith has reviewed all available material, including previously unpublished sources, to produce an excellent,
scholarly, and objective narrative. There are few discern-
ible traces of the evil monster in Hitler's early years, but
the author underlines the influences which left a mark on
his character and personality during the formative years of
his life before 1913.

STEIN, Alfred.
"Adolf Hitler und Gustave Le Bon: der Meister der
Massenbewegung und sein Lehrer". *Geschichte in*
Wissenschaft und Unterricht, vol. 6 (1955), p. 362
—8.
Discusses whether Hitler had read Le Bon's famous work
on mass psychology, *La Psychologie des foules* (1895).
Stein shows that a German translation of the book
appeared in 1908 entitled *Psychologie der Massen*, and that
the Vienna *Hofbibliothek*, which Hitler often used, acquired
a copy the same year. Stein considers it therefore highly
likely, because of the marked resemblance between Hitler's
ideas and Le Bon's, that the former read the book. Hitler,
however, never mentioned the French philosopher in his
writings.

STEIN, George H. (ed.).
Hitler. Englewood Cliffs, New Jersey: Spectrum
Books (1968), 179 pp.
Designed for the general reader and undergraduate.

STELLRECHT, Helmut.
Adolf Hitler: Heil und Unheil; die Verlorene
Revolution. Tübingen: Grabert (1974), 332 pp.
The author is a former high-ranking NSDAP and Hitler
Youth leader and his book is marked by a curious mixture
of disillusionment and nostalgia: it is also historically
worthless.

STERN, J. P.
Hitler: the Führer and the People. London:
Fontana (1975), 254 pp.
A well-written study which shows an impressive degree of
good judgement. Stern analyses the methods by which
Hitler achieved and maintained power, stressing above all
what he calls the "personalization of politics" — Hitler's
uncanny ability to identify himself with the common man
and later with the German nation itself.

TAYLOR, Alan J. P.
"Thus Spake Hitler". In A. J. P. Taylor. *Europe:
Grandeur and Decline.* London: Pelican (1974),
p. 199—203.
A brief, incisive characterization.

TERVEEN, Fritz.
**"Aus einer Wahlrede Hitlers am 27. Juli 1932 in
Eberswalde: ein praktisches Beispiel zur Arbeit an
Filmdokumenten".** *Geschichte in Wissenschaft und
Unterricht,* vol. 10 (1959), p. 215—26.
Examines a speech given by Hitler during the *Reichstag*
election campaign.

TOYNBEE, Arnold J.
Acquaintances. London: Oxford University Press
(1967).
The great man of letters records his impression of Hitler.

TREVOR-ROPER, Hugh R. (ed.).
**Hitler's Table Talk 1941—1944: His Private
Conversations.** London: Weidenfeld & Nicolson
(1973), 746 pp. New ed.
This immensely interesting and important volume contains
references to the development of the NSDAP during the
Kampfzeit, but above all offers a valuable insight into
Hitler's ideas and attitudes on a wide range of political and
non-political subjects. The editor provides in an intro-
duction a brilliant analysis of Hitler's mind.

WAITE, Robert G. L.
**"Adolf Hitler's Guilt Feelings: a Problem in
History and Psychology".** *Journal of Interdisciplinary History,* vol. 1, pt. 2 (1971), p. 229—49.
A speculative and frankly trivial paper. Waite dabbles in
amateur psychology to examine some of Hitler's alleged
"guilt feelings" of the pre-1933 era, for example, his
repeated anxiety about having a Jewish grandmother.

WALDMAN, Morris D.
Sieg Heil! The Story of Adolf Hitler. New York:
Oceana (1962), 318 pp.
The title tells all there is to know.

WATT, Donald C.
**"Die bayerischen Bemühungen um Ausweisung
Hitlers, 1924".** *Vierteljahrshefte für Zeitgeschichte,*
vol. 8, pt. 1 (1958), p. 17—26.
Details the futile attempts of the Bavarian state government
to arrange for Hitler's deportation to Austria. It was not
thanks to the intervention of the pro-National Socialist
Minister of Justice in Bavaria, Franz Gürtner, that the
threat was quashed, as was previously thought. Watt shows
quite clearly that the refusal of Austria to have Hitler was
the decisive factor.

WATT, Donald C.
"New Light on Hitler's Youth". *History Today,*
vol. 8, pt. 1 (1958), p. 17—26.
Notes on Hitler's early life taken from Franz Jetzinger's
book, *Hitlers Jugend: Phantasien, Lügen, und die Wahrheit!*
(see earlier in this section).

WATT, Donald C.
"New Light on Hitler's Apprenticeship". *History
Today,* vol. 9, pt. 11 (1959), p. 711—19.
Again, simply notes from a secondary source summarized
for the general reader.

WIEDEMANN, Fritz.
**Der Mann, der Feldherr werden wollte: Erlebnisse
und Erfahrungen des Vorgesetzten Hitlers im I.
Weltkrieg.** Velbert: Blick und Bild Verlag (1964),
270 pp.
Unrevealing and rather ponderous memoirs of Hitler's
immediate superior officer during the war who later became
his personal aide and adjutant.

WINDELL, George G.
"Hitler, National Socialism, and Richard Wagner".
Journal of Central European Affairs, vol. 22,
pt. 4 (1963), p. 479—97.
The author examines the proposition that Hitler's ideology
was derived in large measure from Wagner, and that Wagner
was therefore the principal intellectual precursor of
National Socialism. His method of answering the question
(basically through a comparison of the writings of the two
men) is not very satisfactory, but his conclusion that the
Wagner-Hitler relationship was tenuous is undoubtedly
correct.

ZIEGLER, Hans S.
Adolf Hitler aus dem Erleben dargestellt.
Göttingen: Schütz-Verlag (1964), 300 pp.
A former top NSDAP member's personal recollections of
the *Führer.*

ZIEGLER, Hans S.
Wer war Hitler? Tübingen: Grabert (1970).
Unscholarly and unworthy of serious consideration.

ZOLLER, Albert.
**Hitler Privat: Erlebnisbericht seiner Geheimsek-
retärin.** Düsseldorf: Droste (1949), 240 pp.
The pseudonymous story of Hitler's private secretary,
Christa Schröder, who was with him until the end in the
Berlin bunker. Her generally reliable and informative
account is an important source for Hitler's private life,
1933—45.

C. OTHERS (A—Z)[1]

1. MARTIN BORMANN

BEZYMENSKI, Lev.
Martin Bormann. Zürich: Aurora Verlag (1965).
A weak study, uninformative and marked by an unfor-
tunate tone of hostility.

---

1. See also relevant parts of section 24B.

McGOVERN, James.
Martin Bormann. London: Barker (1968), 236 pp.
A popular work, replete with careless assumptions. The author's ignorance of the political *ambience* in which Bormann worked is quite appalling.

WULF, Josef.
Martin Bormann, Hitlers Schatten. Gütersloh: Mohn (1962), 254 pp.
A poorly written and wholly inadequate work which comes nowhere near an explanation of the nature and extent of Bormann's role in the NSDAP or of his enigmatic personality.

2. WALTHER DARRÉ[1]

GIES, Horst.
Richard Walther Darré und die national-sozialistische Bauernpolitik 1930 bis 1933. Dissertation, University of Frankfurt (1966).
A most competent and informative study of Darré's contribution to the highly successful NSDAP agrarian campaign before 1933. Darré's ideas are analysed for what they are worth and his personality is effectively assessed (see also section 26B).

3. ARTUR DINTER

FALB, Heinrich.
Artur Dinter als Politiker und Ideologe: ein Beitrag zur Geschichte und Weltanschauung der nationalsozialistischen Bewegung. Dissertation, University of Freiburg (1967).
Dinter is an unpromising subject for a biography: his peculiar brand of religious-racialist fanaticism eventually made him unacceptable even to the NSDAP, which expelled him in the late 1920s. The author of this study has gathered a reasonable amount of relevant material which provides an adequate coverage of Dinter's character. Less satisfactory is Falb's discussion of his political significance.

4. ANTON DREXLER

PHELPS, Reginald H.
"Anton Drexler — der Gründer der NSDAP".
Deutsche Rundschau, vol. 87, pt. 12 (1961), p. 1134—43.
A scholarly and instructive assessment.

5. DIETRICH ECKART

ENGELMANN, Ralph M.
Dietrich Eckart and the Genesis of Nazism.
Dissertation, University of Washington (1971).
Eckart (1868—1923) was, as this study clearly shows, an important influence on Hitler during the early 1920s, particularly as regards anti-semitism and the *Fuhrerprinzip* concept. The book also outlines Eckart's political and publishing activities 1918—23. A useful introduction to a neglected personality, but there is still much filling out of the facts to be done.

PLEWNIA, Margarete.
Auf dem Weg zu Hitler: der völkische Publizist Dietrich Eckart. Bremen: Schünemann (1970), 155 pp.
Useful discussion, particularly of Eckart's early career, but like the previously mentioned work, far from definitive.

1. See also article by C.R. Lovin in section 26B.

6. GOTTFRIED FEDER

HALE, Oron J.
See his article in section 22B.

RIEBE, Manfred.
Gottfried Feder, Wirtschaftsprogrammatiker Hitlers: ein biographischer Beitrag zur Vor- und Frühgeschichte des Nationalsozialismus. Dissertation, University of Erlangen (1971).
This study considers Feder's career from 1883 (his date of birth) to 1923 when he joined the NSDAP. Besides giving interesting biographical data on Feder himself, the work examines his economic ideas, in particular the concept of *Brechung der Zinsknechtschaft* (breaking of the slavery of interest).

7. JOSEF GOEBBELS

BORRESHOLM, Boris von (ed.).
Dr. Goebbels nach Aufzeichnungen aus seiner Umgebung. Berlin (1949).
Consists of a large number of anecdotes about Goebbels, most of which have been reproduced in subsequent biographies. Not a scholarly work, but it has its minor uses for filling out aspects of Goebbels' personality.

BRAMSTED, Ernst K.
See his work and articles in section 28.

EBERMAYER, Erich; **MEISSNER**, Hans-Otto.
Gefährtin des Teufels. Hamburg: Hoffmann & Campe (1952).
Notable only for some details about Goebbels' extra-marital affairs. The remainder of the book is quite useless.

HEIBER, Helmut.
"Joseph Goebbels und seine Redakteure: einige Bemerkungen zu einer neuen Biographie".
Vierteljahrshefte für Zeitgeschichte, vol. 9, pt. 1 (1961), p. 66—75.
This is a scathing attack on journalistic/popular history which is often given a scholarly appearance by the inclusion of footnotes, documentary extracts and so on. Heiber is concerned to expose one outstanding example of this genre, the Manvell-Fraenkel biography of Goebbels (listed below). In particular, Heiber unequivocally reveals how they have disastrously misread and inaccurately translated over one hundred quotations from Goebbels' early diary (1925—26), thus completely altering the meaning of Goebbels' words. This amounts to a staggering indictment of the book's reliability to which there is no retort.

HEIBER, Helmut.
Joseph Goebbels. Berlin: Colloquium Verlag (1962), 433 pp.
A scholarly, balanced, and convincing study — perhaps the best and most up-to-date biography of Goebbels. The different phases in his personality development are convincingly analysed; above all, his actions are shown to have been mainly prompted by an insatiable ego, while politically he was dominated by Hitler's charisma. The *Kampfzeit* era is given good coverage.

HEIBER, Helmut (ed.).
Goebbels-Reden. Vol. I: 1932—1939. Düsseldorf: Droste (1971), 337 pp.
A definitive collection, skilfully edited.

HUNT, Richard M.
Joseph Goebbels: a Study of the Formation of his National Socialist Consciousness (1897—1926).
Dissertation, University of Harvard (1960).
Contains nothing new in terms of factual content or interpretation.

MANVELL, Roger; FRAENKEL, Heinrich.
Dr. Goebbels: His Life and Death. London:
Heinemann (1960), 329 pp.
Written in popular fashion for the commercial market this study is without value for the specialist and misleading for the general reader (except perhaps for the early chapters on Goebbels' youth). The book perpetuates too many falsities, commits a huge number of factual errors, and is incomplete and superficial.

REIMANN, Viktor.
Dr. Joseph Goebbels. Munich: Molden (1971),
383 pp.
Reimann's main thesis that Goebbels is best understood as a social revolutionary and as a reluctant anti-semite is thoroughly unconvincing. Otherwise, the study is apologetic and not always relevant.

REISS, Curt.
Joseph Goebbels: the Devil's Advocate. London:
Hollis & Carter (1948), 383 pp.
This book is very much a racy, journalistic effort, unsupported by any documentary material, and has been superseded by Heiber's work in particular. There is a complete lack of objective analysis of Goebbels' personality and political career, and only minor aspects receive detailed attention.

SCHAUMBURG-LIPPE, Friedrich C. zu.
Dr. G.: ein Porträt des Propagandaministers.
Wiesbaden: Limes Verlag (1963), 288 pp.
Devoted mainly to the post-1933 period, this study fails in its primary aim of assessing Goebbels' role in and contribution to political control in the Third Reich.

SEMMLER, Rudolf.
Goebbels — the Man next to Hitler. Edited by G.S.
Wagner. London: Westhouse (1947), 234 pp.
This is the published version of a diary kept by one of Goebbels' closest associates in the Reich Propaganda Ministry. But there is very little "inside" information of importance here and the notes on Goebbels' personality are pedestrian.

STEPHAN, Werner.
Josef Goebbels: Dämon einer Diktatur. Stuttgart:
Union Verlag (1949).
Very tentative and lacking in objective perspective.

8. HERMANN GOERING

BEWLEY, Charles.
Hermann Goering and the Third Reich. New York:
The Devin-Adair Co. (1962), 517 pp.
Bewley was the Republic of Ireland's representative in Berlin from 1933—39 who befriended Goering. He has written what must surely be the most favourable study ever of the leading National Socialist; it is uncritical and grossly misleading.

BUTLER, Ewan; YOUNG, Gordon.
Marshal Without Glory. London: Hodder &
Stoughton (1951), 287 pp.
Suitably critical in tone, but fails utterly to see Goering in the political context of National Socialism.

FRISCHAUER, Willy.
The Rise and Fall of Hermann Goering. Boston
(1951), 303 pp.
A reasonably accomplished full-length biography, though far from definitive and now needing to be updated in the light of research done on the NSDAP during the last twenty years or so. The narrative is clear and details the major stages of Goering's career, but there are obvious gaps.

GOERING, Emmy.
An der Seite meines Mannes: Begebenheiten und Bekenntnisse. Göttingen: Schütz (1967), 337 pp.
This memoir by Goering's widow has some interesting passages about her husband's private life, but otherwise the book is most disappointing.

MANVELL, Roger; FRAENKEL, Heinrich.
Hermann Göring. London: Heinemann (1962),
429 pp.
This book, intended for the general reader, is fluently written but describes Goering's personality and political role superficially. There are a fair number of factual mistakes and curious interpretations, so even the non-specialist needs to exercise caution when reading it (p. 17—72 deal, badly, with the Weimar period).

MOSLEY, Leonard.
The Reich Marshal: a Biography of Hermann Goering. London: Weidenfeld & Nicolson (1974),
394 pp.
A popular, lavishly illustrated work which, however, is not entirely devoid of merit. Mosley is prepared to argue the significance of certain events in Goering's life, for example the 1923 Putsch, and the smooth narrative does not contain too many errors. The picture that emerges of Goering is rounded, but perhaps sometimes too flattering to him. The specialist will not be detained long by this book, but the general reader should be satisfied.

9. RUDOLF HESS

BIRD, Eugene K.
The Loneliest Man in the World: the Inside Story of the 30-Year Imprisonment of Rudolf Hess.
London: Secker & Warburg (1974), 270 pp.
A most interesting account, written by one of the former American officials responsible for supervising Hess's imprisonment in Berlin's Spandau jail. The author's notes, gathered over the years from private conversations with Hess, add to our knowledge of the former Deputy *Führer's* puzzling personality. The book does not add very much, however, to what we know about the Third Reich or National Socialism.

ENSOR, James.
Rudolf Hess. London (1962).
Probably the most competent full-scale biography available on Hess; it is generally reliable on matters of fact, though tentative in analysis.

HÜTTEN, Bernard J.
Hess: the Man and His Mission. New York: Macmillan (1971), 262 pp.
Concerned exclusively with Hess's motives in flying to Scotland during the war on his famous mission. As such, the book fails to convince.

LEASOR, H. James.
Rudolf Hess: the Uninvited Envoy. London: Allen & Unwin (1962), 239 pp.
Another popular and totally unsatisfactory consideration of Hess's flight to Scotland, his life under arrest in Britain, and his trial at Nuremberg.

MANVELL, Roger; FRAENKEL, Heinrich.
Hess: a Biography. London: MacGibbon & Kee
(1971), 256 pp.
The authors have produced more or less the same kind of
book on Hess as they have produced previously on other
National Socialist leaders; it is general, popular, superficial
and unreliable.

SCHWARZWÄLLER, Wulf.
"Der Stellvertreter des Führers", Rudolf Hess.
Munich: Molden-Verlag (1974), 303 pp.
More satisfactory than most studies of Hess. The narrative
is at least free of important errors and gives a reasonably
full character sketch of the man. However, the right kind of
questions about Hess's political significance have not been
asked.

10. REINHARD HEYDRICH

ARONSON, Shlomo.
**Reinhard Heydrich und die Frühgeschichte von
Gestapo und SD.** Stuttgart: Deutsche Verlagsanstalt
(1971), 340 pp.
An excellent and important study of the founding and
early development of the SS, SD, and *Gestapo* and the contribution made in this respect by Heydrich and Himmler.
For our purposes, the book's first chapter provides a fully
documented description of Heydrich's early life until he
was discharged from the navy and joined the nascent SS.
The author also informs us that, contrary to many previous
opinions, Heydrich was dependent on Himmler from 1931
—35.

WIGHTON, Charles.
Heydrich: Hitler's Most Evil Henchman. London:
Odhams Press (1962), 288 pp.
A rather sensational, journalistic piece.

11. HEINRICH HIMMLER

ACKERMANN, Josef.
Himmler als Ideologe. Göttingen: Musterschmidt
(1970), 320 pp.
A limited work on Himmler's personal *Weltanschauung*.
Although the author has made use of previously unpublished documents and liberally quoted long extracts from
them, he fails to clarify Himmler's fantastic racial and
political theories. This was supposedly the main objective
of the book.

ANGRESS, Werner T.; SMITH, Bradley F.
"Diaries of Heinrich Himmler's Early Years".
Journal of Modern History, vol. 31, pt. 3 (1959),
p. 206—24.
An analysis of fragmented early diaries of Himmler covering 1914—24. They touch upon his home background, his
university days, and his attitudes to politics, but not
mentioned is his involvement with the early NSDAP (he
joined only in August 1923). The diaries also offer some
insight into Himmler's personality, revealing for one thing
that he was apparently "normal", but they do not provide
any clues on how he later became the notorious *Reichsführer* of the SS. Moreover, there are significant gaps in the
diaries: 1916—19; 1920—21; 1922—24. In all, however,
the diaries produce important correctives to previous
accounts of Himmler's early years.

FRISCHAUER, Willy.
Himmler, the Evil Genius of the Third Reich.
London: Odhams (1950).
A poor study, riddled with factual error and false inter-
pretation, and quite incomplete.

LOEWENBERG, Peter.
**"The Unsuccessful Adolescence of Heinrich
Himmler".** *American Historical Review*, vol. 76,
pt. 3 (1971), p. 612—41.
It is interesting to compare this essay's findings with the
paper written by Angress and Smith (see above). In this
psychoanalytic study, Loewenberg uses Himmler's early
diaries to show that his adolescent personality was consistent with the personality of Himmler when head of the
SS. Loewenberg's thesis is vigorously argued but is ultimately unconvincing.

MANVELL, Roger; FRAENKEL, Heinrich.
Heinrich Himmler. London: Heinemann (1965),
285 pp.
In the same category as their previous biographies of the
NSDAP leadership: the book is not for the scholar, and
should be read with care by the general public.

SMITH, Bradley F.
**Heinrich Himmler: a Nazi in the Making, 1900—
1926.** Stanford: Hoover Institution Press (1971),
211 pp.
A scholarly and well researched study of Himmler's early
life and tentative early political involvements. Smith convincingly describes the different facets of Himmler's personality
— he was, for example, pedantic, class-conscious, conservative, and romantic — and the decisive changes brought on
by the war. The book does not explain, however, how
Himmler later developed into a mass murderer: the enigma
remains.

WULF, Josef.
Heinrich Himmler: eine biographische Studie.
Berlin: Arani Verlag (1960), 39 pp.
The aim of this brief survey is to explain what made
Himmler become the head of an extermination programme
unparalleled in modern history. Wulf goes over familiar
ground — Himmler's belief in absurd racial theories, his
lust for power, his ruthlessness — but comes up with no
new answers that are convincing.

12. GRAF ERNST ZU REVENTLOW

BOOG, H.
**Graf Ernst zu Reventlow (1869—1943): eine
Studie zur Krise der deutschen Geschichte seit dem
Ende des 19. Jahrhunderts.** Dissertation, University
of Heidelberg (1965).
Provides a fairly detailed description of Reventlow's
career but does not succeed in establishing in proper per-
spective his political role in the NSDAP.

NEVILLE, Joseph B.
**Count Ernst Reventlow: Revolutionary
Conservatism and the Weimar Republic.** Dissertation, University of Wisconsin (1971).
This brief study concentrates on Reventlow's role in
the *völkisch* movement and the NSDAP after 1918, and on
his ideas, which Neville considers to have been quasi-
nihilistic.

13. ALFRED ROSENBERG[1]

CECIL, Robert.
**The Myth of the Master Race: Alfred Rosenberg
and Nazi Ideology.** London: Batsford (1972), 266
pp.
A disappointing book which is neither a full, let alone
definitive biography of Rosenberg, nor a detailed critique

1. Excluded from consideration are recent studies which
deal exclusively with Rosenberg's position in the Third
Reich; e.g. R. Bollmus, *Das Amt Rosenberg und seine
Gegner*, Stuttgart (1970); and H. D. Loock, *Quisling, Rosenberg und Terboven*, Stuttgart (1970).

of his ideas. Cecil's treatment of the pre-1933 period betrays a fundamental ignorance of the internal development of the NSDAP, so Rosenberg's overall contribution to the rise of the party is inadequately assessed. The work is very general and cannot be seen as anything more than a limited introduction to the theme.

KAISER, Wilhelm J.
Das Rechts- und Staatsdenken Alfred Rosenbergs. Cologne: Wasmund (1964), 161 pp.
An unsatisfactory assessment of the origins and development of Rosenberg's theories in these spheres. The outside influences on his thought require much closer attention.

LANG, Serge; SCHENCK, Ernst von (eds.).
Porträt eines Menschheitsverbrechers nach den hinterlassenen Memoiren des ehemaligen Reichsministers Alfred Rosenberg. St. Gallen: Verlag Zollikofer (1947), 356 pp. (English edition: New York: Ziff-Davis (1949), 328 pp.).
This volume contains fragments of apologetic memoirs written by Rosenberg while in custody at Nuremberg in 1945—46. The editors have carried out the difficult task of preparing the manuscript for publication with considerable skill. The memoirs tell us more about Rosenberg's perverted personality than anything else, but there are also readable sections where Rosenberg accuses some of his former cronies of betraying National Socialist ideology. He also has an interesting note on Gregor Strasser ("Die einzige tragische Grösse" (p. 158)). A valuable study.

14. BALDUR VON SCHIRACH

WHITE, David O.
Hitler's Youth Leader: a Study of the Heroic Imagery in the Major Public Statements of Baldur von Schirach. Dissertation, University of Oregon (1970).
This is a rather odd exercise, overflowing with quasi-philosophical nonsense about Schirach's personality. White seems to tell us that the former Nazi youth leader was romantic, idealistic, authoritarian, narcissistic, heroic, and last but not least, schizophrenic — all of which has been known for quite some time. Schirach's political role in National Socialism is barely analysed.

15. GREGOR STRASSER

DIXON, Joseph M.
Gregor Strasser and the Organization of the Nazi Party 1925—32. Dissertation, Stanford University (1966).
A brief but useful study which stresses Strasser's crucial contribution, as chief party organizer, to the success of the NSDAP. But other aspects of Strasser's career, for example, as an ideologue and contact man with other political parties, are inadequately examined.

KISSENKÖTTER, Udo.
Gregor Strasser und seine Bedeutung für die Spätphase der Weimarer Republik. Dissertation, University of Cologne (1974).
A massively documented study which concentrates on the importance of Strasser's political activity within and outside the NSDAP in 1931—32. The author's arguments are sometimes lost amidst the detail, and besides are open to debate. However, this is a scholarly and able contribution.

STRASSER, P. Bernhard.
Gregor und Otto Strasser. Munich: Verlag Deutsche Freiheit (1965), 30 pp. 2nd ed.
A brief, factual biographical sketch by a third brother of the Strasser family.

WORTZ, U.
See his work in section 22A.

16. OTTO STRASSER

GOTTFRIED, Paul.
"Otto Strasser and National Socialism". *Modern Age*, vol. 13 (1969), p. 142—51.
A very useful assessment and description of Strasser's career and his role in the left wing of the NSDAP before 1930. Based entirely on secondary sources.

PAETEL, Karl O.
"Otto Strasser und die 'Schwarze Front' des 'wahren Nationalsozialismus'". *Politische Studien*, no. 92, vol. 8 (1957), p. 269—82.
An informative and generally sound survey of Otto Strasser's ideas on National Socialism and of the leftist movement within the NSDAP before 1933. Paetel, a close friend of Strasser in the early 1930s, also has a few remarks on the Black Front organization.

REED, Douglas.
Nemesis? The Story of Otto Strasser and the Black Front. London: Jonathan Cape (1952). New ed.
A fragmentary and quite unsatisfactory work which in some instances amounts to a panegyric of Strasser. Lacks any scholarly pretensions and is really worthless.

REED, Douglas.
The Prisoner of Ottawa — Otto Strasser. London: Jonathan Cape (1953).
Like the aforementioned volume, this study is too apologetic on Strasser's behalf to be taken seriously.

THOMA, Peter.
Der Fall Otto Strasser. Cologne (1971), 85 pp.
An uncritical, brief survey of Strasser's political career which adds absolutely nothing to our knowledge of the role he played in the NSDAP before 1930.

WERNER, Alfred.
"Trotsky of the Nazi Party". *Journal of Central European Affairs*, vol. 11, pt. 1 (1951), p. 39—46.
A polemical and unreliable account of Strasser's activities in the National Socialist movement and in his post-1945 *Bund für Deutschlands Erneuerung*. The essay, moreover, is written in a racy journalistic style and contains numerous factual errors and several misrepresentations.

17. JULIUS STREICHER

EHLERS, Carol J.
See her work in section 22D.

LENMAN, Robin.
See his article in section 22D.

RÜHL, Manfred.
See his work in section 28.

VARGA, William P.
Julius Streicher: a Political Biography 1885—1933. Dissertation, Ohio State University (1974).
A rather brief but nonetheless welcome first biographical study of this most repulsive of National Socialist leaders. However, although the factual outline of Streicher's political career is well enough adumbrated, many basic questions regarding his contribution to the success of the NSDAP remain unanswered.

Early Writings of National Socialist Leaders[1]

24

A. ADOLF HITLER

Mein Kampf: eine Abrechnung. Vol. I: Mein Kampf; vol. II: Die nationalsozialistische Bewegung. Munich: Eher-Verlag (1925—26).

The best unexpurgated English edition was published in New York by Hurst and Blackett (1939). A more recent edition with an introduction by D.C. Watt has been made available in London, published by Hutchinson (1969). Despite its obvious shortcomings and vulgarities, *Mein Kampf* remains a vitally important source of information on Hitler's ideas. The extent to which the book is a blueprint for later National Socialist policy and strategy is a matter of controversy among scholars. Some are sceptical because of the abundance of half truths, myths and absurd lies it contains; others, looking beyond these discouraging features, are convinced that here Hitler's *Weltanschauung* is related in embryo. It goes without saying, therefore, that *Mein Kampf* must be used with the greatest caution.

Among the post-1945 works which have specifically commented on *Mein Kampf*, the following should be noted:

BURKE, Kenneth.
Die Rhetorik in Hitlers "Mein Kampf" und andere Essays zur Strategie der Überredung. Frankfurt: Suhrkamp (1967), 153 pp.
A thoughtful discussion.

CASPER, C.
"Mein Kampf — a Best Seller". *Jewish Social Studies*, vol. 20, pt. 1 (1958), p. 3—16.
A useful review of the book's history after publication, including details of the number of copies sold annually, different editions, foreign translations, and royalties accruing to Hitler.

1. Only material published before 1933 has been included; exceptionally, publications of the 1933—45 era which deal substantially with the *Kampfzeit* are listed at the author's discretion. Many of the titles in this section speak for themselves, so that it has not been felt necessary to provide a review for each one as is the practice throughout the rest of this bibliography.

HAMMER, Hermann.
"Die deutschen Ausgaben von Hitlers 'Mein Kampf'". *Vierteljahrshefte für Zeitgeschichte*, vol. 4, pt. 2 (1956), p. 161—78.
An excellent and well documented analysis of the textual alterations which Hitler made for the various editions of the book.

KOCH, Hansjoachim W.
See his article in section 27.

LANGE, Karl.
Hitlers unbeachtete Maximen: "Mein Kampf" und die Öffentlichkeit. Stuttgart: Kohlhammer (1968), 211 pp.
Lange is convinced that *Mein Kampf* is an authentic exposition of Hitler's ideas and on this basis enquires why the book did not provoke controversy or even resistance in Germany and abroad. The old answer seems to apply: very few people bothered to plough through its turgid pages. An informative study.

LANGE, Karl.
"Der Terminus 'Lebensraum' in Hitlers 'Mein Kampf'". *Vierteljahrshefte für Zeitgeschichte*, vol. 13, pt. 4 (1965), p. 426—37.
Traces the development of the term *Lebensraum* from the nineteenth century to the present, showing how interpretations of what it meant were invariably vague, and in any case different from one generation to the next. Against this background, the author analyses Hitler's understanding of the concept, as enunciated in *Mein Kampf*; Lange doubts whether the full implications of it had been marked out by the *Führer* before 1933.

HILDEBRAND, Klaus.
"Hitlers 'Mein Kampf': Propaganda oder Programm? Zur Frühgeschichte der nationalsozialistischen Bewegung". *Neue Politische Literatur*, vol. 14, pt. 1 (1969), p. 72—82.
An intelligently balanced review of recent scholarly publications on the book.

MASER, Werner.
Hitlers "Mein Kampf". Entstehung, Aufbau, Stil, Änderungen, Quellen, Quellenwert, und kommentierte Auszüge. Munich: Bechtle (1966), 344 pp.
Part of the author's purpose is to demonstrate that *Mein Kampf* can be regarded as a legitimate statement of later National Socialist policy. He does succeed to a certain extent, but overlooks or ignores certain passages which appear to contradict his thesis. On this point, therefore, Maser's book must be judged inconclusive. He is also concerned to spotlight the distortions and untruths in the book: again, he is successful to a degree, but the specialist will find some of his interpretations unacceptable. Maser discusses even less well the style and layout of *Mein Kampf*, the significance of amendments made by Hitler in different editions, and finally the sources which may have influenced the *Führer's* ideas. In all, Maser's work is probably to be treated with as much caution as Hitler's.

Die Südtiroler Frage und das deutsche Bündnisproblem. Munich: Eher-Verlag (1926), 47 pp.
Sets out Hitler's thinking on the South Tyrol, which soon caused the party some embarrassment in German rightwing and nationalist circles.

Der Weg zum Wiederaufstieg. Munich (1927).
(Issued privately.)
See H. A. Turner's article in section 26A ("Hitler's Secret Pamphlet for Industrialists, 1927").

Hitlers zweites Buch: ein Dokument aus dem Jahre 1928. Edited by Gerhard L. Weinberg. Stuttgart: Deutsche Verlagsanstalt (1961), 227 pp.
The book was written by Hitler in the summer of 1928 but was never published during his lifetime and only came to light some fifteen years after the war. It is concerned almost entirely with foreign policy; in essence, Hitler expands in slightly more detailed form the ideas in foreign policy already set down in *Mein Kampf*. Thus, for example, the book confirms that Hitler wanted much more than a mere redressing of Versailles, that Germany needed *Lebensraum* at the expense of Russia, and that France was the mortal enemy. The book is more valuable in allowing an insight into Hitler's mind and personality in 1928, while the emphasis on foreign policy may be seen as evidence of the NSDAP's growing rightward course in German politics following the May 1928 *Reichstag* election.[1] Weinberg has provided an extensive and extremely useful editorial annotation.

Readers are also directed to the following article:

BROSZAT, Martin.
"Betrachtungen zu 'Hitlers zweiten Buch'".
Vierteljahrshefte für Zeitgeschichte, vol. 9, pt. 4 (1961), p. 417—29.
In this critical and learned assessment, Broszat weighs up the book's historical importance, particularly of course for the understanding of Hitler's foreign policy during the Third Reich.

Vortrag vor westdeutschen Wirtschaftlern im Industrie-Klub zu Düsseldorf am 27. Januar 1932. Munich: Eher-Verlag (1932), 31 pp.
The text of Hitler's famous speech to the Rhenish industrialists.

Hitlers Auseinandersetzung mit Brüning. Munich: Eher-Verlag (1932), 94 pp.

---

1. This point is expanded in my forthcoming article in the *Vierteljahrshefte für Zeitgeschichte*.

Hitler an Brüning: offener Brief Adolf Hitlers an den Reichskanzler. Munich: Eher-Verlag (1932), 23 pp.

Adolf Hitlers offener Brief an Herrn von Papen: die Antwort des Führers der NSDAP an den Reichskanzler. Berlin: Schleiser (1932), 24 pp.

B. OTHERS (A–Z)

1. PHILIPP BOUHLER

Adolf Hitler: das Werden einer Volksbewegung. Lübeck: Coleman (1932), 48 pp.

2. WALTHER DARRÉ

Das Bauerntum als Lebensquell der nordischen Rasse. Munich: Eher-Verlag (1929), 493 pp.
A definitive statement of Darré's racial-agrarian ideas.

Neuadel aus Blut und Boden. Munich: Lehmann (1930), 231 pp.
On the theme of a regeneration of Germany through the small farmers and peasantry. His ideas are, of course, unoriginal.

Das Schwein als Kriterium für nordische Völker und Semiten. Munich: Lehmann (1933), 35 pp.
(Originally published in 1927).

Erkenntnisse und Werden: Aufsätze aus der Zeit vor der Machtergreifung. Edited by Marie Adelheid Reuss-zur-Lippe. Goslar (1940).
A collection of a score of articles written and published by Darré before he joined the NSDAP. They are all of a nationalist, anti-Marxist, and racialist type which originally appeared in *völkisch* periodicals such as *Deutschlands Erneuerung* and *Volk und Scholle*.

3. ARTUR DINTER

Die Sünden der Zeit. Vol. I: Die Sünde wider das Blut: ein Zeitroman. Leipzig: Matthes (1919). **Vol. II: Die Sünde wider den Geist: ein Zeitroman.** Leipzig: Beust (1921). **Vol. III: Die Sünde wider die Liebe: ein Zeitroman.** Leipzig: Matthes (1922).
A fictional trilogy in which Dinter's cranky racial-religious ideas are expressed in all their absurdity.

"Lichtstrahlen aus dem Talmud": offene Briefe an den Landes-Rabbiner von Sachsen-Weimar-Eisenach Herrn Dr. Wiesen et al. Leipzig: Matthes (1920), 82 pp.

Der Kampf um die Geistlehre. Leipzig: Matthes (1921), 64 pp.
A sequel to his trilogy, in the same vein.

197 Theses zur Vollendung der Reformation: die Wiederherstellung der reinen Heilandeslehre. Leipzig: Beust (1926), 246 pp.
Marked by a vitriolic anti-Catholicism.

Die Entjudung der christlichen Religion: Ziele und Aufgaben der geistchristlichen Reformations- bewegung. Patschkan: Geistchristliche Verlags- anstalt (1932), 28 pp.
Presents his ideas for a purified pagan-Germanic religion.

4. ANTON DREXLER

Mein politisches Erwachen: aus dem Tagebuch eines deutschen sozialistischen Arbeiters. Munich: Deutscher Volksverlag? (1919), 70 pp.
An important source for an understanding of the "socialist" orientation of the German Workers' Party (DAP).

5. DIETRICH ECKART

Das ist der Jude! Laienpredigt über Juden- und Christentum. Munich: Hoheneichen-Verlag (1919), 62 pp.
A specially published anti-semitic piece from his periodical *Auf gut Deutsch.*

Der Bolschewismus von Moses bis Lenin: Zweiges- präch zwischen Adolf Hitler und mir. Munich: Hoheneichen-Verlag (1924), 57 pp.
Arguably one of the most important early anti-semitic influences on Hitler (refer to articles by Ernst Nolte and Shaul Esh in section 23B).

6. GOTTFRIED FEDER

Das Manifest zur Brechung der Zinsknechtschaft des Geldes. Munich: Verlag Huber (1919), 62 pp.
The classical affirmation of his "interest-slavery" theories which were never taken very seriously at any time by the NSDAP.

Der nationalsozialistische deutsche Staat: mit besonderer Berücksichtigung der Finanz- und Wirtschaftspolitik des Nationalsozialismus. Munich: Verlag Deutschvölkische Buchhandlung (1923).
Worth consulting, if only to contrast with the actual financial and economic policies later pursued by the NSDAP.

Der deutsche Staat auf nationaler und sozialer Grundlage: neue Wege im Staat, Finanz und Wirtschaft. Munich: Verlag Deutschvölkische Buchhandlung (1932), 142 pp. 5th ed.

Die Aufwertung. Berlin (1924), 48 pp.

Der Staatsbankerott: die Rettung. Munich: Verlag Huber (1924), 24 pp.

Das Programm der NSDAP und seine weltanschau- liche Grundgedanken. Munich: Eher-Verlag (1927), 60 pp.
A significant early programmatic document.

Der Dawespakt; nach dem Originaltext des Sachverständigenkomitees vom 9. April 1924 mit Kommentaren. Munich: Eher-Verlag (1929), 141 pp.
A bitter attack on international high finance, written during a transitional period in NSDAP development when "leftist" ideas were becoming less and less fashionable in the party as it veered to the right.

Die Wohnungsnot und die soziale Bau- und Wirtschaftsbank, als Retterin aus Wohnungselend, Wirtschaftskrise und Erwerbslosenelend. Munich: Eher-Verlag (1929), 48 pp.
Feder draws attention to the acute housing situation in Weimar — one of the social scandals of the period. The pamphlet apparently reveals that Feder did have a genuine social conscience of sorts.

Was will Adolf Hitler? Das Programm der NSDAP. Munich: Eher-Verlag (1931), 24 pp.

Kampf gegen die Hochfinanz. Munich: Eher-Verlag (1933), 382 pp.
Passes as Feder's magnus opus.

7. WILHELM FRICK

Die Nationalsozialisten im Reichstag 1924—1928. Munich: Eher-Verlag (1928), 63 pp.

Die Tätigkeit der Nationalsozialisten im Reichstag 1928—1930. Munich: Verlag der Nationalsozial- istischen Landtagsfraktion (1930), 117 pp.

Die Nationalsozialisten im Reichstag 1924—1931. Munich: Eher-Verlag (1932), 160 pp.
All three works are most uninformative.

8. JOSEPH GOEBBELS

Das kleine ABC des Nationalsozialismus. Elberfeld: Kampfverlag (1925).
A catechism of simple questions and answers on the aims and meaning of National Socialism.

Der Nazi-Sozi: Fragen und Antworten für den Nationalsozialisten. Berlin: Kampfverlag (1926).
The same format as in the aforementioned work, only slightly enlarged.

Die zweite Revolution: Briefe an Zeitgenossen. Zwickau: Streiter-Verlag (1926), 62 pp.
A collection of open letters on political themes; some are addressed to named individuals like Hitler, Reventlow, and Scheidemann, while others are directed to "narrow-minded intellectuals". A good source for Goebbels' ideas.

Lenin oder Hitler? Eine Rede, gehalten am 19. Februar 1926 im Opernhaus in Königsberg. Zwickau: Streiter-Verlag (1926), 32 pp.
One of his first major public speeches, significant for an understanding of the "socialist" debate in the NSDAP at that time.

Wege ins Dritte Reich: Briefe und Aufsätze für Zeitgenossen. Munich: Eher-Verlag (1927), 64 pp.
Also interesting for an insight into Goebbels' ideas at that time. Note the continuation, despite Bamberg and its aftermath, of the commitment to "socialism".

Das Buch Isidor: ein Zeitbild von Lachen und Hass; von Mjölnir und Dr. Goebbels. Munich: Eher-Verlag (1928), 168 pp.
A collection of violently anti-semitic articles, most of which originally appeared in *Der Angriff*. Mjölnir, the paper's brilliant cartoonist, supplies illustrations.

Michael: ein deutsches Schicksal in Tagebuchblättern. Munich: Eher-Verlag (1929), 158 pp.
Written in 1926 but turned down by every publisher who was offered the manuscript. It is a low quality expressionist novel.

Knorke: ein neues Buch Isidor für Zeitgenossen. Munich: Eher-Verlag (1929), 155 pp.
A sequel along the same lines as the first *Buch Isidor*.

Die verflüchten Hakenkreuzler: etwas zum Nachdenken. Munich: Eher-Verlag (1930).
Thoughts on the withdrawal of the Otto Strasser clique from the party in July 1930.

Signale zum Aufbruch: Rede eines Mannes, dem in Preussen das Reden verboten war; gehalten am 28. März 1931 in Danzig. Munich: Eher-Verlag (1931), 40 pp.
In this speech, he attacks in particular the Jews and Brüning.

Preussen muss wieder preussisch werden. Munich: Eher-Verlag (1932).

Vom Proletariat zum Volk: Rede. Munich: Eher-Verlag (1932).
Goebbels returns to a "socialist" theme here.

Kampf um Berlin: der Anfang. Munich: Eher-Verlag (1932).
An absorbing if not always strictly accurate description of the political struggles of the NSDAP in Berlin under Goebbels' leadership, 1926—28.

Revolution der Deutschen: 14 Jahre Nationalsozialismus. Oldenburg: Stalling Verlag (1933), 229 pp.
A selection of his speeches, 1929—33.

Goebbels spricht: Reden aus Kampf und Sieg. Oldenburg: Stalling Verlag (1933), 104 pp.
A further collection of speeches delivered 1929—33.

Signale der neuen Zeit: 25 ausgewählte Reden von Dr. Joseph Goebbels. Munich: Eher-Verlag, 1934.
Extracts from speeches, 1927—33.

Vom Kaiserhof zur Reichskanzlei: eine historische Darstellung in Tagebuchblättern. Munich: Eher-Verlag (1934), 312 pp.

Provides a readable but not always reliable account of internal party feuding during 1932, including the Gregor Strasser affair.

Der Angriff: Aufsätze aus der Kampfzeit. Munich: Eher-Verlag (1935), 340 pp.
A selection of his articles originally published in *Der Angriff*, 1927—30.

Wetterleuchten: Aufsätze aus der Kampfzeit. Munich: Eher-Verlag (1938), 392 pp.
An interesting volume of editorials, mainly from *Der Angriff*, 1928—33.

Das Tagebuch von Joseph Goebbels, 1925—26. Mit weiteren Dokumenten. Edited by Helmut Heiber. Stuttgart: Deutsche Verlagsanstalt (1961), 144 pp.
The diary, excellently edited and annotated by Heiber, is an important source for insights into Goebbels' personality. There are also valuable references to the intra-party conflict in 1925/26 between the northern "socialist" faction and the conservative-nationalist wing in Munich, and to various personalities such as Hitler, Gregor Strasser and others. As a whole, the diary succeeds in conveying rather well the highly charged atmosphere in the NSDAP at that time, but it does not have anything of significance to say about party organization, structure, etc. Goebbels himself is clearly revealed as an enthusiastic National Socialist.

9. RUDOLF HESS

Tatsachen und Lügen um Hitler. Munich: Eher-Verlag (1932).

10. KONSTANTIN HIERL

Sinn und Gestaltung der Arbeitsdienstpflicht. Munich: Eher-Verlag (1932).
Provides his definition of what the labour service concept should mean in practice.

Ausgewählte Schriften und Reden. Edited by Herbert Freiherr von Stetten-Erb. 2 vols. Munich: Eher-Verlag (1941).
Volume I contains Hierl's speeches and writings of the pre-1933 era.

11. FRIEDRICH HILDEBRANDT

Nationalsozialismus und Landarbeiterschaft. Munich: Eher-Verlag (1930), 45 pp.
Puts forward the case why the rural working class should follow the *Führer*. Hildebrandt was NSDAP *Gauleiter* of the largely agricultural province of Mecklenburg, 1925—30 and 1931—45.

12. HANS HINKEL

Einer unter Hunderttausend. Munich: Knorr und Hirth (1938), 264 pp.
A top official of the Propaganda Ministry relates his "conversion" to the NSDAP before 1933.

13. DIETRICH KLAGGES

Das Urevangelium Jesu, der deutsche Glaube.
Wilster (1926).

**Reichtum und soziale Gerechtigkeit: Grundfragen
einer nationalsozialistischen Volkswirtschaftslehre.**
Leipzig: Armanen-Verlag (1927), 179 pp.

14. REINHOLD MUCHOW

Nationalsozialismus und 'freie' Gewerkschaften.
Munich: Eher-Verlag (1932), 115 pp.
The aims of the National Socialist Factory Cell Organization
(NSBO) are outlined by the deputy leader of that organ-
ization. This is a clear and interesting pamphlet.

15. LUDWIG MÜNCHMEYER

**Der Sieg in der Sache des Borkum-Liedes; als
Anhang und Nachtrag zu der Schrift "Borkum die
deutsche Insel".** Hanover(?) (1924), 18 pp.
A rather crude anti-semitic essay written while Münch-
meyer, later a well-known and effective propagandist for
the Lower Saxony NSDAP from 1928–33, was pastor of
the traditionally anti-semitic resort of Borkum off the coast
of East Friesland.

16. FRITZ REINHARDT

Die Herrschaft der Börse. Munich: Eher-Verlag
(1929), 48 pp.
Reinhardt was a noted member of the NSDAP's left wing
as *Gauleiter* of Upper Bavaria (1928–30). This short brochure outlines the reasons for his anti-capitalism.

17. GRAF ERNST ZU REVENTLOW

Monarchie? Leipzig: Hammer-Verlag (1926),
124 pp.

**Für Christen, Nichtchristen, Antichristen: die
Gottfrage der Deutschen.** Berlin: Verlag der
Reichswart (1928), 330 pp.

Deutscher Sozialismus: Civitas Dei Germanica.
Weimar: Duncker (1930), 310 pp.
The most readable of his books. Many of the views expressed here on "German socialism" coincide with those
held by Gregor Strasser.

**Der deutsche Katholizismus im untergehenden und
im kommenden Reich.** Berlin: Verlag der Reichswart (1932), 32 pp.
Forecasts a gloomy future for Catholicism in Germany. The
pamphlet's tone is in fact more sectarian than political.

18. ERNST RÖHM

Die Geschichte eines Hochverräters. Munich: Eher-
Verlag (1928), 367 pp.
Although Röhm's statements are not consistently accurate,
this memoir is extremely interesting and indeed valuable.
It reveals a good deal about Röhm himself and also provides
a description of his involvement in politics and with the
NSDAP during the early Weimar period. This book and a
later edition (*Die Memoiren des Stabschefs Röhm.* Saarbrücken: Uranus-Verlag (1934), 203 pp.) are discussed and
contrasted by Heinrich Bennecke in "Die Memoiren des
Ernst Röhm: ein Vergleich der verschiedenen Ausgaben und
Auflagen", an article in *Politische Studien*, no. 148, vol. 14
(1963), p. 179–211.

19. ALFRED ROSENBERG

Unmoral im Talmud. Munich: Deutscher Volksverlag (1920), 60 pp.
Viciously anti-semitic.

Die Spur des Juden im Wandel der Zeiten. Munich:
Eher-Verlag (1920), 154 pp.
Also a passionate denunciation of the Jews.

**Das Verbrechen der Freimaurerei: Judentum,
Jesuitismus, deutsches Christentum.** Munich:
Lehmann (1921), 181 pp.
Remarkable that so many prejudices could be packed into
the one book. All Rosenberg's major "hates" (excluding
Marxism) are attacked here: freemasonry, Jews, the
Catholic Church, and Christianity in general.

**Der staatsfeindliche Zionismus, auf Grund
jüdischer Quellen erläutert.** Hamburg: Deutschvölkische Verlagsanstalt (1922), 64 pp.
A good example of Rosenberg's peculiar pseudo-intellectual-
ism.

**Die Protokolle der Weisen von Zion und die
jüdische Weltpolitik.** Munich: Deutscher Volksverlag (1923), 143 pp.

Der völkische Staatsgedanke. Munich: Lehmann
(1924).

Dr. Georg Heim und die Novemberrepublik.
Munich: Deutscher Volksverlag (1924), 16 pp.
An attack on the prominent Bavarian political (BVP) and
peasant leader.

**Der Fall Bettauer: ein Musterbeispiel jüdischer
Zersetzungstätigkeit durch entsittlichendes
Schrifttum.** Munich: Deutscher Volksverlag (1925),
16 pp.

Die internationale Hochfinanz. Munich: Deutscher
Volksverlag (1925).

**Führer zum Reichsparteitag der Nationalsozialist-
ischen Deutschen Arbeiterpartei, Nürnberg,
19./21. August 1927.** Edited by A. Rosenberg &
Wilhelm W. Weiss. Munich: Eher-Verlag (1927).

Der Weltverschwörerkongress zu Basel. Munich: Eher-Verlag (1927), 45 pp.
On the drawing up of the Protocols of the Elders of Zion.

Der Zukunftsweg der deutschen Aussenpolitik. Munich: Eher-Verlag (1927).
A pamphlet which is indicative of the heated debate over foreign policy orientation in the NSDAP at that time. Rosenberg naturally supported an anti-Russian line.

Houston Stewart Chamberlain als Verkünder und Begründer einer deutschen Zukunft. Munich: Bruckmann (1927), 128 pp.

Dietrich Eckart: ein Vermächtnis. Munich: Eher-Verlag (1928), 252 pp.

Führer zum Reichsparteitag der NSDAP zu Nürnberg, vom 1. bis 4. August 1929. Munich: Eher-Verlag (1929).

Freimaurerische Weltpolitik im Lichte der kritischen Forschung. Munich: Eher-Verlag (1929), 75 pp.

Der Mythos des 20. Jahrhunderts: eine Wertung der seelischgeistigen Gestaltenkämpfe unserer Zeit. Munich: Hoheneichen-Verlag (1930), 712 pp.
Rosenberg's major work which, to his deep chagrin, was never accorded official status by the party, and Hitler is reputed not to have read it. The book is boring, verbose, and nonsensical; it attacks Judaism and Christianity as degenerate, while praising the eternal virtues of Aryanism.

Das Parteiprogramm: Wesen, Grundsätze und Ziele der NSDAP. Munich: Eher-Verlag (1930), 64 pp.
Contains the party's agricultural programme, drawn up in early 1930.

Der Sumpf: Querschnitte durch das "Geistes"-Leben der November-Demokratie. Munich: Eher-Verlag (1930), 237 pp.
A polemic against the November "system".

Das Wesensgefüge der Nationalsozialismus: Grundlagen der deutschen Wiedergeburt. Munich: Eher-Verlag (1932), 80 pp.

Kampf um die Macht: Aufsätze von 1921—1932. Edited by Thilo von Trotha. Munich: Eher-Verlag (1937), 797 pp.

Blut und Ehre: ein Kampf für die deutsche Wiedergeburt; Reden und Aufsätze von 1919—1933. Munich: Eher-Verlag (1939), 384 pp.

Schriften und Reden. Vol. I: Schriften aus den Jahren 1917—1921. Vol. II: Schriften aus den Jahren 1921—1923. Munich: Hoheneichen-Verlag (1943).

Letzte Aufzeichnungen: Ideale und Idole der nationalsozialistischen Revolution. Edited by H. Härtle. Göttingen: Plesse Verlag (1955).
This is Rosenberg's posthumously published autobiography; it is overwhelmingly apologetic.

Selected Writings. Edited by Robert Pois. London: Jonathan Cape (1970), 204 pp.

Race and Race History. Edited by Robert Pois. New York: Harper (1974).
Included is a critical assessment of Rosenberg's ideas.

20. FRITZ SAUCKEL

Kampf und Sieg in Thüringen. Weimar (1934).
A fragmentary account, apart from other major failings. Sauckel was the Thuringian *Gauleiter* from 1927—45.

21. HANS SCHEMM

Nationalsozialismus oder Bolschewismus? Der rote Krieg: Mutter oder Genossin? Bayreuth: NS-Kultur-Verlag (1931), 31 pp.

22. GREGOR STRASSER

Freiheit und Brot. Ausgewählte Reden und Schriften eines Nationalsozialisten. Part I: Idee. Berlin: Kampfverlag (1928).
A collection of some of his early speeches, mainly 1924—26.

Hammer und Schwert. Ausgewählte Reden und Schriften eines Nationalsozialisten. Part II: Kampf. Berlin: Kampfverlag (1928).
Speeches 1927—28.

Das Hitlerbüchlein: ein Abriss vom Leben und Wirkens des Führers der nationalsozialistischen Freiheitsbewegung Adolf Hitler. Berlin: Kampfverlag (1928), 22 pp.
A warm appreciation of Hitler.

58 Jahre Young-Plan. Berlin: Kampfverlag (1929).

Der letzte Abwehrkampf des Systems: drei aktuelle Aufsätze. Munich: Eher-Verlag (1931), 22 pp.

Arbeit und Brot! Reichstagsrede Gregor Strassers am 10. Mai 1932. Munich: Eher-Verlag (1932), 31 pp.
Strasser's most famous and effective public speech, which was given extensive coverage by the contemporary media in Germany. Delivered at a time when the NSDAP was already firmly established on a right-wing course, the speech reminded Germany that not all the NSDAP's "socialists" left the party with Otto Strasser in 1930.

Das wirtschaftliche Aufbauprogramm der NSDAP: eine Rede, gehalten vor 15,000 nationalsozialistischen Betriebszellenmitgliedern am 20. Oktober 1932 im Berliner Sportpalast. Berlin: Hempel (1932), 22 pp.

Complements in many ways his *Reichstag* speech of May 1932. It is significant that Strasser chose to announce the economic plans of the party before an audience of National Socialist trade union members: he could be assured of a warm welcome for his decidedly leftist-orientated words.

Wirtschaftliches Sofortprogramm der NSDAP. Ausgearbeitet von der Hauptabteilung IV (Wirtschaft) der Reichsorganisationsleitung der NSDAP. Edited by G. Strasser. Munich: Eher-Verlag (1932), 32 pp.

Kampf um Deutschland: Reden und Aufsätze eines Nationalsozialisten. Munich: Eher-Verlag (1932), 390 pp.

A valuable collection, representative of most important aspects of Strasser's ideological outlook.

23. OTTO STRASSER

14 Theses der deutschen Revolution. Berlin: Kampfverlag (1929).

An unequivocal reaffirmation of Strasser's commitment to "German socialism".

Ministersessel oder Revolution: eine wahrheitsgemässe Darstellung meiner Trennung von der NSDAP. Berlin: Verlag "Der Nationale Sozialist" (1930), 47 pp.

Strasser's not wholly reliable account of his breach with Hitler in the summer of 1930.

Aufbau des deutschen Sozialismus. Leipzig: Linder Verlag (1932).

Contains a definition of Strasser's socialist aims.

24. JULIUS STREICHER

Kampf dem Weltfeind: Reden aus der Kampfzeit. Nuremberg: Verlag Der Stürmer (1938), 148 pp.

A selection of Streicher's choicest anti-semitic diatribes previously published in *Der Stürmer*.

25. OTTO WAGENER

Das Wirtschafts-Programm der NSDAP: Rednermaterial. Munich: Eher-Verlag (1932), 104 pp.

Gives guidelines for NSDAP spokesmen on how to handle the presentation of the party's economic ideas.

25

Ideology and Character of National Socialism[1]

BARBU, Z.
"Die sozialpsychologische Struktur des national-sozialistischen Antisemitismus". In W.E. Mosse (ed.). *Entscheidungsjahr 1932: zur Judenfrage in der Endphase der Weimarer Republik*. Tübingen: Mohr (1966), p. 157—81.
Interesting and toughly argued, but generally inconclusive on several main points.

BARKAI, Avraham.
"Die Wirtschaftsauffassung der NSDAP". *Das Parlament: Aus Politik und Zeitgeschichte*, vol. 25, B9 (1.3.75), p. 3—16.
Argues that although by 1933 the NSDAP did not have a detailed economic programme, it had formulated between 1930—33 a clear, defined, and ideologically orientated economic outlook. The principal elements of this view were the primacy of politics, the right to work, and dominance of agriculture. Such ideas attracted the support of unorthodox reformist theorists during the crisis years at the end of Weimar, and moreover, influenced governmental thinking for a time after 1933. A worthwhile essay which, however, raises too many unanswered questions.

BARRACLOUGH, Geoffrey.
"The Social Dimensions of Crisis". *Social Research*, vol. 39, pt. 2 (1972), p. 341—59.
A valuable interpretative essay on the National Socialist phenomenon set against the conditions which gave rise to its ascendancy in Germany. In his discussion, Barraclough makes judicious reference to some of the principal scholarly works on the Weimar period and the NSDAP.

BIDDISS, Michael D.
Father of Racist Ideology: the Social and Political Thought of Count Gobineau. London: Weidenfeld & Nicolson (1970), 314 pp.
A detailed and scholarly analysis of Gobineau's ideas which reveals that they were anything but original, having become established in Western Europe by the mid-nineteenth century. Gobineau simply systematized theories of Aryan supremacy. More interestingly, Biddiss shows the extent to which German racialists in the late nineteenth century distorted Gobineau's thoughts for their own political and ideological ends. The major weakness of the book is the absence of a convincing analysis of the Gobineau-National Socialist ideological relationship.

1. Cross-refer to relevant titles in the following sections in Part I: 7C, 7D, 11, 15B(iii) (a), 15C(ii); in Part II see especially 23B, 23C, 24, 26B, 27, 29.

BREITLING, Rupert.
Die nationalsozialistische Rassenlehre: Entstehung, Ausbreitung, Nutzen, und Schaden einer politischen Ideologie. Meisenheim: Hain (1971), 76 pp.
A succinct and extremely sensible survey, brief though it may be.

BROSZAT, Martin.
"Die völkische Ideologie und der National-sozialismus". *Deutsche Rundschau*, vol. 84 (1958), p. 53—68.
A distinguished contribution whose conclusion that *völkisch* thought and the National Socialist *Weltanschauung* shared the same origins and content is irrefutable.

BROSZAT, Martin.
Der Nationalsozialismus: Weltanschauung, Programm und Wirklichkeit. Stuttgart: Deutsche Verlagsanstalt (1960), 84 pp. (English ed.: Santa Barbara: ABC-Clio Press (1966), 154 pp.)
A brilliant, penetrating analysis of the nature and substance of National Socialism. The origins of the NSDAP's ideology are clarified, as are the party's political and ideological links with the *völkisch* movement.

BROSZAT, Martin.
"National Socialism, its Social Basis and Psychological Impact". In E.J. Feuchtwanger (ed.). *Upheaval and Continuity: a Century of German History*. London: Oswald Wolff (1973), p. 134—51.
An interpretative essay which, in analysing the indigenous content of European fascist movements on a comparative basis, stresses the economic and socio-cultural factors responsible for the social and psychological disintegration of the German Protestant bourgeoisie and peasantry after 1918. From these classes, National Socialism drew its major support from 1928—33.

CARSTEN, Francis L.
"The Historical Roots of National Socialism". In E.J. Feuchtwanger (ed.). *Upheaval and Continuity: a Century of German History*. London: Oswald Wolff (1973), p. 116—33.
Without saying anything original, this paper argues that the roots of National Socialism can be traced back to the beginning of the nineteenth century when German national-

ism was beginning to develop in its modern form; he rejects the idea that National Socialism was the inevitable outcome of many centuries of historical development in Germany. National Socialism, he concludes, was caused by many factors.

COHN, Norman.
The Pursuit of the Millenium: Revolutionary Millenarians and Mystical Anarchists of the Middle Ages. London: Secker & Warburg (1962), 476 pp.
A most interesting and elegantly written description and analysis of revolutionary chiliasm in the Middle Ages. However, the central thesis of the book is that by studying this medieval phenomenon, additional light is thrown on the sociology and psychology of twentieth century totalitarian movements, including National Socialism. The author makes his point only to a limited extent because the characteristics of modern totalitarianism often compare only generally with those of the messianic groups he describes. For example, to say that National Socialism and the messianic groups were both types of collective paranoiac fanaticism promoted by the same causes requires more elaborate examination to be convincing.

DÖRNER, Klaus.
"Nationalsozialismus and Lebensvernichtung". *Vierteljahrshefte für Zeitgeschichte*, vol. 15, pt. 2 (1967), p. 121—52.
On the chilling theme of the National Socialist policy of extermination of racial groups and certain categories of people deemed to be "unworthy of life". The early part of the essay discusses the racial ideas of the late nineteenth and early twentieth centuries from which National Socialist theory and practice derived. In particular, the development of ideas on euthanasia is analysed.

FETSCHER, Iring.
"Die industrielle Gesellschaft und die Ideologie der Nationalsozialisten". *Gesellschaft, Staat, Erziehung*, vol. 7, pt. 1 (1962), p. 6—23.
Thoughtful and well argued.

FLECHTHEIM, Ossip K.
"Ursachen, Charakter, und Wirkungen des Nationalsozialismus". *Blätter für Deutsch- und Internationale Politik*, vol. 8, pt. 5 (1963), p. 376—83.
Unimportant, and in any case also unsatisfactory.

GABLENTZ, Otto H.
"Um die Idee des Nationalsozialismus". *Deutsche Rundschau*, vol. 69 (1946), p. 100—4.
Trivial.

GASMAN, Daniel.
The Scientific Origins of National Socialism: Social Darwinism in Ernst Haeckel and the German Monist League. New York: Elsevier (1971), 208 pp.
A detailed monograph which depicts Haeckel, the most widely known propagandist of Darwinism in late nineteenth century Germany, as a precursor of the conservative revolution of the Weimar era, and his Monist League as proto-Nazi. Haeckel preached a biological and pseudo-scientific socialism, anti-semitism, ultranationalism, and Pan-Germanism, so that the similarities between his doctrine and National Socialism are undeniable. However, Gasman is much less successful in his effort to show the existence of direct and substantial links between the two; he makes too much of his evidence, and tends to overlook the fact that National Socialism drew from a multiplicity of ideological sources. That Haeckel was a proto-Nazi is therefore not conclusively shown, but the book is scholarly and well written.

GLASER, Hermann.
Spiesser-Ideologie: von der Zerstörung des deutschen Geistes im 19. und 20. Jahrhundert. Freiburg im Breisgau: Verlag Rombach (1964), 280 pp.
Argues that the roots of National Socialism are not to be found in Germany's romanticist tradition but in the distortion of romanticism and idealism by the middle classes. The result, he adds, was a pernicious introspectiveness and callousness from which Hitler later emerged. This is an interesting hypothesis, but Glaser has not developed it fully, nor has he recognized the wider and deeper implications of the points he makes.

GLUM, Friedrich.
Philosophen im Spiegel und Zerrspiegel: Deutschlands Weg in den Nationalismus und Nationalsozialismus. Munich: Isar Verlag (1954), 287 pp.
Examines the reasons for the divergence in attitudes towards the role of the state between Germany and the rest of Western Europe, and for the emergence of an extreme German nationalism which, Glum concludes, culminated in National Socialism. These questions have been asked and answered many times and Glum, who admittedly is writing specifically for the general public, has nothing new to offer. To his credit, however, he does show clearly how much the NSDAP distorted the ideas of nineteenth century philosophers such as Nietzsche for their own base political ends.

GREBING, Helga.
Der Nationalsozialismus: Ursprung und Wesen. Munich: Olzog (1959), 104 pp.
A brief, concise and useful survey of the origins, development and application of National Socialist ideology. The author's discussion of the origins, in particular, needs to be revised, however, in the light of more recent scholarship. There are no original interpretations or conclusions in the book.

HOLBORN, Hajo.
"Origins and Political Character of Nazi Ideology". *Political Science Quarterly*, vol. 79, pt. 4 (1964), p. 542—54.
A rather insipid and disappointing paper. Holborn writes that Hitler's ideas did not change in any way after 1926 (p. 545).

JÄGER, Wolfgang.
Ziele und Praxis des Nationalsozialismus. Hanover: Verlag für Literatur und Zeitgeschehen (1961), 71 pp.
Contains nothing that is significantly new or interesting.

KOEHL, Robert.
"Feudal Aspects of National Socialism". *American Political Science Review*, vol. 54, pt. 4 (1960), p. 921—33.
Sees the National Socialist *Fuhrerprinzip*, the *Blut und Boden* concept, and the stress on the Teutonic Order as reminiscent of certain aspects of feudalism. The analogy is not altogether convincing.

KOHN, Hans.
Political Ideologies of the Twentieth Century. New York: Harper & Row (1966). 3rd revised ed.
Contains a clear assessment of National Socialism; of introductory standard.

LEPPERT-FÖGEN, Annette.
"Der Mittelstandssozialismus der NSDAP".
Frankfurter Hefte, vol. 29 (1974), p. 656—66.
Examines the theoretical and practical relationship between
downward social mobility in an age of economic upheaval
and political counterrevolution, with reference to the Ger-
man middle class of the Weimar era and its support for the
NSDAP. There is a thoughtful discussion of the National
Socialist conception of "socialism" seen against the back-
ground of links between the party and capitalism.

LOVIN, Clifford R.
See his article in section 26B.

McGOVERN, William M.
From Luther to Hitler: the History of Fascist-
Nazi Political Philosophy. London: Harrap (1946),
683 pp.
Chapter XII of this broad survey discusses National Socialism in terms of it being the inevitable culmination of German philosophical and historical development since the
time of Luther. W.L. Shirer is, of course, the most recent
protagonist of this unacceptable thesis, which McGovern
anyway puts forward rather crudely.

MICHALKA, Wolfgang.
"Geplante Utopie: zur Ideologie des National-
sozialismus". *Neue Politische Literatur*, vol. 18
(1973), p. 210—24.
A good discussion of how before 1933 National Socialism
meant something for everyone, but the reasons for its
success were mainly its anti-semitism, anti-Marxism, authoritarianism and aggressive dynamism.

MILLER LANE, Barbara.
"Nazi Ideology: Some Unfinished Business".
Central European History, vol. 7, pt. 1 (1974),
p. 3—30.
A paper which draws attention to the fact that the ideological views of NSDAP leaders before 1933 have not yet
been sufficiently analysed. The author provides an introductory examination of the writings of Dietrich Eckart,
Alfred Rosenberg, Gregor Strasser and others, as well as the
1920 party programme, the party's agricultural statement
of 1930, and its full employment programme of 1932.
However, quite a few of the ideas and interpretations in this
paper are decidedly speculative or erroneous.

MOSSE, George L.
"The Mystical Origins of National Socialism".
Journal of the History of Ideas, vol. 22, pt. 1
(1961), p. 81—96.
Argues that National Socialism was derived in part from
Germany's intellectual rejection of positivist ideology in
favour of the romantic-mystical, elusive, and unconscious
which formed an essential part of German romanticist
tradition.

MOSSE, George L.
The Crisis of German Ideology: Intellectual Origins
of the Third Reich. New York: Grosset & Dunlap
(1964), 373 pp.
An absorbing and important study which examines the elements which constituted the extreme rightist ideology in
Germany in the late nineteenth and early twentieth
centuries, with especial stress on the development and
nature of *völkisch* thought. The author is concerned to
show how National Socialist ideas were part of this
völkisch experience, particularly its racialism and anti-
semitism, which permeated large sections of the bourgeoisie.
A fundamental weakness of the book is that Mosse has not
taken into account the fact that ideas similar to the German
völkisch ideology were to be found in most other European countries at the same time; the uniqueness of the
German case is overstated.

MÜLLER, Hans.
"Der pseudoreligiöse Charakter der national-
sozialistischen Weltanschauung". *Geschichte in*
Wissenschaft und Unterricht, vol. 12, pt. 6 (1961),
p. 337—52.
An interesting paper which looks at the "heroic martyr"
component of National Socialism and how this aspect was
portrayed before and after 1933 in songs and poems.

NEUROHR, Jean.
Der Mythos vom Dritten Reich: zur Geistesgesch-
ichte des Nationalsozialismus. Stuttgart: Cotta
(1957), 288 pp.
The author states that National Socialism represented the
outcome of many intellectual and emotional trends in
Germany since the early nineteenth century, trends which
were sharpened and accentuated by the disturbed political,
social and economic conditions of the 1918—33 period. At
this level, the book provides a solid, clear narrative. However, Neurohr's analysis of connections between the conservative revolution of the 1920s and National Socialism is
unconvincing and indeed contradictory on basic points.

NORTON, Donald H.
Karl Haushofer and His Influence on Nazi
Ideology and German Foreign Policy, 1919—1945.
Dissertation, Clarke University (1965).
A brief but not unmeritorious analysis of Haushofer's
influence on National Socialism, particularly through his
theory of geopolitics. Norton concludes that despite his
close friendship with Rudolf Hess, Haushofer's influence
was virtually non-existent before 1933, and much less than
has been hitherto believed during the Third Reich.[1]

PLESSNER, Helmuth.
Die verspätete Nation: über die politische Ver-
führbarkeit bürgerlichen Geistes. Stuttgart:
Kohlhammer (1959), 174 pp.
In attempting to find an explanation for National Socialism,
Plessner discusses German intellectual development in the
nineteenth century, pinpointing the elements and trends
which he believes produced Hitler: the growth of secularism,
the worship of the *Machtstaat* tradition, the conscious
alienation from the West, the absence of humanitarianism.
In turn, this gave rise to racism and extreme, biological
nationalism, and thence to National Socialism. According
to the author, therefore, Hitler was inevitable. The objections to this thesis have been propounded many times, but
otherwise this book is a well written intellectual history of
modern Germany.

REICHMANN, Eva G.
Hostages of Civilisation: the Social Sources of
National Socialist Antisemitism. London: Gollancz
(1950), 281 pp.
A highly competent and judicious assessment of the history
and development of German anti-semitism. The author
argues that the latter was caused above all by a range of
"negative" influences, including the absence of a real
democratic tradition, a feeling of insecurity and inferiority
in the national psyche, nationalism, and the retardative
power of feudalistic elements such as the *Junker*.

RITTER, Gerhard.
Das deutsche Problem: Grundfragen deutschen
Staatsleben gestern und heute. Munich: Olden-
bourg (1962), 218 pp. Revised ed.
Stresses the European rather than the specifically German
features of National Socialism, arguing that Hitler could

---

1. It would be useful to read this work in conjunction
with Ursula Laack-Michel's *Albrecht Haushofer und der*
Nationalsozialismus: ein Beitrag zur Zeitgeschichte, Stuttgart: Klett (1974), 407 pp. This is a biography of Karl
Haushofer's son, who was murdered by the National Socialists following his peripheral involvement in the July Plot,
1944.

have been the misfortune of other European countries. The book propounds a major thesis on the historical origins of National Socialism and has to be taken seriously. Most scholars, however, would not agree with Ritter.

SAMUEL, R. H.
"The Origin and Development of the Ideology of National Socialism". *Australian Journal of Political History*, vol. 9 (1963), p. 59—77.
A pedestrian survey of some of the ideas in nineteenth century German intellectual and philosophical writing which influenced the content of National Socialism. Based entirely on secondary literature, much of it published since 1945.

SANDVOSS, E.
Hitler und Nietzsche: eine bewusstseingeschicht-liche Studie. Göttingen: Musterschmidt (1969), 208 pp.
A weak study of the extent to which their ideas may be considered similar. Quite unconvincing.

SAUER, Wolfgang.
See his article in section 21.

SCHEFFLER, Wolfgang.
"Faktoren nationalsozialistischen Herrschafts-denkens". In *Faktoren der politischen Entscheidung: Festgabe für Ernst Fraenkel.* Edited by Gerhard Ritter and Gilbert Ziebura. Berlin: de Gruyter (1963), p. 56—72.
A very good paper on the continuity of themes in National Socialist ideology. Scheffler argues that its main features were extreme nationalism, racialism, and a crude social Darwinism. No one would disagree.

SCHIEDER, Theodor.
"Zum Problem der historischen Wurzeln des Nationalsozialismus". *Das Parlament: Aus Politik und Zeitgeschichte* (30.1.1963).
A brief discussion of the different interpretations offered by scholars on the origins of National Socialism. How far back into German history should we look, and to what extent should we stress non-German dimensions of the phenomenon?

SCHULZ, Gerhard.
See his work in section 21.

SNYDER, Louis L.
German Nationalism: the Tragedy of a People. Pennsylvania: The Stackpole Co. (1952), 321 pp.
A work of poor scholarly standard which sees National Socialism as simply the outgrowth of German nationalism since 1815.

STOLL, Gerhard E.
"Evangelische Presse und nationalsozialistische Ideologie 1933". *Publizistik*, vol. 8, pt. 4 (1963), p. 380—9.
Investigates the Protestant Church's attitude to the National Socialist political breakthrough through the pages of its extensive press, as well as its attitude to some of the major aspects of the party's ideology, especially racialism. However, the essay is not particularly instructive.

SZAZ, Zoltan M.
"The Ideological Precursors of National Socialism". *Western Political Quarterly*, vol. 16, pt. 4 (1963), p. 924—45.
Propagates the well-worn thesis that National Socialism was the final product of certain distinctive trends in German intellectual history from the time of the French Revolution, which were given an even more aggressive content under the unstable conditions in the Weimar era. The limitations of this viewpoint are common knowledge.

TONSOR, Stephen J.
National Socialism: Conservative Reaction or Nihilist Revolt? New York: Rinehart (1959), 27 pp.
Attempts to determine the meaning of National Socialism by collecting together extracts from the writings of a number of German writers from Hegel to Rathenau, and from the works of three historians (Friedrich Meinecke, Franz Neumann, Hermann Rauschning). The result is even more unsatisfactory than the method of approach: we have no better idea of what National Socialism was than before we read the book.

VERMEIL, Edmond.
"Quelques aperçus sur les origines du nazisme hitlérien". In Max Beloff (ed.). *On the Track of Tyranny.* London: Vallentine Mitchell (1960), p. 201—10.
An unsatisfactory essay, vague, impressionistic and casual. The author sees National Socialism in terms of previous German intellectual development, stressing the influence of Nietzsche. This eclectic approach is clearly out of date.

VIERECK, Peter.
Metapolitics: the Roots of the Nazi Mind. New York: Capricorn Books (1960). New ed.
In some respects, a fairly provocative survey of conservative -nationalist intellectual trends before 1918. Originally published in 1941, but still worth a look.

VONDUNG, Klaus,
Magie und Manipulation: ideologischer Kult und politische Religion des Nationalsozialismus. Göttingen: Vandenhoeck & Ruprecht (1971), 256 pp.
An interesting discussion of the ceremonial in National Socialism and the way it was exploited to cover up the movement's lack of a substantive ideology.

WHITESIDE, Andrew G.
"The Nature and Origins of National Socialism". *Journal of Central European Affairs*, vol. 17, pt. 1 (1957—58), p. 48—73.
A most useful, well balanced comparative study of the different interpretations of National Socialism put forward by scholars, including those supporting the régime from 1933—45.

ZMARZLIK, Hans-Günter.
"Der Sozialdarwinismus in Deutschland als geschichtliches Problem". *Vierteljahrshefte für Zeitgeschichte*, vol. 11, pt. 3 (1963), p. 246—73.
An examination of the genesis of social Darwinist thought in the nineteenth century, and the importance this thought enjoyed in National Socialist ideology and practice after 1933.

26

The Economy and National Socialism[1]

A. INDUSTRY AND BIG BUSINESS

BARKAI, Avraham.
See his article in section 25.

CZICHON, Eberhard.
Wer verhalf Hitler zur Macht? Zum Anteil der deutschen Industrie an der Zerstörung der Weimarer Republik. Cologne: Pahl-Rugenstein (1967), 105 pp.
The author's objective is to demonstrate that heavy industry supported the NSDAP to an important extent before 1933. However, it must be stated immediately that Czichon has substantially distorted and misinterpreted his evidence to make the picture fit his hypothesis. In consequence, not only does the book contain a plethora of factual errors, it is wholly unreliable and irresponsible. There is abundant evidence available to refute every major assertion of this book.

CZICHON, Eberhard.
"Wer verhalf Hitler zur Macht? Zur politischen Funktion des Keppler-Kreises innerhalb der deutschen Industrie im Jahre 1932". *Blätter für Deutsch- und Internationale Politik*, vol. 11, pt. 10 (1966), p. 873—908.
Czichon's commentary follows the same discredited pattern of his book; of note, however, are thirteen documents in an appendix consisting for the most part of letters exchanged among Hitler, Schacht, Otto Meissner, Kurt von Schröder, and Wilhelm Keppler.

DEUTSCHER GEWERKSCHAFTSBUND (ed.).
Hitler und die Industrie. Düsseldorf: Bundespressestelle des Deutschen Gewerkschaftsbundes (1963), 28 pp.
Contains a few interesting documents on big business-NSDAP relations before 1933. Compare this volume with the following title.

1. See also relevant titles in sections 13, 21, 23C, 24A, and 24B.

DEUTSCHES INDUSTRIEINSTITUT.
Die Legende von Hitler und der Industrie. Cologne: Selbstverlag (1962), 23 pp.
A tentative effort to show that most of industry did not lend funds to Hitler before 1933.

DROBISCH, Klaus.
"Flick und die Nazis". *Zeitschrift für Geschichtswissenschaft*, vol. 14, pt. 3 (1966), p. 378—97.
Concerned mainly with Flick's post-1933 collaboration, but there are a few details of his financial assistance to the NSDAP during the Weimar era.

DROBISCH, Klaus.
"Der Freundeskreis Himmler: ein Beispiel für die Unterordnung der Nazipartei und des faschistischen Staatsapparates durch die Finanzoligarchie". *Zeitschrift für Geschichtswissenschaft*, vol. 8, pt. 2 (1960), p. 304—28.
The first section of this paper on the membership and importance of Himmler's circle of industrial contacts outlines some examples of NSDAP-big business collaboration before 1933. The substance of the article deals with 1933—45 developments.

HALLGARTEN, George W. F.
Hitler, Reichswehr und Industrie: zur Geschichte der Jahre 1918—1933. Frankfurt: Europäische Verlagsanstalt (1955), 130 pp.
A scholarly assessment which, however, must be used with great caution in view of more recent research on NSDAP-big business relations. Hallgarten has exaggerated and predated these relations. His account of NSDAP-army contacts remains more reliable but even so other studies have covered much the same ground in greater depth.

HALLGARTEN, George W. F.
"Adolf Hitler and German Heavy Industry, 1931—1933". *History*, vol. 12, pt. 3 (1952), p. 222—46.
Argues that the large industrial firms which actively supported the NSDAP were mainly those which had been hardest hit by the depression, and which therefore tended to regard Hitler as a "saviour". The help given to the party by the United Steel Works is dealt with at length. As a whole, however, Hallgarten is rightly careful not to ascribe too much responsibility to heavy industry for the victory of National Socialism in 1933.

HEYL, John D.
"Hitler's Economic Thought: a Reappraisal".
Central European History, vol. 6, pt. 1 (1973),
p. 83—96.
An analysis of Hitler's often neglected economic ideas,
discussed within the wider framework of relations
between political leadership and economic policy-making.
Most of the paper considers the 1933—45 period, in particular the depression years.

HILLIARD, Robert B.
**The Genesis of the Economic and Social Program
of the National Socialist Movement.** Dissertation,
State University of Iowa (1957).[1]

PETZINA, Dieter.
"Hitler und die deutsche Industrie". *Geschichte
in Wissenschaft und Unterricht*, vol. 17, pt. 8
(1966), p. 482—91.
A useful discussion of the present state of research in this
field and a review of secondary literature dealing with it.

SAAGE, Richard.
**"Zum Verhältnis von Nationalsozialismus und
Industrie".** *Das Parlament: Aus Politik und
Zeitgeschichte*, vol. 25, B9 (1.3.1975), p. 17—39.
A mature review of the different approaches to the problem of NSDAP-big business relations which have been
adopted by three main schools of thought: the "empirical"
group (Turner, Treue, etc.) which denies there was a
systematic connection; the Soviet-Marxists who posit a
structural identity between monopoly capitalism and
fascism; and the "primacy of politics" historians (Mason,
Petzina, etc.).

STEGMANN, Dirk.
**"Zwischen Repression und Manipulation:
konservative Machteliten und Arbeiter- und
Angestelltenbewegung 1910—1918; ein Beitrag
zur Vorgeschichte der DAP/NSDAP".** *Archiv für
Sozialgeschichte*, vol. 12 (1972), p. 351—432.
A detailed examination of extreme right-wing ideas in
Germany's blue-collar organizations before 1918: the
NSDAP became the primary beneficiary of such developments in the Weimar era. The group which represented
such blue-collar attitudes in 1918—20 was the *Deutsche
Arbeiter- und Angestellten Partei*, the north German variant
of the Munich DAP. While this paper is a valuable contribution to the debate on historical continuity in modern
German history, some of its principal hypotheses are unconvincing. For example, Stegmann does not prove his
point that the DAP/NSDAP became an instrument of conservative power élites, nor does he make his case that between 1919 and 1923 Hitler was controlled by politically
influential but anonymous *Hintermänner*.

STEGMANN, Dirk.
**"Zum Verhältnis von Grossindustrie und
Nationalsozialismus 1930—1933: ein Beitrag zur
Geschichte der sog. Machtergreifung".** *Archiv für
Sozialgeschichte*, vol. 13 (1973), p. 399—482.
The author claims to have reviewed all available evidence
pertaining to this controversial and intriguing topic before
arriving at his conclusions, but in essence he presents mere
variations of well established Marxist interpretations of
the connection between heavy industry and the rise of the
NSDAP. In consequence, his views are highly questionable;

1. I was unable to obtain a copy for review.

they are not substantiated at critical points by concrete
documentary evidence. Hence, what at first sight may
appear to be a major article is in fact a rather misleading
work which should be treated with considerable caution.[2]

TURNER, Henry A.
"Hitler's Secret Pamphlet for Industrialists, 1927".
Journal of Modern History, vol. 40, pt. 3 (1968),
p. 348—74.
Refers to a recently discovered pamphlet written by Hitler
which is published here for the first time; it is entitled *Der
Weg zum Wiederaufstieg*. Hitler had composed it in summer
1927 at the instigation of Emil Kirdorf, the industrialist.
The work, which was not released to the public but
distributed privately to Germany's leading industrialists, reveals Hitler's early attempts to enlist industry's support for
the NSDAP. His tone is moderate and respectable as he
describes Germany's troubles and his solutions to them.
Hitler presents the image of an earnest nationalist of a
conservative-traditionalist type; significantly he makes no
reference to NSDAP "socialism" or to crude anti-semitism.

TURNER, Henry A.
"Emil Kirdorf and the Nazi Party". *Central
European History*, vol. 1, pt. 4 (1968), p. 324—
44.
Describes Emil Kirdorf's career in right-wing politics and
his first involvement with the NSDAP in 1926—27. Kirdorf
joined the party and set out to win industrial support for
Hitler, but he quickly became disillusioned with the party's
"left wing" and resigned his NSDAP membership in 1928,
switching his political allegiance for the remainder of the
Weimar period to the DNVP. Turner's conclusion is that
Kirdorf did not channel huge sums of money into the
NSDAP before 1933 as has often been alleged, nor did he
contribute privately to the party to any large degree. This is
an important revisionist article.

TURNER, Henry A.
"Big Business and the Rise of Hitler". *American
Historical Review*, vol. 75, pt. 1 (1969), p. 56—70.
Another provocative and on the whole convincing paper in
which Turner explodes the myth that big business poured
vast sums into the coffers of the NSDAP. He shows the
diverse nature of political attitudes among industrialists;
there were very few like Fritz Thyssen who were prepared
to back Hitler. Indeed, the bulk of industry's political
funds went to established middle class conservative parties.
Clearly, therefore, the vast majority of industrialists neither
wanted an NSDAP victory nor contributed significantly to
it.

TURNER, Henry A.
"Fritz Thyssen und 'I Paid Hitler'". *Vierteljahrshefte für Zeitgeschichte*, vol. 19, pt. 3 (1971),
p. 225—44.
Turner casts doubt on the validity of Thyssen's book[3] as
an historical source for the relationship between the
NSDAP and big business. He disputes the authenticity of
the book — it is not certain how much of it was actually
written by Thyssen — and questions the reliability of much
of the content. He concludes that the book is now
effectively discredited, and one is certainly inclined to
agree.

2. See H.A. Turner's detailed and convincing critique of
Stegmann in "Grossunternehmertum und Nationalsozialismus 1930—1933. Kritisches und Ergänzendes zu zwei
neuen Forschungsbeiträgen". *Historische Zeitschrift*, no.
221 (1975), p. 18—68.

3. Fritz Thyssen. *I Paid Hitler*. New York (1941).

TURNER, Henry A.
Faschismus und Kapitalismus in Deutschland: Studien zum Verhältnis zwischen Nationalsozialismus und Wirtschaft. Göttingen: Vandenhoeck & Ruprecht (1972), 185 pp.
This volume contains the German translation of the author's work on NSDAP-big business relations which has appeared as articles in learned journals (see the aforementioned titles in this section).

VOGELSANG, Reinhard.
Der Freundeskreis Himmler. Göttingen: Musterschmidt (1972), 182 pp.
A valuable contribution to the topic of NSDAP-big business relations. He shows that the so-called *Kepplerkreis* played a crucial role in helping the NSDAP to power, not by contributing vast sums to the party's treasury, but by exerting pressure on President von Hindenburg. This well researched study goes on to examine the role of the *Kepplerkreis* in the Third Reich.

VOGT, Martin.
See his article in section 22A.

B. AGRICULTURE

GIES, Horst.
See his work in section 23C (under Darré).

GIES, Horst.
"NSDAP und landwirtschaftliche Organisationen in der Endphase der Weimarer Republik". *Vierteljahrshefte für Zeitgeschichte*, vol. 15, pt. 4 (1967), p. 341—76.
An excellent analysis of the nature and extent of the National Socialist agrarian campaign in the countryside, and of the methods employed by the party to infiltrate existing small farmers' and agricultural associations, whereupon they were made ready for *Gleichschaltung*. The key role of the NSDAP's *Agrarpolitische Apparat* is illustrated in detail.

GOSSWEILER, Kurt; **SCHLICHT**, Alfred.
"Junker und NSDAP 1931/32". *Zeitschrift für Geschichtswissenschaft*, vol. 15, pt. 4 (1967), p. 644—62.
Provides details of certain aristocrats who undertook propaganda work for the NSDAP, particularly Friedrich Fürst Eulenburg-Hertefeld and Dietloff Graf von Arnim-Boitzenburg. Nine letters and memoranda written by both men to each other and to fellow *Junker* between January 1931 and March 1932 are reproduced in full in an appendix.

HONIGSHEIM, Paul.
"The Roots of the Nazi Concept of the Ideal German Peasant". *Rural Sociology*, vol. 12, pt. 1 (1947), p. 3—21.
Indicates the existence of a powerful anti-urban trend in German romanticist thought since the nineteenth century. This attitude was kept alive and extended by many rural-orientated organizations so that by 1933 the notion that the rustic life was superior to all others had been firmly established. Thus, even this important element of National Socialist ideology was unoriginal. A well researched and informative paper.

LOOMIS, Charles P; **BEAGLE**, J. Allan.
"The Spread of Nazism in Rural Areas". *American Sociological Review*, vol. 11 (1946), p. 724—34.
Supplies some reasons why the NSDAP was so successful in rural Protestant areas from 1928—33: loss of economic security, social solidarity, frustration, and a longing for the "good old days" among the small farming community.

LOVIN, Clifford R.
"Blut und Boden: the Ideological Basis of the Nazi Agricultural Program". *Journal of the History of Ideas*, vol. 28, pt. 2 (1967), p. 279—88.
A superficial review of the ideas of Walther Darré, the NSDAP agricultural expert, concerning agrarian organization and political agitation. Darré's own writings (which are listed in section 24B) provide the basis for the paper.

Foreign Policy and National Socialism[1]

27

BRADLEY, P. E. Q.
The National Socialist Attack on the Foreign Policies of the German Republic 1919—1933.
Dissertation, Stanford University (1947).[2]

DICKMANN, Fritz.
"Machtwille und Ideologie in Hitlers aussenpolitischen Zielsetzungen vor 1933". In K. Repgen & S. Skalweit (eds.). *Spiegel der Geschichte: Festschrift für Max Braubach.* Münster: Aschendorff (1964), p. 915—41.
A scholarly appraisal of Hitler's aggressive approach to foreign policy.

FRIBERG, A. M.
National Socialist Attitudes toward Foreign Policy 1919—30. Dissertation, Tulane University (1964).
Superficial.

HILDEBRAND, Klaus.
Von Reich zum Weltreich: Hitler, NSDAP, und die koloniale Frage 1919—1945. Munich: Fink-Verlag (1969), 955 pp.
Based on an exhaustive collection of primary and secondary sources, this monumental work is the first serious study of the importance of the colonial question in National Socialism. It is revealed that Hitler's foreign policy programme did contain an element of overseas colonial ambition from 1935 onwards and that two years later he decided to acquire an overseas empire for Germany. The author describes in minute and systematic detail the various stages in Hitler's colonial thought, beginning in the pre-1933 era.

HILDEBRAND, Klaus.
Deutsche Aussenpolitik 1933—1945. Stuttgart: Kohlhammer (1970).
A stimulating, interpretative work in which Hitler is portrayed not as a clever opportunist but as a doctrinaire political leader with a thought-out programme of objectives. As such, the book is a notable contribution to the debate

over the question of continuity in German foreign policy. An early chapter skilfully surveys NSDAP foreign policy attitudes before 1933.

HILLGRUBER, Andreas.
"England in Hitlers aussenpolitischer Konzeption". *Historische Zeitschrift*, no. 218 (1974), p. 65—84.
Chiefly concerned with defining the various different stages in the development of Hitler's policy towards Britain. The early part of the paper discusses some of the foreign policy priorities worked out by Hitler in the 1920s. An interesting outline, also published as "England's Place in Hitler's Plans for World Dominion", in the *Journal of Contemporary History*, vol. 9, pt. 1 (1974), p. 5—22.

JACOBSEN, Hans-Adolf.
Nationalsozialistische Aussenpolitik, 1933—1938. Frankfurt: Metzlar (1968), 944 pp.
A brilliant, exhaustively documented study which is already a standard source. For our purposes, it provides an excellent analysis of the development of NSDAP foreign policy aims before 1933.

JACOBSEN, Hans-Adolf.
"Zur Programmatik und Struktur der nationalsozialistischen Aussenpolitik 1919—1939". *Das Parlament: Aus Politik und Zeitgeschichte* (13. 12.1967).
An interpretative essay anticipatory of the standard set in his aforementioned monograph.

JACOBSEN, Hans-Adolf.
"Die Gründung der Auslandsabteilung der NSDAP (1931—1933)". In E. Schulin (ed.). *Gedenkschrift Martin Göhring: Studien zur europäischen Geschichte.* Wiesbaden: Steiner (1968), p. 353—68.
An interesting paper which describes the origins and activities of the NSDAP's foreign office. An "old fighter" of the party, Bruno Fricke, had taken the initiative for the establishment of the office, but Dr. Hans Nieland was preferred as its head. The paper describes the extent and nature of the office's contacts with German communities abroad before 1933.

---

1. See also relevant titles in sections 22A, 23B, 23C, 24A, 24B and 25.
2. I was unable to see a copy for review.

KOCH, Hansjoachim W.
"Hitler and the Origins of the Second World War: Second Thoughts on the Status of Some of the Documents". *Historical Journal*, vol. 11, pt. 1 (1968), p. 125—43.
Argues that *Mein Kampf* cannot be regarded as a blueprint, let alone a detailed scheme, of Hitler's actions in foreign policy 1933—39. On the contrary, Koch adds, Hitler's foreign policy represents a strong contradiction of the ideas outlined in his book. Koch's essay, however, is one of the least convincing in the whole debate relating to the status of *Mein Kampf*.

KUHN, Axel.
Hitlers aussenpolitisches Programm: Entstehung und Entwicklung 1919—1939. Stuttgart: Klett (1970), 286 pp.
A refreshing, well documented and scholarly analysis. Kuhn shows that Hitler conceived the idea of an alliance with Britain before he developed his concept of *Lebensraum*. The second part of the book concentrates on his unsuccessful relations with Britain, which caused Hitler to drop her from his plans. Kuhn wrongly believes this was the only significant change Hitler ever made in his foreign policy; he overlooks that his relationship with France was also at variance with what he stated about that country in *Mein Kampf*.

LAQUEUR, Walter Z.
See his article in section 19C(i).

MATTHIAS, Erich.
"The Western Powers in Hitler's World of Ideas". In A.J. Nicholls & E. Matthias (eds.). *German Democracy and the Triumph of Hitler*. London: Allen & Unwin (1971), p. 161—74.
A paper based on the findings of other scholars which argues that Hitler's basic ideas in foreign policy had been worked out by 1923, and that he continued to adhere to them despite temporary tactical deviations as future circumstances required. Matthias is concerned to illustrate this point as regards Hitler's attitudes towards France, Italy and Great Britain, and he affirms that *Mein Kampf* contains an explanation of these opinions in essential outline.

PESE, Walter W.
"Hitler und Italien 1920—1926". *Vierteljahrshefte für Zeitgeschichte*, vol. 3, pt. 2 (1955), p. 113—26.
Examines the nature and important aspects of the relationship, but the essay underestimates Mussolini's intrigues with the Bavarian Right as a whole from 1922—25.

SCHUBERT, Günter.
Anfänge nationalsozialistischer Aussenpolitik. Cologne: Verlag Wissenschaft und Politik (1963), 254 pp.
A very good, interesting study of the influences and ideas which formed the core of NSDAP attitudes in foreign policy. A major point to emerge is that Hitler conceived the idea of an alliance between Germany and Britain (1922) before he thought of *Lebensraum* at the expense of Russia (1924). In the latter respect, the influence of Alfred Rosenberg's anti-Bolshevik and anti-semitic feelings is shown to have been of considerable importance.

SMITH, Arthur L.
"Hitler's Gau Ausland". *Political Studies*, vol. 14, pt. 1 (1966), p. 90—5.
Contains a few details on the origins of the NSDAP foreign office in 1931, but the paper is devoted in the main to a brief account of Ernst Wilhelm Bohle, who headed the office 1933—45.

VOIGT, Johannes H.
"Hitler und Indien". *Vierteljahrshefte für Zeitgeschichte*, vol. 19, pt. 1 (1971), p. 33—63.
The early pages of this essay demonstrate that even before 1933 Hitler had expressed thoughts on the Indian nationalist movement and British imperialism, and that the Indian situation exerted a small influence on his overall attitude to Britain.

WEINBERG, Gerhard L.
"Hitler's Image of the United States". *American Historical Review*, vol. 69, pt. 4 (1964), p. 1006—21.
An instructive analysis of Hitler's perception of the United States and the implications of his conclusions for his policies in international affairs. During the early 1920s, Hitler did not pay much attention to the U.S.A. and *Mein Kampf* contains only a few fleeting references to it. But in his *Second Book* (1928), the U.S.A. is mentioned frequently in Hitler's discussion of foreign affairs. This change of heart, argues Weinberg, was due to Hitler's new awareness of the U.S.A.'s economic strength and to his interest in motor cars. Hitler believed therefore that the U.S.A. was a potential threat to Germany, but did not produce any precise formulae on German-American relations before 1933 because of his heavy involvement in Weimar politics. After 1933, his evaluation of the U.S.A. was entirely negative.

WEINBERG, Gerhard L.
"National Socialist Organization and Foreign Policy Aims in 1927". *Journal of Modern History*, vol. 36, pt. 4 (1964), p. 428—33.
Published here is a letter of 30 March 1927 which Rudolf Hess sent to his friend Walter Hewel, an old party comrade, then resident in London. The letter's contents underline the deep interest in and discussion of foreign policy in the NSDAP at that time. Hess disparages the League of Nations as a Jewish-controlled body, stresses the need for *Lebensraum*, and reaffirms Hitler's utter belief in the concept of racially superior and inferior peoples.

Press and Propaganda[1]

28

BALLE, Hermann.
Die propagandistische Auseinandersetzung des Nationalsozialismus mit der Weimarer Republik und ihre Bedeutung für den Aufstieg des Nationalsozialismus. Dissertation, University of Erlangen (1963).
An analysis of the contribution made by NSDAP propaganda to the collapse of the Weimar Republic. Balle shows how the content of the propaganda could be adapted easily because of the flexibility of National Socialist ideology. The methods of NSDAP propagandists are also explained, and no one would quarrel with the author's conclusion that the party's propaganda was a crucial factor in undermining democracy. There is nothing really new in this, and unfortunately Balle does not analyse in detail how the NSDAP's propaganda machine functioned as an organizational body.

BRAMSTED, Ernest K.
"Joseph Goebbels and National Socialist Propaganda 1926—1939: Some Aspects".
Australian Outlook, vol. 8, pt. 2 (1954), p. 65—77.
Goebbels learnt a great deal from Marxist methods of propaganda and put them to good use as *Gauleiter* of Berlin. Above all, he was unscrupulous in his appeal to primitive mass emotions; the only criterion was success. A useful paper.

BRAMSTED, Ernest K.
"Goebbels and His Newspaper 'Der Angriff'".
In Max Beloff (ed.). *On The Track of Tyranny.*
London: Vallentine Mitchell (1960), p. 45—65.
Reviews the unpromising origins of the paper, Goebbels' editorial methods, and the contents. The contribution of Mjölnir, the cartoonist, was important to the success of *Der Angriff*, as was its crude anti-semitism, exemplified in its attacks on the Vice-President of Berlin Police, Dr. Bernhard Weiss — "Isidor".

BRAMSTED, Ernest K.
Goebbels and National Socialist Propaganda, 1925—1945. Michigan: Michigan State University Press (1965), 631 pp.

1. See also relevant titles in sections 23B, 23C, 24A.

A comprehensive but far from definitive study which treats the 1925—33 period unsatisfactorily. The value of the book lies in its detailed description of the organization of the Third Reich's propaganda machinery under Goebbels and the various ways in which it helped sustain the image of the régime and the power of the *Führer*.

BURDEN, Hamilton T.
The Nuremberg Party Rallies, 1923—39. London: Pall Mall (1967), 206 pp.
A most disappointing book; analysis is reduced to a minimum, there are numerous factual errors, and the wider implications of the theme are totally ignored.

HALE, Oron J.
See his work in section 16.

LAYTON, Roland V.
The "Volkischer Beobachter" 1925—1933: a Study of the Nazi Party Newspaper in the Kampfzeit.
Dissertation, University of Virginia (1965).
A wide examination of the origins, content and the contribution of the paper to the NSDAP's success. About half of the book analyses the paper's contents and Layton concludes that it was an effective party organ. Useful.

LAYTON, Roland V.
"The 'Völkischer Beobachter', 1920—1933: the Nazi Party Newspaper in the Weimar Era". *Central European History*, vol. 3, pt. 4 (1970), p. 353—82.
A résumé of the major conclusions and findings of the author's aforementioned dissertation: the paper's financing, circulation figures, brushes with the law, contents. He does not quantify his assertion, however, that the paper was a major propaganda weapon of the NSDAP.

NOLLER, Sonja.
Die Geschichte des "Völkischen Beobachters" von 1920—1923. Dissertation, University of Munich (1956).
A competent survey which supplies more or less the same kind of information for the early period as Layton's study does for 1925—33.

NOLLER, Sonja; **KOTZE,** Hildegard (eds.).
Facsimile Querschnitt durch den "Völkischen Beobachter". Munich: Scherz (1967), 207 pp.
A documentary collection consisting of extracts from the paper: the editorial annotation could have been a lot better.

RAHN, Hans G.
Der nationalsozialistische Typ der Kampfzeitung. Berlin (1959).
A study which is not without value in summarizing the main features of National Socialist aggression in newspaper publishing before 1933, but the wider political context in which the *Kampfzeitung* operated is not explained.

RÜHL, Manfred.
"Der Stürmer" und sein Herausgeber. Dissertation, University of Erlangen (1960).
A useful sketch of the paper's revolting contents and its loathsome editor, Julius Streicher. Rühl actually appears to have manfully waded through most, if not all, editions of this most notorious of NSDAP publications.

SIDMAN, Charles F.
"Die Auflagenkurve des "Völkischen Beobachters" und die Entwicklung des Nationalsozialismus, Dezember 1920—November 1923". *Vierteljahrshefte für Zeitgeschichte*, vol. 13, pt. 1 (1965), p. 112—18.
A graph composed by a friend of Hitler, *Regierungsrat* Fritz Lauböck, and which shows the circulation vicissitudes of the VB in 1921—22 is, Sidman claims, a reliable guide for measuring the popularity and influence of the NSDAP before 1923. Hence, as the party grew stronger, especially following Hitler's "take-over" of July 1921, so the VB prospered: in four years (January 1920—November 1923) the paper developed from a six-page bi-weekly to a six-page daily selling over 25,000 copies per issue.

WILCOX, Larry D.
The National Socialist Party Press in the "Kampfzeit", 1919—1933. Dissertation, University of Virginia (1970).
A sound and interesting study.

ZEMAN, Zbynek A. B.
Nazi Propaganda. London: Oxford University Press (1973), 260 pp. New ed.
A disappointing book full of generalizations. There is very little new information (we are merely reminded that anti-semitism and anti-Marxism were the major themes of NSDAP propaganda), and fundamental problems have been ignored or only fleetingly examined. There are some useful notes about how this propaganda was organized but this is small comfort when the rest of the study is so inadequate.

The Churches and National Socialism[1]

29

BUCHHEIM, Hans.
Glaubenskrise im Dritten Reich. Stuttgart:
Deutsche Verlagsanstalt (1953), 273 pp.
Provides a sound description of the German Christian movement from its pre-1933 origins onwards.

DIRKS, Walter.
See his article in section 10B.

GÖTTE, Karl-Heinz.
See his work in section 16 (article and dissertation).

KINKEL, Walter.
Kirche und Nationalsozialismus: ihre Auseinandersetzung zwischen 1925 und 1945 in Dokumenten dargestellt. Düsseldorf: Patinos (1960),
168 pp.
Concentrates heavily on the post-1933 period, of course, but the author could have done a lot better for the pre-1933 years: there is more documentation available than is presented here, and even what is given requires more competent analysis.

KÜNNETH, Walther.
Der grosse Abfall: eine geschichtstheologische Untersuchung der Begegnung zwischen Nationalsozialismus und Christentum. Hamburg: Wittig-Verlag (1947).
A turgid, ponderous, and basically unsound work.

MEIER, Kurt.
"Die Religionspolitik der NSDAP in der Zeit der Weimarer Republik". In *Zur Geschichte des Kirchenkampfes: Gesammelte Aufsätze, vol. II.*
Göttingen: Vandenhoeck & Ruprecht (1971),
p. 9—24.
A good introductory analysis of the main features of the party's policy, including its attitude to the German Christians.

1. See also relevant titles in sections 22A, 23C, 24B and 25.

MEIER, Kurt.
Die deutschen Christen. Dissertation, University of Halle (1965).
A fairly exhaustive and critical treatment which is relatively free of Marxist-Leninist jargon.

MILLER, Eugene W.
National Socialism and the "Glaubensbewegung Deutsche Christen" 1932—1933: Analysis of a Political Relationship. Dissertation, Pennsylvania State University (1972).
Does not add significantly to previous works on this subject: the origins of the German Christians have been treated in considerable detail before now, as has the NSDAP's fundamental lack of understanding of Protestantism. These latter points constitute the substance of this work, which is really superfluous.

MÜLLER, Hans (ed.).
Katholische Kirche und Nationalsozialismus: Dokumente 1930—1935. Munich: Nymphenburger Verlag (1963), 433 pp.
An important documentary collection divided into three main sections: 1930—32; 1933; 1934—35. The Church's condemnation of National Socialism before 1933 is fully illustrated, but so also is its cautious accommodation with the régime in 1933. The editor has written a useful introduction to each section, this helping to give the documents a proper historical perspective.

REPGEN, Konrad.
See his work in section 10B.

SCHOLDER, Klaus.
See his article in section 10C.

THALMANN, Rita.
"Protestantisme et National-Socialisme: les débuts des 'Chrétiens Allemands'". *Revue d'Histoire Moderne et Contemporaine*, vol. 12, (1965), p. 287—308.
A very informative paper on the significant extent to which Lutheran propaganda for a national and anti-semitic church promoted the success of the NSDAP before 1933. The policies and internal divisions of the German Christians are also convincingly analysed.

VOLK, Ludwig.
See his work in section 10B.

255

30

The Armed Forces and National Socialism[1]

DEUERLEIN, Ernst.
"Hitlers Eintritt in die Politik und die Reichswehr".
Vierteljahrshefte für Zeitgeschichte, vol. 7, pt. 2 (1959), p. 177—227.
An important paper which, together with the 32 documents published here in an appendix, throws light on a previously little known period of Hitler's career — his activities as a member of the army's propaganda and ideological training section 1919—20. In this capacity, Hitler first came into contact with the DAP. The article as a whole also illuminates certain features of Hitler's role in the NSDAP before 1920.

FAVEZ, Jean-Claude.
"Hitler et la Reichswehr en 1923". *Revue d'Histoire Moderne et Contemporaine*, vol. 17, pt. 1 (1970), p. 22—49.
A useful discussion of the Munich Putsch in the context of army politics, but there are no revelations of note. The author is concerned to stress Hitler's disquiet at how the SA and even the NSDAP to a certain extent became militarized during the course of 1923.

HALLGARTEN, George W. F.
See his work in section 26A.

VOGELSANG, Thilo.
"Hitlers Brief an Reichenau vom 4. Dezember 1932". *Vierteljahrshefte für Zeitgeschichte*, vol. 7, pt. 4 (1959), p. 429—37.
Reichenau, German army commander in East Prussia, appealed to Hitler to tone down National Socialist propaganda in that province because of the precarious domestic and foreign situation. In his letter of reply, which is reproduced in full here, Hitler argues that the situation was worrying but that the remedy was to give power to the NSDAP since it was the only party aware of the danger posed to Germany by Russia. In these circumstances, he adds, his followers must be allowed to continue and even intensify their propaganda efforts.

1. See also section 12 in toto.

Author Index

This index also provides references under authors' names to items concerned with the critical discussion of works by them.

Subject Index

References are to page numbers followed by authors' names. Where there is more than one item by a particular author on a page, roman numerals in parentheses after the author's name indicate whether the item referred to is the first, second, etc., on the page.